Lecture Notes in Computer Sc

Edited by G. Goos, J. Hartmanis, and J. v

T0238175

Springer
Berlin
Heidelberg
New York
Hong Kong
London
Milan
Paris
Tokyo

Rei Safavi-Naini   Jennifer Seberry (Eds.)

Information Security and Privacy

8th Australasian Conference, ACISP 2003
Wollongong, Australia, July 9-11, 2003
Proceedings

Springer

Series Editors

Gerhard Goos, Karlsruhe University, Germany
Juris Hartmanis, Cornell University, NY, USA
Jan van Leeuwen, Utrecht University, The Netherlands

Volume Editors

Rei Safavi-Naini
Jennifer Seberry
University of Wollongong
School of Information Technology and Computer Science
Wollongong, NSW 2522, Australia
E-mail: {rei,jennifer_seberry}@uow.edu.au

Cataloging-in-Publication Data applied for

Bibliographic information published by Die Deutsche Bibliothek
 Die Deutsche Bibliothek lists this publication in the Deutsche Nationalbibliografie;

detailed bibliographic data is available in the Internet at <http://dnb.ddb.de>.

CR Subject Classification (1998): E.3, K.6.5, D.4.6, C.2, E.4, F.2.1, K.4.1

ISSN 0302-9743
ISBN 3-540-40515-1 Springer-Verlag Berlin Heidelberg New York

This work is subject to copyright. All rights are reserved, whether the whole or part of the material is
concerned, specifically the rights of translation, reprinting, re-use of illustrations, recitation, broadcasting,
reproduction on microfilms or in any other way, and storage in data banks. Duplication of this publication
or parts thereof is permitted only under the provisions of the German Copyright Law of September 9, 1965,
in its current version, and permission for use must always be obtained from Springer-Verlag. Violations are
liable for prosecution under the German Copyright Law.

Springer-Verlag Berlin Heidelberg New York
a member of BertelsmannSpringer Science+Business Media GmbH

http://www.springer.de

© Springer-Verlag Berlin Heidelberg 2003
Printed in Germany

Typesetting: Camera-ready by author, data conversion by PTP-Berlin GmbH
Printed on acid-free paper   SPIN: 10929049   06/3142   5 4 3 2 1 0

Preface

The 8th Australasian Conference on Information Security and Privacy (ACISP 2003) was held in Wollongong, 9–11 July, 2003. The conference was sponsored by the Australasian Computer Society, the School of Information Technology and Computer Science of the University of Wollongong, and the Smart Internet Technology Collaborative Research Centre. The conference was organized cooperatively with the IEEE-CS Task Force on Information Assurance.

The conference brought together researchers and practitioners, from academia, industry and government, with interests in information security and privacy. The conference program included 42 papers covering a wide range of topics including cryptography and cryptanalysis, network security and system security. The papers were selected from 158 submissions after an extensive and careful refereeing process in which each paper was reviewed by at least 3 members of the program committee. Of the accepted papers there were 11 from Korea, 9 from Japan, 6 from Australia, 3 from Taiwan, 2 each from Singapore and the USA, and 1 each from Canada, China, Denmark, France, Germany, India, Italy, Saudi Arabia, and Spain.

There were four invited speakers for the conference: Prof. Andrew Odlyzko (Digital Media Center, University of Minnesota, USA), Prof. Chris Mitchell (Information Security Group, Royal Holloway, University of London, UK), Dr. Li Gong (Sun Microsystems), and Prof. Gerard Milburn (University of Queensland, Australia).

We appreciate the diligence and hard work of the ACISP 2003 Program Committee. The committee benefited from the reviews and comments of many other experts: Aggelos Kiayias, Alex Dent, Alice Silverberg, Anand Desai, Andrew Clark, Atsuko Miyaji, Atsushi Fujioka, Beatrice Peirani, Bill Millan, Carine Boursier, Chi-Jen Lu, Chieng-Ning Chen, Chong Hee Kim, Christophe Tymen, Claude Carlet, Dae Hyun Yum, Darrel Hankerson, Dong Jin Park, Dong To, Drew Dean, Eiichiro Fujisaki, Eric Brier, Eric Chen, Fabienne Cathala, Gareth Brisbane, Gary Carter, Geraint Price, Gildas Avoine, Glenn Durfee, Gonzalvo Benoit, Greg Maitland, Hao-Chi Wong, Helena Handschu, Hsi-Chung Lin, Huaxiong Wang, Hung-Min Sun, In Kook Park, Jason Crampton, Jason Reid, Jean Monnerat, Jean-Sebastien Coron, Ji Hyun Jeong, John Proos, Jong Hoon Shin, Juan Manuel Gonzalez Nieto, Julien Brouchier, Kapali Viswanathan, Kazumaro Aoki, Khanh Nguyen, Koji Chida, Koji Chida, Koutarou Suzuki, Laurent Gauteron, Lionel Victor, Lu Yi, Ludovic Rousseau, Marc Joye, Mariusz Jakabowski, Mark Bauer, Mark Looi, Matt Henricksen, Min-Shiang Hwang, Nicholas Sheppard, Nicolas Courtois, Oleg Sheyner, Pascal Junod, Pascal Paillier, Philippe Oechslin, Pierre Girard, Ron Steinfeld, Sang Gyoo Sim, Sang Yun Han, Satomi Okazaki, Scarlet Schwiderski-Grosche, Shin'ichiro Matsuo, Simon Blackburn, Siu-Leung Chung, Svein Knapskog, Swee-Huay Heng, Takayuki Yamada, Teresa Lunt, Tetsu Iwata, Thomas Martin, Tung-Shou Chen, Wataru Kishimoto,

Willy Susilo, Xianmo Zhang, Xuli Wang, Yasuhiro Ohtaki, Yeon Hyeong Yang, Yi Lu, Yong Ho Hwang, and Zhi Guo.

The organizing committee was co-chaired by Dr. Willy Susilo and Prof. Jennifer Seberry. Special thanks to Takeyuki Uehara, Rongbo Du and Stephen Haynes for their technical support, to Takeyuki Uehara and Yejing Wang for their help with the local organization, and the following volunteers whose help allowed us to run the conference smoothly: Hartono Kurnio, Luke McAven, Nicholas Sheppard, Tianbing Xia, Nathan Curtis, David Haryanto, Yibing Kong, Gelareh Taban, and Rungrat Wiangsripanawan.

On behalf of all those involved in organizing the conference, we would like to thank the authors of all submitted papers, those who presented their work and those who participated in the conference: their work and contributions made the conference a great success.

July 2003   Rei Safavi-Naini

Australasian Conference on Information Security and Privacy
ACISP 2003

Sponsored by
School of Information Technology and Computer Science of the
University of Wollongong
Australian Computer Society
Smart Internet Technology Cooperative Research Centre

In cooperation with
IEEE-CS Task Force on Information Assurance

General Chairs

Jennifer Seberry   *University of Wollongong, Australia*
Willy Susilo   *University of Wollongong, Australia*

Program Chair

Rei Safavi-Naini   *University of Wollongong, Australia*

Program Committee

Masayuki Abe   *NTT, Japan*
Lynn Batten   *Deakin University, Australia*
Colin Boyd   *Queensland University of Technology, Australia*
Ed Dawson   *Queensland University of Technology, Australia*
Dieter Gollmann   *Microsoft, UK*
Jim Hughes   *StorageTek, US*
Kaoru Kurosawa   *Ibaraki University, Japan*
Kwok-Yan Lam   *Tsinghua University, China*
Chi-Sung Laih   *National Cheng Kung University, Taiwan*
Pil Joong Lee   *Pohang University of Science and Technology, Korea*
Keith Martin   *Royal Holloway, University of London, UK*
Mitsuru Matsui   *Mitsubishi Electric, Japan*
Alfred Menezes   *University of Waterloo, Canada*
Yi Mu   *University of Wollongong, Australia*
David Naccache   *Gemplus, France*

Dingyi Pei	*Chinese Academy of Sciences, China*
Josef Pieprzyk	*Macquarie University, Australia*
Pandu Rangan	*Indian Institute of Technology, Madras, India*
Greg Rose	*Qualcomm, Australia*
Jessica Staddon	*Palo Alto Research Center, US*
Vijay Varharadjan	*Macquarie University, Australia*
Serge Vaudeney	*EPFL (Swiss Fed. Inst. of Tech. Lausanne), Switzerland*
Eric Verheul	*PricewaterhouseCoopers, The Netherlands*
Chee Sun Won	*Dongguk University, Korea*
Sung-Ming Yen	*National Central University, Taiwan*
Moti Yung	*Columbia University, US*

Table of Contents

Mobile and Network Security

Invited Talk (II)

Cryptanalysis (II)

Signature

Cryptosystems (I)

Invited Talk (III)

Cryptosystems (II)

Key Management

Theory and Hash Functions

Author Index

Grouping Verifiable Content for Selective Disclosure

Laurence Bull[1], David McG. Squire[1], Jan Newmarch[2], and Yuliang Zheng[3]

[1] School of Computer Science and Software Engineering,
Monash University, Caulfield East 3145, Australia
{Laurence.Bull, David.Squire}@infotech.monash.edu.au
[2] School of Network Computing,
Monash University, Frankston 3199, Australia
Jan.Newmarch@infotech.monash.edu.au
[3] Department of Software and Information Systems,
University of North Carolina at Charlotte, Charlotte, NC 28223, USA
yzheng@uncc.edu

Abstract. This paper addresses the issue of selective disclosure of verifiable content. It extends previous work relating to Content Extraction Signatures [21] to implement a more complex structure that encodes a richer, more flexible fragment extraction policy, which includes fragment grouping. The new extraction policy enables the signer to specify both optional and mandatory fragment associations (or groupings) for verifying extracted content.

Keywords: Selective content disclosure, content extraction signatures, privacy-enhancing signatures, fragment grouping.

1 Introduction

As the pervasiveness of the Internet grows, so does electronic society. Traditional communication and commerce based on paper documents is being superseded by electronic processes and content.

Documents are merely containers. Traditionally, documents have been viewed and handled as coherent collections of semantically grouped information. More specifically, there are types of documents that represent merely a container of facts, such as a contract, an academic transcript, a non-fiction book, or an encyclopedia. It is with such documents that our main focus lies.

Consider the retrieval and exchange of individual pieces of information contained within a given document, rather than the handling of the whole document. Underlying this activity is the notion that the document itself is not the most important thing to the holder in such cases. The value, rather, lies with the document content, i.e. its constituent pieces of information. Furthermore, this concept is not constrained to small containers of information such as letters, contracts, bank statements or receipts. It is also scalable to very large collections such as books or encyclopedias.

R. Safavi-Naini and J. Seberry (Eds.): ACISP 2003, LNCS 2727, pp. 1–12, 2003.
© Springer-Verlag Berlin Heidelberg 2003

There are everyday situations where, for reasons of relevance or privacy, one wants to disclose only certain parts of a document. Under the current digital signature regime, however, the entire document is signed, thereby forcing the document holder to disclose all of its contents to a third party for the signature to be verifiable.

Stewart Baker, chief counsel for America's National Security Agency (NSA), has warned of the threats to our privacy in an electronic society [1]:

> The biggest threats to our privacy in a digital world come not from what we keep secret but from what we reveal willingly. We lose privacy in a digital world because it becomes cheap and easy to collate and transmit data... Restricting these invasions of privacy is a challenge, but it isn't a job for encryption. Encryption can't protect you from the misuse of data you surrendered willingly.

Blakley claims that digital signatures are quite different from their ink-based predecessors, and suggests that we should "look more closely at every way in which digital signatures differ" so that we may fully realise their worth [5].

We agree with these views. In this paper we propose a means of reducing the erosion of a document holder's privacy in real-world electronic interactions. This is achieved through the use of Content Extraction Signatures (CES) [21], and the further development of a fragment extraction policy that enables the document holder to selectively disclose verifiable content.

1.1 Background

In the physical world commerce is conducted through interactions and transactions. The standard digital signature is well-suited to point-to-point interactions, since party A simply signs the content they wish to send to party B. Not all instances of commerce, however, should be characterised as merely a series of point-to-point interactions. More properly, many instances are multipoint, or multiparty, interactions where information flows from the information signer to the document holder and then to the information consumer(s) as illustrated in Fig. 1. Party A (Alice) produces and signs a document, party B (Bob) receives the document and forwards selected parts thereof to party C (Carol), or party D (Don), who verifies the information.

1.2 Contents of This Paper

After establishing the type of interaction of interest in Section 1, Section 2 introduces two problems relating to electronic multiparty interactions. Section 3 covers related work from a policy and technical perspective. In Section 4, an approach using the current digital signature is discussed to illustrate its limitations and the erosion of the document holder's privacy with its use in these types of interactions. A solution using privacy-enhancing Content Extraction Signatures is then discussed to illustrate their use in multiparty interactions.

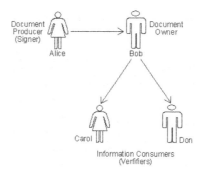

Fig. 1. A Multiparty interaction.

2 The Problems

The elegant concept of public-key cryptosystems [12] and their implementation [20] enabled a content-dependent digital signature to be created for electronic documents. Beth, Frisch and Simmons [4] suggest this changed the information security field and its primary focus from secrecy alone to include broader notions of authentication, identification and integrity verification. With the steady rollout of Public Key Infrastructure (PKI), public, corporate and governmental acceptance of, and confidence in, digital signatures has steadily grown.

Whilst digital signatures are becoming widely accepted, there is privacy erosion attendant on their use in some common multiparty interactions. In other multiparty interactions, the coarse granularity of information signing results in higher and unnecessary usage of bandwidth.

2.1 Granularity versus Privacy

This can be illustrated with a commonplace online transaction where Bob wants to purchase online an academic version of software from the Computer Corporation. Computer Corp. requires proof that Bob is a current student. Bob thus sends his electronic student identification document that has been issued and signed by Ace University. Although he need supply only his name and expiry date to establish that he is a current student, he is forced to reveal all of the other information contained in his student identification document which might include date of birth, address, course enrolment, his photograph, etc.

Ace University signs the information that it sends to Bob, thereby requiring Bob to disclose *all* of this information to Computer Corp.: otherwise it will fail verification. This occurs even if only part of the information is required for the interaction and Bob does not want to reveal all of the information.

Ideally, the information holder should be free to disclose only the minimum information required for the interaction. Bob should be able to disclose only his name, student number and expiry date in support of this transaction. However, this must also be in accordance with the signer's expectations of reasonable use of the document's content. Bob's privacy in this transaction is eroded as the document content is signed with a granularity that is too large for this particular transaction. This demonstrates the tension between verifiable information granularity and the information holder's privacy, as illustrated below in Fig. 3(a).

Our goal is to enhance the document holders' privacy in multiparty interactions, moving from coarser content granularity towards finer granularity.

2.2   Granularity versus Bandwidth

The granularity of signed information in multiparty interactions does not only affect privacy; it also causes unnecessary bandwidth usage. Consider Bob, a document holder, who wants to pass a single item of verifiable information to Carol. Instead of being able to pass this single item of information, Bob is forced to furnish the entire document, which could be significantly greater in size than the single item.

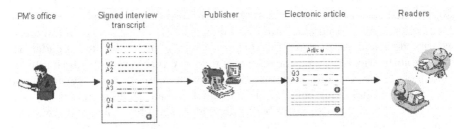

Fig. 2. Example of electronic publishing which includes verifiable content.

To illustrate such a scenario, which is not a privacy issue but one of information relevance, consider an electronically published article, in which some aspect of an interview with the Prime Minister (PM) is reported. As depicted in Fig. 2, the PM's office issues a transcript of the interview involving the PM, which has been signed using the standard digital signature.

The publisher would like to quote only the PM's response to a particular question as there are tight constraints on article size and it is neither appropriate, nor possible, to include the entire transcript of the interview. It is desirable for the reader to be able to verify the quoted content in the article from the signed transcript as it would avoid problems of misinterpretation and misquoting.

If the interview transcript is signed using the standard digital signature, this scenario is not possible. The problem is that the standard digital signature requires all of the signed information to be present: otherwise it will fail verification.

This example illustrates the tension that exists between verifiable content granularity and bandwidth, as illustrated in Fig. 3(b). This tension is likely to arise in many other scenarios as the Internet burgeons. A further goal of this work is to reduce the signed content granularity and move towards reduced bandwidth.

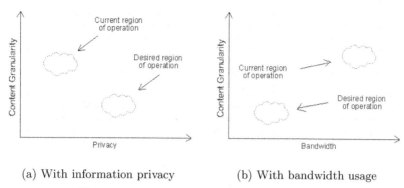

(a) With information privacy   (b) With bandwidth usage

Fig. 3. Tensions with verifiable content granularity

2.3   Selective Content Disclosure Abuse

The potential for abuse accompanies the ability to disclose verifiable information contained in a document more selectively. For example, using the above scenario, to avoid the PM's responses being quoted out of context, it is desirable that the question and the response be linked so that the response is always preceded by the corresponding question. Hence there is a requirement that the information signer be able to exert some control over what verifiable content can be selectively disclosed by the document holder. Conceivably, the document signer would want to be able to specify which fragments: may be extracted in isolation, be extracted only when accompanied by other specified fragments, and never be extracted (i.e. can only ever be provided with the entire document).

3   Related Work

3.1   Policy Initiatives

The ever-increasing adoption of the Internet by government, business and the community has added to existing concerns over privacy arising from the widespread use of information technology. Governments in countries such as Australia have responded by establishing privacy commissioners to develop and administer privacy laws, privacy policies and standards with which organisations must comply [16]. Privacy rights are often expressed in the form of Privacy Principles. In Australia there are ten, which are based on the Organisation for Economic Cooperation and Development (OECD) guidelines and called the National Privacy Principles (NPP) [15]. Australia also has a Privacy Commissioner [10] who is charged with many functions and responsibilities with respect to the Privacy Act.

Whilst the policies and legal framework initiatives are welcome, they are not a panacea. They simply provide a framework within which organisations under their jurisdiction must operate or face sanctions. What about organisations that

operate beyond their jurisdictions? Consider Internet-based gambling. Although
it is now illegal in many countries, it has simply moved offshore and out of the
respective country's jurisdiction.

These initiatives will not prevent breaches of privacy, as illustrated recently
in an incident when customer credit card details were disclosed outside of a
company and were subsequently fraudulently used. After an investigation, the
Federal Privacy Commissioner stated that "It is important to note that addressing the privacy risks identified would not necessarily prevent a breach such as
the one that occurred ..." [17]

Once private information is released, you cannot recall it. In the above example, all the credit cards had to be cancelled and new ones issued. Perhaps not a
particularly great inconvenience—what, however, if the privacy breach involved
much more sensitive information such as a digital identity, or private key?

Policies alone cannot ensure privacy. There needs to be technical support
for privacy and it needs to be put back into the hands of the people to allow
them a role in their own privacy.

3.2   The XML Signature

The XML-Signature (XMLsig) specification [2], also from the W3C, defines a
scheme for creating digital signatures that can be applied to digital content, or
data objects, which may be within the same XML document as the signature,
or located externally in other documents on various sites across the web. The
XMLsig enables the signer to sign anything that can be referenced by a URI,
along with any transforms of the information, so that other users can verify the
signature. In essence, the thrust of XMLsig is to enable a signer to efficiently
sign multiple objects that may be located on physically different servers and
to enable a verifier to verify the available objects even though the entire set of
signed objects may not be available.

Whilst the basic XMLsig's functionality is similar to our first CES scheme,
CommitVector [21, §4.1], it is not designed to provide the CES *privacy* security
for blinded content nor does it allow the signer to specify an extraction policy.
Nonetheless, it has been shown that the functionality of the XMLsig can be
extended to include CES functionality [9], including a richer extraction policy
to handle fragment grouping, which is described in this paper. Due to space
constraints this could not be included with the work reported in this short version
of the paper, however, the interested reader is referred to the full version where
it is included [8].

3.3   Other Work

A general concept, proposed by Rivest [19], which has since been referred to
as "... signature schemes that admit forgery of signatures derived by some specific operation on previous signatures but resist other forgeries." [3]. Micali and
Rivest introduced transitive signature schemes in this area [14], while Bellare and
Niven presented schemes that provided performance improvements [3]. Johnson,

Molnar, Song and Wagner have investigated a general approach to homomorphic signature schemes for some binary operations such as: addition, subtraction, union, intersection [13].

Brands has performed extensive work on enhancing the privacy of document owners and has proposed "Digital Credentials", which are issued by trusted "Credential Authorities", along with associated protocols that have the capability for selective disclosure of the data fields in the credential [6,7].

A different approach was taken by Orman [18] who proposes using the XML-sig for an authorisation and validation model for mildly active content in web pages. This enables the content owner's intentions with respect to document modification to be embodied in the document so that any party can validate the document with respect to these intentions. It permits the document owner to delegate modification rights verifiably by signing the URL: a form of "late binding".

Other work has focussed on certain types of path and selection queries over XML documents that can be run on untrusted servers. Devanbu, Gertz, Kwong et al. [11] have proposed a new approach to signing XML documents so that answers to arbitrary queries can be certified.

4   Solutions

4.1   Using Standard Digital Signatures

A simplistic approach to the content granularity problem is for Alice, the signer, to sign the individual document fragments using the standard digital signature and to forward all these signed fragments to Bob, the information holder, for use. If there are n content fragments, then the computational overhead would be n signatures.

Bob does not need to perform any further computation as all that is required is simply to forward the required fragment(s) along with their associated signature(s) to Carol, the information consumer, for verification. For peace of mind, however, it is likely that Bob would first verify each fragment received from the signer, thus requiring n signature verifications.

Carol, upon receipt of the fragment(s) would have to perform m signature verifications where $m < n$ and m is the number of fragments forwarded by Bob.

How could Alice protect against the potential of disclosure abuse?
If Alice follows the scheme described above, she *cannot* protect against disclosure abuse. Her alternative is to decide upon allowed subsets of fragments, corresponding to various permissable fragment associations, or groupings. Each of these subsets could be signed and issued as a separate document. There is an upper bound of 2^n possible subsets, which implies a considerable document management challenge for both Alice and Bob.

Using the standard digital signature in this manner departs from the conventional single document/container approach and involves many signed items.

This would require more storage space and complicate the handling required by Bob. Notwithstanding the storage problem, the prospect of searching through the many items to find the desired combination of fragments to disclose would be daunting.

4.2 Using Content Extraction Signatures

Content Extraction Signatures can be verified for a subdocument which has been generated by blinding or removing portions of the original signed document, in accordance with the signer's policy for blinding the document content [21]. The communications and/or computational cost of CES is lower than that of the simple multiple signature solution using the standard digital signature described above.

The same general structure initially proposed for CES will be used. However, in this work we substantially extend the Content Extraction Access Structure (CEAS) encoding to enable the signer to specify a *richer extraction policy* for the document fragments.

Fragment Extraction Policy. In [21] we did not specify an encoding scheme for the CEAS. In this paper, we focus on the ability to select and extract particular fragments and their associations, or grouping, with any other fragments. Thus, we have a multidimensional view of the fragment. This presents a challenge: how to achieve this flexibility in the fragment extraction policy whilst constraining the size of the extraction signature. For a document containing n fragments there are 2^n subdocuments possible (although the number of useful subdocuments would be smaller) and 2^{2^n} permutations of the CEAS for the relationships of the n fragments with each other.

The CEAS provides a mechanism for the document signer to avoid the abuse of extracted content by specifying which fragments and groupings (via fragment associations) can be extracted. It is an encoding of the subsets of fragment groupings for which the document holder is 'allowed' to extract valid signatures. All associations are relative to a 'primary target' fragment, asymmetric and non-transitive. Association transitivity has not been included in this work and has been left for further work.

A fragment that is allowed to be extracted in its own right is considered to be a *primary* target. Only primary targets may be directly selected for extraction. If a fragment is not a primary target, then it is called a *secondary* target and may only be extracted through an association with a primary target. If a fragment has a mandatory association with a primary target, this means that the associated fragment *must* accompany the primary target fragment if it is extracted. A fragment which has an optional association with a primary target fragment *may* accompany the primary target fragment if it is extracted. A fragment cannot have a mandatory and optional association with the same fragment.

We will now describe fragment policy options and their use by the document owner. A fragment type and its extraction permissions can be identified as:

- a secondary target with no associations—it can never be extracted;
- a secondary target with mandatory associations—can only be extracted when accompanying a primary target fragment via a mandatory association;
- a secondary target with optional associations—it can only be extracted when accompanying a primary target fragment through an optional association;
- a primary target with no associations—it can be extracted by itself;
- a primary target with mandatory associations—if extracted it must be accompanied by its associated mandatory fragments;
- a primary target with optional associations—if extracted it may be accompanied by its associated optional fragments; or
- a primary target with mandatory associations from *all* other primary targets—a mandatory fragment which must accompany any primary fragment that is extracted.

CEAS Using Byte Lists. A simple approach to storing the signer's fragment extraction policy is to use lists for the fragment associations. We implement for each fragment a list for its mandatory associations and a list for its optional associations. A target's type is determined by which list its own number is located in: primary target if in the mandatory list, otherwise secondary target if in the optional list.

With a 32 bit fragment identifier, the size of the CEAS for a document containing 100 fragments with an average of, say, 20 associations per fragment would be 64kbits.

CEAS Using Bit Vectors. Bit vectors could be used as an alternative to using lists, where for a document with n fragments, we allocate a vector of n bits for each fragment. This can be seen as a $n \times n$ bit matrix, irrespective of the number of associations. As there are n bits available per fragment, we use:

- *the self-referent bit*—to specify if the fragment is a primary target or a secondary target; and
- *the non self-referent bits (or other bits)*—to specify the mandatory and optional fragment associations.

The type of association specified by the other bits depends on whether the fragment is a primary or secondary target. For primary targets the other bits define the mandatory associations, while for secondary targets they define the optional associations. Also, there are no optional associations between two primary fragments. This would be redundant, as you can simply extract the two primary fragments, or not, as required.

A simple CEAS for a document with six fragments is illustrated in Table 1. This simple example illustrates the encoding of the various fragment types as identified above. However, it is expected that an actual extraction policy would likely involve a good deal more associations. Following is an explanation of the fragment extraction policy for the document.

Table 1. Sample CEAS for a document with 6 fragments

Fragment no.	CEAS
1	0 0 0 0 0 0
2	0 0 0 0 0 0
3	0 0 0 0 1 0
4	0 1 0 1 0 1
5	0 0 0 0 1 1
6	0 0 0 0 0 1

Frag1 is a secondary target and can never be extracted as no other fragments are associated with it, ie. $CEAS_1[1] \lor \ldots \lor CEAS_n[1] = F$

Frag2 is a secondary target and can only be extracted through its mandatory association with frag4. If frag4 is extracted, then frag2 must accompany it.

Frag3 is a secondary target and can only be extracted via its optional association with frag5. If frag5 is extracted, frag3 may optionally accompany it.

Frag4 is a primary target with some mandatory fragment associations that must accompany it should it be extracted. If frag4 is extracted, then frag2 and frag6 must accompany it.

Frag5 is a primary target with mandatory and optional fragment associations. Should frag5 be extracted, then frag6 must accompany it, while frag3 may optionally accompany it.

Frag6 is a primary target with no associations that must accompany it should it be extracted. Frag6 can be extracted by itself.

Frag6 is also a mandatory fragment, which must always be extracted, as every primary target has a mandatory association with it, ie.

$b_1 \land b_2 \land \ldots b_n = T$

where $b_i = \neg CEAS_i[i] \lor CEAS_i[6]$ and i indexes the fragments.

As the bit matrix hints, the CEAS is in fact a labelled directed graph, the matrix in Table 1 corresponding to the connectivity matrix. The node labels indicate fragment identity, and edges represent associations. Primary targets are represented by nodes that are connected to themselves. Nodes corresponding to primary targets have edges directed to the nodes with which they have mandatory associations. Nodes corresponding to secondary targets have edges directed to nodes with which they have optional associations.

List-based representations are most efficient when the average number of associations (i.e. edges) per fragment (i.e. node) is low. The bit matrix will be the better encoding when the association density is high. Let f be the size of the fragment identifier in bits and $\bar{a}$ be the average number of associations per fragment. The size of the list encoding is $n\bar{a}f$ bits and the matrix encoding is n^2 bits. The matrix encoding will thus be the more efficient when $\bar{a} > n/f$. For the example in Section 4.2, the matrix representation would cost 10kbits.

Signing the Document. Signing the document using Content Extraction Signatures involves a two step process: (i) define the fragments, and (ii) specify the fragment extraction policy. The process of defining a fragment includes specifying the content itself as well as whether it is a primary or secondary target. Once the fragments have all been defined, the signer specifies the mandatory and optional fragment associations for each fragment. This information is included as part of the extraction signature. On completion of signing, the document and its extraction signature is forwarded to the document holder.

5   Conclusion

In an electronic society where the use of paper is more the exception than the norm, we have shown that the use of the current digital signature can erode privacy and increase bandwidth usage in multiparty interactions. We have introduced a new, more powerful, approach for encoding the signer's fragment extraction policy. This approach is tailored more for selective fragment grouping rather than selective fragment blinding, as was the emphasis in our earlier paper. This different perspective for the use of CES presents the concept of handling verifiable information selectively for paperless commerce in an online and a mobile environment. Content Extraction Signatures can be used for almost any multiparty interaction involving the selective disclosure of information.

In a digital world, which promises far richer functionality than the paper-based world, we seek more flexible applications of digital signatures. With this work we are striving for additional functionality, beyond that which a simple analogue of the humble and longstanding hand-written signature provides.

References

1. S. Baker. Don't worry be happy. Available online, June 1994. [Last accessed: July 27, 2002].
   URL: http://www.wired.com/wired/archive/2.06/nsa.clipper_pr.html
2. M. Bartel, J. Boyer, B. Fox, B. LaMacchia, and E. Simon. XML-signature syntax and processing. In D. Eastlake, J. Reagle, and D. Solo, editors, *W3C Recommendation*. Feb. 12 2002. [Last accessed: September 18, 2002].
   URL: http://www.w3.org/TR/2002/REC-xmldsig-core-20020212/
3. M. Bellare and G. Neven. Transitive signatures based on factoring and RSA. In Y. Zheng, editor, *Proceedings of The 8th International Conference on the Theory and Application of Cryptology and Information Security (ASIACRYPT 2002)*, volume 2501 of *Lecture Notes in Computer Science*, pages 397–414. Springer, December 2003.
4. T. Beth, M. Frisch, and G. Simmons, editors. *Public-Key Cryptography: State of the Art and Future Directions*, volume 578 of *Lecture Notes in Computer Science*. Springer, July 1992. E.I.S.S. Workshop Oberwolfach Final Report.
5. G. Blakley. Twenty years of cryptography in the open literature. In *Proceedings of 1999 IEEE Symposium on Security and Privacy*, pages 106–7. IEEE Computer Society, May 1999.
6. S. Brands. *Rethinking Public Key Infrastructures and Digital Certificates: Building in Privacy*. MIT Press, Cambridge, MA, 2000.

7. S. Brands. A technical overview of digital credentials. Available online, Feb. 20 2002. [Last accessed: February 18, 2003].
   URL: http://www.credentica.com/technology/overview.pdf

8. L. Bull, D. M. Squire, J. Newmarch, and Y. Zheng. Grouping verifiable content for selective disclosure using XML signatures. Technical Report, School of Computer Science and Software Engineering, Monash University, 900 Dandenong Road, Caulfield East, Victoria 3145 Australia, April 2003.

9. L. Bull, P. Stanski, and D. M. Squire. Content extraction signatures using XML digital signatures and custom transforms on-demand. In *Proceedings of The 12th International World Wide Web Conference (WWW2003)*, Budapest, Hungary, 20–24 May 2003. (to appear).

10. M. Crompton. The privacy act and the Australian federal privacy commissioner's functions. In *Proceedings of the tenth conference on computers, freedom and privacy*, pages 145–8. ACM Press, 2000.

11. P. T. Devanbu, M. Gertz, A. Kwong, C. Martel, G. Nuckolls, and S. G. Stubblebine. Flexible authentication of XML documents. In *ACM Conference on Computer and Communications Security*, pages 136–45, 2001.

12. W. Diffie and M. Hellman. New directions in cryptography. *IEEE Transactions on Information Theory*, IT-22(6):644–54, 1976.

13. R. Johnson, D. Molnar, D. Song, and D. Wagner. Homomorphic signature schemes. In *Proceedings of the RSA Security Conference Cryptographers Track*, volume 2271 of *Lecture Notes in Computer Science*, pages 244–62. Springer, February 2002.

14. S. Micali and R. L. Rivest. Transitive signature schemes. In B. Preneel, editor, *Proceedings of The Cryptographer's Track at the RSA Conference (CT-RSA 2002)*, volume 2271 of *Lecture Notes in Computer Science*, pages 236–243. Springer, December 2002.

15. Office of the Federal Privacy Commissioner. My privacy my choice - your new privacy rights. Available online. [Last accessed: July 31, 2002].
    URL: http://www.privacy.gov.au/privacy_rights/npr.html

16. Office of the Federal Privacy Commissioner. Privacy in Australia. Available online, October 2001. [Last accessed: July 12, 2002].
    URL: http://www.privacy.gov.au/publications/pia.html

17. Office of the Federal Privacy Commissioner. Announcement: Transurban privacy review completed. Available online, May 2002. [Last accessed: July 31, 2002].
    URL: http://www.privacy.gov.au/news/media/02_9.html

18. H. Orman. Data integrity for mildly active content. In *Proceedings of Third Annual International Workshop on Active Middleware Services*, pages 73–7. IEEE Computer Society, March 2002.

19. R. Rivest. Two signature schemes. Available online, October 2000. Slides from talk given at Cambridge University. [Last accessed: February 19, 2003].
    URL: http://theory.lcs.mit.edu/ rivest/publications.html

20. R. Rivest, A. Shamir, and L. Adleman. A method for obtaining digital signatures and public-key cryptosystems. *Communications of the ACM*, 21(2):120–8, 1978.

21. R. Steinfeld, L. Bull, and Y. Zheng. Content extraction signatures. In *Proceedings of The 4th International Conference on Information Security and Cryptology (ICISC 2001)*, volume 2288 of *Lecture Notes in Computer Science*, pages 285–304. Springer, December 2001.

Evaluation of Anonymity of Practical Anonymous Communication Networks

Shigeki Kitazawa[1], Masakazu Soshi[2], and Atsuko Miyaji[2]

[1] Mitsubishi Electric Corporation Information Technology R&D Center
5-1-1 Ofuna, Kamakura, Kanagawa, 247-8501 JAPAN
shigeki@iss.isl.melco.co.jp
[2] School of Information Science, Japan Advanced Institute of Science and Technology
1-1 Asahidai, Tatsunokuchi, Nomi, Ishikawa 923-1292, JAPAN
{soshi,miyaji}@jaist.ac.jp

Abstract. In the paper we shall evaluate various aspects of anonymity properties afforded by practical anonymous communication networks. For that purpose, first we propose two novel anonymity metrics for practical anonymous communication networks. Next we shall discuss whether or not deterministic protocols can provide anonymity efficiently in terms of computational complexity. Unfortunately, we can show that it is difficult to build efficient anonymous networks only by means of deterministic approaches. We also run simulation experiments and discuss the results.

1 Introduction

Anonymous communication networks are indispensable to protect privacy of users in open networks such as the Internet. Therefore they have wide application, e.g., electronic voting, and enormous research has been conducted on them [1,2,3,4,5,6,7,8]. The simplest way of establishing anonymous networks is given as follows. When Alice sends a message to Bob anonymously, she first dispatches it to a trusted *proxy* (or anonymizer) and then the proxy forwards the message to Bob. Consequently Bob cannot know who originally injected the message into the network and thus anonymous communication is achieved. This is essentially the same as what Anonymizer does [2]. In this paper, an entity which initiates anonymous communication is called an *initiator*, and an entity for which messages of the initiator are destined is called a *responder*. Furthermore, we use the terms 'proxy' and 'node' interchangeably in this paper.

Anonymous networks, however, could not be useful unless we can evaluate anonymity properties provided by them. Unfortunately, although we can analyze anonymity of some anonymous protocols in a rigorous manner [1,4,5], from a practical point of view, such protocols often degrade efficiency or incurs some cost. For example, [5] requires a lot of servers and [4] is quite ineffective.

On the other hand, with respect to practical anonymous communication networks [2,6,7], it is difficult to evaluate anonymity attained in the networks. This is mainly due to the lack of *anonymity metrics* for practical anonymous networks. However, since it is difficult to devise general anonymity metrics for practical

R. Safavi-Naini and J. Seberry (Eds.): ACISP 2003, LNCS 2727, pp. 13–26, 2003.
© Springer-Verlag Berlin Heidelberg 2003

anonymous networks such as Crowds [7], few attempts have been made so far to evaluate anonymity provided by anonymous networks [7,10,11]. Consequently it is difficult to discuss advantages and disadvantages of various practical anonymous networks proposed so far. Therefore in this paper we shall evaluate various aspects of anonymity properties afforded by practical anonymous communication networks.

For that purpose, first we propose two novel anonymity metrics for practical anonymous communication networks. Anonymity metrics proposed in this paper are based on the following observations:

1. Generally speaking, anonymous networks have several intermediate proxies en route from an initiator to a responder. In such a case, as the number of the intermediate proxies increases, i.e., the path that messages in anonymous communication follows becomes longer, anonymity provided by the anonymous protocols becomes higher [3,6,7,8]. On the other hand, communication costs, which can be represented by communication paths, cannot be infinitely high. Due to performance reasons, constraints by network architectures, and so on, the costs are under restriction to some degree.
2. As discussed above, the most primitive form of anonymous communication is via one or more proxies. Hence if an initiator can choose a trusted proxy to which she first dispatches her messages whenever she initiates anonymous communication with various responders, then such anonymous networks can afford desirable anonymity.

Later in this paper, from the viewpoints as discussed above, we formalize the anonymity metrics for practical anonymous networks.

Next we shall discuss whether or not deterministic anonymous networks can provide anonymity efficiently in terms of computational complexity. Unfortunately, we can show that we have little hope of efficient anonymous networks only by means of deterministic approaches.

As a result we need to invent practical anonymous networks by probabilistic or heuristic means. Hence we consider several possible (practical) anonymous protocols, run simulation experiments for them, and discuss the results. Simulation results show that we can enhance anonymity only by taking into consideration the neighborhood nodes. Especially, anonymous protocols considered in the experiments suggest some possible extensions to the famous Crowds anonymous system.

The rest of the paper is organized as follows. In Sect. 2 we propose novel anonymous metrics and discuss various aspects of them. In Sect. 3 we run simulation experiments to investigate heuristic approaches. Finally, we conclude this paper in Sect. 4.

2   Proposed Anonymity Metrics and Evaluation

In this section, we propose and discuss two anonymity metrics for practical anonymous networks.

As stated in Sect. 1, our proposed metrics are briefly summarized as follows:

1. anonymity properties with respect to communication paths, and
2. anonymity properties with respect to the possibility of selecting trusted proxies.

In this section, we first present the background of each anonymity metrics and then formalize the two metrics. Next we discuss whether or not deterministic protocols can provide anonymity efficiently in terms of computational complexity. Unfortunately, we can show that we have little hope of efficient anonymous networks only by means of deterministic approaches.

2.1   Anonymity Metric (1)

Background

1. Generally speaking, as the number of the intermediate proxies on anonymous communication path increases, anonymity provided by the anonymous network becomes higher.
2. On the other hand, communication costs cannot be infinitely high. Due to performance reasons, constraints by network architectures, and so on, the costs are under restriction to some length.

Now we model anonymity properties just discussed. First, in order to develop an abstract model for evaluating anonymity from the viewpoint of the item 1 above, assume that some value is assigned to each node in the network. Moreover, assume that anonymity afforded by anonymous communication can be estimated by adding the value of each node on the path. In other words, a larger value of the sum indicates a higher level of anonymity. Henceforth we suppose that we are given a function which assigns the value to each node and we call the function *privacy function*. The assigned values are called *privacy values*.

On the other hand, communication costs are usually constrained from the viewpoint of the item 2. To express such a situation, let us assume that some value, which is apart from the privacy value of the node, is assigned to each node. Then as the sum of the values on a path becomes larger, the cost of the path becomes larger. Henceforth we suppose that we are given a function which assigns the value to each node and we call the function *cost function*[1]. The assigned values are called *cost values*.

Given a network system, it would be straightforward to define cost functions. With respect to privacy functions, we can consider various ways of deriving them. For instance, we can take advantage of various available rating methods such as those used in reputation systems [12,13].

For another example, ISO defines the international standard for security system evaluation, i.e., ISO 15408 [14]. In the standard, 'Security Functional Requirements' prescribes several privacy conditions, that is,

---

[1] Alternatively, we can assign a cost value to a communication link. However, for simplicity, in this paper we model it as is given above.

FPR_AANO.1 Anonymity, FPR_PSE Pseudonymity, FPR_UNO.1 Unobservability, and FPR_UNL.1 Unlinkability. They are good candidates for the basis on which privacy functions are developed.

In summary, privacy and cost functions provide abstraction for anonymity properties as mentioned above. In the rest of this paper, we suppose that these two functions are given in advance. However, as shown later, it is shown that even if such functions are available, effective anonymous communication networks can hardly be built only by means of deterministic methods.

Formalization and Evaluation. In this section, we formalize the anonymity metric discussed in Sect. 2.1.

First, a network is supposed to be represented by a directed graph $G = (V, E)$. Here V is a set of nodes (proxies) and E is a set of directed edges. In general $E \subseteq V \times V$ holds.

Hereinafter in this paper we denote an initiator and a responder by s and d ($\in V$), respectively, unless explicitly stated. Moreover, as discussed in Sect. 2.1, we assume that privacy function $\mathcal{P} : V \to N$ and cost function $\mathcal{C} : V \to N$ are given. Here N is a set of non-negative integers.

Now we are ready to define the anonymity metric as follows:

Definition 1. *In a directed graph G, with respect to a path $v_1 \ (= s)$, v_2, ..., $v_n \ (= d)$, if $\sum_{i=1}^{n} \mathcal{P}(v_i) \geq p$ and $\sum_{i=1}^{n} \mathcal{C}(v_i) \leq c$, then we call the path (p, c)-anonymous.*

Next we shall discuss whether or not deterministic protocols can efficiently provide anonymity in terms of the metric. For that purpose, we define a decision problem corresponding to the anonymity metric as follows:

Problem 1. ((p, c)-anonymity)

[**INSTANCE**] A directed graph $G = (V, E)$, $s, d \in V$, and privacy function $\mathcal{P} : V \to N$ and cost function $\mathcal{C} : V \to N$.

[**QUESTION**] Is there a (p, c)-anonymous path from s to d?

Now we can prove Theorem 1.

Theorem 1. *(p, c)-anonymity is NP complete.*

Proof. Given G, privacy function $\mathcal{P}$, cost function $\mathcal{C}$, and a path $v_1 \ (= s)$, v_2, ..., $v_n \ (= d)$, it should be obvious that in polynomial time we can determine whether or not the path is (p, c)-anonymous. Thus we can construct a non-deterministic algorithm to solve (p, c)-anonymity in polynomial time and consequently (p, c)-anonymity is in NP.

Now we show that "PARTITION", which is known to be NP-complete, is polynomially reducible to (p, c)-anonymity. PARTITION is defined as follows [15]:

Problem 2. (PARTITION)

[**INSTANCE**] A finite set $A = \{a_1, a_2, \ldots, a_n\}$ and a size function $w : A \to N$.

[**QUESTION**] Is there a subset $A' \subseteq A$ such that $\sum_{a \in A'} w(a) = \sum_{a \in A-A'} w(a)$?

When we are given an arbitrary instance of PARTITION, we construct the following graph $G = (V, E)$, and define privacy function $\mathcal{P}$, cost function $\mathcal{C}$, and the privacy and cost values p and c respectively.

$$V = \{a_{1,0}, a_{2,0}, \ldots, a_{n,0}, a_{(n+1),0}\} \cup \left(\bigcup_{i=1}^{n} \{a_{i,1}, a_{i,2}\} \right)$$

$$E = \left(\bigcup_{i=1}^{n} \{(a_{i,0}, a_{i,1})\} \right) \cup \left(\bigcup_{i=1}^{n} \{(a_{i,0}, a_{i,2})\} \right) \cup \left(\bigcup_{i=1}^{n} \{(a_{i,1}, a_{(i+1),0})\} \right)$$
$$\cup \left(\bigcup_{i=1}^{n} \{(a_{i,2}, a_{(i+1),0})\} \right)$$

$$\begin{aligned}
\mathcal{P}(a_{i,1}) = \mathcal{C}(a_{i,1}) = w(a_i) & \quad (i = 1, \ldots, n) \\
\mathcal{P}(a_{i,2}) = \mathcal{C}(a_{i,2}) = 0 & \quad (i = 1, \ldots, n) \\
\mathcal{P}(a_{i,0}) = \mathcal{C}(a_{i,0}) = 0 & \quad (i = 1, \ldots, n+1) \\
p = c = \frac{1}{2} \sum_{i=1}^{n} w(a_i) &
\end{aligned}$$

where $a_{i,0} = s$ and $a_{(n+1),0} = d$.

To illustrate the above reduction, for example we depict in Fig. 1 the reduction where the instance of PARTITION is $A = \{a_1, a_2, a_3\}$, $w(a_1) = 3$, $w(a_2) = 5$, $w(a_3) = 2$.

Let us now suppose that PARTITION has a solution $A' = \{a_{i_1}, a_{i_2}, \ldots, a_{i_j}\}$. Without loss of generality, assume that $i_1 < i_2 \ldots < i_j$. In such a case we define a function δ as follows:

$$\delta(k) = \begin{cases} 1 & \text{if } k = i_l \text{ for some } l \\ 2 & \text{otherwise} \end{cases}$$

By using function δ, consider a path $P = a_{1,0}, a_{1,\delta(1)}, a_{2,0}, a_{2,\delta(2)}, \ldots, a_{n,\delta(n)}, a_{(n+1),0}$. We can readily see that P is (p, c)-anonymous in G. This is because $\sum_{a \in P} \mathcal{P}(a) = \sum_{a \in P} \mathcal{C}(a) = \frac{1}{2} \sum_{i=1}^{n} w(a_i) (= p = c)$. For example, in Fig. 1, the path corresponds to $a_{1,0}, a_{1,1}, a_{2,0}, a_{2,2}, a_{3,0}, a_{3,1}, a_{4,0}$.

Conversely, assume that graph G has a (p, c)-anonymous path. Let us further assume that $a_{i_1,1}, a_{i_2,1}, \ldots, a_{i_j,1}$ are all nodes such that the second subscript is one. It is now clear that $\{a_{i_1}, a_{i_2}, \ldots, a_{i_j}\}$ $(= A')$ is a solution of PARTITION. $\qquad \square$

It is well-known that in some NP-complete problems there exist algorithms to find solutions which are never far from optimal ones by more than some

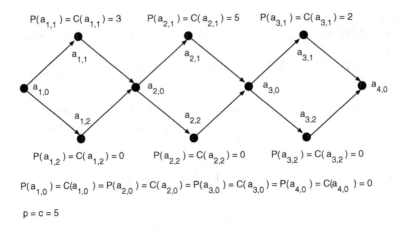

$P(a_{1,1}) = C(a_{1,1}) = 3$ $P(a_{2,1}) = C(a_{2,1}) = 5$ $P(a_{3,1}) = C(a_{3,1}) = 2$

$P(a_{1,2}) = C(a_{1,2}) = 0$ $P(a_{2,2}) = C(a_{2,2}) = 0$ $P(a_{3,2}) = C(a_{3,2}) = 0$

$P(a_{1,0}) = C(a_{1,0}) = P(a_{2,0}) = C(a_{2,0}) = P(a_{3,0}) = C(a_{3,0}) = P(a_{4,0}) = C(a_{4,0}) = 0$

$p = c = 5$

Fig. 1. Reduction from PARTITION

specific bounds. They are called *approximation algorithms* [15]. Unfortunately, (p, c)-anonymity is so difficult that there does not exist such an approximation algorithm. This will be shown below.

We denote by I an instance of (p, c)-anonymity with some fixed c. Furthermore, a solution by an optimization algorithm that maximizes $\sum_{i=1}^{n} \mathcal{P}(v_i)$ of I is denoted by $OPT(I)$ (such problems are called *optimization problems*). Obviously (p, c)-anonymity is no more difficult than a problem to find $OPT(I)$ and the latter problem is thus NP-hard.

Now we can prove Theorem 2.

Theorem 2. *If $P \neq NP$, then there does not exist a deterministic polynomial algorithm (approximation algorithm) A which can guarantee $|OPT(I) - A(I)| \leq p'$ for a fixed p' and all instances I of the optimization problems for (p, c)-anonymity.*

Proof. We prove this theorem by contradiction. Without loss of generality, assume that p' is a positive integer.

Suppose that there is an A in Theorem 2. In such a case, by using A, we can construct a deterministic polynomial algorithm B which can solve (p, c)-anonymity, which contradicts the assumption $P \neq NP$.

B is actually constructed as follows. First we denote by I' a new instance where privacy function $\mathcal{P}$ is replaced by $\mathcal{P}'$, which is defined as $\mathcal{P}'(v) = (p' + 1)\mathcal{P}(v)$.

Then candidate solutions for I' are clearly the same as those for I and the privacy value of a solution for I' is $(p' + 1)$ times the corresponding value for I. Now note that every solution for I' is a multiple of $p' + 1$ and that $|OPT(I') - A(I')| \leq p'$ holds. So it must hold that $|OPT(I') - A(I')| = 0$ and finally we can conclude that $|OPT(I) - B(I)| = |OPT(I') - A(I')| / (p' + 1) = 0$. However, the fact also means that we can find $OPT(I)$ in polynomial time. This is a contradiction. □

2.2   Anonymity Metric (2)

In this section we propose and discuss another anonymity metric.

Background. As discussed in Sect. 1, the most primitive form of anonymous communication is via one or more proxies. However, in practical anonymous communication networks, it is not always possible to select a trusted proxy when an initiator anonymously sends messages to a responder because of the network topology or the locations of the initiator or responder. Moreover, we cannot trust all proxies in the network.

Hence if an initiator can choose a trusted proxy to which she first dispatches her messages whenever she initiates anonymous communication with various responders, then such anonymous networks can afford a desired level of anonymity. Therefore we can consider anonymity metric whether or not we can arrange trusted proxies in the anonymous network in such a way as stated above.

Formalization and Evaluation. Here we formalize anonymity metric discussed in Sect. 2.2.

First, as in Sect. 1, we regard a network as a directed graph $G = (V, E)$. Moreover, let $s \in V$ and a set of nodes $\{d_1, d_2, ..., d_j\} \subseteq V$ be an initiator and a set of responders, respectively.

Now we can formalize anonymity metric discussed in Sect. 2.2 as follows:

Definition 2. *Suppose that we are given a directed graph $G = (V, E)$, $s \in V$, and a set of nodes $\{d_1, d_2, ..., d_j\} \subseteq V$. In such a case, if for a fixed positive value t ($\leq |V|$) there exist a subset $T \subseteq V$, $|T| \leq t$ such that we can always find some $n \in T$ on paths from s to every $d \in \{d_1, ..., d_j\}$, then we call G is t-locatable with respect to s and $\{d_1, ..., d_j\}$.*

Next we shall discuss whether or not deterministic protocols can efficiently provide anonymity in terms of the metric. For that purpose, we define a decision problem corresponding to the anonymity metric as follows:

Problem 3. (t-locatability)

[**INSTANCE**] A directed graph $G = (V, E)$, $s \in V$, a responder set $\{d_1, d_2, ..., d_j\} \subseteq V$, and a positive value t ($\leq |V|$).

[**QUESTION**] Is a graph G is t-locatable with respect to initiator s and a responder set $\{d_1, d_2, ..., d_j\}$?

Based on the above definitions, we can now prove Theorem 3.

Theorem 3. *t-locatability is NP-complete.*

Proof. t-locatability is in NP. This is because we can construct a nondeterministic polynomial algorithm which arbitrarily chooses a subset of V and determines whether or not the subset satisfies the condition of t-locatability.

Next we show that an NP-complete problem, "VERTEX COVER", is in polynomial time reduced to t-locatability. VERTEX COVER is defined below [15]:

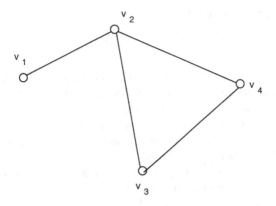

Fig. 2. An Instance of VERTEX COVER

Problem 4. (VERTEX COVER)

   [INSTANCE] Graph $G = (V, E)$, positive integer $K \leq |V|$.

   [QUESTION] Is there a vertex cover of size K or less for G, i.e., a subset $V' \subseteq V$ with $|V'| \leq K$ such that for each edge $\{u, v\} \in E$ at least one of u and v belongs to V'?

where G is an undirected graph.

   Given an instance of VERTEX COVER, we transform it into an instance of t-locatability, which is defined as follows:

- Graph $G'' = (V'', E'')$, where $V'' = \{s\} \cup V \cup \{v_1 v_2 \mid (v_1, v_2) \in E\}$ and $E'' = \{(s, v) \mid v \in V\} \cup \{(v_1, v_1 v_2), (v_2, v_1 v_2) \mid (v_1, v_2) \in E\}$.
- initiator $= s$,
- responder set $= \{v_1 v_2 \mid (v_1, v_2) \in E\}$
- $t = K$

Note that in the above reduction, $v_1 v_2$ $((v_1, v_2) \in E)$ represents a single node in G''.

To demonstrate an example of the reduction, we pay attention to an instance of VERTEX COVER as shown in Fig. 2. The instance is reduced to the instance of t-locatability depicted in Fig. 3.

   Below we show that the reduction given above is actually polynomial time reduction from VERTEX COVER to t-locatability.

   First let us suppose that VERTEX COVER has a solution $V' = \{v_{i_1}, v_{i_2}, ..., v_{i_j}\}$ $(j \leq K)$. In such a case $T = V'$ $(\subseteq V'')$ is a solution for the corresponding instance of t-locatability. The reason is as follows. Let $R = \{v_1 v_2 \mid (v_1, v_2) \in E\}$ be a responder set of G''. Then a path from s to a responder $v_1 v_2 \in R$ is either $s \to v_1 \to v_1 v_2$ or $s \to v_2 \to v_1 v_2$. Keeping in mind that $(v_1, v_2) \in E$ and V' is a solution of VERTEX COVER, we can see that either $v_1 \in V'$ $(= T)$ or $v_2 \in V'$ $(= T)$ holds. Consequently all we have to do is to place a proxy on v_1 $(\in V'')$ or v_2 $(\in V'')$, respectively in the former case or the latter.

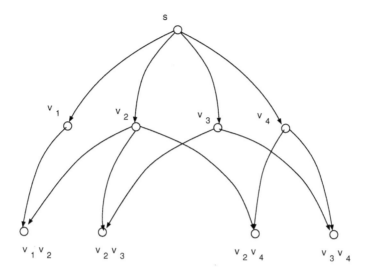

Fig. 3. Reduction from VERTEX COVER

Conversely, if an instance of t-locatability given above has a solution $T = \{v_{i_1}, v_{i_2}, ..., v_{i_j}\}$, then we can conclude that $V' = T$ in a similar manner.

At this stage it should be clear that the above reduction can be done in polynomial time.   □

Now we consider an approximation algorithm to the optimization problem for t-locatability. In a similar way as in the case of (p, c)-anonymity, given an instance I of the optimization problem for t-locatability, we denote by $OPT(I)$ a solution found by an optimization algorithm of the problem that minimizes t. Then we can show that it is difficult to even find a solution approximate to the optimal one.

Theorem 4. *If $P \neq NP$, then no polynomial time approximation algorithm A for t-locatability can guarantee $|OPT(I) - A(I)| \leq t'$ for a fixed constant t'.*

Proof. We can show this theorem again by contradiction as Theorem 2. Without loss of generality, we assume that t' is a positive integer.

Suppose that A is actually such an approximate algorithm in Theorem 4. Then by using A we can construct a deterministic polynomial time algorithm B which can solve t-locatability.

B is constructed as follows. First we consider a new instance I' of t-locatability, where graph G is replaced by a new graph $G' = (V', E')$. G' has the same s as I and consists of $(t' + 1)$ graphs, each of which is isomorphic to G.

More precisely, G' is defined as follows:

$$V' = \{s\} \cup \{v[i] \mid v \in V, 1 \le i \le t' + 1\}$$
$$\cup \{v_1[i]v_2[i] \mid v_1v_2 \in V, 1 \le i \le t' + 1\}$$
$$E' = \{(s, v[i]) \mid v \in V, 1 \le i \le t' + 1\}$$
$$\cup \{(v_1[i], v_1[i]v_2[i]) \mid v_1v_2 \in V, 1 \le i \le t' + 1\}$$
$$\cup \{(v_2[i], v_1[i]v_2[i]) \mid v_1v_2 \in V, 1 \le i \le t' + 1\}$$

Then the corresponding nodes in G to candidate solutions for I' are clearly the candidate solutions for I and the number of proxies of a solution for I' is $(t' + 1)$ times the corresponding value for I. Now note that every solution for I' is a multiple of $t' + 1$ and that $|OPT(I') - A(I')| \le t'$ holds. So it must hold that $|OPT(I') - A(I')| = 0$ and finally we can conclude that $|OPT(I) - B(I)| = |OPT(I') - A(I')| / (t' + 1) = 0$. However, the fact also means that we can find $OPT(I)$ in polynomial time. Contradiction.   □

2.3 Discussion

So far we have proposed and thoroughly discussed two new anonymity metrics for practical anonymous networks ((p, c)-anonymity, t-locatability). It is also possible to develop other anonymity metrics. In this section we take into consideration some anonymity metrics other than (p, c)-anonymity and t-locatability.

For example, as mentioned before, it is the most intuitive to adopt anonymity metric which considers anonymity properties where the level of anonymity becomes higher as the path which anonymous communication follows becomes longer. Generally speaking, this can be formalized by a decision problem "LONGEST PATH" [15].

Problem 5. (LONGEST PATH)

[INSTANCE] Graph $G = (V, E)$, length $l(e) \in Z^+$ for each $e \in E$, positive integer K, specified vertices $s, t \in V$.

[QUESTION] Is there a simple path in G from s to t of length K or more, i.e., whose edge lengths sum to at least K?

LONGEST PATH is also known to be NP-complete [15].

Let us consider another anonymity metric. When an initiator sends many messages to a responder anonymously, as the number of paths the messages follow becomes larger, it becomes more difficult for attackers to gather information about the initiator and the responder and thus more anonymity would be provided.

Anonymity metric for the case just mentioned can be formalized by (bounded) disjoint paths [15]. Bounded disjoint paths are a set of paths whose lengths are limited by some bound and no pair of which have a node in common. More formally, the problem is defined as follows.

Problem 6. (MAXIMUM LENGTH-BOUNDED DISJOINT PATHS)

[**INSTANCE**] Graph $G = (V, E)$, specified vertices s and t, positive integers $J, K \leq |V|$.

[**QUESTION**] Does G contain J or more mutually vertex disjoint paths from s to t, none involving more than K edges?

MAXIMUM LENGTH-BOUNDED DISJOINT PATHS is NP-complete [15].

We also considered other anonymity metrics, which are omitted from this paper due to the lack of space, most of which are in NP-complete. Needless to say, it is strongly believed that it is almost impossible to solve NP-complete problems efficiently (i.e., in polynomial time). This implies that NP $\neq$ P.

Therefore based on the discussion so far, generally speaking, it is difficult to establish effective practical anonymous networks only by means of deterministic approaches. Hence practical anonymous networks should be built with probabilistic or heuristic approaches.

3   Simulation Experiments

Based on the previous section, we consider several practical anonymous protocols and run the simulation experiments for them in this section. As a result of the experiments, we can show that heuristic approaches for anonymous networks work fine in terms of our anonymity metrics.

3.1   Descriptions of Simulations

In this section we discuss the background for our simulation experiments.

In order to conduct network simulation, first we have to generate network topologies which conform to the existing networks. In our simulation experiments, we have used Inet topology generator developed in Michigan University [16].

Next we focus our attention on privacy and cost functions. Although we can suppose various privacy and cost functions, in the simulation we define the functions according to the following policies:

N1 Privacy and cost values are generated at random.

N2 Larger cost and smaller privacy values are assigned to articulation nodes[2]. Intuitively speaking, articulation nodes are the points where various paths join and so the attacks to such nodes can pose a serious threat to anonymity properties. In other words, N2 is one example scenario in favor of attackers. In our simulation, we assign every articulation node and its adjacent node (i.e., connected through an edge) to more than 0.8 times the maximum cost value with probability 0.8. Furthermore, with probability 0.8, we assign every articulation node and its adjacent node to less than 0.2 times the maximum privacy value.

---

[2] Articulation nodes are what increase the number of connected components of the graph if they are removed [17].

Table 1. Simulation results (N1)

	P1+N1	P2+N1	P3+N1	P4+N1	P5+N1
length	5.68	5.55	5.86	3.93	3.86
cost	2968.53	2390.54	3112.20	1790.56	2174.50
privacy	3119.67	2973.76	3818.19	2259.76	2232.12

Table 2. Simulation results (N2)

	P1+N2	P2+N2	P3+N2	P4+N2	P5+N2
length	5.51	5.71	5.59	3.77	3.88
cost	5392.66	4893.18	5132.26	3670.01	4019.74
privacy	1125.10	1512.52	1751.69	1039.15	843.36

Furthermore, in our simulation we implement the following anonymous communication protocols.

P1 Crowds protocol [7]
P2 Crowds protocol with a strategy to choose a node with the smallest cost value when forwarding messages.
P3 Crowds protocol with a strategy to choose a node with the largest anonymity value when forwarding messages.
P4 protocol to choose a path with the smallest sum of the cost values of the nodes on the path.
P5 shortest path (just for comparison)

3.2   Evaluation

As stated in Sect. 3.1, there are two ways of network conditions (N1 and N2) and five ways of protocols (P1, P2, P3, P4, and P5). Thus we combinedly have ten ways of simulation experiments. Henceforth we call each of them P1+N1, P1+N2, P2+N1, P2+N2, P3+N1, P3+N2, P4+N1, P4+N2, P5+N1, and P5+N2, respectively.

The network topology used in our simulation was generated by Inet and the number of the nodes is 3037. Privacy and cost values are integers from 0 to 1000. The forwarding probability of Crowds is 2/3. Finally, initiators and responders were chosen randomly and each experiment was run 1000 times. We show the averages of the simulation experiments in Table 1 and 2.

In the following evaluation, we regard P1+N1, i.e., Crowds protocol on a network with random privacy and cost values, as the base for comparison.

First consider the case in Fig. 1. In comparison of P2+N1 with P1+N1, since P2 selects a node with the smallest cost value, the average of the value decreases by 19.5%. At the same time, the average privacy value also decreases by 4.7%. However, the rate of decrease of the cost value is greater than that of the privacy and consequently it shows the effectiveness of P2.

Similarly, in comparison of P3+N1 with P1+N1, since P3 selects a node with the largest privacy value, the average of the value increases by 22.4%. On the other hand, the average cost value also increases, but only by 4.8%. Hence we can see that P3 is also a promising heuristic.

With respect to P4+N1, since P4 selects a path with the smallest sum of the cost values of the nodes on the path, the rate of decrease of cost values is the largest (39.7% decrease in comparison with P1+N1). However, the rate of decrease of the privacy values is also large (27.6% decrease in comparison with P1+N1). This is partly because paths with smaller cost values are often shorter and hence privacy values also become smaller.

This consideration is supported by the comparison of P5+N1 with P1+N1. That is, generally speaking, as a path becomes shorter, the sums of privacy and cost values on the path also become smaller. Consequently it is not obvious whether or not P4 and P5 are useful.

In the case in Table 2, we can evaluate the experiments in a similar way as in Table 1. However, in Table 2, we can immediately see that cost and privacy ratios of P2+N2, P3+N2 and P4+N2 with respect to P1+N2 are better than those of P2+N1, P3+N1 and P4+N1 with respect to P1+N1, respectively. This is because N2 is a scenario in favor of attackers and we can obtain greater effects from anonymous protocols which try to enhance anonymity. On the other hand, it is not clear whether or not P5+N2 is more effective than P5+N1.

Note that P1 (Crowds), P2, and P3 do not need information about a whole network, but only about the neighborhood nodes. In other words, from the simulation experiments, we can see that if we monitor only the neighbors and assign appropriate privacy and cost values to the nodes, then we can get significant effects. In particular, since Crowds does not take into consideration such cases, if we slightly modify it as P2 or P3, then we can get more effective version of Crowds anonymous communication protocols.

4   Conclusion

Anonymous communication networks are indispensable to protect users' privacy in open networks such as the Internet. In the paper we have evaluated various aspects of anonymity properties afforded by practical anonymous communication networks.

In this paper we proposed two novel anonymity metrics for practical anonymous communication networks. Furthermore we discussed whether or not deterministic protocols can provide anonymity efficiently in terms of computational complexity. Unfortunately, we can show that we have little hope of efficient anonymous networks only by means of deterministic approaches.

Finally we run simulation experiments and discussed the results. Simulation results show that we can enhance anonymity only by taking into consideration the neighborhood nodes. Especially, anonymous protocols considered in the experiments suggest some possible extensions to the famous Crowds anonymous system.

References

1. Abe, M.: Universally verifiable Mix-net with verification work independent of the number of Mix-servers. IEICE Trans. Fundamentals **E83-A** (2000) 1431–1440
2. Anonymizer: http://www.anonymizer.com/
3. Chaum, D.: Untraceable electronic mail, return addresses, and digital pseudonyms. CACM **24** (1981) 84–88
4. Chaum, D.: The dining cryptographers problem: Unconditional sender and recipient untraceability. Journal of Cryptography **1** (1988) 65–75
5. Desmedt, Y., Kurosawa, K.: How to break a practical MIX and design a new one. EUROCRYPT 2000. Vol. 1807 of LNCS, Springer-Verlag (2000) 557–572
6. Pfitzmann, A.: A switched/broadcast ISDN to decrease user observability. Proc. of 1984 International Zurich Seminar on Digital Communications, Applications of Coding, Channel Coding and Secrecy Coding. (1984) 183–190
7. Reiter, M.K., Rubin, A.D.: Crowds: anonymity for web transactions. ACM Trans. Information and System Security **1** (1998) 66–92
8. Syverson, P.F., Goldschlag, D.M., Reed, M.G.: Anonymous connections and Onion routing. IEEE Symposium on Security and Privacy. (1997) 44–54
9. Mitomo, M., Kurosawa, K.: Attack for flash MIX. ASIACRYPT 2000. Vol. 1976 of LNCS, Springer-Verlag (2000) 192–204
10. Syverson, P.F., Tsudik, G., Reed, M.G., Landwehr, C.E.: Towards an analysis of onion routing security. Workshop on Design Issues in Anonymity and Unobservability. (2000)
11. Wright, M., Adler, M., Levine, B.N., Shields, C.: An analysis of the degradation of anonymous protocols. Network and Distributed System Security Symposium. (2002)
12. Dingledine, R., Freedman, M.J., Hopwood, D., Molnar, D.: A reputation system to increase MIX-net reliability. Information Hiding: 4th International Workshop, IHW 2001. Volume 2137 of LNCS. (2001) 126–140
13. Dingledine, R., Syverson, P.: Reliable MIX cascade networks through reputation. Sixth International Financial Cryptography Conference (FC 2002). (2002)
14. International Organization of Standardization (ISO): International standard ISO/IEC 15408 (1999) Technically identical to Common Criteria version 2.1.
15. Garey, M.R., Johnson, D.S.: Computers and Intractability – A Guide to the Theory of NP-completeness. W. H. Freeman and Co. (1979)
16. Winick, J., Jamin, S.: Inet-3.0: Internet topology generator. Technical Report CSE-TR-456-02, University of Michigan (2002)
17. Harary, F.: Graph Theory. Perseus Publishing (1995)

An Anonymous Credential System and a Privacy-Aware PKI

Pino Persiano* and Ivan Visconti *

Dipartimento di Informatica ed Applicazioni
Università di Salerno
Via S. Allende, 84081 Baronissi (SA), Italy
{giuper, visconti}@dia.unisa.it

Abstract. In this paper we present a non-transferable anonymous credential system that is based on the concept of a chameleon certificate. A chameleon certificate is a special certificate that enjoys two interesting properties. Firstly, the owner can choose which attributes of the certificate to disclose. Moreover, a chameleon certificate is multi-show in the sense that several uses of the same chameleon certificate by the same user cannot be linked together.

We adopt the framework of Brands [2] and our construction improves the results of Camenisch *et al.* [5] and Verheul [16] since it allows the owner of a certificate to prove general statements on the attributes encoded in the certificate and our certificates enjoy the multi-show property.

1 Introduction

The protection of private information in access-control based applications is a challenge that can be postponed no longer.

In this work we present new cryptographic techniques to allow the deployment of an anonymous credential system and a privacy-aware PKI that protect both the privacy of the users and the security of the services. The protection of user privacy is based on the disclosure of only the private information strictly necessary for a given transaction. For example, a user that has a credential specifying the year of birth can prove that he was not born in 1974 without disclosing his year of birth. This is achieved by using techniques similar to those of [2] and the result cannot be derived from those of [5,16] in which one of the following cases happens: 1) the year of the birth must be disclosed; 2) the possession of an ad-hoc credential that states that the year of the birth is different from 1974 is required. In the first case, more information than needed is released since the exact year of the birth is not required. In the second case the user must possess a credential that exactly fits the requirement of the access control policy of the service provider. This last case is not reasonable since an access control policy of a service provider can be short-lived while the process of obtaining a credential

---

* Supported by a grant from the Università di Salerno and by Young Researchers grants from the CNR.

R. Safavi-Naini and J. Seberry (Eds.): ACISP 2003, LNCS 2727, pp. 27–38, 2003.
© Springer-Verlag Berlin Heidelberg 2003

from a trusted organization requires longer (*e.g.*, when some form of personal identification is required). Moreover, if a user has a credential for each possible access-control based service then the number of credentials he has to deal with becomes impractical.

2   Contributions and Related Work

Related Work. Our work follows the lead of Brands [2] that constructed a certificate system in which a user has control over what is known about the attributes of his certificate. Moreover, within the settings of Brands, it is possible for a user to give interactive or non-interactive proofs that the attributes encoded in a certificate enjoy a given property as encoded by a linear Boolean formula. The main drawback of Brands' certificates is that they are *one-show* in the sense that using the same certificate twice makes the two transactions linkable even though the attributes are still hidden. In the rest of the paper we call *multi-show* a certificate that can be used several times and still guarantees unlinkability. We will base our construction on some techniques proposed in [2] in order to achieve proofs of possession of attributes that satisfy a linear Boolean formula and we extend such schemes in order to achieve the *multi-show* property.

Recently, Verheul [16] proposed a new solution for multi-show digital certificates. In his model, that supports a multi-show property similar to the one that we adopt in this paper, the owner of a certificate can construct by himself another certificate with the same attributes of the original one and such that they are unlinkable. The result is based on the assumption that for some groups the Decisional version of the Diffie-Hellman (DDH) problem is easy while its Computational version (CDH) is hard and on an additional *ad-hoc* assumption. However, Verheul's certificates do not allow the user to prove in a zero-knowledge fashion properties of the attributes of his certificate as in the case of Brands' certificates (see our discussion at the end of Section 1).

Another approach to prove possession of attributes has been addressed as *Anonymous Credentials*. In this approach the user is the owner of some credentials released by trusted organizations. In order to achieve anonymity, credentials should change their aspect so that different proofs of possession are unlinkable. The first implementation of anonymous credentials is presented in [10] where an interaction with a third party is always necessary in order to achieve unlinkability. Lysyanskaya *et al.* [14] proposed a general credential system that, however, is impractical being based on general zero-knowledge proofs. Several papers have then improved on these pioneering work, most notably the work of Camenisch and Lysyanskaya [5] that proposed a practical anonymous credential system that is based on the strong RSA assumption and the DDH assumption. In the system of [5] it is possible to unlinkably prove possession of a credential supporting the multi-show property and the entities that release credentials can independently choose their cryptographic keys. However the approach is subject to the lending problem and the proposed solution based on a new primitive called *circular encryption* affects intensively the performances and it is not possible to prove possession of attributes that satisfy a given linear Boolean formula.

Contributions of the paper. In this paper we present a system based on the concept of a *chameleon certificate*. A chameleon certificate is a digital certificate similar to the one proposed by Brands in [2] and thus conceptually similar to an X509 v.3 [13] digital certificate. Chameleon certificates enjoy the following two important properties: 1) the owner of a certificate has complete control on the amount of information about its attributes that is released; 2) different uses of the same certificate are unlinkable. The second property is not enjoyed by Brands' certificates, while the first property is not enjoyed by the anonymous credential system of [5] and by the credential certificate system of [16].

Being conceptually similar to X509 v.3 certificates, chameleon certificates can be easily adapted to work in a PKIX-like scenario even though the protocols to be implemented are obviously different. Moreover, we show that it is possible to prove properties of credentials encoded in a chameleon certificate provided that they could be expressed as a linear Boolean formula. Such proof systems were first considered (and shown to exist) in the framework of a general work on zero-knowledge proof systems for Boolean formula by [11].

We will use both the terms of credential and attribute in order to refer to a private information of a user, since the term credential is typically used in credential systems while the term attribute is typically used in a PKI context.

3   Background and Assumptions

In this section we summarize the main cryptographic techniques and assumptions that we use in our constructions. For details see [15].

RSA malleability. The RSA signature scheme is multiplicative:

$$m_1^d \pmod{n} \cdot m_2^d \pmod{n} \equiv (m_1 \cdot m_2)^d \pmod{n}.$$

A consequence of this property is that having the signatures of two different messages it is possible to compute the signature of their product without using the private key. Moreover having just one signature it is possible by using exponentiations to compute the signatures of other related messages. The malleability property is sometimes seen as a drawback for security properties but it has been heavily used (*e.g.*, for privacy [9]).

Assumptions. We give now some assumptions that will be used in our constructions.

Definition 1. *The* discrete logarithm problem (DL problem) *is the following: let q be a prime and Z_q^* be the finite cyclic group of the first $q-1$ positive integers. Let g be a generator of Z_q^*, and let $y \in Z_q^*$. Find the unique integer x, such that $0 \leq x \leq q-1$ and $y = g^x \bmod q$.*

Definition 2. *The* discrete logarithm representation problem (DLREP problem) *is the following: let q be a prime and Z_q^* be the finite cyclic group of the first $q - 1$ positive integers. Let $g_0, g_1, \cdots, g_l \neq 1$ be elements of Z_q^* and let $y \in Z_q^*$. Find a tuple $(x_0, x_1, \ldots, x_l)$ called $(q, g_0, g_1, \cdots, g_l)$-representation of $y \in Z_q^*$ such that $y = g_0^{x_0} g_1^{x_1} \cdots g_l^{x_l} \bmod q$.*

The following proposition states that if the DL problem is hard then the DLREP problem is hard.

Proposition 1. *Given an instance of the DL problem it is possible to construct an instance of the DLREP problem such that if there is an efficient algorithm A that solves with non-negligible probability the DLREP instance then there is another efficient algorithm A' that solves with non-negligible probability the DL instance.*

The following proposition states that the discrete logarithm problem and the discrete logarithm representation problem are hard also with respect to Z_n^* with n composite. For details see [15].

Proposition 2. *Let n be a composite integer. If the discrete logarithm problem in Z_n^* can be solved in polynomial time, then n can be factored in expected polynomial time.*

In [8] Camenisch and Stadler base the security of a group signature scheme on the assumption that, on input an integer $n = pq$ where p and q are primes of the same length, an integer e such that $(e, \phi(n)) = 1$ and $a \in Z_n^*$, it is hard to find in probabilistic polynomial time a pair (v, x) such that $v^e = a^x + 1 \bmod n$. Moreover, in [8] it is assumed that a pair (v, x) is hard to find even if several other pairs are known. This property is used in order to prove the unforgeability with respect to coalitions of users. Subsequently, in [1] the assumption described above has been shown to be fallacious and in [4] a new assumption, sufficient to prove correctness of a modified group signature scheme, is introduced: given an integer $n = pq$ where p and q are primes of the same length, an integer e such that $(e, \phi(n)) = 1$ and two integers $a, c \in Z_n^*$, it is hard to find in probabilistic polynomial time a pair (v, x) such that $v^e = a^x + c \bmod n$.

In this paper we shall use a generalization of the (modified) Camenisch-Stadler assumption to prove some security properties of our scheme.

We introduce now two assumptions that will be used in order to prove unlinkability and unforgeability properties of our construction. The first assumption states that it is not possible for an efficient algorithm on input $g_1, g_2 \in_R Z_n^*$, where $n = pq$ and p, q are primes, to establish if $g_1 \in \langle g_2 \rangle$ (we denote by $\langle g \rangle$ the group generated by g) even if the factorization of n is known.

More precisely, we define *success probability* $\mathrm{Succ}_1^{A_1}(k)$ of a probabilistic algorithm A_1 as the following probability:

$$\mathrm{Succ}_1^{A_1}(k) = Pr((n, p, q, g_1, g_2) \leftarrow \mathrm{GenPrimes}(1^k);$$
$$b \in \{0, 1\} \leftarrow A_1(n, p, q, g_1, g_2) : b = 0 \text{ if } g_2 \in \langle g_1 \rangle \text{ or } b = 1 \text{ if } g_2 \notin \langle g_1 \rangle)$$

where GenPrimes is an algorithm that, on input 1^k, outputs two randomly chosen primes p, q of length k, their product n and two randomly chosen elements $g_1, g_2 \in Z_n^*$.

Assumption 1 *For all efficient algorithms A_1, for all constants c and for all sufficiently large k*

$$\mathrm{Succ}_1^{A_1}(k) \leq 1/2 + k^{-c}.$$

For our second assumption, we consider a probabilistic polynomial-time algorithm A_2 that receives as input

1. an integer n such that $n = pq$ where p and q are primes of length k;
2. $e \in Z_n^*$ such that $(e, \phi(n)) = 1$;
3. $g, g_0, g_1, \ldots, g_l \in Z_n^*$;
4. s such that $g = s^e \bmod n$.

and has access to an oracle $\mathcal{O}$ that on input $(x_0, \ldots, x_{l-2})$ outputs $(v, x_0, x_1, \ldots, x_l)$ such that x_{l-1} and x_l are uniformly distributed over Z_n^* and $v^e = g_0^{x_0} g_1^{x_1} \cdots g_{l-1}^{x_{l-1}} + g_l^{x_l} \bmod n$.

We denote by $\mathrm{Succ}_2^{A_2}(k)$ the probability that algorithm A_2, on input randomly chosen $(n, e, g, g_0, \cdots, g_l, s)$ with n product of two primes of length k and having access to $\mathcal{O}$ outputs a tuple $(v, x, y, x_0, x_1, \ldots, x_l)$ such that $v^e = g^x g_0^{x_0} g_1^{x_1} \cdots g_{l-1}^{x_{l-1}} + g_l^{x_l} g^y \bmod n$ and $(x_0, x_1, \ldots, x_l)$ is not part of one of the oracle's replies.

Assumption 2 *For all efficient algorithms A_2, for all constants c and for all sufficiently large k*

$$\mathrm{Succ}_2^{A_2}(k) \leq k^{-c}.$$

We observe that it is very easy, given a tuple $(v, x_0, x_1, \ldots, x_l)$, to output a new tuple $(v', x, x, x_0, x_1, \ldots, x_l)$. Indeed we will use exactly this property in order to achieve unlinkability. However, we stress that in order to break our assumption it is necessary to produce a new tuple in which the sequence $x_0, x_1, \ldots, x_l$ is different from that of each original tuple. We notice that our non-standard intractability assumption is similar to the Camenisch-Stadler one. We are neither aware of any corroboration that it should be hard, nor can we break it. The following three obvious attacks do not seem to work:

1. if the adversary first chooses $x, x_0, x_1, \ldots, x_l$, then, to compute the value v, the adversary has to break the RSA assumption;
2. if the adversary randomly chooses a pair (v, z) such that $z = v^e \pmod{n}$ then he has to compute two representations with respect to the given bases whose sum is z, and this seems to be an intractable problem;
3. if the adversary uses the malleability of RSA multiplying elements for which he knows the representations and the RSA signatures (as we stated in the assumption), he does not obtain a new valid tuple $(v, x, y, x_0, \ldots, x_l)$.

Brands' results. In [2], a mechanism to prove knowledge of a $(n, g_0, g_1, \ldots, g_m)$-representation of an integer y satisfying a given linear Boolean formula is presented. This is achieved by showing that the knowledge of a $(n, g_0, g_1, \ldots, g_m)$-representation can be used to prove the knowledge of another specific representation if and only if the values satisfy a given linear Boolean formula. In particular Brands' interactive proofs of knowledge are honest verifier zero-knowledge while the non-interactive proofs of knowledge are secure in the random oracle model. We will use these results to guarantee the privacy property of our construction.

Proofs over committed values. In [7] the authors present a proof system for proving that the sum of two committed integers is equal to a third committed integer modulo a fourth committed integer is presented. For details see Section 3 of [7]. We will use this result to guarantee the unlinkability property of our construction.

4   Chameleon Certificates

Our model consists of three types of players:

1. The *organizations*, that release *master chameleon certificates* to users.
2. The *users*, each with has a set of attributes and a private key. A user receives a master chameleon certificate encoding his attributes from an organization that he will then use to construct unlinkable *slave* chameleon certificates. Slave chameleon certificates are then used to prove possession of credentials.
3. The *service providers*, that use access control policies in order to protect their resources. Each service provider discriminates between legitimate users of the service and users that do not have the rights to access the service. We assume that the access control policy for each resource of each service provider is represented by a formula Φ over the credentials of the users.

Next, we summarize the procedures executed by the parties in the system for which we are going to present an implementation in the next section.

1. **System set-up**: this step is performed only once by each organization in order to establish publicly verifiable parameters that will be used by the next procedures. At the end of this phase, the organization is ready to release chameleon certificates.
2. **User enrollment**: this step is performed by the user and by an organization. The user asks for a *master* chameleon certificate corresponding to a set of credentials. The organization verifies the credentials and then releases the master chameleon certificate.
3. **Refreshing**: this step is performed by a user that holds a master chameleon certificates in order to obtain a *slave* chameleon certificate that contains the same attributes and public key of the master chameleon certificate but such that the slave and the master chameleon certificates cannot be linked together.

4. **Showing possession of credentials**: this step is performed by a user that interacts with a service provider in order to gain access to a service restricted to legitimate users.

We wish to guarantee the following properties:

1. **Unforgeability**: it is computationally infeasible for a coalition of users to generate a new master chameleon certificate without the help of an organization or to generate a slave (or a master) chameleon certificate whose encoded credentials are different from one of the master chameleon certificates received from an organization.
2. **Unlinkability**: a slave chameleon certificate cannot be linked to the master chameleon certificate or to other slave chameleon certificates.
3. **Privacy**: it is infeasible for a service provider to compute the value of any attribute hidden by a master or a slave chameleon certificate or to gain more information with respect to the one disclosed by the user by proving the satisfaction of a linear Boolean formula.
4. **Malleability**: the refreshing procedure can be executed by the client without interacting with any organization.
5. **Usability**: a slave chameleon certificate can be verified as authentic by the service provider.
6. **Lending**: it is inconvenient for a legitimate user to share its credentials with other users.

Let us discuss the properties listed above. When a user receives the master chameleon certificate from an organization he can construct other certificates (*i.e.*, slave chameleon certificates) such that they are unlinkable (property 2) to the first one (*i.e.*, there is privacy with respect to the organization) and unlinkable among themselves (*i.e.*, there is privacy with respect to a coalition of organizations and service providers that share the issued/received chameleon certificates). In particular the construction of usable slave chameleon certificates can be performed without interacting with other parties (properties 4 and 5), thus it can be distributed over time as the user prefers (*i.e.*, this implies the multi-show property). A master chameleon certificate and its corresponding slave chameleon certificates do not expose directly information stored in them, selective disclosure of user information and satisfaction of linear Boolean formulas is possible, while the construction of a user profile by an organization or a coalition of organizations is hard to perform (properties 2 and 3). A coalition of users cannot construct a new valid chameleon certificate whose credentials are different from the ones encoded in at least one of the released master chameleon certificates (property 1). Of course a user can always give all his private information to another one lending the secrets that correspond to his certificate, so we require that the lending of private credential is inconvenient (property 6).

5   A Construction for Chameleon Certificates

System set-up. For the sake of ease of exposition, we now present our system only for the case in which a chameleon certificate carries two credentials. We stress that modifying the system in order to support more than two credentials is straightforward.

Organization O performs the following steps:

1. randomly picks a pair $(P_O = (n,e), S_O = (n,d))$ of RSA public and private keys where $n = pq$ and p, q are k-bit prime integers;
2. randomly picks 5 elements $g_0, g_1, g_2, g_3, g_4 \in Z_n^*$ and an element $g \in Z_n^*$ such that the order of g is unknown (e.g., it can be taken from a public random string);
3. computes a signature $s = g^d \bmod n$ of g;
4. publicizes public(O)$= (P_O, g, s, g_0, g_1, g_2, g_3, g_4)$.

The bases g_1, g_2 are used to encode the 2 credentials of a certificate, g and s are used in order to achieve unlinkability, g_0 is used to encode user key, g_3 and g_4 are used against adaptive attacks.

User enrollment. In this phase user U asks to the organization O for a chameleon certificate with encoded values x_1, x_2 of the 2 credentials and the public key $P_u = g_0^{x_0}$. The values x_1, x_2 of the credentials are sent in clear to O while the secret key x_0 is kept secret and only P_u along with a proof of knowledge of its discrete logarithm with respect to the base g_0 is sent to O.

Once the attributes of the user have been verified in accordance to the policies of the organization, O randomly chooses $x_3, x_4 \in Z_n^*$ and releases a master chameleon certificate that consists of the pair (C, S) where

$$C = P_u g_1^{x_1} g_2^{x_2} g_3^{x_3} + g_4^{x_4} \bmod n \text{ and } S = C^d \bmod n.$$

The user U receives $(C, S), x_3, x_4$ and verifies that the master chameleon certificate has been correctly computed.

Refreshing. Now we present our *refreshing* procedure that is executed by the user each time he needs to exhibit a slave chameleon certificate. Starting from a chameleon certificate (C, S) a new slave chameleon certificate is generated by the user in the following way:

1. pick a random value $x \in Z_n^*$ and computes $C' = g^x \cdot C \bmod n$;
2. compute a signature S' of C' as $S' = s^x \cdot S \bmod n$;
3. the slave chameleon certificate is (C', S').

Showing possession of credentials. In this phase a user proves to a service provider the possession of a master chameleon certificate (C', S') in order to obtain access to a service. The access control policy of the service provider for a given resource is described by a linear Boolean formula Φ and the user proves that the credentials encoded in the master chameleon certificates satisfy the formula Φ. More precisely, the following steps are performed by the user and the service provider.

1. The user generates a slave chameleon certificates (C', S') by picking a random x and setting $C_0' = g^x g_0^{x_0} g_1^{x_1} g_2^{x_2} g_3^{x_3}$ and $C_1' = g_4^{x_4} g^x$ (so that $C' = C_0' + C_1'$ (mod n));

2. The user computes commitments $(\hat{C}_0', \hat{C}_1', \hat{C}')$ of C_0', C_1', C' using the techniques of [7] and sends them to the service provider.

3. The service provider sends $b \in_R \{0, 1, 2\}$ as challenge.

4. If b is 0 then the user proves that $(\hat{C}_0', \hat{C}_1', \hat{C}')$ are well computed, i.e., $\hat{C}'$ is the commitment of the sum modulo n of two values whose commitments are $\hat{C}_0'$ and $\hat{C}_1'$ and that $\hat{C}'$ is the commitment of C'. This is achieved by using the proof systems described in [7]. Moreover the user sends S' and the service provider verifies that S' is a correct signature of C'.

5. If b is 1 then the user opens $\hat{C}_0'$ and both parties engage in a PoK in which the user proves to know a $(n, g, g_0, g_1, g_2, g_3)$-representation (x, x_0, x_1, x_2, x_3) of C_0' such that $\Phi(x, x_0, x_1, x_2, x_3) = 1$. This is achieved by using the results described in [2].

6. If $b = 2$ then the user opens $\hat{C}_1'$ and proves that it knows the (n, g, g_4)-representation (x, x_4) of C_1'. This is achieved by using the proof of knowledge of a representation.

Notice that only the owner of the certificate knows the (n, g, g_4)-representation of C_1' and the $(n, g, g_0, g_1, g_2, g_3)$-representation of C_0', thus only the legitimate owner of the certificate can use the certificate, since it is the only party that knows the private key x_0.

The steps described above must be repeated several times in order to gain a satisfying soundness. At each iteration a new slave chameleon certificate is used.

Security of the system. We now discuss the security of our proposal with respect to the properties that we described in Section 4.

Unforgeability. A coalition of users can share the secrets of their master/slave chameleon certificates in order to obtains a new master/slave chameleon certificate whose attributes $x_0, x_1, \ldots, x_4$ are different with respect to any shared master/slave chameleon certificate. However if such an algorithm exists, another algorithm that uses the first one and exploits the malleability property of RSA can easily break Assumption 2.

Unlinkability. Suppose that there exists an algorithm A that guesses whether a given slave chameleon certificate (C', S') is related to a given master chameleon certificate (C, S). More precisely, algorithm A receives as input the information publicized at set-up phase by O along with the transcript of a transaction in which the slave chameleon certificate has been used. A has to distinguish between two cases: (C', S') has been obtained by running the refreshing procedure on input master chameleon certificate (C, S) or by running the refreshing procedure on input a randomly chosen master chameleon certificate (C^*, S^*). We say that the adversary succeeds if it has probability of guessing correctly significantly better than $1/2$. We show that A can be used to break Assumption 1. Consider now an algorithm A' that receives two primes p, q of the same length and $y, g \in Z_n^*$ where $n = pq$ and has to output a guess to whether $y \in \langle g \rangle$. A' generates an RSA key $((n,d),(n,e))$, randomly chooses $g_0, \ldots, g_l, x_0, x_1, x_2, x_3, x_4$, computes a master chameleon certificate

$$(C'' = g_0^{x_0} g_1^{x_1} g_2^{x_2} g_3^{x_3} + g_4^{x_4} \bmod n, S'' = C''^d \bmod n)$$

and runs

$$A((C'', S''), (C'' \cdot y, S'' \cdot y^d \bmod n), (n, d, e, p, q, g_0, g_1, g_2, g_3, g_4, x_0, x_1, x_2, x_3, x_4)).$$

If the output of A is true then A' can establish that $y \in \langle g \rangle$ else $y \notin \langle g \rangle$. Thus A contradicts Assumption 1.

A similar result can be given for the case of the linking of two slave chameleon certificates.

Privacy. Using the interactive honest-verifier ZKPoK or the non-interactive PoK in the random oracle model of the $(n, g, g_0, g_1, g_2, g_3)$-representation of the first component of a slave chameleon certificate and the proof of knowledge of satisfaction of linear Boolean formula over its attributes presented in [2] we have that the selective disclosure property of our scheme holds.

Malleability. Each step of the refreshing procedure can be executed by the user without interacting with any party. Moreover such operations can be performed in any moment since data extracted from an on-line interaction are not required.

Usability. It is easy to verify that by the malleability property of RSA signatures, in the output of the refreshing procedure (C', S') on input a master chameleon certificate (C, S), S' is a valid RSA signature of C'. We stress that this procedure does not require interaction with any party.

Lending. When a user shares his private information regarding a chameleon certificate with other users then they can use the certificate for their purposes since there is a complete sharing of user identity. Even if the presence of the private key is a first deterrent to this drawback a more sophisticate strategy to discourage such sharing can be achieved by adding attributes that typically are not shared by their owners. For example another base $g_c \in Z_n^*$ could be considered and inserted in each certificate to represent a credit card number. Using this mechanism each user that tries to use such a master chameleon certificate or one of its corresponding slaves needs to know the owner's credit card number to convince the verifier during the PoK.

5.1 Applications

Based on the concept of a chameleon certificate, we can design a system for non-transferable anonymous credential system including the following parties:

1. the organizations that release credentials;
2. the users that get the credentials and give proofs of possession;
3. the service providers that trust the organizations and restrict their services to the users that possess some credentials.

Each organization that releases credentials publicizes the list of *supported* credentials. The credentials are released by encoding them in chameleon certificates and thus the corresponding public information are publicized too.

Each service provider publicizes the list of trusted organizations. Moreover for each restricted resource there is a corresponding linear Boolean formula over some credentials. The service provider knows the list of credentials released by each of his trusted organizations and thus the case that a linear Boolean formula refers to credentials that are not totally released by at least a trusted organization cannot happen.

A user needs at least one master chameleon certificate released by one organization. However the organizations do not necessarily grant on the same credentials, in this case a user could receive some master chameleon certificates from different organizations. Moreover the service providers do not necessarily trust the same organizations and thus the same credentials could be repeated in different master chameleon certificates so that the right one is selected during user enrollment.

In order to prove possession of some credentials, the user performs the *refreshing* procedure on the master chameleon certificate in order to obtain the slave chameleon certificates (this step can be executed off-line). Then the user proves the possession of credentials that satisfy the linear Boolean formula that corresponds to the requested resource as we discussed in Section 5.

Privacy-aware PKI. A privacy-aware PKI is obtained by using chameleon certificates. The role of organizations is played by the certification authorities. The credentials encoded in the certificate are the attributes that are assigned to the owner. The master chameleon certificate (C, S) can be publicized along with the two shares C_0 and C_1 such that $C_0 + C_1 = C \bmod n$ and such that the owner knows the representations of C_0 and C_1 with respect to the appropriate bases.

Certificate revocation. The revocation of a chameleon certificate is possible in different ways. Following the approach of Verheul it is possible to use short-lived certificates. Another possibility is to use standard CRLs represented by sequences of serial numbers, in this case the serial number can be encoded as an attribute of the chameleon certificate and during their use it is necessary to prove that the corresponding attribute is different from each serial number contained in a CRL. Of course when the size of the CRL increases the performances of the protocols decrease. Finally, we can use the general technique of [6] to make revocable a chameleon certificates.

The PKI discussed above is similar to the one proposed in [2], but in our case the owner of a certificate can use it for anonymous identification or to prove possession attributes in such a way that different transactions are not linkable.

6   Conclusions

In this paper we have introduced the concept of a *chameleon certificate*. Moreover, we have presented a construction for chameleon certificates that is based on a generalization of the assumption of [8]. We have shown a non-transferable anonymous credential system and a PKI based on chameleon certificates. Finally, we remark that the proof systems of [3] can also be used in our construction.

References

1. G. Ateniese and G. Tsudik, Some open issues and new directions in group signatures. *Financial Cryptography 1999*, volume 1648 of LNCS.
2. S. Brands, *Rethinking Public Key Infrastructures and Digital Certificates; Building in Privacy.* MIT Press, 2000.
3. E. Bresson and J. Stern., Proofs of knowledge for non-monotone discrete-log formulae and applications. In *Proceedings of International Security Conference (ISC 2002)*, volume 2433 of LNCS.
4. J. Camenisch., A note on one of the assumptions. Jan Camenisch Home Page - Selected Publications.
5. J. Camenisch and A. Lysyanskaya. An efficient non-transferable anonymous multi-show credential system with optional anonymity revocation, *Eurocrypt 2001*, volume 2045 of LNCS.
6. J. Camenisch and A. Lysyanskaya. Dynamic accumulators and application to efficient revocation of anonymous credentials. *Crypto 2002*, volume 2442 of LNCS.
7. J. Camenisch and M. Michels. Proving in zero-knowledge that a number is the product of two safe primes. *Eurocrypt 99*, volume 1592 of LNCS.
8. J. Camenisch and M. Stadler. Efficient group signature schemes for large groups. *Crypto 97*, volume 1294 of LNCS.
9. D. Chaum. Blind signatures for untraceable payments. *Crypto 82*.
10. D. Chaum and J. Evertse. A secure and privacy-protecting protocol for transmitting personal information between organizations. *Crypto '86*, volume 263 of LNCS.
11. A. De Santis, G. Di Crescenzo, G. Persiano, and M. Yung. On monotone formula closure of SZK. FOCS 1994.
12. A. Fiat and A. Shamir. How to prove yourself: Practical solutions to identification and signature problems. *Crypto '86*, volume 263 of LNCS.
13. R. Housley, W. Polk, W. Ford, and D. Solo. Internet X509 public key infrastructure: Certificate and Certificate Revocation List (CRL) Profile. Network Working Group, RFC 3280, April 2002.
14. A. Lysyanskaya, R. Rivest, A. Sahai, and S. Wolf. Pseudonym systems. *Proceedings of Selected Areas in Cryptography 1999*, volume 1758 of LNCS.
15. A. Menezes, P. C. van Oorschot, and S. A. Vanstone. *Handbook of Applied Cryptography.* CRC Press, 1996.
16. E. Verheul. Self-blindable credential certificates from the weil pairing. *ASIACRYPT 2001*, volume 2248 of LNCS.

Flaws in Some Robust Optimistic Mix-Nets

Masayuki Abe[1] and Hideki Imai[2]

[1] NTT Laboratories
abe@isl.ntt.co.jp
[2] Information & Systems, Institute of Industrial Science, University of Tokyo
imai@iis.u-tokyo.ac.jp

Abstract. This paper introduces weaknesses of two robust Mix-nets proposed in [10] and [7]. First, we show that [10] can lose anonymity in the presence of a malicious user even though all servers are honest. Second, we show that [7] can lose anonymity through the collaboration of a malicious user and the first server. The user can identify the plaintext sent from the targeted user by invoking two mix sessions at the risk of the colluding server receiving an accusation. We also point out that in a certain case, anonymity is violated solely by the user without colluding to any server. Practical repairs are provided for both schemes. Since such flaws are due to their weak security definitions, we present a stronger security definition by regarding a Mix-net as a batch decryption algorithm of a CCA secure public-key encryption scheme.

1 Introduction

Mix-net [4] is a central tool for many electronic voting systems. It establishes an anonymous channel between the voters and the ballot box. Intensive research has been done to realize a robust Mix-net that withstands the malicious behavior of servers and users. While many papers present *publicly verifiable* Mix-nets [14, 2,6,11], the interesting attempt of [9] introduces a *privately convincing* Mix-net where only the mix-servers can convince themselves of correctness. This kind of Mix-net provides better efficiency in exchange for this limitation. Although the particular construction has been attacked [5], the principle is adopted by several latest schemes such as [10]. Another interesting attempt is described in [7] where the processing is very fast as long as the servers are honest. If a malfunctioning server is detected, the input data is processed by a full-fledged (and thus slow) robust Mix-net. Although one has to implement both types of Mix-net, such optimistic construction has a certain practical value.

This paper shows some weaknesses in the optimistic Mix-nets presented in [10] and [7] (referred as JJ01 and GZ$^+$02, respectively). In particular, we show that JJ01 can lose anonymity in the presence of a malicious user even though all servers are honest. For GZ$^+$02, we show that a malicious user colluding with the first mix-server can break anonymity at the risk of having the server accused. We also point out that in a certain case, a malicious user can solely mount an attack to trace a specific message at the cost of receiving accusation to himself. Our

R. Safavi-Naini and J. Seberry (Eds.): ACISP 2003, LNCS 2727, pp. 39–50, 2003.
© Springer-Verlag Berlin Heidelberg 2003

attack against GZ$^+$02 is also introduced independently by [16], which includes rather subtle attacks.

Since both JJ01 and GZ$^+$02 have been considered as secure with regard to particular definitions of security, the presence of the practical attacks means that the definitions must be re-considered. We present a security definition in which a Mix-net is considered as a batch decryption algorithm of a CCA secure public-key encryption scheme.

2   Attack on JJ01

2.1   Review

JJ01 is based on hybrid encryption with a message authentication code (MAC) that assures the integrity of the internal results. The Mix-net consists of n mix-servers and one additional server located at the tail of the sequence of servers. The additional server is actually simulated by the servers in a distributed manner. The role of this simulated server is decryption only (it does not shuffle the results).

By using the key-scheduling technique of [12], each user shares symmetric encryption key k_i with server i. This is done by sending server i a hint, say y_{i-1}, through the previous servers. That is, the user sends $y_0 (= g^\rho)$ to the first server and it is then randomized and passed to the second server as y_1. This procedure is continued to the last server. Please refer to [12] for details but we stress that this key-scheduling is done in a deterministic way and every symmetric-key k_i is determined from just y_0 (and the public-keys of servers that determine the randomness used for randomizing y_0). It is also important to note that the key-scheduling allows these symmetric-keys to be verifiably shared among the servers and so ensure robustness. In JJ01, server i derives a MAC-key, say z_i, from the same hint y_i. Using symmetric encryption E and message authentication code MAC, message m is encrypted by computing

$$c_n = E_{k_{n+1}}(m)$$
$$c_i = E_{k_{i+1}}(c_{i+1} \| \mu_{i+1}) \qquad 0 \leq i \leq n-1$$
$$\mu_i = MAC_{z_{i+1}}(c_i \| \mathsf{SID}) \qquad 0 \leq i \leq n$$

where SID is a session identifier uniquely assigned to each execution of Mix-net probably provided by the Mix-net or determined by system environment such as current date. The ciphertext is a triple (c_0, μ_0, y_0).

Mix-net decrypts each ciphertext as follows. Let L_0 be the list of N cipher-texts given to the first server. Similarly, let L_{i-1} be the input to server i given from server $i - 1$. For each ciphertext $(c_i, \mu_i, y_i) \in L_i$, server $i + 1$ first verifies $\mu_i \overset{?}{=} MAC_{z_{i+1}}(c_i \| \mathsf{SID})$, then decrypts c_i by using symmetric-key k_{i+1} to obtain $(c_{i+1} \| \mu_{i+1})$. The triple $(c_{i+1}, u_{i+1}, y_{i+1})$ is the result of internal decryption. The results are randomly ordered in list L_{i+1} and given to the next server.

Now, if the MAC verification fails, the server claims so by publishing MAC-key z_{i+1}. (In fact, it is verifiably reconstructed by the rest of servers. For simplicity, we assume that servers honestly publish the correct keys by themselves. The same is true hereafter.) If the MAC is really wrong, it might have been caused by the previous server i. Hence server i proves its honesty *by publishing correspond-ing encryption-key* k_i and the corresponding input ciphertext $(c_{i+1}, u_{i+1}, y_{i+1})$. If key k_i does not correctly decrypt c_{i+1} into c_{i+1}, u_{i+1}, the server i is disquali-fied. Otherwise, it continues until all previous servers prove their honesty in the same way. If this cycle reaches the first server, the user who has posted the orig-inal ciphertext is disqualified. One important observation in this disqualification process is that the MAC-key z_{i+1} and encryption-key k_i is revealed in public. Our attack abuses this information leakage.

2.2   Attack

Let $C_0 = (c_0, \mu_0, y_0) \in L_0^0$ be an input ciphertext for session $\mathsf{SID} = 0$ posted by the targeted user. The purpose of the adversary is to identify the plaintext embedded in C. For this, it is sufficient to distinguish internal ciphertext $C_n = (c_n, \mu_n, y_n)$ that corresponds to C_0 among the ciphertexts in L_n^0. (Remember that the simulated server at the tail does not shuffle its inputs.) The attack proceeds as follows.

- Given C_0, the adversary (a user who can post a ciphertext to the same Mix) composes $\tilde{C}_0 = (c_0, \tilde{\mu}_0, y_0)$ where $\tilde{\mu}_0$ is a random string that looks like a MAC. $\tilde{C}_0$ is sent to the Mix at new session $\mathsf{SID} = 1$.
- Server 1 rejects $\tilde{C}_0$ with high probability since MAC $\tilde{\mu}_0$ is wrong. To show that it is really wrong, server 1 publishes MAC-key z_1 derived from y_0, which is the correct MAC-key used for computing μ_0.
- By using this z_1, the adversary re-computes $\tilde{\mu}_0$ as $\tilde{\mu}_0 = MAC_{z_1}(c_0 \| 2)$ and sends $\tilde{C}_1 = (c_0, \tilde{\mu}_0, y_0)$ to the Mix at $\mathsf{SID} = 2$.
- Since $\tilde{\mu}_0$ is now correct, server 1 derives symmetric-key k_1 from y_0 and per-forms decryption. Resulting ciphertext (c_1, μ_1, y_1) is passed to server 2.
- Server 2 now rejects the ciphertext because μ_1 is wrong with regard to $c_1 \| 2$. (Notice that MAC μ_1 was issued for $c_1 \| 0$.) Thus, server 2 will publish z_2 and accuse server 1. (Note that the rejected ciphertext (c_1, μ_1, y_1) is exactly the same as the one appeared in L_1^0, which is the output of server 1 in session 0. Thus, by seeing which one is rejected, the adversary can successfully trace the target ciphertext shuffled by server 1.)
- To prove honesty, server 1 publishes symmetric-key k_1 with regard to the rejected ciphertext. By back-tracing the process, the bad user is eventually found and his input ciphertext is removed from the rest of the process.
- Up to this point, the adversary has obtained (z_1, k_1, z_2). By using these keys, he computes $\tilde{C}_2 = (\tilde{c}_0, \tilde{\mu}_0, y_0)$ where

$$\tilde{\mu}_1 = MAC_{z_2}(c_1 \| 3),$$
$$\tilde{c}_0 = E_{k_1}(c_1 \| \tilde{\mu}_1), \text{ and}$$
$$\tilde{\mu}_0 = MAC_{z_1}(\tilde{c}_0 \| 3).$$

Then $\tilde{C}_2$ is posted to the Mix-net at $\mathsf{SID} = 3$.

- In session 3, the second server outputs (c_2, μ_2, y_2) which will be rejected by the third server. However, the adversary now successfully identifies the target ciphertext $(c_2, \mu_2, y_2) \in L_2^0$ in the original session, and obtains k_2 and z_3.
- It is now easy to see that, by repeating this procedure for up to session n+1, the adversary can eventually identify $C_n = (c_n, \mu_n, y_n) \in L_n^0$ that corresponds to C_0.

Observe that the adversary can mount this attack by himself if he is allowed to join to $n+1$ sessions. Even if a disqualified user is excluded from all subsequent sessions, $n + 1$ colluding users are sufficient for the attack to be successful.

2.3 Repair

A trivial repair is to hide symmetric-keys by using zero-knowledge proofs to show the honesty in the accusation procedure. However, general zero-knowledge proofs for correct symmetric-decryption and MAC would be unacceptably expensive in terms of computation cost. Even worse, such accusation process can be invoked solely by malicious user who posts a garbage ciphertext in order to slow down the servers.

A more practical repair would be to force every user to prove that he knows the secret used for key-delivery. That is, a user proves, in zero-knowledge manner, that he knows ρ of $y_0 = g^\rho$. For efficiency, the zero-knowledge proof will be replaced with a Schnorr signature with public-key y_0 and private-key ρ. The security of this variant can be argued in the generic model combined with random oracle model (see [15] for details about this model). We note that, as well as the original scheme, the repaired scheme allows a user and the first server cooperatively change the content of the ciphertext sent from the user after the mix processing is started. As discussed in JJ01, such an act may be harmless depending on applications, but it does not meet our definition of strong robustness introduced in Section 4.

3   Attack on GZ$^+$02

3.1   Review

Let (M, G) be an ElGamal ciphertext of message m. Let $H = h(M\|G)$, where h is a hash function. An input ciphertext C of message m is a triple $C = (E(M), E(G), E(H))$ where $E(\cdot)$ is also ElGamal encryption. Namely, the ciphertext C doubly envelopes message m with ElGamal encryption adding a hash value to the message of the outer encryption.

The servers first sequentially re-encrypt and shuffle the input ciphertexts. The outer layer encryption of the shuffled ciphertexts are then decrypted by the collaboration of a quorum of servers. If all the resulting triples, $\{(M, G, H)\}$, contain a consistent hash value, the inner ElGamal encryption, (M, G), is decrypted by the quorum of servers to obtain the plaintext.

In the re-encryption and shuffling stage, each mix-server has to prove correctness. This is done by proving that the embedded plaintexts are unchanged except for the order. In general, however, it is an expensive task. In GZ$^+$02 scheme, the servers only prove that the *product* of all plaintexts are unchanged. In this way, one can design very efficient zero-knowledge proof system that abuses the multiplicative property of ElGamal ciphertext. It is, of course, easy for a cheating server to modify embedded plaintexts so that their product remain unchanged. However, such an attempt would result in an inconsistent hash value H and eventually the malicious sever would be detected by back-tracing. (Once such an actively deviating server is detected, the rest of servers cooperatively remove the outer layer encryption from the input ciphertexts and input the inner layer ElGamal ciphertexts to a full-fledged robust Mix-net such as [11].)

Observe that an input ciphertext $C = (E(M), E(G), E(H))$ is malleable since it is just a triple of ElGamal encryption. Hence, in order to prevent copied and re-encrypted ciphertexts from being posted, the user has to prove his knowledge about the embedded message (M, G, H) in a zero-knowledge manner. In fact, the proof and encryption are done at the same time by using so called Signed ElGamal encryption for computing each of $E(M), E(G), E(H)$ so that finding the correct ciphertext implies the knowledge of (M, G, H). In this way, the outer encryption becomes non-malleable in the generic model and the random oracle model. In the next section, however, we show that this non-malleable encryption (and its original interactive version) is not secure enough in the Mix-net scenario because it does not guarantee the knowledge of the inner message m.

3.2   Attack 1

Suppose that an attacker (a user) is colluding with the first mix-server. Let $C = (E(M), E(G), E(H))$ be the target input ciphertext to trace. The attack proceeds as follows.

- The attacker creates a ciphertext $C' = (E(M'), E(G'), E(H'))$ correctly from an arbitrary message and sends it to the Mix-net.
- The first server re-encrypts and shuffles correctly except that the re-encrypted hash values of C, C' are interchanged. More precisely, it outputs $(\tilde{E}(M), \tilde{E}(G), \tilde{E}(H'))$ and $(\tilde{E}(M'), \tilde{E}(G'), \tilde{E}(H))$ where $\tilde{E}(X)$ denotes a re-encryption of ciphertext $E(X)$. Clearly, this does not affect to the proof of equality of product message and the process flows as it is. Eventually, (M, G, H') and (M', G', H) appear after decrypting the outer layer encryption. The user now obtains correct (M, G, H) that corresponds to C. (The servers notice the inconsistent hash values and the first server will be disqualified as a result of back-tracing. The remaining servers then abandon this internal result and go into the full-fledged mix process. But this is no longer relevant to this attack.)
- The user encrypts (M, G, H) to $C'' = (E(M''), E(G''), E(H''))$ and sends C'' to a new Mix session. Observe that the user can correctly prove his knowledge of (M, G, H) because he indeed knows it (though he does not

know m embedded in (M, G)). Accordingly, (M, G, H) appears as a result of outer layer decryption and the corresponding message m is output without permutation at the end of this session.

Note that even if the first server is removed, the Mix-net remains functional in subsequent sessions as long as a quorum of servers are honest. In particular, since re-encryption can be done without knowing the secret-key, anyone can work as a server in the re-encryption and shuffling stage instead of the disqualified server.

3.3 Attack 2

In GZ$^+$02, it is noted that one can omit the proof of knowledge about r_3 to reduce the computational cost. However, we point out that such an attempt leads to another attack that can be mounted solely by a malicious user.

Let $C = (E(M), E(G), E(H))$ be the target ciphertext to trace. The attacker correctly computes ElGamal ciphertext (M', G') of arbitrary message m'. He then computes the input ciphertext $C' = (E(M'), E(G'), E(H))$ whose third part is the same as that of C (or, it can be re-encrypted as $\tilde{E}(H)$). Now, assume that the proof about the knowledge about H is omitted. This means that C' will be accepted as the attacker can correctly show proof of knowledge about m' since he indeed knows m' relative to (M, G). As the process proceeds, (M', G', H) will come out and be rejected. At this point, the adversary can identify target ciphertext (M, G, H) by using H observed in the rejected ciphertext. Although the input from the attacker will be ejected from this process, no servers are in collusion and the process goes ahead. Hence the target ciphertext (M, G, H) will be decrypted by the collaboration of servers without being shuffled, and the plaintext will be straightforwardly exposed. This attack shows the importance of making the entire input non-malleable.

3.4 Repair

A straightforward repair is to force the user to prove his knowledge about inner message m. Let $C = (E(M), E(G), E(H))$ be an input ciphertext where

$$(M_0, G_0) = (my^{r_0}, g^{r_0})$$
$$H = h(M_0, G_0)$$
$$E(M) = (M_1, G_1) = (My^{r_1}, g^{r_1}) = (my^{r_0 + r_1}, g^{r_1})$$
$$E(G) = (M_2, G_2) = (Gy^{r_2}, g^{r_2}) = (g^{r_0}y^{r_2}, g^{r_2}) \text{ and,}$$
$$E(H) = (M_3, G_3) = (Hy^{r_3}, g^{r_3}).$$

Proving one's knowledge about (r_0, r_1, r_2, r_3) in the above representation is sufficient to show his knowledge about message m. (It seems that proof of r_3 is unnecessary as mentioned in the original description of GZ$^+$02. But this is necessary as is shown in the sequel.) The proof can be done by combining two Schnorr proofs of knowledge and a proof of representation as follows.

- Select $(w_0, w_1, w_2, w_3) \leftarrow \mathbb{Z}_q^4$.
- Compute $A_1 = g^{w_1}$, $A_2 = g^{w_0} y^{w_2}$, and $A_3 = g^{w_2}$, $A_4 = g^{w_3}$, .
- Compute $c = h(A_1, A_2, A_3, A_4, C, \mathsf{SID})$.
- Compute $z_0 = w_0 - cr_0 \bmod q$, $z_1 = w_1 - cr_1 \bmod q$, $z_2 = w_2 - cr_2 \bmod q$, and $z_3 = w_3 - cr_3 \bmod q$.

The output is (c, z_0, z_1, z_2, z_3). This is verified by computing $A_1' = g^{z_1} G_1{}^c$, $A_2' = g^{z_0} y^{z_2} M_2{}^c$, $A_3' = g^{z_2} G_2{}^c$, $A_4' = g^{z_3} G_3{}^c$, and checking $c \stackrel{?}{=} h(A_1', A_2', A_3', A_4', C, \mathsf{SID})$.

This modification is quite costly in terms of computation. If desired, a straightforward modification allows one to batch verify the predicate to minimize the computational impact in trade-off against communication cost. We also remark that this repair only prevents so called relation attacks [13] mounted by malicious users. Indeed, due to [16], it remains vulnerable against corruption of the last mix-server. Hence it does not provide the strong security defined in the next section.

4   Security of Mix-Net

Since both JJ01 and GZ$^+$02 have been considered as secure with regard to particular definitions of security, the presence of practical attacks means that more appropriate definitions are needed. Among several definitions considered, this section reviews the security definition of Mix-net given in [1].

In a narrow sense, Mix-net can be seen as a batch decryption function accompanied by random permutation performed by several servers. Including key-generation and encryption function, a Mix-net scheme could be considered as a public-key encryption scheme featuring batch decryption and random permutation. Thus, it would be reasonable to define security by following the strongest notion of security as a public-key encryption scheme, i.e., indistinguishability against adaptive chosen ciphertext attacks. Definitions in the subsequent sections follow this understanding.

4.1   Model

Mix-net: The ideal system is illustrated in Figure 1; Each user is connected to a tamper-proof shuffling-box that takes a list of messages, say $(\mu_1, \ldots, \mu_n)$ from each user via a physically secure (i.e., untappable) channel, and outputs a list of randomly re-ordered messages, say $(v_1, \ldots, v_n)$. We refer to such a system as the ideal shuffling-box.

We represent a practical Mix-net as a system that mimics "private channel + shuffling-box" over a public network as outlined in Figure 2. Let $[n]$ denote $\{1, \ldots, n\}$. Let Π_n denote a set of permutation over $[n]$.

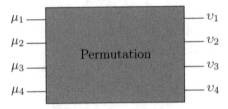

Fig. 1. The ideal shuffling box. A single trusted server connected to each user via physically secure channel permutes the input messages.

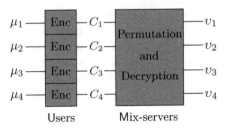

Fig. 2. Mix-net system. Users and Mix-servers are connected via a public channel which may be wiretapped. Each user sends a message in an encrypted form and the servers permute and decrypt them in collaboration.

Definition 1 (Mix-net). *Mix-net is a triple, $(\mathcal{G}^{mix}, \mathcal{E}^{mix}, M)$, such that*

- $\mathcal{G}^{mix}$ *is a probabilistic algorithm that takes security parameter κ, and access structure Γ for m party, and outputs a public encryption key, say y, and a set of private decryption keys $x = (x_1, \ldots, x_m)$. The public-key set may contain a set of local public-keys $(y_1, \ldots, y_m)$ that corresponds to x. Public-key y determines message space $\mathcal{M}_y$.*
- $\mathcal{E}^{mix}$ *is a probabilistic algorithm that takes message $\mu \in \mathcal{M}_y$ and public-key y and outputs a ciphertext C. We require that, for any μ and μ' in $\mathcal{M}_y$, $\mathcal{E}_y^{mix}(\mu) \cap \mathcal{E}_y^{mix}(\mu') = \emptyset$ if $\mu \neq \mu'$. (Here, $\mathcal{E}_y^{mix}(\mu)$ denotes an output of function $\mathcal{E}_y^{mix}(\mu)$ and also denotes the distribution of the outputs according to the randomness used in the function. Such notation will be used for conciseness hereafter.)*
- M *is a set of probabilistic polynomial-time interactive Turing machines, say $\{M_1, \ldots, M_m\}$, called mix-servers. Each mix-server is given a list of ciphertexts, $\{C_1, \ldots, C_n\}$ and public-key y as common inputs. Private-key x_i is a private input. Mix-servers interact with each other and output a list of messages $(v_1, \ldots, v_n)$ on their output tape. It is required that there exists permutation $\pi \in \Pi_n$ such that $v_{\pi(i)} = \mu_i$ if there exists $\mu_i \in \mathcal{M}_y$ such that $C_i \in \mathcal{E}_y^{mix}(\mu_i)$, Otherwise, $v_{\pi(i)} = \perp$. Here, $\perp$ is a special letter that is not in $\mathcal{M}_y$.*

Note that $\mathcal{E}^{\mathsf{mix}}$ *must* be probabilistic. Otherwise, one can easily find the correspondence between resulting plaintexts and input ciphertexts. For convenience, we define the decryption algorithm $\mathcal{D}^{\mathsf{mix}}$ that corresponds to $\mathcal{E}^{\mathsf{mix}}$ in such a way that $\mathcal{D}_x^{\mathsf{mix}}(\mathcal{E}_y^{\mathsf{mix}}(\mu)) = \mu$ for all $\mu \in \mathcal{M}_y$, and $\mathcal{D}_x^{\mathsf{mix}}(C) = \bot$ if $C \notin \mathcal{E}_y^{\mathsf{mix}}(\mu)$ for any $\mu \in \mathcal{M}_y$. Note that the decryption algorithm corresponds to M when M consist of a single mix-server and only one input ciphertext is given.

Additional information, such as the maximum number of input ciphertexts, may be provided to each algorithm. Typically, $\mathcal{G}^{\mathsf{mix}}$ is performed by Mix-servers themselves so that each piece of the private key is known only to the relevant server according to the access structure. In a narrow sense, Mix-net refers to Mix-servers or their algorithms. According to the standard scenario, each input ciphertext is created by an entity called a *user*. Let U_i denote a user who has message μ_i and posts a ciphertext, say C_i. By U we denote a set of users, $\mathsf{U} = \{\mathsf{U}_1, \ldots, \mathsf{U}_n\}$.

Communication Channel: For simplicity, we assume that all communication between all M and all U is done via a bulletin board, denoted by BB. The bulletin board BB is a public memory where everyone can read and write in authenticated manner but no one erase or overwrite any information once written. This is equivalent to a complete, synchronous, authenticated network with broadcast function. When a private channel is needed, we implicitly assume public-key encryption.

Adversary: We follow the central adversary model; There is a polynomial-time adversary $\mathcal{A}$ that can corrupt subsets of mix-servers and users. We say that $\mathcal{A}$ is (t_u, t_m)-limited if it corrupts up to t_u users and t_m servers. (More general and detailed notation will specify the collusion structure among the servers and users. We restrict ourselves to this simple notation.) Let $\mathsf{U_A}$ and $\mathsf{M_A}$ denote the set of corrupt users and servers, respectively. Similarly, let $\mathsf{U_H}$ and $\mathsf{M_H}$ denote honest users and servers, respectively. *Active* adversary controls $\mathsf{U_A}$ and $\mathsf{M_A}$ in an arbitrary way to break the anonymity of $\mathsf{U_H}$ or to lead $\mathsf{M_H}$ to issue an incorrect output. If the adversary is considered to be *passive*, it can obtain only the internal state of the corrupt players. *Adaptive* adversary decides the target of corruption at an arbitrary time while *static* adversary is restricted to setting the target before any protocol (including the key generation protocol) starts.

4.2 Security Definitions

Let L_y denote a language such that

$$L_y \stackrel{\mathsf{def}}{=} \{C_1, \ldots, C_n, v_1, \ldots, v_n \mid$$
$$\exists \pi \in \Pi_n \text{ s.t. } v_{\pi(i)} = \mathcal{D}_x^{\mathsf{mix}}(C_i)\}$$

with regard to (y, x) generated by $\mathcal{G}^{\mathsf{mix}}(1^\kappa)$.

Definition 2. $(v_1, \ldots, v_n)$ *is correct with regard to y and $(C_1, \ldots, C_n)$ if*

$$(C_1, \ldots, C_n, v_1, \ldots, v_n) \in L_y.$$

Definition 3 (Anonymity). *Let $\mathcal{A}$ be an adversary that plays the following game. At any moment of the game, $\mathcal{A}$ is allowed to corrupt up to t_u users and t_m servers. Once corrupted, the user or the server is thoroughly controlled by $\mathcal{A}$.*

1. $(y, x) \leftarrow \mathcal{G}^{mix}(1^\kappa)$. *Public-key y and each shared decryption key x_i is given to M_i.*
2. *$\mathcal{A}$ is given y and allowed to invoke M an arbitrary number of times for arbitrary chosen input ciphertexts (i.e., $\mathcal{A}$ can use M as a decryption oracle).*
3. *$\mathcal{A}$ outputs $L_C = (\mu_1, \ldots, \mu_n)$ that is a list of messages chosen from $\mathcal{M}_y$.*
4. *Choose a permutation, $\pi \leftarrow \Pi_n$. Each U_i is given $\mu_{\pi(i)}$ privately and outputs ciphertext C_i. If U_i is corrupted and outputs nothing, let C_i be an empty string. Let $\mathbf{C} = \{C_1, \ldots, C_n\}$.*
5. *M performs mix processing on $\mathbf{C}$.*
6. *$\mathcal{A}$ is again allowed to invoke M an arbitrary number of times for arbitrarily chosen input ciphertexts except for the ones included in $\mathbf{C}$.*
7. *$\mathcal{A}$ outputs $(i^\star, j^\star) \in \{1, \ldots, n\}^2$. The restriction is that $U_{i^\star} \notin U_\mathcal{A}$ (i.e., $U_{i^\star}$ has never been corrupted).*

$\mathcal{A}$ wins the game if $\pi(i^\star) = j^\star$. Mix-net is anonymous against (t_u, t_m)-limited adaptive and active adversary $\mathcal{A}$ if the probability that any polynomial-time (t_u, t_m)-limited adaptive and active adversary $\mathcal{A}$ wins the above game is at most $\frac{1}{n-t_u} + \epsilon$ where ϵ is negligible in κ. Probability is taken over the coin flips of $\mathcal{G}^{mix}$, U, M, $\mathcal{A}$ and the choice of π.

Remark 1. In step 5, the mix protocol may be disrupted by corrupt servers. It is irrelevant, however, whether the mix protocol completes or not at this step.

Remark 2. With only one mix-server ($m = 1$) and two users ($n = 2$), the above definition is almost the same as that of indistinguishability against adaptive chosen ciphertext attacks. A slight difference is that, in this case, two ciphertexts are given to the adversary. It is known, however, that such a *matching problem* is basically equivalent to a decision problem where only one ciphertext is given to the adversary [8].

Remark 3. An adversary who plays the analogue anonymity game with the ideal shuffling box has a winning probability of $\frac{1}{n-t_u}$.

Remark 4. The definition can be extended so that ϵ depends also on the number of inputs. Remember that some schemes efficiently preserve anonymity only if the number of inputs is huge.

Next we define robustness. Intuitively, Mix-net is robust if it always outputs correct results in the presence of corrupt servers and users up to some limit.

Definition 4 (Robustness). *A Mix-net is robust against (t_u, t_m)-limited adaptive and active adversary if, for any of such polynomial-time adversary, M_H terminates in polynomial-time with a correct output with overwhelming probability in κ. The probability is taken over the coin flips of $\mathcal{A}$, U, and M.*

Definition 4 does not address anonymity, though it can be made to include anonymity at the same time. Our separate definitions are useful in describing Mix-nets with different boundary parameters. For instance, some Mix-nets may output correct results but loose anonymity with some parameter settings. (One may desire to have correct output after detecting malicious players even though anonymity is lost. Such a treatment would be needed for optimistic schemes.)

Definitions considering more restricted (i.e. static and/or passive) adversaries can be obtained by appropriately restricting the adversary in definition 3 and 4.

5   Conclusion

These attacks remind us that the input ciphertext must be non-malleable against chosen ciphertext attacks. Since the attacked schemes have been proven secure with regard to some security definitions, the presence of concrete attacks means that stronger definitions are needed. We have presented security definitions based on the thought that Mix-net is a form of batch decryption and hence should provide indistinguishability against adaptive chosen ciphertext attacks. One could develop other possibly equivalent definitions based on, for instance, the framework of multi-party computation [3].

References

1. M. Abe. *Efficient Components for Cryptographic Applications in the Discrete-Log Setting*. PhD thesis, University of Tokyo, 2002.
2. M. Abe and F. Hoshino. Remarks on mix-network based on permutation network. In K. Kim, editor, *PKC 2001*, volume 1992 of *Lecture Notes in Computer Science*, pages 317–324. Springer-Verlag, 2001.
3. R. Canetti. Security and composition of multiparty cryptographic protocols. *Journal of Cryptology*, 13(1):143–202, Winter 2000.
4. D. L. Chaum. Untraceable electronic mail, return address, and digital pseudonyms. *Communications of the ACM*, 24:84–88, 1981.
5. Y. Desmedt and K. Kurosawa. How to break a practical MIX and design a new one. In Bart Preneel, editor, *Advances in Cryptology — EUROCRYPT 2000*, volume 1807 of *Lecture Notes in Computer Science*, pages 557–572. Springer-Verlag, 2000.
6. J. Furukawa and K. Sako. An efficient scheme for proving a shuffle. In J. Killian, editor, *Advances in Cryptology – Crypto 2001*, volume 2139 of *Lecture Notes in Computer Science*, pages 368–387. Springer-Verlag, 2001.

7. P. Golle, S. Zhong, D. Boneh, M. Jakobsson, and A. Juels. Optimistic mixing for exit-polls. In Y. Zheng, editor, *Advances in Cryptology – Asiacrypt 2002*, volume 2501 of *Lecture Notes in Computer Science*, pages 451–465. Springer-Verlag, 2002.

8. H. Handschuh, Y. Tsiounis, and M. Yung. Decision oracles are equivalent to matching oracles. In H. Imai and Y. Zheng, editors, *Second International Workshop on Practice and Theory in Public Key Cryptography*, volume 1560 of *Lecture Notes in Computer Science*, pages 276–289. Springer-Verlag, 1999.

9. M. Jakobsson. A practical mix. In K. Nyberg, editor, *Advances in Cryptology — EUROCRYPT '98*, volume 1403 of *Lecture Notes in Computer Science*, pages 448–461. Springer-Verlag, 1998.

10. A. Juels and M. Jakobsson. An optimally robust hybrid mix network. In *Proceedings of the 20th annual ACM Symposium on Principles of Distributed Computation*, 2001.

11. A. Neff. A verifiable secret shuffle and its application to e-voting. In *ACM CCS'01*, pages 116–125. ACM, 2001.

12. M. Ohkubo and M. Abe. A length-invariant hybrid mix. In T. Okamoto, editor, *Advances in Cryptology — ASIACRYPT 2000*, volume 1976 of *Lecture Notes in Computer Science*, pages 178–191. Springer-Verlag, 2000.

13. B. Pfitzmann. Breaking an efficient anonymous channel. In Alfredo De Santis, editor, *Advances in Cryptology — EUROCRYPT '94*, volume 950 of *Lecture Notes in Computer Science*, pages 339–348. Springer-Verlag, 1995.

14. K. Sako and J. Killian. Receipt-free mix-type voting scheme — a practical solution to the implementation of a voting booth —. In L. C. Guillou and J.-J. Quisquater, editors, *Advances in Cryptology — EUROCRYPT '95*, volume 921 of *Lecture Notes in Computer Science*, pages 393–403. Springer-Verlag, 1995.

15. C. P. Schnorr and M. Jakobsson. Security of signed Elgamal encryption. In T. Okamoto, editor, *Advances in Cryptology — ASIACRYPT 2000*, volume 1976 of *Lecture Notes in Computer Science*, pages 73–89. Springer-Verlag, 2000.

16. D. Wikström. Four practical attacks for "optimistic mixing for exit-polls". Technical Report SICS-T-2003/04-SE, Swedish Institute of Computer Science (SICS), February 2003. (Preliminary SICS-T-2002/24-SE, Dec. 2002).

The Unsolvable Privacy Problem and Its Implications for Security Technologies

Andrew Odlyzko

Digital Technology Center, University of Minnesota,
499 Walter Library, 117 Pleasant St. SE,
Minneapolis, MN 55455, USA
odlyzko@umn.edu
http://www.dtc.umn.edu/~odlyzko

Abstract. Privacy presents many puzzles. In particular, why is it eroding, given the high value people assign to their privacy? This extended abstract argues that there are strong incentives for decreasing privacy, rooted in the economic benefits of price discrimination. As a result, the privacy problem is unsolvable. The conflict between incentives to price discriminate and the public dislike of this practice will influence what security technologies are likely to succeed.

1   Introduction

This is an extended abstract of the invited lecture by this title at the 2003 Australasian Conference on Information Security and Privacy.

What causes the steady erosion of privacy we experience? Some of the push comes from government agencies, and their incentives are easy to understand. Moreover, in democratic societies it is understood how to control government privacy intrusions. However, most of the developments that reduce privacy are coming from corporations, which care about money, not politics. And on the private enterprise side, there are many puzzles. First of all, although huge amounts of data are being collected, overall not much use is being made of it right now. Second, given most people's concern about their privacy, why is there this insistence on very intrusive data collection?

The consumer side of the privacy issue also presents puzzles. People are extremely concerned about their privacy, often citing this as a reason they are reluctant to engage in ecommerce. On the other hand, these same people appear unwilling to do much to protect their privacy, and rather freely share detailed information about their activities. Are they just paranoid, or is there something yet unseen that they have reason to fear?

The thesis that is reported on very briefly here (with full details being written up in a series of papers) resolves these puzzles. The erosion of privacy is caused by the incentives to price discriminate. Privacy intrusions enable more effective price discrimination. The public's fears about decreased privacy are likely to prove justified from their personal perspective, since evidence shows

R. Safavi-Naini and J. Seberry (Eds.): ACISP 2003, LNCS 2727, pp. 51–54, 2003.
© Springer-Verlag Berlin Heidelberg 2003

that people strongly dislike price discrimination. This thesis is supported be extensive data and analysis, with some of the most illustrative examples coming from comparisons of 19th century railroad pricing practices with those in the modern economy. In particular, the railroad example then helps explain why the spread of price discrimination is taking place in a stealthy manner.

2   Benefits of Price Discrimination

Price discrimination is the charging of varying prices when there are no cost justifications for the differences. The benefits of this practice have been understood in economics ever since the work of the French "econoengineers" on railroad pricing in the middle of the 19th century. It is part of the universally accepted economic theory that price discrimination increases the efficiency of the economy by enabling transaction that would not take place otherwise.

3   Increasing Incentives for Price Discrimination

The increasing upfront costs of providing goods and services, and declining marginal costs, combine to increase incentives to price discriminate, as is well established in the economics literature.

Railroads were the major industry of the 19th century, and they had huge fixed and relatively low marginal costs, which again produced huge incentives to price discriminate. (These incentives were also present, sometimes to an even greater extent, in canals and some other industries. While the development of price discrimination did take place in those fields, and is part of the fascinating historical record, those industries were nowhere near as large and noticeable a part of the economy as railroads.)

4   Increasing Ability to Price Discriminate

One of the most important results of the development of improved information and communication technologies, especially the Internet, is the great improvement in the ability to price discriminate. It is possible to obtain much better information about customers' willingness to pay, and it is possible to control their usage much better than before. The comparison of 19th century railroads with airlines at the end of the 20th century is especially instructive. Railroad passenger tickets were transferable, which limited the extent of price discrimination that was feasible. On the other hand, airline tickets are contracts for service between a particular passenger named on the ticket and the airline. Therefore, with the help of "positive passenger identification" systems, airlines can engage in their "yield management" schemes. The benefits of these schemes are derived primarily from price discrimination, as in charging business travelers unwilling to stay over a Saturday night much higher fares than discretionary vacation travelers.

5   Competition and Price Discrimination

The general thinking, often deeply embedded in legal doctrines, has long been that price discrimination comes from monopoly power. However, historically there have been many instances of very competitive markets where price discrimination was widely practiced, and such examples are growing increasingly numerous. (The development of airline "yield management" after deregulation is just one such development.)

One of the most notable features of the evolving "New Economy" (as opposed to the discredited "New Economy" that had been widely forecasted a few years ago) will likely be the growth of price discrimination in competitive markets. This will require revisions in legal and economic doctrines. Among other upsets to "conventional wisdom," first degree price discrimination will come to be seen as feasible.

6   Public Hate of Price Discrimination

There is extensive evidence of the spread of price discrimination. This spread would undoubtedly be even more rapid if it were not for the public's hate and fear of rice discrimination. Again, the comparison with 19th century railroads is instructive. It was not profiteering by railroads that brought about intrusive government regulation, but price discrimination. (In the United States, the Interstate Commerce Act of 1887, the first serious federal government intrusion into commercial conduct, was aimed almost exclusively at railroad price discrimination.) Similar negative reaction to overt price discrimination have been seen in more recent times.

The public dislike of price discrimination provides incentive to hide it. As it turns out, practices such as bundling and site licensing provide a way to attain the same end as explicit price discrimination, by reducing consumer surplus while appearing to offer great bargains to buyers.

7   Conclusions

There is no easy resolution to the conflict between sellers' incentives to price discriminate and buyers' resistance to such measures. The continuing tension between these two factors will have important consequences for the nature of the economy. It will also determine which technologies will be adopted widely. Governments will likely play a role in controlling pricing, although their roles will probably be ambiguous. Sellers are likely to rely on bundling, since that allows them to extract more consumer surplus and also to conceal the extent of price discrimination. Micropayments and auctions are likely to play a smaller role than is often expected. In general, because of the strong conflicting influences, privacy is likely to prove an intractable problem that will be prominent on the the public agenda for the foreseeable future.

More details will be available in a series of papers that are in preparation and which will be available on my home page, at ⟨http://www.dtc.umn.edu/~odlyzko/doc/recent.html⟩. Some of the main theses of this lecture were already outlined in the earlier paper [1]. There are also several sets of presentation slides (especially "The New Economy and old economics: What 19th century railroads can tell us about the future of ecommerce") available at ⟨http://www.dtc.umn.edu/~odlyzko/talks/index.html⟩ that cover some of the material in this extended abstract.

References

1. Odlyzko, A.M.: The Bumpy Road of Electronic Commerce. In: Maurer, H. (ed.): WebNet 96 – World Conf. Web Soc. Proc. AACE (1996) 378–389. Available at ⟨http://www.dtc.umn.edu/~odlyzko/doc/recent.html⟩.

The Security of Fixed versus Random Elliptic Curves in Cryptography

Yvonne Hitchcock[1], Paul Montague[2], Gary Carter[3], and Ed Dawson[1]

[1] Information Security Research Centre, Queensland University of Technology
GPO Box 2434, Brisbane Q 4001, Australia
{y.hitchcock, e.dawson}@qut.edu.au
[2] Motorola Australia Software Centre
2 Second Ave, Mawson Lakes, SA 5095, Australia
pmontagu@asc.corp.mot.com
[3] School of Mathematics, Queensland University of Technology
GPO Box 2434, Brisbane Q 4001, Australia
g.carter@qut.edu.au

Abstract. This paper examines the cryptographic security of fixed versus random elliptic curves over the field $GF(p)$. Its basic assumption is that a large precomputation to aid in breaking the elliptic curve discrete logarithm problem (ECDLP) can be made for a fixed curve. We take this into account when examining curve security as well as considering a variation of Pollard's rho method where computations from solutions of previous ECDLPs can be used to solve subsequent ECDLPs on the same curve. We present a lower bound on the expected time to solve such ECDLPs using this method, as well as an approximation of the expected time remaining to solve an ECDLP when a given size of precomputation is available. We conclude that adding 5 bits to the size of a fixed curve to avoid general software attacks and an extra 6 bits to avoid attacks on special moduli and a parameters provides an equivalent level of security.

1 Introduction

Elliptic curves were first proposed as a basis for public key cryptography in the mid 1980's independently by Koblitz and Miller. Elliptic curves provide a discrete log based public key cryptosystem and can use a much shorter key length than other public key cryptosystems to provide an equivalent level of security. Elliptic curve cryptosystems (ECCs) can also provide a faster implementation than RSA or discrete log (DL) systems, and use less bandwidth and power [3]. These issues can be crucial in lightweight applications such as smart cards. In the last few years, ECCs have been included or proposed for inclusion in internationally recognized standards (specifically IEEE 1363, WAP (Wireless Application Protocol), ANSI X9.62, ANSI X9.63 and ISO CD 14888-3). Thus ECCs are set to become an integral part of lightweight applications in the immediate future.

One drawback of an ECC is the complexity of generating a secure elliptic curve, which renders it infeasible to generate a randomly chosen but secure

R. Safavi-Naini and J. Seberry (Eds.): ACISP 2003, LNCS 2727, pp. 55–66, 2003.
© Springer-Verlag Berlin Heidelberg 2003

elliptic curve on a mobile device (e.g. telephones, PDAs, smart cards, etc.). This is due to the time required to count the points on the curve and ensure other security requirements [1, Sect. V.7] are met. Even if a mobile device could generate a secure elliptic curve, there would be other costs, such as the bandwidth required to transmit the new curve and a substantially increased code size.

Alternatively, if a fixed curve is used, an implementation on a mobile device is certainly feasible since various implementations have been reported (eg. [3]). In this case, the mobile device is only required to generate a secret key and transmit the corresponding public key to the other parties. Since the necessary random number generator and scalar multiplication routine are both likely to be required by the protocols the mobile device utilizes, any extra code associated with curve generation or key selection is minimal. Also, the bandwidth required is much lower as only the mobile device's compressed public key must be transmitted. Note that the curve parameters of both fixed and random curves must be published before use, so such publication is not a disadvantage specific to fixed curves. While these issues may not be major for all mobile devices (eg. devices for which a server generates the random curve and bandwidth usage is not a problem), the difficulties associated with using random curves have caused fixed curves to be included in standards such as WAP [13] and NIST [9].

Whilst a fixed curve is attractive for efficiency reasons, it also offers a single target for people all over the world to attack. If random curves are used instead, there are many more curves in use throughout the world, particularly if the curves in use are constantly changed. Attackers must then split their resources amongst many targets, instead of one. Furthermore, attacking one curve will not provide any advantage for a later attack on a different curve. Thus the computational power deployed to break a fixed curve is likely to be much greater than that deployed to break a random curve. In addition, if a random curve used by a small number of people is broken, the overall impact is much less than that of breaking a fixed curve used by many people all over the world.

Given the above observations, it appears intuitively obvious that it is more secure to use a random curve than a fixed curve. However, the exact amount and significance of any extra security provided by a random curve is much less clear. Previously, there have been no publications examining whether the decision to use a fixed curve compromises the security of a cryptosystem, and the significance of any such compromise. This paper therefore investigates these issues.

The discussion is restricted to curves over the field $GF(p)$ where p is a large prime. These curves consist of the set of points (x, y) satisfying the equation $y^2 \equiv x^3 + ax + b \pmod{p}$ where a and b are constants such that $4a^3 + 27b^2 \not\equiv 0 \pmod{p}$. The paper firstly examines existing methods of software attack and their impact on fixed curve security, including a variant of Pollard's rho method which can be used to break more than one ECDLP on the one curve. We then present a lower bound on the expected number of iterations required to solve a subsequent ECDLP using this method, as well as an approximation for the number of remaining iterations to solve an ECDLP when a given number of iterations have already been performed. We also investigate threats from hardware attacks and optimizations for curves with special properties. Finally, recommendations are made for the size increase required for a fixed curve to have an equivalent security level to a random curve.

2   Existing Methods of Attack

In this section the different methods available to attack the ECDLP on an arbitrary elliptic curve are examined. They are then used in the following section to analyse the security of fixed curves compared to random curves.

2.1   Pohlig-Hellman Algorithm

The Pohlig-Hellman algorithm breaks the ECDLP down into several different ECDLPs, one in each prime order subgroup of the elliptic curve group [11]. Obviously, the hardest one of these to solve is in the subgroup of largest prime order, and thus the attack is resisted by requiring the order of this subgroup to be at least 160 bits [1, p.98]. For the rest of this paper, we assume that (if applicable) the Pohlig-Hellman algorithm has been used to reduce the ECDLP to an ECDLP in the subgroup of largest prime order.

2.2   Index Calculus and Related Methods

There are currently no Index Calculus or related methods applicable to elliptic curves. Indeed, it is believed to be unlikely that such attacks will ever be possible [1]. Therefore these methods are considered no further in this paper.

2.3   Shanks's Baby-Step Giant-Step Method

The baby-step giant-step (BSGS) method of Shanks [10] has a precomputation for each curve. A balanced version is often given in the literature (eg. [1]). We give an unbalanced version below which takes advantage of the fact that the negative of an elliptic curve point can be calculated "for free," in a similar manner to Shanks's original proposal. Let n, Q, z, m, R and d be defined as follows:

$$n = \text{The prime order of the base point } P,$$
$$Q = \text{The point whose ECDL is to be found,} \qquad d = \left\lceil \frac{n}{2m} \right\rceil,$$
$$z = \text{The value of the ECDLP; that is, } Q = [z]P, \qquad R = [d]P.$$
$$m = \text{Number of points in the precomputation,}$$

The precomputation of giant steps can be calculated as $S_\alpha = [\alpha] R$ for $0 \leq \alpha$ and $\alpha < m$, and it is then possible to solve the ECDLP by finding the baby steps $R_\beta = Q - [\beta] P$ for $0 \leq \beta$ and $\beta < d$ until an R_β value is found which is the same as S_α or $-S_\alpha$ for some α. The solution to the ECDLP is then $z = (\alpha d + \beta)$ if $R_\beta = S_\alpha$, or $z = (n - \alpha d + \beta)$ if $R_\beta = -S_\alpha$.

There are approximately m elliptic curve additions required in the precomputation, and on average $\frac{d}{2}$ further elliptic curve additions required to solve the ECDLP. Thus, on average, it requires approximately $\frac{4m^2+n}{4m}$ operations to solve one ECDLP. This value is at its minimum of $\sqrt{n}$ operations when $m \approx \frac{\sqrt{n}}{2}$.

Table 1. Definitions for Pollard's rho method

n = The prime order of the base point P.
Q_k = The points whose ECDLs are to be found. That is, $Q_k = [z_k]P$, where we wish to find z_k for $k \geq 0$.
$R_{k,0} = [u_{k,0}]P + [w_{k,0}]Q_k$, where $u_{k,0}$ and $w_{k,0}$ are randomly chosen constants from $\mathbb{Z}_p$ and $w_{k,0} \neq 0$.
$R_{k,i}$ = The ith point in the pseudo-random walk to solve the ECDLP for Q_k. Note that $R_{k,i} = [u_{k,i}]P + [w_{k,i}]Q_k$.
s = The number of equations defining the pseudo-random walk.
$f(R)$ = A function mapping a point R to an integer between 1 and s.
$g(R_{k,i}) = R_{k,i+1} = [h_{f(R_{k,i})}]R_{k,i} + [c_{f(R_{k,i})}]P$ (this is the next value in the pseudo-random walk), where c_j and h_j are constants for $1 \leq j \leq s$.
$u_{k,i+1} \equiv h_{f(R_{k,i})}u_{k,i} + c_{f(R_{k,i})}$ (mod n)   for $0 \leq i$.
$w_{k,i+1} \equiv h_{f(R_{k,i})}w_{k,i}$ (mod n)   for $0 \leq i$.

2.4   Pollard's Rho Method

Pollard's rho method is currently the best method known for solving the general ECDLP [12]. The method searches for a collision in a pseudo-random walk through the points on the curve. If the iterating function defining the pseudo-random walk is independent of the point whose discrete logarithm is to be found, then the same calculations can be used to find more than one discrete logarithm on the one curve. Kuhn and Struik [5] provide an analysis of the expected running time of such a method, which is described as follows. Let the definitions in Table 1 be given. The pseudo-random walk function to solve the kth ECDLP, $g(R_{k,i})$, is defined to be as follows:

$$g(R_{k,i}) = [h_{f(R_{k,i})}]R_{k,i} + [c_{f(R_{k,i})}]P$$

where h_j and c_j are constants. Note that the next value in the pseudo-random walk to solve the kth ECDLP, $R_{k,i+1}$, is determined only by P and $R_{k,i}$, not P, Q_k and $R_{k,i}$. In order to maximize efficiency, h_j can be set to 1 for all but one of the possible values of j, in which case h_j is set to 2 and c_j is set to zero. Each iteration of the method will then require only one elliptic curve addition. This random walk is similar to a special case of the "combined walk" proposed by Teske [11]. We note that currently there is no proof that the above random walk is sufficiently random for the theoretical results (which assume the randomness of the walk) to hold. However, since it differs from the random walk with such a proof proposed by Teske in approximately $1/s$ cases where s is the number of equations defining the pseudo-random walk and $s \approx 20$ gives optimal performance [11], it is expected to perform randomly enough.

A collision can occur either with a point on the current pseudo-random walk or with a point on a previous pseudo-random walk and can be solved as follows:

If $R_{k,i} = R_{k,j}$ then $[u_{k,i}]P + [w_{k,i}]Q_k = [u_{k,j}]P + [w_{k,j}]Q_k$

with a solution of $Q_k = \left[\dfrac{u_{k,j} - u_{k,i}}{w_{k,i} - w_{k,j}} \right] P$.

Otherwise, $R_{k,i} = R_{l,j}$ where $R_{l,j} = [u_{l,j}]P + [w_{l,j}]Q_l$ and $Q_l = [z_l]P$.

Therefore, $[u_{k,i}]P + [w_{k,i}]Q_k = [u_{l,j}]P + [w_{l,j}z_l]P$

with a solution of $Q_k = \left[\dfrac{u_{l,j} + w_{l,j}z_l - u_{k,i}}{w_{k,i}} \right] P$.

In order to detect collisions, the current point on the random walk must be compared with previous (stored) points. In order to save storage space, $R_{k,i}$, $u_{k,i}$ and $w_{k,i}$ are only stored if $R_{k,i}$ is a *distinguished point* (a point with some easily checkable property, such as having ten leading zeros in the x coordinate). Because only distinguished points are stored, a collision will not be detected as soon as it occurs, but rather at the next distinguished point on the pseudo-random walk. This is so because $R_{k,i+1}$ only depends on $R_{k,i}$ and P, and once a collision between $R_{k,i}$ and $R_{l,j}$ occurs, $R_{k,i+m} = R_{l,j+m}$ for all $m \geq 0$.

It is emphasized that if distinguished points are used, the random walk definition *must* be independent of the values $Q_1, Q_2, \ldots$ in order for the results in this section to hold. Note that the particular random walk recommended by Kuhn and Struik in [5] to solve a single ECDLP should not be used to solve multiple ECDLPs because it depends on Q_i. Although Kuhn and Struik provide an analysis of the time required to solve multiple ECDLPs, they do not specify a suitable random walk to use in this situation. The problem with the random walk depending on any Q_i is that a different random walk must be used for each ECDLP to be solved. Thus any collisions of non-distinguished points from different random walks are not detected because the random walks take different paths after the collision; only collisions of distinguished points are detected. Of course, if all points are distinguished then the random walk may depend on Q_i, but this will not be the case in most practical situations. Figure 1 shows the results of using a different random walk for each ECDLP compared to using the one random walk described above. It is easily seen that while some advantage is gained from the distinguished points of previous (different) random walks, it is quite small compared to that from using only one random walk.

We now wish to know how much of an improvement previous calculations can offer to the speed with which the solution to a subsequent ECDLP is found.

Let Z_i = The number of iterations required to solve the ith ECDLP.

T_i = The total number of iterations to solve the first i ECDLPs.

(Note that $T_i \geq i + 1$.) Obviously, the expected value of Z_1, $E(Z_1)$, is the same as that of the traditional Pollard's rho method, namely [11]:

$$E(T_1) = E(Z_1) \approx \sqrt{\frac{\pi n}{2}} .$$

Wiener and Zuccherato [12] have improved this figure by a factor of $\sqrt{2}$ by restricting the random walk to points with distinct x coordinates. For simplicity, the optimization has not been included in this section. However, by changing n to $n/2$ in the following discussion, its effect can be taken into consideration. Note that calculations in Sect. 3 do account for this optimization. It is also possible to parallelize Pollard's rho algorithm [1] to obtain a linear speedup. However, such parallelization is not directly included in the model since it can be taken into account by linearly increasing the speed at which calculations are made.

We now wish to find $E(T_i)$ and $E(Z_i)$ for $i > 1$. Kuhn and Struik [5] provide an approximation for the expected value of Z_{i+1} as:

$$E(Z_{i+1}) \approx \sqrt{\frac{\pi n}{2}} \binom{2i}{i} \frac{1}{4^i} \quad \text{for } i \ll n^{\frac{1}{4}} \tag{1}$$

and the expected value of T_{i+1} as:

$$E(T_{i+1}) \approx \sqrt{\frac{\pi n}{2}} \sum_{t=0}^{i-1} \frac{\binom{2t}{t}}{4^t} \quad \left(\text{for } i \ll n^{\frac{1}{4}} \right) \approx 2\sqrt{\frac{i}{\pi}} E(Z_1) . \tag{2}$$

We note that if $\sqrt{\frac{\pi n}{2}}$ is replaced with $E(Z_1)$, the above are not only approximations of the expected values (as shown by Kuhn and Struik), but also lower bounds on the expected values. The proofs of the following lower bounds are omitted for lack of space, but can be found in [4]:

$$E(Z_{i+1}) \geq \binom{2i}{i} \frac{1}{4^i} E(Z_1) \quad \text{for } i \geq 1 \tag{3}$$

$$E(Z_{i+1}) \geq \frac{1}{2i} E(T_i) .$$

Note that the bound is reached when $i = 1$ so that $E(Z_2) = \frac{1}{2}E(Z_1)$ and that (3) can be approximated using Stirling's formula [4] as:

$$E(Z_i) \geq \frac{1}{\sqrt{\pi i}} E(Z_1) \quad \text{for large } i .$$

As stated in [5], (1) and (2) are good approximations. We provide experimental evidence of this in Fig. 1, which shows the actual number of iterations to solve 50 ECDLPs on a 32-bit curve averaged over 200 trials, as well as the bound in (3). Note that since $E(Z_1)$ has been taken to be $\sqrt{\frac{\pi n}{2}}$, the bound is the same as the expected value provided in (1).

We also use $E(Z_i \mid r \text{ previous iterations})$ in our analysis in the following section. It can be approximated using integration [4] to give the result:

$$E(Z_i \mid r \text{ previous iterations}) \approx \sqrt{\frac{\pi n}{2}} e^{\frac{r^2}{2n}} \left(1 - \Phi\left(\frac{r}{\sqrt{2n}} \right) \right) \tag{4}$$

$$\text{where } \Phi(x) = \frac{2}{\sqrt{\pi}} \int_0^x e^{-t^2} dt .$$

Taking into account the Wiener and Zuccherato optimization [12], (4) becomes:

$$E(Z_i \mid r \text{ previous iterations}) \approx \frac{\sqrt{\pi n}}{2} e^{\frac{r^2}{n}} \left(1 - \Phi\left(\frac{r}{\sqrt{n}} \right) \right) . \tag{5}$$

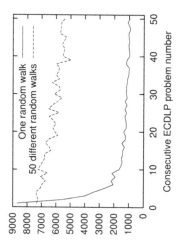
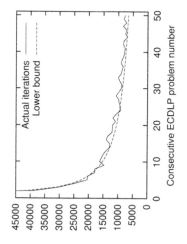

Actual iterations to solve 50 ECDLPs on a 25-bit curve with 1 in 400 points distinguished, averaged over 200 trials

Actual iterations to solve 50 ECDLPs on a 32-bit curve, averaged over 200 trials, with the theoretical bound from (3)

Fig. 1. Results of implementation of Pollard's rho method

3 Security Comparison

3.1 Equivalent Security Definition

In order to compare the security of fixed and random curves, a definition of *"equivalent security"* is required. Firstly, suppose that $S(t)$ iterations per year can be made at time t, where $t = 0$ corresponds to the creation of the fixed curve. Using Moore's law (the efficiency of computers increases exponentially over time) [6], we set $S(t) = \kappa_1 e^{\kappa_2 t}$ and find the number of iterations performed in τ years as:

$$\text{Iterations in } \tau \text{ years} = I(\tau) = \int_0^\tau S(t)dt = \frac{\kappa_1 e^{\kappa_2 \tau}}{\kappa_2} - \frac{\kappa_1}{\kappa_2}. \tag{6}$$

Definition 1 (Equivalent Security). *The value obtained in (6) can be taken as the number of iterations used to create a precomputation available τ years after the release of the fixed curve, and can be used to find the expected iterations to solve the first ECDLP. A calculation can then be made to determine how many extra bits need to be added to the order of the fixed curve to ensure that at time τ, the first ECDLP on the fixed curve (using a precomputation) is as hard as an ECDLP on a random curve. A fixed curve and a random curve with curve orders satisfying these conditions will have* equivalent security (ES).

It is stressed that there is no significant improvement of the time to solve the first ECDLP on a fixed curve compared to a random curve if the precomputation time is included. Kuhn and Struik [5] show this by proving $E(Z_1) - k \leq E(Z_{(1:k)})$ and $E(Z_{(1:k)}) \leq E(Z_1)$ where $Z_{(1:k)}$ is the time to solve one out of k ECDLPs. Since k is much less than $E(Z_1)$, we can approximate $E(Z_{(1:k)})$ with $E(Z_1)$. The precomputation time is ignored when calculating ES because there is a greater incentive to break ECDLPs on a fixed curve than a random curve (this is because more ECDLPs may be solved for the same effort).

In the following examples, n_F and n_R denote the orders of prime (sub)groups of fixed and random curves having ES. The table by Lenstra and Verheul [6] is also used, which gives the minimum secure key size in a certain year. In particular, they give a minimum key size of 135 bits for 2002. To estimate how many iterations of a precomputation could be made per year, we assume it would take the entire year of 2002 to break a 135 bit ECC using Pollard's rho method. Since a 135 bit ECC is considered to be secure in 2002, this is a very optimistic estimation of the current computing power available. As in [6], we also assume that available computing power per dollar is doubling every 18 months and the available budget to spend on such computing power is doubling every ten years. To satisfy these budget and computing power requirements, we must solve:

$$S(t) = S(0) \cdot 2^{\frac{t}{1.5}} \cdot 2^{\frac{t}{10}}, \qquad \text{or} \qquad e^{\kappa_2 t} = 2^{\frac{t}{1.5} + \frac{t}{10}}$$

for κ_2, giving $\kappa_2 = \frac{23}{30} \ln(2)$. To allow a 135 bit elliptic curve to be solved in 2002, the number of iterations in the first year, $I(1)$ (where $I(\tau)$ is defined in (6)), is set to be the number of iterations expected to be required to solve such a curve. That is, we set:

$$I(1) = \frac{\sqrt{\pi \, 2^{135}}}{2} \; ; \qquad \text{that is,} \quad \frac{\kappa_1}{\kappa_2}\left(e^{\kappa_2 \cdot 1} - 1\right) = \frac{\sqrt{\pi \, 2^{135}}}{2}$$

$$\therefore \kappa_1 = \frac{\frac{23}{30} \ln(2) \sqrt{\pi \, 2^{133}}}{2^{\frac{23}{30}} - 1} \approx 1.343018162 \sqrt{2^{133}}.$$

Note that with this value of κ_1, $t = 0$ corresponds to the beginning of 2002.

For a curve of size v bits, we multiply κ_1 by $\frac{135^2}{v^2}$ because the modular multiplication operations used by the point addition in each iteration have a complexity proportional to the square of the number of bits in the curve. This takes account of the fact that each iteration on a curve larger than 135 bits is slower than an iteration on a 135 bit curve.

Table 2 shows the sizes of various fixed curves and the number of bits fewer a random curve satisfying ES would have. To determine the precomputation size, the last year in which the fixed curve would be considered secure was obtained from Table 1 of [6]. The shorter precomputation ends at the beginning of that year and starts at the beginning of 2002, allowing one year after the completion of the precomputation to break any ECDLPs. The longer precomputation finishes at the same time the curve becomes insecure. While conservative users may wish to use the longer precomputation, we believe the shorter precomputation is adequate.

An example calculation from Table 2 for a fixed curve with order $n \approx 2^{160}$ bits is now performed. Since a 160 bit curve is secure until 2019, we allow 2019 - 2002 = 17 years to find the precomputation of size m iterations where:

Table 2. Loss in security of a fixed curve according to ES

Fixed curve size (bits)	136	144	152	160	168	176	184	192	200
Last year curve is secure (γ)	2003	2008	2014	2019	2024	2030	2035	2041	2046
Precomputation time of γ - 2002 years									
Precomp. size	$2^{67.3}$	$2^{72.2}$	$2^{76.7}$	$2^{80.4}$	$2^{84.1}$	$2^{88.5}$	$2^{92.2}$	$2^{96.7}$	$2^{100.4}$
BSGS bits lost	2.3	4.0	5.0	4.4	3.8	4.7	4.1	5.1	4.5
Pollard bits lost	1.7	2.7	3.4	3.0	2.5	3.2	2.8	3.5	3.1
Precomputation time of $\gamma + 1$ - 2002 years									
Precomp. size	$2^{68.7}$	$2^{73.0}$	$2^{77.5}$	$2^{81.1}$	$2^{84.8}$	$2^{89.3}$	$2^{93.0}$	$2^{97.5}$	$2^{101.2}$
BSGS bits lost	5.1	5.6	6.6	5.9	5.3	6.3	5.7	6.6	6.1
Pollard bits lost	3.5	3.9	4.7	4.2	3.7	4.5	4.0	4.8	4.3

$$m = \frac{\kappa_1}{\kappa_2}\left(e^{\kappa_2 \tau} - 1\right) = \frac{135^2}{160^2}1.34\sqrt{2^{133}}\frac{30}{23\ln(2)}\left(e^{\frac{23}{30}\ln(2)\cdot 17} - 1\right) = 2^{80.38} \; .$$

For the BSGS method, any ECDL can then be found using an average of $\frac{n}{4m} = \frac{2^{160}}{2^{80.38+2}} = 2^{77.62}$ iterations. We then set this equivalent to the number of iterations required to solve an ECDLP on a random curve for an unknown size using Pollard's rho method (since it is faster than the BSGS method):

$$2^{77.62} = \sqrt{\pi n_R}/2 \qquad \text{or} \qquad n_R = 2^{155.6} \; .$$

Therefore about five bits of security have been lost in seventeen years. Note that while the time for each iteration on the fixed curve will be slightly different to that required on the random curve, because the curves are close in size, the effect is minimal (about 0.2 fewer bits are actually lost).

For Pollard's rho method, we find how much loss in security occurs for the same curve and precomputation as were used for the BSGS method. We substitute the size of the seventeen year precomputation ($2^{80.38}$) as r in (5) to find how many iterations are expected to remain to solve the ECDLP.

$$E(Z_1) \approx \frac{\sqrt{2^{160}\pi}}{2}\left(e^{(2^{-160})(2^{160.76})}\right)\left(1 - \Phi\left(\frac{2^{80.38}}{2^{80}}\right)\right) \approx 2^{78.34} \; .$$

The size of a random curve generated in 2019 with ES is then found by:

$$2^{78.34} = \frac{\sqrt{\pi n_R}}{2} \qquad \text{or} \qquad n_R \approx 2^{157.0} \; .$$

Therefore, using Pollard's rho method, only 3 bits of security are lost, as opposed to 5 bits using the BSGS method. In fact, Table 2 shows that using the BSGS method causes a greater decrease in the security of a fixed curve.

Given the above assumptions, adding five bits to a fixed curve compared to a random curve will give approximately the same level of security as defined by ES when attacks are performed using the BSGS or Pollard's rho methods.

3.2   Curves with Special Properties

Standardized fixed curves often have special properties in order to increase the speed at which ECCs can operate. For example, the curves specified by NIST [9] use primes with fast modular reduction algorithms and set the a parameter to -3 for faster point addition. On the other hand, the WAP specification [13] sometimes sets the a parameter to 0 for the same reason. Unfortunately, these settings mean that attacks can also be performed at a faster rate.

Using one of the generalized Mersenne primes specified by NIST can make an implementation up to 3.7 times as fast, based on figures from [2]. Even if the modular reduction took no time at all, then this would only lead to an implementation up to 4.5 times as fast. Therefore, based on the relationship between curve size and the complexity of the BSGS and Pollard's rho methods, adding $2 \cdot \log_2(4.5) = 4.34$ bits to the curve size would overcome this problem.

Using an a parameter of -3 can reduce the number of squares and multiplies required for a point addition from 10 to 8, so that addition is about 1.25 times as fast. Using an a parameter of 0 can reduce the number of squares and multiplies to 7 instead of 10, so that addition is about 1.43 times as fast. An increase of $2 \cdot \log_2(1.43) = 1.03$ bits to the curve size would overcome problems due to special values for the a parameter.

To avoid any attacker obtaining an advantage when attacking a fixed curve with a special modulus or a parameter, we suggest that an increase of 5.4 bits $(1.03 + 4.34)$ will provide a more than adequate level of security.

3.3   Special Purpose Hardware

It is possible to build special purpose hardware to attack elliptic curve cryptosystems which would be considerably faster than a software attack using equipment of the same value. Lenstra and Verheul [6, Section 3.2.5] conclude that in the elliptic curve case, for curves over the field $GF(p)$, software is more than $2,000 \approx 2^{11}$ times more expensive than hardware.

As another example, an MPC190 security processor from Motorola [7] running at 66 MHz can perform 1000 internet key exchanges on a 155 bit elliptic curve per second. Therefore, one scalar multiplication takes less than 1 ms. A Pentium IV 1.8 GHz takes 2.66 ms for a scalar multiplication on a 160 bit curve; that is about $73 \approx 2^{6.2}$ times slower taking into account the processor speed.

Hardware availability forms an equal threat to both fixed and random curves because hardware such as the MPC190 is able to perform calculations for any elliptic curve. If attackers are able to invest in hardware to attack fixed curves, then that hardware can just as easily be used to attack random curves. While those who see hardware as a greater threat to fixed curves may suggest adding some extra bits to the fixed curve (22 bits based on [6] or 13-15 bits based on the MPC190 speed), we believe that such an action is unnecessary, given the equal susceptibility of fixed and random curves to these attacks.

Table 3. Time (in ms) of elliptic curve scalar multiplication on a Pentium IV 1.8 GHz

Bit size	Random curve	Fixed curve
160	2.66	
192	4.46	2.19
224	6.76	3.34

3.4   Results of Analysis and Performance Effects

By combining the results of the previous subsections we can determine how many extra bits should be added to a fixed curve for security equivalent to a random curve. Approximately 11 bits should be added to fixed curves over $GF(p)$ (being 5 bits to achieve ES and 6 bits for special curve attacks). Of course, if the fixed curve has neither a special modulus nor a special a parameter, only an extra 5 extra bits are required for the fixed curve.

While adding extra bits to a fixed curve increases the time required to perform elliptic curve operations, the increase is still small enough for fixed curves to be attractive. For comparison, Table 3 shows timings using the MIRACL library [8] for a single scalar multiplication on both a fixed and random curve. In all cases, the Comba optimization from the MIRACL library has been used which unravels and reorganizes the programme loops implicit in the field multiplication and reduction processes. The curves recommended by NIST [9] were used as the fixed curves and have an a parameter of -3 and a generalized Mersenne prime as the modulus. The table shows that a fixed curve with these properties is still faster than a random curve 32 bits smaller than it. Therefore, if fixed curves take advantage of the availability of special moduli and parameters, the 11 extra bits we recommend adding to the size of a fixed curve will not have any serious impact on performance compared to random curves. In fact, the fixed curve may be faster than a random curve implementation not using these special features but with an equivalent level of security. Although in practice 32 (rather than 11) bits are likely to be added to make the modulus size a multiple of the word size of the processor being used, this does not change our conclusion.

4   Conclusion

It was found that if the order of a fixed curve over $GF(p)$ is 11 bits larger than that of a random curve, an equivalent level of security is achieved if previously published attacks are used to solve the ECDLP.

A lower bound on the expected value to solve more than one ECDLP on a curve using Pollard's rho method was given a definition of *"equivalent security"* (ES) proposed. It was concluded that 5 bits must be added to achieve ES.

Attacks taking advantage of special purpose hardware were considered, but since special purpose hardware forms an equal threat to both fixed and random curves, this attack does not require the size of fixed curves to be increased compared to random curves. Also, attacks taking advantage of fixed curves using a special modulus or a parameter have been investigated, and a recommendation made to add 6 bits to the size of the fixed curve to resist these attacks.

Taking all attacks into consideration, we recommend adding 11 bits to the size of a fixed curve compared to a random curve, being 6 bits to resist attacks due to a special modulus or a parameter, and 5 bits to achieve ES.

References

1. Ian Blake, Gadiel Seroussi, and Nigel Smart. *Elliptic Curves in Cryptography*, volume 265 of *London Mathematical Society Lecture Note Series*. Cambridge University Press, Cambridge, 1999.
2. M. Brown, D. Hankerson, J. López, and A. Menezes. Software implementation of the NIST elliptic curves over prime fields. In *Topics in Cryptology—CT-RSA 2001*, volume 2020 of *Lecture Notes in Computer Science*, pages 250–265. Springer-Verlag, 2001.
3. Toshio Hasegawa, Junko Nakajima, and Mitsuru Matsui. A practical implementation of elliptic curve cryptosystems over $GF(p)$ on a 16-bit microcomputer. In *Public Key Cryptography—PKC '98, Proceedings*, volume 1431 of *Lecture Notes in Computer Science*, pages 182–194. Springer-Verlag, 1998.
4. Yvonne Hitchcock, Paul Montague, Gary Carter, and Ed Dawson. Details omitted due to lack of space but available on request. Email: y.hitchcock@qut.edu.au.
5. Fabian Kuhn and René Struik. Random walks revisited: Extensions of Pollard's rho algorithm for computing multiple discrete logarithms. In *Selected Areas in Cryptography—SAC 2001, Proceedings*, volume 2259 of *Lecture Notes in Computer Science*, pages 212–29. Springer-Verlag, 2001.
6. Arjen K. Lenstra and Eric R. Verheul. Selecting cryptographic key sizes. *Journal of Cryptology: the journal of the International Association for Cryptologic Research*, 14(4):255–293, 2001.
7. Motorola, Inc. MPC190 : Security processor. URL: http://e-www.motorola.com /webapp/sps/site/prod_summary.jsp?code=MPC190&nodeId=01DFTQ42497721 (accessed 13/02/2003).
8. Multiprecision Integer and Rational Arithmetic C/C++ Library (MIRACL). URL: http://indigo.ie/~mscott/ (accessed 23/6/2000).
9. National Institute of Standards and Technology. Digital signature standard (DSS), January 2000. URL: http://www.csrc.nist.gov/publications/fips/ (accessed 07/06/2001).
10. Daniel Shanks. Class number, A theory of factorization, and genera. In Donald J. Lewis, editor, *Proceedings of Symposia in Pure Mathematics 1969 Number Theory Institute*, volume XX, pages 415–440, Providence, 1971. AMS.
11. Edlyn Teske. Speeding up pollard's rho method for computing discrete logarithms. In *Algorithmic Number Theory: Third International Symposium—ANTS-III 1998, Proceedings*, volume 1423 of *Lecture Notes in Computer Science*, pages 541–554. Springer-Verlag, 1998.
12. Michael J. Wiener and Robert J. Zuccherato. Faster attacks on elliptic curve cryptosystems. In *Selected Areas in Cryptography—SAC '98, Proceedings*, volume 1556 of *Lecture Notes in Computer Science*, pages 190–200. Springer-Verlag, 1999.
13. Wireless Application Protocol Forum Ltd. Wireless application protocol: Wireless transport layer security, 2001. URL: http://www1.wapforum.org /tech/terms.asp?doc=WAP-261-WTLS-20010406-a.pdf (accessed 31/07/2002).

Cryptanalysis of the Full Version Randomized Addition-Subtraction Chains

Dong-Guk Han[1], Nam Su Chang[1], Seok Won Jung[1],
Young-Ho Park[2]*, Chang Han Kim[3], and Heuisu Ryu[4]

[1] Center for Information and Security Technologies(CIST),
Korea Univ., Seoul, KOREA
{christa,michael,jsw}@cist.korea.ac.kr,
[2] Dept. of Information Security, Sejong Cyber Univ., Seoul, KOREA
youngho@cybersejong.ac.kr
[3] Dept. of Information Security, Semyung Univ., Jechon, KOREA
chkim@venus.semyung.ac.kr
[4] Electronics and Telecommunications Research Institute(ETRI)
hsryu@etri.re.kr

Abstract. In [12], Okeya and Sakurai showed that the simple version randomized addition-subtraction chains countermeasure [14] is vulnerable to SPA attack. But their analysis method is not able to be applicable to the complex version [14]. In this paper, we show that Okeya and Sakurai's attack algorithm has two latent problems which need to be considered. We further propose new powerful concrete attack algorithms which are different from [12,15]. By using our proposed attack algorithms, we can totally break the full version randomized addition-subtraction chains [14]. From our implementation results for standard 163-bit keys, the success probability for the simple version with *20* AD sequences is about 94% and with *30* AD sequences is about 99%. Also, the success probability for the complex version with *40* AD sequences is about 94% and with *70* AD sequences is about 99%.

Keywords: Elliptic curve cryptosystems, Side-channel attack, SPA attack, Randomized addition-subtraction chains countermeasure.

1 Introduction

Elliptic curve groups were first proposed as a primitive for public key cryptography independently by Koblitz [5] and Miller [9]. Elliptic curve is used in the discrete log based public key cryptosystem and this system uses much shorter key length than that of other public key cryptosystems to provide an equivalent level of security. The small key size of ECC is suitable for implementing on low-power devices like smart cards. More recently, Kocher et al. [7] have described side-channel attacks on smart card implementation of cryptosystems. Side-channel

---

* The fourth author is corresponding author and this work was supported by Korea Research Foundation Grant(KRF-2002-015-CP0049)

R. Safavi-Naini and J. Seberry (Eds.): ACISP 2003, LNCS 2727, pp. 67–78, 2003.
© Springer-Verlag Berlin Heidelberg 2003

attacks on the implementation of cryptosystems observe computation timings [6] or power consumption measurements in order to obtain information that is supposed to be kept secret. Both power-analysis variants, the simple power analysis(SPA) and the differential power analysis(DPA), are effective against unprotected implementation of an elliptic curve scalar point multiplication. The basic principles of how to apply the power analysis attacks on elliptic curve cryptosystem have been discussed by Coron in [1]. In [1], he introduced three countermeasures against power attacks; randomization of the private exponent, blinding the point and randomization of the projective coordinates. But in [11], Okeya and Sakurai discussed some weakness of the Coron's first and second countermeasures against DPA. Also, Goubin showed that a power analysis attack is still possible even if the Coron's third countermeasure is used [2]. Thus, Goubin recommended message blinding method before entering the "scalar multiplication" primitive with "random projective coordinates [1]", "random elliptic curve isomorphism [4]" or "random fields isomorphism [4]" to resist DPA. There are two approach to resist the SPA. The first one uses the indistinguishable addition and doubling in the scalar multiplication. For example, elliptic curves of Hesse and Jacobi form achieve the indistinguishability by using the same formula for both addition and doubling [3,8]. The second one uses the add-and-double-always method to mask the scalar dependency. For instance, there are Coron's dummy inserted algorithm [1] and Montgomery form [13].

In [14], Oswald and Aigner proposed **two** randomized addition-subtraction chains as countermeasures against SPA and DPA. They inserted a random decision in the process of building addition-subtraction chain, which had been originally utilized for speeding up the ordinary binary scalar multiplication of an elliptic curve point. A speeding up chain method was first introduced in 1990 by Morain and Olivos [10]. The randomized addition-subtraction chains countermeasure [14] had been considered to be effective in preventing side channel attacks. However, Okeya and Sakurai showed that the randomized addition-subtraction chains countermeasure is vulnerable to SPA attack [12]. But their attack algorithm is just for simple version countermeasure. Namely, their attack algorithm is not able to be applicable to the complex version of the countermeasure against power attacks. So, SPA attack to the complex version is remained as an **open question**. In [15], Walter also analyzed the Oswald-Aigner's randomized addition-subtraction chains with the transition matrix. But in his reconstructing secret value method, there exist undetermined bits of secret value. Namely, Walter's analysis method is just reducing the key space. Also, he didn't give the concrete attack algorithm, which recovers the secret value and his method is much complicated to implement than the Okeya and Sakurai's one.

In this paper, we show that Okeya and Sakurai's attack algorithm [12] has two latent problems that need to be considered. The first one is that an attacker should know the bit length of the secret value d to decide whether their attack algorithm is finished or not. But it isn't a strong assumption for an attacker, who has the capability of distinguishing between addition and doubling operation, to know the bit length of the secret value exactly. The other one is that Okeya and Sakurai overlooked the case that in point addition, one of the points is the point at infinity. In these, the finite field operation in point addition does not take place generally. So their attack algorithm should be modified to detect the secret value completely. The more detailed explanation is contained in Section 3.

We further propose new powerful concrete attack algorithms which are different from the Okeya and Sakurai's one [12] and the Walter's method [15]. By using our proposed attack algorithms, we can break the full version Randomized Addition-Subtraction Chains. Namely, our proposed attack algorithms can be directly applicable to the complex version [14] which was remained as an open question in [12]. By using our attack algorithms, an attacker can find the whole secret value with n AD sequences, which does not leave undetermined bits of the secret value. The worst error probability is $(\frac{3}{4})^{n|d|/2}$. Moreover, our proposed attack algorithm for the simple version can be easily converted into the attack algorithm for the complex version. From our implementation results for standard 163-bit keys, the success probability for the simple version with 20 AD sequences is about 94% and with 30 AD sequences is about 99%. Also, the success probability for the complex version with 40 AD sequences is about 94% and with 70 AD sequences is about 99%. In fact, the success probability 99% with 30 AD sequences means that if an attacker repeatedly obtains 30 AD sequences 100 times for the same secret value, then he can accurately detect the secret value 99 times.

Therefore, we show that all the randomized addition-subtraction chains countermeasures [14], simple version and complex version, are vulnerable to SPA attack. In Section 4, properties of the algorithms [14] and our proposed concrete attack algorithm are mentioned. Implementation results are also contained in Section 4.

2   Randomized Addition-Subtraction Chains Countermeasure

In [14], Oswald and Aigner proposed two randomized addition-subtraction chains as countermeasures against SPA and DPA. A point P on an elliptic curve and a scalar value d are inputted to the randomized addition-subtraction chains, which then computes and outputs a scalar-multiplied point dP as follows:

Note that in this section, we only deal with the Randomized Automaton 2 which is the complex version of the Randomized Automaton 1. So we will cover the Randomized Automaton 1 in Appendix.

▶ **Randomized Automaton 2 (Complex version)**

(Initialization) Set P ← $\mathcal{O}$, Q ← P and j ← 0, and set **state = 0**, where $\mathcal{O}$ is the point at infinity.

■ In case of **state = 0**

- If $d_j = 1$; set P ← P+Q, Q ← 2Q and j ← $j+1$; and set **state =1**.
- If $d_j = 0$; set Q ← 2Q and j ← $j+1$; and set **state =0**.

■ In case of **state = 1**

- If $j = |d|$; output P as dP.
- If $d_j = 1$ and a random number e = 1; set P ← P+Q, Q ← 2Q and j ← $j+1$; and set **state** =1.
- If $d_j = 1$ and a random number e = 0; set P ← P−Q, Q ← 2Q and j ← $j+1$; and set **state** =11.
- If $d_j = 0$; set Q ← 2Q and j ← $j+1$; and set **state** =0.

■ In case of **state = 11**

- If $j = |d|$; output P+Q as dP.
- If $d_j = 1$ and a random number e = 1; set Q ← 2Q and j ← $j+1$; and set **state** =11.
- If $d_j = 1$ and a random number e = 0; set Q ← 2Q, P ← P+Q and j ← $j+1$; and set **state** =1.
- If $d_j = 0$; set P ← P+Q, Q ← 2Q and j ← $j+1$; and set **state** =110.

■ In case of **state = 110**

- If $d_j = 1$ and a random number e = 1; set P ← P+Q, Q ← 2Q and j ← $j+1$; and set **state** =1.
- If $d_j = 1$ and a random number e = 0; set P ← P−Q, Q ← 2Q and j ← $j+1$; and set **state** =11.
- If $d_j = 0$; set Q ← 2Q and j ← $j+1$; and set **state** =0.

Here, $|d|$ denotes the bit length of d, and d_j is the j−th bit of d. That is, $d = \sum_{j=0}^{|d|-1} d_j 2^j$, $d_j \in \{0,1\}$. In addition, the most significant bit $d_{|d|-1} = 1$.

3   Consideration of the Attack Algorithm Proposed by Okeya and Sakurai in [12]

Okeya and Sakurai showed that the simple version algorithm [14] is vulnerable to SPA attack under distinguishability between addition and doubling [12]. Their attack algorithm used the fact that $d_j = 0$ implies **state=0**. But $d_j = 0$ does not imply **state=0** in the complex version. So, SPA attack to the complex version is remained as an open question. Okeya and Sakurai's attack algorithm consists of three steps; determining bits of the scalar value d, determining a position of an AD sequence, and determining information of **state**.

However, their attack algorithm [12] has two latent problems which need to be considered as follows:

- **Attacker should know the bit length $|d|$ of the secret value d :** In the attack algorithm, the bit length $|d|$ is always used except in **step (a)**. This problem can be easily solved for an attacker who has the capability of distinguishing addition from doubling operation. Every bit of the scalar value d is associated with a corresponding doubling operation. This means that the number of doublings is fixed. So the number of doublings is the length of the scalar value d.

- They overlook the case that in point addition, one of the points is the point at infinity : In the implementation of scalar multiplication dP, such special cases of point doubling and point addition as Q=2*$\mathcal{O}$ or Q=P + $\mathcal{O}$ can be avoided. In the ordinary implementation, instead of doubling or addition operation, the point duplication or assignment can be used. A problem comes from neglecting such point addition that one of the points is the point at infinity.

4   Analysis of Randomized Addition-Subtraction Chains Countermeasure

In a simple power analysis attack, an attacker is assumed to be able to monitor the power consumption of one scalar point multiplication. His goal is to find the key using the information obtained from carefully observing the power trace of a complete scalar point multiplication. Such a scalar point multiplication consists of a sequence of point addition, subtraction and doubling operations. The point addition operation has a different power-consumption pattern from the point doubling operation. Since point addition and point subtraction only differ slightly, they can be implemented in such a way that they are indistinguishable for an attacker. Throughout this paper, we thus assume that point addition and point doubling are distinguishable by one-time measurement of power consumption, whereas point addition and point subtraction are indistinguishable. From now on, we briefly say point addition(subtraction) as addition(subtraction) and point doubling as doubling. In the randomized addition-subtraction chains proposed by Oswald-Aigner [14], there are more difficult relations between certain occurrences of operations in the measurement of power consumption and specific bits (or maybe combination of bits) because addition(or doubling) operation corresponds to both 0 and 1 in a digit of d. Namely, when a digit of d is 1(or 0), addition operation may be occurred in some cases and doubling operation also may be occurred in some cases. So, in [12], Okeya and Sakurai analyzed the Randomized Automaton 1, but their proposed attack was not applicable to the Randomized Automaton 2 which is complex version of the Randomized Automaton 1.

However, in this paper we propose a new "*if and only if*" relation between **bits** and **operations** which are obtained by measurements of power consumption. By using this relation, we will show that how an attacker can detect the scalar value d with n measurements of power consumption for scalar multiplication. Our proposed attack algorithms eliminate weak points described beforehand and also can be directly applicable to the Randomized Automaton 2.

Notations : Let S be an AD sequence, i.e., it is a sequence consisting of only addition **A** and doubling **D**. We call **A**(or **D**) as the AD sequence's element. $S_i[k]$ denotes the k-th value of the i-th sequence S_i where $S_i[0]$ denotes the leading value from left to right. $S_i[k_i, n]$ denotes the AD sequence which is the n consecutive values from the k_i-th value of the i-th sequence S_i. $|S|$ denotes the number of character **A,D**. If $S_i[k]$ is empty then we denote $S_i[k]$ = NULL.

Attacker's Task : An attacker has the ability to observe a sequence of elliptic curve operations and his aim is to derive a relation between key bits and AD sequence's values given AD sequences. Using the information of such relation, the attacker can induce attack algorithms for detecting the scalar value d.

4.1   Properties of Randomized Addition-Subtraction Chains Countermeasure

Let us review the properties of randomized addition-subtraction chains proposed by Oswald-Aigner [14]. We will derive a relation between key bits and AD sequence's values from the following proposed Tables 1,2, and 3 in Section 4.1.

Assumption :   An attacker inputs an elliptic curve point into a cryptographic device with the randomized addition-subtraction chains countermeasure, and obtains an AD sequence. He repeats this procedure n times and gathers n AD sequences. Let S_i be an i-th AD sequence where $1 \leq i \leq n$. We follow the notations of Okeya and Sakurai's one [12].

Let the j-th bit d_j of the secret value d be a present bit which should be decided at this time.

Property 1. If for all i_1, $S_{i_1}[k_{i_1}]=\mathbf{A}$, $S_{i_1}[l]=\mathbf{D}$ $(0 \leq l \leq k_{i_1} - 1)$, $S_{i_2}[k_{i_2} + 2]=\mathbf{A}$, and $S_{i_3}[k_{i_3} + 2]=\mathbf{D}$ for some i_2, i_3, then $d_{j-1} = \mathbf{1}$, $d_j = \mathbf{1}$ and $\{d_0, \cdots, d_{j-2}\}$ are all 0 if $j > 1$.

Property 2. If for all i_1, $S_{i_1}[k_{i_1}]=\mathbf{A}$, $S_{i_1}[l]=\mathbf{D}$ $(0 \leq l \leq k_{i_1} - 1)$, and $S_{i_2}[k_{i_2} + 2]=\mathbf{A}$ (or $S_{i_3}[k_{i_3} + 2]=\mathbf{D}$) for all $i_2(i_3)$, then $d_{j-1} = \mathbf{0}$, $d_j = \mathbf{1}$. If $j = 2$ then $d_0 = 1$, otherwise, exactly only one $d_l = 1(0 \leq l \leq j - 2)$ and others are all 0.

These two properties are derived from point addition for the case that one of the points is the point at infinity. In the case that the variable P is the point at infinity and the next bit is 1, the point addition does not operated. Merely, point doubling is operated. If $\mathbf{A}$ firstly appears in the AD sequence, then the present bit d_j is 1, exactly only one d_l is 1 $(0 \leq l \leq j - 1)$ and others are all 0. Properties 1 and 2 can be easily verified by using the previous comment and Property 3.

Theorem 1. *If a current* **state** = **0** *or* **state** = **110***(in the Randomized Automaton 2), then the key bit d_i = 0 if and only if $S_{i_1}[k_{i_1}]=\mathbf{D}$ for all i_1.*

Theorem 2. *If a current* **state** = **0** *or* **state** = **110***(in the Randomized Automaton 2), then the key bit d_i = 1 if and only if $S_{i_1}[k_{i_1}]=\mathbf{A}$ for all i_1 when the variable P is not the point at infinity.*

Theorems 1 and 2 are clear from the Randomized Automata 1 and 2. Note that Properties 1 and 2, and Theorems 1 and 2 are applied to both Randomized Automata 1 and 2.

Table 1. AD sequences if the previous consecutive bits are 11 or 01(the $j-1$-th **state** is not all **1**)

d_{j-2}, d_{j-1}	d_j, d_{j+1}	AD sequence	Probability
11 or 01	11	DAAD	1/4
		DDA	1/8
		DD	1/8
		ADDA	1/8
		ADD	1/8
		ADAD	1/4
	10	DAD	1/2
		ADAD	1/4
		ADD	1/4
	01	ADAD	1/2
		DAD	1/2
	00	ADD	1/2
		DD	1/2

Table 1 shows AD sequences and probability after the computation for two bits d_j, d_{j+1} when the previous consecutive bits are 11 or 01(the $j-1$-th **state** is not all **1**) and the variable P is not the point at infinity.

For instance, the second row and the fourth column's probability $\frac{1}{4}$ means as follows:

$$\mathbf{Pr[DAAD} \text{ and } (d_j, d_{j+1}) = (1,1) \mid (d_{j-2}, d_{j-1}) = (1,1)] = \frac{1}{4}.$$

Table 2 shows AD sequences and probability after the computation for three bits of the scalar value d when the previous consecutive bits are 11 or 01(the $j-1$-th **state** is not all **1**), $d_j=1$, and the variable P is not the point at infinity. Note that Table 1 and Table 2 can be also applied to both Randomized Automaton 1 and 2.

Property of Algorithm for Randomized Automaton 2

Property 3. If $S_{i_1}[k_{i_1}]=\mathbf{D}$ and $S_{i_2}[k_{i_2}]=\mathbf{A}$ for some i_1, i_2, then the previous two bits d_{j-2}, d_{j-1} are all 1 or the previous two bits are $d_{j-2} = 0$, $d_{j-1} = 1$ with the $(j-2)$-th **state** = **110**.

Property 3 implies that an attacker can't determinately detect the next bit from given AD sequences whenever the previous consecutive two bits are all 1 or the previous consecutive three bits are 110 with the present bit $d_j = 1$. The reason of the first case is as follows:

$$\mathbf{Pr}[D_j \mid (d_{j-2}, d_{j-1}, d_j) = (1,1,1)] = \mathbf{Pr}[A_j \mid (d_{j-2}, d_{j-1}, d_j) = (1,1,1)] = \frac{1}{2},$$

$$\mathbf{Pr}[D_j \mid (d_{j-2}, d_{j-1}, d_j) = (1,1,0)] = \mathbf{Pr}[A_j \mid (d_{j-2}, d_{j-1}, d_j) = (1,1,0)] = \frac{1}{2},$$

where an AD sequence's element D_j(or A_j) corresponds to the j-th bit d_j.

Table 2. AD sequences if the previous consecutive two bits are 11 or 01(the $j - 1$-th state is not all **1**) and $d_j = 1$

d_{j-2}, d_{j-1}	d_j, d_{j+1}, d_{j+2}	AD sequence	Probability
11 or 01	111	ADDAAD	1/8
		ADDDA	1/16
		ADDD	1/16
		ADADDA	1/16
		ADADD	1/16
		ADADAD	1/8
		DAADDA	1/16
		DAADD	1/16
		DAADAD	1/8
		DDAAD	1/8
		DDDA	1/16
		DDD	1/16
	110	ADDAD	1/4
		ADADAD	1/8
		ADADD	1/8
		DAADAD	1/8
		DAADD	1/8
		DDAD	1/4

The reason of the second case is as follows:

$$\mathbf{Pr}[D_{j+1} \mid (d_{j-3}, d_{j-2}, d_{j-1}, d_j, d_{j+1}) = (\mathbf{1}, \mathbf{1}, \mathbf{0}, \mathbf{1}, \mathbf{1})] = \frac{1}{3},$$

$$\mathbf{Pr}[A_{j+1} \mid (d_{j-3}, d_{j-2}, d_{j-1}, d_j, d_{j+1}) = (\mathbf{1}, \mathbf{1}, \mathbf{0}, \mathbf{1}, \mathbf{1})] = \frac{2}{3},$$

$$\mathbf{Pr}[D_{j+1} \mid (d_{j-3}, d_{j-2}, d_{j-1}, d_j, d_{j+1}) = (\mathbf{1}, \mathbf{1}, \mathbf{0}, \mathbf{1}, \mathbf{0})] = \frac{2}{3},$$

$$\mathbf{Pr}[A_{j+1} \mid (d_{j-3}, d_{j-2}, d_{j-1}, d_j, d_{j+1}) = (\mathbf{1}, \mathbf{1}, \mathbf{0}, \mathbf{1}, \mathbf{0})] = \frac{1}{3}.$$

However, if the previous two bits are not all 1 or the previous two bits are $d_{j-2} = 0$, $d_{j-1} = 1$ with the $(j-2)$-th **state** $\neq$ **110**, the next bit can be decided determinately from Theorems 1 and 2. Property 3 is always true from Table 3 and Theorems 1 and 2. But the inverse of Property 3 is not always true. The probability of this event is less than $(\frac{2}{3})^n$.

Theorem 3. $S_{i_1}[k_{i_1}] = D$ and $S_{i_2}[k_{i_2}] = A$ for some i_1, i_2 if and only if the previous two bits d_{j-2}, d_{j-1} are all 1 or the previous two bits are $d_{j-2} = 0$, $d_{j-1} = 1$ with the $(j-2)$-th **state** = **110**. The error probability of the necessary condition is less than $(\frac{2}{3})^n$.

Table 3 shows AD sequences and probability after the computation for two bits d_j, d_{j+1} when the previous consecutive bits are 110 and the variable P is not the point at infinity.

Table 3. AD sequences if the previous consecutive three bits are 110

$d_{j-3}, d_{j-2}, d_{j-1}$	d_j, d_{j+1}	AD sequence	Probability
110	11	**ADAD**	2/3
		ADDA	1/6
		ADD	1/6
	10	**ADD**	2/3
		ADAD	1/3
	01	**DAD**	1
	00	**DD**	1

4.2   The Proposed Attack Algorithm

An attacker inputs an elliptic point into a cryptographic device with the randomized addition-subtraction chains countermeasure and obtains an AD sequence. He repeats this procedure n times and gathers n AD sequences. He then detects the secret value d under n AD sequences S_i as follows.

Our proposed attack algorithm consists of two steps. The one is to determine bits of the scalar value d, and the another is to determine position of the value of S. The attack algorithm doesn't need the information of **state** unlike Okeya and Sakurai's one. Due to space limitations, we omit our proposed new attack algorithm for the Randomized Automaton.

Attack Algorithm for Randomized Automaton 2:   The Attack algorithm for Randomized Automaton 2 consists of following four algorithms.

(INITIALIZATION) $k_i = 0$ for each i, and $j = 0$; then go to Key Finding Algorithm 0. Note that the variable k_i is related with the position of the AD sequences and j with the bit of the scalar value d.

▶ *Key Finding Algorithm 1*

☐ If $S_{i_1}[k_{i_1}]$= NULL for some i_1, then d_j is 1 and others bits $\{d_0, \cdots, d_{j-1}\}$ are all 0. (Algorithm is finished)

☐ If $S_{i_1}[k_{i_1}] = \mathbf{A}$ for all i_1 and $S_{i_2}[k_{i_2} + 2]$= NULL for some i_2, then set $d_j = 1$. And exactly only one d_l is 1 where $0 \leq l \leq j - 1$ and others are all 0. We can determine d_l where $0 \leq l \leq j - 1$ by just j-th exhaustive searching. (Algorithm is finished)

☐ If $S_{i_1}[k_{i_1}] = \mathbf{D}$ for all i_1; set $j \leftarrow j+1$; set $k_i \leftarrow k_i +1$ for all i; then go to Algorithm 1.

☐ If $S_{i_1}[k_{i_1}] = \mathbf{A}$ for all i_1,
- If $S_{i_2}[k_{i_2} + 2]$=$\mathbf{A}$ and $S_{i_3}[k_{i_3} + 2]$=$\mathbf{D}$ for some i_2, i_3; set $d_{j-1} = 1$, $d_j = 1$ and if $j > 1$ then $\{d_0, \cdots, d_{j-2}\}$ are all 0; set $j \leftarrow j+1$; set $k_i \leftarrow k_i +2$ for all i; then go to *Sub-Algorithm 1-1*.
- Else
  set $d_{j-1} = 0$, $d_j = 1$. If $j = 2$ then set $d_0 = 1$, otherwise, exactly only

one d_l is 1 where $0 \le l \le j-2$ and others are all 0. We can determine d_l where $0 \le l \le j-2$ by just $j-1$-th exhaustive searching. Set $j \leftarrow j+1$; set $k_i \leftarrow k_i+2$ for all i; then go to *Algorithm 1*.

▶ *Key Finding Algorithm 1*

☐ If $S_{i_1}[k_{i_1}]=$ NULL for some i_1, then $d=\sum_{k=0}^{j-1} d_k 2^k$. (Algorithm is finished)

☐ If $S_{i_1}[k_{i_1}] = \mathbf{D}$ for all i_1; set $d_j = 0$, $j \leftarrow j+1$; set $k_i \leftarrow k_i +1$ for all i, then go to *Algorithm 1*.

☐ Else
  - If $S_{i_1}[k_{i_1}] = \mathbf{A}$ for all i_1, set $d_j = 1$, $j \leftarrow j+1$, $k_i \leftarrow k_i +2$ for all i, then go to *Algorithm 1*.
  - Else
    go to *Sub-Algorithm 1-1*.

▶ *Key Finding Sub-Algorithm 1-1*

☐ If $S_{i_1}[k_{i_1}]=$ NULL for some i_1, then $d=\sum_{k=0}^{j-1} d_k 2^k$. (Algorithm is finished)

☐ If $S_{i_1}[k_{i_1} + 2]=$ NULL for some i_1, then set $d_j = 1$ and $d=\sum_{k=0}^{j} d_k 2^k$. (Algorithm is finished)

☐ If $S_{i_1}[k_{i_1},3] = \mathbf{DAA}$ and $S_{i_2}[k_{i_2} + 5]=$ NULL for all i_1, i_2, then set $d_j = 1, d_{j+1} = 1$ and $d=\sum_{k=0}^{j+1} d_k 2^k$. (Algorithm is finished)

☐ If $S_{i_1}[k_{i_1},3]=\mathbf{DAA}$ for some i_1,
  - If $S_{i_2}[k_{i_2},4]=\mathbf{DDAD}$ or $S_{i_2}[k_{i_2},5]=\mathbf{ADDAD}$ for some i_2; set $d_j = 1$, $d_{j+1} = 1$, $d_{j+2} = 0$, $j \leftarrow j+3$; set $k_i \leftarrow k_i +4$ for all i such that $S_i[k_i,4]=\mathbf{DDAD}$, $k_i \leftarrow k_i +5$ for all i such that $S_i[k_i,5]=\mathbf{DAADD}$, $\mathbf{ADDAD}$, or $\mathbf{ADADD}$, and $k_i \leftarrow k_i +6$ for the others; then go to *Sub-Algorithm 1-2*.
  - Else
    set $d_j = 1$, $d_{j+1} = 1$ ($d_{j+2} = 1$), $j \leftarrow j+2$; set $k_i \leftarrow k_i +2$ for all i such that $S_i[k_i,3]=\mathbf{DDD}$, $k_i \leftarrow k_i +3$ for all i such that $S_i[k_i,3]=\mathbf{DDA}$ or $S_i[k_i,4]=\mathbf{ADDD}$, and $k_i \leftarrow k_i +4$ for the others ; then go to *Sub-Algorithm 1-1*.

☐ Else
  - If $S_{i_1}[k_{i_1},3]=\mathbf{DAD}$ for some i_1,
    * If $S_{i_2}[k_{i_2},3]=\mathbf{ADD}$ for some i_2; set $d_j = 1$, $d_{j+1} = 0$, $j \leftarrow j+2$; set $k_i \leftarrow k_i +4$ for all i such that $S_i[k_i,4]=\mathbf{ADAD}$, and $k_i \leftarrow k_i +3$ for the others; then go to *Sub-Algorithm 1-2*.
    * Else
      set $d_j = 0$, $d_{j+1} = 1$, $j \leftarrow j+2$; set $k_i \leftarrow k_i +3$ for all i such that $S_i[k_i,3]=\mathbf{DAD}$, and $k_i \leftarrow k_i +4$ for the others; then go to *Sub-Algorithm 1-1*.
  - Else
    set $d_j = 0$, $d_{j+1} = 0$, $j \leftarrow j+2$; set $k_i \leftarrow k_i +2$ for all i such that $S_i[k_i,2]=\mathbf{DD}$, and $k_i \leftarrow k_i +3$ for the others; then go to *Algorithm 1*.

▶ *Key Finding Sub-Algorithm 1-2*

☐ If $S_{i_1}[k_{i_1}]=\mathbf{A}$ for some i_1; set $d_j = 1$, $j \leftarrow j+1$; set $k_i \leftarrow k_i +2$ for all i; then go to *Sub-Algorithm 1-1*.

☐ Else set $d_j = 0$, $j \leftarrow j+1$; set $k_i \leftarrow k_i +1$ for all i; then go to *Sub-Algorithm 1*.

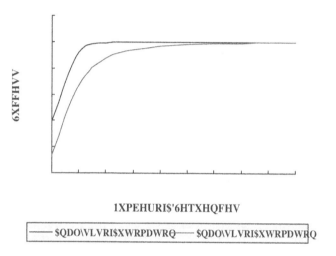

1XPEHURI$'6HTXHQFH

| ——— $QDO\VLVRI$XWRPDWRQ | ——— $QDO\VLVRI$XWRPDWRQ |

Fig. 1. Comparison of the success probability between the Randomized Automaton 1 and the Randomized Automaton 2

4.3   Implementation Results

We experimentally applied our attack algorithm to both the Randomized Automata 1 and 2. The implementation results for standard 163-bit keys are shown in Figure 1. From Figure 1, the success probability for the simple version with *20* AD sequences is about 94% and with *30* AD sequences is about 99%. And the success probability for the complex version with *40* AD sequences is about 94% and with *70* AD sequences is about 99%. For instance, the success probability 99% with *30* AD sequences means that if an attacker repeatedly obtains *30* AD sequences 100 times for the same secret value, then he can accurately detect the secret value 99 times. Actually, we have tested for many different secret values.

References

1. J.S.Coron, *Resistance against Differential Power Analysis for Elliptic Curve Crytosystems*, In Workshop on Cryptographic Hardware and Embedded Systems(CHES'99), LNCS1717, (1999),292–302.

2. L.Goubin, *A Refined Power-Analysis Attack on Elliptic Curve Cryptosystems*, Public Key Cryptography (PKC 2003), LNCS2567, (2003),199–211.
3. M.Joye and J.Quisquater, *Hessian ellitpic curves and side-channel attacks*, In Workshop on Cryptographic Hardware and Embedded Systems(CHES'01), LNCS2162, (2001),402–410.
4. M.Joye and C.Tymen, *Protections against differential analysis for elliptic curve cryptography*, In Workshop on Cryptographic Hardware and Embedded Systems(CHES'01), LNCS2162, (2001),377–390.
5. N.Koblitz, *Elliptic curve cryptosystems*, In Mathematics of Computation, volume 48,(1987),203–209.
6. P.Kocher, *Timing attacks on implementations of Diffie-Hellman, RSA, DSS, and other systems*, In Advances in Cryptology- CRYPTO'96, LNCS1109,(1996),104–113.
7. P.Kocher, J.Jaffe, and B.Jun, *Differential power analysis*, In Advances in Cryptology- CRYPTO'99, LNCS1666,(1999),388–397.
8. P.Liardet and N.Smart, *Preventing SPA/DPA in ECC systems using the Jacobi form*, In Workshop on Cryptographic Hardware and Embedded Systems(CHES'01), LNCS2162, (2001),391–401.
9. V.S.Miller, *Use of elliptic curves in cryptography*, In Advances in Cryptology-CRYPTO'85, LNCS218,(1986),417–426.
10. F.Morain and J.Olivos, *Speeding up the computation on an elliptic curve using addition-subtraction chains*, Inform Theory Appl., vol 24,(1990),531–543.
11. K.Okeya, K.Sakurai, *Power analysis breaks elliptic curve cryptosystems even secure against the timing attack*, Indocrypt 2000, LNCS1977, (2000),178–190.
12. K.Okeya, K.Sakurai, *On Insecurity of the Side Channel Attack Countermeasure Using Addition-Subtraction Chains under Distinguishability between Addition and Doubling*, Information Security and Privacy (ACISP'02), LNCS2384, (2002),420–435.
13. K.Okeya, H.Kurumatani and K.Sakurai, *Elliptic curves with the Montgomery form and their cryptographic applications*, Public Key Cryptography (PKC 2000), LNCS1751, (2000),446–465.
14. E.Oswald, M.Aigner, *Randomized Addition-Subtraction Chains as a Countermeasure against Power Attacks*, In Workshop on Cryptographic Hardware and Embedded Systems(CHES'01), LNCS2162, (2001),39–50.
15. C.D. Walter, *Security Constraints on the Oswald-Aigner Exponentiation Algorithm*, Cryptology ePrint Archive, Report 2003/013, (2003).http//eprint.iacr.org/.

Generic GF(2^m) Arithmetic in Software and Its Application to ECC

André Weimerskirch[1*], Douglas Stebila[2*], and Sheueling Chang Shantz[3]

[1] Communication Security Group, Ruhr-Universität Bochum, Germany
weika@crypto.rub.de
[2] Department of Combinatorics & Optimization, University of Waterloo, Ontario,
Canada
dstebila@uwaterloo.ca
[3] Sun Microsystems Laboratories, Mountain View, California, USA
sheueling.chang@sun.com

Abstract. This work discusses generic arithmetic for arbitrary binary fields in the context of elliptic curve cryptography (ECC). ECC is an attractive public-key cryptosystem recently endorsed by the US government for mobile/wireless environments which are limited in terms of their CPU, power, and network connectivity. Its efficiency enables constrained, mobile devices to establish secure end-to-end connections. Hence the server side has to be enabled to perform ECC operations for a vast number of mobile devices that use variable parameters in an efficient way to reduce cost. We present algorithms that are especially suited to high-performance devices like large-scaled server computers. We show how to perform an efficient field multiplication for operands of arbitrary size, and how to achieve efficient field reduction for dense polynomials. We also give running times of our implementation for both general elliptic curves and Koblitz curves on various platforms, and analyze the results. Our new algorithms are the fastest algorithms for arbitrary binary fields in literature.

Keywords: Binary Fields, Dense Field Polynomials, Field Multiplication, Field Reduction, Elliptic Curves, Koblitz Curves

1 Introduction

In recent years Elliptic Curve Cryptography (ECC) has received increased acceptance. ECC has been included in standards from bodies such as ANSI, IEEE, ISO, and NIST. Further evidence of widespread acceptance are the inclusion of ECC in IPsec, TLS, and OpenSSL [17]. Compared to traditional cryptosystems like RSA, ECC offers smaller key sizes and more efficient arithmetic which results in faster computations, lower power consumption, as well as memory and bandwidth savings. This is especially useful for mobile, constrained devices.

---

* The research was done at and sponsored by Sun Microsystems Laboratories, Mountain View, CA, USA.

R. Safavi-Naini and J. Seberry (Eds.): ACISP 2003, LNCS 2727, pp. 79–92, 2003.
© Springer-Verlag Berlin Heidelberg 2003

Hence ECC enables wireless mobile devices to perform secure communications efficiently and establish secure end-to-end connections.

In this paper we focus on binary field arithmetic and its application to ECC. Many software implementations have been reported in recent years. These works range from implementations in very constrained environments [1][23] to broad surveys [6]. However, all of these implementations are done for specific fields and cannot handle arbitrary fields and curves. While there is value in constructing a highly specialized implementation for constrained devices such as PDAs and smart cards, there is a need to handle arbitrary curves on the server side efficiently. As ECC becomes more important and more widely used, we foresee the following scenario. Commercial entities such as financial services or online stores will carry out transactions with users. The servers are required to perform cryptographic operations such as signature generation and verification, and key exchange. Most of these operations will employ standardized settings such as the NIST recommended elliptic curves [16]. However, there may be users that generate curves themselves, or Certificate Authorities that issue certificates over non-standardized curves that promise a performance gain. For example, they might want to use a curve defined over $GF(2^{155})$ as described in [18], a curve over $GF(2^{178})$ as presented in [19], or curves suited to special field element representations as in [2]. There may also be standards which are rarely used and thus do not justify the implementation of a special case, and future standards may introduce new curves. Still, a server must be able to handle all requests efficiently to reduce computing time and hence cost.

Our approach and motivation is based on this scenario. We present a binary field implementation for arbitrary fields $GF(2^m)$ in the context of ECC which works for CPUs with different word sizes. Our implementation is a complete software package which is part of the ECC support for binary fields of OpenSSL [17][1]. We present algorithms that are especially suited to high-performance devices like large-scaled server computers. We show how to perform an efficient field multiplication for operands of arbitrary size, and how to achieve efficient field reduction for dense polynomials. We give performance numbers that show the efficiency of our implementation, and analyze the results. We implemented both general curves and Koblitz curves. The results show that our algorithms are the fastest methods for arbitrary binary field arithmetic in existing literature.

The remainder of this paper is organized as follows. Related work is presented in the next section. Section 3 presents the algorithms that we used for the binary field arithmetic and the ECC operations, and Section 4 presents results and an analysis of our implementation.

2   Related Work

Since the introduction of elliptic curves to cryptography in 1985 by Koblitz and Miller a vast amount of research has been done. When implementing ECC in

---

[1] Note that this paper describes a highly optimized and adapted version of the ECC library available in OpenSSL 0.9.8.

software there are several choices to make. We categorize these parameter choices as follows:

- Underlying field type, field representation, and field operation algorithms
- Elliptic curve point representation and point operation algorithms
- Protocol algorithms

The literature contains significant research on each of these issues. As our goal is a generic implementation of ECC, we focus on the optimization of the operations of the underlying field. We think it is easier to optimize a generic ECC implementation over binary fields than over prime fields. As the results in [1] suggest, the efficient use of prime fields requires platform dependent assembly code. Therefore we restrict our attention here to binary fields.

A comprehensive survey of binary field and elliptic curve arithmetic for the NIST recommended elliptic curves was done in [6]. A specialized implementation was done for the field $GF(2^{155})$ [18]. There are also implementations available for constrained devices. PGP was ported to constrained devices in [1] while [23] optimizes an ECC implementation for a Palm PDA. López and Dahab presented a Montgomery field multiplication for binary fields in [14]. They also did research on binary field multiplication [15] and ECC over binary fields [13]. More point multiplication algorithms can be found in [10] and [12]. Further work was done for special field choices like composite fields, e.g., in [2] and [4]. There were, however, recent attacks [3] on these fields. Finally, Solinas developed efficient algorithms for Koblitz curves over binary fields using complex multiplication [22].

3 Arithmetic

3.1 Binary Field $GF(2^m)$

In the following we present new algorithms that are suitable for performing efficient general binary field arithmetic. For the field representation we chose a polynomial basis as it is most widely used and as it yields a simple but fast implementation in software. Let $f(x) = x^m + f'(x)$ be an irreducible binary polynomial of degree m. The elements of $GF(2^m)$ are represented by binary polynomials of degree at most $m - 1$. Operations in $GF(2^m)$ are performed modulo $f(x)$. We represent a field element $a(x) = \sum_{i=0}^{m-1} a_i x^i \in GF(2^m)$ as a binary vector $a = (a_{m-1}, \ldots, a_0)$ of length m. As we use word arithmetic, where the register size is noted as W, we also write $A = (A[s-1], \ldots, A[0])$ with $A[i] = (a_{iW+W-1}, \ldots, a_{iW+1}, a_{iW})$ and $s = \lceil m/W \rceil$. Note that $A[s-1]$ is padded on the left with zeros as needed. The expression $A\{i\}$ denotes the sub array $A\{i\} = (A[s-1], \ldots, A[i])$.

There are two main strategies for implementing general binary fields. The first one is to use the Montgomery multiplication and squaring as presented in [9]. The Montgomery multiplication roughly requires two polynomial multiplications but omits the reduction step. The other possibility is to perform field operations in two steps, namely the polynomial operation and reduction. Since we estimate as described later that a general reduction for an arbitrary field polynomial can be done with our new method in time roughly 1/3 of a polynomial multiplication at the cost of memory storage we decided to use this technique.

Addition of field elements is done as word-wise XOR. Since the field size is not fixed we do not know the operand's length at implementation time. We use a jump table to unroll the loop as shown in Algorithm 1 as it gave us a speed-up in our experiments. However, this technique does not necessarily improve running time on all platforms.

Algorithm 1 Addition using jump table

INPUT: Binary polynomials $a(x)$ and $b(x)$ of degree at most $m-1$ and s words.
OUTPUT: The binary polynomial $c(x) = a(x) \oplus b(x)$.

1: **switch (s)**
2:   **case 40:** $C[39] \leftarrow A[39]$ XOR $B[39]$
3:   ...
4:   **case 1:** $C[0] \leftarrow A[0]$ XOR $B[0]$
5:   **break**
6:   **default:** do standard addition with loop
7: **end switch**
8: **Return** $c(x)$

We perform division according to [20] and squaring in linear time complexity by a table lookup as presented in [18]. In the following we focus on the multiplication and reduction operation.

Multiplication. Modular multiplication is done in two phases. First we compute the polynomial product $c'(x) = a(x) \cdot b(x)$ and then we reduce the result $c(x) \equiv c'(x) \bmod f(x)$. We look at the reduction step in the next section and consider the first step here.

We implemented the Karatsuba Algorithm (KA) and the comb method [15]. The comb method can be implemented as presented in Algorithm 2. Note that W describes the word size, so typical values for W are $8, 16, 32$ and 64. The comb multiplication requires a table of size $2^w s$ where w is the window size. For an efficient implementation one should choose a window size that is a divisor of the word size. We selected $w = 4$ which requires $16s$ table entries for all typical word sizes. Obviously $w = 2$ and $w = 8$ is not optimal for operand sizes as they are used in ECC. We implemented the left shift operation in Steps 1 and 9 as a jump table in a manner similar to the field addition to achieve loop unrolling while still having a general implementation. Note that the left shift of Step 9 is done over the double-sized result operand. Thus, for large word sizes W it might be more efficient to decrease the number of runs of the outer loop in Step 3 by "emulating" smaller word sizes. For instance, operands of 64-bit words might be considered as operands of twice as many 32-bit words. Then the outer loop is executed only 3 times instead of 7 times whereas the instructions, namely the XOR operation, would still be performed over 64-bit words to utilize the advantage of larger word sizes. However, this might lead to alignment errors at run time on several hardware platforms and thus cannot be seen as a general approach.

Algorithm 2 Comb method with window size $w = 4$

INPUT: Binary polynomials $a(x)$ and $b(x)$ of degree at most $m - 1$.
OUTPUT: The binary polynomial $c'(x) = a(x) \cdot b(x)$.
1: Compute $B_u(x) = u(x) \cdot b(x)$ for all polynomials $u(x)$ of degree at most 3.
2: $C' \leftarrow 0$
3: **for** $i = W/4 - 1$ down to 0 **do**
4:     **for** $j = 0$ to $s - 1$ **do**
5:         Let $u = (u_3, u_2, u_1, u_0)$, where u_k is bit $(4i + k)$ of $A[j]$.
6:         $C'\{j\} \leftarrow C'\{j\} \oplus B_u$
7:     **end for**
8:     **if** $i \neq 0$ **then**
9:         $C' \leftarrow C'x^4$
10:     **end if**
11: **end for**
12: **Return** $c'(x)$

The basic KA works as follows. Consider two operands $A(x)$ and $B(x)$.

$$A(x) = A[1]x^W + A[0], \ B(x) = B[1]x^W + B[0]$$

Let $D_0, D_1, D_{0,1}$ be auxiliary variables with

$$D_0 = A[0] \ B[0], \quad D_1 = B[1] \ B[1]$$
$$D_{0,1} = (A[0] \ \text{XOR} \ A[1])(B[0] \ \text{XOR} \ B[1])$$

Then the polynomial $C(x) = A(x) \ B(x)$ can be calculated in the following way:

$$C(x) = D_1 x^{2W} + (D_{0,1} \oplus D_0 \oplus D_1)x^W + D_0 \tag{1}$$

The KA can easily be expanded in a recursive way, or by splitting the operands into more than two words [24]. For example, to multiply operands of three words using the KA, compute

$$C(x) = D_2 x^{4W} + (D_{1,2} \oplus D_1 \oplus D_2)x^{3W} + (D_{0,2} \oplus D_2 \oplus D_0 \oplus D_1)x^{2W} \tag{2}$$
$$+ (D_{0,1} \oplus D_1 \oplus D_0)x^W + D_0$$

where

$$D_0 = A[0] \ B[0], D_1 = A[1] \ B[1], D_2 = A[2] \ B[2]$$
$$D_{0,1} = (A[0] \ \text{XOR} \ A[1])(B[0] \ \text{XOR} \ B[1])$$
$$D_{0,2} = (A[0] \ \text{XOR} \ A[2])(B[0] \ \text{XOR} \ B[2])$$
$$D_{1,2} = (A[1] \ \text{XOR} \ A[2])(B[1] \ \text{XOR} \ B[2])$$

Obviously this can also be done in a recursive manner.

We implemented the KA as follows. First we multiply two words using a slightly modified comb method that does not require a multi-word shift operation. The complexity of the comb method [15] can be generalized to $s\left(\frac{m}{w} + 2^w - w - 1\right)$ XOR and $w - 1 + 2(\frac{W}{w} - 1)$ SHIFT operations. In our case $s = 1$ and $m = W$. Since we avoid a shift over multiple words this reduces to $\frac{W}{w} + 2^w - w - 1$ XOR and $w + \frac{2W}{w} - 3$ SHIFT operations. Assuming that an XOR and a SHIFT operation needs the same execution time we obtain the following optimum window sizes w. For 8-bit and 16-bit hardware we use a window size of 2, for 32-bit a size of 3,[2] and for 64-bit CPUs a size of 4. We call the corresponding macro 1x1_MUL. Based on this elementary multiplication we realized hard-coded macros to compute the product of 2, 3, and 4 words[3]. We call these macros 2x2_MUL, 3x3_MUL and 4x4_MUL, which call the 1x1_MUL macro 3, 6, and 9 times, respectively. The cost of the addition operation is negligible for binary fields and is not considered in the following. Our field multiplication is implemented in a way that different functions can be plugged in for different field sizes. To multiply operands that consist of $s = 1, \ldots, 8$ words, we use specialized methods whereas for operands with $s \geq 9$ words, we use a general approach. The cases $s = 1, \ldots, 4$ are mapped onto the hard coded macros. For $s = 5$ we split the operands into two parts of size 3 and 2 words, respectively. This requires $2 \cdot 6 + 3 = 15$ 1x1_MULs. The cases $s = 6, \ldots, 8$ are executed in similar ways. Table 1 presents the cost of the specialized cases in terms of the number of 1x1_MULs executed.

Table 1. Cost (in number of 1x1_MULs) of KA for $n =$2-8 words

n	1	2	3	4	5	6	7	8
cost	1	3	6	9	15	18	24	27

For the general case we implemented a recursive method as shown in Algorithm 3. Note that a_i and b_i in Steps 10, 12 and 14 describe the sub-polynomials of a and b, respectively. Clearly, the algorithm could be extended such that the recursion ends in more than the four multiplication macros and the recursive selection handles more cases of s than only those divisible by 2 and 3. We call this the *KA factor basis*. We used a simulation to evaluate the improvements gained by increasing the number of primes in the factor basis: we compared the number of operations for a range of $s = 5, \ldots, 40$ and computed the average cost for the different factor bases. We found that on average a performance gain of 8% is realized when going from the factor basis of 2 to that of 2 and 3, and no performance gain is achieved when adding 5, 7, or 11 to the factor basis. The

---

[2] Contrary to our earlier statement we use a window size that is not a divisor of the word-size since we are only working on one register.

[3] The method for 4 words has the same complexity as a recursive version computing products of two words but saves some overhead. However, this comes at the cost of a larger code-size.

factors 5, 7, and 11 can optimally be expressed by the factor basis of 2 and 3. For example, the best method to perform KA for 7 words is to split the operand into two portions of 3 and 4 words, respectively. These can optimally be computed by the KA using a prime basis of 2 and 3. Thus these larger factors in the prime basis do not give an additional speed-up. In practice there still might be a performance gain from enlarging the KA factor basis since the recursion overhead is reduced. On the other hand, the code complexity and size increases. We also note that the performance improvement is for the average case. There are some cases, in which a smaller factor basis executes faster. For example, for $s = 15$ words a factor basis of 2 and 3 requires 90 elementary 1x1_MUL operations while a factor basis of 2 only needs 78 such operations.

Algorithm 3 General Karatsuba Algorithm GEN_KA(a,b,s)

INPUT: Binary polynomials $a(x)$ and $b(x)$ of s words.
OUTPUT: The binary polynomial $c'(x) = a(x) \cdot b(x)$.

1: **if** $s = 4$ **then**
2:     Return 4x4_MUL(a,b)
3: **else if** $s = 3$ **then**
4:     Return 3x3_MUL(a,b)
5: **else if** $s = 2$ **then**
6:     Return 2x2_MUL(a,b)
7: **else if** $s = 1$ **then**
8:     Return 1x1_MUL(a,b)
9: **else if** $s \bmod 3 = 0$ **then**
10:     Split a and b each into three sub polynomials a_i, $i = 1, 2, 3$, of size $s/3$, and b_i, respectively. Perform GEN_KA($a_i, b_i, s/3$) 6 times according to the elementary 3-word KA (2), and put the result together.
11: **else if** $s \bmod 2 = 0$ **then**
12:     Split a and b each into two sub polynomials a_i, $i = 1, 2$, of size $s/2$, and b_i, respectively. Perform GEN_KA($a_i, b_i, s/2$) 3 times according to the elementary 2-word KA (1), and put the result together.
13: **else**
14:     Split a and b each into two sub polynomials a_i, $i = 1, 2$, of size $\lfloor s/2 \rfloor$ and $\lceil s/2 \rceil$, and b_i, respectively. Perform GEN_KA($a_i, b_i, \lceil s/2 \rceil$) twice and GEN_KA($a_i, b_i, \lfloor s/2 \rfloor$) once according to the elementary 2-word KA (1), and put the result together.
15: **end if**

Reduction. Reduction can be performed efficiently for trinomials and pentanomials with middle terms close to each other. All standardized curves use these kinds of field polynomials. It is known that for all binary fields $GF(2^m)$ up to at least $m = 1000$ there exists such an irreducible polynomial [11]. While reduction can be hard-coded for a fixed field polynomial and executed at negligible cost, this is not the case for a generic implementation.

As before we decided to offer different reduction methods which can be plugged in for different fields. We offer a reduction method for trinomials as well as for pentanomials which performs a word-wise reduction for general trinomials and pentanomials, respectively [6]. Furthermore we implemented a general version that can handle arbitrary field polynomials. However, it becomes very expensive for dense irreducible polynomials. It is clear that even the specialized methods for trinomials and pentanomials cannot be nearly as efficient as hard coded methods for a given irreducible polynomial. Another universal method to perform reduction is division with remainder which usually is expensive.

We propose a third reduction method using a window technique as described in Algorithm 4. This algorithm contains a precomputation step in which all possible window values are computed and stored in a table, and a computation step in which the polynomial is reduced by one window segment at a time. The algorithm can be best explained with the following example. Let $f(x) = x^m + f'(x) = x^{163} + x^7 + x^6 + x + 1$, $W = 32$, $s = 6$, and let $\ll t$ and $\gg t$ be a shift to the left or right by t bit positions, respectively. Furthermore, let $PreF_i$ be the table entry at index i. First, we insert the polynomial $f'(x)$ into the table at index $2^{163 \bmod 32}$. Since we will perform shifts of this table entry to the right in order to obtain further values we attach a zero-word below the least significant bit, i.e., we store $PreF_8 = f'(x) \cdot x^W$. The remaining table entries can now be computed as $PreF_1 = PreF_8 \gg 3$, $PreF_2 = PreF_1 \ll 1$, $PreF_3 = PreF_2 \oplus PreF_1$, and so on. Further speed-up can be achieved by computing table entries $PreF_{j \cdot t}$ with $j \in \{1, \ldots, W/w\}$ and $t \in \{1, \ldots, 2^w - 1\}$ where w is the window size. This avoids shifting operations in the computation step. In the computational phase the polynomials are reduced by a window segment in each step. Let $c(x)$ be a polynomial of order larger than 162, and let $(c_{iW+jw+w-1}, \ldots, c_{iW+jw})$ be a window of $C[i]$ with $iW + jw \geq 163$. Then this window segment can be reduced by XORing $C\{i - s\}$ with $PreF_{(j+1)(iW+jw+w-1,\ldots,iW+jw)_2}$, where $C\{i - s\}$ denotes the sub array $C\{i - s\} = (C[i], \ldots, C[i - s])$. The addition in Step 6 can be done efficiently by only performing an XOR operation for values not equal to 0. The last word $C[s - 1]$ is reduced separately to take into account that only a part of it is reduced, namely $(c_{(s-1)W+W-1}, \ldots, c_{(s-1)W+(m \bmod W)}, 0, \ldots, 0)$. Note that in the last step we XOR $(PreF_{j \cdot t} \gg W)$ to C.

The technique is very similar to the comb method for polynomial multiplication [15]. Each table entry $PreF_u(x)$ requires $s + 1$ words. Thus the memory requirement is $(W/w)(2^w - 1)(s + 1)$ words. Algorithm 4 uses window size $w = 8$ as it is most suitable for a server application and needs a memory size of $255(W/8)(s + 1)$ words[4]. The precomputation step is done only once per field and can be done off-line. Our reduction method does not require any shift operations. Assuming that the precomputation is done off-line the method requires $(m/w)(s + 1)$ XORs. Thus a reduction step costs $(m/8)(s + 1)$ XOR operations in our case. The comb method requires $s(m/4 + 11)$ XORs and $3 + 2(W/4 - 1)$ SHIFTs over multiple words [15]. Hence the cost of a reduction step for arbi-

---

[4] A window size of $w = 8$ requires for a 32-bit CPU ($W = 32$) and a 163-bit curve ($s = 6$) 28 KB while a window size of $w = 16$ needs 3.5 MB.

trary field polynomials is less than $1/2$ of a comb polynomial multiplication. For typical field sizes of $m = 163$ our reduction method has a running time of approximately $1/3$ of a comb multiplication. We expect this to be the fastest general reduction algorithm at the cost of memory storage.

Further improvements could be made by doing a partial reduction [5] as follows. Usually we reduce an operand $c'(x)$ of size $2s$ to $c(x)$ such that $degree(c) < m$. However, we can save some calculations by reducing $c'(x)$ to $c''(x)$ such that $degree(c''(x)) < sW$. The binary field operations are able to handle this operand size without any further cost. Algorithm 4 can easily be adjusted to this fact by omitting Steps $9 - 12$.

Algorithm 4 Window reduction method with window size $w = 8$

INPUT: A binary polynomial $c'(x)$ of $2s$ words and an irreducible binary polynomial $f(x) = x^m + f'(x)$ of s words.
OUTPUT: The binary polynomial $c(x) \equiv c'(x) \bmod f(x)$.

1: Precompute $PreF_u$ for all $u = jt$ with $j \in \{1, \ldots, W/8\}$ and $t \in \{1, \ldots, 2^8 - 1\}$:
  $PreF_1 = (f'(x) \cdot x^W) \gg (m \bmod W)$
  $PreF_{2^v} = PreF_{2^{v-1}} \ll 1$ for $0 < v < 8$
  $PreF_t = PreF_{2^v} \oplus PreF_{t-2^v}$ for $2^{v+1} < t < 2^v, 0 < t < 2^8$
  $PreF_{jt} = PreF_t << 8(j - 1)$ for $j \in \{2, \ldots, W/8\}$ and $t \in \{1, \ldots, 2^8 - 1\}$
2: $C \leftarrow C'$
3: **for** $i = 2s - 1$ down to s **do**
4:   **for** $j = W/8 - 1$ down to 0 **do**
5:     Let $t = (t_7, t_6, t_5, t_4, t_3, t_2, t_1, t_0)$, where t_k is bit $(8j + k)$ of $C[i]$.
6:     $C\{i - s\} = C\{i - s\} \oplus PreF_{j \cdot t}$
7:   **end for**
8: **end for**
9: **for** $j = W/8 - 1$ down to 0 **do**
10:   Let $t = (t_7, t_6, t_5, t_4, t_3, t_2, t_1, t_0)$, where t_k is bit $(8j + k)$ of $C[s - 1]$ if $(8j + k) \geq (m \bmod W)$ and $t_k = 0$ otherwise.
11:   $C\{0\} = C\{0\} \oplus (PreF_{j \cdot t} \gg W)$
12: **end for**
13: **Return** $c(x)$

3.2   Elliptic Curve $E(GF(2^m))$

We chose standard algorithms to implement the general elliptic curves. We use the projective Montgomery point multiplication as introduced in [14]. We also implemented standard point addition and point doubling [7].

Koblitz Curves. We implemented Koblitz Curves as described in [22]. We chose the windowed NAF technique for point multiplication using projective coordinates as introduced in [13]. Most of the values needed for the computation can be computed on the fly at initialization time. However, obtaining the window coefficients α_i [22] requires operations such as complex number arithmetic that are not supported by our software library. There are two kinds of Koblitz curves, namely for curve parameter $a = 0$ and $a = 1$. We decided to support window sizes of $w = 5$ and $w = 6$. The windowed NAF technique performs a point multiplication at the cost of $2^{w-2} - 1 + \frac{m}{w+1}$ point additions for fields $GF(2^m)$. Thus for $m < 336$ we use a window size of $w = 5$ whereas for $m \geq 336$ we choose $w = 6$. A window size of $w = 4$ is efficient for $m < 120$ and a window size of $w = 7$ for $m > 896$. Since these field sizes are not relevant for ECC we do not support these window sizes. We precomputed all possible window coefficient values α_i for the four combinations off-line, namely $a = 0$ and $a = 1$ combined with $w = 5$ and $w = 6$. The memory storage for the precomputed values is negligible and would easily fit into the storage of a smart card.

4   Implementation

In this section we give timings for our implementation and analyze the results. We did our timings for the NIST recommended binary fields and curves over $GF(2^{163})$, $GF(2^{233})$, $GF(2^{283})$, $GF(2^{409})$ and $GF(2^{571})$ [16]. We considered general curves and Koblitz curves which are denoted as B-163, B-233, B-283, B-409, B-571 and K-163, K-233, K-283, K-409, and K-571, respectively. The fields of bit-size 163, 283, and 571 use pentanomials while fields of bit-size 233 and 409 use trinomials as field polynomials. We compiled our code on a SPARC 32-bit and 64-bit workstation and on an Intel workstation. The SPARC timings were done on a 900 MHz UltraSPARC III CPU running Solaris 9, and gcc version 3.1. The UltraSPARC III is a 64-bit CPU which can also emulate a 32-bit mode. The Intel timings were performed on a 1 GHz Pentium III and gcc version 2.95.3 under Linux. We implemented all algorithms in C and did not use any assembly code.

Table 2 presents our timings of the field operations. The field operations always include the reduction step which is performed by the word-wise method for general trinomials as well as general pentanomials. It is worth noticing that a squaring, which is usually considered to have little cost, is no longer negligible for unknown field polynomials. The cost is especially considerable for small field sizes.

We experienced in our tests that the running time of the comb method is very dependent on the hardware platform and even the compiler. While KA performs similarly on different platforms we were unable to predict the running time of the comb method. It also seemed difficult to implement the comb method in a general fashion. We did some testings by implementing a special comb method for 6 words as needed for B-163. We unrolled all the loops, and used special addition and shifting macros for the given operand's length. The obtained timings are comparable to the KA times. However, we did not find a way to implement the comb method faster in a general way. Having specialized methods for each size results in large and complex code, while plugging in different methods for

Table 2. Timings in μs for one field operation (for trinomials and pentanomials as field polynomial)

Field Size	Operation		SPARC 32-bit 900 MHz	SPARC 64-bit 900 MHz	Intel 1 GHz
163	Multiplication	Comb Method	3.9	3.4	2.8
		Karatsuba	2.3	1.3	1.9
	Reduction		0.7	0.4	0.4
	Squaring		0.8	0.5	0.5
233	Multiplication	Comb Method	5.8	4.8	3.8
		Karatsuba	2.8	1.5	2.9
	Reduction		0.3	0.2	0.3
	Squaring		0.5	0.4	0.4
283	Multiplication	Comb Method	6.6	5.8	4.5
		Karatsuba	4.5	3.3	4.4
	Reduction		0.7	0.5	0.5
	Squaring		1.0	0.8	0.6
409	Multiplication	Comb Method	10.7	8.9	6.9
		Karatsuba	8.5	4.7	8.1
	Reduction		0.5	0.3	0.4
	Squaring		0.8	0.6	0.6
571	Multiplication	Comb Method	17.7	12.8	10.6
		Karatsuba	16.4	7.0	13.4
	Reduction		1.3	0.9	0.9
	Squaring		1.8	1.2	1.2

different cases requires expensive function calls and cannot be done as compile-time macros. However, it seems that the comb method outperforms the KA for large operand sizes. For a server implementation one could implement both the comb method and KA, do some test runs when a new field comes into use and plug in the faster method.

Now we want to point the reader's attention to the 64-bit multiplication. While the KA performs nearly twice as fast as the 32-bit version, the comb method gets only slightly faster. Our 1x1_MUL for 64-bit requires about 65% more operations than the 32-bit version. However, the number of multiplications required for the KA applied to operands of half the size decreases by a factor of up to 3. Thus the KA becomes almost twice as fast, i.e., by a factor of around $3/1.65 = 1.82$. However, the comb method requires $W/4 - 1$ left shifts of the double-sized result operand. Since the number of shifts doubles and the number of words is halved the overall computational cost remains unimproved. For instance, if the operand's length is s words on a 32-bit machine and $s' = s/2$ words on a 64-bit computer, the number of shifts evaluates to $3s$ and $7s' = 3.5s$, respectively. Since shifting has linear time complexity, i.e. a shift over $2t$ words takes twice as long as a shift over t words, the number of executable CPU instructions roughly remains the same. Thus there is only little speed gain due to the accelerated XOR operations for the comb method on a 64-bit CPU.

We compared our numbers to NTL 5.3 [21] which is considered to be one of the fastest number arithmetic libraries publicly available. The results for the Intel platform are presented in Table 3. Both multiplication and squaring include the modulo reduction. Note that we compare the timings to our KA implementation although on the Intel platform it is slower than the comb method for large field sizes. Our results are considerably faster for the essential field multiplication. One can guess that this is due to our polynomial multiplication method.

Table 3. Timings in μs for one field operation on 1 GHz Intel

Field Size	Operation	NTL	GEN_KA
163	Multiplication	4.7	1.9
	Reduction	0.8	0.4
	Squaring	1.1	0.5
233	Multiplication	5.5	2.9
	Reduction	1.0	0.3
	Squaring	1.1	0.4
283	Multiplication	9.7	4.4
	Reduction	1.1	0.5
	Squaring	1.8	0.6
409	Multiplication	14.6	8.1
	Reduction	1.1	0.4
	Squaring	1.3	0.6
571	Multiplication	27.4	13.4
	Reduction	1.2	0.9
	Squaring	3.1	1.2

Table 4 presents the timings for the elliptic curve point multiplication. For each platform, the first column is based on the KA while the second one uses the comb method. When comparing our timings to the numbers for fixed fields presented in [6] one can see that our flexible implementation still is slower than such a specialized implementation.

5   Conclusions

In this paper we presented an industry implementation of ECC as part of OpenSSL. Our implementation takes a general approach to implement binary field arithmetic and does not depend on any choice of field size or field polynomial. We showed that we achieve running times that are in the range of previously reported implementation results for fixed field sizes. Furthermore we showed that our implementation is faster than other implementations for arbitrary field sizes.

Table 4. Timings in ms for one point multiplication

Curve	SPARC 32-bit 900 MHz KA	Comb	SPARC 64-bit 900 MHz KA	Comb	Intel 1 GHz KA	Comb
B-163	3.0	4.9	1.8	4.1	2.3	3.6
B-233	4.8	8.7	2.8	7.3	4.7	6.4
B-283	10.0	13.9	6.8	12.0	9.5	9.7
B-409	24.9	30.0	14.1	24.3	23.6	19.8
B-571	66.6	71.5	30.3	51.3	54.3	44.9
K-163	1.6	2.0	1.0	1.7	1.2	1.4
K-233	2.2	3.3	1.5	2.6	2.0	2.5
K-283	4.6	5.4	3.1	4.3	3.7	3.8
K-409	9.6	10.9	5.4	7.7	8.0	7.2
K-571	22.5	23.8	11.4	15.9	17.2	15.3

Acknowledgments. We thank the anonymous referees for their helpful and detailed remarks. We are also grateful to the people of Sun Microsystems Laboratories at Mountain View for their support.

References

1. M. Brown, D. Cheung, D. Hankerson, J. L. Hernandez, M. Kirkup, and A. Menezes. PGP in Constrained Wireless Devices. *Proceedings of the 9th USENIX Security Symposium*, 2000.
2. E. De Win, A. Bosselaers, S. Vandenberghe, P. De Gersem and J. Vandewalle. A fast software implementation for arithmetic operations in $GF(2^n)$. *Advances in Cryptology – ASIACRYPT '96*, LNCS 1163, Springer-Verlag, 65–76, 1996.
3. P. Gaudry, F. Hess, and N. Smart. Constructive and Destructive Facets of Weil Descent on Elliptic Curves. *Journal of Cryptology*, 15, 19–46, 2002.
4. J. Guajardo and C. Paar. Efficient algorithms for elliptic curve cryptosystems. *Advances in Cryptology – CRYPTO '97*, LNCS 1294, Springer-Verlag, 342–356, 1997.
5. N. Gura, H. Eberle, and S. Chang Shantz. Generic Implementations of Elliptic Curve Cryptography using Partial Reduction. *9th ACM Conference on Computer and Communications Security*, 2002.
6. D. Hankerson, J. L. Hernandez and A. Menezes. Software Implementation of Elliptic Curve Cryptography Over Binary Fields. *Cryptographic Hardware and Embedded Systems, CHES 2000*, LNCS 1965, Springer-Verlag, 1–24, 2000.
7. IEEE P1363. *Standard Specifications for Public-Key Cryptography*, 2000.
8. ISO/IEC 15946. *Information Technology – Security Techniques – Cryptographic Techniques Based on Elliptic Curves*, 1999.
9. C. Koç and T. Acar. Montgomery multiplication in $GF(2^k)$. *Designs, Codes and Cryptography*, 14, 57–69, 1998.
10. K. Koyama and Y. Tsuruoka. Speeding up elliptic curve cryptosystems by using a signed binary window method. *Advances in Cryptology – Crypto '92*, LNCS 740, Springer-Verlag, 345–357, 1993.

11. R. Lidl and H. Niederreiter. *Introduction to Finite Fields and their Applications, Revised Edition.* Cambridge Unversity Press, Cambridge, United Kingdom, 1994.
12. C. Lim and P. Lee. More flexible exponentiation with precomputation. *Advances in Cryptology – Crypto '94*, LNCS 839, Springer-Verlag, 95–107, 1994.
13. J. López and R. Dahab. Improved Algorithms for Elliptic Curve Arithmetic in $GF(2^n)$. *Selected Areas in Crytography – SAC '98*, LNCS 1556, Springer-Verlag, 201–212, 1999.
14. J. López and R. Dahab. Fast multiplication on Elliptic Curves over $GF(2^n)$ without Precomputation, *Cryptographic Hardware and Embedded Systems-CHES '99*, LNCS 1717, Springer-Verlag, 316–327, 1999.
15. J. López and R. Dahab. High-speed Software Multiplication in $\mathbb{F}_{2^m}$. *Indocrypt 2000*, LNCS 1977, Springer-Verlag, 203–212, 2000.
16. National Institute of Standards and Technolgy. *Recommended Elliptic Curves for Federal Government Use*, May 1999, available from http://csrc.nist.gov/encryption.
17. OpenSSL, http://www.openssl.org.
18. R. Schroeppel, H. Orman, S. O'Malley and O. Spatscheck. Fast Key Exchange with Elliptic Curve Systems. *Advances in Cryptology – Crypto '95*, LNCS 963, Springer-Verlag, 43–56, 1995.
19. R. Schroeppel, C. Beaver, R. Gonzales, R. Miller, and T. Draelos. A Low-Power Design for an Elliptic Curve Digital Signature Chip. Presented at *Cryptographic Hardware and Embedded Systems (CHES) 2002*.
20. S. Shantz. From Euclid's GCD to Montgomery Multiplication to the Great Divide, preprint, 2000.
21. V. Shoup. NTL: A Library for doing Number Theory, available from http://www.shoup.net/ntl/.
22. J. A. Solinas. Efficient Arithmetic on Koblitz Curves. *Designs, Codes and Cryptography*, 19(2/3), 195–249, 2000.
23. A. Weimerskirch, C. Paar, and S. Chang Shantz. Elliptic Curve Cryptography on a Palm OS Device. *The 6th Australasian Conference on Information Security and Privacy (ACISP 2001)*, LNCS 2119, Springer-Verlag, 502–513, 2001.
24. A. Weimerskirch and C. Paar. Generalizations of the Karatsuba Algorithm for Polynomial Multiplication. *Technical Report*, Ruhr-University Bochum, 2002, Available from http://www.crypto.rub.de.

Sun, Sun Microsystems, the Sun logo, and Solaris are trademarks or registered trademarks of Sun Microsystems, Inc. in the United States and other countries.

UltraSPARC III is a trademark or registered trademark of SPARC International, Inc. in the United States and other countries. Products bearing SPARC trademarks are based upon an architecture developed by Sun Microsystems, Inc.

An Addition Algorithm in Jacobian of C_{34} Curve

Seigo Arita

Internet Systems Research Laboratories, NEC, Kawasaki Kanagawa, Japan,
s-arita@ab.jp.nec.com

Abstract. *This paper gives an efficient algorithm to compute addition in Jacobian of C_{34} curves. The paper modifies the addition algorithm of [1], by classifying the forms of Groebner bases of all ideals involved in the addition in Jacobian, and by computing Groebner bases of ideals without using Buchberger algorithm. The algorithm computes the addition in Jacobian of C_{34} curves in about 3 times amount of computation of the one in elliptic curves, when the sizes of groups are set to be the same.*

1 Introduction

Although now elliptic curve cryptosystems are widely used, discrete logarithm based cryptosystem with Jacobian group of more general algebraic curves, such as hyperelliptic, superelliptic[3] and C_{ab} curve[10,8], are not used. One of the main reasons for that is large computational amount of addition in Jacobian of such non-elliptic curves.

Surprisingly, Harley[5], by carefully optimizing Cantor's algorithm[2], gives an addition algorithm in Jacobian of hyperelliptic curves of genus two, which computes the addition on the hyperelliptic curve almost in the same time as that on elliptic curves, when the sizes of groups are same. Harley's algorithm is being modified by Matsuo and Chao[9] and by Lange[7].

This paper treats C_{34} curves which are special cases of C_{ab} curves. C_{34} curves are non-hyperelliptic and of genus three. We classify all of the forms of Groebner bases of ideals involved in the addition in Jacobian of C_{34} curve. With the classification, we can modify the addition algorithm of [1] to obtain Groebner bases of ideals without using Buchberger algorithm. We show our algorithm computes the addition in Jacobian of C_{34} curves in about 3 times amount of computation of that in elliptic curves, when the sizes of groups are same.

We note that Harasawa and Suzuki[4] also gives an addition algorithm on Jacobian of C_{ab} curves, by extending the addition algorithm on superelliptic curves of Galbraith, Paulus, and Smart[3]. Their algorithms use LLL-algorithm to reduce ideals. Although [4] gives an asymptotic evaluation of the amount of computation of their algorithm, the evaluation of O-constants is not given.

2 C_{34} Curve and Its Jacobian Group

C_{34} curve, which is a special case of C_{ab} curve[10,8], is a nonsingular plan curve defined by the following form of polynomial $F(X, Y)$:

R. Safavi-Naini and J. Seberry (Eds.): ACISP 2003, LNCS 2727, pp. 93–105, 2003.
© Springer-Verlag Berlin Heidelberg 2003

$$F(X,Y) = Y^3 + a_0 X^4 + a_1 XY^2 + a_2 X^2 Y + a_3 X^3 + a_4 Y^2 + a_5 XY + a_6 X^2 + a_7 Y + a_8 X + a_9,$$
(1)

with a_i's in the definition field k and $a_0 \neq 0$.

C_{34} curve C has a unique point ∞ at the infinity. The function Y and X has the unique pole at ∞ of order four and three, respectively. Gap sequence at ∞ is $\mathbb{N}_0 - <3,4> = \{1,2,5\}$, and the genus of C_{34} is three.

Let $D_C^0(k)$ denote the group of divisors of degree 0 on C defined over k, and $P_C(k)$ be the group of principal divisors on C defined over k. As well known, Jacobian group $J_C(k)$ on C is defined to be the factor

$$J_C(k) = D_C^0(k)/P_C(k).$$

On the other hand, let $R = k[X,Y]/F$ be the coordinate ring of C. Since C_{34} curve C is nonsingular by the definition, R is a Dedekind domain. Hence, all of the nonzero fractional ideals of R compose a group $I_R(k)$. Putting the group of principal ideals of R $P_R(k)$, the ideal class group $H_R(k)$ of R is defined to be the factor

$$H_R(k) = I_R(k)/P_R(k).$$

In general, for a nonsingular curve, we can identify divisors on the curve and ideals of the coordinate ring, and its Jacobian group $J_C(k)$ is naturally isomorphic to the ideal class group $H_R(k)$ (Example 6.3.2 of [6]):

$$J_C(k) \cong H_R(k)$$
$$[E - n\infty] \mapsto [\bigcup_{n=0}^{\infty} L(m\infty - E)],$$

where E is a positive divisor prime to ∞. In the below, we treat Jacobian group $J_C(k)$ as the ideal class group $H_R(k)$ of the coordinate ring R.

3 Δ-Set of Ideals

Let '$<$' be a monomial order in a polynomial ring $S = k[X_1, \cdots, X_n]$. Let I be an ideal of S. The set of monomials (or their multi-degrees) not belonging to LM(I) (which is an ideal generated by leading monomials in I) is called a Δ-set of I and denoted by $\Delta(I)$. $\Delta(I)$ gives a basis of the vector space S/I over k. When we plot monomials $X_1^{m_1} X_2^{m_2} \cdots$, or their multi-degrees $(m_1, m_2, \cdots)$ in $\Delta(I)$ on the $(m_1, m_2, \cdots)$-space, there appears a convex set, of which surrounding lattice points correspond to leading monomials of polynomials in Groebner base of I.

Let $R = S/F$ be a coordinate ring of a C_{34} curve defined by F. By identifying ideals of R with ideals of S including F, we can consider Groebner bases for ideals of R. For a 0-dimensional ideal I (i.e. the zero set of I is finite), we define its *order* $\delta(I)$ as $\delta(I) = \dim_k R/I$. We see $\delta(I) = \sharp\Delta(I)$. Since C_{34} curve is nonsingular, $\delta(IJ) = \delta(I)\delta(J)$. If $I = (f)$ is a principal ideal in R, we have $\delta(I) = -v_\infty(f)$.

4   An Addition Algorithm in Jacobian of C_{34} Curve — Abstract Level

Let $R = k[X, Y]/F$ be a coordinate ring of a C_{34} curve C defined by the polynomial F (1). We can define a monomial order '$>$', called C_{34} order, by the pole number of monomials at ∞. That is,

$$X^{m_1}Y^{n_1} > X^{m_2}Y^{n_2} \overset{\text{def}}{\Longleftrightarrow} 3m_1 + 4n_1 > 3m_2 + 4n_2$$
$$\text{or } 3m_1 + 4n_1 = 3m_2 + 4n_2, \; m_1 < m_2$$

Hereafter, we always use C_{34} order to compare monomials in R.

For an ideal I in R, let f_I be the nonzero 'monic' polynomial with the smallest leading monomial in I. We define I^* as $I^* = (f_I) : I \; (= \{g \in R \mid gI \subset (f_I)\})$. Then, we have

Proposition 1 *Let I, J be any ideals in the coordinate ring R. We have*

(1) I is equivalent to I^{**}.
(2) I^{**} is an ideal equivalent to I with the smallest order.
(3) If I and J are equivalent, then we have $I^* = J^*$. In particular, $I^{**} = (I^{**})^{**}$.

Proof *(1) I^* is equivalent to the inverse ideal of I from definition.*

(2) Let J be an (integral) ideal equivalent to I^{-1}. There is a $f \in R$ satisfying $JI = (f)$. From the definition of I^*, $I^*I = (f_I)$. So, we have

$$\delta(J)\delta(I) - \delta(I^*)\delta(I) = -v_\infty(f) + v_\infty(f_I) \geq 0,$$

by the definition of f_I. Therefore, I^* is an (integral) ideal equivalent to I^{-1} with the smallest order. So, I^{**} is an (integral) ideal equivalent to I with the smallest order.

(3) If I and J are equivalent, there are $j, h \in R$ satisfying $J = \frac{j}{h}I$. Then, we have $f_J = \frac{j}{h}f_I$. So, for $g \in R$,

$$gJ \subset (f_J) \Leftrightarrow g\frac{j}{h}I \subset (\frac{j}{h}f_I) \Leftrightarrow gI \subset (f_I)$$

□

An ideal I in the coordinate ring R is called *reduced* when we have $I^{**} = I$. By Proposition1(1),(3), any ideal in R is equivalent to the unique reduced ideal. That is, reduced ideals compose a complete representative system of ideal classes. Moreover, by Proposition1(2), we see that a reduced ideal has the smallest order among ideals in the same ideal class. This property should be a merit to implement algorithms.

Using reduced ideals as a representative system of ideal classes, we get the following addition algorithm in Jacobian of C_{34} curve.

Algorithm 1 (Addition in Jacobian of C_{34} curve – abstract version)
Inputs: reduced ideals I_1, I_2 in the coordinate ring R
Output: reduced ideal I_3 equivalent to the ideal product $I_1 \cdot I_2$

$1°$ $J \leftarrow I_1 \cdot I_2$
$2°$ $J^* \leftarrow (f_J) : J$
$3°$ $I_3 \leftarrow (f_{J^*}) : J^*$

5   Ideal Classification

Now, we classify ideals involved in Algorithm1. Since the genus of C_{34} curve is three, the orders of those ideals are not greater than six. Hereafter, even if the defining polynomial F (Equation (1)) of C_{34} curve C appears in Groebner base of an ideal, we do not show it. Let a_i, b_j, c_k denote coefficients of polynomials in Groebner bases.

5.1   Ideals of Order 6

Let I be an ideal in R of order 6. By the definition of order, $V = R/I$ is a sixth dimensional vector space over the definition field k.

Type 61. An ideal I of order six has six zero points including multiplicities. When those six points are in 'general' positions, the first six monomials $1, X, Y, X^2, XY, Y^2$ with respect to the C_{34} order are linearly independent on those six points. So, the set of monomials $M = \{1, X, Y, X^2, XY, Y^2\}$ is a basis of the vector space $V = R/I$. In this case, we call I an ideal of *type 61*.

It is easily seen that the fact that the set of monomials M is linearly dependent in $V = R/I$ is equivalent to the fact that there is a monomial in M belonging to LM(I). So, If I is an ideal of type 61, then the set of monomials M is nothing but $\Delta(I)$. Using notation of multi-degrees, we have $\Delta(I) = \{(0,0), (1,0), (0,1), (2,0), (1,1), (0,2)\}$. It is easily seen that lattice points surrounding $\Delta(I)$ are $\{(0,3), (1,2), (2,1), (3,0)\}$. So, Groebner base of an ideal I of type 61 has the form in Table 1. Those three polynomials correspond to the lattice points $(3,0),(2,1),(1,2)$ (Note the lattice point $(0,3)$ corresponds to the defining polynomial F).

Type 62 and 63. In general, six monomials $1, X, Y, X^2, XY, Y^2$ are not linearly independent in $V = R/I$. First, we consider the case that the first five monomials $1, X, Y, X^2, XY$ with respect to the C_{34} order are linearly independent, but the sixth monomial Y^2 is equal to a linear sum of them in V.

In that case, $\Delta(I)$ is a convex set of order 6, which includes $\{(0,0), (1,0), (0,1), (2,0), (1,1)\}$, but does not include $(0,2)$. From this, we can easily see that $\Delta(I) = \{(0,0), (1,0), (0,1), (2,0), (1,1), (2,1)\}$, or

$\Delta(I) = \{(0,0),(1,0),(0,1),(2,0),(1,1),(3,0)\}$. In the former case we call I an ideal of *type 62*, and in the latter case , we call I an ideal of *type 63*.

Lattice points surrounding $\Delta(I)$ are $\{(0,2),(3,0)\}$ for I of type 62, and $\{(0,2),(2,1),(4,0)\}$ for I of type 63. So, forms of their Grobner bases are as in Table 1. Note there should be a polynomial corresponding to the lattice point $(4,0)$ in Groebner base for I of type 63. However, the polynomial can be immediately obtained as $F - Yf$ with the defining polynomial F and the polynomial $f = Y^2 + a_5 XY + a_4 X^2 + a_3 Y + a_2 X + a_1$. So, we omit it.

Type 64. Next, suppose the first four monomials $1, X, Y, X^2$ are linearly independent, but the fifth monomial XY is a linear sum of them in $V = R/I$. That is, $\Delta(I)$ includes $\{(0,0),(1,0),(0,1),(2,0)\}$, but does not include $(1,1)$.

Then, if $\Delta(I)$ does not include $(0,2)$, we must have $\Delta(I) = \{(0,0),(1,0),(0,1),(2,0),(3,0),(4,0)\}$. However, by the assumption, I includes a polynomial $f = Y^2 + \cdots$ with the leading monomial Y^2, so I includes $Yf - F = -a_0 X^4 + \cdots$. This means $(4,0) \notin \Delta(I)$, a contradiction. Thus, we see that $\Delta(I)$ must include $(0,2)$, and $\Delta(I) = \{(0,0),(1,0),(0,1),(2,0),(0,2),(3,0)\}$. In this case, we call I an ideal of *type 64*.

Lattice points surrounding $\Delta(I)$ are $\{(0,3),(1,1),(4,0)\}$. Hence, the form of Groebner base of I of type 64 is as in Table 1.

Type 65. Next suppose the first three monomials $1, X, Y$ are linearly independent, but the fourth monomial X^2 is a linear sum of them in $V = R/I$. Then, the ideal I include a polynomial f with the leading term X^2. And we have $\Delta(I) = \{(0,0),(1,0),(0,1),(1,1),(0,2),(1,2)\}$. In this case, we call I an ideal of *type 65*. Since lattice points surrounding $\Delta(I)$ are $\{(0,3),(2,0)\}$, we know I is a principal ideal generated by f as in Table 1 (note the lattice point $(0,3)$ corresponds to the defining polynomial F).

A polynomial f with the leading term Y does not vanish on the six points corresponding to I, because $\deg(f)_0 = -v_{P_\infty}(f) = 4 < 6$. Hence, the first three monomials $1, X, Y$ are always linearly independent in $V = R/I$.

Now classification of ideals of order 6 is completed.

5.2 All Ideal Types of Order Not Greater than 6

Ideals of order less than 6 are also similarly classified. We only show the result of classification in Table 1. Ideals of type 65, 44 and 33 are principal ideals, units in Jacobian. Among all of the ideal types, only ideals of type 31, 21, 22 and 11 are reduced. For example, we can see that ideals of type 32 are not reduced as follows. Let I be an ideal of type 32. Then $f_I = Y + a_2 X + a_1$. So, $\delta(I^*) = -v_\infty(f_I) - \delta(I) = 4 - 3 = 1$. We know I^* is of type 11 and $f_{I^*} = X + a_1'$. So, $\delta(I^{**}) = -v_\infty(f_{I^*}) - \delta(I^*) = 3 - 1 = 2$. Since orders are distinct, $I \neq I^{**}$.

Table 1. All ideal types of order not greater than 6

Order	Type	Form of Groebner base
6	61	$\{X^3 + a_6 Y^2 + a_5 XY + a_4 X^2 + a_3 Y + a_2 X + a_1, X^2 Y + b_6 Y^2 + b_5 XY + b_4 X^2 + b_3 Y + b_2 X + b_1, XY^2 + c_6 Y^2 + c_5 XY + c_4 X^2 + c_3 Y + c_2 X + c_1\}$
6	62	$\{Y^2 + a_5 XY + a_4 X^2 + a_3 Y + a_2 X + a_1, X^3 + b_5 XY + b_4 X^2 + b_3 Y + b_2 X + b_1\}$
6	63	$\{Y^2 + a_5 XY + a_4 X^2 + a_3 Y + a_2 X + a_1, X^2 Y + b_6 X^3 + b_5 XY + b_4 X^2 + b_3 Y + b_2 X + b_1\}$
6	64	$\{XY + a_4 X^2 + a_3 Y + a_2 X + a_1, X^4 + b_6 X^3 + b_5 Y^2 + b_4 X^2 + b_3 Y + b_2 X + b_1\}$
6	65	$\{X^2 + a_3 Y + a_2 X + a_1\}$
5	51	$\{Y^2 + a_5 XY + a_4 X^2 + a_3 Y + a_2 X + a_1, X^3 + b_5 XY + b_4 X^2 + b_3 Y + b_2 X + b_1, X^2 Y + c_5 XY + c_4 X^2 + c_3 Y + c_2 X + c_1\}$
5	52	$\{XY + a_4 X^2 + a_3 Y + a_2 X + a_1, Y^2 + b_4 X^2 + b_3 Y + b_2 X + b_1\}$
5	53	$\{XY + a_4 X^2 + a_3 Y + a_2 X + a_1, X^3 + b_5 Y^2 + b_4 X^2 + b_3 Y + b_2 X + b_1\}$
5	54	$\{X^2 + a_3 Y + a_2 X + a_1, XY^2 + b_5 Y^2 + b_4 XY + b_3 Y + b_2 X + b_1\}$
4	41	$\{XY + a_4 X^2 + a_3 Y + a_2 X + a_1, Y^2 + b_4 X^2 + b_3 Y + b_2 X + b_1, X^3 + c_4 X^2 + c_3 Y + c_2 X + c_1\}$
4	42	$\{X^2 + a_3 Y + a_2 X + a_1, XY + b_3 Y + b_2 X + b_1\}$
4	43	$\{X^2 + a_3 Y + a_2 X + a_1, Y^2 + b_4 XY + b_3 Y + b_2 X + b_1\}$
4	44	$\{Y + a_2 X + a_1\}$
3	31	$\{X^2 + a_3 Y + a_2 X + a_1, XY + b_3 Y + b_2 X + b_1, Y^2 + c_3 Y + c_2 X + c_1\}$
3	32	$\{Y + a_2 X + a_1, X^3 + b_3 X^2 + b_2 X + b_1\}$
3	33	$\{X + a_1\}$
2	21	$\{Y + a_2 X + a_1, X^2 + b_2 X + b_1\}$
2	22	$\{X + a_1, Y^2 + b_2 Y + b_1\}$
1	11	$\{X + a_1, Y + b_1\}$

6 An Addition Algorithm in Jacobian of C_{34} Curve — Concrete Level

Let $R = k[X,Y]/F$ be the coordinate ring of a C_{34} curve C defined by a polynomial F(Equation (1)) over a finite field k. In this section, we put Algorithm 1 into more concrete shape and estimate its efficiency. In the below, bearing an application for cryptography in mind, we assume the order of the definition field k is large enough.

6.1 Composition1

First, we deal with the first step of Algorithm 1 for distinct ideals I_1, I_2. That is, we compute f_J for the ideal product $J = I_1 \cdot I_2$. For that sake, it is sufficient to find Groebner base of J with respect to C_{34} order (f_J is the first element of it).

Since the genus of C_{34} curves is three, types of input ideals for Algorithm 1 are either 11,21,22,31 or 32. Here, we only discuss the case in which ideals I_1, I_2 are both of type 31. Another cases are dealt with similarly.

Suppose we choose distinct ideals I_1, I_2 of type 31 at random from Jacobian group. Then since we assume the order q of k is large enough, almost always (with the probability approximately $(q - 1)/q$) we have

$$V(I_1) \cap V(I_2) = \emptyset \tag{2}$$

where $V(I)$ denotes the zero set of an ideal I. So, first we assume the condition (2).

Let $J = I_1 I_2$ be the ideal product of I_1 and I_2. Since the order of J is 6, the type of J is either 61,62,63,64 or 65. To determine which it is, by Table 1, we see it is sufficient to find linear relations among 10 monomials

$$1, X, Y, X^2, XY, Y^2, X^3, X^2Y, XY^2, X^4 \tag{3}$$

in the vector space R/J over k.

Since I_i ($i = 1, 2$) is of type 31, we have

$$R/I_i \simeq k \cdot 1 \oplus k \cdot X \oplus k \cdot Y. \tag{4}$$
$$m \mapsto v_m^{(i)} \tag{5}$$

By condition (2), we have

$$R/J \simeq \qquad R/I_1 \oplus R/I_2 \qquad \simeq \oplus_{i=1}^6 k,$$
$$m \mapsto (m \bmod (I_1), m \bmod (I_2)) \mapsto v_m^{(1)} : v_m^{(2)} \tag{6}$$

where $v_m^{(1)} : v_m^{(2)}$ denotes the sixth dimensional vector over k obtained by connecting two vectors $v_m^{(i)}$ ($i = 1, 2$).

Thus, to obtain linear relations in R/J among 10 monomials m_i in equation (3), it is sufficient to find linear relations among rows of the 10×6 matrix M_C which is obtained by lining up vectors $v_{m_i}^{(1)} : v_{m_i}^{(2)}$ ($i = 1, 2, \cdots 10$)

Linear relations among rows of M_C can be obtained by making M_C triangular using the row reduce procedure as well known, and we get the type of ideal J and its Groebner base. More details are shown through the following example.

When condition (2) does not hold for ideals I_1, I_2, the rank M_C becomes less than 6. After making M_C triangular, if we know the rank of M_C is less than 6, then we generate R_i satisfying $R_1 + R_2 = 0$, and compute $(I_1 + R_1) + (I_2 + R_2)$ instead of $I_1 + I_2$. Here, '+' denotes the addition in Jacobian.

Example. For example, we deal with C_{34} curve $Y^3 + X^4 + 7X = 0$ on the prime field of characteristics $p = 1009$. Take the following two ideals of type 31:

$I_1 = \{X^2 + 726Y + 836X + 355, XY + 36Y + 428X + 477, Y^2 + 746Y + 425X + 865\}$
$I_2 = \{X^2 + 838Y + 784X + 97, XY + 602Y + 450X + 291, Y^2 + 506Y + 524X + 497\}$

We would like to compute Groebner base of $J = I_1 I_2$ to find f_J. By computing the remainder of each m_i in equation (3) modulo I_1 and I_2 respectively, we get the matrix M_C for I_1, I_2:

$$M_C = \begin{pmatrix} 1 & 0 & 0 & 1 & 0 & 0 \\ 0 & 1 & 0 & 0 & 1 & 0 \\ 0 & 0 & 1 & 0 & 0 & 1 \\ 654 & 173 & 283 & 912 & 225 & 171 \\ 532 & 581 & 973 & 718 & 559 & 407 \\ 144 & 584 & 263 & 512 & 485 & 503 \\ 349 & 269 & 429 & 53 & 821 & 109 \\ 609 & 418 & 243 & 888 & 856 & 916 \\ 199 & 720 & 418 & 310 & 331 & 91 \\ 554 & 498 & 143 & 643 & 522 & 107 \end{pmatrix}.$$

To obtain linear relations among rows of M_C, we connect M_C and 10-th unit matrix I_{10} to get $M_C' = M_C : I_{10}$. Against M_C', we apply the row reduce procedure up to the sixth row:

$$m = \begin{pmatrix} 1 & 0 & 0 & 1 & 0 & 0 & 1 & 0 & 0 & 0 & 0 & 0 & 0 & 0 & 0 & 0 \\ 0 & 1 & 0 & 0 & 1 & 0 & 0 & 1 & 0 & 0 & 0 & 0 & 0 & 0 & 0 & 0 \\ 0 & 0 & 1 & 0 & 0 & 1 & 0 & 0 & 1 & 0 & 0 & 0 & 0 & 0 & 0 & 0 \\ 0 & 0 & 0 & 258 & 52 & 897 & 355 & 836 & 726 & 1 & 0 & 0 & 0 & 0 & 0 & 0 \\ 0 & 0 & 0 & 0 & 621 & 688 & 268 & 365 & 592 & 187 & 1 & 0 & 0 & 0 & 0 & 0 \\ 0 & 0 & 0 & 0 & 0 & 31 & 514 & 469 & 637 & 669 & 155 & 1 & 0 & 0 & 0 & 0 \\ 0 & 0 & 0 & 0 & 0 & 0 & 28 & 132 & 31 & 271 & 469 & 166 & 1 & 0 & 0 & 0 \\ 0 & 0 & 0 & 0 & 0 & 0 & 856 & 618 & 747 & 909 & 132 & 636 & 0 & 1 & 0 & 0 \\ 0 & 0 & 0 & 0 & 0 & 0 & 652 & 322 & 240 & 978 & 826 & 846 & 0 & 0 & 1 & 0 \\ 0 & 0 & 0 & 0 & 0 & 0 & 333 & 346 & 980 & 935 & 824 & 614 & 0 & 0 & 0 & 1 \end{pmatrix}.$$

The result shows the first six rows of M_C are linearly independent. This means monomials $1, X, Y, X^2, XY, Y^2$ are linearly independent in R/J and the product J is of type 61.

Moreover, the right 10 elements of the seventh, eighth and ninth rows of m represents liner expressions of the seventh, eighth and ninth rows of M_C by the first six rows of M_C, respectively. From this, we know linear expressions of $X^3, X^2 Y, XY^2$ by $1, X, Y, X^2, XY, Y^2$ in R/J, respectively, and we get the following Groebner base of J:

$$J = \{28 + 132X + 31Y + 271X^2 + 469XY + 166Y^2 + X^3,$$
$$856 + 618X + 747Y + 909X^2 + 132XY + 636Y^2 + X^2 Y,$$
$$652 + 322X + 240Y + 978X^2 + 826XY + 846Y^2 + XY^2\}$$

Hence, we have $f_J = 28 + 132X + 31Y + 271X^2 + 469XY + 166Y^2 + X^3$.

6.2   Composition2

We consider the first step of Algorithm 1 for the same two ideals $I_1 = I, I_2 = I$ in R. That is, we compute Groebner base of the ideal product $J = I^2$ to get

f_J. As in section 6.1, we only deal with an ideal I of type 31. Other cases are handled similarly.

Since we assume the order q of k is large enough, almost always (with the probability approximately $(q-1)/q$) it holds that

$$V(I) \text{ has no multiple point.} \tag{7}$$

So, first we assume the condition (7).

Since the order of $J = I^2$ is also 6, it is sufficient to find linear relations in R/J among monomials in equation (3). By condition (7), the necessary and sufficient condition to $f(\in R)$ belongs to $J = I^2$ is

$$f \in I, \; f_X F_Y - f_Y F_X \in I.$$

So, we have

$$R/J \simeq \qquad\qquad R/I \oplus R/I \qquad\qquad \simeq \oplus_{i=1}^{6} k,$$
$$m \mapsto (m \bmod (I), m_X F_Y - m_Y F_X \bmod (I)) \mapsto v_m : v_{(m_X F_Y - m_Y F_X)} \tag{8}$$

where $v_m : v_{(m_X F_Y - m_Y F_X)}$ is a sixth dimensional vector over k obtained by connecting two vectors $v_m, v_{(m_X F_Y - m_Y F_X)}$.

Thus, to obtain linear relations in R/J among m_i in equation (3), it is sufficient to find linear relations among rows of 10×6 matrix M_D which is obtained by lining up vectors $v_{m_i} : v_{(m_{iX} F_Y - m_{iY} F_X)}$ $(i = 1, 2, \cdots, 10)$.

Just as in section 6.1, we make M_D triangular by the row reduce procedure to obtain the type of J and its Groebner base.

If condition (7) does not hold for I, the rank of M_D is less than 6. After making M_D triangular, if we know the rank of M_D is less than 6, then we generate R_i satisfying $R_1 + R_2 = 0$, and compute $(I + R_1) + (I + R_2)$ instead of $I + I$. Here, '+' denotes the addition in Jacobian.

6.3 Reduction

We consider the second (and the third) step of Algorithm 1. That is, we compute Grobner base of $J^* = f_J : J$ for an ideal J of order not greater than 6. Here we only deal with J of type 61. Other types of J are dealt with similarly.

Since J is of type 61, J can be written as

$$\{f_J = X^3 + a_6 Y^2 + \cdots, g = X^2 Y + b_6 Y^2 + \cdots, h = XY^2 + c_6 Y^2 + \cdots\}.$$

Since $J^* = f_J : J$ from definition, we have $\delta(J^*) = -v_\infty(f_J) - \delta(J) = 3$. Moreover J^* is reduced by Proposition 1, so the type of J^* must be 31 (see Remark in section 5).

Hence, to find Groebner base of J^*, it is sufficient to find linear relations $\sum_i d_i m_i$ for m_i in

$$1, X, Y, X^2, XY, Y^2 \tag{9}$$

such that both $\sum_i d_i m_i g$ and $\sum_i d_i m_i h$ are equal to 0 in R/f_J.

Since $LM(F) = Y^3$, $LM(f_J) = X^3$, we have

$$R/f_J R \simeq k \cdot 1 \oplus k \cdot X \oplus k \cdot Y \oplus k \cdot X^2 \oplus k \cdot XY \oplus k \cdot Y^2 \oplus k \cdot X^2 Y \oplus k \cdot XY^2 \oplus k \cdot X^2 Y^2.$$
$$f \mapsto w_f$$

So, to find those linear relations among m_i in equation (9), it is sufficient to find linear relations among rows of 6×18 matrix M_R which is obtained by lining up vectors $w_{m_i g} : w_{m_i h}$ $(i = 1, 2, \cdots 6)$.

Just as in section 6.1, we make M_R triangular by the row reduce procedure to obtain the type of J^* and its Groebner base.

However, in the almost all cases, it is sufficient to make 6×3 sub-matrix M_r of M_R triangular, instead of the whole matrix M_R. Details are shown in the next section.

7   Formal Description of the Algorithm and Estimates of Its Efficiency

By the discussion of the last section, we get a concrete algorithm for addition in Jacobian of C_{34} curve.

Now we estimate the amount of computation of the algorithm with an explanation of using the sub-matrix M_r instead of M_R. Let q be the order of the definition field k. A random element in Jacobian is represented by an ideal of type 31 with the probability about $(q-1)/q$. Also, outputs of Compose 1,2 for ideals of type 31 are ideals of type 61 with the probability about $(q-1)/q$. So, to estimate the efficiency of the algorithm, it is sufficient to estimate the amount of computation of Compose1, 2 for ideals of type 31 and the amount of computation of Reduce for ideals of type 61 and 31. In the below, we describe the amount of computation by the number of times of multiplication and inverse of elements in k.

First, we see the amount of computation of Compose1. Let I_1, I_2 be ideals of type 31:

$$I_1 = \{X^2 + a_3 Y + a_2 X + a_1, XY + b_3 Y + b_2 X + b_1, Y^2 + c_3 Y + c_2 X + c_1\}$$
$$I_2 = \{X^2 + s_3 Y + s_2 X + s_1, XY + t_3 Y + t_2 X + t_1, Y^2 + u_3 Y + u_2 X + u_1\}$$

For ideals I_1, I_2, the matrix M_C is represented as

$$M_C = \left\{ \begin{array}{ccc}
1 & 0 & 0 \\
0 & 1 & 0 \\
0 & 0 & 1 \\
-a_1 & -a_2 & -a_3 \\
-b_1 & -b_2 & -b_3 \\
-c_1 & -c_2 & -c_3 \\
a_1a_2 + a_3b_1 & -a_1 + a_2^2 + a_3b_2 & a_2a_3 + a_3b_3 \\
a_2b_1 + a_3c_1 & a_2b_2 + a_3c_2 & -a_1 + a_2b_3 + a_3c_3 \\
b_1b_2 + b_3c_1 & b_2^2 + b_3c_2 & -b_1 + b_2b_3 + b_3c_3 \\
e_{10,1} & e_{10,2} & e_{10,3} \\
1 & 0 & 0 \\
0 & 1 & 0 \\
0 & 0 & 1 \\
-s_1 & -s_2 & -s_3 \\
-t_1 & -t_2 & -t_3 \\
-u_1 & -u_2 & -u_3 \\
s_1s_2 + s_3t_1 & -s_1 + s_2^2 + s_3t_2 & s_2s_3 + s_3t_3 \\
s_2t_1 + s_3u_1 & s_2t_2 + s_3u_2 & -s_1 + s_2t_3 + s_3u_3 \\
t_1t_2 + t_3u_1 & t_2^2 + t_3u_2 & -t_1 + t_2t_3 + t_3u_3 \\
e_{10,4} & e_{10,5} & e_{10,6}
\end{array} \right\}$$

$e_{10,1} = a_1^2 - a_1a_2^2 - 2a_2a_3b_1 - a_3^2c_1$, $\quad e_{10,2} = 2a_1a_2 - a_2^3 - 2a_2a_3b_2 - a_3^2c_2$

$e_{10,3} = 2a_1a_3 - a_2^2a_3 - 2a_2a_3b_3 - a_3^2c_3$, $\quad e_{10,4} = s_1^2 - s_1s_2^2 - 2s_2s_3t_1 - s_3^2u_1$

$e_{10,5} = 2s_1s_2 - s_2^3 - 2s_2s_3t_2 - s_3^2u_2$, $\quad e_{10,6} = 2s_1s_3 - s_2^2s_3 - 2s_2s_3t_3 - s_3^2u_3$

From this representation, we see the matrix M_C can be constructed in at most 44 multiplications, removing duplication adequately. Knowing the first three rows of M_C' are already row-reduced, and elements of them are 0 or 1, and assuming the output ideal would be of type 61, we see RowReduce for M_C' can be performed in 3 inverses and at most $6 \cdot 6 + 6 \cdot 5 + 6 \cdot 4 = 90$ times multiplications. Thus, Compose1 are performed in at most 3 inverses and 134 multiplications.

Similarly, we can see Compose2 are performed in at most 3 inverses and 214 multiplications. As M_D is more complicated than M_C, times of multiplication is increased.

Next we estimate the amount of computation of Reduce for an ideal of type 61. Let J be an ideal of type 61:

$$J = \{X^3 + a_6Y^2 + a_5XY + a_4X^2 + a_3Y + a_2X + a_1,$$
$$X^2Y + b_6Y^2 + b_5XY + b_4X^2 + b_3Y + b_2X + b_1,$$
$$XY^2 + c_6Y^2 + c_5XY + c_4X^2 + c_3Y + c_2X + c_1\}$$

The 6×3 sub-matrix M_r, obtained by extracting the seventh, eighth and ninth columns of M_R for J, is represented as

$$M_r = \begin{pmatrix}
1 & 0 & 0 \\
-a_4 - a_5a_6 + b_5 & -a_5 - a_6^2 + b_6 & 0 \\
b_4 + a_5b_6 & b_5 + a_6b_6 & 1 \\
e_{4,1} & e_{4,2} & -a_5 - a_6^2 + b_6 \\
e_{5,1} & e_{5,2} & e_{5,3} \\
e_{6,1} & e_{6,2} & e_{6,3}
\end{pmatrix} \tag{10}$$

$e_{4,1} = -a_2 + a_4^2 - a_3a_6 + 3a_4a_5a_6 + a_5^2a_6^2 + b_3 - a_5b_4 - a_4b_5 - a_5a_6b_5$

$e_{4,2} = -a_3 + a_4a_5 + a_5^2a_6 + 2a_4a_6^2 + a_5a_6^3 - a_6b_4 - a_5b_5 - a_6^2b_5$

$e_{5,1} = -2a_3a_5 + 2a_4a_5^2 - a_2a_6 + a_4^2a_6 + a_5^3a_6 - a_3a_6^2 + 3a_4a_5a_6^2 + a_5^2a_6^3 + b2 - a_4b_4 - a_5a_6b_4$
$\qquad + a_3b_6 - 2a_4a_5b_6 - a_5^2a_6b_6$

$e_{5,2} = -a_2 + a_5^3 - 2a_3a_6 + 2a_4a_5a_6 + 2a_5^2a_6^2 + 2a_4a_6^3 + a_5a_6^4 + b_3 - a_5b_4 - a_6^2b_4 - a_5^2b_6$
$\qquad - a_4a_6b_6 - a_5a_6^2b_6$

$$e_{5,3} = -a_4 - 2a_5 a_6 - a_6^3 + b_5 + a_6 b_6$$

$$e_{6,1} = -2a_3 a_4 - 2a_2 a_5 + 3a_4^2 a_5 - 4a_3 a_5 a_6 + 6a_4 a_5^2 a_6 - a_2 a_6^2 + a_4^2 a_6^2 + 2a_5^3 a_6^2 - a_3 a_6^3 + 3a_4 a_5 a_6^3$$
$$\quad + a_5^2 a_6^4 + a_5 b_3 + a_3 b_5 - 2a_4 a_5 b_5 - a_5^2 a_6 b_5 + a_2 b_6 - a_4^2 b_6 + a_3 a_6 b_6 - 3a_4 a_5 a_6 b_6 - a_5^2 a_6^2 b_6$$

$$e_{6,2} = -2a_3 a_5 + 2a_4 a_5^2 - 2a_2 a_6 + a_4^2 a_6 + 2a_5^3 a_6 - 3a_3 a_6^2 + 5a_4 a_5 a_6^2 + 3a_5^3 a_6^3 + 2a_4 a_6^4 + a_5 a_6^5$$
$$\quad + b2 + a_6 b_3 - a_5^2 b_5 - a_4 a_6 b_5 - a_5 a_6^2 b_5 + a_3 b_6 - a_4 a_5 b_6 - a_5^2 a_6 b_6 - 2a_4 a_6^2 b_6 - a_5 a_6^3 b_6$$

$$e_{6,3} = -a_5^2 - 2a_4 a_6 - 3a_5 a_6^2 - a_6^4 + b_4 + a_6 b_5 + a_5 b_6 + a_6^2 b_6$$

Using this representation we know that if the $(2, 2)$-element $d = -a_5 - a_6^2 + b_6$ of M_r is not equal to zero, the rank of M_r must be 3. So, if $d \neq 0$, we can use 6×3 matrix M_r instead of 6×18 matrix M_R. As the probability of $d = 0$ is about $1/q$, we can assume $d \neq 0$ to estimate the efficiency of the algorithm.

By equation (10), we see that the matrix M_r can be constructed in at most 40 multiplications, removing duplication adequately. Knowing the first three rows of M_r has the triangular form and its $(1, 1)$ and $(3, 3)$ elements are 1, we see RowReduce for M_r' can be performed in 1 inverse and at most $2 \cdot 4 + 2 \cdot 3 = 14$ times multiplications. Thus, Reduce for an ideal of type 61 can be performed in at most 1 inverses and 54 multiplications. Similarly, we can see that Reduce for an ideal of type 31 can be performed in at most 1 inverses and 16 multiplications.

Summarizing the above discussion, the amount of computation of the concrete algorithm is given in the following Table 2. In the table, I and M denotes the operation of inverse and multiplication of elements in k, respectively.

Table 2. Amount of computation of the concrete algorithm

	Addition	Doubling
Compose	134M+3I	214M+3I
Reduce for the type 61	54M+I	54M+I
Reduce for the type 31	16M+I	16M+I
Total	204M+5I	284M+5I

We can add two points on an elliptic curve with one inverse and three multiplications of elements in the definition field, and can double a point with one inverse and four multiplications. Note to obtain the same size of Jacobian, elliptic curves require the definition field of 3 times of bits length of the one for C_{34} curve. Assuming the amount of computation of one inverse is equal to the amount of 10 times multiplication, and assuming the amount of computation of inverse or multiplication grows in the order of square of bit lengths, the amount of computation of the addition on C_{34} curve is $254/(13 \times 9) \approx 2.17$ times of the one for an elliptic curve, and the one of the double is $334/(14 \times 9) \approx 2.65$ times of the one for an elliptic curve.

References

1. S. Arita, "Algorithms for computations in Jacobian group of C_{ab} curve and their application to discrete-log-based public key cryptosystems," IEICE TRANS., VOL.J82-A, NO.8, pp.1291–1299, 1999.
2. D.G.Cantor, "Computing in the Jacobian of a hyperelliptic curve", Mathematics of Computation, 48(177), pp.95–101,1987.
3. S.D.Galbraith, S.Paulus, and N.P.Smart "Arithmetic on Superelliptic Curves", J. Cryptology (1999) 12, 193–196.
4. R.Harasawa, J.Suzuki, "A Fast Jacobian Group Arithmetic Scheme for Algebraic Curve Cryptography", IEICE TRANS., Vol.E84-A No.1, pp.130–139, 2001
5. R. Harley, http://cristal.inria.fr/ harley/hyper/adding.text
6. R.Hartshorne, "Algebraic Geometry", Springer-Verlag, 1977.
7. T. Lange, "Weighted Coordinates on Genus 2 Hyperelliptic Curves", preprint.
8. R. Matsumoto, "The Cab Curve — a generalization of the Weierstrass form to arbitrary plane curves", http://www.rmatsumoto.org/cab.html
9. K. Matsuo, J. Chao, "Fast Cryptosystems Using Genus 2 Hyperelliptic curves", preprint.
10. S. Miura, "Linear Codes on Affine Algebraic Curves", Trans. of IEICE, vol. J81-A, No. 10, 1398–1421, Oct. 1998.

Amplified Differential Power Cryptanalysis on Rijndael Implementations with Exponentially Fewer Power Traces*

Sung-Ming Yen

Laboratory of Cryptography and Information Security (LCIS)
Dept of Computer Science and Information Engineering
National Central University, Chung-Li, Taiwan 320, R.O.C.
yensm@csie.ncu.edu.tw
http://www.csie.ncu.edu.tw/~yensm/

Abstract. Recently, many research works have been conducted about how to carry out physical cryptanalysis on cryptographic devices by exploiting any possible leaked information through side channels. Research results were also reported on how to develop countermeasures against existing physical cryptanalysis. However, very little attention has been paid to deal with the possible mutual relationship between different kinds of physical cryptanalysis when designing a specific countermeasure. In this paper, it is pointed out that enhanced implementations of the Rijndael cipher (AES) against timing cryptanalysis and simple power cryptanalysis (SPA) may unfortunately become more vulnerable to the differential power cryptanalysis (DPA). Technically speaking, based on Sommer's work and experiments presented in CHES 2000, this new DPA on the above mentioned Rijndael implementations enables a much more significant observable peak within the differential power trace. This makes the DPA attack be more easier with fewer required power traces.

1 Introduction

Smart IC cards are frequently employed as tamper-proof devices when developing and implementing a large variety of modern cryptographic schemes. Previously, smart IC cards were assumed to provide high reliability and security based on the embedded central processing unit to control data input/output and to prevent unauthorized access. Due to this popular usage of smart IC cards, much attention has recently been paid to the security issues of implementing cryptosystems based on tamper-proof devices. There is a tremendous difference between this new branch of cryptanalysis and the conventional mathematical or theoretical approaches, the former is specifically called the *physical cryptanalysis*.

---

* Supported by the National Science Council of the Republic of China under contract NSC 91-2213-E-008-032 and also by the Ministry of Education Program for Promoting Academic Excellent of Universities of the Republic of China under the grant number EX-92-E-FA06-4-4.

R. Safavi-Naini and J. Seberry (Eds.): ACISP 2003, LNCS 2727, pp. 106–117, 2003.
© Springer-Verlag Berlin Heidelberg 2003

Active physical cryptanalysis based on the presence of hardware faults have been studied extensively [1,2,3,4]. These attacks exploit the presence of some kinds of transient or permanent faults. Therefore, based on a set of collected incorrect outputs from a device, an adversary can extract the secret key embedded inside the tamper-proof device.

Two well known and extensively studied passive attacks have been reported in the literature, i.e., the timing cryptanalysis and the power analysis attack. The *timing cryptanalysis* was originally proposed by Kocher [5] in 1996 and was further studied in [6,7]. Based on a set of collected timing information and some simple statistical analysis, an adversary can extract the embedded secret key.

The *power analysis attack* is another category of passive attack and was also originally proposed by Kocher [8] in which both simple power analysis (SPA) and differential power analysis (DPA) were considered. SPA tries to extract the secret key by observing a single power consumption trace of the device. DPA is conducted by collecting a large set of power consumption traces and performing some simple statistical analysis. Many research results on power analysis attack can be found in the literature; among them, some works specific for public key cryptosystems are [9,10] and some works specific for symmetric key cryptosystems are [11,12,13].

During the past years, much attention has been paid to propose new physical attacks and also to develop possible countermeasures against existing physical cryptanalysis. A few research works pointed out a straightforward result that a countermeasure against one physical attack does not necessarily thwart another kind of physical attack. However, extremely little attention has been paid to consider the possible *mutual* relationship between different kinds of physical cryptanalysis when designing a specific countermeasure.

The main contribution of this paper is to point out that some enhanced and popular implementations of the Rijndael cipher (AES) [14] against timing cryptanalysis unfortunately becomes more vulnerable to the proposed DPA, say the *amplified DPA*. Feasibility analysis of this new DPA on these popular Rijndael implementations will be considered. The primary result is that this amplified DPA enables a much more significant observable peak within a differential power trace. This makes DPA be more easy with fewer collected power traces.

2   The Rijndael Cipher

The Rijndael cipher [14] has been selected to be the final candidate of AES in the early 2001. During the evaluation process, the issues of physical cryptanalysis on Rijndael were reported in [7,11].

2.1   Rijndael Operation

Detailed description of the Rijndael cipher is out of the scope of this article. Only some preliminary knowledge about Rijndael is necessary to understand the attack proposed in this paper. For a complete description of Rijndael, the reader can refer to [14].

The Rijndael cipher consists of an initial round key addition, followed by N usual rounds of transformation; and the final round is slightly different from other usual rounds. In the cipher, a 'State' denotes a matrix of bytes representing an intermediate result. In an encryption, the initial value of 'State' is a block of plaintext. In the following, only the initial round and the first round are listed:

(0)   AddRoundKey(State, RoundKey): This is the initial round key addition performed by XOR operation.

(1.A) ByteSub(State): A byte-by-byte fixed substitution is performed for each byte in a State.

(1.B) ShiftRow(State): Bytes in a State are rotated on each row (except the first row) in a fixed approach.

(1.C) MixColumn(State): Each column of a State (considered as a 3rd order polynomial with its coefficients from $GF(2^8)$) is multiplied with $(03h)x^3 + (01h)x^2 + (01h)x + (02h)$, then modulo $(01h)x^4 + (01h)$ (both polynomials with their coefficients from $GF(2^8)$). One of the primary operations in this step is the xtime operation.

(1.D) AddRoundKey(State, RoundKey): Similar to the step (0) but using another block of key bytes.

2.2   Two Implementations of xtime in Rijndael

Given an element $a(x)$ in $GF(2^8)$ (with standard polynomial representation), the xtime operation computes $a(x) \cdot x \bmod m(x)$ where $m(x) = x^8 + x^4 + x^3 + x + 1$ is an irreducible polynomial. A straightforward implementation (using pseudo code) of xtime is given in Fig. 1 where the register A initially stores the eight binary coefficients of $a(x)$.

```
xtime:
        SL   A
        JR   NC, NEXT
        XOR  PRI        % PRI=1Bh (in hexadecimal)
NEXT:
```

Fig. 1. An implementation of xtime.

The instruction "XOR PRI" (realizes modulo $m(x)$ and the constant PRI=1Bh stores $x^4 + x^3 + x + 1$) will execute only if the carry bit is one. Evidently, this enables an attacker to verify his guess of the carry bit by exploiting the execution time of xtime. For the details of how to mount a successful timing cryptanalysis on a Rijndael implementation (under the adoption of xtime in Fig. 1) by exploiting the above timing difference in xtime, please refer to [7]. It is well known that direct secret data (e.g., key) dependent conditional branch instructions and steps should be avoided in order to be immune from a timing cryptanalysis. In fact, avoiding secret data dependent decisions and branch instructions are also necessary to resist the simple power cryptanalysis (SPA) [8]. In order to resist against timing

cryptanalysis (and also SPA), a novel modified implementation of xtime as shown in Fig. 2 was suggested by Sano *et al* [15], and has been adopted in some Rijndael implementations.

```
xtime:
        SL    A
        LD    B, A
        SBC   A, A    % A ← A-(A+cf)
        AND   PRI
        XOR   B
```

Fig. 2. The first timing attack resistant implementation of xtime.

In this novel implementation of xtime, depending on the value of carry flag cf, after executing the instruction "SBC A, A" the value of register A will become ffh if cf=1; otherwise, the value of register A will be 00h. These two possible extreme values in A will be used as masks in the instruction "AND PRI", and after that register A becomes either PRI or 00h if cf=1 or cf=0, respectively. This realizes the conditional modulo $m(x)$ operation without using any conditional instruction.

3   Amplified Differential Power Cryptanalysis on the First Modified xtime Implementation

3.1   Process of the Proposed Amplified DPA

Similar to DPA on other symmetric key cryptosystem implementation, a set of power monitoring traces and their related information (e.g., the plaintext in the following context) are collected. The power traces and the plaintexts are denoted as Tr_i and M_i $(i = 1, 2, \ldots, n)$. In this paper, we consider the case of recovering the initial round key used in the step (0). After recovering the initial round key (and some part of the round key used in the first round), the other round keys can be derived based on the property of Rijndael key schedule design.

Without losing any general property of the proposed DPA, it is assumed in the following that there are four rows and four columns in the Rijndael State; it is also the case for each round key. Some notations are listed to help the explanation of the following DPA. In the initial round, the plaintext with the format of a matrix of 16 bytes $a_{i,j}$ $(i, j \in \{0, 1, 2, 3\})$ are bitwise XORed with the initial round key $k_{i,j}$ such that $b_{i,j} = a_{i,j} \oplus k_{i,j}$. Then, each $b_{i,j}$ is substituted by $c_{i,j}$ in the step (1.A). The step (1.B) rotates $c_{i,j}$ left with some specific bytes as defined in AES. This rotated $c_{i,j}$ will be operated by step (1.C) MixColumn in a four-byte column approach which can be implemented by using the algorithm listed in Fig. 3 where the first column of State is considered.

Input: first column of State before MixColumn $\{c_{0,0}, c_{1,1}, c_{2,2}, c_{3,3}\}$
Output: first column of State after MixColumn $\{d_{0,0}, d_{1,0}, d_{2,0}, d_{3,0}\}$
$$Com = c_{0,0} \oplus c_{1,1} \oplus c_{2,2} \oplus c_{3,3}$$
$$Tm = c_{0,0} \oplus c_{1,1}$$
$$Tm = \text{xtime}(Tm) \qquad \cdots\cdots \text{first xtime}$$
$$d_{0,0} = c_{0,0} \oplus Com \oplus Tm$$
$$Tm = c_{1,1} \oplus c_{2,2}$$
$$Tm = \text{xtime}(Tm) \qquad \cdots\cdots \text{second xtime}$$
$$d_{1,0} = c_{1,1} \oplus Com \oplus Tm$$
$$Tm = c_{2,2} \oplus c_{3,3}$$
$$Tm = \text{xtime}(Tm) \qquad \cdots\cdots \text{third xtime}$$
$$d_{2,0} = c_{2,2} \oplus Com \oplus Tm$$
$$Tm = c_{3,3} \oplus c_{0,0}$$
$$Tm = \text{xtime}(Tm) \qquad \cdots\cdots \text{fourth xtime}$$
$$d_{3,0} = c_{3,3} \oplus Com \oplus Tm$$

Fig. 3. An implementation of MixColumn – the case of first column.

The following paragraph describes the steps of the amplified DPA on the above Rijndael implementation. Here, the two key bytes $k_{0,0}$ and $k_{1,1}$ are under attack.

Guess initial round key. The attacker randomly guesses both $k_{0,0}$ and $k_{1,1}$ and computes (through the steps (0), (1.A), and (1.B)) the related $c_{0,0}$ and $c_{1,1}$ for all collected plaintexts M_i. Notice that the attacker does not need to compute other unnecessary bytes $c_{i,j}$ since they are not required in the following attack.

Carry bit derivation. Within the implementation of step (1.C) (refer to Fig. 3), the attacker first computes $Tm = c_{0,0} \oplus c_{1,1}$ and obtains the most significant bit (MSB) of Tm. A MSB of "1" in Tm will lead to a value of ffh in the register A after executing "SBC A, A" in Fig. 2; otherwise, the value of register A becomes 00h. The attacker does not need to compute other unnecessary values, e.g., Com, the value of $\text{xtime}(Tm)$, and other parts, since they are not required in this attack.

Power trace classification. Similar to an ordinary DPA, for all M_i's which lead to a MSB=1 in Tm, the related power traces Tr_i are collected and the average trace of these Tr_i is computed which is denoted as $Tr^{(1)}$. On the other hand, all other traces with a related MSB=0 in Tm, are also collected and the average trace $Tr^{(0)}$ is computed. Then, a differential trace $Tr^{(diff)}$ between $Tr^{(1)}$ and $Tr^{(0)}$ is computed and analyzed. If a significant peak can be found within this differential trace, then the guessed key bytes $k_{0,0}$ and $k_{1,1}$ are correct; otherwise, the attacker tries another possibility of $k_{0,0}$ and $k_{1,1}$ in the step of **Guess initial round key** and performs the remaining computation again.

Once $k_{0,0}$ and $k_{1,1}$ are derived in the above amplified DPA attack, the attacker can now attack $k_{2,2}$ and $k_{3,3}$ in a similar approach by analyzing and observing the "third" xtime operation in Fig. 3.

However, a much better approach is that only $k_{2,2}$ is derived (recall that now $k_{1,1}$ is already available) in a similar approach by analyzing and observing the "second" xtime operation in Fig. 3. Then, $k_{3,3}$ is derived by analyzing the "third" xtime operation after obtaining $k_{2,2}$. The above separated attack on $k_{2,2}$ and then on $k_{3,3}$ reduces cryptanalysis complexity substantially. In the combined attack on $k_{2,2}$ and $k_{3,3}$ together (each with eight bits), the computational complexity by exhaustive search is $O(2^{16})$, while the separated approach takes a complexity of $O(2^9)$. This evidently simplifies the attack.

Finally, we found that the "fourth" xtime operation in Fig. 3 can be employed as a double check to identify any possible error when deriving $k_{0,0}$ and $k_{3,3}$, or indirectly to verify the entire attack procedure.

All other key bytes in the "initial" round key can be derived in a similar approach.

3.2 Feasibility Analysis and Major Advantage of the Proposed Attack

A major difficulty of any previous DPA on other symmetric key cryptosystem implementations, e.g., DES, is that an observable peak within the differential trace $Tr^{(diff)}$ between $Tr^{(1)}$ and $Tr^{(0)}$ will not be very significant if a *single-bit* DPA is adopted, i.e., a two-way partitioning is employed. In this case, minor measurement errors can reduce the feasibility of the attack. Therefore, *multiple-bit* DPA was suggested to enhance the significance of the expected peak within some differential traces among all possible trace groups. The reason is straightforward that power consumption of a specific processor instruction (especially for boolean instruction executions and power consumption used to drive data bus between ALU and a register or memory) is more or less proportional to the Hamming weight of either the operands or the instruction's output.

Unfortunately, the multiple-bit approach also brings another major disadvantage that much more power traces should be collected for a successful DPA. This is because that a multiple-bit approach leads to exponentially more groupings (basically 2^b groups for a b-bit approach). Therefore, *exponentially* more power traces are required to be distributed among these 2^b groups. This often makes the DPA be infeasible or at least be impractical; say in the real world it would be difficult to collect too many power traces of a specific smart IC card under attack. Recall that DPA (in fact, also timing attack or hardware fault attack) does not assume the permanent possession of the IC card under attack. So, only reasonable amount of collected power traces are possible.

Therefore, a DPA with less or reasonable amount of recorded power traces is always important and required by the attackers. Noticeable that the considered DPA on a popular Rijndael implementation using the xtime listed in Fig. 2 does not suffer from the above difficulty. As described previously, depending on the value of MSB of $a(x) \cdot x$ (i.e., the carry flag cf after the operation "SL A"), the value of register A will be either ffh or 00h after executing the instruction "SBC A, A".

In the work by Sommer [16], it clearly revealed that power consumption characteristic of a microprocessor chip is highly correlated to the Hamming weight of instruction arguments. Her work showed that this high correlation (or power consumption proportionality) happens especially when an instruction argument is transferred over the internal bus before getting involved with a mathematical or a logical operation in the ALU. In fact, this may also happen when the operation result will be moved into a specific location, say a register.

Therefore, the major advantage of the proposed DPA is that even if a *single-bit* (i.e., cf or the MSB of $a(x) \cdot x$) differential power analysis is employed, a much more significant peak can be expected within the differential power trace without collecting exponentially more power traces, because that *multiple-bit* difference between ffh and 00h can be achieved in both of the following operations:

(1) when storing the result back to register A after executing the instruction "SBC A, A";
(2) when accessing the operand from register A prior to executing the instruction "AND PRI".

Because of the different features apart from ordinary *single-bit* and *multiple-bit* DPA, the above proposed DPA is called an *amplified single-bit* DPA in this paper. Theoretically, based on Sommer's work and experiments [16], this new DPA will enable the observable peak within $Tr^{(diff)}$ to eight times of amplitude as in ordinary DPA if: (1) an eight-bit processor will be considered; (2) power consumption difference for different instruction operands is assumed to be directly proportional to the Hamming weight difference of the operands. At least, a much more significant peak can be expected within $Tr^{(diff)}$. Nowadays, 16-bit processors have already been widely adopted even in the smart IC card implementation; the situation will become worse, because that a much more significant peak can be expected in this situation. This will enable a very successful DPA with much fewer collected power traces.

The following Definition 1 summarizes and concludes the importance of the proposed amplified single-bit DPA which needs *exponentially* fewer power traces when compared with a conventional DPA.

Definition 1 *Theoretically, an amplified single-bit DPA with b times of differential peak amplitude amplification needs $1/2^b$ times of collected power traces of employing a conventional b-bit DPA. This assumes the model and experimental results by Sommer [16].*

4   Amplified Differential Power Cryptanalysis on Another Modified xtime Implementation

In this section, another real enhanced implementation of xtime trying to be immune from timing and SPA cryptanalysis will be shown to be more vulnerable to the proposed amplified DPA.

In [17], Blömer and Seifert considered an enhanced xtime implementation which was originally designed to be immune from timing and SPA attacks. The algorithm was written in an extended 8051 assembler language (see Fig. 4) since the extended 8051 microcontroller is still the most commonly employed controller in contemporary smart cards. They showed that the implementation in Fig. 4 is vulnerable to the hardware fault attack based on the idea of *safe-error* proposed in [4].

```
xtime:
        MOV   B, A
        SLL   B                    % B ← (a₆, a₅, ..., a₀, 0)
        DIV   A, #10000000b        % A ← (0, 0, ..., 0, a₇)
        MUL   A, #00011011b
        XRL   A, B                 % A ← A ⊕ B
```

$$\text{SLL} \quad \text{B} \qquad \% \; B \leftarrow (a_6, a_5, \ldots, a_0, 0)$$
$$\text{DIV} \quad \text{A, \#10000000b} \quad \% \; A \leftarrow (0, 0, \ldots, 0, a_7)$$
$$\text{XRL} \quad \text{A, B} \qquad \% \; A \leftarrow A \oplus B$$

Fig. 4. The second timing attack resistant implementation of xtime.

The implementation realizes the conditional modulo $m(x)$ operation without using any conditional instruction. In this xtime implementation, after the execution of "DIV A, #10000000b" the register A becomes either 00h or 01h depending on the value of a_7. Based on this result, the value of register A becomes either 00h or 00011011b after the execution of "MUL A, #00011011b". These two possible values in A with large difference of Hamming weight, i.e., four, enables our proposed amplified DPA.

4.1   Process of the Proposed DPA

The attack goes in the same way as the previous amplified DPA which consists of (1) guess initial round key; (2) carry bit derivation; and (3) power trace classification.

As previously, this attack takes the advantage that even if a single-bit difference in the highest order coefficient of $a(x) \cdot x$ (which is initially stored in the MSB of register A and then stored in the LSB of A after executing "DIV A, #10000000b"), a much more significant peak can be expected than in the conventional single-bit DPA. The reason is that *multiple-bit* difference between 00h and 00011011b can be achieved in both of the following operations:

(1) when storing the result back to register A after executing the instruction "MUL A, #00011011b";
(2) when accessing the operand from register A prior to executing the instruction "XRL A, B".

Theoretically, based on Sommer's work [16], this amplified DPA will enable the observable peak within $Tr^{(diff)}$ to four times of amplitude as in an ordinary DPA.

5   Some Remarks on Countermeasures without Secret Key Dependent Jump Instruction

It was widely believed and employed that secret key dependent conditional jump instructions should be totally removed from the implementations in order to be immune from the timing attack and SPA [8]. Therefore, enhanced implementations were developed (such as the enhanced xtime considered in this paper) in which *explicit* secret key dependent conditional jumps were usually replaced by a set of routine instructions running with constant time but not with constant power consumption.

In fact, in all implementations, secret key (or any secret information, like the MSB of register A of a xtime routine) based conditional operations still exist in the following approach.

(1) **Secret key/information extraction.** The required secret information is extracted by some means and moved to some location within the CPU. In Fig. 2, the original value of a_7 is moved to the flag bit by using a left shift instruction "SL A". In Fig. 4, the instruction "DIV A, #10000000b" is employed to extract a_7 and to store it at the LSB of the destination register, i.e., still the register A.

(2) **Secret key/information dependent intermediate data generation.** At least one secret information controlled intermediate data will be generated by using the previously extracted secret information which is already stored somewhere. In Fig. 2, a mask of value 00h or ffh (depending on the secret information) is computed by executing "SBC A, A". In Fig. 4, the instruction "MUL A, #00011011b" is employed to generate either 00h or #00011011b depending on the secret information.

(3) **Secret key/information dependent cryptographic operation.** In Fig. 2, the instruction "XOR B" performs a conditional modulo $m(x)$ indirectly. On the other hand, in Fig. 4, the instruction "XRL A, B" performs a conditional modulo $m(x)$ indirectly.

In the above approach, it is easy to prove the immunity of an implementation against the timing attack when each of the involved instructions can be executed with a specific constant time. Basically, this is easy to achieve in a conventional *synchronous* circuit design even for most of the arithmetic instructions.

As for differential power attack, a countermeasure designed to improve its immunity against some physical attacks, e.g., timing attack, should avoid to enlarge the Hamming weight of the related secret key or secret information during the Step (2) and Step (3) of the above mentioned unconditional instructions execution. By the way, we notice that a negative property of employing a constant time routine is possible when considering DPA. A routine without secret key dependent conditional jump benefits DPA, because it becomes more easier to conduct the statistical analysis on the collected power traces since the routine will be executed with a constant time.

6   Yet Another Amplified Differential Power Cryptanalysis – Second-Order Amplified DPA

In [17], another timing attack immune implementation of xtime was considered on its immunity against glitch attack (a hardware fault attack). The implementation was described in a high level language as shown in Fig. 5.

```
xtime:
        f  := a7
        A  := (a6, a5, a4, a3, a2, a1, a0, 0)
        xtime[0]  := A ⊕ (0,0,0,0,0,0,0,0)
        xtime[1]  := A ⊕ (0,0,0,1,1,0,1,1)
        return(xtime[f])
```

Fig. 5. The third timing attack resistant implementation of xtime.

In fact, the statement xtime[0] := A ⊕ (0,0,0,0,0,0,0,0) can be simplified and be replaced by only xtime[0] := A without damaging its security against timing attack and SPA.

At the first look, it appears that the implementation in Fig. 5 can be secure against the proposed amplified DPA. This is because that there is no single operand or computation result of the statement (or instruction) within the implementation which will demonstrate a big difference of Hamming weight depending on the status of a_7. However, the implementation is still vulnerable to the following more advanced amplified DPA.

6.1   Process of the Proposed Second-Order Amplified DPA

In [12], Messerges proposed the idea of second-order DPA which employs the statistics of power consumption on two time instants but not only on one time instant of all power traces. The concept can be generalized into the more higher-order DPA. Based on this technique, the following second-order amplified DPA can be developed.

In Fig. 5, if $a_7 = 0$ (now stored in the variable f), then the result storing into xtime[0] and the value returned from the called function return(xtime[f])[1] are identical. Hence, based on Sommer's experiments and observation [16, see p.91 of §4 Concluding Remarks], power consumption taken by the chip to transfer these data over the internal bus will be very similar when the operands are the same even if the instructions are not identical[2].

On the other hand, if $a_7 = 1$, then the result storing into xtime[0] and the value returned from the called function return(xtime[f]) will always have a

---

[1] Note that returning a result from a called function or an assembler routine consists of storing the value into a specific location.

[2] In our attack, the instructions can be the same one, e.g., both are MOV or LD instructions.

difference on Hamming weight of "four" since A $\oplus$ (A $\oplus$ (0,0,0,1,1,0,1,1)) =(0,0,0,1,1,0,1,1).

Therefore, the attacker computes the difference between the power consumptions of both (1) storing a result into `xtime[0]`, and (2) returning a result by `return(xtime[f])` for all collected power traces. The difference computed for the ith power trace will be denoted as Tr_i^D. The difference is actually computed near both the two specific instants, so each Tr_i^D may consist of a small sequence of sampling values. As in an ordinary second-order DPA, this attack assumes more detailed implementation knowledge, especially the right time instants for the above two data movement instructions. The attack then goes as follows:

(1) **Guess initial round key**
(2) **Carry bit derivation**
(3) **Power trace classification.** In fact, now only the difference value Tr_i^D classification is sufficient. If a significant observable peak within the differential power trace $Tr^{(diff)}$ can be identified, then the guessed key bytes are correct.

The above second-order amplified DPA may enable a more significant peak for a successful attack than in an ordinary second-order DPA. Of course, both the enhanced implementations of Fig. 2 and Fig. 4 are vulnerable to the above proposed second-order amplified DPA. However, in those scenarios we do not have to conduct the second-order amplified DPA since the ordinary (or first-order) amplified DPA suffices for a successful attack and assumes less knowledge about the exact implementation details.

7   Concluding Remarks

It is already a well known result that a countermeasure developed against one physical attack does not necessarily thwart another kind of physical attack. More interestingly, a countermeasure developed

against one physical attack if not carefully examined will sometimes benefit another physical attack which was originally impossible. Furthermore, the most important thing we wish to emphasize is that the above mentioned new induced attack (by exploiting a countermeasure) may *substantially* benefit another physical attack, i.e., to amplify the attack. A reason to bring the above conclusion is that very little attention has been paid to deal with the possible mutual relationship between different kinds of physical cryptanalysis when designing a specific countermeasure.

The amplified first-order and second-order DPA found in this paper reveal that an overall design and analysis of countermeasures against physical cryptanalysis will become quite complex and difficult in its essence. This may especially be true if the attacker considers a *combined* physical cryptanalysis (it means a new physical attack taking the key idea of two or more physical attacks simultaneously) which is still a yet well studied area but may become a very powerful technique.

References

1. D. Boneh, R.A. DeMillo, and R.J. Lipton, "On the importance of checking cryptographic protocols for faults," In *Advances in Cryptology – EUROCRYPT '97*, LNCS 1233, pp. 37–51, Springer-Verlag, 1997.
2. E. Biham and A. Shamir, "Differential fault analysis of secret key cryptosystems," In *Advances in Cryptology – CRYPTO '97*, LNCS 1294, pp. 513–525, Springer-Verlag, Berlin, 1997.
3. M. Joye, A.K. Lenstra, and J.-J. Quisquater, "Chinese remaindering based cryptosystems in the presence of faults," *Journal of Cryptology*, vol. 12, no. 4, pp. 241–245, 1999.
4. S.M. Yen and M. Joye, "Checking before output may not be enough against fault-based cryptanalysis," *IEEE Trans. on Computers*, vol. 49, no. 9, pp. 967–970, Sept. 2000.
5. P. Kocher, "Timing attacks on implementations of Diffie-Hellman, RSA, DSS, and other systems," In *Advances in Cryptology – CRYPTO '96*, LNCS 1109, pp. 104–113, Springer-Verlag, 1996.
6. J.F. Dhem, F. Koeune, P.A. Leroux, P. Mestre, J.J. Quisquater, and J.L. Willems, "A practical implementation of the timing attack," In *Proceedings of CARDIS '98 – Third Smart Card Research and Advanced Application Conference*, UCL, Louvain-la-Neuve, Belgium, Sep. 14–16, 1998.
7. F. Koeune and J.-J. Quisquater, "A timing attack against Rijndael," *Technical Report CG-1999/1*, Université catholique de Louvain, June 1999.
8. P. Kocher, J. Jaffe and B. Jun, "Differential power analysis," In *Advances in Cryptology – CRYPTO '99*, LNCS 1666, pp. 388–397, Springer-Verlag, 1999.
9. T.S. Messerges, E.A. Dabbish, and R.H. Sloan, "Power analysis attacks of modular exponentiation in smartcards," In *Cryptographic Hardware and Embedded Systems – CHES '99*, LNCS 1717, pp. 144–157, Springer-Verlag, 1999.
10. C. Clavier, J.-S. Coron, and N. Dabbous, "Differential power analysis in the presence of hardware countermeasures," In *Cryptographic Hardware and Embedded Systems – CHES 2000*, LNCS 1965, pp. 252–263, Springer-Verlag, 2000.
11. T.S. Messerges, "Securing the AES finalists against power analysis attacks," In *Proceedings of Fast Software Encryption Workshop – FSE 2000*, LNCS 1978, pp. 150–164, Springer-Verlag, 2001.
12. T.S. Messerges, "Using second-order power analysis to attack DPA resistant software," In *Cryptographic Hardware and Embedded Systems – CHES 2000*, LNCS 1965, pp. 238–251, Springer-Verlag, 2000.
13. M. Akkar and C. Giraud, "An implementation of DES and AES, secure against some attacks," In *Cryptographic Hardware and Embedded Systems – CHES 2001*, LNCS 2162, pp. 309–318, Springer-Verlag, 2001.
14. J. Daemen and V. Rijmen, "AES Proposal: Rijndael," AES submission, 1998, available at URL <http://csrc.nist.gov/encryption/aes/aes_home.htm>.
15. F. Sano, M. Koike, S. Kawamura, and M. Shiba, "Performance evaluation of AES finalists on the high-end smart card," In *Proceedings of the Third Advanced Encryption Standard (AES) Candidate Conference*, pp. 82–93, April 13–14, 2000.
16. R.M. Sommer, "Smartly analyzing the simplicity and the power of SPA on smartcards," In *Cryptographic Hardware and Embedded Systems – CHES 2000*, LNCS 1965, pp. 78–92, Springer-Verlag, 2000.
17. J. Blömer and J.P. Seifert, "Fault based cryptanalysis of the Advanced Encryption Standard (AES)," Cryptology ePrint Archive of IACR, No. 075, 2002, available at URL <http://eprint.iacr.org/2002/075>.

Differential Fault Analysis on AES Key Schedule and Some Countermeasures[*]

Chien-Ning Chen and Sung-Ming Yen

Laboratory of Cryptography and Information Security (LCIS)
Dept of Computer Science and Information Engineering
National Central University, Chung-Li, Taiwan 320, R.O.C.
{ning;yensm}@csie.ncu.edu.tw
http://www.csie.ncu.edu.tw/~yensm/

Abstract. This paper describes a DFA attack on the AES key schedule. This fault model assumes that the attacker can induce a single byte fault on the round key. It efficiently finds the key of AES-128 with feasible computation and less than thirty pairs of correct and faulty ciphertexts. Several countermeasures are also proposed. This weakness can be resolved without modifying the structure of the AES algorithm and without decreasing the efficiency.

Keywords: AES, Differential fault analysis (DFA), Physical cryptanalysis, Rijndael, Smart cards.

1 Introduction

Since physical cryptanalysis [1,2,3,4] was first considered a few years ago, secure implementations of cryptographic systems have received much attention. Conventional cryptanalysis deals with only the mathematical properties of a system, but physical cryptanalysis focuses on the physical behavior of a system when an implementation executes.

Differential fault analysis (DFA) is one category of physical cryptanalysis and was originally proposed by Biham and Shamir in 1997 [5]. It assumes that an attacker can induce faults into a system and collect the correct as well as the faulty behaviors. The attacker compares the behaviors in order to retrieve the secret information embedded inside a system (more precisely, an implementation). As to the reality of DFA attacks or other kind of hardware fault attacks, it was once considered to be more or less theoretical work. However, more and more researchers in this field warn people of the danger of hardware fault attacks.

The most important thing is that extremely few attention has ever been paid to DFA on AES and we have the first result in early 2002 [6] which was motivated by our another unpublished work in 2000 of DFA on IDEA [7]. In [6], it assumes that a single bit fault can be induced on the temporary result within the cipher.

---

[*] Supported in part by the National Science Council of the Republic of China under contract NSC 91-2213-E-008-032.

R. Safavi-Naini and J. Seberry (Eds.): ACISP 2003, LNCS 2727, pp. 118–129, 2003.
© Springer-Verlag Berlin Heidelberg 2003

By comparing the correct and the faulty decryption outputs, the attacker can retrieve possible values of one byte of the last round key. The unique value of the byte can be retrieved by intersecting several sets of those possible values. However, the DFA considered in [6] has its limitation in practice because the operands of most computers are 'byte' or 'word', but not 'bit'. In practice, it is not easy to induce a fault within only one bit. The result in this paper is much important than our result in [6] since the new attack needs fewer faulty ciphertexts to mount the attack and makes more reasonable assumption.

Another DFA attack on the AES algorithm was proposed in 2003 [8]. Its fault module is to induce a fault within one byte of the temporary result before the ninth round's MixColumns. The MixColumns will propagate the fault to four bytes, which will cause four-byte differences in the input of the last round's SubBytes. Possible values of the differences in the input of SubBytes can be derived from the relationships between them. After retrieving the differences in the input and output of SubBytes, the remaining process is similar to [6].

Not only the temporary result, the AES key schedule has similar weakness, because both of them employ the same non-linear function, SubBytes. Giraud proposed another DFA on AES based on this observation [9]. It was announced that the key of AES-128 can be resolved with about 250 faulty ciphertexts in five days by using a modern personal computer. Thus not only the temporary result but also the key schedule is vulnerable under the DFA attacks.

The main contribution of this paper is that we extend Giraud's DFA and develop a novel methodology to recover the encryption key with fewer faulty ciphertexts and with extremely less computational complexity. The first two steps of our method are similar to Giraud's. But in the second step of our method, only three bytes of the round key are retrieved in order to reduce the number of samples required. The third step of Giraud's method requires a huge amount of computation, on the contrary, the third step of ours focuses on the inverse SubBytes and requires only very few samples and computations. The requirement of samples is analyzed rigorously in this paper. Finally, three countermeasures are proposed. All of them are compatible with the standard of AES-128.

All other parts of this paper are organized as follows. In Sect. 2, the AES algorithm will be briefly reviewed and some necessary notations will be defined. The proposed DFA on the AES key schedule will be described in Sect. 3 with rigorous analysis on the correctness and its attack performance. Finally, three possible countermeasures will be provided in Sect. 4.

2   The AES Specification

The AES algorithm [10,11] was published by NIST in Nov 2001. Figure 1 is the block diagram of the last two rounds. The key schedule is split into the linear part, L_i, and the non-linear part, N_i.

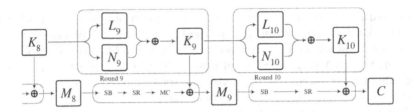

Fig. 1. The last two rounds of AES-128.

2.1   The Key Schedule of the AES Algorithm

The KeyExpansion function in Fig. 2 generates the round keys for AES-128. There are two sub functions and one table in the KeyExpansion. They are SubWord(), RotWord(), and Rcon[].

$key[]$: The input 16-byte key.
$w[]$: The resulting round keys, stored in an array of four-byte words.

```
01  KeyExpansion(byte key[16], word w[44]){
02      word temp;
03      for (i = 0; i < 4; i++)
04        w[i] = (key[4*i], key[4*i+1], key[4*i+2], key[4*i+3]);
05      for (i = 4; i < 11; i++){
06        temp = w[i-1];
07        if (i mod 4 == 0)
08          temp = SubWord(RotWord(temp)) ⊕ Rcon[i/4];
09        w[i] = w[i-4] ⊕ temp;
10      }
11  }
```

Fig. 2. Pseudo codes for the key expansion of AES-128.

SubWord() is a function that takes a word input and applies the SubBytes() to each of those four bytes to produce a word output. RotWord() takes a word (a_0, a_1, a_2, a_3) as its input, performs a cyclic permutation, and returns the word (a_1, a_2, a_3, a_0). Rcon[] is a four-byte table and Rcon[i] contains the values, $(2^{i-1}, 0, 0, 0)$, where 2^{i-1} is the power of 2 $(= 1 \cdot x)$ in the defined field.

2.2   Notations

Necessary notations are defined in the following.

M_i is the temporary result of message after the ith round. M_i' is the temporary result with fault. C is the ciphertext, and the faulty ciphertext is D.
(Note: The subscript, "Byte" or "Word", means that the size of the elements in the bracket is 8-bit or 32-bit.)

$$M_i = (m_i[0], \cdots, m_i[15])_{\texttt{Byte}}, \text{ and } C = M_{N_r} = (c[0], \cdots, c[15])_{\texttt{Byte}}.$$
$$M'_i = (m'_i[0], \cdots, m'_i[15])_{\texttt{Byte}}, \text{ and } D = M'_{N_r} = (d[0], \cdots, d[15])_{\texttt{Byte}}.$$

K_i is the ith round key and K'_i is the ith round key with fault.

$$K_i = (k_i[0], \cdots, k_i[15])_{\texttt{Byte}} = (w[4i], \cdots, w[4i+3])_{\texttt{Word}}, \text{ and}$$
$$K'_i = (k'_i[0], \cdots, k'_i[15])_{\texttt{Byte}}.$$

In addition, L_i is the linear part of the key schedule, and N_i is the non-linear part. $K_i = L_i \oplus N_i$. In AES-128, L_i and N_i are defined as

$$
\begin{aligned}
L_i &= (l_i[0], \cdots, l_i[15])_{\texttt{Byte}} \\
&= (w[4i-4], \\
&\quad\ w[4i-4] \oplus w[4i-3], \\
&\quad\ w[4i-4] \oplus w[4i-3] \oplus w[4i-2], \\
&\quad\ w[4i-4] \oplus w[4i-3] \oplus w[4i-2] \oplus w[4i-1])_{\texttt{Word}} \text{ and}
\end{aligned}
$$

$$
\begin{aligned}
N_i &= (n_i[0], \cdots, n_i[15])_{\texttt{Byte}} \\
&= (\texttt{SubWord}(\texttt{RotWord}(w[4i-1])) \oplus \texttt{Rcon}[i], \\
&\quad\ \texttt{SubWord}(\texttt{RotWord}(w[4i-1])) \oplus \texttt{Rcon}[i], \\
&\quad\ \texttt{SubWord}(\texttt{RotWord}(w[4i-1])) \oplus \texttt{Rcon}[i], \\
&\quad\ \texttt{SubWord}(\texttt{RotWord}(w[4i-1])) \oplus \texttt{Rcon}[i])_{\texttt{Word}}.
\end{aligned}
$$

$L'_i = (l'_i[0], \cdots, l'_i[15])_{\texttt{Byte}}$ is the faulty L_i, and
$N'_i = (n'_i[0], \cdots, n'_i[15])_{\texttt{Byte}}$ is the faulty N_i.

3   The DFA Attack on the AES-128 Key Schedule

This section describes DFA on AES-128 with round keys generated on the fly. It assumes that the attacker can induce a single byte fault on the round key and collect the correct ciphertext C as well as the faulty ciphertext D. The idea of this attack is also suitable for AES-192 and AES-256, but the attacker can retrieve only a part of round keys.

3.1   Faults on the Last Four Bytes of K_9

In order to retrieve the last four bytes of K_9, a fault is induced only on one of last four bytes in K_9. When the single one-byte fault occurs, there are five non-zero bytes in $C \oplus D$. Four bytes of them are equal and lay on the same row. The remaining one is placed on the particular byte corresponded to where the fault is induced on. If the faults occur on more bytes, there will be more non-zero rows in $C \oplus D$. Inducing faults on more bytes doesn't mean that this attack will fail. It may reduce the required samples but need analyze case by case. When

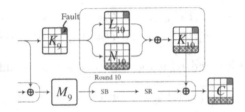

Fig. 3. Fault induced on the twelfth byte of K_9.

the difference is the specified form, the probability that the fault occurs on more bytes is extremely low.

The fault, $\delta_9[i]$ ($i = 12 \sim 15$), induced on the ith byte of K_9 can be derived from $c[i] \oplus d[i] = k_{10}[i] \oplus k'_{10}[i] = l_{10}[i] \oplus l'_{10}[i] = k_9[i] \oplus k'_9[i] = \delta_9[i]$. The possible values of $k_9[i]$ can be deduced from

$$c[i-1] \oplus d[i-1] = k_{10}[i-1] \oplus k'_{10}[i-1] = n_{10}[i-1] \oplus n'_{10}[i-1]$$
$$= \texttt{SubBytes}(k_9[i]) \oplus \texttt{SubBytes}(k_9[i] \oplus \delta_9[i]). \tag{1}$$

The unique value of $k_9[i]$ can be retrieved by intersecting several sets of the possible values caused by different induced faults. $k_9[12 \sim 15]$ can be retrieved in this step.

3.2 Faults on the Last Three Bytes of K_8

In the second step, a fault is induced on a single one-byte of $w[35]$. When the single byte fault occurs, there are nine or ten non-zero bytes in $C \oplus D$. Eight of them lay on two rows.

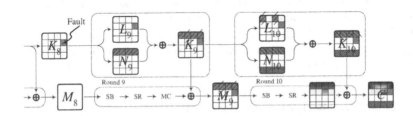

Fig. 4. Fault induced on the thirteenth byte of K_8.

If the fault occurs on one of $w[35]$'s last three bytes, the induced fault, $\delta_8[i]$ ($i = 13 \sim 15$), can be derived from $c[i] \oplus d[i]$. In following equations, $f_{\text{iSR}}(i)$ denotes the location for $k_x[i]$ before $\texttt{ShiftRows}()$, i.e., the $f_{\text{iSR}}(i)$-th byte will be rotated to the ith byte by $\texttt{ShiftRows}()$.

$$c[i] \oplus d[i] = (\texttt{SubBytes}(m_9[f_{\text{ISR}}(i)]) \oplus k_{10}[i]) \oplus (\texttt{SubBytes}(m_9[f_{\text{ISR}}(i)]) \oplus k'_{10}[i])$$

$$= k_{10}[i] \oplus k'_{10}[i] = l_{10}[i] \oplus l'_{10}[i] = k_9[i] \oplus k'_9[i] = l_9[i] \oplus l'_9[i]$$

$$= k_8[i] \oplus k'_8[i] = \delta_8[i]. \tag{2}$$

$k'_9[i-1]$ can be derived from $c[i-2]$, $d[i-2]$, and $k_9[12 \sim 15]$. For each $(c[i-2], d[i-2], c[i] \oplus d[i])$ pair, some possible values of $k_8[i]$ can be deduced from the following equatioin. The unique value of $k_8[i]$ can be retrieved by comparing several sets of those possible values, $(i = 13 \sim 15)$.

$$c[i-2] \oplus d[i-2] = (\texttt{SubBytes}(m_9[f_{\text{ISR}}(i-2)]) \oplus k_{10}[i-2]) \oplus$$

$$(\texttt{SubBytes}(m_9[f_{\text{ISR}}(i-2)]) \oplus k'_{10}[i-2])$$

$$= n_{10}[i-2] \oplus n'_{10}[i-2]$$

$$= \texttt{SubBytes}(k_9[i-1]) \oplus \texttt{SubBytes}(k'_9[i-1]), \text{ so}$$

$$k'_9[i-1] = \texttt{SubBytes}^{-1}(c[i-2] \oplus d[i-2] \oplus \texttt{SubBytes}(k_9[i-1])).$$

$$k_9[i-1] \oplus k'_9[i-1] = n_9[i-1] \oplus n'_9[i-1]$$

$$= \texttt{SubBytes}(k_8[i]) \oplus \texttt{SubBytes}(k_8[i] \oplus \delta_8[i]). \tag{3}$$

But the behavior is different when the fault occurs on $k_8[12]$. Because the rotation amount of the $\texttt{ShiftRows}$ in the first row is 0, $\delta_8[12]$ can not be derived directly from (2). Without the value of $\delta_8[12]$, $k_8[12]$ can not be retrieved.

3.3   Faults on the Eighth to Eleventh Bytes of K_8

In the third step, a fault is induced on the single byte of $w[34]$, $k_8[8 \sim 11]$. When the fault occurs on only one byte, there are six or seven non-zero bytes in $C \oplus D$. Four of them appear in the same row with the equal value.

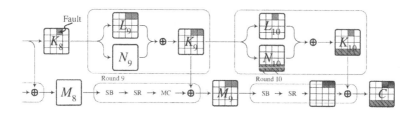

Fig. 5. Fault induced on the eighth byte of K_8.

If the fault occurs on the ith byte of K_8 $(i = 8 \sim 11)$, it raises

$$c[i-5] \oplus d[i-5] = \texttt{SubBytes}(k_9[i+4]) \oplus \texttt{SubBytes}(k'_9[i+4])$$

$$= \texttt{SubBytes}(k_9[i+4]) \oplus \texttt{SubBytes}(k_9[i+4] \oplus \delta_8[i]) \text{ and}$$

$$\delta_8[i] = \texttt{SubBytes}^{-1}(c[i-5] \oplus d[i-5] \oplus$$

$$\texttt{SubBytes}(k_9[i+4])) \oplus k_9[i+4].$$

$$c[f_{\text{SR}}(i)] = \text{SubBytes}(m_9[i]) \oplus k_{10}[f_{\text{SR}}(i)] \text{ and}$$
$$d[f_{\text{SR}}(i)] = \text{SubBytes}(m_9'[i]) \oplus k_{10}'[f_{\text{SR}}(i)]$$
$$= \text{SubBytes}(m_9[i] \oplus \delta_8[i]) \oplus k_{10}'[f_{\text{SR}}(i)].$$
$$\delta_8[i] = \text{SubBytes}^{-1}(c[f_{\text{SR}}(i)] \oplus k_{10}[f_{\text{SR}}(i)]) \oplus$$
$$\text{SubBytes}^{-1}(d[f_{\text{SR}}(i)] \oplus k_{10}'[f_{\text{SR}}(i)]). \text{ Similarly,} \qquad (4)$$
$$\delta_8[i] = \text{SubBytes}^{-1}(c[f_{\text{SR}}(i+4)] \oplus k_{10}[f_{\text{SR}}(i+4)]) \oplus$$
$$\text{SubBytes}^{-1}(d[f_{\text{SR}}(i+4)] \oplus k_{10}'[f_{\text{SR}}(i+4)]). \qquad (5)$$

$\delta_8[i]$ can be derived easily from above equations. $k_{10}[8]$, $k_{10}[12]$, $k_{10}[5]$, $k_{10}[9]$, $k_{10}[2]$, $k_{10}[6]$, $k_{10}[15]$, $k_{10}[3]$ can be retrieved from (4) and (5). These deductions use the same technique that deduces the last four bytes of K_9 in Section 3.1.

3.4   The Whole of K_{10}

The last four bytes of K_9 and the last three bytes of K_8 are retrieved in Sects. 3.1 and 3.2. The ninth to eleventh bytes of K_9 can be derived from $k_9[i] = k_8[i+4] \oplus k_9[i+4]$, $(i = 9 \sim 11)$. In Sect. 3.3, we retrieve eight bytes of K_{10}, $k_{10}[2, 3, 5, 6, 8, 9, 12, 15]$. Another five bytes of K_{10}, $k_{10}[7, 10, 11, 13, 14]$, can be deduced by the relationship between ninth and tenth round keys. The remaining three bytes of K_{10} can be efficiently retrieved by exhaustive search.

3.5   Performance Evaluation

This proposed DFA attack is based on retrieving possible values of keys from the differences inside and outside the $\text{SubBytes}()$. The set of the possible values is defined by

Definition 1. $\text{SubBytes}()$ *is the S-Box of AES. δ_x and δ_y are the differences inside and outside the $\text{SubBytes}()$. Let $\mathcal{F}(\delta_x, \delta_y)$ is the set associated the δ_x and δ_y by $\mathcal{F}(\delta_x, \delta_y) = \{x \mid \text{SubBytes}(x) \oplus \text{SubBytes}(x \oplus \delta_x) = \delta_y\}$.* ◇

The requirement of samples is affected by the size of the set or the intersection of several sets. The following propositions are necessary to evaluate the requirement.

Proposition 1. *If δ_x, $\delta_y \neq 0$, then the size of $\mathcal{F}(\delta_x, \delta_y)$ is zero, two, or four.* ◇

Proposition 2. $x \in \mathcal{F}(\delta_x, \delta_y)$ *if and only if $(x \oplus \delta_x) \in \mathcal{F}(\delta_x, \delta_y)$.* ◇

Proposition 3. *When δ_x, $\delta_y \neq 0$, $|\mathcal{F}(\delta_x, \delta_y)| = 4$ iff $\{0, \delta_x\} \subset \mathcal{F}(\delta_x, \delta_y)$. Moreover, $\mathcal{F}(\delta_x, \delta_y) = \{0, \delta_x, \delta_x \cdot \text{0xBC}, \delta_x \cdot \text{0xBD}\}$ and $\delta_y = \text{SubBytes}(0) \oplus \text{SubBytes}(\delta_x)$.* ◇

Proposition 4. *If* $|\mathcal{F}(\delta_x, \delta_y) \cap \mathcal{F}(\delta'_x, \delta'_y)| > 1$, $(\delta_x, \delta'_x \neq 0 \text{ and } \delta_x \neq \delta'_x)$, *then* $\mathcal{F}(\delta_x, \delta_y) = \mathcal{F}(\delta'_x, \delta'_y) = \{0, \delta_x, \delta'_x, \delta_x \oplus \delta'_x\}$. ⋄

Proposition 5. *If* $\mathcal{F}(\delta_x, \delta_y) = \{0, \delta_x, x_2, x_3\}$, *then* $\mathcal{F}(\delta_x, \delta_y) = \mathcal{F}(x_2, \delta'_y) = \mathcal{F}(x_3, \delta''_y)$ *where* $\delta'_y = \texttt{SubBytes}(0) \oplus \texttt{SubBytes}(x_2)$ *and* $\delta''_y = \texttt{SubBytes}(0) \oplus \texttt{SubBytes}(x_3)$. *In addition,* $x_2 \oplus x_3 = \delta_x$. ⋄

Proposition 6. *If* $\mathcal{F}(x_1, \delta_y) = \{0, x_1, x_2, x_3\}$ *and* $\mathcal{F}(x, \delta'_y) = \mathcal{F}(x_1, \delta_y)$. *Then* $x \in \{x_1, x_2, x_3\}$. ⋄

Proposition 7. *There are 85 various sets whose size is 4.* ⋄

Definition 2. *Similar to the definition of* $\mathcal{F}(\delta_x, \delta_y)$, $\mathcal{G}(\delta_x, \delta_y)$ *is defined by* $\mathcal{G}(\delta_x, \delta_y) = \{y \mid \texttt{SubBytes}^{-1}(y) \oplus \texttt{SubBytes}^{-1}(y \oplus \delta_y) = \delta_x\}$. ⋄

Proposition 8. *The properties of* $\mathcal{G}(\delta_x, \delta_y)$ *are similar to* $\mathcal{F}(\delta_x, \delta_y)$. *And* $\mathcal{G}(\delta_x, \delta_y) = \{y \mid \texttt{SubBytes}^{-1}(y) \in \mathcal{F}(\delta_x, \delta_y)\}$. ⋄

Because of the above propositions, the probability that the size of two sets' intersection equals one is approximately 100%. The probability that the size is larger than one is $1/127$ if the corresponding unknown byte of the round key is '0', or $3/(255 * 127)$ if the byte is not '0'. In general, this means that an unique solution can be retrieved by intersecting two sets. In the worst case, intersecting four sets can determine the unique byte.

Seven bytes of the round keys can be retrieved by (1) and (3) in Sects. 3.1 and 3.2. Each byte requires two, three, or four faulty samples. In Sect. 3.3, (4) and (5) can share the faulty ciphertexts, so the attacker can retrieve four bytes by (4) and four bytes by (5) in parallel. Therefore, one correct ciphertext and less than forty-four faulty ones are sufficient if the fault can be induced accurately. In most cases, twenty-two faulty ciphertexts are enough.

The table, $\{\delta_x, \delta_y, \mathcal{F}(\delta_x, \delta_y)\}$ $(\delta_x, \delta_y \in [1, 255])$ can be constructed by checking if $\delta_y = \texttt{SubBytes}(x) \oplus \texttt{SubBytes}(x \oplus \delta_x)$ for all values of δ_x, δ_y, and x. Because the equation contains only simple exclusive-OR and $\texttt{SubBytes}()$-table lookup, this table can be constructed very efficiently. When simulating, this can be completed within one second on a Pentium 4 computer.

The thirteen bytes of the last round key can be obtained easily because the set associated with δ_x and δ_y can be found simply by a table lookup. The remaining three bytes require a search on the 2^{24} possibilities. The time required by this exhaustive search is similar to decrypting 2^{24} blocks which can be completed within one minute on a Pentium 4 computer. Thus, the computational cost of this attack is extremely small.

4   Possible Countermeasures

4.1   The First Approach – Storing the Round Key

The first proposed countermeasure is to avoid generating the round key on the temper-proof device. Storing the round keys requires more flash memory but can eliminate the code that generates the round keys. Removing the key schedule will decrease the code size in ROM and increase the performance.

However, some systems need to update the key frequently. For those systems, two countermeasures are suggested and described in the following.

4.2   The Second Approach – Generating the Round Key Once

The proposed fault model has three stages, and each of the stages requires various faults induced. If the round key is generated only once when updating the key, the attack has only one chance to induce the fault on the key schedule. It is impossible to collect sufficient pairs to satisfy the requirement.

Furthermore, the deduction in Sect. 3.1 only depends on the induced fault, i.e., it is independent of the value of the corresponding plaintext. With only one chance to induce the fault, the attacker can only recover partial information about the last four bytes of K_9. Without the accurate values of the last four bytes of K_9, the remaining deductions in Sects. 3.2 and 3.3 are infeasible.

4.3   The Third Approach – Parity Checking for Round Keys

Under some circumstance, the system designer still wishes to generate the round keys on the fly. For example, to parallel the round and the key expansion is a countermeasure to protect the key expansion against the SPA attacks [12]. In this case, the third approach can be employed to detect if faults are induced.

Before describing this countermeasure, the linear part and the non-linear part of the key expansion are reorganized as

$$L_i = \begin{bmatrix} l_i[0] & l_i[4] & l_i[8] & l_i[12] \\ l_i[1] & l_i[5] & l_i[9] & l_i[13] \\ l_i[2] & l_i[6] & l_i[10] & l_i[14] \\ l_i[3] & l_i[7] & l_i[11] & l_i[15] \end{bmatrix} = K_{i-1} \begin{bmatrix} 1 & 1 & 1 & 1 \\ 0 & 1 & 1 & 1 \\ 0 & 0 & 1 & 1 \\ 0 & 0 & 0 & 1 \end{bmatrix} = K_{i-1}T.$$

$$N_i = \begin{bmatrix} n_i[0] & n_i[1] & n_i[2] & n_i[3] \end{bmatrix}^t \begin{bmatrix} 1 & 1 & 1 & 1 \end{bmatrix}, \text{ and}$$

$$\mathcal{N}_i = N_i \begin{bmatrix} 1 & 0 & 0 & 0 \end{bmatrix}^t = \begin{bmatrix} n_i[0] & n_i[1] & n_i[2] & n_i[3] \end{bmatrix}^t.$$

T is the transformation matrix and $T^4 = I_4$. Since each column of N_i is equal, the extra notations, $\mathcal{N}_i$, is defined to simplify the expressions. The round keys are reorganized as

$$K_1 = K_0 T \oplus N_1.$$
$$K_2 = K_1 T \oplus N_2 = K_0 T^2 \oplus N_1 T \oplus N_2.$$
$$\cdots\cdots\cdots$$

$$K_{10} = K_0 T^{10} \oplus \bigoplus_{i=1}^{10} (N_i T^{10-i})$$

$$= K_0 T^2 \oplus (N_2 \oplus N_6 \oplus N_{10}) \begin{bmatrix} 1 & 1 & 1 & 1 \end{bmatrix} \oplus (N_1 \oplus N_5 \oplus N_9) \begin{bmatrix} 1 & 0 & 1 & 0 \end{bmatrix}$$
$$\oplus (N_4 \oplus N_8) \begin{bmatrix} 1 & 1 & 0 & 0 \end{bmatrix} \oplus (N_3 \oplus N_7) \begin{bmatrix} 1 & 0 & 0 & 0 \end{bmatrix}.$$

$$w[40] = w[0] \oplus \bigoplus_{i=1}^{10} N_i,$$

$$w[41] = w[1] \oplus N_2 \oplus N_4 \oplus N_6 \oplus N_8 \oplus N_{10},$$

$$w[42] = w[0] \oplus w[2] \oplus N_1 \oplus N_2 \oplus N_5 \oplus N_6 \oplus N_9 \oplus N_{10}, \text{ and}$$

$$w[43] = w[1] \oplus w[3] \oplus N_2 \oplus N_6 \oplus N_{10}.$$

So, $w[40] \oplus w[41] \oplus w[42] \oplus w[43] = w[2] \oplus w[3] \oplus N_3 \oplus N_7$ and the parity check for the ith row of the last round key is

$$k_{10}[i] \oplus k_{10}[4+i] \oplus k_{10}[8+i] \oplus k_{10}[12+i] = k_0[8+i] \oplus k_0[12+i] \oplus n_3[i] \oplus n_7[i].$$

The value only depends on the master key and the non-linear part of the third and seventh round keys. The row parity check can detect the fault induced on the eighth to tenth round keys. In a similar way, the column parity check is constructed. For example, the equation for the last column of K_{10} is

$$\bigoplus_{i=12}^{15} k_{10}[i] = \left(\bigoplus_{i=4}^{7} k_0[i] \right) \oplus \left(\bigoplus_{i=12}^{15} k_0[i] \right) \oplus \left(\bigoplus_{i=0}^{3} (n_2[i] \oplus n_6[i] \oplus n_{10}[i]) \right).$$

Both of the row and column parity checks can verify the correctness of the round key. This method only requires few additional resources and is suitable for both software and hardware implementations.

5   Conclusions

This paper describes the DFA attack on the AES-128 key schedule. This method can retrieve thirteen bytes of the round key efficiently with an acceptable amount of samples. Another three bytes are derived by exhaustive search with feasible computation. In most cases, it only requires one correct and twenty-two faulty ciphertexts. And forty-four samples are sufficient in the worst case.

This paper also recommends three possible countermeasures against the proposed DFA. The first and the second countermeasures are to avoid generating the round key on the fly. The last countermeasure is a parity check method, i.e., a method to verify the correctness of the round key. None of these three countermeasures need to modify the AES algorithm.

In fact, it is hard to say whether any physical attack can be served as a tool or indicator to tell us which cipher is more secure in a smart card. This is much relevant to the real implementation of the cipher we consider. Basically, all assumptions for all kinds of physical attacks apply (although may not be always equally) to all ciphers when they are implemented. Each attack may be extremely different from others depending on the real implementation and maybe also a little bit depending on the basic property of the cipher itself. For example, when selecting the final AES candidate, people also considered the resistance against every kind of physical attack when it will be implemented. But unfortunately when evaluating Rijndael, most people believed that Rijndael can be implemented easily to be physical attack immune. The authors of Rijndael also claimed such in their book about the design of Rijndael cipher [13] (at the end of the book). But, this is not really true as shown in this paper and in another paper of these proceedings [14].

Acknowledgments. The authors wish to thank Dr. Greg Rose for his kindness to provide many useful discussions and assistance on editing the paper which improve both presentation and technical content.

References

1. D. Boneh, R.A. DeMillo, and R.J. Lipton, "On the importance of checking cryptographic protocols for faults," In *Advances in Cryptology – EUROCRYPT '97*, LNCS 1233, pp. 37–51, Springer-Verlag, 1997.
2. P. Kocher, "Timing attacks on implementations of Diffie-Hellman, RSA, DSS, and other systems," In *Advances in Cryptology – CRYPTO '96*, LNCS 1109, pp. 104–113, Springer-Verlag, 1996.
3. P. Kocher, J. Jaffe and B. Jun, "Introduction to differential power analysis and related attacks," 1998, available at URL
   <http://www.cryptography.com/dpa/technical>.
4. P. Kocher, J. Jaffe and B. Jun, "Differential power analysis," In *Advances in Cryptology – CRYPTO '99*, LNCS 1666, pp. 388–397, Springer-Verlag, 1999.
5. E. Biham and A. Shamir, "Differential fault analysis of secret key cryptosystems," In *Advances in Cryptology – CRYPTO '97*, LNCS 1294, pp. 513–525, Springer-Verlag, 1997.
6. S.M. Yen and J.Z. Chen, "A DFA on Rijndael," In *Information Security Conference 2002*, Taiwan, May 2002.
7. X. Lai, *On the Design and security of Block Ciphers*, Ph.D. thesis, Swiss Federal Institue of Technology, Zurich, 1992.
8. P. Dusart, G. Letourneux and O. Vivolo, "Differential Fault Analysis on A.E.S.," Cryptology ePrint Archive of IACR, No. 010, 2003, available at URL
   <http://eprint.iacr.org/2003/010>.
9. C. Giraud, "DFA on AES," Cryptology ePrint Archive of IACR, No. 008, 2003, available at URL <http://eprint.iacr.org/2003/008>.
10. J. Daemen and V. Rijmen, "AES Proposal: Rijndael," AES submission, 1998, available at URL <http://csrc.nist.gov/encryption/aes/aes_home.htm>.
11. NIST, "Federal Information Processing Standards Publication 197 – Announcing the ADVANCED ENCRYPTION STANDARD (AES)," 2001, available at URL
   <http://csrc.nist.gov/publications/fips/fips197/fips-197.pdf>.
12. S. Mangard, "A simple power-analysis (SPA) attack on implementations of the AES key expansion," In *Information Security and Cryptology – ICISC 2002*, LNCS 2587, pp. 343–358, Springer-Verlag, 2003.
13. J. Daemen and V. Rijmen, *The Design of Rijndael, AES – The Advanced Encryption Standard*, Springer-Verlag, Berlin, 2002.

14. S.M. Yen, "Amplified differential power cryptanalysis of some enhanced Rijndael implementations," In the Eighth Australasian Conference on Information Security and Privacy – ACISP 2003, 2003.
15. J.B. Fraleigh, *A First Course in Abstract Algebra*, / 5th Edition, Addison-Wesley Publishing Company, 1994. (Corollary 2 of Section 5.6, p.322)

A   The Proofs of the Propositions in Section 3.5

Proof (of Proposition 1). If $x \in \mathcal{F}(\delta_x, \delta_y)$, then x satisfies the equation,

$$\delta_y = \text{SubBytes}(x) \oplus \text{SubBytes}(x \oplus \delta_x) \tag{6}$$
$$= \left(M(x^{-1}) \oplus \text{0x63} \right) \oplus \left(M((x \oplus \delta_x)^{-1}) \oplus \text{0x63} \right) = M(x^{-1}) \oplus M((x \oplus \delta_x)^{-1}),$$

where M is the transformation matrix and 0x63 is the constant vector.

If $\delta_y = M(0^{-1}) \oplus M(\delta_x^{-1}) = M(\delta_x^{-1})$, then 0 and δ_x are two solutions of Eq 6. ($0^{-1} = 0$ is defined in AES.) When $x \neq 0, \delta_x$, we also have

$$M^{-1}(\delta_y) = x^{-1} \oplus (x \oplus \delta_x)^{-1}$$
$$x^2 \oplus \delta_x x = (M^{-1}(\delta_y))^{-1}\delta_x. \tag{7}$$

Because of the theorem in [15], (7) has at most two solutions. If x is a solution, $x \oplus \delta_x$ will be another one. Thus, (6) has zero, two, or four solutions.   □

Proof (of Proposition 3). "only if" part can be retrieved in the proof of Proposition 1. If $\{0, \delta_x\} \not\subset \mathcal{F}(\delta_x, \delta_y)$, then the size of $\mathcal{F}(\delta_x, \delta_y)$ is most two.

"if" part: Because $\{0, \delta_x\} \subset \mathcal{F}(\delta_x, \delta_y)$, we have $\delta_y = M(\delta_x^{-1})$ and (7) can be reduced to $x^2 \oplus \delta_x x \oplus \delta_x^2 = 0$. Since $x = \text{0xBC}$ and $x = \text{0xBD}$ are two solutions of $x^2 + x + 1 = 0$, $x = \delta_x \cdot \text{0xBC}$ and $x = \delta_x \cdot \text{0xBD}$ are two solution of (7).   □

Proof (of Proposition 4). We assume $\{x_1, x_1 \oplus \delta_x\} \in \mathcal{F}(\delta_x, \delta_y)$ and $\{x_2, x_2 \oplus \delta_x'\} \in \mathcal{F}(\delta_x', \delta_y')$. Because $\delta_x \neq \delta_x'$, we have $\{x_1, x_1 \oplus \delta_x\} \neq \{x_2, x_2 \oplus \delta_x'\}$. Thus, the size of one of the two sets is four. Without loss of generality, we assume $\mathcal{F}(\delta_x, \delta_y) = \{0, \delta_x, \delta_x \cdot \text{0xBC}, \delta_x \cdot \text{0xBD}\}$. Moreover, one of 0 and δ_x belongs to $\mathcal{F}(\delta_x', \delta_y')$, and one of $\delta_x \cdot \text{0xBC}$ and $\delta_x \cdot \text{0xBD}$ belongs to $\mathcal{F}(\delta_x', \delta_y')$. Therefore, $\mathcal{F}(\delta_x', \delta_y') = \{0, \delta_x, \delta_x \cdot \text{0xBC}, \delta_x \cdot \text{0xBD}\}$ can be retrieved by one of the two equations, $\text{SubBytes}(0) \oplus \text{SubBytes}(\delta_x \cdot \text{0xBC}) = \text{SubBytes}(\delta_x) \oplus \text{SubBytes}(\delta_x \cdot \text{0xBD})$ and $\text{SubBytes}(0) \oplus \text{SubBytes}(\delta_x \cdot \text{0xBD}) = \text{SubBytes}(\delta_x) \oplus \text{SubBytes}(\delta_x \cdot \text{0xBC})$.   □

Proof (of Proposition 5). This proposition can be proved by Proposition 4. Since $\{0, x_2\} \in \mathcal{F}(x_2, \text{SubBytes}(0) \oplus \text{SubBytes}(x_2))$, $\mathcal{F}(x_2, \text{SubBytes}(0) \oplus \text{SubBytes}(x_2)) = \mathcal{F}(\delta_x, \delta_y) = \{0, \delta_x, x_2, x_3\}$.   □

Proof (of Proposition 6). Since $0 \in \mathcal{F}(x, \delta_y')$, $\mathcal{F}(x, \delta_y') = \{0, x, x', x''\}$. Thus, $\{x, x', x''\} = \{x_1, x_2, x_3\}$ and $x \in \{x_1, x_2, x_3\}$.   □

Proof (of Proposition 7). There are one '0' and three nonzero elements in the set whose size is four. And if 0 and a nonzero x belong to two sets, $\mathcal{F}(\delta_x, \delta_y)$ and $\mathcal{F}(\delta_x', \delta_y')$, then $\mathcal{F}(\delta_x, \delta_y) = \mathcal{F}(\delta_x', \delta_y')$. Therefore, $85 = 255/3$.   □

On the Pseudorandomness of KASUMI Type Permutations[*]

Tetsu Iwata[1], Tohru Yagi[2], and Kaoru Kurosawa[1]

[1] Department of Computer and Information Sciences,
Ibaraki University
4–12–1 Nakanarusawa, Hitachi, Ibaraki 316-8511, Japan
{iwata, kurosawa}@cis.ibaraki.ac.jp
[2] Department of Communications and Integrated Systems,
Tokyo Institute of Technology
2–12–1 O-okayama, Meguro, Tokyo 152-8552, Japan

Abstract. KASUMI is a block cipher which has been adopted as a standard of 3GPP. In this paper, we study the pseudorandomness of idealized KASUMI type permutations for adaptive adversaries. We show that

- the four round version is pseudorandom and
- the six round version is super-pseudorandom.

1 Introduction

1.1 Pseudorandomness

Let R be a randomly chosen permutation and Ψ be a block cipher such that a key is randomly chosen. We then say that

- Ψ is pseudorandom if Ψ and R are indistinguishable and
- Ψ is super-pseudorandom if (Ψ, Ψ^{-1}) and (R, R^{-1}) are indistinguishable.

Luby and Rackoff studied the pseudorandomness of idealized Feistel permutations, where each round function is an independent (pseudo)random function. They proved that

- the three round version is pseudorandom and
- the four round version is super-pseudorandom

for adaptive adversaries [8].

---

[*] See [5] for a long version. Most of the proofs are omitted in this proceedings version.

R. Safavi-Naini and J. Seberry (Eds.): ACISP 2003, LNCS 2727, pp. 130–141, 2003.
© Springer-Verlag Berlin Heidelberg 2003

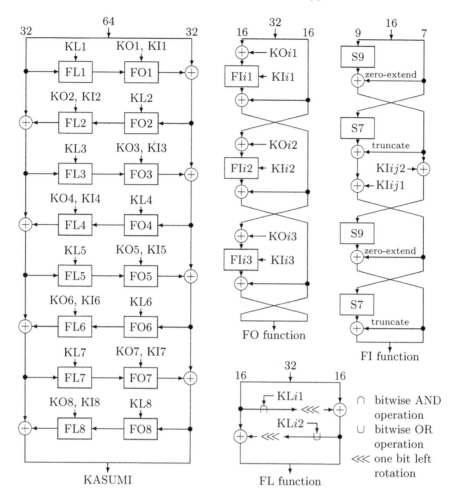

Fig. 1. KASUMI

1.2   KASUMI

KASUMI is a block cipher which has been adopted as a standard of 3GPP [2], where 3GPP is the body standardizing the next generation of mobile telephony. The structure of KASUMI is illustrated in Fig. 1. (See [1] for details.)

- The overall structure of KASUMI is a Feistel permutation.
- Each round function consists of two functions, FL function and FO function.
- Each FO function consists of a three round MISTY type permutation, where each round function is called an FI function.
- Each FI function consists of a four round MISTY type permutation.

The initial security evaluation of KASUMI can be found in [3]. Blunden and Escott showed related key attacks on five round and six round KASUMI [4].

1.3 Previous Work (Non-adaptive)

We idealize KASUMI as follows.

- Each FL function is ignored. (In [7], the authors stated that the security of KASUMI is mainly based on FO functions.)
- Each FI function is idealized by an independent (pseudo)random permutation.

We call such an idealized KASUMI a "KASUMI type permutation."

However, we do not assume that each FO function is a random permutation. This implies that we can not apply the result of Luby and Rackoff to KASUMI type permutations. (Indeed, Sakurai and Zheng showed that a three round MISTY type permutation is not pseudorandom [11].)

Kang et al. then showed that

- the three round version is not pseudorandom and
- the four round version is pseudorandom

for non-adaptive adversaries [7].

1.4 Our Contribution (Adaptive)

In this paper, we study the pseudorandomness of KASUMI type permutations for adaptive adversaries. We prove that

- the four round version is pseudorandom and
- the six round version is super-pseudorandom.

See the following table, where $\times$ comes from [7], $\bigcirc^1$ comes from [7] and $\bigcirc^2$ is proved in this paper.

Table 1. Summary of the previous results and our contributions.

Number of rounds	Three	Four	Five	Six
Pseudorandomness (non-adaptive)	$\times$	$\bigcirc^1$	$\bigcirc^1$	$\bigcirc^1$
Pseudorandomness	$\times$	$\bigcirc^2$	$\bigcirc^2$	$\bigcirc^2$
Super-pseudorandomness	$\times$	?	?	$\bigcirc^2$

(We cannot idealize MISTY1 [9,10] like KASUMI type permutations because each FI function of MISTY1 is a three round MISTY type permutation and three round MISTY type permutation is not pseudorandom [11].)

1.5 Flaw of the Previous Work

Kang et al. claimed that the four round KASUMI type permutation is pseudorandom for adaptive adversaries [6]. However, we show that their proof is wrong in Appendix A.

2   Preliminaries

2.1   Notation

For a bit string $x \in \{0,1\}^{2n}$, we denote the first (left) n bits of x by x_L and the last (right) n bits of x by x_R. Similarly, for a bit string $x \in \{0,1\}^{4n}$, we denote the first (left) n bits of x by x_{LL}, the next n bits of x by x_{LR}, the third n bits of x by x_{RL}, and the last (right) n bits of x by x_{RR}. That is, $x = (x_{LL}, x_{LR}, x_{RL}, x_{RR})$. For a set of l-bit strings $\{x^{(i)} \mid x^{(i)} \in \{0,1\}^l\}_{1 \le i \le q}$, we say $\{x^{(i)}\}_{1 \le i \le q}$ are *distinct* to mean $x^{(i)} \ne x^{(j)}$ for $1 \le \forall i < \forall j \le q$.

If S is a set, then $s \xleftarrow{R} S$ denotes the process of picking an element from S uniformly at random.

Denote by P_n the set of all permutations over $\{0,1\}^n$, which consists of $(2^n)!$ permutations in total. For functions f and g, $g \circ f$ denotes the function $x \mapsto g(f(x))$.

2.2   KASUMI Type Permutation [2]

We define KASUMI type permutations as follows.

Definition 2.1 (The basic KASUMI type permutation). *Let* $x \in \{0,1\}^{4n}$. *For any permutations* $p_1, p_2, p_3 \in P_n$, *define the basic KASUMI type permutation* $\psi_{p_1, p_2, p_3} \in P_{4n}$ *as* $\psi_{p_1, p_2, p_3}(x) \stackrel{\text{def}}{=} y$, *where*

$$
\begin{cases}
y_{LL} \stackrel{\text{def}}{=} x_{RL}, \\
y_{LR} \stackrel{\text{def}}{=} x_{RR}, \\
y_{RL} \stackrel{\text{def}}{=} x_{RL} \oplus p_1(x_{RR}) \oplus p_2(x_{RL}) \oplus p_3(x_{RL} \oplus p_1(x_{RR})) \oplus x_{LL}, \quad \text{and} \\
y_{RR} \stackrel{\text{def}}{=} x_{RL} \oplus p_1(x_{RR}) \oplus p_2(x_{RL}) \oplus x_{LR}.
\end{cases}
$$

Note that it is a permutation since $\psi_{p_1, p_2, p_3}^{-1}(y) = x$, *where*

$$
\begin{cases}
x_{LL} = y_{LL} \oplus p_1(y_{LR}) \oplus p_2(y_{LL}) \oplus p_3(y_{LL} \oplus p_1(y_{LR})) \oplus y_{RL}, \\
x_{LR} = y_{LL} \oplus p_1(y_{LR}) \oplus p_2(y_{LL}) \oplus y_{RR}, \\
x_{RL} = y_{LL}, \quad \text{and} \\
x_{RR} = y_{LR}.
\end{cases}
$$

Definition 2.2 (The r round KASUMI type permutation). *Let* $r \ge 1$ *be an integer,* $p_1, p_2, \ldots, p_{3r} \in P_n$ *be permutations. Define the r round KASUMI type permutation* $\psi(p_1, p_2, \ldots, p_{3r}) \in P_{4n}$ *as*

$$
\psi(p_1, p_2, \ldots, p_{3r}) \stackrel{\text{def}}{=} \psi_{p_{3r-2}, p_{3r-1}, p_{3r}} \circ \psi_{p_{3r-5}, p_{3r-4}, p_{3r-3}} \circ \cdots \circ \psi_{p_1, p_2, p_3} \ .
$$

See Fig. 2 for illustrations. For simplicity, swaps are omitted.

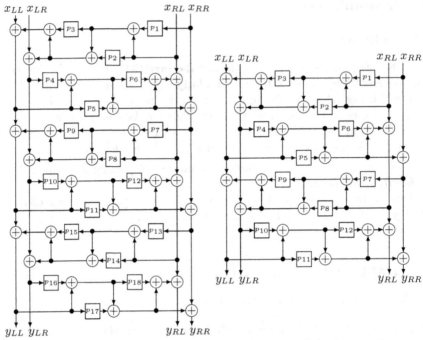

Fig. 2. A six round KASUMI type permutation $\psi(p_1, \ldots, p_{18})$ (left) and a four round KASUMI type permutation $\psi(p_1, \ldots, p_{15})$ (right).

2.3   Pseudorandom and Super-Pseudorandom Permutations [8]

Our adaptive adversary $\mathcal{A}$ is modeled as a Turing machine that has black-box access to an oracle (or oracles). The computational power of $\mathcal{A}$ is unlimited, but the total number of oracle calls is limited to a parameter q. After making at most q queries to the oracle(s) adaptively, $\mathcal{A}$ outputs a bit.

The pseudorandomness of a block cipher Ψ over $\{0,1\}^{4n}$ captures its computational indistinguishability from P_{4n}, where the adversary is given access to the forward direction of the permutation. In other words, it measures security of a block cipher against adaptive chosen plaintext attack.

Definition 2.3 (Advantage, prp). *Let a block cipher Ψ be a family of permutations over $\{0,1\}^{4n}$. Let $\mathcal{A}$ be an adversary. Then $\mathcal{A}$'s advantage is defined by*

$$\mathsf{Adv}_{\Psi}^{\mathsf{prp}}(\mathcal{A}) \stackrel{\text{def}}{=} \left| \Pr(\psi \stackrel{R}{\leftarrow} \Psi : \mathcal{A}^{\psi} = 1) - \Pr(R \stackrel{R}{\leftarrow} P_{4n} : \mathcal{A}^{R} = 1) \right| .$$

The notation $\mathcal{A}^{\psi}$ indicates $\mathcal{A}$ with an oracle which, in response to a query x, returns $y \leftarrow \psi(x)$. The notation $\mathcal{A}^{R}$ indicates $\mathcal{A}$ with an oracle which, in response to a query x, returns $y \leftarrow R(x)$.

The super-pseudorandomness of a block cipher Ψ over $\{0,1\}^{4n}$ captures its computational indistinguishability from P_{4n}, where the adversary is given access to both directions of the permutation. In other words, it measures security of a block cipher against adaptive chosen plaintext and chosen ciphertext attacks.

Definition 2.4 (Advantage, sprp). *Let a block cipher Ψ be a family of permutations over $\{0,1\}^{4n}$. Let $\mathcal{A}$ be an adversary. Then $\mathcal{A}$'s advantage is defined by*

$$\mathsf{Adv}_\Psi^{\mathsf{sprp}}(\mathcal{A}) \stackrel{\mathrm{def}}{=} \left| \Pr(\psi \stackrel{R}{\leftarrow} \Psi : \mathcal{A}^{\psi, \psi^{-1}} = 1) - \Pr(R \stackrel{R}{\leftarrow} P_{4n} : \mathcal{A}^{R, R^{-1}} = 1) \right| .$$

The notation $\mathcal{A}^{\psi, \psi^{-1}}$ indicates $\mathcal{A}$ with an oracle which, in response to a query $(+, x)$, returns $y \leftarrow \psi(x)$, and in response to a query $(-, y)$, returns $x \leftarrow \psi^{-1}(y)$. The notation $\mathcal{A}^{R, R^{-1}}$ indicates $\mathcal{A}$ with an oracle which, in response to a query $(+, x)$, returns $y \leftarrow R(x)$, and in response to a query $(-, y)$, returns $x \leftarrow R^{-1}(y)$.

3   A Four Round KASUMI Type Permutation Is Pseudorandom

Theorem 3.1. *For $1 \le i \le 12$, let $p_i \in P_n$ be a random permutation. Let $\psi = \psi(p_1, \ldots, p_{12})$ be a four round KASUMI type permutation, $R \in P_{4n}$ be a random permutation, and $\Psi \stackrel{\mathrm{def}}{=} \{\psi \mid \psi = \psi(p_1, \ldots, p_{12}), p_i \in P_n \text{ for } 1 \le i \le 12\}$. Then for any adversary $\mathcal{A}$ that makes at most q queries in total,*

$$\mathsf{Adv}_\Psi^{\mathsf{prp}}(\mathcal{A}) \le \frac{15}{2} \cdot \frac{q(q-1)}{2^n - 1} .$$

Proof. Let $\mathcal{O}$ be either R or ψ. The adversary $\mathcal{A}$ has oracle access to $\mathcal{O}$. $\mathcal{A}$ can make a query x and the oracle returns $y = \mathcal{O}(x)$. For the i-th query $\mathcal{A}$ makes to $\mathcal{O}$, define the query-answer pair $(x^{(i)}, y^{(i)}) \in \{0,1\}^{4n} \times \{0,1\}^{4n}$, where $\mathcal{A}$'s query was $x^{(i)}$ and the answer it got was $y^{(i)}$. Define view v of $\mathcal{A}$ as $v = \langle (x^{(1)}, y^{(1)}), \ldots, (x^{(q)}, y^{(q)}) \rangle$. We say that $v = \langle (x^{(1)}, y^{(1)}), \ldots, (x^{(q)}, y^{(q)}) \rangle$ is a *possible view* if there exists some permutation $p \in P_{4n}$ such that $p(x^{(i)}) = y^{(i)}$ for $1 \le \forall i \le q$ (or, equivalently, $v = \langle (x^{(1)}, y^{(1)}), \ldots, (x^{(q)}, y^{(q)}) \rangle$ is a possible view if $\{x^{(i)}\}_{1 \le i \le q}$ are distinct and $\{y^{(i)}\}_{1 \le i \le q}$ are distinct).

Since $\mathcal{A}$ is computationally unbounded, we may without loss of generality assume that $\mathcal{A}$ is deterministic. This implies that for every $1 \le i \le q$ the i-th query $x^{(i)}$ is fully determined by the first $i - 1$ query-answer pairs, and the final output of $\mathcal{A}$ (0 or 1) depends only on v. Therefore, there exists a function $\mathcal{C}_\mathcal{A}(\cdot)$ such that

$$\begin{cases} \mathcal{C}_\mathcal{A}(x^{(1)}, y^{(1)}, \ldots, x^{(i-1)}, y^{(i-1)}) = x^{(i)} \text{ for } 1 \le i \le q \text{ and} \\ \mathcal{C}_\mathcal{A}(v) = \mathcal{A}\text{'s final output.} \end{cases}$$

Let $\boldsymbol{v}_{one} \stackrel{\mathrm{def}}{=} \{v \mid \mathcal{C}_\mathcal{A}(v) = 1\}$ and $N_{one} \stackrel{\mathrm{def}}{=} \#\boldsymbol{v}_{one}$. Further, we let $\boldsymbol{v}_{good}$ be a set of all possible view $v = \langle (x^{(1)}, y^{(1)}), \ldots, (x^{(q)}, y^{(q)}) \rangle$ which satisfies the following four conditions:

- $C_{\mathcal{A}}(v) = 1$,
- $\{y_{LL}^{(i)}\}_{1 \le i \le q}$ are distinct,
- $\{y_{LR}^{(i)}\}_{1 \le i \le q}$ are distinct, and
- $\{x_{LL}^{(i)} \oplus x_{LR}^{(i)} \oplus y_{LL}^{(i)} \oplus y_{LR}^{(i)}\}_{1 \le i \le q}$ are distinct.

We also let $N_{good} \stackrel{\text{def}}{=} \#\boldsymbol{v}_{good}$.

Evaluation of p_R. We first evaluate $p_R \stackrel{\text{def}}{=} \Pr(R \stackrel{R}{\leftarrow} P_{4n} : \mathcal{A}^R = 1)$. We have $p_R = \frac{\#\{R | \mathcal{A}^R = 1\}}{(2^{4n})!}$. For each $v \in \boldsymbol{v}_{one}$, the number of R such that

$$R(x^{(i)}) = y^{(i)} \text{ for } 1 \le \forall i \le q \tag{1}$$

is exactly $(2^{4n} - q)!$. Therefore, we have $p_R = \sum_{v \in \boldsymbol{v}_{one}} \frac{\#\{R | R \text{ satisfying (1)}\}}{(2^{4n})!} = N_{one} \cdot \frac{(2^{4n} - q)!}{(2^{4n})!}$.

Evaluation of p_ψ. We evaluate $p_\psi \stackrel{\text{def}}{=} \Pr(\psi \stackrel{R}{\leftarrow} \Psi : \mathcal{A}^{\psi, \psi^{-1}} = 1)$. Note that "$\psi \stackrel{R}{\leftarrow} \Psi$" is equivalent to "$p_i \stackrel{R}{\leftarrow} P_n$ for $1 \le i \le 12$ and then let $\psi \leftarrow \psi(p_1, \ldots, p_{12})$." We have $p_\psi = \frac{\#\{(p_1, \ldots, p_{12}) | \mathcal{A}^{\psi, \psi^{-1}} = 1\}}{\{(2^n)!\}^{12}}$.

We have the following lemma. A proof of this lemma is given in [5].

Lemma 3.1 (Main Lemma for $\psi(p_1, \ldots, p_{12})$). *For any fixed possible view $v = \langle (x^{(1)}, y^{(1)}), \ldots, (x^{(q)}, y^{(q)}) \rangle$ such that $\{y_{LL}^{(i)}\}_{1 \le i \le q}$ are distinct, $\{y_{LR}^{(i)}\}_{1 \le i \le q}$ are distinct, and $\{x_{LL}^{(i)} \oplus x_{LR}^{(i)} \oplus y_{LL}^{(i)} \oplus y_{LR}^{(i)}\}_{1 \le i \le q}$ are distinct, the number of $(p_1, \ldots, p_{12})$ which satisfies*

$$\psi(x^{(i)}) = y^{(i)} \text{ for } 1 \le \forall i \le q \tag{2}$$

is at least $\left(1 - \frac{6q(q-1)}{2^n - 1}\right) \cdot \{(2^n)!\}^8 \cdot \{(2^n - q)!\}^4$.

Then from Lemma 3.1, we have

$$p_\psi \ge \sum_{v \in \boldsymbol{v}_{good}} \frac{\#\{(p_1, \ldots, p_{12}) | (p_1, \ldots, p_{12}) \text{ satisfying (2)}\}}{\{(2^n)!\}^{12}}$$

$$\ge \sum_{v \in \boldsymbol{v}_{good}} \left(1 - \frac{6q(q-1)}{2^n - 1}\right) \cdot \frac{\{(2^n - q)!\}^4}{\{(2^n)!\}^4}.$$

Now we have the following lemma. A proof of this lemma is given in Appendix B

Lemma 3.2. $N_{good} \ge N_{one} - \frac{3}{2} \cdot \frac{q(q-1)}{2^n - 1} \cdot \frac{(2^{4n})!}{(2^{4n} - q)!}$.

From Lemma 3.2, we have

$$p_\psi \geq \left(N_{one} - \frac{3}{2} \cdot \frac{q(q-1)}{2^n-1} \cdot \frac{(2^{4n})!}{(2^{4n}-q)!}\right) \cdot \left(1 - \frac{6q(q-1)}{2^n-1}\right) \cdot \frac{\{(2^n-q)!\}^4}{\{(2^n)!\}^4}$$

$$= \left(p_R - \frac{3}{2} \cdot \frac{q(q-1)}{2^n-1}\right) \cdot \left(1 - \frac{6q(q-1)}{2^n-1}\right) \cdot \frac{\{(2^n-q)!\}^4}{\{(2^n)!\}^4} \cdot \frac{\{(2^{4n})!\}}{\{(2^{4n}-q)!\}} .$$

Now it is easy to see that $\frac{\{(2^n-q)!\}^4}{\{(2^n)!\}^4} \cdot \frac{\{(2^{4n})!\}}{\{(2^{4n}-q)!\}} \geq 1$ (this can be shown easily by an induction on q). Then $p_\psi \geq \left(p_R - \frac{3}{2} \cdot \frac{q(q-1)}{2^n-1}\right) \cdot \left(1 - \frac{6q(q-1)}{2^n-1}\right) \geq p_R - \frac{15}{2} \cdot \frac{q(q-1)}{2^n-1}$. Applying the same argument to $1 - p_\psi$ and $1 - p_R$ yields that $1 - p_\psi \geq 1 - p_R - \frac{15}{2} \cdot \frac{q(q-1)}{2^n-1}$, and we have $|p_\psi - p_R| \leq \frac{15}{2} \cdot \frac{q(q-1)}{2^n-1}$.   □

From Theorem 3.1, it is straightforward to show that $\psi = \psi(p_1, \ldots, p_{12})$ is pseudorandom even if each p_i is a pseudorandom permutation by using a standard hybrid argument. For example, see [8].

4   A Six Round KASUMI Type Permutation Is Super-Pseudorandom

Theorem 4.1. For $1 \leq i \leq 18$, let $p_i \in P_n$ be a random permutation. Let $\psi = \psi(p_1, \ldots, p_{18})$ be a six round KASUMI type permutation, $R \in P_{4n}$ be a random permutation, and $\Psi \stackrel{def}{=} \{\psi \mid \psi = \psi(p_1, \ldots, p_{18}), p_i \in P_n \text{ for } 1 \leq i \leq 18\}$. Then for any adversary A that makes at most q queries in total,

$$\mathsf{Adv}_\Psi^{\mathsf{sprp}}(A) \leq \frac{9q(q-1)}{2^n-1} .$$

Proof. Let $\mathcal{O}$ be either R or ψ. The adversary A has oracle access to $\mathcal{O}$ and $\mathcal{O}^{-1}$.

There are two types of queries A can make: either $(+, x)$ or $(-, y)$. For the i-th query A makes to $\mathcal{O}$ or $\mathcal{O}^{-1}$, define the query-answer pair $(x^{(i)}, y^{(i)}) \in \{0,1\}^{4n} \times \{0,1\}^{4n}$, where either A's query was $(+, x^{(i)})$ and the answer it got was $y^{(i)} = \mathcal{O}(x^{(i)})$ or A's query was $(-, y^{(i)})$ and the answer it got was $x^{(i)} = \mathcal{O}^{-1}(y^{(i)})$. Define view v of A as $v = \langle (x^{(1)}, y^{(1)}), \ldots, (x^{(q)}, y^{(q)}) \rangle$.

Since A has unbounded computational power, A can be assumed to be deterministic. This implies that there exists a function $\mathcal{C}_A$ such that

$$\begin{cases} \mathcal{C}_A(x^{(1)}, y^{(1)}, \ldots, x^{(i-1)}, y^{(i-1)}) = \text{either } (+, x^{(i)}) \text{ or } (-, y^{(i)}) \text{ for } 1 \leq i \leq q \text{ and} \\ \mathcal{C}_A(v) = A\text{'s final output.} \end{cases}$$

Let $v_{one} \stackrel{def}{=} \{v \mid \mathcal{C}_A(v) = 1\}$ and $N_{one} \stackrel{def}{=} \#v_{one}$.

Evaluation of p_R. We first evaluate $p_R \stackrel{def}{=} \Pr(R \stackrel{R}{\leftarrow} P_{4n} : A^{R,R^{-1}} = 1)$. We have $p_R = N_{one} \cdot \frac{(2^{4n}-q)!}{(2^{4n})!}$ as was done in the proof of Theorem 3.1

Evaluation of p_ψ. We evaluate $p_\psi \stackrel{\text{def}}{=} \Pr(\psi \stackrel{R}{\leftarrow} \Psi : \mathcal{A}^{\psi, \psi^{-1}} = 1)$. Note that "$\psi \stackrel{R}{\leftarrow} \Psi$" is equivalent to "$p_i \stackrel{R}{\leftarrow} P_n$ for $1 \leq i \leq 18$ and then let $\psi \leftarrow \psi(p_1, \ldots, p_{18})$."

We have $p_\psi = \frac{\#\{(p_1, \ldots, p_{18}) | \mathcal{A}^{\psi, \psi^{-1}} = 1\}}{\{(2^n)!\}^{18}}$.

We have the following lemma. A proof of this lemma is given in [5].

Lemma 4.1 (Main Lemma for $\psi(p_1, \ldots, p_{18})$). *For any fixed possible view $v = \langle (x^{(1)}, y^{(1)}), \ldots, (x^{(q)}, y^{(q)}) \rangle$, the number of $(p_1, \ldots, p_{18})$ such that*

$$\psi(x^{(i)}) = y^{(i)} \text{ for } 1 \leq \forall i \leq q \tag{3}$$

is at least $\left(1 - \frac{9q(q-1)}{2^n - 1}\right) \cdot \{(2^n)!\}^{14} \cdot \{(2^n - q)!\}^4$.

Then from Lemma 4.1, we have

$$
\begin{aligned}
p_\psi &= \sum_{v \in v_{one}} \frac{\#\left\{(p_1, \ldots, p_{18}) \mid (p_1, \ldots, p_{18}) \text{ satisfying } (3)\right\}}{\{(2^n)!\}^{18}} \\
&\geq \sum_{v \in v_{one}} \left(1 - \frac{9q(q-1)}{2^n - 1}\right) \cdot \frac{\{(2^n - q)!\}^4}{\{(2^n)!\}^4} \\
&\geq N_{one} \cdot \left(1 - \frac{9q(q-1)}{2^n - 1}\right) \cdot \frac{\{(2^n - q)!\}^4}{\{(2^n)!\}^4} \\
&= p_R \cdot \left(1 - \frac{9q(q-1)}{2^n - 1}\right) \cdot \frac{\{(2^n - q)!\}^4}{\{(2^n)!\}^4} \cdot \frac{\{(2^{4n})!\}}{\{(2^{4n} - q)!\}} .
\end{aligned}
$$

Since $\frac{\{(2^n - q)!\}^4}{\{(2^n)!\}^4} \cdot \frac{\{(2^{4n})!\}}{\{(2^{4n} - q)!\}} \geq 1$, $p_\psi \geq p_R \cdot \left(1 - \frac{9q(q-1)}{2^n - 1}\right) \geq p_R - \frac{9q(q-1)}{2^n - 1}$. Applying the same argument to $1 - p_\psi$ and $1 - p_R$ yields that $1 - p_\psi \geq 1 - p_R - \frac{9q(q-1)}{2^n - 1}$ and we have $|p_\psi - p_R| \leq \frac{9q(q-1)}{2^n - 1}$. $\qquad \square$

From Theorem 4.1, it is straightforward to show that $\psi = \psi(p_1, \ldots, p_{18})$ is super-pseudorandom even if each p_i is a pseudorandom permutation. Note that we do *not* need the super-pseudorandomness of p_i to derive this result, since KASUMI type permutation does *not* use p_i^{-1} in both encryption and decryption. That is, we can "simulate" both ψ and ψ^{-1} *without* using p_i^{-1}.

5   Conclusion

In this paper, we showed that a four round KASUMI type permutation is pseudorandom (Theorem 3.1). We proved that the advantage is at most $\frac{15}{2} \cdot \frac{q(q-1)}{2^n - 1}$. We also showed that a six round KASUMI type permutation is super-pseudorandom (Theorem 4.1). We proved that the advantage is at most $\frac{9q(q-1)}{2^n - 1}$.

It is an important open question to prove (or disprove) the super-pseudorandomness of the five round KASUMI type permutation. We conjecture that it *is* super-pseudorandom.

References

1. http://www.3gpp.org/.
2. 3GPP TS 35.202 v 3.1.1. Specification of the 3GPP confidentiality and integrity algorithms, Document 2: KASUMI specification. Available at http://www.3gpp.org/tb/other/algorithms.htm.
3. Evaluation report (version 2.0). Specification of the 3GPP confidentiality and integrity algorithms, Report on the evaluation of 3GPP confidentiality and integrity algorithms. Available at http://www.3gpp.org/tb/other/algorithms.htm.
4. M. Blunden and A. Escott. Related key attacks on reduced round KASUMI. *Fast Software Encryption, FSE 2001, LNCS 2355*, pp. 277–285, Springer-Verlag, 2002.
5. T. Iwata, T. Yagi, and K. Kurosawa. On the pseudorandomness of KASUMI type permutations. A long version of this paper. Available from the authors and Cryptology ePrint Archive, http://eprint.iacr.org/.
6. J. S. Kang, S. U. Shin, D. Hong, and O. Yi. Provable security of KASUMI and 3GPP encryption mode $f8$. *Advances in Cryptology — ASIACRYPT 2001, LNCS 2248*, pp. 255–271, Springer-Verlag, 2001.
7. J. S. Kang, O. Yi, D. Hong, and H. Cho. Pseudorandomness of MISTY-type transformations and the block cipher KASUMI. *Information Security and Privacy, The 6th Australasian Conference, ACISP 2001, LNCS 2119*, pp. 60–73, Springer-Verlag, 2001.
8. M. Luby and C. Rackoff. How to construct pseudorandom permutations from pseudorandom functions. *SIAM J. Comput.*, vol. 17, no. 2, pp. 373–386, April 1988.
9. M. Matsui. New structure of block ciphers with provable security against differential and linear cryptanalysis. *Fast Software Encryption, FSE '96, LNCS 1039*, pp. 206–218, Springer-Verlag.
10. M. Matsui. New block encryption algorithm MISTY. *Fast Software Encryption, FSE '97, LNCS 1267*, pp. 54–68, Springer-Verlag.
11. K. Sakurai and Y. Zheng. On non-pseudorandomness from block ciphers with provable immunity against linear cryptanalysis. *IEICE Trans. Fundamentals*, vol. E80-A, no. 1, pp. 19–24, April 1997.

A   Flaws in the Proof of [6]

Kang et al. claimed that:

- the four round MISTY type permutation is pseudorandom for adaptive adversaries [6, Theorem 1] and
- the four round KASUMI type permutation is pseudorandom for adaptive adversaries [6, Theorem 3].

In this section, we show that both proofs are wrong. In what follows, we use the same notation as in [6].

A.1   Flaws on Theorem 1

On advantage. In [6, Proof of Theorem 1, p.262], it is stated that

$$\left|\Pr(T_{\Lambda_{n+m}} = \sigma \mid \sigma \notin \mathrm{BAD}(f_1, f_2)) - \Pr(T_{\mathcal{P}_{n+m}} = \sigma)\right| \le \varepsilon_{n,m,q} \ ,$$

and then

$$\sum_{\sigma \in \Theta} \Pr(\sigma \notin \mathrm{BAD}(f_1, f_2))$$
$$\cdot \left|\Pr(T_{\Lambda_{n+m}} = \sigma \mid \sigma \notin \mathrm{BAD}(f_1, f_2)) - \Pr(T_{\mathcal{P}_{n+m}} = \sigma)\right| \le \varepsilon_{n,m,q} \ ,$$

where $\varepsilon_{n,m,q} = \{2^{n+m}(2^n - 1)(2^m - 1)\cdots(2^n - q + 1)(2^m - q + 1)\}^{-1}$.

However, we can only say that there are at most $1/\varepsilon_{n,m,q}$ σ such that $\sigma \in \Theta$. This implies only that

$$\sum_{\sigma \in \Theta} \Pr(\sigma \notin \mathrm{BAD}(f_1, f_2))$$
$$\cdot \left|\Pr(T_{\Lambda_{n+m}} = \sigma \mid \sigma \notin \mathrm{BAD}(f_1, f_2)) - \Pr(T_{\mathcal{P}_{n+m}} = \sigma)\right| \le 1$$

and $ADV_{\mathcal{D}} < 1$. Hence it does not prove that $ADV_{\mathcal{D}}$ is negligible.

On collision. In [6, Lemma 4, p.261], it is stated that

$$\Pr(f_3(L_2^{(i)}) = y_L^{(i)} \oplus \overline{R_2^{(i)}} \text{ for } 1 \le \forall i \le q) = \frac{(2^n - q)!}{(2^n)!}, \tag{4}$$

where:

- f_3 is a random permutation over $\{0,1\}^n$,
- $L_2^{(i)}$ is a fixed n-bit string such that $L_2^{(i)} \ne L_2^{(j)}$ for $1 \le \forall i < \forall j \le q$,
- $y_L^{(i)}$ is a fixed n-bit string such that $y_L^{(i)} \ne y_L^{(j)}$ for $1 \le \forall i < \forall j \le q$, and
- $R_2^{(i)}$ is a fixed n-bit string such that $\overline{R_2^{(i)}} \ne \overline{R_2^{(j)}}$ for $1 \le \forall i < \forall j \le q$.

However eq.(4) does not hold because in general, $y_L^{(i)} \oplus \overline{R_2^{(i)}} \ne y_L^{(j)} \oplus \overline{R_2^{(j)}}$ does not hold even if $y_L^{(i)} \ne y_L^{(j)}$ and $\overline{R_2^{(i)}} \ne \overline{R_2^{(j)}}$. For example, $y_L^{(i)} = 0^n, y_L^{(j)} = 10^{n-1}, \overline{R_2^{(i)}} = 0^n, \overline{R_2^{(j)}} = 10^{n-1}$.

Exactly the same problem occurs in the analysis of f_4 in [6, Lemma 4, p.261].

A.2   Flaws on Theorem 3

In [6, p.266] it is stated that "Theorem 3 is proved straightforwardly by the similar process in the proof of Theorem 1." However, the proof of Theorem 1 is wrong as shown above. Therefore, the proof of Theorem 3 is also wrong. (In addition, the proof of Lemma 6 is wrong similarly to above.)

B   Proof of Lemma 3.2

For any fixed i and j such that $1 \leq i < j \leq q$, the number of $\{y^{(i)}\}_{1 \leq i \leq q}$ such that $y_{LL}^{(i)} = y_{LL}^{(j)}$ is at most $\frac{2^{3n}-1}{2^{4n}-(j-1)} \cdot \frac{(2^{4n})!}{(2^{4n}-q)!} \leq \frac{2^{3n}-1}{2^{4n}-(q-1)} \cdot \frac{(2^{4n})!}{(2^{4n}-q)!}$, since we have: $(2^{4n})(2^{4n}-1)\cdots(2^{4n}-(j-2))$ choice of $y^{(1)}, \ldots, y^{(j-1)}$, which uniquely determines $y_{LL}^{(j)} = y_{LL}^{(i)}$; at most $2^{3n}-1$ choice of $y_{LR}^{(j)}, y_{RL}^{(j)}, y_{RR}^{(j)}$; and $(2^{4n}-j)(2^{4n}-j-1)\cdots(2^{4n}-(q-1))$ choice of $y^{(j+1)}, \ldots, y^{(q)}$.

Similarly, for any fixed i and j such that $1 \leq i < j \leq q$, the number of $\{y^{(i)}\}_{1 \leq i \leq q}$ such that $y_{LR}^{(i)} = y_{LR}^{(j)}$ is at most $\frac{2^{3n}-1}{2^{4n}-(q-1)} \cdot \frac{(2^{4n})!}{(2^{4n}-q)!}$.

Next, for any fixed i and j such that $1 \leq i < j \leq q$, the number of $\{y^{(i)}\}_{1 \leq i \leq q}$ such that $x_{LL}^{(i)} \oplus x_{LR}^{(i)} \oplus y_{LL}^{(i)} \oplus y_{LR}^{(i)} = x_{LL}^{(j)} \oplus x_{LR}^{(j)} \oplus y_{LL}^{(j)} \oplus y_{LR}^{(j)}$ is at most $\frac{2^{3n}}{2^{4n}-(j-1)} \cdot \frac{(2^{4n})!}{(2^{4n}-q)!} \leq \frac{2^{3n}}{2^{4n}-(q-1)} \cdot \frac{(2^{4n})!}{(2^{4n}-q)!}$, since we have: $(2^{4n})(2^{4n}-1)\cdots(2^{4n}-(j-2))$ choice of $y^{(1)}, \ldots, y^{(j-1)}$; 2^n choice of $y_{LR}^{(j)}$, which uniquely determines $y_{LL}^{(j)} = x_{LL}^{(i)} \oplus x_{LR}^{(i)} \oplus y_{LL}^{(i)} \oplus y_{LR}^{(i)} \oplus x_{LL}^{(j)} \oplus x_{LR}^{(j)} \oplus y_{LR}^{(j)}$; at most 2^{2n} choice of $y_{RL}^{(j)}, y_{RR}^{(j)}$; and $(2^{4n}-j)(2^{4n}-j-1)\cdots(2^{4n}-(q-1))$ choice of $y^{(j+1)}, \ldots, y^{(q)}$.

Therefore, the number of $y^{(1)}, \ldots, y^{(q)}$ such that

- $y_{LL}^{(i)} = y_{LL}^{(j)}$ for $1 \leq \exists i < \exists j \leq q$,
- $y_{LR}^{(i)} = y_{LR}^{(j)}$ for $1 \leq \exists i < \exists j \leq q$, or
- $x_{LL}^{(i)} \oplus x_{LR}^{(i)} \oplus y_{LL}^{(i)} \oplus y_{LR}^{(i)} = x_{LL}^{(j)} \oplus x_{LR}^{(j)} \oplus y_{LL}^{(j)} \oplus y_{LR}^{(j)}$ for $1 \leq \exists i < \exists j \leq q$

is at most $\binom{q}{2} \cdot \frac{3 \cdot 2^{3n}-2}{2^{4n}-(q-1)} \cdot \frac{\{(2^{4n})!\}}{\{(2^{4n}-q)!\}}$, which is at most $\frac{3}{2} \cdot \frac{q(q-1)}{2^n-1} \cdot \frac{\{(2^{4n})!\}}{\{(2^{4n}-q)!\}}$. $\square$

Theoretical Analysis of χ^2 Attack on RC6

Masahiko Takenaka, Takeshi Shimoyama, and Takeshi Koshiba

Secure Computing Lab., Fujitsu Laboratories Ltd.,
4-1-1 Kamikodanaka, Nakahara-ku, Kawasaki 211-8588, Japan
{takenaka,shimo,koshiba}@labs.fujitsu.com

Abstract. In this paper, we give a theoretical analysis of χ^2 attack proposed by Knudsen and Meier on the RC6 block cipher. To this end, we propose the method of security evaluation against χ^2 attack precisely including key dependency by introducing a method "Transition Matrix Computing." Previously, no theoretical security evaluation against χ^2 attack was known, it has been done by computer experiments. We should note that this is the first results that a theoretical evaluation against χ^2 attack is shown.

Keyword: RC6, χ^2 attack, Transition Matrix,

1 Introduction

The block cipher RC6 was proposed by Rivest et al. in [9] to meet the requirements of the Advanced Encryption Standard (AES) and is one of the finalists of the AES candidates. It has been admired for its high-level security and high-speed software implementation especially on Intel CPU.

RC6 is designed based on the block cipher RC5 [8] which makes essential use of arithmetic key additions and data-dependent rotations. As additional primitive operations to RC6, the inclusion of arithmetic multiplications and fixed rotations is believed to contribute to the strength of the security of RC6. Several cryptanalyses of RC6 have been already known: resistance against Differential Attack, Related Key Attack [2,3], Linear Attack [1,2,3], Mod n Attack [5], and Statistical Attack [4]. Shimoyama *et al.* [10] evaluated the resistance of RC6 with 256-bit key against multiple linear attack and showed that the target key of 14-round RC6 can be recovered and also that the target key of 18-round RC6 with weak keys, which exists with probability $1/2^{90}$ at least, can be recovered.

One of the most effective attacks is an attack based on χ^2 test. This attack was originally proposed by Vaudenay [11], and was applied to RC6 by Gilbert et al. [4] and Knudsen and Meier [6], independently. In [6], Knudsen and Meier can cryptanalyze up to 15-round RC6 with general keys and 17-round RC6 with weak keys. Additionally Minier and Gilbert applied this attack to truncated linear cryptanalysis against Crypton by using a transition matrix [7]. We enumerate attacks on RC6 in Table 1.

In this paper, we study the attack based on χ^2 statistic attack against RC6 more precisely. We call this attack "χ^2 attack" shortly in this paper. Knudsen

R. Safavi-Naini and J. Seberry (Eds.): ACISP 2003, LNCS 2727, pp. 142–153, 2003.
© Springer-Verlag Berlin Heidelberg 2003

Table 1. Previous Attacks on RC6

Attack	Rounds	Data size	Comments
Linear Attack [1]	16	2^{119}	Upper bound of complexity
Differential Attack [2]	12	2^{117}	Upper bound of complexity
Mod n Attack [5]	—	—	—
χ^2 Attack [6]	15	$2^{119.0}$	Lower bound of complexity (estimation)
	17	$\leq 2^{118}$	Lower bound (estimation, $1/2^{80}$ weak keys)
Multiple Linear Attack [10]	14	$2^{119.68}$	Lower bound
	18	$2^{126.936}$	Lower bound ($1/2^{90}$ weak keys)

Table 2. The results of Knudsen-Meier's experiment on RC6-8 and RC6-32

rounds	♯$Texts$	χ^2	♯$Tests$	rounds	♯$Texts$	χ^2	♯$Tests$
2	2^8	77	20	2	2^{13}	1096	20
2	2^9	107	20	2	2^{14}	1196	20
4	2^{16}	68	20	2	2^{15}	1332	20
4	2^{17}	73	20	4	2^{29}	1096	20
4	2^{18}	83	20	4	2^{30}	1163	20
6	2^{26}	78	20	4	2^{31}	1314	20
	RC6-8				RC6-32		

and Meier [6] experimented with 2-, 4- and 6-round RC6 by χ^2 test and estimated the sample complexity necessary to distinguish $(2r+1)$-round RC6 from random permutation at $2^{16.2r-2.4}$. However, no theoretical evaluation against χ^2 attack was known, it has previously been done by computer experiments. We analyze the sample complexity (in the sense of chosen plaintext) of Knudsen and Meier's χ^2 attack on RC6 more precisely. We introduce a novel technique "Transition Matrix Computing" to evaluate the expected χ^2 value, and to estimate the sample complexity with respect to any fixed key. We show that the sample complexity with respect to the average key to distinguish $(2r + 1)$-round RC6 from a random permutation is at most $2^{16.0198r-2.9104}$. We note that the sample complexity $2^{16.2r-2.4}$ estimated by Knudsen and Meier is quite close to our results though their value is drawn from 20 trials. (See Table 2.)

2   Preliminary

In this section, we define notations referred for this paper. RC6 is a block cipher proposed by Rivest et al. [9]. A version of RC6 is more accurately specified as RC6-$w/r/b$ where the word size is w bits, encryption consists of a nonnegative number of rounds r, and b denotes the length of the encryption key in bytes.

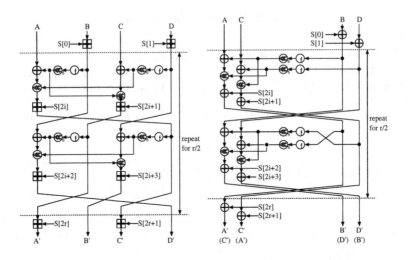

Fig. 1. RC6 structure and its transformation

Currently RC6 with $r = 20$, $4w = 128$ and $8b = 128, 192, 256$ is recommended to give sufficient resistance against known attacks. (See Table 1.)

Let (A, B, C, D) be an input to RC6 and (A', B', C', D') the corresponding output. Let $S[0], \cdots, S[2r + 1]$ be w-bit extended keys for RC6.

In this paper, we use a Feistel-like description of RC6 as described in [10]. (See Figure 1.) For $a \in GF(2)^{32}$, we denote by $lsb_5(a)$ the least significant five bits of a. And we denote by $lsb_5(a, b)$ the concatenation $(lsb_5(a)|lsb_5(b))$ of the couple of each least significant five bits of a and b. For $a, b \in GF(2)^8$, we define $lsb_3(a)$ and $lsb_3(a, b)$, similarly.

We let the sample space be $\Omega = \{(P, RC6(P)) \mid lsb_5(A, C) = 0, P = (A, B, C, D)\}$ and X_n some sample of n examples. We define the χ^2 statistic for the sample X_n as follows. We note that the user key is implicitly assumed and we omit the user key unless otherwise stated.

$$\chi^2(X_n) = \frac{m}{n} \sum_{a=0}^{m-1} \left(N_a(X_n) - \frac{n}{m} \right)^2,$$

where $N_a(X_n)$ is the cardinality of the set $\{(P, RC6(P)) \in X_n \mid lsb_5(A', C') = a, RC6(P) = (A', B', C', D')\}$, and the value a in the summation is over 0 to 1023 ($= m - 1$). We note that $lsb_5(a, b)$ (resp., $lsb_3(a, b)$) is a string of 10 bits (resp., 6 bits) and the possibilities for $lsb_5(a, b)$ (resp., $lsb_3(a, b)$) are 2^{10} (resp., 2^6.) Therefore, degrees of freedom m is 2^{10} (resp., 2^6.)

3   Expected χ^2 Value and χ^2 Attack

In this section, we consider the expected χ^2 value $E[\chi^2(X_n)]$ and derive it theoretically.

First, we consider the probability distributed on the least significant five bits of the output with respect to RC6 ($lsb_5(A', C')$.) Let $p(a) = \frac{N_a(\Omega)}{\sharp\Omega}$ be occurrence probability. We note that $\sum p(a) = 1$.

Proposition 1. *We have the following equality,*

$$E[\chi^2(X_n)] = mn \sum_{a=0}^{m-1} \left(p(a) - \frac{1}{m} \right)^2 + \frac{(\sharp\Omega - n)}{(\sharp\Omega - 1)} \left(m - m \sum_{a=0}^{m-1} p(a)^2 \right).$$

Proof. (This proof is omitted due to the space limitation.)

In addition, when $\sharp\Omega$ is sufficiently large with respect to n and the value of each $p(a)$ is close to $1/m$, the expected χ^2 value can be approximated as follows. (See [5,11].)

Corollary 1. *If $\sharp\Omega \gg n$ and $\sum p(a)^2 \approx 1/m$, then we have*

$$E[\chi^2(X_n)] \approx mn \sum_{a=0}^{m-1} \left(p(a) - \frac{1}{m} \right)^2 + m - 1.$$

Especially, the expected value $E[\chi^2(X_n)]$ is almost proportional to n.

In [6], Knudsen and Meier obtained the experimental values of $p(a)$ by computer experiments, and estimated the value of $E[\chi^2(X_n)]$. In the next section, we propose a new method to obtain the theoretical value of $p(a)$. And we evaluate the value of $E[\chi^2(X_n)]$ precisely.

4 χ^2 Attack

In this section, we review the attack based on χ^2 test, which is proposed by Knudsen and Meier. In this paper, we call this attack "χ^2 attack" for simplicity. On χ^2 attack, the least significant 5 bits in words B and D of input to RC6 are fixed to zero, and the other bits of input are randomly chosen. And we observe the χ^2 values of the 10-bit integer as obtained by concatenating the least significant bits in words (A', C') that is the output of $(2r + 1)$-round RC6. If the output of RC6 is perfectly random, the χ^2 value follows the χ^2 distribution with 1023 degrees of freedom. When this χ^2 value is larger than 1098, the output of RC6 is possible to be distinguished from the uniformly random number with probability of 95%.

Knudsen and Meier experimented χ^2 attack against versions of RC6 with word size $w = 8, 16, 32$ bits. Using the results, they estimated the necessary number of plaintexts to distinguish $(2r + 1)$-round RC6-32 from random permutations. And they estimated that necessary number of plaintexts against 15-round RC6-32 is $2^{111.0}$. Their results of the computer experiment with word size $w = 8, 32$ bits is shown in Table 2.

Moreover, expanding this Distinguishing Attack, they proposed the key recovery algorithm and estimated the sample complexity and the computational

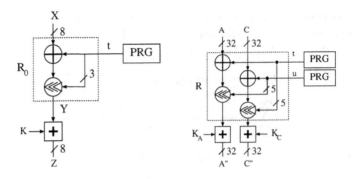

Fig. 2. Basic Model and RC6 Model of the round function

complexity to derive key. We note that although we discuss only the necessary number of plaintexts theoretically, we omit discussion of the key recovery. (They are up to [6].)

5   Density Computation Using Transition Matrix

5.1   Basic Model

In this section, we briefly sketch our idea of analysis of RC6. First, we consider the following simple model. Let R_0 be a function whose input, denoted by X, t, and output, denoted by Y, are both 8-bit wide.

$$Y = R_0(X, t) = ((X \oplus t) \lll lsb_3(t))$$
$$Z = Add_K(Y) = Y + K \bmod 2^8,$$

where $a \lll lsb_3(t)$ is a rotation of a and the number of rotation times is corresponding to the least significant three bits of t. (See Figure 2.)

Matrix Representation of the Input-Output Transition of R_0. For the sake of simplicity, we consider the case $lsb_3(X) = 0$. Since $lsb_3(X \oplus t) = lsb_3(t)$, we have an input-output transition of R_0 (See Table 3.) In [11], Vaudenay mentioned a similar transition matrix for consideration of the generalized linear test.

The symbols "*" corresponds with the most significant five bits of $X \oplus t$. If we assume that t are randomly and independently given from X, the most significant five bits of $X \oplus t$ is uniformly random for any X. Under the assumption, we can treat the symbol "*" as either 0 or 1 with the equal probability $1/2$. Thus, we can calculate the distribution on Y that depends on the value $lsb_3(t)$. And, we can say that $Y = R(X, t)$ is biased if and only if $lsb_3(X)$ is biased. Moreover, since we take into account that the output Y from R_0 flows to the next R_0, we may consider the least significant three bits of Y.

Table 3. Output $Y = R_0(X, t)$ and the distribution on $lsb_3(Y)$ (in the case $lsb_3(X) = 0$)($\times 1/64$)

$lsb_3(t)$	Y	$lsb_3(Y)$							
		000	001	010	011	100	101	110	111
000	*****000	8	0	0	0	0	0	0	0
001	****001*	0	0	4	4	0	0	0	0
010	***010**	2	2	2	2	0	0	0	0
011	**011***	1	1	1	1	1	1	1	1
100	*100****	1	1	1	1	1	1	1	1
101	101*****	1	1	1	1	1	1	1	1
110	10*****1	0	2	0	2	0	2	0	2
111	1****11	0	0	0	4	0	0	0	4
Prob.		13	7	9	15	3	5	3	9

Table 4. Transition probability matrix between the lsb_3 of input to R_0 and lsb_3 of output from R_0 ($\times 1/64$)

$lsb_3(Y)$	$lsb_3(X)$							
	000	001	010	011	100	101	110	111
000	13	7	5	3	7	9	11	9
001	7	17	7	5	9	11	5	3
010	9	3	17	7	11	5	7	5
011	15	9	7	13	9	3	5	3
100	3	5	3	9	13	7	9	15
101	5	7	5	11	7	17	3	9
110	3	5	11	9	5	7	17	7
111	9	11	9	7	3	5	7	13

In case that $lsb_3(t) = 0 = (0,0,0)$, which occurs with probability $1/8$, $lsb_3(Y)$ is always equal to $0 = (0,0,0)$. In case that $lsb_3(t) = 1 = (0,0,1)$, which occurs with probability $1/8$, $lsb_3(Y)$ is distributed on $2 = (010)$ and $3 = (0,1,1)$ with each probability $1/2$.

It is easy to compute the distribution on $lsb_3(Y)$ in any other cases. (See Table 3.)

Now, by the Table 3, we can easily see that $lsb_3(Y)$ is biased. Similarly, we consider the other cases than $lsb_3(X) = 0$ and have the transition probability matrix between the $lsb_3(X)$ of input to R_0 and $lsb_3(Y)$ of output from R_0 in Table 4. We note that the distribution on $lsb_3(Y)$, which is seen in Table 4, can be easily calculated using the value of $lsb_3(X)$ and the independent uniform randomness of t, and the most significant five bits of X does not affect the distribution of $lsb_3(Y)$.

Let M_{R_0} be the matrix given in Table 4 and $p_{R0}(x)$ be the probability that the least significant three bits $lsb_3(X)$ of X which is input of R_0 is equal to x. We denote, by ϕ_x, the column vector consisting of $p_{R0}(0), ..., p_{R0}(7)$. (For example,

if the least significant three bits of X is always equal to 0 then $\phi_x = {}^t(1, 0, ..., 0)$.)
Similarly, we denote, by ϕ_y, the column vector of the occurrence probabilities of
$0, ..., 7$ in $lsb_3(Y)$. Then, we have the following equation.

$$\phi_y = M_{R_0}\phi_x$$

Matrix Representation of Key Addition. Next, we consider the matrix
representation of key addition $Z = Add_K(Y) = Y + K \bmod 2^8$ when restricted
on the least significant three bits in the simple model. (See Figure 2.) Since the
least significant three bits of output Z from Add_K is just an additive result of the
least significant three bits of Y and key K. For example, if the key satisfies that
$lsb_3(K) = 1$ then the probability that $lsb_3(Z) = 1$ is the one that $lsb_3(Y) = 0$.
Let ϕ_z be the column vector of the occurrence probability of $0,...,7$ in $z = lsb_3(Z)$.
Then it is easy to see that ϕ_z is the vector whose elements coincide with a rotation
of elements in ϕ_y. Thus, the key addition in case that the least significant three
bits of the key K is equal to 1 is represented by the following 8×8 matrix T_0
and the equation $\phi_z = T_0\phi_y$ holds.

$$T_0 = \begin{pmatrix} 0 & 0 & 0 & 0 & 0 & 0 & 0 & 1 \\ 1 & 0 & 0 & 0 & 0 & 0 & 0 & 0 \\ 0 & 1 & 0 & 0 & 0 & 0 & 0 & 0 \\ 0 & 0 & 1 & 0 & 0 & 0 & 0 & 0 \\ 0 & 0 & 0 & 1 & 0 & 0 & 0 & 0 \\ 0 & 0 & 0 & 0 & 1 & 0 & 0 & 0 \\ 0 & 0 & 0 & 0 & 0 & 1 & 0 & 0 \\ 0 & 0 & 0 & 0 & 0 & 0 & 1 & 0 \end{pmatrix}$$

Moreover, if the least significant three bits of the key K is equal to k then
the transition by the key addition is represented as follows.

$$\phi_z = T_0{}^k\phi_y$$

5.2 RC6 Model

In this subsection, we expand the Basic Model, which has been considered in the
previous subsection, into a generalized model in which we can handle the functions in RC6. For simplicity, we consider RC6-8, which is a variant of RC6 of the
block size 32-bit (and of the word size 8-bit). We note that the following discussion is applicable to RC6-32 with a block size equal to 128-bit. Let (A, C, t, u) be
an input to RC6-8 and (K_A, K_C) be a key of RC6-8, where A, C, t, u, K_A, K_C are
some 8-bit words. Then, a function R in RC6-8 and the key addition $Add_{(K_A, K_C)}$
in RC6-8 are defined as follows.

$$(A', C') = R(A, C, t, u) = ((A \oplus t) \lll lsb_3(u), (C \oplus u) \lll lsb_3(t))$$
$$(A'', C'') = Add_{(K_A, K_C)}(A', C') = (A' + K_A \bmod 2^8, C' + K_C \bmod 2^8)$$

In this paper, we assume that t and u are random numbers. The values t and
u are the results of the multiplication operation $Y = X(2X + 1) \lll 5$ in RC6.
Even if there is small bias in the distribution of input value X, it is expected that
there is negligible bias in the distribution of the value of Y (, especially $lsb_3(Y)$).
(See Figure 2.)

Table 5. Output of R-function (in the case that each of the least significant three bits of A and C is 0)

$lsb_3(t,u)$ $(a'|c')$	$lsb_3(t,u)$ $(a'|c')$	$lsb_3(t,u)$ $(a'|c')$	$lsb_3(t,u)$ $(a'|c')$
000000 000000	010000 0100**	100000 100***	110000 110**0
000001 00*001	010001 10*1**	100001 00****	110001 10***0
000010 0**010	010010 0**0**	100010 0*****	110010 0****0
000011 ***011	010011 ***1**	100011 ******	110011 *****0
000100 ***100	010100 ***0**	100100 ******	110100 *****1
000101 ***101	010101 ***1**	100101 ******	110101 *****1
000110 **0110	010110 **00**	100110 **1***	110110 **1**1
000111 *00111	010111 *011**	100111 *10***	110111 *11**1
001000 00100*	011000 011***	101000 101***	111000 111*00
001001 01*01*	011001 11****	101001 01****	111001 11**00
001010 1**10*	011010 1*****	101010 1*****	111010 1***01
001011 ***11*	011011 ******	101011 ******	111011 ****01
001100 ***00*	011100 ******	101100 ******	111100 ****10
001101 ***01*	011101 ******	101101 ******	111101 ****10
001110 **010*	011110 **0***	101110 **1***	111110 **1*11
001111 *0011*	011111 *01***	101111 *10***	111111 *11*11

Table 6. Distribution on $(a'|c')$ (in the case that each of the least significant three bits of A and C is 0)($\times 1/2^{12}$)

$(0|0)$ 1616	$(1|0)$ 1136	$(2|0)$ 976	$(3|0)$ 688	$(4|0)$ 688	$(5|0)$ 720	$(6|0)$ 1136	$(7|0)$ 1232
$(0|1)$ 1136	$(1|1)$ 1744	$(2|1)$ 1008	$(3|1)$ 912	$(4|1)$ 784	$(5|1)$ 880	$(6|1)$ 848	$(7|1)$ 880
$(0|2)$ 976	$(1|2)$ 1008	$(2|2)$ 1616	$(3|2)$ 1328	$(4|2)$ 816	$(5|2)$ 848	$(6|2)$ 1008	$(7|2)$ 592
$(0|3)$ 688	$(1|3)$ 912	$(2|3)$ 1328	$(3|3)$ 1616	$(4|3)$ 720	$(5|3)$ 944	$(6|3)$ 784	$(7|3)$ 1200
$(0|4)$ 688	$(1|4)$ 784	$(2|4)$ 816	$(3|4)$ 720	$(4|4)$ 1104	$(5|4)$ 1200	$(6|4)$ 1424	$(7|4)$ 1456
$(0|5)$ 720	$(1|5)$ 880	$(2|5)$ 848	$(3|5)$ 944	$(4|5)$ 1200	$(5|5)$ 1360	$(6|5)$ 1136	$(7|5)$ 1104
$(0|6)$ 1136	$(1|6)$ 848	$(2|6)$ 1008	$(3|6)$ 784	$(4|6)$ 1424	$(5|6)$ 1136	$(6|6)$ 1232	$(7|6)$ 624
$(0|7)$ 1232	$(1|7)$ 880	$(2|7)$ 592	$(3|7)$ 1200	$(4|7)$ 1456	$(5|7)$ 1104	$(6|7)$ 624	$(7|7)$ 1104

Matrix Computation of Input-Output Transition. As in the RC6 Model, we assume that t, u and A, C are distributed uniformly and independently and given to R. Let a (resp., c) be the least significant three bits $lsb_3(A)$ (resp., $lsb_3(C)$) of A (resp., C). We consider the case of $a = c = 0$. Then, we have $lsb_3(A \oplus t) = lsb_3(t)$, $lsb_3(C \oplus u) = lsb_3(u)$. Let $(a'|c') = lsb_3(A', C')$, where $(A', C') = R(A, C, t, u)$. Then, the values of $(a'|c')$ are calculated as in Table 5.

The symbols in "*" in Table 5 correspond to some bits in the most significant 27 bits of either $A \oplus t$ or $C \oplus u$. Since we assume that t, u are uniformly random values and chosen independently from A, C, we can treat the symbol "*" as either 0 or 1 with the equal probability $1/2$. As in Basic Model, we can calculate the distribution on $(a'|c')$. (See Table 6.)

As in the case of $(a|c) = (0|0)$, it is not hard to calculate the distribution of $(a'|c')$ in any other cases than $(a|c) = (0|0)$. Let M_R be the transition probability

64×64 matrix from $(a|c)$ to $(a'|c')$. That is, the element which is in the ith row and in the jth column of M_R represents the probability that $(a'|c') = i$ occurs when $(a|c) = j$. As in Basic Model, ϕ denotes the column vector of occurrence probabilities of values on $(a|c)$ and ψ denotes the column vector of occurrence probabilities of values on $(a'|c')$. Then we have the following equation.

$$\psi = M_R\phi$$

Key Addition in RC6 Model. We consider the matrix representation of the key addition $Add_{(K_A,K_C)}$ in $RC6$. For example, if the least significant three bits k_1 of the key K_A is equal to 1 and the least significant three bits k_2 of the key K_C is equal to 0, then the input-output transition matrix T_1 (64×64) by the key addition is the following, where E is the 8×8 identity matrix. We note that the transition matrix T_2 (64×64) in the case $k_1 = 0$ and $k_2 = 1$ is represented in the following, where T_0 is the matrix considered in Basic Model.

$$
T_1 = \begin{pmatrix}
0 & 0 & 0 & 0 & 0 & 0 & 0 & E \\
E & 0 & 0 & 0 & 0 & 0 & 0 & 0 \\
0 & E & 0 & 0 & 0 & 0 & 0 & 0 \\
0 & 0 & E & 0 & 0 & 0 & 0 & 0 \\
0 & 0 & 0 & E & 0 & 0 & 0 & 0 \\
0 & 0 & 0 & 0 & E & 0 & 0 & 0 \\
0 & 0 & 0 & 0 & 0 & E & 0 & 0 \\
0 & 0 & 0 & 0 & 0 & 0 & E & 0
\end{pmatrix},
\quad
T_2 = \begin{pmatrix}
T_0 & 0 & 0 & 0 & 0 & 0 & 0 & 0 \\
0 & T_0 & 0 & 0 & 0 & 0 & 0 & 0 \\
0 & 0 & T_0 & 0 & 0 & 0 & 0 & 0 \\
0 & 0 & 0 & T_0 & 0 & 0 & 0 & 0 \\
0 & 0 & 0 & 0 & T_0 & 0 & 0 & 0 \\
0 & 0 & 0 & 0 & 0 & T_0 & 0 & 0 \\
0 & 0 & 0 & 0 & 0 & 0 & T_0 & 0 \\
0 & 0 & 0 & 0 & 0 & 0 & 0 & T_0
\end{pmatrix}.
$$

Let ψ be the column vector of occurrence probabilities on $(a'|c')$, the least significant three bits of inputs to the key addition $Add_{(K_A,K_C)}$, and ω be the column vector of probabilities on $(a''|c'')$, the least significant three bits of outputs from the key addition. Then, we have the following equation.

$$\omega = T_1{}^{k_1} T_2{}^{k_2} \psi$$

2r-Round RC6 Model. In discussion so far, we have assumed that t and u that are inputs to R-function are uniformly distributed. We comment on the validity of this assumption. The values on t and u in the original RC6 are calculated as follows: $t = (B(2B + 1))\lll 5$ and $u = (D(2D + 1))\lll 5$. It is easy to see that these functions are one-to-one w.r.t. B and D respectively. Furthermore, each least significant three bits of t and u is a value obtained by a multiplication. In general, the most significant bits of a value obtained by a multiplication are highly randomized. Thus, we regard our assumption as being appropriate.

Let $(A^{(r)}, C^{(r)}, B^{(r)}, D^{(r)})$ be output from 2r-round RC6-8. For convenience, let $(A^{(0)}, C^{(0)}, B^{(0)}, D^{(0)})$ be input (i.e., plaintexts) to 2r-round RC6-8. Let $\phi^{(0)}$ be the column vector of occurrence probabilities on $(a^{(0)}, c^{(0)})$, pair of the least significant three bits of $A^{(0)}$ and $C^{(0)}$. For example, if $(a^{(0)}, c^{(0)}) = (0,0)$ then $\phi^{(0)} = {}^t(1,0,...,0) \in \mathcal{R}^{64}$. Using the discussion in this section, we have the following equation w.r.t. $\phi^{(0)}$ and $\phi^{(1)}$.

$$\phi^{(1)} = T_1{}^{lsb_3(S[2])} T_2{}^{lsb_3(S[3])} M_R\phi^{(0)}$$

Using similar discussion, we can calculate the output distribution on $2r$-round RC6 (w.r.t. any fixed extended key $S[i]$) as follows.

$$\phi^{(r)} = \prod_{i=1}^{r} (T_1^{lsb_3(S[4i+2])} T_2^{lsb_3(S[4i+3])} M_R) \phi^{(0)}$$

6 χ^2 Statistic with Transition Matrix Computation

In the previous section, we consider RC6-8 of the block size 32-bit. The similar discussion is applicable to RC6-32 of the block size 128-bit. A major difference is the size of transition matrices. The size of matrices T_1, T_2 and M_R is 1024×1024 in case of RC6-32.[1] In this section, we calculate the distribution on the least significant five bits of output from each round in RC6-32 by using the way shown in the previous section. We also exactly calculate the expected χ^2 value from the resulting distribution and compare with experimental results in Knudsen and Meier [6].

Using the fixed user key, we calculate round keys $S[i]$ that is generated from the key schedule function of RC6. Then, we calculate the value of $\phi^{(r)}$ with the below matrix equation, which is obtained in the previous section.

$$\phi^{(r)} = \prod_{i=1}^{r} (T_1^{lsb_5(S[4i+2])} T_2^{lsb_5(S[4i+3])} M_R) \begin{pmatrix} 1 \\ 0 \\ \vdots \\ 0 \end{pmatrix}$$

Proposition 1 in Section 3 implies that the expected value $E[\chi^2(X_n)]$ of $\chi^2(X_n)$ can be computed from m and probability $\phi_x^{(r)}$ for each x and that the expected value is almost proportional to n. Where, $\phi_x^{(r)}$ is the x-th element of vector $\phi^{(r)}$.

$$\theta(\phi^{(r)}) = m \sum_{x=0}^{m-1} (\phi_x^{(r)} - 1/m)^2$$

$$E[\chi^2(X_n)] = \theta(\phi^{(r)}) \cdot n + m - 1$$

We set $m = 1024$ and $\#\Omega = 2^{118}$ and compute $\theta(\phi^{(r)})$ from randomly chosen 1000 user keys. We also compute the averages and the derivations from the experimental data. By using these averages, we calculate the value of n satisfying that $E[\chi^2(X_n)] = \theta(\phi^{(r)}) \cdot n + 1023 = 1098$, that means the average sample complexity which the χ^2 value exceeds 1098. (See Table 7.) The logarithm of the sample complexity to distinguish $2r$-round RC6-32 from random permutation is almost linear in r. Using a least square method, we obtain that the sample complexity to distinguish $(2r + 1)$-round RC6-32 from random permutation is $2^{16.0198r-2.9104}$. We note that the sample complexity $2^{16.2r-2.4}$ to distinguish

---

[1] Since the whole matrix (1024×1024) is too large to show in this paper, we note only that the $(0,0)$-element of M_R is $1813/2^{20}$.

Table 7. The average value for $log_2(\theta(\phi^{(r)}))$ and the sample complexity to distinguish $(2r+1)$-round RC6 from random permutation $(log_2)(\sharp round = 2r+1)$

round	r	$log_2(\theta(\phi^{(r)}))$	$\sharp$text (log_2)	
			average	weak
3	1	-6.7566	12.9854	12.9854
5	2	-22.9979	29.2067	27.8251
7	3	-39.0473	45.2761	42.3149
9	4	-55.0994	61.3282	56.3422
11	5	-71.1414	77.3702	70.4079
13	6	-87.1729	93.4017	84.3690
15	7	-103.2145	109.4433	98.2064
17	8	-119.2522	125.4810	112.0031
19	9	-135.2883	141.5171	125.8010

$(2r+1)$-round RC6-32 estimated by Knudsen and Meier [2] is quite close to the theoretical value though their value is drawn from the 20 trials for 2- and 4-round RC6-32.

In [6], Knudsen and Meier estimated the sample complexity in case of 2-round RC6-32 at 2^{13}. They also experimented with 4-round RC6-32 and claimed that $2^{16.2}$ times sample complexity should be required to distinguish two more rounds of RC6-32 from random permutation. From the estimation they had, they calculated the sample complexity to distinguish $2r$-round RC6-32 from random permutation by the linear interpolation. In Figure 3, we illustrate the theoretical χ^2 values, our experimental χ^2 values, and Knudsen-Meier's experimental χ^2 values on RC6-8. (w.r.t. RC6-8 as a simple case in which we explain our theory.) We note that these experimental results endorse our theory.

From Table 7, we can show that 15-round RC6-32 using the random keys can be distinguished by using sample complexity less than 2^{118}. And we can also show that 17-round RC6-32 using "weak key" mentioned in [6] can be distinguished. (We omit the discussion about the "weak key" in this paper.)

7   Conclusion

In this paper we had given a theoretical analysis of χ^2 attack by Knudsen and Meier on the RC6 block cipher. For this, we had proposed a method of security evaluation against the χ^2 attack precisely including key dependency by introducing the technique "Transition Matrix Computing." Previously, no theoretical security evaluation against χ^2 attack was known, it has been done by computer experiments. We had shown the way of security evaluation theoretically.

---

[2] In [6], they said that sample complexity to distinguish $(2r+3)$-round RC6-32 is $2^{16.2r+13.8}$. We note that we translate their values in order to suit then to our setting.

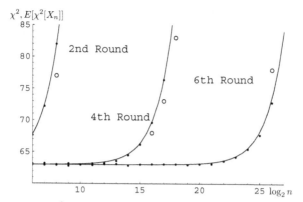

Theoretical χ^2 values obtained from the matrix computation(-)
Experimental χ^2 values from our 1000 tests($\bullet$)
Knudsen and Meier's χ^2 value with 20 experiments($\circ$)

Fig. 3. Theoretical χ^2 values, our experimental χ^2 values, and Knudsen-Meier's experimental χ^2 values on RC6-8

References

1. J. Borst, B. Preneel, and J. Vandewalle. Linear cryptanalysis of RC5 and RC6. FSE'99, LNCS 1636, pp.16–30, 1999.
2. S. Contini, R.L. Rivest, M.J.B. Robshaw, and Y.L. Yin. The security of the RC6 block cipher. v.1.0, August 20, 1998.
   Available at http://www.rsasecurity.com/rsalabs/rc6/.
3. S. Contini, R.L. Rivest, M.J.B. Robshaw, and Y.L. Yin. Improved analysis of some simplified variants of RC6. FSE'99, LNCS 1636, pp.1–15, 1999.
4. H. Gilbert, H. Handschuh, A. Joux and S. Vaudenay, A Statistical Attack on RC6. FSE 2000, LNCS 1978, pp.64–74, 2001.
5. J. Kelsey, B. Schneier, and D. Wagner. Mod n cryptanalysis, with applications against RC5P and M6. FSE'99, LNCS 1363, pp.139–155, 1999.
6. L.R. Knudsen and W. Meier. Correlations in RC6 with a reduced number of rounds. FSE 2000, LNCS 1978, pp.94–108, 2001.
7. M. Minier and H. Gilbert. Stochastic Cryptanalysis of Crypton. FSE 2000, LNCS 1978, pp.121–133, 2001.
8. R.L. Rivest. The RC5 encryption algorithm. FSE'94, LNCS 1008, pp.86–96, 1995.
9. R.L. Rivest, M.J.B. Robshaw, R. Sidney and Y.L. Yin. The RC6 block cipher. v1.1, August 20, 1998. Available at http://www.rsasecurity.com/rsalabs/rc6/.
10. T. Shimoyama, M. Takenaka and T. Koshiba. Multiple linear cryptanalysis of a reduced round RC6. FSE 2002, LNCS 2365, pp.76–88, 2002.
11. S. Vaudenay. An Experiment on DES Statistical Cryptanalysis. *3rd ACM Conference on Computer and Communications Security*, ACM Press, pp. 139–147, 1996.

A Typed Theory for Access Control and Information Flow Control in Mobile Systems*

Libin Wang and Kefei Chen

Department of Computer Science and Engineering,
Shanghai Jiaotong University, Shanghai 200030, PR China
{wang-lb, chen-kf}@cs.sjtu.edu.cn
http://www.cs.sjtu.edu.cn/index.html

Abstract. We propose a novel security type system for the π-calculus in which a fine-grained access control mechanism is guaranteed by static type checking and secure information flow can be characterized by a new form of non-interference property based on typed behavioral equivalence. In this paper, we present the syntax, subtyping rules, and typing rules of the type system, and explain how the secure data access can be controlled by typing. And then we elaborate a framework of *typed level bisimulation* to construct the secure information flow property named as *non-interference at level*. Moreover, some results are presented to indicate that our theory is an efficient enforceable model to support the specification and analysis of secure mobile systems.

1 Introduction

Security model, formalism to characterize the confidentiality of multilevel systems, mainly concerns two related but distinct topics:

- access control, the mechanism to prevent unauthorized subjects from accessing the confidential objects;
- information flow control, the mechanism to restrict what unauthorized subjects can infer about confidential objects from observing system behavior.

However, it is well-known that conventional access control mechanisms do not address the enforcement of fine-grained access control, and more severely, they do not address the enforcement of information flow control. The idea of implicit information channel is illustrated in Figure 1 which depicts an unauthorized(low-level) process infers the information from an malicious(high-level) process by observing the low-level channel.

In the past years, a number of models which relied on non-interference to formulate the information-flow security have been published [4,7,11,15,8,2,12]. Non-interference, due to Goguen and Meseguer [4], the restriction that the input

---

* Work partially supported by National Natural Science Foundation of China (#90104005, #60173032, #60273049).

© Springer-Verlag Berlin Heidelberg 2003

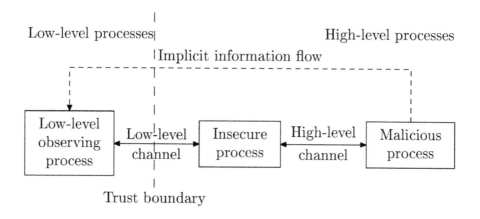

Fig. 1. Implicit Information Flow

of the high level users can not interfere with the output of low level users, is a simple but general concept to provide a formal foundation to formalize system information flow.

In the notable works of Focardi et al. [2] and Ryan et al. [12], researchers reduce the characterization of non-interference to characterizing the equivalence of certain processes in a process algebraic setting, which is CCS [9] and CSP [6] respectively. We believe that reducing the characterization of non-interference to characterizing the equivalence of certain processes and using process algebra to define and analyze security is an elegant and illuminating idea because process algebras, provide a general framework for describing interacting systems, so security models in process algebra setting can be easily generalized and compared. Another advantage of using a process algebraic framework is that it allows us to apply a number of established results, such as the completeness of unwinding rules, and compositionality. On the other hand, there are still many subtleties lurking, models should be modified and extended to have more expressiveness, e.g., mobility.

Addressing to that problems, we choose π-calculus [10,13], a very expressive language for describing mobile system, as the formalism to characterize security framework. We elaborate our theory by two phases. At first, aiming at the access control, a type system with security levels is proposed and the *Subject Reduction Theorem* under labelled transition system is proved. By typing systems with security levels, we annotate every name in system with a security level, and all the names follow the principles that low level channels can not input or output a high level name and low level channels can not read from a high level name. Our typing system is based on the type judgement of the form:

$$\Gamma \vdash^{\sigma} P$$

indicates process P is well-typed in the type environment Γ and P uses names with security level at most σ and the security property is preserved as it evolves.

Thus our typing system ensures the *no read-up/no write-down* security property of Bell and LaPadula [1] by statically type checking, and it promises an efficient enforcement of fine-grained access control mechanism.

Second, aiming at the information flow control, by reducing the characterization of non-interference security to characterizing typed behavioral equivalence of certain processes, we present our non-interference property which is named as *Non-interference at Security Level*(NIS), to specify and analyze the information flow control.

$P \in \mathcal{NIS}^\delta$ if and only if there is $\Gamma \vdash^\sigma P$, and $\delta \sqsubseteq \sigma$ such that $\Gamma \rhd P \approx^\delta [\![P]\!]^\delta$.

The basic idea is that to determine the security property of process P we should check the process P under a particular type environment Γ, which includes the potential threat(malicious processes) of environment. If the δ-level view of P, denoted as $[\![P]\!]^\delta$, is typed behavioral equivalent at level δ to P, then we assert that there are no malicious processes can interfere with the δ-level views of P, say that process P is non-interference security at level σ. In this framework, system security properties at different levels can be easily rephrased and evaluated, and new security properties can also be flexibly defined by using different type environments and behavioral equivalence relations in future. Moreover, we present and prove a security property of our framework which says the security state will be preserved as the system evolving. That results show that our framework is a flexible and enforceable security model.

This paper is structured as follows: in Section 2, we briefly recall the syntax and operational semantics of π-calculus. In Section 3, we present a type system with security levels, included subtyping rules and typing rules, at the same time we explain the construction of our type system and prove its *Type Consistency* and *Subject Reduction*. In Section 4, we construct the framework of *non-interference security at Security level*, and precise statement of our framework is presented and some results are given. The last section presents some conclusions.

2   The Syntax and Operational Semantics of π-Calculus

In this section we briefly recall the π-calculus, a model of concurrent communicating processes based on the notion of *naming*.

Definition 1. *(π-calculus)Let x, y, z, $\cdots$ range over a denumerable set $\mathcal{N}$. The processes evolve four kinds of actions which are expressed via the prefixes:*

$$\pi ::= \bar{x}y \quad | \quad x(z) \quad | \quad \tau \quad | \quad [x = y]\pi$$

The processes and the summations of the π-calculus, denoted by a set $\mathcal{P}^\pi$, are given respectively by

$$P ::= M \quad | \quad P|P' \quad | \quad \nu z P \quad | \quad !P$$

$$M ::= 0 \quad | \quad \pi.P \quad | \quad M + M'$$

Below we will give a brief, informal account of the intended interpretation of processes.

(1) 0 is inaction; it is a process that can do nothing.

(2) The prefix $\pi \cdot P$ has a single capability, expressed by π; the process P cannot proceed until that capability has been exercised. The output prefix $\bar{x}y \cdot P$ can send the name y via the name x and continue as P. The input prefix $x(z) \cdot P$ can receive any name via x and continue as P with the received name substituted for z. The unobservable prefix $\tau \cdot P$ can evolve invisibly to P. As in CCS, τ can be thought of as expressing an internal action of a process. The match prefix $[x = y]\pi \cdot P$ can evolve as $\pi \cdot P$ if x and y are the same name, and can do nothing otherwise.

(3) The capabilities of the sum $P + P'$ are those of P together with those of P'. When a sum exercises one of its capabilities, the others are rendered void.

(4) In the composition $P|P'$, the components P and P' can proceed independently and can interact via shared names.

(5) In the restriction $\nu z P$, the scope of the name z is restricted to P. Components of P can use z to interact with one another but not with other processes.

(6) Finally, the replication $!P$ can be thought of as an infinite composition $P|P| \cdots$ or, equivalently, a process satisfying the equation $!P = P|!P$. Replication is the operator that makes it possible to express infinite behaviors.

We write $\pi(P)$ for a set of names which represents all the names of process P, and write $Subject(\alpha)$ for the prefix of action α. In this paper, we use the standard syntax of π-calculus as well as its standard operational semantics [13] which is defined in Table 3(see appendix). We will also use the standard α-conversion rules, structure congruence which are not reported in this paper because of space limitation.

3   The Type System with Security Levels

3.1   Syntax of Types

We now introduce a type system for the π-calculus by extending an existing type system [13] with security levels. We present a security lattice $\langle \mathcal{L}, \sqsubseteq, top, bot \rangle$ of arbitrary security levels which denotes partial order. The security levels are ranged over by $\sigma, \delta, \cdots$, the top and bot denotes the most top level and most low level respectively, and with ordering $bot \sqsubseteq top$. We write $lev(x)$ for x's security level, where x is an arbitrary name or type. As in [13], every channel type carries a polarity which tells whether the channel may be used for input($\downarrow$), output($\uparrow$), or both($\updownarrow$) and annotated with a security level $\sigma \in \mathcal{L}$. The secure types are defined by the grammar:

$$V ::= (\mathbf{B}, \sigma)$$
$$| \ (L, \sigma) \qquad\qquad\qquad where \quad lev(L) \sqsubseteq \sigma$$
$$L ::= (V^{\downarrow}, \sigma) \ | \ (V^{\uparrow}, \sigma) \ | \ (V^{\updownarrow}, \sigma) \qquad where \quad lev(V) \sqsubseteq \sigma$$

where we use V to range over value types, L over link types. The set of basic types $\mathbf{B}$ is left unspecified. In this definition, we annotate every type with a security level, and the type is nested, but one type's security level is always higher than its nested type's level. The i/o typing have following informal meanings:

- $(T^{\uparrow}, \sigma)$ is the type of a name with security level σ that can be used only in output and that carries values of a lower level type T, that is $lev(T) \sqsubseteq \sigma$.
- $(T^{\downarrow}, \sigma)$ is the type of a name with security level σ that can be used only in input and that carries values of a lower level type T, that is $lev(T) \sqsubseteq \sigma$.

Table 1. Subtyping rules

$$\text{SUB-REFL} \frac{}{T \leqslant T} \qquad \text{SUB-TRANS} \frac{S \leqslant S', \quad S' \leqslant T}{S \leqslant T} \qquad \text{SUB-DATA1} \frac{\sigma \sqsubseteq \delta}{(T,\sigma) \leqslant (T,\delta)}$$

$$\text{SUB-DATA2} \frac{S \leqslant T}{(S,\sigma) \leqslant (T,\sigma)} \qquad \text{SUB-}\updownarrow\text{I} \frac{}{(T^{\updownarrow},\sigma) \leqslant (T^{\downarrow},\sigma)} \qquad \text{SUB-}\updownarrow\text{O} \frac{}{(T^{\updownarrow},\sigma) \leqslant (T^{\uparrow},\sigma)}$$

$$\text{SUB-II} \frac{S \leqslant T}{(S^{\downarrow},\sigma) \leqslant (T^{\downarrow},\sigma)} \qquad \text{SUB-OO} \frac{T \leqslant S}{(S^{\uparrow},\sigma) \leqslant (T^{\uparrow},\sigma)} \qquad \text{SUB-BB} \frac{T \leqslant S, \quad S \leqslant T}{(S^{\updownarrow},\sigma) \leqslant (T^{\updownarrow},\sigma)}$$

$$\text{SUB-RD} \frac{\sigma \sqsubseteq \delta}{(T^{\downarrow},\sigma) \leqslant (T^{\downarrow},\delta)}$$

3.2 Subtyping

The subtyping rules appear in Table 1. A *subtype judgement* has the form $S \leqslant T$; it asserts that S is a subtype of T. For simplicity, we use letters S and T to stand for arbitrary type in below typing and subtyping rules as well as in discussions and proofs.

We briefly comment on the subtyping rules. The rules SUB-REFL and SUB-TRANS show that $\leqslant$ is a preorder. Showing the subtyping of value types, rule SUB-DATA1 says that if security level δ is higher then level σ then type (T,δ) is the supertype of the type (T,σ), and the rule SUB-DATA2 says that if type S is the subtype of T, then type (S,σ) is the subtype of (T,σ).

The i/o subtyping rules follow the well-known principles in [13], the rule SUB-II says that $\downarrow$ is a covariant construct, SUB-OO says $\uparrow$ is a contravariant and SUB-BB says that $\updownarrow$ is an invariant. The rules SUB-$\updownarrow$I and SUB-$\updownarrow$O show that $\updownarrow$ can construct a type which possesses both the input and output capability.

The most contributing rule for security property is SUB-RD, it says that an input type is the supertype of another input type when they both input the same type value but the former with a higher security level. SUB-RD is the only i/o subtyping rule with different security levels, in other words, we do not allow a name for output can change its security level by using subtyping. The rule SUB-RD ensures the *no read-up/no write-down* principle of Bell and LaPadula Model. To show this, we present the *Type Consistency Lemma* which says that if input type $(T_1^\downarrow,\sigma_1)$ and output type $(T_2^\uparrow,\sigma_2)$ belong to a same name, then $T_2 \leqslant T_1$ and $\sigma_2 \sqsubseteq \sigma_1$.

Lemma 1. *(Type Consistency Lemma) If $S \leqslant (T_1^\downarrow,\sigma_1)$ and $S \leqslant (T_2^\uparrow,\sigma_2)$ then $T_2 \leqslant T_1$ and $\sigma_2 \sqsubseteq \sigma_1$*

Proof. Type S is of the form $(T^?,\delta)$. By $S \leqslant (T_1^\downarrow,\sigma_1)$, we infer that $? \in \{\updownarrow,\downarrow\}$, $T \leqslant T_1$ and $\delta \sqsubseteq \sigma_1$. By $S \leqslant (T_2^\uparrow,\sigma_2)$, we infer that $? \in \{\updownarrow,\uparrow\}$, $T_2 \leqslant T$ and $\delta = \sigma_2$. Hence, $? = \updownarrow$, and by transitivity of subtyping, we have $T_2 \leqslant T_1$ and $\sigma_2 \sqsubseteq \sigma_1$.

Table 2. Typing rules for π-calculus

Value typing	
TV-BASE $\dfrac{}{\Gamma \vdash bv:B}\ bv \in B$	TV-NAME $\dfrac{}{\Gamma,x:T \vdash x:T}$

Process typing		
T-PAR $\dfrac{\Gamma \vDash^\sigma P:\diamond \quad \Gamma \vDash^\sigma Q:\diamond}{\Gamma \vDash^\sigma P|Q:\diamond}$	T-SUM $\dfrac{\Gamma \vDash^\sigma P:\diamond \quad \Gamma \vDash^\sigma Q:\diamond}{\Gamma \vDash^\sigma P+Q:\diamond}$	
T-MAT $\dfrac{\Gamma \vdash v:(T^\updownarrow,\delta) \quad \Gamma \vdash w:(T^\updownarrow,\delta) \quad \Gamma \vDash^\sigma P:\diamond \quad \delta \sqsubseteq \sigma}{\Gamma \vDash^\sigma [v=w]P:\diamond}$		T-NIL $\dfrac{}{\Gamma \vDash^\sigma 0}$
T-REP $\dfrac{\Gamma \vDash^\sigma P:\diamond}{\Gamma \vDash^\sigma !P:\diamond}$	T-RES $\dfrac{\Gamma,x:R \vDash^\sigma P:\diamond}{\Gamma \vDash^\sigma (\nu x:R)P:\diamond}$	T-TAU $\dfrac{\Gamma \vDash^\sigma P:\diamond}{\Gamma \vDash^\sigma \tau\cdot P:\diamond}$
T-INP $\dfrac{\Gamma \vdash a:(T^\downarrow,\delta) \quad \Gamma,x:(T,\delta) \vDash^\sigma P:\diamond \quad \delta \sqsubseteq \sigma}{\Gamma \vDash^\sigma a(x)\cdot P:\diamond}$		
T-OUT $\dfrac{\Gamma \vdash a:(T^\uparrow,\delta) \quad \Gamma \vdash w:(T,\delta) \quad \Gamma \vDash^\sigma P:\diamond \quad \delta \sqsubseteq \sigma}{\Gamma \vDash^\sigma \bar{a}w\cdot P:\diamond}$		
T-SUB-NAME $\dfrac{\Gamma \vdash v:T \quad T \leqslant T'}{\Gamma \vdash v:T'}$	T-SUB-LEVEL $\dfrac{\Gamma \vDash^\delta P \quad \delta \sqsubseteq \sigma}{\Gamma \vDash^\sigma P:\diamond}$	

3.3   The Typing System

A *type environment* is a finite set of assignments of types to names, we use Γ, Δ to range over type environment. In general, *type judgements* are of the form $\Gamma \vdash E : T$, where E may be a process or a name. If E is a process then T is $\diamond$, the behavior type. A process type judgement $\Gamma \vdash P : \diamond$ asserts that process P respects the type assumptions in Γ, and a name type judgement $\Gamma \vdash v : T$ asserts that name v has the type R under the type assumptions Γ. Our typing rules are presented in Table 2 where the process type judgements take the form:

$$\Gamma \vDash^\sigma P : \diamond$$

This judgement means not only the process P respects the type assumptions in Γ but in addition it uses names with security level at most σ, abbreviated to P *at level σ*. In this paper, for simplicity and without confusion, sometimes we omit the behavior type $\diamond$.

The purpose of our type judgement is to differentiate the processes by security levels. The value typing and the rule T-SUB-NAME are standard. The rule T-NIL says that process 0 is well typed in any typing and any level. The rule T-PAR and rule T-SUM say that two processes are well typed and at level σ if each is well typed and at level σ in isolation. The rules T-REP, T-TAU and T-RES are similar. The rule T-MAT says that a process at σ ia allowed to test equality between names of the same connection type with a lower level than σ. The most interesting cases are T-INP, T-OUT and T-SUB-LEVEL. In an input process $a(x) \cdot P$ at level σ, the subject a should have a link type with level δ and $\delta \sqsubseteq \sigma$; moreover, the type of x is determined and then the process P at level σ is required to be well typed under the resulting extension of Γ. The case for output is similar: the output process $\bar{a}w \cdot P$ at level σ is well typed if $\bar{a}$ has a link type with level δ and $\delta \sqsubseteq \sigma$; moreover the type of a is compatible with that of w, and P should be well typed at level σ. The rule T-SUB-LEVEL indicates that if P is a process at level δ then it is also a process at a higher level σ.

To prove the main theorem our typing system, we need some easy lemmas which can proved by straightforward deduction on the depth of the derivation of the judgement in the hypothesis. Proofs are omitted here.

Lemma 2. *(Strengthening Lemma) If* $\Gamma, x : S \vdash^\sigma E : T$ *and* x *is not free in* E *then also* $\Gamma \vdash^\sigma E : T$

Lemma 3. *(Weakening Lemma) If* $\Gamma \vdash^\sigma E : T$ *then* $\Gamma, x : S \vdash^\sigma E : T$ *for any type* S *and any name* x *on which* Γ *is not defined.*

Lemma 4. *(Substitution Lemma)* $\Gamma, y : R \vdash^\sigma P : \diamond$, $\Gamma \vdash z : R$ *imply* $\Gamma \vdash^\sigma P\{z/y\} : \diamond$.

Above lemmas allow us to prove the *Subject Reduction Theorem* which expresses a consistency between the operational semantics and the typing rules, show how the typing of a process evolves under transitions and how the typing can be used to obtain information about the process's possible transitions. Here, the only requirement on *closed* processes is that their free names have link types.

Theorem 1. *(Subject Reduction) Suppose* $\Gamma \vdash^\sigma P$ *with* Γ *is closed, and* $P \xrightarrow{\alpha} P'$.

1. *If* $\alpha = \tau$ *then* $\Gamma \vdash^\sigma P'$
2. *If* $\alpha = av$ *then there is* T *and* $\delta \sqsubseteq \sigma$ *such that*
    a) $\Gamma \vdash a : (T^\downarrow, \delta)$
    b) *if* $\Gamma \vdash v : (T, \delta)$ *then* $\Gamma \vdash^\sigma P'$
3. *If* $\alpha = (\nu \tilde{x} : \tilde{S})\bar{a}v$ *then there is* T *and* $\delta \sqsubseteq \sigma$ *such that*
    a) $\Gamma \vdash a : (T^\uparrow, \delta)$
    b) $\Gamma, \tilde{x} : \tilde{S} \vdash v : (T, \delta)$
    c) $\Gamma, \tilde{x} : \tilde{S} \vdash^\sigma P'$
    d) *each component of* $\tilde{S}$ *is a link type.*

Proof. By induction on the derivation of $P \xrightarrow{\alpha} P'$, the proof is similar to that of Theorem 6.3.7 of [13]. Most cases are simple, we examine only below cases.

The rule INP: In this case, $P = a(x) \cdot Q$ and $P' = Q\{v/x\}$. From $\Gamma \vdash^\sigma P$, we infer that $\Gamma \vdash a : (T^\downarrow, \delta)$ and $\Gamma, x : (T, \delta) \vdash^\sigma Q$, for some T and $\delta \sqsubseteq \sigma$. We have to show that if $\Gamma \vdash v : (T, \delta)$ then $\Gamma \vdash^\sigma Q\{v/x\}$. From $\Gamma \vdash v : (T, \delta)$ and Weakening, $\Gamma, x : (T, \delta) \vdash v : (T, \delta)$. It also holds that $(\Gamma, x : (T, \delta))(x) = (T, \delta)$ and $\Gamma, x : (T, \delta) \vdash^\sigma Q$. We can therefore apply the Substitution Lemma and infer $\Gamma, x : (T, \delta) \vdash^\sigma Q\{v/x\}$. Since x is not free in $Q\{v/x\}$, by Strengthening Lemma, $\Gamma \vdash^\sigma Q\{v/x\}$.

The rule COMML-L: Suppose $P = P_1 | P_2$, $P_1 \xrightarrow{(\nu \tilde{x}:\tilde{S})\bar{a}v} P_1'$, $P_2 \xrightarrow{av} P_2'$, and $P' = (\nu \tilde{x} : \tilde{S})(P_1' | P_2')$. Let Γ^+ be $\Gamma, \tilde{x} : \tilde{S}$. Since $\Gamma \vdash^\sigma P_1$, by the inductive assumption on P_1 there is T and $\delta_1 \sqsubseteq \sigma$ such that

$$\Gamma \vdash a : (T^\uparrow, \delta_1), \tag{1}$$
$$\Gamma^+ \vdash v : (T, \delta_1), \tag{2}$$

and $\Gamma^+ \vdash^\sigma P_1'$. Since $\Gamma \vdash^\sigma P_2$, also $\Gamma^+ \vdash^\sigma P_2$. By the inductive assumption on P_2 and Γ^+, there is S and $\delta_2 \sqsubseteq \sigma$ such that

$$\Gamma^+ \vdash a : (S^\downarrow, \delta_2), \tag{3}$$

and

$$if \quad \Gamma^+ \vdash v : (S, \delta_2), \quad then \quad also \quad \Gamma^+ \vdash^\sigma P_2'. \tag{4}$$

Because of (1), it holds that $\Gamma(a) \leqslant (T^\uparrow, \delta_1)$; similarly, because of (3), it holds that $\Gamma(a) \leqslant (S^\downarrow, \delta_2)$. By Lemma 1, we have $T \leqslant S$ and $\delta_1 \sqsubseteq \delta_2$, then we get $(T, \delta_1) \leqslant (S, \delta_2)$ by using subtyping rules. Therefore we can apply rule T-SUB-NAME to (2) and infer $\Gamma^+ \vdash v : (S, \delta_2)$. By (4), we get $\Gamma^+ \vdash^\sigma P_2'$. Finally using rules T-PAR and T-RES, we have $\Gamma \vdash^\sigma (\nu \tilde{x} : \tilde{S})(P_1' | P_2')$.

4   Information Flow Control

In this section, we will propose a novel framework for non-interference properties in typed π-calculus setting, the basic idea is inspirited by the concept of *BNDC* which is studied in [2,3]. A process P is *BNDC* if what a low level user sees of the system is not modified by composing any high level process Π to P. However, this non-interference properties in CCS setting can not be transformed in π-calculus setting trivially because π-calculus is a mobile theory with name-passing, it is impossible to restrict any arbitrary high level process not to change the views of low level, and the universal quantification over all the possible high level processes is difficult to check. To express our framework, besides the typing system in last section, we need some auxiliary definitions, and count on a new definition of typed behavioral bisimulation.

Definition 2. *(Observability Predicates)For each name or co-name μ, the observability predicate $\downarrow_\mu$ is defined by*

1. $P \downarrow_x$ *if P can perform an input action with subject x*
2. $P \downarrow_{\bar{x}}$ *if P can perform an output action with subject x*

Informally, μ ranges over names and co-names, and observability predicates of one process express which names of the process can interact with the environment.

A typed relation is a set of quadruples $(\Delta; \sigma; P; Q)$ where Δ is a closed typing and $\Delta \vdash^\sigma P, Q$. We say that Γ is a closed σ-extension of Δ if Γ is closed and extends Δ with some names which security level is at most σ. In below definition, '$\Gamma \vdash a : S$ and $\mathcal{O}(S) = T$' means that a can carry values of type T.

Definition 3. *(Typed Level-Bisimilarity) Typed Level-Bisimilarity is the largest symmetric typed relation $\mathcal{R}$ such that $(\Delta; \sigma; P; Q) \in \mathcal{R}$ implies:*

1. *if $P \downarrow_a$, there is Γ is a closed σ-extension of Δ, $\Gamma \vdash a : S$ and $\mathcal{O}(S) = T$ and $\Gamma \vdash v : T$*
   a) *if $lev(a) \sqsubseteq \sigma$, whenever $P \xrightarrow{av} P'$*
      there is Q' such that $Q \stackrel{av}{\Longrightarrow} Q'$ and $(\Gamma; \sigma; P'; Q') \in \mathcal{R}$
   b) *if $\sigma \sqsubseteq lev(a)$ and $\sigma \neq lev(a)$*
      i. *there is $\Gamma \vdash \bar{a}w$*
      ii. *whenever $P|\bar{a}w \xrightarrow{\tau} P'$*
         there is Q' such that $Q \Longrightarrow Q'$ and $(\Gamma; \sigma; P'; Q') \in \mathcal{R}$
2. *if $P \downarrow_{\bar{a}}$*
   a) *if $lev(a) \sqsubseteq \sigma$, whenever $P \xrightarrow{(\nu\tilde{b}:T)\bar{a}v} P'$*
      there is Q' such that $Q \stackrel{(\nu\tilde{b}:T)\bar{a}v}{\Longrightarrow} Q'$ and $(\Delta, \tilde{b} : \tilde{T}; P'; Q') \in \mathcal{R}$
   b) *if $\sigma \sqsubseteq lev(a)$ and $\sigma \neq lev(a)$*
      i. *there is $\Gamma \vdash aw$*
      ii. *whenever $P|aw \xrightarrow{\tau} P'$*
         there is Q' such that $Q \Longrightarrow Q'$ and $(\Delta; \sigma; P'; Q') \in \mathcal{R}$
3. *whenever $P \xrightarrow{\tau} P'$ there is Q' such that $Q \Longrightarrow Q'$ and $(\Delta; \sigma; P'; Q') \in \mathcal{R}$.*

Let Δ be a closed typing with $\Delta \vdash^\sigma P, Q$. We say that P and Q are typed σ-bisimilar at Δ, written $\Delta \rhd P \approx^\sigma Q$, if $(\Delta; \sigma; P; Q)$ is in some typed level-bisimulation.

Definition 4. *Function $Act_H : (\mathcal{P}^\pi, \sigma) \mapsto \mathcal{N}, \forall P \in \mathcal{P}^\pi$ and $\forall \sigma \in \mathcal{L}$, if there is a type environment Γ, such that $\Gamma \vdash^\sigma P$, $Act_H(P, \sigma) \triangleq \{x \mid x \in \pi(P), \sigma \sqsubseteq lev(\Gamma(x))$ and $\sigma \neq lev(\Gamma(x))\}$.*

Definition 5. *The σ-level view of process P is a function denoted as $[\![P]\!]^\sigma$: $(\mathcal{P}^\pi, \sigma) \mapsto \mathcal{P}^\pi$, such that $\forall \sigma \in \mathcal{L}$ and $\forall P \in \mathcal{P}^\pi$, $[\![P]\!]^\sigma \triangleq (\nu\tilde{H})P$, where $\tilde{H} = a_1, a_2, \cdots, a_n$ includes all the name of $Act_H(P, \sigma)$.*

Intuitively, $Act_H(P, \sigma)$ denotes the set of names which security level is strictly higher than σ, and $[\![P]\!]^\sigma$ denotes the behaviors of process P which can be viewed by the users whose security level is at most σ.

Definition 6. *(Non-interference at Security Level δ) We say process P is non-interference security at level δ, written $P \in \mathcal{NIS}^\delta$, if and only if, there is $\Gamma \vdash^\sigma P$, and $\delta \sqsubseteq \sigma$ such that $\Gamma \rhd P \approx^\delta [\![P]\!]^\delta$.*

The basic idea is that to determine the security property of process P we should check the process P under a particular type environment Γ, which includes the potential threat(malicious processes) of environment, then we avoid the universal quantification over all possible high level behaviors. If the δ-level view of P, denoted as $[\![P]\!]^\delta$, is typed behavioral equivalent at level δ to P, then we assert that there are no malicious process can interfere with the δ-level views of P, say that process P is non-interference security at level δ. In other words, if $P \in \mathcal{NIS}^\delta$, then from the view at level δ, we can not distinguish P from $[\![P]\!]^\delta$. *Typed level-bisimulation* playes an important role in our definition, because it ensures we only check the behaviors of P at level δ, and it also ensures P only interact with particular names at a δ-extension environment. In the future study, we can refine our framework by choosing different type environment and/or equivalent relation in the definition. Below we will present a property which says that all possible reachable processes of a secure process are still 'secure'.

Definition 7. *(Insecure State)We say process P is in an insecure state at level σ if P can only perform actions which security levels are higher than σ and there is $x \in \pi(P)$ and $lev(Subject(x)) \sqsubseteq \sigma$.*

Definition 8. *(Closed Transition at security level) If $\Gamma \vdash^\sigma P$ and $P \downarrow_\alpha$, we say that P' is reached from P by a closed transition at level δ if there is $\delta \sqsubseteq \sigma$ and the following hold:*

1. *if $lev(Subject(\alpha)) \sqsubseteq \delta$ or $\alpha = \tau$ then $P \xrightarrow{\alpha} P'$*
2. *if $\delta \sqsubseteq lev(Subject(\alpha))$ and $\delta \neq lev(Subject(\alpha))$ then there is a $\Delta \vdash \bar{\alpha}$ when Δ is a δ-extension of Γ, such that $P|\bar{\alpha} \xrightarrow{\tau} P'$.*

Theorem 2. *If process $P \in \mathcal{NIS}^\delta$ and for any P' is reached from P by finite closed transitions at level δ, then P' can not be an insecure state at δ.*

Proof. It can be proved by reduction to absurdity. Suppose there is a P' which is evolved from P by finite closed transition at level δ and P' is an insecure state at δ. Because $P \in \mathcal{NIS}^\delta$ then $P \approx^\delta [\![P]\!]^\delta$. Because P' is reached from P by finite closed transition at level δ, then there is a $[\![Q]\!]^\delta$ which is reached from $[\![P]\!]^\delta$ in finite steps, and $P' \approx^\delta [\![Q]\!]^\delta$, but this is impossible, because we note that P' is an insecure state at δ, whenever $P' \xrightarrow{\hat{x}} P''$, $lev(x) \sqsubseteq \delta$, correspondingly $[\![Q]\!]^\delta \xrightarrow{\hat{x}} Q'$, but on the contrary, whenever $[\![P]\!]^\delta \xrightarrow{\hat{x}} Q'$, P' has not a corresponding action.

5   Conclusions

Recently, there is a vast studies on the topic of our paper, and the most particularly relevant works are Hennessy et al.'s [5]. Although their works share some basic mechanisms with ours, there are some major differences can be noted. Firstly, their type system uses sets of so called read or write 'capability' while our type system is an extension of the existing type system of Sangiorgi [13] which makes our system more understandable. Secondly, essentially their type system ensures the non-interference property while our non-interference property badly counts on the typed behavior bisimulation. Lastly, their non-interference is defined in terms of testing equivalence while ours depend on a typed bisimilarity and there are universal σ-free processes H and K in their *Non-interference Theorem*, while our non-interference property, depended on a particular type environment, tends to be 'local'. In summary, it appears that our theory constructs a security model in programming language level while the theory of Hennessy et al.'s addresses information flow control within the core π-calculus.

Here, we propose a novel security type system for the π-calculus in which a fine-grained access control mechanism is guaranteed and secure information flow can be characterized. Our framework is an efficient enforceable formalism to support security specification and analysis, it can be viewed as a rather appealing step towards providing language-based security [14] in real systems. However, a number of issues should be investigated further in our theory. Firstly, the type system we presented is static, but the security of channels change dynamically. Secondly, our type system can not handle integrity properties which is crucial in some e-commerce systems, and it also does not address to the advanced types, which play a key role in the analysis of complicated process behavior. Thirdly, the security property defined in our framework, can not express the temporal and probabilistic security properties.

References

1. D. Elliott Bell and Leonard J. LaPadula. Secure computer system: Mathematical foundations and model. Technical Report 2547, MITRE Corporation, March 1975.
2. Riccardo Focardi and Roberto Gorrieri. A classification of security properties for process algebra. *Journal of Computer Security*, 3(1):5–33, 1995.
3. Riccardo Focardi and Sabina Rossi. Information flow security in dynamic contexts. In *Proceedings of 15th IEEE Computer Security Foundations Workshop*. IEEE Press, 2002.
4. Joseph Goguen and Jose Meseguer. Security policies and security models. In *Proceedings of IEEE Symposium on Research in Security and Privacy*, pages 11–20. IEEE Press, 1982.
5. Matthew Hennessy. The security pi-calculus and non-interference. Technical Report CSR Technical Report 05/2000, University of Sussex, May 2000.
6. C.A.R Hoare. *Communication Sequential Processes*. Prentice-Hall, 1985.
7. Daryl McCullough. Specification for mulit-level security and a hook-up property. In *Proceedings of IEEE Symposium on Research in Security and Privacy*. IEEE Press, 1987.
8. John McLean. A general theory of composition for a class of possibility composability. *IEEE Transaction on Software Engineering*, 22(1):53–67, Jan 1996.
9. Robin Milner. *Communication and Concurrency*. Prentice-Hall, 1989.
10. Robin Milner. *Communicating and Mobile Systems: the π-calculus*. Cambridge University Press, 1999.
11. Colin O'Halloran. A calculus of information flow. In *Proceedings of the European Symposium on Research in Computer Security*, 1990.

12. Peter Ryan and Steve Schneider. Process algebra and noninterference. In *Proceedings of 12th IEEE Computer Security Foundations Workshop*. IEEE Press, 1999.
13. Davide Sangiorgi and David Walker. *The pi-calculus: A Theory of Mobile Processes*. Cambridge University Press, 2001.
14. Fred B. Schneider, Greg Morrisett, and Robert Harper. *A language-based approach to security*. Springer LNCS 2000, 2000.
15. D. Sutherland. A model of information. In *Proceedings of Ninth National Computer Security Conference*. National Bureau of Standars/National Computer Security Center, 1986.

Appendix: The Transition Rules for π-Calculus

Table 3. The Transition Rules for π-Calculus

$$\text{OUT}\dfrac{}{\bar{a}w\cdot P\xrightarrow{\bar{a}w}P} \qquad \text{INP}\dfrac{}{a(x)\cdot P\xrightarrow{aw}P\{w/x\}} \qquad \text{TAU}\dfrac{}{\tau\cdot P\xrightarrow{\tau}P}$$

$$\text{MAT}\dfrac{P\xrightarrow{\alpha}P'}{[x{=}x]P\xrightarrow{\alpha}P'} \qquad \text{SUM-L}\dfrac{P\xrightarrow{\alpha}P'}{P+Q\xrightarrow{\alpha}P'}$$

$$\text{PAR-L}\dfrac{P\xrightarrow{\alpha}P'}{P|Q\xrightarrow{\alpha}P'|Q}\,bn(\alpha)\cap fn(\alpha)=\varnothing$$

$$\text{COMM-L}\dfrac{P\xrightarrow{(\nu\tilde{z}:\tilde{T})\bar{a}v}P' \qquad Q\xrightarrow{av}Q'}{P|Q\xrightarrow{\tau}(\nu\tilde{z}:\tilde{T})(P'|Q')}\,\tilde{z}\cap fn(Q)=\varnothing$$

$$\text{RES}\dfrac{P\xrightarrow{\alpha}P'}{(\nu x{:}T)P\xrightarrow{\alpha}(\nu x{:}T)P'}\,x\notin n(\alpha)$$

$$\text{OPEN}\dfrac{P\xrightarrow{(\nu\tilde{z}:\tilde{T})\bar{a}v}P'}{(\nu\tilde{x}:\tilde{T})P\xrightarrow{(\nu\tilde{z}:\tilde{T},x:T)\bar{a}v}P'}\,x\in fn(v),x\notin\{\tilde{z},a\}$$

$$\text{REP-ACT}\dfrac{P\xrightarrow{\alpha}P'}{!P\xrightarrow{\alpha}P'|!P}$$

$$\text{REP-COMM}\dfrac{P\xrightarrow{(\nu\tilde{z}:\tilde{T})\bar{a}v}P' \qquad P\xrightarrow{av}P''}{!P\xrightarrow{\tau}(\nu\tilde{z}:\tilde{T})(P'|P'')|!P}\,\tilde{z}\cap fn(Q)=\varnothing$$

Provably Secure Mobile Key Exchange: Applying the Canetti-Krawczyk Approach

Yiu Shing Terry Tin, Colin Boyd, and Juan Manuel González Nieto

Information Security Research Centre,
Queensland University of Technology.
PO Box 2434, Brisbane, QLD 4001, Australia.
{t.tin,c.boyd,j.gonzaleznieto}@qut.edu.au

Abstract. Practical use of the Canetti and Krawczyk approach to development of proven secure key exchange protocols is explored. The suite of protocols that can be developed using existing building blocks is discussed. An additional building block is provided by proving a new protocol secure in the ideal model of the approach. In the application area of wireless protocols it is shown that the best existing protocols can be matched with versions carrying security proofs. We conclude that building a library of building blocks will allow protocols with proven security to become the norm rather than the exception.

1 Introduction

Informal analysis of authenticated key-exchange (AKE) protocols can provide some confidence in their correctness. However, experience has shown time and again that AKE protocols are likely to contain flaws even after an informal analysis is completed. In recent years it has become increasingly common to expect a formal analysis, and preferably a mathematical proof, of any published AKE protocol in order to obtain increased confidence in its security.

Proofs for AKE protocols were first provided by Bellare and Rogaway [3, 4]. Although their initial model only covered the case where two parties already share a long-term secret it has been extended, by themselves and others, to cover all the main types of AKE protocols. The proofs follow the style of most proofs in modern cryptography by reducing the security of the protocol to the security of some underlying primitive. A limitation of these proofs is that they tend to be complex and difficult for practitioners. Even more important from our viewpoint is that they are monolithic and fragile. A small change in the protocol structure can destroy the proof and leave no indication of how to repair it.

A modular approach to proving security was introduced by Bellare, Canetti and Krawczyk [1] in 1998. There were some drawbacks with the original formulation [16], and subsequently the model was modified and extended by Canetti and Krawczyk [7] at Eurocrypt 2001; this is what we refer to as the *Canetti–Krawczyk (CK) approach* in this paper. Roughly the idea is that the confidentiality and authentication elements of the protocol are separated so that they can be analysed independently and combined in a modular fashion.

R. Safavi-Naini and J. Seberry (Eds.): ACISP 2003, LNCS 2727, pp. 166–179, 2003.
© Springer-Verlag Berlin Heidelberg 2003

There are two types of fundamental building blocks that are used in the CK approach. The first type are protocols that are secure in an idealised model, the so-called *authenticated-links adversarial model (AM)*, where all communications between parties are "magically" authenticated. We call these protocols *AM protocols*. The second type of building blocks are protocol translators known as *authenticators*. Authenticators are used to transform AM protocols into protocols that are secure in a more realistic model, the so-called *unauthenticated-links adversarial model (UM)*. In principle any authenticator (possibly more than one) can be used with any AM protocol, so that there is a multiplying effect as new building blocks are found of either type.

Bellare *et al.* [1] introduced two authenticators based on public key primitives, one using encryption and one using signatures. Canetti and Krawczyk [7] added a third authenticator which relies on the existence of shared keys. Only two AM protocols are provided in the previous work; one of these is the basic Diffie-Hellman key agreement and the other is key transport through public key encryption. One of the main contributions of this paper is to propose and prove secure a new AM protocol. By applying the two public key based authenticators mentioned above this results immediately in two new proven secure protocols.

Application to Mobile Security. Not all protocols are well-suited for use in a mobile environment because of the limited computational capabilities of user devices. Therefore many researchers have developed protocols which take into account the special requirements. One useful technique is to arrange a computational imbalance between the two protocol principals so that the user device has a smaller computational load than the server. Another trick is to rely on pre-computation of certain cryptographic values which can be calculated by mobile devices during idle time. Despite such measures, protocols frequently sacrifice security properties in order to achieve greater efficiency. For example, AKE protocols for mobile devices often do not possess the *forward secrecy* property which protects old session keys when a long-term secret is compromised.

As an application of the CK approach we explore the development of secure AKE protocols suitable for the mobile environment. We use as a benchmark a recent study by Horn, Martin and Mitchell [10] of protocols suitable for the mobile environment. They identify two protocols, from those proposed in the literature, which provide most of the desirable properties for mobile communications.

Main Contributions. We regard the following as the main contributions.

- A new basic protocol proven secure in the ideal model or so-called authenticated links model of Canetti and Krawczyk.
- New applications of the modular approach of Canetti and Krawczyk in the mobile environment.
- Two examples of protocols optimised for the mobile environment which hold formal proofs of security.

Organisation. The rest of this paper has three main sections. Section 2 provides an outline of the CK approach. We illustrate in Sect. 3 how to apply the method to obtain a protocol not included in the original papers. Section 4 describes our new protocol in the ideal (AM) model and provides a security proof. We then apply the signature-based authenticator to our new AM-secure protocol to obtain a new secure protocol in the real world (UM). Section 5 compares the suitability and performance of the protocols derived in the previous two sections with the two best protocols identified by Horn, Martin and Mitchell [10] as most suitable for the mobile environment followed by conclusion.

Notation. The following notation is used throughout this paper. $\mathcal{E}_K$ and $\mathcal{D}_K$ denote encryption and decryption, respectively, under the symmetric key K. Similarly, $\mathcal{E}_{PK_A}$ and $\mathcal{D}_{SK_A}$ denote encryption and decryption under the public and private key pairs (PK_A, SK_A) of an entity A. The signature on a message m by entity A is denoted by $Sig_A(m)$ and a hash function is denoted by h. $r \in_R \{0,1\}^\kappa$ denotes a string chosen at random from the set of all strings of bit-length κ. We use $x \in_R \mathbb{Z}$ to denote that x is chosen uniformly at random from the set $\mathbb{Z}$.

2   The Model

In the CK model the definition of security for key-exchange (KE) protocols follows the tradition of Bellare and Rogaway [2], and is based on a game played between the adversary and the parties $P_1, \ldots, P_n$. In this game, protocol π is modeled as a collection of n programs running at different parties $P_1, \ldots, P_n$. Each program is an interactive probabilistic polynomial-time (PPT) machine. Each invocation of π within a party is defined as a *session*, and each party may have multiple sessions running concurrently. The communications network is controlled by an adversary $\mathcal{A}$, also a PPT machine, which schedules and mediates all sessions between the parties. $\mathcal{A}$ may activate a party P_i in two ways:

1. By means of an establish-session(P_i, P_j, s) request, where P_j is another party with whom the key is to be established, and s is a session-id string which uniquely identifies a session between the participants. Note that session-id is chosen by the adversary, with the restriction that it has to be unique among all sessions between the two parties involved. This allows the delivery of messages to the right protocol instantiation within a party. In practice, the session-id is negotiated by the communicating parties during a preamble to the actual KE protocol.
2. By means of an *incoming message* m with a specified sender P_j.

A restriction on how the adversary activates parties exists depending on which of the following two adversarial models is being considered:

- *Authenticated-links adversarial Model (AM)* defines an idealised adversary that is not allowed to generate, inject, modify, replay and deliver messages of its choice except if the message is purported to come from a corrupted party. Thus, an *AM–adversary* can only activate parties using incoming messages that were generated by other parties in π.

- *The Unauthenticated-links adversarial Model (UM)* is a more realistic model in which the adversary does not have the above restriction. Thus, a *UM–adversary* can fabricate messages and deliver any messages of its choice.

Upon activation, the parties do some computations, update their internal state, and may output messages which include the identity of the intended receiver. Two activated parties P_i and P_j are said to have a *matching session* if they have sessions whose session-ids are identical and they recognised each other as their respective communicating partner for the session. In addition to the activation of parties, A can perform the following actions:

1. A may *corrupt* a party P_i at will, by issuing the query corrupt(P_i), and learn the entire current state of P_i including long-term secrets, session internal states and session keys. From this point on, A may issue any message in which P_i is specified as the sender and play the role of P_i;
2. A may issue the query session-key(P_i, s), which returns the session key (if any) accepted by P_i during a given session s;
3. A may issue the query session-state(P_i, s), which returns all the internal state information of party P_i associated to a particular session s;
4. A may issue the query test-session(P_i, s). To respond to this query, a random bit $b \in_R \{0,1\}$ is selected. If $b = 1$ then the session key is returned. Otherwise, return a random key chosen from the probability distribution of keys generated by the protocol. This query can only be issued to a session that has not been *exposed*, i.e that has not been the subject of a session-state or session-key queries, and whose involved parties have not been corrupted.

During the game, the adversary performs a test-session query to a party and session of its choice. After that, the adversary is not allowed to expose the test-session. A may continue with its regular actions with the exception that no more test-session queries can be issued. Eventually A outputs a bit b' as its guess on whether the value returned value is the session key or a random number, then halts. A wins the game if $b = b'$. The definition of security follows.

Definition 1. *A KE protocol π is called* SK-secure *without perfect forward secrecy in the AM if the following properties are satisfied for any AM-adversary A.*

1. *If two uncorrupted parties complete matching sessions then they both output the same key;*
2. *The probability that A guesses correctly the bit b is no more than $\frac{1}{2}$ plus a negligible fraction in the security parameter.*

The definition of SK-secure protocols in the UM is done analogously. In this paper we only consider KE protocols without *forward secrecy*. We refer the reader to [7] for definitions of SK-security with forward secrecy. By distinguishing between the AM and the UM, Canetti and Krawczyk allow for a modular approach to the design of SK-secure protocols. Protocols that are SK-secure in the AM can be converted into SK-secure protocols in the UM by applying a so-called *authenticator*. An authenticator is a protocol translator $\mathcal{C}$ that takes as input a protocol π and outputs another protocol $\pi' = \mathcal{C}(\pi)$, with the property that if π is SK-secure in the AM, then π' is SK-secure in the UM. Authenticators can be constructed by applying a *message transmission (MT) authenticator* to each of the messages of the input protocol. Bellare *et al.* [1] and Canetti and Krawczyk [7] provide three examples of MT-authenticators. In the next section we describe one of them and illustrate how it can be used to obtain a SK-secure protocol in the UM from a SK-secure protocol in the AM.

3   Example of Modularly Designed KE Protocol

The CK approach to the design of SK-secure protocols in the UM consists of the following three steps:

CK1. Design a basic protocol and prove it SK-secure in the AM.

CK2. Design an authenticator and prove that it is valid.

CK3. Apply the authenticator to the basic protocol to produce a protocol that is automatically secure in the UM. If necessary, re-order and re-use message components to optimise the resulting protocol.

We illustrate the use of the approach by applying the three step process to derive a proven secure protocol which will be useful in Sect. 5 for protocol comparison. For step CK1 we need an AM protocol with a security proof. In this case we will use the protocol ENC, shown in Fig. 1 which was proven secure in the AM by Canetti and Krawczyk. As specified in Sect. 2, s denotes a session identifier known by both parties.

$$
\begin{array}{ccc}
P_i & & P_j \\
x \in_R \{0,1\}^\kappa & & \\
c = \mathcal{E}_{PK_{P_j}}(x) & \xrightarrow{P_i, s, c} & x' = \mathcal{D}_{SK_{P_j}}(c) \\
K = h(x, P_i, P_j, s) & & K' = h(x', P_i, P_j, s)
\end{array}
$$

Fig. 1. The AM Protocol ENC

Theorem 1 ([7]). *If the encryption scheme is secure against chosen ciphertext attack and h is pseudorandom, then protocol ENC is SK-secure without forward secrecy in the AM.*

For step CK2 we need an appropriate authenticator. We will construct the authenticator by applying an MT-authenticator to each of the messages exchanged in the protocol of Fig. 1. For practical reasons, it is useful to have a signed message as part of the protocol interaction in the mobile security application. This is because there are payment instructions that needs to be signed which can be included inside the signature used for key exchange. We therefore choose to use the signature based MT-authenticator of Bellare *et al.* [1] shown in Fig. 2.

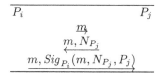

$$P_i \qquad\qquad\qquad\qquad\qquad P_j$$
$$\overset{m}{\longrightarrow}$$
$$\overset{m, N_{P_j}}{\longleftarrow}$$
$$\overset{m, Sig_{P_i}(m, N_{P_j}, P_j)}{\longrightarrow}$$

Fig. 2. Signature Based MT-authenticator

Since the AM-protocol ENC has only one message, step CK3 is completely straightforward. The message m and the nonce N_{P_j} is replaced by (P_i, s, c) and y respectively for generating a three move protocol in the UM. Some of the protocol elements such as fields in m have been eliminated in the second and third messages because of their redundancy. The session-id s remains in the protocol for supporting concurrent sessions. The resultant SK-secure protocol is illustrated in Fig. 3, named SIG-ENC.

P_i		P_j
$x \in_R \{0,1\}^\kappa$		$y \in_R \{0,1\}^\kappa$
$c = \mathcal{E}_{PK_{P_j}}(x)$	$\overset{P_i, s, c}{\longrightarrow}$	
$K = h(x, P_i, P_j, s)$	$\overset{s, y}{\longleftarrow}$	$x' = \mathcal{D}_{SK_{P_j}}(c)$
	$\overset{s, Sig_{P_i}(P_i, s, c, y, P_j)}{\longrightarrow}$	$K' = h(x', P_i, P_j, s)$

Fig. 3. The SK-secure Protocol SIG-ENC in the UM

Both parties are assumed to known s before running the protocol. This can be achieved during a prologue message exchange between the two parties prior to the execution of the actual protocol. For example, P_i sends a nonce s_i to P_j, similarly P_j sends a nonce s_j to P_i, and both make $s = (s_i, s_j)$. This is quite practical, without incurring into much extra communications overhead, since most implementation of KE protocols require a protocol preamble in which parties exchange parameters such as cryptographic capabilities. Alternatively, Canetti and Krawczyk suggest that s can be generated in real time during the execution of the protocol without compromising its security by having P_i include s_i in the first message, P_j include s_j in the second message and making sure that $s = (s_i, s_j)$ is included in the signature of third message. In our case we can make $s_i = c$, and $s_j = y$. Apart from being inputs to the generation of the session-id, c is a challenge computed by P_i for P_j and y is a random number generated by P_j for P_i. We replace s with (c, y) and remove redundant protocol elements.

Note that both parties have partial knowledge of s before the protocol execution, P_i knows c and P_j knows y. The knowledge of the *complete* s at both parties becomes possible only after the arrival of the second flow at P_i.

4   A New Provably Secure Protocol

In this section we propose a new basic protocol and prove it SK-secure in the AM. It is a new building block which can be used many times for designing provably secure protocols. An example of its use is shown in Sect. 4.2.

Jakobsson and Pointcheval [12] proposed a secure key exchange with mutual authentication for low-power mobile devices, and provided a security proof in the UM based on same assumptions as our new protocol. Unfortunately, the protocol in the pre-proceedings was vulnerable to a variant of interleaving attacks [?,9], a so-called "hijacking attack" by Wong and Chan [17].

As a countermeasure, Wong and Chan [17] proposed a new protocol scheme with a security proof within a variant of Bellare-Rogaway model [3,4] which is also in the UM. The published protocol was later found to be vulnerable to a variant of unknown key share attacks [5].

The above two scenarios suggested that providing proofs in the real world is more error-prone due to the complexity of the model. The real world model often deals with both authentication and key agreement at the same time and increases complexity and difficulty. In addition, the proofs done in the real world can not be reused as a minor change in the protocol may destroy the validation of the proofs. In comparison, proofs done in the ideal world can be reused as a building block such that applying an authenticator generates a new proven secure protocol in the real world.

4.1   A New SK-Secure Protocol in the AM

Figure 4 shows the protocol that we are going to prove SK-secure in the AM. It is a Diffie-Hellman [8] variant without providing forward secrecy. Hereafter, we refer to it as the DHM protocol. The notation used in the protocol is as follows. Let p and q be two primes such that $q|(p-1)$. $G = \langle g \rangle$ is a subgroup of order q of the multiplicative group $\mathbb{Z}_p^*$ of integers modulo a prime p. (y_j, g^{y_j}) is the private-public key pair of P_j. The public keys and g,p and q are publicly known.

P_i		P_j
$x \in_R \mathbb{Z}_q$		
$a = (g^{y_j})^x$	$\xrightarrow{\;P_i, s, g^x\;}$	$a' = (g^x)^{y_j}$
$K = h(a, P_i, P_j, s, g^x)$		$K' = h(a', P_i, P_j, s, g^x)$

Fig. 4. The Protocol DHM

In what follows, we show that the DHM protocol is SK-secure in the AM provided that the so-called Gap Diffie-Hellman (GDH) problem [13] is hard and that

h is an ideal hash function in the tradition of the *random oracle model* of Bellare and Rogaway [2]. Informally, the GDH problem entails breaking the Computational Diffie-Hellman (CDH) having the assistance of a Decisional Diffie-Hellman (DDH) oracle. Given a triplet (g, g^u, g^v) of elements in G, the CDH problem entails finding g^{uv}. A DDH oracle, given a quadruple (g, g^u, g^v, g^w) of elements in G, outputs 1 if $w = uv \mod q$ and 0 otherwise. A more formal definition of the GDH assumption is as follows.

Assumption 1 (GDH) *Let p, q be primes, where q is of length κ bits and $q|p-1$. Let G be the subgroup of $\mathbb{Z}_p^*$ generated by an element g of order q, and $\mathcal{DDH}$ be a DDH oracle for G. Then, for any probabilistic polynomial time (in κ) algorithm $\mathcal{X}$,*

$$\Pr[\mathcal{X}^{\mathcal{DDH}}(p, g, g^u, g^v) = g^{uv}] \leq \epsilon(\kappa),$$

where $u, v \in_R \mathbb{Z}_q$, and where $\epsilon(\kappa)$ is negligible. The superscript in $\mathcal{X}^{\mathcal{DDH}}$ denotes that $\mathcal{X}$ has oracle access to $\mathcal{DDH}$. The probability is taken over the coin tosses of $\mathcal{X}$, the choice of p, q, g and the random choices of u and v in $\mathbb{Z}_q$.

Remark 1. The security of protocol DHM assumes that operations related to the computation of session keys are executed in a separate secure module. In other words only the value K (resp. K') is revealed by the session-state query, but not a (resp. a') and the long-term secret y_j. This assumption is required for protocol DHM to be secure in the model due to the lack of forward secrecy, otherwise the protocol allows an attacker $\mathcal{A}$ to answer test-session queries correctly with non-negligible probability using the following mechanism. Assuming that a test-session query has been made for communications between parties P_i and P_j where P_i sent (P_i, s, g^x) to P_j, $\mathcal{A}$ proceeds as follows:

1. $\mathcal{A}$ corrupts a party $P_{l \neq i,j}$ and takes control of the party;
2. $\mathcal{A}$ then impersonates as P_l and sends $P_l, s' \neq s, g^x$ to P_j;
3. Once P_j accepts the values P_l, s', g^x sent by $\mathcal{A}$ and stores the temporary value $a'_{lj} = g^{xy_j}$ in the state of session s', the attacker $\mathcal{A}$ issues a session-state query to P_j for session s' and learns a'_{lj};
4. With the knowledge of a'_{lj}, $\mathcal{A}$ computes $K_{\mathcal{A}} = h(a'_{lj}, P_i, P_j, s, g^x)$ which is the session key corresponding to the unexposed session s between P_i and P_j since $a'_{lj} = a_{ij}$.

Alternatively, without the use of a separate module a weakened model can be used where session-state queries are not allowed so that all internal state values are only accessible via corrupt queries which expose all sessions associated with the party. Remember that once a party is corrupted, no test-session query can be made to sessions involving the corrupted party.

Remark 2. As mentioned in the beginning of Sect. 4, a protocol was proven secure by Jakobsson and Pointcheval [12] in the UM. Their protocol applies the same mechanism for deriving a session key as our new protocol in the AM. More precisely our new protocol is the core for key agreement and can be used for deriving their protocol by adding mutual authentication. We stress that their proof cannot be reused for other protocols as a minor change in the protocol requires a complete revision of the proof. In comparison our new protocol is reusable as an AM building block for generating secure protocols in the UM without providing security proofs again, thus increasing efficiency.

Theorem 2. *Under the GDH assumption and assuming that h behaves as a random oracle, protocol DHM is SK-secure without forward secrecy in the AM.*

Proof. Protocol DHM satisfies both properties of Definition 1 and hence it is SK-secure in the AM (without forward secrecy). The first property of Definition 1 is easy to verify. Thus, we concentrate on demonstrating the second property.

Let $\mathcal{A}$ be an adversary that has a non-negligible success probability $\nu(\kappa)$ in the AM against protocol DHM. We construct another algorithm $\mathcal{X}$ that uses $\mathcal{A}$ as a subroutine and with access to a DDH oracle, that on input a test instance for the CDH problem, $(p, g, A = g^u, B = g^v)$, where A and B are randomly and independently generated as required in Assumption 1, outputs g^{uv} with non-negligible probability, thus contradicting the assumption.

Let q_s be the maximum number of sessions that can be invoked by $\mathcal{A}$ in a simulated interaction with all parties $P_1, \ldots, P_n$. Both q_s and n are polynomial in κ. Out of the n principals, $\mathcal{X}$ selects at random one of them, P^*. This represents $\mathcal{X}$'s guess at the party that will play the role of responder in the test-session (the session on which $\mathcal{A}$ decides to be tested). Similarly, $\mathcal{X}$ tries to guess the test-session by choosing an integer r at random in $\{1, \ldots, q_s\}$, representing the rth session invoked by $\mathcal{A}$.

When $\mathcal{X}$ executes $\mathcal{A}$, $\mathcal{X}$ simulates the participants in the protocol and answers all queries performed by $\mathcal{A}$. We model the hash function in the protocol as a random oracle. Each new hash query is answered with a random value. If the query was asked previously, then the same value as before is returned. All hash queries and their answers are stored by $\mathcal{X}$ in a table H in the form of $m = h(a, P_i, P_j, s, g^x)$. $\mathcal{X}$ also maintains a table T in which entries are stored in the form of $t = h(P_i, P_j, s, g^x)$ where t is a random value of the same length as m. $\mathcal{X}$ assigns long term keys to the parties as follows. Each principal P_i different from P^* is assigned private and public key-pairs (y_i, g^{y_i}) where y_i is chosen randomly from $\mathbb{Z}_q$. Participant P^* is assigned a public key $B = g^v$ with no private key. $\mathcal{X}$ keeps a record of all protocol runs. $\mathcal{A}$ is then run on input (p, q, g) and the public keys of $P_1, \ldots, P_n$. All queries made by $\mathcal{A}$ are answered by $\mathcal{X}$ as follows.

- Whenever $\mathcal{A}$ activates a party to send or receive a message in a session different from the rth session, $\mathcal{X}$ responds normally as per protocol DHM specification. Thus, when session (P_i, P_j, s) is activated within P_i to establish a key with P_j, $\mathcal{X}$ chooses x at random and computes g^x on behalf of P_i, and then returns the message (P_i, s, g^x) to $\mathcal{A}$. $\mathcal{X}$ simulates the responder P_j by simply accepting the message. Note that there is no need for $\mathcal{X}$ to compute the session key at this stage.

- If the rth session, say $(P_{i'}, P_{j'}, s')$ is invoked within a party $P_{i'}$ to establish a key with party $P_{j'}$, then if $P_{j'} \neq P^*$, $\mathcal{X}$ terminates the execution of $\mathcal{A}$ and fails. Otherwise, $\mathcal{X}$ returns the message $(P_{i'}, s', A)$ to $\mathcal{A}$.
- If $\mathcal{A}$ tries to expose the rth session by issuing a session-key or session-state query to its partner oracles, then $\mathcal{X}$ terminates the execution of $\mathcal{A}$ and fails.
- All exposures for sessions different from the rth session that do not involve P^* as the responder can be answered in a straight-forward way by $\mathcal{X}$, since $\mathcal{X}$ knows the private key of the responder. (Recall that operations related to the computation of session keys are executed in a separate secure module as discussed in Remark 1.) Exposures of sessions different from the rth session in which the responder is P^* are dealt by $\mathcal{X}$ as follows. Let P_i be the initiator of the session and s be the session identifier.
  - If P_i was uncorrupted for the session, then $\mathcal{X}$ chose x and hence it can answer the query as normal.
  - If P_i was corrupted for the session, then $\mathcal{X}$ does not know x but it can obtain g^x from the record of protocol runs and responds as follows. $\mathcal{X}$ looks up the table H for an entry where $m = h(a, P_i, P^*, s, g^x)$ for some a satisfying $\mathcal{DDH}(g, g^x, B, a) = 1$. If such an entry exists then $\mathcal{X}$ returns m. Otherwise $\mathcal{X}$ returns a random value t of the same size of m and creates a new entry in T as $t = h(P_i, P^*, s, g^x)$. This value will be returned if a hash query $h(a, P_i, P^*, s, g^x)$ is made such that $\mathcal{DDH}(g, g^x, B, a) = 1$.
- If a corruption query is made against $P_{i'}$ or P^*, $\mathcal{X}$ terminates the execution of $\mathcal{A}$ and fails. All other corruption queries to principals different from $P_{i'}$ and P^* can be answered by $\mathcal{X}$ since it knows the corresponding private keys.
- If $\mathcal{A}$ selects a session different from the rth session as the test-session, then $\mathcal{X}$ aborts the execution of $\mathcal{A}$ and fails. If $\mathcal{A}$ issues a test-session query against a participant of the rth session, $\mathcal{X}$ answers the query by returning a random session key value.

At some stage, if not aborted by $\mathcal{X}$, $\mathcal{A}$ completes. It is not difficult to see that, unless $\mathcal{A}$ is aborted by $\mathcal{X}$, the above simulation is perfect. The above interaction allows prediction of the Diffie-Hellman of A and B. By assumption $\mathcal{A}$ has a non-negligible success probability $\nu(\kappa)$ against DHM. As $\mathcal{A}$ can gain no advantage in guessing any key for which the random oracle is not queried, $\mathcal{X}$ examines all queries made by $\mathcal{A}$ of the form $h(C, P_{i'}, P_{j'}, s', D)$ for any value C satisfying $\mathcal{DDH}(g, D, B, C) = 1$ and outputs the corresponding C. Otherwise it returns 'fail'. The probability that $\mathcal{X}$ correctly guesses the correct session and session responder for the test query is $1/(nq_s)$. Hence, $\mathcal{X}$'s success probability is

$$\Pr[\mathcal{X}(p, g, A, B) = g^{uv}] = \frac{\nu(\kappa)}{nq_s}$$

which, as we wanted to show, is non-negligible.

4.2   A New SK-Secure Protocol in the UM

We now demonstrate the practical usefulness of the AM-secure protocol DHM of Fig. 4. Since the protocol DHM is SK-secure in the AM, any authenticators can be applied. As mentioned in Sect. 3 we will use the signature-based MT-authenticator of Fig. 2 for deriving UM protocols in this paper. As a result, we obtain a UM SK-secure protocol SIG-DHM of Fig. 5 which provides unilateral authentication and implicit mutual authentication.

P_i		P_j
$x \in_R \mathbb{Z}_q$		$r \in_R \mathbb{Z}_q$
$a = (g^y)^x$	$\xrightarrow{P_i, s, g^x}$	
	$\xleftarrow{s, r}$	$a' = (g^x)^y$
$K = h(a, P_i, P_j, s, g^x)$	$\xrightarrow{s, Sig_{P_i}(P_i, s, g^x, r, P_j)}$	$K' = h(a', P_i, P_j, s, g^x)$

Fig. 5. The Protocol SIG-DHM

Without losing generality, the protocol performance is measured in terms of number of times the cryptographic operations have to be performed of both the client (protocol initiator) and server (protocol responder). The certificate of the server is assumed to be transmitted via an out-of-band channel before running the protocol and thus is not included as part of our performance measurement.

5   Protocol Comparison for Mobile Communications

Horn, Martin and Mitchell [10] compared and analysed seven protocols designed for the mobile environment in order to determine their suitability in terms of security, efficiency and the ability to support payment mechanisms. Their security analysis was informal, based on the systematic inspection of a list of common attacks. Two protocol candidates were identified as being particularly suitable for mobile communications. They are the Boyd-Park [6] and ASPeCT [11] protocols because of their minimal computational requirements. The latter was regarded as the best of the seven candidates. We use their evaluations on Boyd-Park and ASPeCT protocols to compare against SIG-ENC of Fig. 3 and SIG-DHM of Fig. 5, respectively. In particular, we compare their suitability for mobile communications in regards of the following goals:

1. Mutual entity authentication of participants.
2. Mutual key agreement between participants with joint key control.
3. Mutual assurance of key freshness of participants.
4. Support of payment mechanism and non-repudiation of payments.

Protocol Goals of the Boyd-Park and SIG-ENC Protocol. The Boyd-Park protocol assessed by Horn et al. [10] was different to that in the original paper of Boyd and Park [6]. They removed the detection field [14] for cloning fraud in mobile handsets from the protocol. We illustrate the modified version in Fig. 6 and use it for our needs.

$$
\begin{array}{ll}
P_i & P_j \\
x \in_R \{0,1\}^\kappa & y \in_R \{0,1\}^\kappa
\end{array}
$$

$$\xrightarrow{\mathcal{E}_{PK_{P_j}}(P_i, x)}$$

$$\xleftarrow{y, \mathcal{E}_K(x)}$$

$$K' = h(x,y) \quad \xrightarrow{Sig_{P_i}[P_j, h(y, K')]} \quad K = h(x,y)$$

Fig. 6. The Boyd-Park Protocol

Both the Boyd-Park and SIG-ENC protocol seem to satisfy all goals except the last one which can be achieved by including payment parameters as part of the signature. The former supports explicit key confirmation by $\mathcal{E}_K(x)$ for P_j to P_i and $h(y, K')$ for P_i to P_j and the latter achieves mutual authentication implicitly. Both protocols use a hash function to derive session keys and are capable of providing user anonymity if an appropriate signature scheme such as Schnorr [15] type signature or a suitable variant is used.

Protocol Goals of the ASPeCT and SIG-DHM Protocol. The simplified version of the ASPeCT protocol [11] is shown in Fig. 7 in which the certified public keys and other parameters used for charging and payment data are eliminated. Let g^y and y be the public and private keys of P_j, the function h_1 be preimage resistant, h_2 be partial-preimage resistant and h_3 be collision resistant.

$$
\begin{array}{ll}
P_i & P_j \\
x \in_R \mathbb{Z}_q & r \in_R \mathbb{Z}_q
\end{array}
$$

$$\xrightarrow{g^x}$$

$$K' = h_1[r, (g^y)^x] \quad \xleftarrow{r, h_2(K, r, P_j)} \quad K = h_1[r, (g^x)^y]$$

$$H = h_3(g^x, g^y, r, P_j) \quad \xrightarrow{\mathcal{E}_{K'}[Sig_{P_i}(H)]}$$

Fig. 7. Simplified ASPeCT Protocol

Although the ASPeCT and SIG-DHM protocol seem to be different, they both apply the same mechanism for key agreement. The former supports explicit key confirmation and mutual authentication by using three different hash functions while the latter supports implicit mutual authentication without key confirmation. We stress that the latter can easily be modified for supporting the same features as the former, but with the cost of increased protocol complexity and higher cryptographic tools requirements.

Performance of Protocols. Table 1 lists the number of computational operations that protocol participants perform. We denote I the protocol initiator (client) and R the protocol responder (server). (1) indicates the operation that can be computed offline and the participant is required to perform it once.

Table 1. Computational Loads of the Protocols

Computational Operation	Protocol							
	Boyd-Park		SIG-ENC		ASPeCT		SIG-DHM	
	I	R	I	R	I	R	I	R
Exponentiation	0	0	0	0	(2)	1	(2)	1
Asymmetric Encryption	(1)	0	(1)	0	0	0	0	0
Asymmetric Decryption	0	1	0	1	0	0	0	0
Signature Generation	1	0	1	0	1	0	1	0
Signature Verification	0	1	0	1	0	1	0	1

For the sake of simplicity, the table does not include the count of hash functions, symmetric encryption and decryption operations, but only operations regarded as expensive. In that regard, the performance of SIG-ENC is exactly the same as Boyd-Park protocol so as the pair SIG-DHM and ASPeCT protocols.

6   Conclusion

According to the comparison performed in Sect. 5, we have demonstrated that the use of modular approach for designing secure protocols will not introduce a negative impact on protocol performance and usability. Protocols carrying security proofs are as efficient as some of the most efficient protocols without security proofs. We may alter SIG-DHM to reproduce ASPeCT protocol by adding key conformation and explicit mutual authentication to it. An additional bonus of designing secure protocols modularly is that building blocks are reusable without providing a new proof. More building blocks imply more possible combinations of provably secure protocols in the UM.

References

1. Mihir Bellare, Ran Canetti, and Hugo Krawczyk. A modular approach to the design and analysis of authentication and key exchange protocols. In *Proceedings of the 30th Annual Symposium on the Theory of Computing, ACM*, pages 412–428, 1998. Full version at http://www-cse.ucsd.edu/users/mihir/papers/modular.pdf.
2. Mihir Bellare and Phillip Rogaway. Random oracles are practical: A paradigm for designing efficient protocols. In *First ACM Conference on Computer and Communications Security*, pages 62–73, 1993.

3. Mihir Bellare and Phillip Rogaway. Entity authentication and key distribution. In *Advances in Cryptology - Crypto 1993*, volume 773 of *LNCS*, pages 232–249. Springer-Verlag, 1994. Full version at `http://www-cse.ucsd.edu/users/mihir/papers/eakd.pdf`.
4. Mihir Bellare and Phillip Rogaway. Provably secure session key distribution - the three party case. In *Proceedings of the 27th ACM Symposium on the Theory of Computing*, pages 57–66, May 1995.
5. Simon Blake-Wilson and Alfred Menezes. Unknown key-share attacks on the station-to-station (sts) protocol. In *Public Key Cryptography 1999*, volume 1560 of *LNCS*, pages 154–170. Springer-Verlag, 1999.
6. C. Boyd and D.-G. Park. Public key protocols for wireless communications. *The 1998 International Conference on Information Security and Cryptology (ICISC '98)*, pages 47–57, 1998. Seoul, Korea.
7. Ran Canetti and Hugo Krawczyk. Analysis of key-exchange protocols and their use for building secure channels. In *Advances in Cryptology – Eurocrypt 2001*, volume 2045 of *LNCS*, pages 453–474. Springer-Verlag, 2001. Full version at `http://eprint.iacr.org/2001/040.ps`.
8. W. Diffie and M. Hellman. New direction in cryptography. *IEEE Transactions on Information Theory*, 22:644–654, 1976.
9. W. Diffie, P.C. van Oorschot, and M.J. Wiener. Authentication and authenticated key exchanges. *Designs, Codes and Cryptography*, 2:107–125, 1992.
10. Günther Horn, Keith M. Martin, and Chris J. Mitchell. Authentication protocols for mobile network environment value-added services. *IEEE Transactions on Vechicular Technology*, 51(2):383–392, 2002.
11. Günther Horn and Bart Preneel. Authentication and payment in future mobile systems. In *European Symposium on Research in Computer Security (ESORICS)*, volume 1485 of *LNCS*, pages 277–293. Springer-Verlag, 1998.
12. Markus Jakobsson and David Pointcheval. Mutual authentication for low-power mobile devices. In *Proceedings of Financial Cryptography 2001*, volume 2339 of *LNCS*, pages 178–195. Springer-Verlag, 2001.
13. Tatsuaki Okamoto and David Pointcheval. The gap-problems: a new class of problems for the security of cryptographic schemes. In *Public Key Cryptography 2001*, volume 1992 of *LNCS*, pages 104–118. Springer-Verlag, February 2001.
14. D.-G. Park, M.-N. Oh, and M. Looi. A fraud detection method and its application to third generation wireless systems. In *Proceedings of Globecom 98*, pages 1984–1989, 1998.
15. Claus P. Schnorr. Efficient signature generation by smart cards. *Journal of Cryptology 4*, pages 161–174, 1991.
16. Victor Shoup. On formal models for secure key exchange. Research Report RZ 3120, IBM Zurich Research Lab, 1999. Version 4 of 1999 revision of IBM Research Report RZ 3120 at `http://www.shoup.net/papers/skey.pdf`.
17. Duncan S. Wong and Agnes H. Chan. Efficient and mutually authenticated key exchange for low power computing devices. In *Advances in Cryptology – Asiacrypt 2001*, volume 2248 of *LNCS*, pages 272–289. Springer-Verlag, 2001.

Mobile PKI: A PKI-Based Authentication Framework for the Next Generation Mobile Communications*

Jabeom Gu[1], Sehyun Park[1], Ohyoung Song[1], Jaeil Lee[2],
Jaehoon Nah[3], and Sungwon Sohn[3]

[1] School of Electrical and Electronics Engineering,
Chung-Ang University, Seoul 156-756, Korea
jabeom@ms.cau.ac.kr, {shpark, song}@cau.ac.kr
[2] Korea Information Security Agency (KISA)
jilee@kisa.or.kr
[3] Electronics and Telecommunications Research Institute (ETRI)
{jhnah, swsohn}etri.re.kr

Abstract. The next generation mobile Internet is expected to develop towards "Always Best Connected (ABC)", or "Any Time, Any Where, Any Service", and provide completely open environments for interconnection with the external world through the IP-enabled structure. In addition to this, the support for new kinds of management such as service provisioning, customization, and personalization will lead to a more complicated network revolution. In the paper, we propose an authentication framework, which use PKI-based mutual authentication to establish trust relations between the communication entities and to guarantee minimized handover delay by extending the trust relations. The simulation results, in conjunction with the experiment conducted on a WLAN testbed, are presented that illustrate how the framework can best be applied to the next generation mobile environments.

1 Introduction

The dynamic growth of mobile communication technologies has fueled the efforts to realize "Any Where, Any Time, Any Service" in the next generation mobile Internet. Since these efforts are mainly intended to meet the demand of high quality of multimedia services, the importance of various kinds of contents and contents aware services as well as lower layer improvements will be more evident than ever [1-3, 17]. Furthermore, the 3rd Generation Partnership Project (3GPP) is planning to adopt the all-IP structure as its core network protocol to accommodate various software that are at present realized in wired networks, and integrate various kinds of hardware interface in the next generation mobile communication [4-6].

---

* This work was supported by the Information Telecommunication Researching Institute of Chung-Ang University in 2003.

R. Safavi-Naini and J. Seberry (Eds.): ACISP 2003, LNCS 2727, pp. 180–191, 2003.
© Springer-Verlag Berlin Heidelberg 2003

The mobile communication environments will make data highly available by providing various types of network architecture and enhanced quality of service in open environments. However, the advantage of these open mobile communication environments can be a liability unless well thought-out security is put into place to supplement the *openness*. The diversity of the network architecture and the all-IP structure adopted in the new environment will increase the complexity and the entities will unwillingly be exposed to the external. The openness implies that the vulnerabilities and attacks that exist in the wired networks can also be exploited for the new environment.

In the paper, we propose Mobile PKI to overcome the weakness of security structure in 'open' mobile communication environment. In addition, we will show the strength and practical feasibility of our new framework through performance analysis of several scenarios.

The rest of this paper is organized as follows: Section 2 discuss environmental features and new security requirements. Section 3 describes our network model and the concepts of trust and token. Section 4 details the Mobile PKI framework. Section 5 presents performance analyses of the proposed framework. We conclude the paper in Section 6.

2   New Security Requirements

Three major features of the next generation mobile communication model, outlined by the ITU, are as follows [7]:

- *Many network operators and global roaming*: The network domain consists of various types of service nodes and ranges from an office at the smallest, to a hot spot, a school, an industry, or a nation at the largest. Various network operators draw logical boundary of the domain. Since the mobile terminal should get seamless service while moving around between various domains, mutual authentication with an arbitrary entity should be possible. Furthermore, because different operator who has different security policy manages the domain, very complex interwork schemes between one domain and the other as well as between mobile terminal and domain are required.
- *Multiple wireless interfaces*: The open environment is not based on just one standard interface but various kinds of interfaces (for example, Bluetooth, Wireless LAN, and UMTS, etc.). Each interface suggests its own standard for security structure appropriate to the interface so that security between interfaces can not be guaranteed to extend during interwork in open environment.
- *All-IP structure*: It is not too much to say that All-IP is a must for open network structure to interconnect various software and hardware-interfaces. The weakness and the attacks existing in the wired IP network hold true to the next generation mobile communication.

Because of the weakness of physical security, the mobile communication system should include such security services as authentication, secrecy, privilege grant, accounting, and access control [7]. But the *opneness* of the next generation mobile communication system also intimates special security requirements such as:

- *Secure association supporting mutual authentication*: Continuous mutual authentication in various kinds of domains enables mobile terminals to get reliable service.
- *Security between network domains*: Secrecy should be kept by mutual authentication and encryption because information for communication connection is transmitted through all-IP network.
- *AAA extensible to the global*: It will be a very common situation that the mobile terminal is served from foreign domain, which requires indirect-billing between two different network operators, service provisioning without any pre-established user authentication or authorization. Consequently, to support the global roaming and meet the AAA requirements [18], the authentication and non-repudiation should be enforced in any place.

In the paper, we use the hierarchical PKI model [12] as a solution to satisfy these security requirements. It has been generally understood that the PKI achieves very strong functions at the cost of computation overhead. We propose a method to maximize the efficiency of PKI by *trust* and *token* and a framework suitable to use PKI in mobile communication environment.

3   Trust and Token for Mobile PKI

3.1   Mobile PKI Network Model

Fig. 1 shows the simplified network model of the mobile communication system. The network domains are classified into the *local domain*, which provides services to mobile terminals and the *home domain*, which manages authentication and accounting information for mobile terminals. We define the *domain controller* (DC) as the core nodes in the local domain. Since the domain controller contains such functions as location management, accounting, and authentication for mobile terminals, it works like GGSN (or SGSN) in GSM/UMTS [8, 9] and FA (Foreign Agent) in Mobile IP [14]. In order to control the access of the mobile terminal, the AP requests authentication result for the mobile terminal to the domain controller. The home domain manages mobile terminal information, and contains the nodes managing accounting and location. We define the *home environment* (HE) as th core nodes in the home domain. The functionality of the HE and the DC are exactly same, but are distinguished by where the mobile terminal is located and which HE it belongs to. It is assumed without loss of generality that the same Certification Authority (CA) that has certified the HE also certifies the mobile terminal that belongs to that HE. Fig. 1 shows this by a tree shaped certification path. It is also assumed that core networks are based on all-IP. All control information between the local domain and the home domain are transferred through the IP-network.

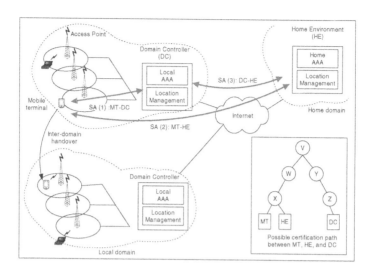

Fig. 1. Mobile PKI network model and secure associations between MT, DC, and HE. A possible certification path from DC to MT and HE is shown in the small box in the bottom. Certification path from MT to DC, for example, can be expressed as: X<W> W<V> V<Y> Y<Z> Z<DC>

All participating entities should establish trust relations with each other by secure association as shown in Fig. 1. In general, these secure associations should re-establish the trust relations and resume communication with the other peer whenever handover occurs. Consequently, repeated authentication, encryption, and decryption in the handover procedure will result in waste of resources for the all entities involved. In the paper, we propose *trust* and *token*, which are efficient mobility management scheme for the secure association with arbitrary domain controller and the frequent re-authentication that occur during the handover procedure.

3.2   Trust

To use the PKI for the purpose of authentication and access control, the access controller (AP) requires to assure whether the private key belongs to someone who claims and the certification path is valid. A valid certification path means that none of the certificates in the certification path has been revoked or has had its validity period expire. In this paper, we use the phrase "the *trust* for one entity has been generated" to mean that the identity of that entity has been confirmed, certificate path is valid, and then AAA requirements can be satisfied. A hypothetical certification path between the mobile terminal, the domain controller, and the home environment is shown in Fig. 1, where the V, X, X, Y, and Z represent the CA's. The certification path between the three entities changes depending on which domain the mobile terminal is located in.

Mutual authentication between the mobile terminal and the home environment can be easily enforced because we assumed that they have been certified by the same CA. For the mutual authentication between other entities, we use the 'indirect trust generation', which has two dimensions. First, indirect trust generation occurs when the mobile terminal tries to generate a trust for the domain controller. That is, the trust for the domain controller is generated 'indirectly' by the home environment rather than by the mobile terminal, considering trust generation process for the domain controller by the home environment has the same certification path as one by the mobile terminal, and the mobile terminal has limited resources. The home environment carries out the trust generation procedure as proxy for the mobile terminal, encrypts it, and transfers it to the mobile terminal. Second, indirect trust generation also occurs during the handover procedure, where the domain controller requires to generate trust for both the mobile terminal and the home environment. While the domain controller generates trust 'directly' in the initial authentication procedure, indirect trust generation is used for the re-authentication in the handover procedure. If an inter-domain handover occurs, the domain controller in the new domain receives the trust that the domain controller in the previous domain generated instead of generating new trust. This indirect trust generation relies on the trust relations between the two domain controllers involved, which can be pre-established because of their locality.

3.3   Token

The *token* is used to reduce the burden of repeated identification and authentication when the mobile terminal moves between AP's in a domain. While the domain controller generates the trust for the mobile terminal, it also grants a token to the mobile terminal for further access control in intra-domain handover. If the token is valid, the mobile terminal is allowed to move from AP to AP with seamless and efficient manner. The security of the token depends on the trust relation that has been established during the direct or indirect trust generation procedures. The lifetime of the token is limited to the domain boundary. In the inter-domain handover, a new token should be granted to the mobile terminal.

4   Mobile PKI Framework

4.1   Trust Based Full Authentication

We define the *full authentication* (FA) as the access control method by secure association and authentication between the mobile terminal, the domain controller, and the home environment using the *trust*. When a naive PKI based mutual authentication scheme is used between the three entities, the main problem is the limited computation power of the mobile terminal. The certification path between the mobile terminal and the domain controller may be so long that it can cause to exhaust the resources severely. Furthermore, data transfer for acquiring the certificates and the CRL's, which requires a lot of network bandwidth,

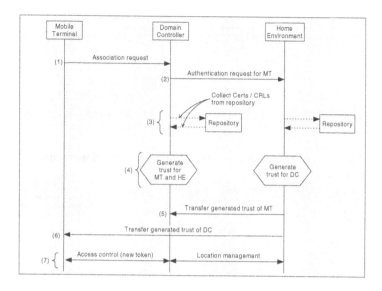

Fig. 2. Trust based full authentication procedure

is required even before the mobile terminal receives the access privilege to the network.

The full authentication shown in Fig. 2 proceeds as follows: (1) The domain controller receives the request from the mobile terminal, and (2) transfers it to the home environment. (3) The domain controller acquires the certificates and CRL's in the certification path for the home environment to verify the home environment. (4) The domain controller generates the trust for the home environment. The home environment generates the trust for the domain controller in similar way. (5) The home environment transfers the trust for the mobile terminal to the domain controller and (6) the trust for the domain controller to the mobile terminal. Since the domain controller has already generated the trust for home environment, it trusts the data that the home environment transfers. As a result, the domain controller additionally acquires the trust for the mobile terminal from the home environment and the mobile terminal does the trust for the domain controller. (7) The final step of the full authentication is for the domain controller to generate the token and grant it to the mobile terminal for further intra-domain handover. The trust based full association makes it unnecessary for the mobile terminal to acquire the certificates and the CRL's and verify them.

4.2   Simple and Extended Authentication

During the handover in the domain or between domains, the mobile terminal should be re-authenticated because access control, accounting, and its location management require new association. Fig. 3 shows the *simple authentication* that is used for the mobile terminal to move from AP to AP in the domain.

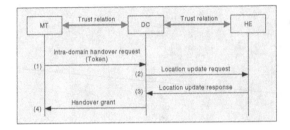

Fig. 3. Token based simple authentication for inter-domain handover

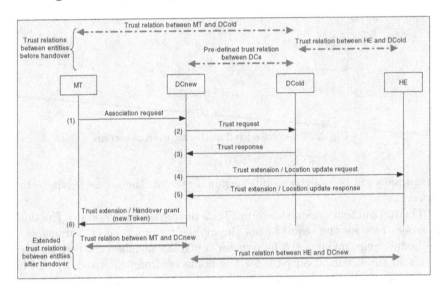

Fig. 4. Trust based extended authentication for inter-domain handover

(1) The mobile terminal transfers the token to the domain controller. (2) The domain controller confirms the token, and (3) modifies the location information. (4) The domain controller allows the mobile terminal to access the network if the token is valid. Even the simple authentication guarantees the security between the domain controller and the mobile terminal because the trust relation has been established by the full authentication. Fig. 4 shows how the *extended authentication* is used to reduce the authentication procedures for inter-domain handover. The figure explains the procedures the mobile terminal takes to move from DC_{old} to DC_{new}. (1) When DC_{new} receives handover request, (2) it sends a trust request to DC_{old}, and (3) receives the trust response (trust for the MT and HE) from DC_{old}. (4)(5) Also the predefined trust relation between DC_{new} and DC_{old} is informed to the home environment. Otherwise the home environment should authenticate the DC_{new}. (6) DC_{new} grants new token to the mobile terminal. Fig. 4 also shows the trust relations before and after handover. The trust relations before handover lie in $< MT \leftrightarrow DC_{old} >$, $< DC_{new} \leftrightarrow DC_{old} >$,

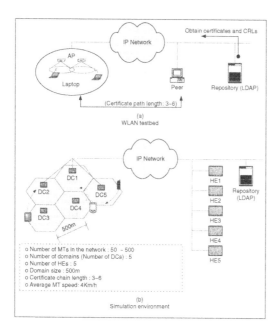

Fig. 5. Testbed and simulation environment

and $< DC_{old} \leftrightarrow HE >$. The trust relations after handover are newly formed in $< MT \leftrightarrow DC_{new} >$ and $< DC_{new} \leftrightarrow HE >$.

5 Performance Evaluation

5.1 Testbed and Simulation Environment

Fig. 5 shows testbed and simulation environment. The testbed was set up, as shown in Fig. 5(a), in the WLAN environment and tests were run to determine the simulation variables such as certificate-chain-validation-time when the chain length of the hierarchical X.509 structure is varied. In the testbed, a WLAN laptop that is equipped with Pentium III-450MHz acts as a mobile terminal and one desktop functions as a Domain Controller, which validate the authenticity of each other. The performance of the mobile terminal in our testbed is a bit higher than the PDA-class devices that are available today. But the recent improvement in functionality and performance of leading PDA platform and cell phone technology is likely to give more horsepower to various types of mobile terminals in the near future. The experiment results of our testbed could accordingly be applied to wide variety of mobile terminals such as cell phones and PDAs as well as laptops. The repository is implemented with LDAP (Lightweight Directory Access Protocol) located in the external network. The OpenSSL [11] library was modified to implement the certificate chain validation.

The experimental values obtained from the testbed and other simulation parameters are used to simulate and analyze the Mobile PKI. The OPNET [13] simulator is used for the simulation. Fig. 5(b) show the simulation environment. The network is consists of five equal sized domains (500 meters in diameter) and ten to twenty APs are placed in each domain. The Initial number of MTs in the entire network is varied from 50 to 500, and the speed of each MT has normal distribution from 1 to 7 kilometers per hour. A brief summary of simulation variable is given in the Table 1.

Table 1. Simulation parameters

Simulation parameter	Remark	Value
Hash function	MD5	100.7 MB/sec
Average digital signature time	RSA (512bits)	4.92 ms
Average digital signature verification time	RSA (512bits)	0.43 ms
	Chain length = 2	30 ms
Certificate chain validation time	Chain length = 3	43 ms
	Chain length = 4	60 ms
	Chain length = 5	76 ms
Average repository (LDAP) access time	CRL access	170 ms

5.2 Simulation Results

Full Authentication. Fig. 6(a) shows the distribution of delay caused during simulation of full authentication, where the initial number of mobile terminals in the network is 50, and the length of certification path is set from 2 to 6. The delays are randomly distributed ranging from 1.0 to 2.2 seconds. The delay characteristic becomes obvious when the delay is categorized by the certificate chain length and the number of MT's in the network as shown in Fig. 6(b). This figure shows that the increased delay gap due to the increase in certificate chain length outmeasure the one caused from the increased number of MT's in the network. (Every length increase by 1 adds about 20ms delay.) Although the full authentication procedure and consequent network traffic may have greater burden to both the network and the entities than they could afford when the number of MT's and certificate chain length are increased, it sets up a security association and trust relations between three entities in the initial association procedure. Furthermore, the use of the full authentication procedure is enforced only in the initial trust generation, which reduces the load of each entity once the trust is generated. Another advantage of the full authentication is that the minimum resources of the mobile terminal and the wireless link are used at the time of initial authentication.

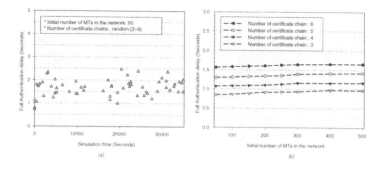

Fig. 6. Full authentication. (a) Distribution of full authentication delay. (b) Averaged full authentication delay vs. initial number of MT's in the network

Simple and Extended Authentication. Delay distributions of handover procedure are shown in Fig. 7(a). The intra-domain handover using simple authentication shows delay from 18 to 25 ms, while inter-domain handover based on the extend authentication shows delay from 40 to 50 ms. This means that the trust and token that are generated from the full authentication procedure increase the performance as we expected. Fig. 7(b) shows the handover delays of the two cases and delays of IEEE 802.11b [14] based open authentication and IEEE 802.1X [15] based authentication. Since IEEE 802.11b based open authentication uses simple request/response for association and the procedures for handover are not explicitly defined, the mobile terminal always performs the same association procedures whenever it moves to new AP. The delay of IEEE 802.11b based open authentication measured as 7-9ms and is shown for reference in Fig. 7(b) IEEE 802.1X also doesn't have any explicit procedure for handover. IEEE 802.1X based authenticated is simulated in the domain structure similar to that of our framework and the results are shown in Fig. 7(b). The delay of extended authentication is almost same as that of the IEEE 802.1X; while the delay of the simple authentication is reduced to about 50 percent. This represents valuable benefits: reduced handover delay, tight trust relation, and its extension.

Efficiency of Delegated Authentication Using Trust in Full Authentication. Table 2 shows the processing times spent on full authentication at the home environment (or the domain controller), and the mobile terminal with certification path length changed. Since the home environment and the domain controller should verify the certification path to generate the trust, the processing time increases as the certification path length does. On the other hand, since the mobile terminal processes indirect authentication using the information received from the home environment, even increasing certification path length does not add more burden. In the simulation, the delay is held constant at about 15ms.

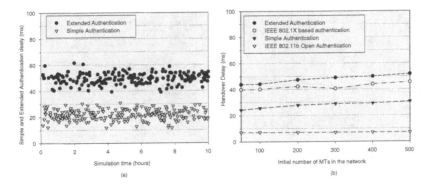

Fig. 7. Simple and extended authentication. (a) Distribution of simple and extended authentication delay in handover procedure. (b) Average handover delay as a function of number of MT's in the network. Delay of IEEE 802.11b open authentication for one MT is shown for reference

This result presents that our framework can be efficiently applicable to mobile terminals with limited system resources.

6   Conclusion

In the paper, we discussed the security requirements of the next generation mobile communication. In order to satisfy the requirements, we proposed a new security framework based on PKI called Mobile PKI. To evaluate the performance of the Mobile PKI, we set up and experimental testbed and measured the performance of PKI related functions such as certificate acquisition, verification, and encryption. These experiment results are sued to simulate the mobile terminal, the domain controller, and the home environment work with the full, the simple, and the extended authentication procedures. The simulation results show that the proposed framework is very promising in that it is able to reduce the load of the mobile terminal and the wireless link, and minimize the handover delay efficiently. Therefore, when the Mobile PKI framework is applied to mobile communication system such as pervasive computing environment, it is expected to make various multimedia services possible while support AAA efficiently.

Table 2. Efficiency of delegated trust generation

Certification chain length	2	3	4	5	6
Full Authentication processing time in HE or DC (in Seconds)	0.6401	0.7479	1.0638	1.2539	1.4622
Full Authentication request processing time in MT (in Seconds)	0.0141	0.0162	0.0158	0.0167	0.0148

References

1. M. Frodigh, S. Parkvall, C. Roobol, P. Johansson, P. Larsson: Future Generation Wireless Networks. IEEE Personal Communications, Vol. 8, No. 5, October 2001.
2. T. Otsu, I. Okajima, N. Umeda, Y. Yamao: Network Architecture for Mobile Communications Systems Beyond IMT-2000. IEEE Personal Communications, Vol.8, No. 5, October 2001.
3. K. W. Richardson: UMTS overview. Electronics & Communication Engineering Journal, Vol. 12, No. 3, June 2000.
4. G. Patel, S Dennett: The 3GPP and 3GPP2 Movements Toward an All-IP Mobile Network. IEEE Personal Communications, Vol. 7, Issue 4, August 2000.
5. T. Robles, A. Kadelka: QoS Support for an All-IP System Beyond 3G. IEEE Communications Interactive, Vol. 39, No. 8, August 2001.
6. T. Zhang, P. Agrawal, J. C. Chen: IP-Based Base Stations and Soft Handoff in All-IP Wireless Networks. IEEE Personal Communications, Vol. 8, No. 5, October 2001.
7. ITU-R Recommendations M.1078 (09/94): Security Principles for International Mobile Telecommunications-2000 (IMT-2000).
8. UMTS 33.21: Universal Telecommunications System (UMTS); Security Requirements.
9. GSM 03.20: Digital Cellular Telecommunications System; Security Related Network Functions.
10. 3GPP TS 33.102: 3GPP Technical Specification Group Service and System Aspects; Security Architecture.
11. OpenSSL Project (http://www.openssl.org)
12. ITU-T Recommendation X.509: Information Technology – Open Systems Interconnection – The Directory: Authentication Framework.
13. IEEE Standards for Local and Metropolitan Area Networks: Port based Network Access Control, IEEE Std 802.1X-2001, June 2001.
14. C. Perkins: IP Mobility Support for IPv4. IETF RFC 3220, August 2002.
15. Information technology – Telecommunications and information exchange between systems – Local and metropolitan area networks – Specific Requirements Part 11: Wireless LAN Medium Access Control (MAC) and Physical Layer (PHY) Specifications, IEEE Std. 802.11–1997, 1997.
16. OPNET (http://www.opnet.com)
17. M. Satyanarayanan: Pervasive computing: vision and challenges. IEEE Personal Communications, Vol. 8, Issue 4, August 2001.
18. C. Perkins: Mobile IP Joins Forces with AAA. IEEE Personal Communications, Vol. 7, Issue 4, August 2000.

Practical Pay TV Schemes

Arvind Narayanan[1], C. Pandu Rangan[1][*], and Kwangjo Kim[2]

[1] Department of Computer Science and Engineering,
Indian Institute of Technology, Madras,
Chennai-600036, INDIA.
arvindn@meenakshi.iitm.ernet.in,rangan@iitm.ernet.in
[2] IRIS(International Center for Information Security)
ICU(Information and Communications University)
58-4, Hwaam-Dong, Yusong-gu, Taejon, 305-732, South Korea.
kkj@icu.ac.kr

Abstract. We propose an efficient and robust *Pay TV* scheme for the case when there are a number of streams, as opposed to just one. In our model, the broadcast is divided into *billing periods*; during each billing period the entitlement of the users does not change. We achieve *full flexibility* with only a constant factor data redundancy. Our scheme has very little secure memory requirements and does not require the users' secure keys to be changed once they have been written into the secure memory. There is also no upper limit on the number of subscribers. We extend this scheme to have the *cracker identification* property: If a collusion of less than t users crack their *set-top terminals* and produce a new decryption key, the *exact set* of crackers can be efficiently identified with high probability. This property is similar to but different from the *traitor tracing* schemes of Chor et al [5].

Keywords: Broadcast Encryption, Pay TV, Set-top terminal, Cracker Identification.

1 Introduction

A *Pay TV* system consists of a set of *services* or *streams* $S_1, S_2..., S_m$ and a set of *users* $U_1, U_2, ..., U_n$. Each user is *subscribed* or *entitled* to some subset of the set of services. The *Broadcaster* encrypts the content of the streams and sends them over the *Broadcast Channel*. Every user is provided with a *Set-top terminal (STT)*, which receives the broadcasted content. A typical STT holds a very limited number of decryption keys in secure, tamper-proof and non-volatile memory. Users can change their entitlement by subscribing to or unsubscribing from a service.

In modeling the system properties, we will stick as closely as possible to actual practice. Accordingly, we assume that the channel is insecure but authenticated.

[*] Financial support from Ministry of Information Technology, Government of Korea is acknowledged.

R. Safavi-Naini and J. Seberry (Eds.): ACISP 2003, LNCS 2727, pp. 192–203, 2003.
© Springer-Verlag Berlin Heidelberg 2003

That is, Eve can receive all messages that are broadcast but cannot herself insert, delete or alter any messages. An important assumption we have made implicitly is that each message sent on the channel belongs to one of a small number of streams, instead of being associated with an arbitrary subset of the users.

One obvious requirement of a Pay TV system is that any user Alice should be able to decrypt exactly those streams to which she has subscribed. Another important requirement is *full flexibility*: by this we mean that the scheme must impose no restrictions on the set of services to which Alice can subscribe.

We note that the use of an STT containing a secure chip along with tamper-proof memory for storing the users' keys is unavoidable: if we merely give Alice's decryption keys to her, there is nothing to prevent her from sharing them with Oscar who can subsequently view all the streams that Alice is entitled to. It may be argued that this problem is insoluble anyway: Oscar could simply download content off Alice even when STTs are used. There is a crucial difference, however: while sharing of keys is a one time transaction, sharing of content needs to be done continuously. The latter is much easier to detect and is costly for Oscar. In fact, Oscar might find it more economical to subscribe with the broadcaster (Bob) directly. Content sharing is sufficiently difficult in practice to be a non-issue [5].

The STT needs to keep its decryption keys in non-volatile, secure and tamper proof memory. Because of these stringent requirements, the amount of secure memory available is very limited, typically a few kilobytes. In addition, the STT also has a (large) store of non-volatile memory which is neither secure nor tamper-proof.

The tamper proof nature of STTs should not be taken for granted; indeed, STTs have been extensively cracked in practice [9]. A very desirable property to have is that if Alice's STT is cracked, the cracker should not be able to decrypt any streams to which Alice is not currently subscribed.

Clearly, the STT is vulnerable to known-plaintext attack; however, it is infeasible for an attacker to mount a chosen plaintext attack. Further, an adversary can feed in ciphertext and observe the plaintext without requiring broadcast of the ciphertext; thus the STT must also be secure against *chosen-ciphertext* attacks.

Some schemes that have been used in STTs, the *bit-vector scheme* and the *block-by-block scheme* are discussed in [12], in which it is pointed out that these fare poorly both in terms of security and in terms of flexibility and efficient use of bandwidth.

1.1   Related Work

Broadcast encryption was introduced by Fiat and Naor in [7]. They consider the problem of securely broadcasting a secret to a *dynamically changing* subset of the users. Extensions to this work are found in [2] and [3]. The trade-off between transmission length in broadcast encryption and the number of keys per user is studied in [8].

Pay TV is a specific application of broadcast encryption in which the set to which the secret is to be broadcast is associated with one of a small number of services. Therefore, focusing on Pay TV allows one to construct more efficient protocols than by adopting a generic broadcast encryption protocol to Pay TV. Another difference is that in the case of Pay TV, legitimate users may volunteer to help users in the non-privileged set learn the secret. Therefore techniques such as tamper-proof decoding boxes and traitor tracing are used.

Pay TV schemes have been proposed by [12] and [10]. The former work describes schemes which allow the broadcaster to offer a hierarchy of packages to the users. The latter has focused on unsubscription process being totally transparent to the users. To achieve this they use techniques that associate multiple decryption keys with one encryption key.

Schemes for controlling the number of users who are not entitled to the broadcast but can still receive it can be found in [1].

Some of the literature deals with single-stream schemes. We note that such a scheme can not be trivially extended to an m-stream case since this would involve an m-fold increase in the users' secure as well as non-secure keys.

Traitor tracing has been studied in [5] and [11]. These schemes work by distributing some subset of a master set of keys to every authorized user; if a pirate constructs a decoding box using information from a threshold number of users, by observing the behavior of the box on various inputs (and *without* examining its internals), it is possible to identify at least one user who co-operated with the pirate. These protocols need to be combined with a broadcast encryption protocol to obtain a Pay TV scheme.

More recently Boneh and Franklin ([4]) have proposed a deterministic public-key traitor tracing scheme which identifies all traitors. Their scheme has a computational complexity of $O(k)$ modular exponentiations. This constitutes a significant improvement in efficiency over previous traitor tracing schemes.

1.2   Contributions

In this paper we consider the broadcast to be divided into *billing periods*. All subscription and unsubscription happens only at the end of each billing period. This closely models actual practice. It has the further advantage that the revocation problem no longer exists: the key re-transmission associated with unsubscription gets amortized over the set of users. Our model differs from that of the broadcast encryption schemes in [7] because we do not require each message to be sent to an arbitrary subset of the users.

In this model we present an RSA based system in which the message expansion is by a constant factor, independent of the number of users or services. Only a constant number of keys need to be stored in the secure memory. Further, these keys need never be changed once they have been written. Each user is also given a set of non-secret keys; these alone are changed by subscription/unsubscription. Adding or removing a service can be done at any time with no overhead. Subscription can also occur at any time without involving other users.

Our scheme is also very robust. If Alice cracks her STT, she can still decrypt only the streams to which she is entitled. Therefore, the only harm that she can do is to publish information that would allow everyone to decrypt the streams that Alice is entitled to; the information she publishes, however, can be directly traced to her. Also, no collusion of crackers can compromise system security or decrypt more streams than they are together entitled to.

We consider the problem of a collusion of crackers producing a new decryption key. We extend our protocol in such a way that no collusion of crackers smaller than a given threshold can untraceably publish enough information to decode the broadcast. To achieve this, we make use of the following construction:

Construct n $(t+1)$-tuples of integers such that given any linear combination of any $s < t$ of the tuples, it is possible to efficiently identify (with high probability) the exact set of tuples that were used.

Our scheme shares certain similarities with that of [4] (which is based on the hardness of the discrete log problem). In both schemes the computational complexity and the message expansion factor are $O(t)$, where t is minimum number of STTs to be cracked to circumvent the scheme. The main advantage of our scheme is that it works with multiple streams (it uses a common RSA modulus for all streams). Thus, the total size of the keys that each STT needs to store becomes $O(m + t)$, instead of $O(mt)$.

Finally we discuss several practical issues that arise in the implementation of our scheme.

2   The New Pay TV Scheme

Our scheme is based on RSA. In the next subsection, we describe a basic protocol to present the essentials of our scheme in a simple setting. We demonstrate the security of this protocol against a single cracker and show how a collusion of three crackers is enough to compromise system security. In protocol P2, this weakness is removed; however, it is possible for a collusion of three crackers to untraceably publish information that would enable everyone to decode the broadcast. This motivates the cracker identification algorithm of section 4.

2.1   Basic Protocol P1

We represent the entitlements of the users as a $m \times n$ matrix *Subsc* where $Subsc[i, j]$ is 1 if U_j is entitled to S_i. Each user U_j has a set of secure keys e_{rj} and a set of non-secure keys, one for each service S_i that she is entitled to.

Our scheme consists algorithms *Setup, AddUser, AddStream, Broadcast, Receive, Subscribe,* and *Unsubscribe*.

Algorithm Setup1

Bob selects two large primes p and q and sets $N = pq$ as in RSA. He selects two decryption keys d_1, d_2 such that $0 \leq d_1, d_2 < \phi(N)$ and d_2 is coprime to $\phi(N)$. Bob makes N public while p, q, d_1 and d_2 are kept secret.

Algorithm AddStream1

To add a new service S_i, Bob randomly selects $g_i \in Z_N^*$ such that g_i has high order modulo N. $Subsc[i,j]$ is set to 0 for each j. g_i is kept secret.

Algorithm AddUser1

To add a new user U_j, Bob randomly chooses e_{1j}, $0 < e_{1j} < \phi(N)$ and sets e_{2j} to the smallest positive residue of $(1 - d_1 e_{1j}) d_2^{-1}$ modulo $\phi(N)$. U_j is given an STT whose secure key is the pair (e_{1j}, e_{2j}). The secure chip of the STT allows raising an arbitrary input to the power of e_{1j} or e_{2j} modulo N.[1] $Subsc[i,j]$ is set to 0 for each i.

Algorithm Subscribe1

When U_j subscribes to S_i, Bob gives her the non-secure key $g_i^{e_{1j}}$ and sets $Subsc[i,j]$ to 1.

Algorithm Unsubscribe1

When U_j unsubscribes from S_i, Bob sets $Subsc[i,j]$ to 0, picks a new value for g_i as in Algorithm AddStream1, and sends $g_i^{e_{1j}}$ to each user U_j having $Subsc[i,j] = 1$.

Algorithm Broadcast1

To broadcast a message M belonging to the stream S_i, Bob picks a random x coprime to $\phi(N)$ and sends the ciphertext $C = (x, C_1, C_2)$ where $C_1 = M^{d_1} g_i^x$ and $C_2 = M^{d_2}$ over the broadcast channel.

Algorithm Receive1

To decrypt the ciphertext $C = (x, C_1, C_2)$ belonging to the stream S_i, U_j computes $C_1^{e_{1j}} C_2^{e_{2j}} / (g_i^{e_{1j}})^x$.

It is easy to see that the Algorithm Receive1 works correctly: If $Subsc[i,j] = 0$, U_j does not know $g_i^{e_{1j}}$ and hence can not execute Receive1 for service S_i. If $Subsc[i,j] = 1$, $C_1^{e_{1j}} C_2^{e_{2j}} / (g_i^{e_{1j}})^x = (M^{d_1} g_i^x)^{e_{1j}} (M^{d_2})^{e_{2j}} / g_i^{x e_{1j}} = M^{d_1 e_{1j} + d_2 e_{2j}} = M$.

The last equality holds because e_{1j} and e_{2j} are chosen in such a way that $d_1 e_{1j} + d_2 e_{2j} \equiv 1 (mod\ \phi(N))$.

2.2   Security

We consider two types of adversaries: *Honest but curious* or *Semi-honest* users are willing to deviate from the protocol and share information with other users about their (non-secure) keys. However, they will not tamper with their STTs. Malicious users, in addition to this, will also actively crack their STTs and discover their secure keys. An important assumption regarding security is that the algorithms used are publicly specified and only the keys are secret, even though the algorithms to be executed by the users are implemented in a secure chip and hence not directly accessible.

It is obvious that a collusion of semi-honest users can not crack the system: $g_i^{e_{1j}}$ gives no information because e_{1j} are not known to the users. Also, a semi-honest user U_j can not decrypt a message M belonging to a channel i to which

---

[1] Henceforth, we omit the modulus N when it is obvious.

she is not entitled: She can compute $C_1^{e_{1j}} C_2^{e_{2j}} = M g_i^{x e_{1j}}$, but can not obtain M from this as she does not know $g_i^{e_{1j}}$. Further U_j cannot get any information about a combination of two messages M_1 and M_2 in stream i: she can compute $M_1 g_i^{x_1 e_{1j}}$ and $M_2 g_i^{x_2 e_{1j}}$, but since x_1 and x_2 are different she does not get any information about M_1 / M_2.

Security against a single cracker: If U_j cracks her STT, she knows e_{1j} and e_{2j} in the equation $d_1 e_{1j} + d_2 e_{2j} \equiv 1 \ (mod \ \phi(N))$. However, this gives her no new information since she does not know $\phi(N)$. U_j can publish the triple $(e_{1j}, e_{2j}, g_i^{e_{1j}})$ enabling everyone to decrypt stream S_i, but she can not do this without revealing her identity to the broadcaster. Publishing g_i would enable everyone possessing an STT to decrypt stream S_i, but she can not get g_i from $g_i^{e_{1j}}$ since g_i has high order.

2.3 Weaknesses

Protocol P1 is not secure against the collusion of three crackers. To see this, we eliminate d_1 and d_2 from the equations $d_1 e_{11} + d_2 e_{21} \equiv d_1 e_{12} + d_2 e_{22} \equiv d_1 e_{13} + d_2 e_{23} (mod \ \phi(N))$ to get

$$(e_{12} e_{21} - e_{11} e_{22})(e_{12} - e_{13}) - (e_{12} e_{23} - e_{13} e_{22})(e_{12} - e_{11}) \equiv 0 \ (mod \ \phi(N))$$

If U_1, U_2 and U_3 all crack their STTs, then they can compute the left hand side of the above congruence. The left hand side is a multiple of $\phi(N)$. The chance that this multiple is 0 is negligible, since e_{1j} were randomly chosen. Note that if Oscar knows some (nonzero) multiple of $\phi(N)$, he can invert modulo $\phi(N)$, and hence the system is irreparably broken.

A further weakness is as follows: If U_1 and U_2 crack their STTs, there is a non-negligible probability that e_{11} and e_{12} are coprime. If that is the case, there are integers u_1 and u_2 such that $u_1 e_{11} + u_2 e_{12} = 1$. Therefore, $g_i = (g_i^{e_{11}})^{u_1} (g_i^{e_{12}})^{u_2}$ can be obtained for all i having $Subsc[i, j_1] = Subsc[i, j_2] = 1$.

3   A Cracker Proof Protocol

In this section we extend protocol P1 such that system security can not be compromised by cracking STTs.

3.1 Protocol P2

Algorithm Setup2

  Bob chooses N, p, q as in Algorithm Setup1. Let l be the number of bits of N. Bob selects a random l bit number R such that $R\phi(N) + 1$ has a divisor d of roughly l bits in length. Bob also selects $2l$ bit numbers d_1, d_2, d_3 which are divisible by d such that $\frac{d_2}{d}$ and $\frac{d_3}{d}$ are coprime.

Algorithm AddUser2

  Bob chooses e_{1j} randomly such that it is even. e_{2j} and e_{3j} are chosen in order that $\sum_{r=1}^{3} e_{rj} d_r = R\phi(N) + 1$. (This is possible because $\frac{d_2}{d}$ and $\frac{d_3}{d}$ are coprime.) U_j's secure keys are e_{1j}, e_{2j}, e_{3j}.

Algorithm Broadcast2

To broadcast a message M belonging to the stream S_i, Bob picks a random x coprime to $\phi(N)$ and sends the ciphertext $C = (x, C_1, C_2, C_3)$ where $C_1 = M^{d_1} g_i^x$, $C_2 = M^{d_2}$, $C_3 = M^{d_3}$.

Algorithm Receive2

To decrypt the ciphertext $C = (x, C_1, C_2, C_3)$ belonging to the stream S_i, U_j computes

$$(\textstyle\prod_{r=1}^{3} C_r^{e_{rj}})/(g_i^{e_{1j}})^x.$$

The other algorithms are the same as the corresponding algorithms for Protocol P1.

Algorithm Receive2 is correct because of the identity $(\prod_{r=1}^{3} C_r^{e_{rj}})/g_i^{x e_{1j}} = M^{\sum_{r=1}^{3} e_{rj} d_r} = M^{R\phi(N)+1} = M$.

3.2   Security

The results pertaining to semi-honest users proved for the previous protocol carry over to this one, too. We proceed to show how this protocol is secure against a collusion of crackers. We need to show that a collusion of crackers can not break the system, i.e, find $\phi(N)$ or allow semi-honest users to decrypt streams to which they are not entitled, i.e, find g_i.

Claim. No collusion of crackers can discover (a multiple of) $\phi(N)$.

If $U_1, U_2, \ldots U_s$ crack their STTs, then they know the values of e_{rj} in the equation $\sum_{r=1}^{3} d_r e_{r1} = \sum_{r=1}^{3} d_r e_{r2} = \ldots \sum_{r=1}^{3} d_r e_{rs}$. This equation is not a congruence modulo $\phi(N)$ but instead an exact equality. This fact is the key to the security of the protocol. For any integer x, the tuple $(x\frac{d_1}{d}, x\frac{d_2}{d}, x\frac{d_3}{d})$ in place of (d_1, d_2, d_3) also satisfies the above equation. Therefore, while a collusion of crackers might be able to find $(\frac{d_1}{d}, \frac{d_2}{d}, \frac{d_3}{d})$, and hence $\frac{R\phi(N)+1}{d}$, finding $R\phi(N)+1$ itself would involve guessing d and is hence infeasible.[2]   □

As a consequence, an attack similar to the one in section 2.3 would fail because the resulting multiple of $\phi(N)$ would in fact be 0.

Claim. No collusion of crackers can find g_i.

Suppose that $U_{j_1}, U_{j_2}, \ldots U_{j_s}$ all crack their STTs, and are all subscribed to the service S_i. It is clear that they can compute g_i^e for exactly those e which are an integral linear combination of the $e_{j_1}, e_{j_2}, \ldots e_{j_s}$. Since all the e_j are even, no odd power of g_i can be computed. In particular, g_i cannot be found. Note that publishing g_i^2 will enable any cracker to decrypt S_i. However, knowledge of g_i^2 is of no use to an honest user U_j because she does not know e_{1j}.   □

---

[2] For guessing d to be infeasible, it is enough for d to be a k-bit number, where k is a security parameter. However, this will not work if k is smaller than $\frac{l}{2}$: If an attacker knows $\frac{R\phi(N)+1}{d}$, then $\frac{R\phi(N)+1}{Nd}$ gives her a very good approximation to $\frac{R}{d}$ since the first $\frac{l}{2}$ bits of N and $\phi(N)$ are the same. This approximation is sufficient to find both R and d since R and d are coprime.

3.3   Weakness

Cracking 3 STTs gives 2 homogeneous linear equations in d_1, d_2, d_3. From this one can obtain the ratios $d_i/d_j (1 \leq i, j \leq 3)$. Once these are known, it is easy to enumerate *all* tuples (e_1, e_2, e_3) such that $\sum_{r=1}^{3} d_r e_r = R\phi(N) + 1$. In addition, if g_i^2 is known $g_i^{e_1}$ is known as well. Publishing $(e_1, e_2, e_3, g_i^{e_1})$ allows *anyone* to decrypt stream S_i, not just users possessing an STT. Further, this information is not traceable to any of the cracked STTs.

On the other hand, if only 2 STTs are cracked, not all possible tuples (e_1, e_2, e_3) can be generated, and thus the two cracked STTs can be identified (with high probability).[3] If we generalize the above protocol so that there are α secret keys, $d_1, d_2, \ldots d_\alpha$, and $\beta < \alpha$ STTs are cracked, then the crackers can be identified. However, the naive way of doing this has a time complexity of $\theta(n^\beta)$ where n is the number of users. What we need to do is to use e_{rj} of some special form such that the cracker identification algorithm becomes efficient.

4   Cracker Identification

Our technique for cracker identification is based on the following construction:
Construct n $(t+1)$-tuples of integers $\mathbf{x_1}, \mathbf{x_2}, \ldots \mathbf{x_n}$ such that given any linear combination of any $s < t$ of the vectors, it is possible to efficiently identify (with high probability) the exact set of vectors that were used.
In the following, k is a security parameter and δ is a tolerance bound such that the probability of our algorithm producing incorrect output is less than δ.

Vector generation algorithm

– *Constraint generation:* First we generate $et\ log \frac{n}{\delta}$ constraints, in $h = e\ log \frac{n}{\delta}$ groups of t constraints each.[4] The constraint $\gamma = (\mu_0, \mu_1, \mu_2, \ldots \mu_t, P)$ represents the equation $\sum_{i=0}^{t} \mu_i x_i \equiv 0 (mod\ P)$
  For each i, $1 \leq i \leq h$, we generate the ith group of constraints as follows:
  Select a random k bit prime P_i and a matrix $\mathbf{M_i}$ with t rows and $t + 1$ columns whose entries are uniformly selected modulo P_i. This gives t linear constraints on the (column) vector $\mathbf{x}$, one corresponding to each row of $\mathbf{M_i}$ in the equation $\mathbf{M_i x} \equiv \mathbf{0}(mod\ P_i)$.
– To generate a new vector $\mathbf{x} = (x_0, x_1, x_2, \ldots x_t)$, we select each of the constraints with probability $1 - \frac{1}{t}$; $\mathbf{x}$ is constructed so as to satisfy all the selected constraints.
  For each i, $1 \leq i \leq h$, let $r \leq t$ be the number of constraints in the ith group of constraints that are selected. Fix $x_0, x_1, \ldots x_{t-r}$ randomly modulo P_i and

---

[3] The probability that the same tuple (e_1, e_2, e_3) can be generated from 2 different pairs of cracked STTs is negligibly small.
[4] Here *log* refers to the natural logarithm.

solve (uniquely) for the remaining r x_j's modulo P_i using the r linear equations. (Since the coefficients of the linear equations were randomly generated and P_i is large, the probability that there is no solution is negligible.)

Thus the values of $x_0, x_1, \ldots x_t$ modulo each of the primes P_i are obtained; these are combined using the Chinese Remainder Theorem to get $\mathbf{x} = (x_0, x_1, x_2, \ldots x_t)$.

Identification algorithm

Input: A vector $\mathbf{y}$ that is a linear combination of some $s < t$ of the $\mathbf{x_j}$.

- Set the "suspect set" S to $\{\mathbf{x_1}, \mathbf{x_2}, \ldots \mathbf{x_n}\}$.
- For each constraint γ that is satisfied by $\mathbf{y}$
    For each $\mathbf{x_j} \in S$
        If $\mathbf{x_j}$ does not satisfy γ, remove it from S.
- Output S.

Correctness

In the following we refer to the vectors used in the given linear combination as "guilty" and the other vectors as "innocent".

We will prove that at the end of the identification algorithm, the probability that any $\mathbf{x_j} \in S$ is innocent is negligible.

We observe that if all the guilty vectors satisfy a constraint γ, then so does $\mathbf{y}$ (since the constraints are linear, and $\mathbf{y}$ is a linear combination of the guilty vectors). Conversely, suppose that at least one of the guilty vectors $\mathbf{x} = (x_0, x_1, x_2, \ldots x_t)$ does not satisfy $\gamma = (\mu_0, \mu_1, \mu_2, \ldots \mu_t, P)$. Then $\sum_{i=0}^{t} \mu_i x_i$ is uniformly distributed modulo P and therefore $\sum_{i=0}^{t} \mu_i y_i$ is also uniformly distributed modulo P. The probability that this value is zero is negligibly small, since P is large, and hence $\mathbf{y}$ does not satisfy γ with very high probability.

Let s be the number of guilty vectors and let $\mathbf{x}$ be one of the vectors that is innocent. For each constraint γ, the probability that all of the guilty vectors satisfy γ is $(1 - \frac{1}{t})^s$ and the probability that $\mathbf{x}$ does not satisfy γ is $\frac{1}{t}$. Therefore the probability that $\mathbf{x}$ is eliminated by γ is $\frac{1}{t}(1 - \frac{1}{t})^s \geq \frac{1}{t}(1 - \frac{1}{t})^{t-1} > \frac{1}{et}$. There are $et \, log \frac{n}{\delta}$ constraints; the probability that all of them fail to eliminate $\mathbf{x}$ is $(1 - \frac{1}{et})^{et \, log \frac{n}{\delta}} \approx \frac{\delta}{n}$. Hence, the probability that at least one of the innocent vectors is declared guilty is at most $1 - (1 - \frac{\delta}{n})^n < \delta$, establishing the claim.

We are now ready to describe Protocol P3.

4.1   Protocol P3

In the following, let t be a threshold such that we want at least t STTs to be cracked in order for the crackers to be unidentifiable and δ the error probability we are willing to tolerate.

Algorithm Setup3
    Bob selects $N = pq, d_1, d_2, d_3, R$ as in Algorithm Setup2. He further selects $d_r \in_R \{1, 2, \ldots, \phi(N)\}$ for $4 \leq r \leq 4+t$. Bob also runs the constraint generation part of the vector generation algorithm described above to obtain $et \, log(n/\delta)$ constraints.

Algorithm AddUser3

U_j's secure key is a $(t+4)$-tuple $(e_{1j}, e_{2j}, \ldots e_{t+4,j})$. Of these, e_{1j} is selected randomly so that it is even. $e_{4j}, e_{5j}, \ldots e_{t+4,j}$ are generated by executing the vector generation algorithm above, using the constraints generated in Algorithm Setup3. Finally e_{2j} and e_{3j} are chosen so that the equation $\sum_{r=1}^{t+4} e_{rj} d_r = R\phi(N) + 1$ is satisfied.

The other algorithms are essentially the same as in Protocol P2, the difference being that the ciphertext that is broadcast is a $(t+4)$-tuple instead of a 3 tuple.

4.2   Security

The proof of system security under a collusion of arbitrary many crackers is similar to the proof for protocol P2, and we omit it. The cracker identification property is a direct consequence of the correctness of the identification algorithm above: as long as less than t STTs are cracked, the only way to generate a new decryption vector is as a rational linear combination of the cracked vectors (with the sum of the coefficients being unity). If $(e_1, e_2, \ldots e_{t+4})$ is the new vector, then by running the identification algorithm with $(e_4, e_5, \ldots e_{t+4})$ as input, we can identify the cracked STTs with high probability.

We note that the identification algorithm depends on certain linear combinations being uniformly distributed modulo P_i. Therefore, to ensure security it is necessary for the primes P_i and the matrices $\mathbf{M_i}$ to be kept secret by the broadcaster.

4.3   Size of the Users' Secure Keys

It is essential that choosing $\mathbf{e} = (e_4, e_5, \ldots e_{t+4})$ satisfying all the constraints does not increase its size unacceptably. To estimate the size, we recall that in the Chinese Remainder Theorem, the solution is unique modulo the product of the individual moduli. Therefore, the size of the solution is roughly the sum of the sizes of the moduli. In the constraint generation algorithm, satisfying each of the $e \, log\frac{n}{\delta}$ groups of constraints fixes each component of the vector modulo a k bit prime; therefore each e_r has $ek \, log\frac{n}{\delta}$ bits. Importantly, this number is independent of t and only weakly dependent on n. For typical values of n, δ and k: 10^6, 10^{-3} and 128 respectively, we find that this number is about 900 bytes, which is reasonable.

5   Issues in Practice

In this section, we discuss several issues pertaining to the implementation of a Pay TV system using our scheme.

In a Pay TV system, subscription and unsubscription can happen only at the end of a fixed time unit called the *billing period*. This is very important because it amortizes the communication overhead of the unsubscription algorithm. At the start of each billing period, the broadcaster simply sends to each user her non-secure keys for each service that she is entitled to. The billing period is typically a week or a month.

We have assumed all messages to belong to some service. In practice, a service is either a "channel", or a single pay-per-view event (such as movies). We might have to use a smaller billing period for the latter category of service than for the former. We also note that unsubscription is not meaningful for pay-per-view events.

The *power-on latency* is the maximum time between Alice switching on her STT and the start of decoding of broadcast. The broadcast is divided into *sessions*, each of which lasts for a time equal to the power-on latency. During each session, the broadcast is encrypted using some *symmetric key* algorithm; the protocols we have proposed are used only for the broadcast of these symmetric keys. This achieves the following:

- Content sharing between users remains unfeasible.
- The bandwidth inefficiency of broadcast protocols is amortized.
- Costly public key operations need to be performed only once per session.

5.1   Key Distribution

The users' non-secret keys can be transmitted in-band with the broadcast. However, Alice's STT must be switched on during key broadcast in order for her to be able to receive her keys. In the following we give several techniques to address this problem.

1. **Physical transfer.** A simple approach is to physically transfer to the user at the start of each billing period a removable chip containing the user's non-secure keys that can be plugged into and read by the STT.
2. **Uplink.** If an STT has uplink capability [6], it would be easy to request a key from the broadcast center whenever one is required. For example, the STT sends i to the broadcast center whenever the user switches channels to service i, upon which the center broadcasts that user's non-secure key for service i.
3. **Synchronization.** The broadcaster transmits all keys of all users exactly once (say) every day. Then the STT can easily be equipped with a clock that "wakes up" the STT once every day and downloads the users' keys. Of course the STT's clock needs to be high precision and synchronized with the broadcaster's clock.
4. **Caching.** Caching of the user's non-secure keys by the STT can be used in combination with other strategies. The STT caches the non-secure keys in its non-volatile memory even when switched off.

6   Conclusion

We have considered a model for Pay TV in which the target set of users is not arbitrary but is associated with one of a small number of services or streams.

We have also assumed that the users' decoding boxes are provided with a secure chip and that entitlements of users are fixed for each billing period. Under these assumptions, we are able to achieve full flexibility with a constant data redundancy and a constant number of secure keys per user. We believe that this model is the most appropriate one in practice.

Our cracker identification algorithm is motivated by the need to prevent a collusion of crackers from untraceably publishing a decryption key. It would be interesting to see if our construction has other applications apart from Pay TV. We suggest a value for t of between 20 and 50 to realize a robust system (this value is sufficient because of the use of tamper proof decoding boxes). There appears to be scope for further work in our this algorithm - in particular, it might be possible to reduce the message expansion factor. Another possibility is to construct a scheme under our model in which it is impossible for crackers to construct a new decryption key.

Acknowledgements. The authors would like to thank K. Srinathan for useful discussions and suggestions.

References

1. M. Abdalla, Y. Shavitt, and A. Wool. Towards making broadcast encryption practical. In *Financial Cryptography*, volume 1648 of *LNCS*, pages 140–157, 1999.
2. C. Blundo and A. Cresti. Space requirements for broadcast encryption. In *Advances in Cryptology, Eurocrypt '94*, volume 950 of *LNCS*, pages 287–298, 1994.
3. C. Blundo, L. A. Frotta Mattos, and D. R. Stinson. Trade-offs between communication and storage in unconditionally secure schemes for broadcast encryption and interactive key distribution. In *Advances in Cryptography, CRYPTO '96*, LNCS, pages 387–400, 1996.
4. D. Boneh and M. Franklin. An efficient public key traitor tracing scheme. In *Proc. 19th International Advances in Cryptology Conference – CRYPTO '99*, pages 338–353, 1999.
5. B. Chor, A. Fiat, and M. Naor. Tracing traitors. In *Advances in cryptology – CRYPTO'94*, volume 839 of *LNCS*, pages 257–270, 1994.
6. J. L. Cohen, M. H. Etzel, D. W. Faucher, and D. N. Heer. Security for broadband digital networks. In *Communications Technology*, pages 58–69, 1995.
7. A. Fiat and M. Naor. Broadcast encryption. In *Advances in Cryptology, CRYPTO '93*, volume 773 of *LNCS*, 1994.
8. M. Luby and J. Staddon. Combinatorial bounds for broadcast encryption. In *Advances in Cryptology, Eurocrypt '98*, volume 1403 of *LNCS*, pages 512–526, 1998.
9. J. McCormac. European scrambling systems 5. *Waterford University Press, Waterford, Ireland*, 1996.
10. Y. Mu and V. Varadharajan. Robust and secure broadcast. In *Progress In Cryptology – Indocrypt 2001*, volume 2247 of *LNCS*, pages 223–231, 2001.
11. M. Naor and B. Pinkas. Threshold traitor tracing. In *Advances in cryptology – CRYPTO'98*, volume 1462 of *Lecture Notes in Computer Science (LNCS)*, pages 502–517, 1998.
12. A. Wool. Key management for encrypted broadcast. In *5th ACM conference on Computer and Communications Security*, pages 7–16, 1998.

Cooperative Routers against DoS Attacks

Ha Yoon Song and Han-gyoo Kim

College of Information and Computer Engineering, Hongik University, Seoul, Korea
{song, hkim}@cs.hongik.ac.kr

Abstract. In order to protect network from the Denial of Service attacks which sends excessive traffic to a host, it is required for network components to throttle unauthorized traffics. The attacker must be identified through the cooperation of routers and must be isolated by the nearest router. It is the most important to identify and isolate the attacker since the nearest router can make ideal blocking of the DoS attacks. In this research, we will present a protocol which can identify the attacker of DoS by the request of victim in cooperation of routers on the attacking path between a victim and the attacker. The performance of our protocol will be verified by simulations and the experiments show that it takes considerably small time to identify the location of attacker.

1   Introduction

With the explosive growth of the Internet, the importance of Internet security has been increased since vicious attacks on networks have also been increased in order to prevent the normal operation of networks and to harm the availability. The most prominent one has been the Denial of Service (DoS) attack that sends huge numbers of extra packets in order to overheat the host so that services to normal users will be unavailable. The distributed version of DoS attack, termed as DDoS, makes the problem more malignant [1].

Many research efforts to defense DoS and DDoS have been made to invent methods of tracing back the IP addresses of sources of attackers [2] [3] [4] [5] [6]. However, mere back-tracing the attackers' IP addresses does not cure the problem. It is more desirable to identify the attacker paths effectively and efficiently so that the attacker can be isolated [7] [3].

Isolating attackers is intrinsically a matter of routers and requires intensive cooperation among the routers involved on the victim-attacker path (attack path). Routers on the attacker path must cooperate with each other to track the attacker in order to block the attack and therefore isolate the attacker. In this paper, such a protocol named as RCPaD (Router Cooperative Protocol against DoS) will be presented in detail. The protocol will force the identified attacker down the traffic amount by the initiation of a victim whenever the victim finds suspected DoS attack. We verified the protocol by simulation using NS-2 with several possible attacking scenarios.

RCPaD is a distributed protocol that premises cooperation among the routers in order to isolate the attacker paths efficiently when the victim senses possible

R. Safavi-Naini and J. Seberry (Eds.): ACISP 2003, LNCS 2727, pp. 204–213, 2003.
© Springer-Verlag Berlin Heidelberg 2003

ongoing DoS or DDoS attacks. Among the four phases of detection, traceback, response, termination of usual DoS defense mechanism [5], we will concentrate on traceback mechanism throughout this paper. RCPaD is simple but effective and requires no extra data objects that are not defined in standard network management protocol such as SNMP. Therefore, RCPaD can be implemented and deployed without extra overhead of network resources or difficulties of implementation. The structure of this paper is as follows. Section 2 will discuss the RCPaD with the SNMP (Simple Network Management Protocol) [8] as well as the definition of router status and RCPaD messages for RCPaD. Section 3 will show the performance results of RCPaD operations by simulation. Finally, sections 4 with future works will conclude this paper.

2   Protocol

Several questions have been addressed to develop the RCPaD protocol.

- How can the victim sense the possible DoS attack?
- How can the victim differentiate honest router from the malicious router?
- How can the routers sense the amount of traffic?
- What are the formats of messages exchanged for the RCPaD protocol?

In this section, we will answer questions above in order to design the RCPaD protocol.

2.1   Category of Router Status

For the RCPaD, we must categorize the status of routers. Victims and attackers are clear however routers on the attacker-victim path must be ramified further. The status of routers can be categorized as follows.

Router Status	Description
Attacker	A router which is in charge of a DoS attacking host. It could just forward attacking packets or aggressively assist the attack.
Victim	A router connected to a victim host.
Suspected Router (SR)	A router emitting superfluous traffic. Once a router is a suspected router, it maybe on the attack path or it maybe the attacker itself. The innocence of SR must be proven by itself and verified by other routers.
Uncertain Router (UR)	Every router is initially regarded as an uncertain router, since it is not yet identified whether it is attacker or not.
Innocent Router (IR)	A router proved to be a non-attacker. For an uncertain router, innocence can be proven after exchanging the messages regardless whether it is on the attack path or not.

Any UR could be regarded as an SR by victim or IRs. Every SR must be proven its innocence by the request of victims or IRs. The proof process must be done by exchanging RCPaD messages by RCPaD protocol on each router. SRs will be marked as IRs after the proof of their innocence.

2.2   Detection of DoS Attacks by SNMP Traffic Metrics

RCPaD protocol requires a direct measure of traffic amount in order to find a suspected router (SR). Among the various methods to measure the traffic, we will use a method provided by SNMP. Various monitoring schemes are allowed through SNMP such as MRTG (Multi Router Traffic Grapher).

Traffic measurement and network management with SNMP can be done by referring MIB (Management Information Base), which is a set of information for the operations of SNMP. Currently, System group, Interface group, IP group, ICMP group, TCP group, and UDP group have their own MIB. IP group's *ipForwDatagrams* shows the number of passed packets by SNMP agent, so that traffics measurement can be done with ipForwDatagrams which is 1.3.6.1.2.1.4.6. The check of traffic is done through *GetRequest* of SNMP to check ipForwDatagrams.

The ipForwDatagrams on an agent is not in a traffic amount per unit time but in a cumulative amount of forwarded datagrams. Therefore, traffic amount can be identified like the following when ipForwDatagrams at time t_1 be $ipForwDatagrams_1$ and ipForwDatagrams at time t_2 be $ipForwDatagrams_2$ where $t_2 > t_1$.

$$TrafficAmount = \frac{ipForwDiagrams_2 - ipForwDiagrams_1}{t_2 - t_1}$$

For the environment where SNMP does not fit, another MIB based approach [6] can be replaced for the detection of DoS attacks.

2.3   Message Definitions for RCPaD

Messages defined for RCPaD have similar structures. There are only three types of messages defined for RCPaD: SM (Suspicion Message), EM (Elucidation Message), and CM (Command Message).

Suspicion Message. SM will be sent to the router under the suspicion of an attacker. The structure of SM is like follows.

IP address of victim: IP address of a victim			
IP address of sender: IP address of a router sending this suspicion message			
Traffic threshold: threshold of normal traffic. Traffic amount over this value be regarded as superfluous.			
Attack path (optional): IP address of routers on the Attacker path.			

0	8	16	24	32
Type=0		Traffic threshold	Length of attack path	
IP address of Victim				
IP address of Sender				
IP address of attack path				
....				

Elucidation Message. A router is supposed to send an EM in response to the SM in order to prove its innocence. Receiver of EM must check its validity.

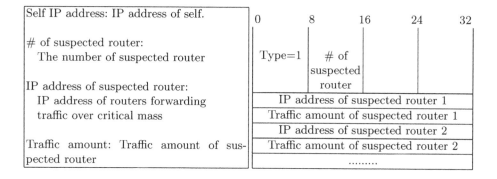

Self IP address: IP address of self.	0	8	16	24	32

Fields:
- # of suspected router: The number of suspected router
- IP address of suspected router: IP address of routers forwarding traffic over critical mass
- Traffic amount: Traffic amount of suspected router

Packet layout:
- Type=1 | # of suspected router
- IP address of suspected router 1
- Traffic amount of suspected router 1
- IP address of suspected router 2
- Traffic amount of suspected router 2
- ....

Command Message. Command Message (CM) is sent to the attacker to block or decrease the traffic after the attacker is identified.

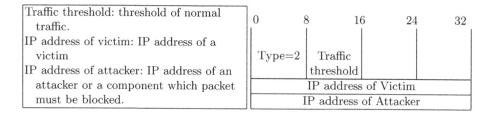

Traffic threshold: threshold of normal traffic.	0	8	16	24	32

Fields:
- IP address of victim: IP address of a victim
- IP address of attacker: IP address of an attacker or a component which packet must be blocked.

Packet layout:
- Type=2 | Traffic threshold
- IP address of Victim
- IP address of Attacker

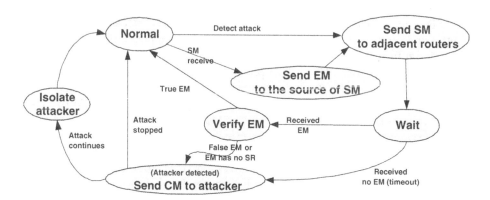

Fig. 1. State transition diagram

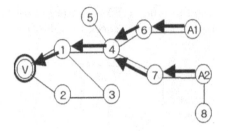

Fig. 2. Victim is under attack.

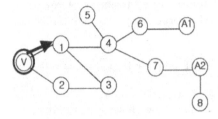

Fig. 3. V sends SM to router 1.

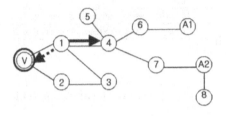

Fig. 4. Router 1 replies with EM and sends
SM to router 4.

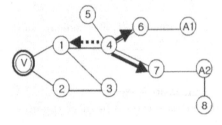

Fig. 5. RCPaD operations of router 4.

2.4 Protocol Operation

RCPaD will start immediately if it probes superfluous traffic or it receives SM.
Figure 1 shows the state transition diagram of RCPaD. Protocol on a router
exchanges messages to decide if its SR is attacker or not. Once the victim sends
SM, the receiving routers adjacent repeats the same operations subsequently. If
the SR is an attacker, RCPaD reports the catch of the attacker to the initial
victim and sends CM to the attacker. Figure 2 shows an example of the attacks
to a victim in progression on a network.

Protocol starts once V (victim) probes an attack. V discovers a router that
sends superfluous traffic. In figure 2, both router 1 and router 2 are uncertain,
however, router 1 is suspicious. V regards router 1 as SR and sends SM to router
1 as shown in figure 3. Router 1 receives SM, adds itself on the attacker path,
and discovers its SRs to which SMs are to be sent. Also, router 1 replies with
EM, which contains proof that it is not an attacker but an innocent repeater of
traffic as shown in figure 4. Victim receives EM from router 1 and checks the
traffic of router 4 with SNMP to check if router 1 is honest (EM verification).
Router 1 will be regarded as innocent with the certainty of its EM if the traffic
of router 4 measured by victim and traffic reported by router 1 are within a
tolerable range. There are two conditions for SNMP packet checking:

- The direct destination of the packet must be router 1. It can be checked by
  the IP *strict source router* protocol.

– TTL value is restricted (set) to two or replied TTL must not be decreased by more than two from the default value and be returned via router 1 (It can be done by referring *ipdefaultTTL*).

The default value of TTL is defined as 64 by RFC 1812 [9] but not absolutely. Once TTL value is restricted to 2, timeout must be long enough to tolerate the longest latency over the network. IP protocol provides record router function and it can be checked if the reply packet returned via router 1. That is, the router which sends EM can assert direct adjacent routers as an SR. Router 1, identified as innocent, repeats the protocol as victim did to it.

It is router 4 that sends superfluous traffic to router 1. Router 4 sends EM to router 1 after router 1 sent SM to router 4. In addition, router 4 adds itself to attack path and send the attack path to victim as it is under attack by router 6 and router 7. As shown in figure 5, it sends SM to router 6 and router 7. Router 1 receives EM from router 4 and checks the traffic of router 6 and router 7 by itself to verify the EM from router 4. Router 6 and router 7 send EM to router 4 and send SM to A1 and A2. Attacker can take one out of three actions - not reply (sending no EM), reply with honest EM, reply with fake EM:

1. The router not replying with EM is regarded as an attacker after the timeout.
2. The sender of honest EM can be regarded as an attacker. The EM has zero as a value of number of SR, asserting that there is no SR. It stands that sender of honest SM asserts no router sending superfluous traffic to itself since it is the attacker.
3. A malignant attacker can modify EM. This fake EM can be checked its validity by SNMP protocol according to the modification style of EM by the attacker: Normal *GetResponse* messages can be replied from the non-existing SR by *GetRequest* of SNMP. The next hop of SNMP packet must be the attacker and the TTL is restricted by 2 or must not be decrease by 2 from the default value if the attacker asserts a fake SR by EM. The fake EM can be checked if no normal response has been received in timeout or if TTL value decrease is more than two.

In figure 6, even though A1 asserts fake SM as (non-existing) router 9 by sending fake EM to router 6, other routers cannot get normal response from router 9 so that check the fake EM from A1. *i*)Asserting the non-existing router (or non-adjacent router) as its SR: *ii*)Reporting fake SR as its neighbor and fake traffic amount of the SR: If there are differences between the traffic on EM and replied traffic from each SR on the EM by sending GetRequest, the EM can be regarded as fake. In figure 6, A2 can lie that router 8 is an SR with 10000 packet/sec traffic. Router 7 can check and reveal that traffic of router 8 is 40 packet/sec. Thus, EM from A2 can be checked as fake. *iii*.)Reporting honest traffic amount of fake SR as its neighbor: The sender of EM can be regarded as an attacker as if it sends honest EM since every SR in this EM has record of traffic under the traffic threshold. Thus, router 6 and 7 can identify the attacker. They send CM to A1 and A2. Attacker checks the IP address of attacking node on CM. If the IP address and its IP address are coincident, it

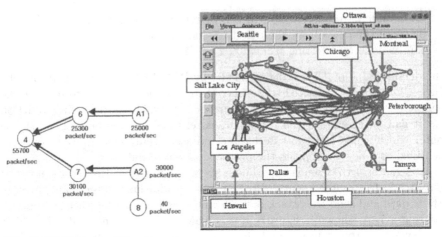

Fig. 6. RCPaD identifies the attacker.

Fig. 7. Scenario testbed

blocks the host sending superfluous amount or throttle the packet amount to the victim by traffic threshold. If the attacking node denies throttling the traffic, the host must be isolated. Other routers on the attack path (since they received SM from the victim) can throttle the packets to the victim among the packets from the attacker if they probe no decrease of packet traffic after the sending of CM. The RCPaD can be reapplied if the attacker chooses another attack path in order to continue the attack.

3 Performance Evaluation

In this section, the performance of RCPaD to identify the attacker will be shown in time to identify (TTI). We will discuss experimental setup first.

3.1 Experimental Environment

The experiments for performance evaluation of RCPaD are done with NS-2 (Network Simulator-2) [10] on the Linux platform. NS-2 is a simulator designed and developed by Network Research Group of Lawrence Berkeley National Research Center, based on the UNIX with C++ and Tcl/Tk for high scalability [11]. NS-2 package is composed of simulation engine, NAM (Network ANimator) for graphical result presentation and X-graph for graph generation, and it supports various packet types and protocols on IP level. NS-2 regards packets as stack of headers. Each packet header has attribute variables such as *uid, ptype, size, ttl,* and *sequence number* that can be controlled artificially by users. We developed a set of codes to demonstrate and generated scenarios with various attacker and victim patterns and paths in order to verify the RCPaD protocol.

3.2   Performance of Attacker Identification

The scenario is based on the continental networks topology over North America [12] as shown in figure 7. Nodes represent the major cities over North America and links between nodes have the same bandwidth with real network. There are 73 nodes, and delays between nodes are proportional to the geographical distance between cities except Hawaii and Honolulu.

In the following experiments, attackers are allowed to generate any types of fake EMs. We will list scenarios for experiments and results for various possible cases. The scenario includes victims, attackers, and related assumptions. Results must show TTI (Time to Identify) as an important parameter for the validity of the RCPaD.

Experiment 1.   Single Attacker. Enabled fake EM. (1)

Victim	Los Angeles		
Attacker	One in Peterborough, Ottawa, Montreal	**Attacker**	**TTI (sec)**
		Peterborough	8.500032
Assumption	Attacker reports fake EMs in timeout.	Ottawa	8.840066
		Montreal	9.060079

Experiment 2.   Single Attacker. Enabled fake EM (2). TTI varies according to the contents of fake EM from attacker, reporting non-existing router as an SR. With timeout mechanism, TTI contains time for timeout to figure out fake EMs. With TTL decrement algorithm, TTI increases with the distance to SR reported by fake EM.

Victim	Los Angeles		
Attacker	Ottawa		
	Attacker reports fake EM in timeout with different SRs from time to time.	**SR**	**TTI for Ottawa**(sec)
		New York	5.430003
		Chicago	5.970002
Assumption		Vancouver	10.370010
	Attacking paths has length more than 5.	Honolulu	14.070014

Experiment 3.   Single Attacker, Honest EM. With the same situations in the experiments above, honest EM can be reported otherwise. Victim can receive honest EM when the attacking router does not obey attacker host. The received EM has zero as a number of SRs once the SM have been reached to the terminal of attacker path. This EM can be used to identify attacker without validating its honesty, thus drastically decrease TTI comparing to experiment 1.

Victim	Los Angeles		
Attacker	One of Peterborough, Ottawa, Montreal	**Attacker**	**TTI** (sec)
		Peterborough	2.760023
Assumption	Attacker takes shortest path possible. Honest EMs will be replied.	Ottawa	2.820035
		Montreal	2.840025

Experiment 4. Single Attacker, Varying attack paths. With the same attacker and the same victim, TTI varies according to the situation of links and the length of paths with varying attack path. However, it is always possible to identify every attacker.

Victim	Los Angeles
Attacker	Toronto
Assumption	Attacker Toronto reports with fake EM and changed attacker path three times. **Attack 1 :** Toronto → Calgary → Vancouver → Seattle → Santa Clara → Los Angeles (TTI: 6.710011) **Attack 2 :** Toronto → New York → Washington DC → Dallas → Los Angeles (TTI: 10.280102) **Attack 3 :** Toronto → Tysons Corner → Washington DC → Dallas → Los Angeles (TTI: 10.480012)

Experiment 5. Multiple Attacker (1). Four attacker attacks single victim concurrently. Victim sends SM for each path.

Victim	Dallas		Attacker	TTI (sec)
Attacker	Portland, Tampa, Chicago, Ottawa		Chicago	6.670010
			Tampa	9.710014
Assumption	Attacker reports fake EMs in timeout.		Ottawa	11.530416
			Portland	14.470010

Experiment 6. Multiple Attacker (2). Six attackers attack single victim similar to experiment 5. Attacker reports fake EMs.

Victim	Dallas		Attacker	TTI (sec)
Attacker	Seattle, Tampa, Chicago, San Antonio, Hawaii, Salt Lake City		Seattle	4.630007
			Chicago	4.810001
			Tampa	5.450005
Assumption	Each attacker reports fake EMs.		San Antonio	12.280009
			Hawaii	13.630016
			Salt Lake City	14.230003

Experiment 7. Multiple Attacker (3). Six attackers attack single victim similar to experiment 6. However, each attacker can report honest EMs.

Victim	Dallas		Attacker	TTI (sec)
Attacker	Seattle, Tampa, Chicago, San Antonio, Hawaii, Salt Lake City		San Antonio	0.400002
			Chicago	1.310001
			Tampa	2.090004
Assumption	Each attacker reports with honest EMs.		Salt Lake City	2.810000
			Seattle	4.130001
			Hawaii	5.010012

4   Conclusion

RCPaD protocol presented in this paper provides a mechanism to block DoS attacks. The simulation study shows that RCPaD can identify the attacker paths against any types of DoS or DDoS attacks within few seconds regardless that attackers send back fake EMs or no EM. RCPaD is also proved to be effective even in case that the attacking paths are changing from the initial paths. RCPaD effectively reconfigures whenever the attacker exploits various attacking paths so that the attackers can be isolated eventually. The effectiveness of RCPaD comes from the fact that the protocol fully takes advantage of cooperation among the routers involved. RCPaD, however, requires minimal degree of computation and communication yet provides effective method for isolating attacker paths in dynamic environment. All the necessary traffic metrics for RCPaD are obtained from pre-existing SNMP, thus the effort of protocol construction can be minimized. It has been believed that the cooperation among the routers plays most important role in providing effective tools for various QoS control. The RCPaD protocol presented in this paper can be applied other types of network attacks than DoS but with similar attacking patterns [13].

References

1. Felix Lau, Stuart H. Rubin, Michael H. Smith, and Ljiljana Trajkovic. *Distributed Denial of Service Attacks*. McGraw-Hill, 2000.
2. Dawn Song and Adrian Perrig. Advanced and authenticated marking schemes for IP traceback. In *IEEE Infocomm*, 2001.
3. Stefan Savage, David Wetherall, Anna Karlin, and Tom Anderson. Practical network support for IP traceback. *ACM SIGCOMM*, 2000.
4. Vern Paxon. An analysis using reflectors for distributed Denial-of-Service attacks. *ACM SIGCOMM*, 31(3), July 2001.
5. Eric Y. Chen. Aegis: An active-network-powered defense mechanism against ddos attacks. *Lecvure Notes in Computer Science*, 2207, 2001.
6. J. B. D. Cabrera, L. Lewis, Xinzhou Qin, Wenke Lee, R. K. Prasanth, B. Ravichandran, and R. K. Mehra. Proactive detection of distributed denial of service attacks using MIB traffic variables - a feasibility study. In *Proceedings of 2001 IEEE/IFIP International Symposium on Integrated Network Management*, 2001.
7. Drew Dean, Matt Franklin, and Adam Stubblefield. An algebraic approach to IP traceback. *ACM Transactions on Information and System Security*, 5(2):199–137, May 2002.
8. J. D. Case et al. SNMP v2. *RFC 1441*, 1993.
9. F. Baker. Requirements for IP version 4 routers. *RFC 1812*, 1995.
10. http://www.isi.edu/nsnam/ns/. *The Network Simulator -ns-2*.
11. Kevin Fall and Kannan Varadhan. *The NS Manual*. UC Berkeley, 2001.
12. http://www.uu.net/network/maps/northam/index.xml. *WorldCom's UUNET network maps*.
13. P. Ferguson. Network ingress filtering: Defeating denial of service attacks which employ IP source address spoofing. *RFC 2267*, 1998.

Detecting Distributed Denial of Service Attacks by Sharing Distributed Beliefs

Tao Peng[1], Christopher Leckie[1,2], and Kotagiri Ramamohanarao[1,2]

[1] ARC Special Research Center for Ultra-Broadband Information Networks
Department of Electrical and Electronic Engineering
The University of Melbourne
Victoria 3010, Australia
{t.peng,c.leckie}@ee.mu.oz.au
http://www.ee.mu.oz.au/cubin
[2] Department of Computer Science and Software Engineering
The University of Melbourne
Victoria 3010, Australia
rao@cs.mu.oz.au

Abstract. We propose a distributed approach to detect distributed denial of service attacks by monitoring the increase of new IP addresses. Unlike previous proposals for bandwidth attack detection schemes which are based on monitoring the traffic volume, our scheme is very effective for highly distributed denial of service attacks. Our scheme exploits an inherent feature of DDoS attacks, which makes it hard for the attacker to counter this detection scheme by changing their attack signature. Our scheme uses a sequential nonparametric change point detection method to improve the detection accuracy without requiring a detailed model of normal and attack traffic. In a multi-agent scenario, we show that by sharing the distributed beliefs, we can improve the detection efficiency.

1 Introduction

A denial-of-service (DoS) attack is a malicious attempt by a single person or a group of people to cripple an online service. The impact of these attacks can vary from minor inconvenience to users of a website, to serious financial losses for companies that rely on their on-line availability to do business. As emergency and essential services become more reliant on the Internet as part of their communication infrastructure, the consequences of denial-of-service attacks could even become life-threatening. There are many indications that since September 11, the number of DoS attacks have greatly increased [3].

Attackers can instruct computers under their control to send bogus data to a victim. Simultaneously, the resulting traffic can clog links, and cause routers near the victim or the victim itself to fail under the load. The type of DoS attack that causes problems by overloading the victim with useless traffic is known as a *bandwidth attack*. This paper focuses on curtailing bandwidth attacks.

A key problem to tackle when solving bandwidth attacks is *attack detection*. There are two challenges for detecting bandwidth attacks. The first challenge is

R. Safavi-Naini and J. Seberry (Eds.): ACISP 2003, LNCS 2727, pp. 214–225, 2003.
© Springer-Verlag Berlin Heidelberg 2003

how to detect malicious traffic close to its source. This is particularly difficult when the attack is highly distributed, since the attack traffic from each source may be small compared to the normal background traffic. The second challenge is to detect the bandwidth attack as soon as possible without raising a false alarm, so that the victim has more time to take action against the attacker.

Previous approaches rely on monitoring the volume of traffic that is received by the victim [10]. Due to the inherently bursty nature of Internet traffic, a sudden increase in traffic may be mistaken as an attack. If we delay our response in order to ensure that the traffic increase is not just a transient burst, then we risk allowing the victim to be overwhelmed by a real attack. Moreover, some persistent increases in traffic may not be attacks, but actually "flash crowd" events, where a large number of legitimate users access the same website simultaneously. We need to distinguish between these events.

A better approach is to monitor the number of new source IP addresses, rather than the local traffic volume. Jung et al. [7] have observed that during bandwidth attacks, most source IP addresses are new to the victim, whereas most source IP addresses in a flash crowd appeared at the victim before. Previously, this observation has been used as the basis for a mechanism to filter out attack traffic at the victim [13]. In our previous paper [12], we proposed to monitor the number of new IP addresses in a given time period in order to detect bandwidth attacks. In this paper, we proposed a distributed detection scheme based on the source IP address monitoring.

Our main contribution in this paper is that we describe how machine learning can be used to improve the efficiency of a multi-agent system for distributed attack detection. We show that this approach is much more effective than earlier schemes, especially when there are multiple attack sources and the attack traffic is highly distributed. We adapt the detection scheme proposed by Wang et al. [16], which is based on an advanced non-parametric change detection scheme, CUSUM, and demonstrate that this approach detects a wide range of attacks quickly and with high accuracy.

The rest of the paper is organized as follows. Section 2 gives an overview of our solution to this problem. Section 3 explains the methodologies we used for attack detection. Section 4 presents the simulation results of our detection mechanism. Section 5 discusses related work.

2   Our Solution: Source IP Address Monitoring

We propose a scheme called Source IP address Monitoring (SIM) to detect the Highly Distributed Denial of Service (HDDoS). This detection scheme uses an intrinsic feature of HDDoS attacks, namely the huge number of new IP addresses in the attack traffic to the victim. This novel approach has the advantage that it can detect attacks close to their sources in the early stages of the attack.

SIM contains two parts: *off-line training*, and *detection and learning*. The first part is the *off-line training*, where a learning engine adds legitimate IP addresses into an IP Address Database (IAD) and keeps the IAD updated by adding new legitimate IP addresses and deleting expired IP addresses. This is done off-line to make sure the traffic data used for training does not contain any bandwidth attacks. A simple rule can be used to decide whether a new IP address is legitimate or not. For example, a TCP connection with less than 3 packets is considered to be an abnormal IP flow. How to build an efficient IAD is discussed in detail in [13].

The second part is *detection and learning*. During this period, we collect several statistics of incoming traffic for the current time interval Δ_n. For example, by analyzing the number of new IP addresses, we can detect whether a HDDoS attack is occurring. In [12], more details are discussed. More importantly, in a multi-agent scenario, the detection performance can be improved by sharing the information among the agents using a machine learning scheme.

3   Methodology

Our detection mechanism has two key parts. The first is a scheme for individual detection agents to detect the abnormal network behavior. The second is to develop a rule to decide *when* to broadcast the warning message.

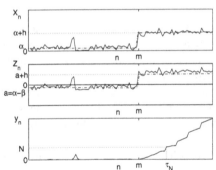

Fig. 1. The CUSUM algorithm   **Fig. 2.** Distributed detection model

3.1   The CUSUM Algorithm

Let X_n represent the fraction of new IP addresses during time interval Δ_n. Consider the illustrative example in Figure 1. For the random sequence $\{X_n\}$, there is a step change of the mean value at m from α to $\alpha + h$. We require an algorithm to detect changes of at least step size h and estimate m in a sequential manner so that the detection delay and false positive rate are both minimized. In our experiment, we applied the non-parametric CUSUM (Cumulative Sum) method [2] in our detection algorithm. This general approach is based on the model presented in Wang et al. [16] for attack detection using CUSUM. The main idea behind the non-parametric CUSUM algorithm is that we accumulate values of X_n that are significantly higher than the mean level under normal operation. One of the advantages of this algorithm is that it monitors the input random variables in a sequential manner so that real-time detection is achieved.

Let us begin by defining our notation before we give a formal definition of our algorithm. As we mentioned before, X_n represents the fraction of new IP addresses in the measurement interval Δ_n. The top graph in Figure 1 shows an illustrative example of $\{X_n\}$. In normal operation, this fraction will be close to 0, i.e. $E(X_n) = \alpha \ll 1$, since there is only a small proportion of IP addresses that are new to the network under normal conditions [7] [13]. However, one of the assumptions for the nonparametric CUSUM algorithm [2] is that mean value of the random sequence is negative during normal conditions, and becomes positive when a change occurs. Thus, without loss of any statistical feature, $\{X_n\}$ is transformed into another random sequence $\{Z_n\}$ with negative mean a, i.e. $Z_n = X_n - \beta$, where $a = \alpha - \beta$ (See the middle graph of Figure 1). Parameter β is a constant value for a given network condition, and it helps to produce a random sequence $\{Z_n\}$ with a negative mean so that all the negative values of $\{Z_n\}$ will not accumulate according to time. When an attack happens, Z_n will suddenly become large and positive, i.e. $h + a > 0$, where h can be viewed as a lower bound of the increase in Z_n during an attack. Hence, Z_n with a positive value $(h + a > 0)$ is accumulated to indicate whether an attack happens or not (See the bottom graph of Figure 1). One thing worth noting is that h is defined as the minimum increase of the mean value during an attack and it is not the threshold for the bandwidth attack detection. The attack detection threshold N is used for the y_n, accumulated positive values of Z_n, which is illustrated in Figure 1. Our change detection is based on the observation of $h \gg \beta$.

For efficiency, we use the recursive version of non-parametric CUSUM algorithm [1][2][16] which is shown as follows:

$$y_n = (y_{n-1} + Z_n)^+,$$
$$y_0 = 0, \tag{1}$$

where x^+ is equal to x if $x > 0$ and 0 otherwise. A large y_n is a strong indication of an attack.

As we see in the bottom graph of Figure 1, y_n represents the cumulative positive values of Z_n. We consider the change to have occurred at time τ_N if $y_{\tau_N} \geq N$. The decision function can be described as follows:

$$d_N(y_n) = \begin{cases} 0 \text{ if } y_n \leq N; \\ 1 \text{ if } y_n > N. \end{cases}$$

N is the threshold for attack detection and $d_N(y_n)$ represents the decision at time n: '1' if the test statistic y_n is larger than N, which indicates an attack, and '0' otherwise, which indicates the normal operation. Further details can be found in [12].

3.2   Detection by Sharing the Distributed Beliefs

As the distributed denial of service (DDoS) attack traffic transmits across the Internet towards the victim, the victim can detect the attack easily by observing the degraded services. However, it is hard for the victim to locate the attack sources to filter the DDoS attack traffic. The key role for the intrusion detection system is to detect the DDoS attack traffic as close to the attack source as possible. As we analyzed before, the DDoS attack traffic will cause the increase of a large number of new IP addresses. However, since the transit network will only see part of the DDoS attack traffic, the number of increased new IP addresses might not be large enough to raise a alarm. As shown in Figure 2, let y_l and y_r be the detection variables that Intrusion Detection System (IDS) agent **L** and **R** will observe and let N_l and N_r be the detection thresholds for the IDS agent **L** and **R** respectively. Then, $y_l < N_l$ and $y_r < N_r$. Thus, each agent acting in isolation has insufficient evidence to consider the traffic to be suspicious.

In order to detect this distributed denial of service attack, the two agents need to cooperate by sharing their beliefs about potentially suspicious traffic. This raises two challenges. First, we need a framework for combining different agents' beliefs about the incoming traffic. Second, we need a function that decides when to share beliefs about the incoming traffic.

Combining beliefs. It is important that our model for combining beliefs should use summary information about the traffic rather than raw measurements about each new IP address in the incoming traffic, in order to minimize the communication overhead. Without loss of generality, we consider there are two transit networks where the DDoS attack passing through, each with its own intrusion detection agent. It is a trivial matter to apply our model to larger numbers of agents. Let $\mathcal{D}^L$ and $\mathcal{D}^R$ denote the set of hosts in the left and right transit networks, respectively. Let $P_n(\mathcal{D}^L)$ and $P_n(\mathcal{D}^R)$ represent the percentage of new IP addresses that pass the transition network L and R. As we analyzed in Section 3.1, the decision function is based on monitoring the percentage of new IP addresses during the designated time interval. If one IDS agent can update the percentage of new IP addresses by sharing the distributed beliefs, it can recalculate the detection variable y_n using CUSUM algorithm. Therefore, the IDS agent can make a decision by combining beliefs from other IDS agents.

The first step to realize our distributed model is to calculate the percentage of new IP addresses by sharing the distributed beliefs. Let $\mathcal{F}^L$ and $\mathcal{F}^R$ represent the collection of the frequent IP addresses which are stored in the IP Address Database (IAD). Let $\mathcal{M}^L$ and $\mathcal{M}^R$ represent the collection of the incoming IP addresses during the monitoring period. Thus, we have $P_n(\mathcal{D}^L) = \frac{|\mathcal{M}^L| - |\mathcal{M}^L \cap \mathcal{F}^L|}{|\mathcal{F}^L|}$ and $P_n(\mathcal{D}^R) = \frac{|\mathcal{M}^R| - |\mathcal{M}^R \cap \mathcal{F}^R|}{|\mathcal{F}^R|}$. Ideally, when we combine the belief, the percentage of new IP addresses to two transition network should be $P_n(\mathcal{D}) = \frac{|\mathcal{M}^L \cup \mathcal{M}^R| - |(\mathcal{M}^L \cup \mathcal{M}^R) \cap (\mathcal{F}^L \cup \mathcal{F}^R)|}{|\mathcal{F}^L \cup \mathcal{F}^R|}$. However, in order to get an accurate value of $P_n(\mathcal{D})$ we need raw measurement, for example, $\mathcal{M}^L$ and $\mathcal{F}^L$, which takes a huge communication overhead. In order to simplify the implementation of this scheme, we make the following assumptions. First, the IADs of the two transition networks have a big overlap, i.e., $|\mathcal{F}^L \cup \mathcal{F}^R| \simeq max(|\mathcal{F}^L|, |\mathcal{F}^R|)$. Second, $\mathcal{M}^L$ and $\mathcal{M}^R$ are disjoint collections. Thus, the simplified calculation is $P_n(\mathcal{D}) = \frac{|\mathcal{M}^L| + |\mathcal{M}^R| - |\mathcal{M}^L \cap \mathcal{F}^L| - |\mathcal{M}^R \cap \mathcal{F}^R|}{max(|\mathcal{F}^L|, |\mathcal{F}^R|)}$.

Given this method for combining beliefs about the incoming traffic from different agents, we need to formulate a technique for deciding *when* to broadcast this information, and hence combine beliefs between agents.

Learning when to broadcast the warning message. Our aim is to find a decision function that can be used by agents to decide when they should share the beliefs. Agents should share information when there is a significant change in belief that is likely to help confirm a hypothesis. Our approach is based on the learning scheme described in [9].

We have used a decision function based on the CUSUM algorithm described in the previous sections. Recall that an agent L considers an attack happens if

$$N_l < y_l.$$

Our decision function should trigger a broadcast before the agent has confirmed that the incoming traffic is attack traffic. The key issue is how small this difference in likelihoods should be before we broadcast.

We introduce a parameter T that represents the threshold at which we should broadcast. Thus, our decision function is:

$$\text{Broadcast if } N_l - y_l < T.$$

If T is large then the agent will broadcast early, when it has seen few new IP addresses and y_l is small. Conversely, if T is small, then the agent will delay broadcasting until it has seen sufficient new IP addresses to increase y_l in comparison to N_l.

The aim of learning is to find an optimum broadcast threshold T, so that we avoid wasting broadcasts while minimizing the detection delay. We need to adjust T in response to feedback about how our multi-agent system performs in comparison to a centralized monitoring approach. Each time a DDoS attack occurs, we record how many new IP addresses (γ_m) were needed before our multi-agent system detected the DDoS attack. We can also determine how many new IP addresses (γ_s) would have been needed by a centralized system using a single agent to analyze all the incoming IP addresses. Note that $\gamma_m \geq \gamma_s$. We refer to the difference $\delta = \gamma_m - \gamma_s$ as the *confirmation delay* of using a distributed approach. We can also record whether an agent issued a broadcast in the course of analyzing the number of new IP addresses of the incoming traffic. Let $\sigma = 1$ if a broadcast was made, otherwise $\sigma = 0$.

In order to measure the performance of our multi-agent system, we can average δ and σ over a large number of DDoS attacks. Let $\bar{\delta}$ and $\bar{\sigma}$ denote the average confirmation delay and the average number of broadcasts over a set of

DDoS attacks. Given that we want to minimize both these quantities, we define our feedback function as

$$f(T) = \sqrt{u(\bar{\delta})^2 + v(\bar{\sigma})^2},$$

where u and v can be any functions. In our case, we have used the identity function for u and v.

For a given setting of the threshold T in our decision function, we can observe the feedback function $f(T)$ by averaging over a set of DDoS attacks. Consequently, we can use $f(T)$ as our objective function to optimize T. This is an example of a stochastic optimization problem, where the objective function and its gradient can only be estimated by observation. We can solve this problem using a technique known as stochastic approximation (see [14] for an overview). We use the current value of T_k at the kth iteration to estimate T_{k+1} using:

$$T_{k+1} = T_k - a_k \hat{g}_k(T_k),$$

where $\hat{g}_k(T_k)$ is an estimate of the gradient of the objective function at $f(T_k)$, and a_k is a step size co-efficient. The gradient is estimated using perturbations $\pm c_k$ around T_k:

$$\hat{g}_k(T_k) = \frac{f(T_k + c_k) - f(T_k - c_k)}{2c_k}.$$

We choose the perturbations and step size based on a scheme by Spall [15]. Based on Spall's recommendations, we found that a global minimum was obtained using $a_k = 10/\sqrt{k}$ and $c_k = 1/\sqrt{k}$.

Using this scheme, we can learn an optimum value of T that minimizes both the communication overhead and the confirmation delay. In our test domain, we observed that there was a well-defined global minimum for T. We have used this approach in a centralized learning scheme, where each agent uses the same threshold value. It is a simple matter for agents to archive measurements of confirmed attacks, so that they can be downloaded later as training examples for learning. In order to provide a basis for comparison with our machine learning approach, we have developed a default decision function that is based on random broadcasts. Our default decision function is to broadcast after an agent has received M new measurements relating to a hypothesis, where M is uniformly distributed $Uniform(1, M_{max})$.

Random broadcasts: Broadcast belief in a hypotheses each time the detection variable reaches M, where $M := Uniform(0, M_{max})$ is reset after each broadcast.

We use this decision function as a benchmark to explore the trade-off between communication overhead and confirmation delay by varying M_{max}.

4   Performance Evaluation

To evaluate the efficacy of our detection scheme SIM, we created different types of DDoS attack traffic and merged them with the normal traffic. SIM was then applied to detect the attacks from the merged traffic. The normal traffic traces used in our study are collected at the University of Auckland [6] with an OC3 (155.52 Mbps) Internet access link in March 2001.

4.1   Performance of SIM

To test the detection sensitivity for DDoS attacks with different numbers of new IP addresses, we conducted the following experiment. We used the incoming traffic to the University of Auckland as the background traffic for the last-mile router detection evaluation, and outgoing traffic from the University of Auckland as the background traffic for the first-mile router detection evaluation. As mentioned before, our detection algorithm is not affected by whether the attack traffic is bursty or constant since the detection is based on the cumulative effect of the attack traffic. For the simplicity of the experiment design, we assume the attack traffic rate to be constant. The attack period is set to be 5 minutes, which is a commonly observed attack period in the Internet [11]. The attack traffic rate for the last-mile router is set to be 500 Kbps [1] in order to constitute an effective bandwidth attack to medium-size victim networks, which in our case is the network of the University of Auckland.

Let W represent the number IP addresses in the attack traffic which are new to the network. The detection performance for the first and last-mile routers using different values of W are shown in Tables 1 and 2.

As we can see from the simulation results, our detection algorithm is very robust in both the first-mile and last-mile routers. For the last-mile router, we can detect the DDoS attack with $W = 18$ within 81.1 seconds with 100% accuracy, and detect the DDoS attack with $W = 15$ within 127.3 seconds with 90% accuracy. Given the attack traffic length is no more than 5 minutes, only the attack traffic with $W < 18$ has the possibility of sometimes avoiding our detection. However, by forcing the attacker to use a small number of new IP addresses, we can detect the attack by observing the abrupt change in the number of packets per IP source address.

For the first-mile router, we can achieve 99% detection accuracy even when there are only 2 new IP addresses in the attack traffic. This is because the background traffic for the first-mile router is very clear. Generally, there will be very few IP addresses that are new to the network since all the valid IP packets originated from within the same network. Since the IP addresses in the *IP Address Database* (IAD) will expire and be removed after a certain time period, the IP addresses within the subnetworks which have not been used recently will be new to IAD. This is very similar to ingress filtering [4]. However, ingress filtering cannot detect the attack when the spoofed IP addresses are within the subnetworks. In contrast, our first-mile router detection algorithm can detect the spoofed IP addresses within the subnetworks if they are new to the IAD. In our experiment we used a conservative detection interval $\Delta_n = 10s$. If we decrease

---

[1] We set the attack traffic volume to be low in order to test the sensitivity and robustness of our scheme.

the detection interval by using more computing resources, we can reduce the detection time accordingly.

Table 1. Detection performance of first-mile router

W	Accuracy	Detection Time
2	99%	69.7s
4	100%	20.1s
6	100%	18.9s
8	100%	10s
10	100%	10s

Table 2. Detection performance of last-mile router

W	Accuracy	Detection Time
15	90%	127.3s
18	100%	81.1s
40	100%	18.9s
60	100%	10s
200	100%	10s

4.2 Performance of Combining Beliefs

We have evaluated our learning technique by testing its performance on a set of simulated distributed denial of service attacks, and comparing its performance to a default decision function that is based on random broadcasts. We measure the performance of these two approaches in terms of the average confirmation delay and the average number of broadcasts made by our multi-agent system on the set of simulated DDoS attcks.

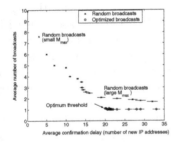

Fig. 3. The distributed detection model

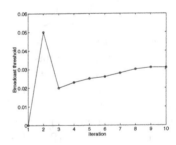

Fig. 4. Convergence of the distributed detection model

We introduce two types of costs for learning. The first cost is the cost of sharing information by broadcasting. The second cost is confirmation delay. When an attacker starts a DDoS attack, it is initially classified as normal until it has created enough new IP addresses to be classified as an attack. The same attack takes longer to detect in a multi-agent system compared to a centralized system, because each agent sees only a subset of the attack traffic. Given enough new IP addresses, the multi-agent system will reach the same conclusion as the centralized system. Hence, it is important to measure this confirmation delay.

In order to measure these two costs, we have tested our multi-agent approach on a set of known DDoS attacks, and compared its performance to our centralized approach. We have generated DDoS attacks with sufficiently large volume so that they are always detected by the centralized approach, and almost always detected by the multi-agent approach. On the rare occasions when our multi-agent approach is unable to detect the DDoS attack in the given number of new IP addresses, the cost of misclassification is reflected by setting the confirmation delay to the total length of the DDoS attack.

We have based our simulated DDoS attacks on the Auckland traces. In the data traces, all the IP addresses have been mapped into 10.*.*.* using one-to-one hash mapping for privacy. Let IP prefix 10.1.*.* represent transit network L and IP prefix 10.2.*.* represent transit network R. For all the traffic with the destination IP address 10.1.*.* and 10.2.*.* are analyzed by the intrusion detection agent L and R respectively. Each agent monitors the percentage of new IP addresses and calculates the CUSUM variable y_n to decide whether it is an attack. If any evidence has been broadcast from the other agent, then it is included in this evaluation. The agent also uses its decision function to determine if it should share its beliefs with the other agent.

Once an agent has confirmed that the traffic is attack traffic, we record the total number of new IP addresses that were generated by the DDoS attack before it was detected, as well as the number of broadcasts received by the agent before it reached its conclusion. We also determined the number of new IP addresses that would have been required by a centralized agent in order to confirm that a DDoS attack happens. The difference between the number of new IP addresses needed by the multi-agent system and the centralized system represents the confirmation delay in using a distributed approach.

We used this procedure to evaluate our optimized and default decision functions in terms of the number of broadcasts needed and the confirmation delay. For the optimized decision function, our feedback function $f(T)$ was averaged over 1000 trials, where each trial is defined as a new simulated DDoS attack with a random assignment of attack traffic volume. It was necessary to average over a large number of trials in order to eliminate random variations in individual DDoS attacks. For the default decision function using random broadcasts, we tried 17 different settings of M_{max} from 0.01 to 0.05. At each setting, we averaged the results over 1000 random trials.

The results are shown in Figure 3. Each point in the graph corresponds to the average of 1000 trials using the indicated decision function. The 95% confidence intervals for these averages are shown at each point. Note that there are separate confidence intervals for the average number of broadcasts and the average confirmation delay, since these are both dependent variables of the given settings of the decision function. The results using random broadcasts form a curve, with small values of M_{max} on the left, and large values on the right. If an optimized decision function is to be considered acceptable, it should fall below the envelope formed by the random broadcasts.

Our learning technique found an optimum value of $T = 0.03$, which resulted in an average of 1.1 broadcasts per agent and an average confirmation delay of 20 new IP addresses. The optimization converged after 10 iterations, as shown in Figure 4. Figure 3 shows the trajectory of successive T_k values moving from right to left, with the results for the optimum value of T_k indicated. Note that all the values of T_k performed better than the random broadcasts.

In summary, our results demonstrate that we can learn a decision function for when to share beliefs without requiring any prior knowledge of the domain. Furthermore, we can learn a decision function that outperforms a default decision function based on random broadcast periods.

5   Related Work

Gil proposes a scheme called MULTOPS [5] to detect DoS attacks by monitoring the packet rate in both the up and down links. However, MULTOPS assumes that packet rates between two hosts are proportional and the IP addresses are not spoofed. Wang et al. [16] developed a scheme to detect SYN flood attacks by observing the ratio of SYN packets to FIN packets. However, the attacker can bypass the detection by sending SYN and FIN packets together.

Distributed intrusion detection has been studied in a number of systems. Krugel et al. [8] have developed a system for distributed pattern detection, and analyzed its throughput and bandwidth requirements. In contrast to our probabilistic approach, they use constraint-based correlation. Consequently, they do not model uncertain beliefs.

6   Conclusion

In this paper we proposed a multi-agent scheme to detect distributed denial of service attacks by monitoring the increase of new IP addresses. We have also presented a machine learning scheme to optimize the communication between the agents while sharing the distributed beliefs.

We demonstrated the efficiency and robustness of this scheme by using trace-driven simulations. The experimental results in the Auckland traces show that we can detect DDoS attacks with 100% accuracy using as few as 18 new IP addresses in the last-mile router and DDoS attacks using as few as 2 new IP address in the first-mile router. Our online detection algorithm is fast and has a very low computing overhead. Furthermore, our first-mile router SIM has the advantage over ingress filtering [4] that it can detect attack traffic with spoofed source IP addresses within the subnetworks.

We have evaluated our learning technique using extensive simulations of DDoS attacks based on packet trace data from a real network. This evaluation demonstrated that we can reduce both the delay and communication overhead required to detect network intrusions, in comparison to a default decision function that relies on arbitrarily chosen broadcast periods.

Acknowledgement. We thank the Waikato Applied Network Dynamics Research Group for their data traces. This work was supported by the Australia Research Council.

References

1. M. Basseville and I. V. Nikiforov. *Detection of Abrupt Changes: Theory and Application*. Prentice Hall, 1993.
2. B. E. Brodsky and B. S. Darkhovsky. *Nonparametric Methods in Change-point Problems*. Kluwer Academic Publishers, 1993.
3. Anirban Chakrabarti and G. Manimaran. Internet infrastructure security: A taxonomy. *IEEE Network*, 16:13–21, 2002.
4. P. Ferguson and D. Senie. *Network ingress filtering: Defeating denial of service attacks which employ IP source address spoofing.* RFC2267, IETF, January 1998.
5. Thomer M. Gil and Massimiliano Poletto. Multops: a data-structure for bandwidth attack detection. In *Proceedings of the 10th USENIX Security Symposium*, 2001.
6. Waikato Applied Network Dynamics Research Group. Auckland university data traces. http://wand.cs.waikato.ac.nz/wand/wits/.
7. Jaeyeon Jung, Balachander Krishnamurthy, and Michael Rabinovich. Flash crowds and denial of service attacks: Characterization and implications for CDNs and web sites. *Proceeding of 11th World Wide Web conference*, 2002. May 7–11, 2002, Honolulu, Hawaii, USA.
8. C. Krugel and T. Toth. Distributed pattern detection for intrusion detection. In *Proceedings of Network and Distributed System Security Symposium*, 2002.
9. C. Leckie and R. Kotagiri. Learning to share distributed probabilistic beliefs. In *Proceedings of the Nineteenth International Conference on Machine Learning (ICML-2002)*, Sydney, Australia, July 2002.
10. Ratul Mahajan, Steven M. Bellovin, Sally Floyd, John Ioannidis, Vern Paxson, and Scott Shenker. Controlling high bandwidth aggregates in the network. Technical report, AT&T Center for Internet Research at ICSI (ACIRI) and AT&T Labs Research, February 2001.
11. David Moore, Geoffrey M. Voeker, and Stefan Savage. Inferring internet Denial-of-Service acitivity. In *Proceedings of the USENIX Security Symposium*, pages 9–22, August 2001.
12. Tao Peng, Christopher Leckie, and Kotagiri Ramamohanarao. Detecting distributed denial of service attacks using source IP address monitoring. draft, November 2002.
13. Tao Peng, Christopher Leckie, and Kotagiri Ramamohanarao. Prevention from distributed denial of service attacks using history-based IP filtering. In *Proceeding of ICC 2003 (to appear)*, Anchorage, Alaska, USA, August 2003.
14. J.S. Rustagi. *Optimization techniques in statistics*. Boston : Academic Press, 1994.
15. J.C. Spall. Implementation of the simultaneous perturbation algorithm for stochastic optimization. In *IEEE Trans. on Aerospace and Electronic Systems*, volume 34, pages 817–823, 1998.
16. Haining Wang, Danlu Zhang, and Kang G. Shin. Detecting SYN flooding attacks. In *Proceedings of IEEE Infocom'2002*, June 2002.

Malicious ICMP Tunneling: Defense against the Vulnerability

Abhishek Singh, Ola Nordström, Chenghuai Lu, and Andre L.M. dos Santos

Georgia Tech. Information Security Center (GTISC)
Center for Experimental Research in Computer Systems (CERCS)
College of Computing
Georgia Institute of Technology
Atlanta, GA 30332
{abhi,nalo,lulu,andre}@cc.gatech.edu

Abstract. This paper presents a systematic solution to the problem of using ICMP tunneling for covert channel. ICMP is not multiplexed via port numbers and the data part of the ICMP packet provides considerable bandwidth for malicious covert channels. These factors make it an integral part of many malicious software like remote access and denial of service attack tools. These tools use ICMP to establish covert communication channels. In this paper a stateless model is proposed to prevent ICMP tunneling. A Linux kernel module was implemented to demonstrate the proposed stateless solution. The module enforces a fixed payload policy for ICMP packets and virtually eliminates ICMP tunneling which arises due to the data carrying capability of ICMP. The performance impact on end hosts and routers due to the stateless monitoring model is described.

1 Introduction

The Internet and the World Wide Web (WWW) have had a phenomenal growth during the past few years, interconnecting average users and average user to expert users who are not always good neighbors. Many Internet attacks, both simulated and real, have been described by the security community and have appeared in mainstream media. Two factors that have contributed to widespread Internet attacks are the lack of security as an initial design consideration for the Internet and the average user's inadequate knowledge of threats faced every time their computer is connected to the Internet. Although the attacks vary on their form, most of them have a common goal of leaving a back door open for a future communication with a victim machine.

Internet communication is based, in addition to the Internet Protocol (IP), on three basic protocols: Transmission Control Protocol (TCP), User Datagram Protocol (UDP), and Internet Control Message Protocol (ICMP). Firewalls, depending on the services required by their internal networks, totally block or partially filter Internet packets using one or more of these protocols. An attacker has to decide which protocol or protocols they will use to communicate

R. Safavi-Naini and J. Seberry (Eds.): ACISP 2003, LNCS 2727, pp. 226–236, 2003.
© Springer-Verlag Berlin Heidelberg 2003

with a backdoor installed on a host that has been compromised. The attacker's objective is to make the traffic generated by the backdoor appear as much as possible to be normal traffic so it is not blocked by the firewall. TCP and UDP, the most widely used protocols by application servers, are the ones that can be abused with the greatest chance of allowing the traffic to pass through. TCP and UDP packets can carry information either manipulating unused parts of the packet or making the payload look legitimate. For example, various header fields like ACK flags and port number can be used to establish covert communication using TCP or UDP [10]. Knowing about the possibility of this kind of attacks, firewalls like IP Filter can prevent covert channels that make use of TCP/UDP header fields for its communication. IP Filter [9] uses stateful packet filtering. The state engine not only inspects the presence of ACK flags in TCP packets but also includes sequence numbers and window sizes in its decision to block or to allow packets. However, IP Filter does not check the content of ICMP packets and hence fails to prevent covert channels that can arise due to misuse of the payload of ICMP packets. Therefore, although TCP and UDP continue to be a subject for studies in vulnerabilities, ICMP also provides several means for stealth traffic.

ICMP tunneling was first reported in the 1997 [8] [7]. Initial versions of ICMP tunneling enabled an attacker to execute remote commands and steal information from a compromised machine. Although ICMP tunneling has been used for user-user and user - machine communication, its most damaging usage has been for coordination of distributed denial of service attacks. In early February 2000, a distributed denial of service attack was launched against Yahoo, Amazon, eBay and other popular Internet sites. The attacks on Yahoo, eBay, Amazon.com and E*Trade resulted in a loss of approximately $1.2 billion, according to The Yankee Group, a Boston consulting firm. It is reported in [11] that almost all of the tools used on the distributed denial of service (DDOS) attacks on Yahoo, Amazon, eBay, and E*Trade internet sites, have used ICMP for covert communications between the DDOS clients and the attacker's handler program. Some of the most widely known distributed denial of service attack tools like Tribe Flood Net2K [1] and Stacheldraht rely on ICMP tunneling to establish communication channels between the compromised machines and the hacker's machine. Since ICMP tunneling is very simple to deploy and can cause a significant amount of damage it has been classified as a high risk security threat by Internet Security Services [4] and SANS [12].

The rest of the paper is organized as follows. Section 2 presents the solutions that are currently being used to prevent ICMP tunneling. Section 3 presents experimental result of a modified application using ICMP tunneling. Section 4 discusses the proposed solution and its performance impact on routers and on end hosts. Finally, in section 5 conclusion and future work are presented.

2   ICMP Tunneling Vulnerability

Most types of ICMP packets like echo_request/echo_reply (commonly used for ping) have the capability of carrying data in its payload. This data carrying capability of ICMP can be used to establish covert channels. Various malicious applications like "Loki" [8] [7] use the data carrying capability of ICMP to establish covert channels. The use of ICMP for covert communication presents one big advantage over the use of TCP or UDP. ICMP packets use fewer parameters than TCP or UDP. For example, ICMP does not use port numbers. Port number gives an additional parameter for firewalls to filter suspicious traffic. The first 64 bits of the original IP datagram's data are used by the host to match ICMP error messages to the appropriate application level process. The simplicity and lack of parameters used in ICMP have made it popular for hackers designing tools that require covert communication.

Many solutions have been proposed to prevent ICMP tunneling. Some of the proposed solutions currently being used to prevent ICMP tunneling are discussed in the following paragraphs.

Disable all ICMP traffic. Disabling all ICMP traffic prevents covert communication using ICMP packets. However, ICMP messages are required to check the status of a network and communicate IP packet errors. Therefore, disabling all ICMP messages prevents covert communication, but also prevents users on one side of the network protected by the firewall to check the status of machines on the other side or receive valid ICMP packets related to transient network problems. This limitation is not acceptable in some environments and is not a general solution.

Disable part of the ICMP traffic allowed by a firewall. For example, disable incoming echo_request, while allowing outgoing echo_request. If naively implemented, policies like this will still allow covert communication, limiting only which host needs to start a communication. In addition, outgoing ICMP packets could be used to establish a unidirectional channel to send compromised information. A modified server can periodically send ICMP packets containing sensitive information. For example, an e- commerce web server could switch to ICMP mode of communication for 10 second after every 30 minutes. During these 10 seconds it could send to a receiving machine, credit card information that has been captured during the previous 30 minutes.

Limit the size of ICMP packets. Large ICMP packet can be seen as suspicious by an IDS system that could inspect the ICMP packet and raise an alarm. However, since there are legitimate uses for large ICMP packets it is difficult to determine if a large ICMP packet is malicious. For example, large echo_request packets are used to check if a network is able to carry large packets. Differentiating legal from illegal large packets is even more difficult if covert communication is encrypted. An IDS needs to be able to determine if a packet is encrypted or not. Distinguishing encrypted from non-encrypted packet still remains an open interesting research problem.

Preserve the state of ICMP packet to check for covert channel. Some firewalls like Raptor use state preservation technique to prevent ICMP tunneling. A dae-

mon called pingd runs as an application process on the firewall. If the firewall is
the target of ping then pingd responds to the client normally. If the firewall is
not the target of ping then pingd will construct a new echo request with a new
sequence number, new time to live, and a new payload (with new checksum).
When the reply is received it is ensured that the data is the same as what had
been sent, and the sequence number and responders IP address are valid and as
expected. After a successful check the firewall transmits the echo_reply to the
original client. Although state preserving technique can easily prevent ICMP
tunneling, it is a computing intensive process. Therefore, currently application
level personal firewalls do not use state preserving techniques. Application level
personal firewalls [8] running on personal computers only monitor inbound and
outbound Internet traffic and alerts the user when an application is attempting
access their personal computer or their machine is trying to access something on
the Internet. As per the configuration rule, personal firewalls can either block
ICMP or allow it irrespective of the fact that the ICMP is being used for tunneling. Protecting personal machines from ICMP tunneling is very important since
there are a large number of personal machines connected to high speed links
which in turn can be used to launch DDOS attacks.

Although some of the solutions presented above can be acceptable, ideally
the prevention of ICMP misuse due to their data carrying capabilities should be
able to provide the following.

- It should enable users to use ICMP messages for administrative purposes
  freely.
- It should allow large size of ICMP so users can find out if the network can
  carry large size of data packets.
- It should be able to prevent personal machines that are not behind powerful
  state preserving firewalls from being used as DDOS slaves.

3   ICMP Tunneling: Case Study

An application that uses ICMP tunneling was implemented and studied to better
understand the ICMP tunneling efficiency and capabilities. The application, a
remote access tool, is described in this section.

Remote Access Tools allows a user to access data and control a remote computer. Back Orifice (BO2K) [2] was used to test ICMP tunneling due to the
easy availability of its source code. The communication infrastructure of BO2K
was moved to ICMP. An ICMP echo_request contained the remote command
issued by a client of BO2K and an echo_reply contained the information from
the machine that was running BO2K server. Strong authentication and encryption was also implemented to evaluate the impact of these features. The Bellovin
and Merritt [2] key exchange known for its strong authentication and establishment of session keys was implemented in the BO2K communication protocol.
The session key generated by the Bellovin and Merritt protocol was then used
to encrypt the data using 3DES. The server and the client of the modified BO2K

were installed on a pair of personal computers. The machines were connected via the Internet and were using the personal firewall as their application level firewall.

3.1   Results

Since ICMP uses raw sockets for its communication, root (administrator) privileges are required. For the experimentation purposes it was assumed that the root privileges could be obtained. More details about getting the root permission can be found in [3]. However, in most of the commonly used operating systems like Windows ME/98 root permission is not required. In addition, it was also assumed that the firewall is customized to allow ICMP packets.

The personal firewall used in the machines was set up such that it raise an alarm in the form of a pop up window each and every time it sees an incoming or an outgoing data packet. For an incoming connection, the pop up window displays the IP address of the machine initiating the connection and the protocol, which is being used for the connection. For an outgoing connection, the pop up window shows the IP address of the destination machine along with the protocol used for the communication. A server and a client BO2K were installed on machines running the Windows ME operating system. Snapshots of the connection initiation steps and the real time interaction steps are omitted due to limited space. However as per our observation the ICMP mode of communication provides false information to the firewall. Even though ICMP packets are being sent by the application, the firewall infers them to be sent by the operating system. The real time interactions enabled by the modified application shows that ICMP tunneling is highly efficient and can be used in many malicious applications. Even though ICMP packets are being used by the application, the personal firewall infers these ICMP packets as the control messages issued by the operating system.

4   Proposed Solution

The solution to prevent ICMP tunneling should:

- Enable administrators to use ICMP messages freely.
- Enable large size of ICMP to be used.
- Work for every machine connected to the Internet.

Instead of the expensive and centralized state preserving model used by industrial firewalls, a simple stateless model is proposed to prevent tunneling. The stateless model caters to the above mentioned requirements. The proposed solution, which requires a common agreement upon the allowable payload of ICMP messages, should be implemented in the ICMP protocol implementation of the kernel. It should be enforced either when an ICMP packet is going up the network stack or when it is going down the stack. The solution uses the algorithm shown in Figure 6. This algorithm first scans the content of the payload of the

ICMP packet against a predefined set. If any malicious content is found in the payload an alarm is raised. The algorithm then zeros out the entire data carrying field irrespective of the ICMP type.

Linux was chosen for the implementation of the proposed solution because of its freely available source code. The Netfilter framework was used to extend existing functionality within the kernel. Netfilter [15] is a set of hooks inside the Linux 2.4.x kernel's network stack which allows kernel modules to register callback functions, called when a network packet traverses one of the predefined hooks. The handlers will execute as if they were part of the packet processing pipeline directly. Netfilter allows a module to register the IP_POST_ROUTING hook that is called after a packet has been through the routing table and right before it is delivered to the outgoing interface (typically an Ethernet device). The ICMP monitor (icmp_mon) is registered with the IP_POST_ROUTING handler, and thus allowing icmp_mon to process all locally outbound packets as well as forward packets since all packets go through the post routing hooks. The icmp_mon module at runtime calls icmp_mon_erase and icmp_mon_scan to perform a combination of actions.

- icmp_mon_erase; Zeros out unused portions of ICMP messages.
- icmp _mon _scan; Scans packets for predefined strings

The icmp_mon_scan module raises an alarm when it detects some suspicious content in the data portion of the packet. The packet is then forwarded to the icmp_mon_erase module. Irrespective of the fact that it is carrying some malicious strings the data field of ICMP is filled with zeros. Thus the proposed solution can stop even encrypted traffic. Since the packet is analyzed when it is outbound, the proposed solution will work in the case of packets that are locally generated or are forwarded on behalf of another machine. Hence this patch can work in machines that are acting as a gateway, router, sensor or as a host.

```
ICMP_MON (ICMP packet)
Begin
    input : ICMP Packet
    for every ICMP packet
    Begin
        icmp_mon_scan (data portion of ICMP packet)
        If the data field matches with the signature
            Raise an alarm.
    End
    icmp_mon_erase{data portion of the ICMP packet}
    Begin
        Fill in the data portion with zeros.
    End
End
```

The module can be compiled directly into a monolithic kernel. The filter hooks are registered when the modules init routines are called at the boot time if it is compiled into the kernel. The proposed module cannot be bypassed by user space applications since it does not interact with any. Iptables is the user space command that is used to modify Linux firewalling rules. Iptables is typically used to add and remove filtering rules pertaining to regular TCP/IP packets. Because icmp_mon is not part of iptables, the only way to disable the scanning is to remove the module (using rmmod), which is not possible in this scenario since the module is statically compiled into a monolithic kernel. When using a monolithic kernel the machine would have to be rebooted into a different kernel to disable the icmp_mon from operating. This is not trivial to do on a compromised host machine. In addition, if the proposed patch is running on a gateway or at a sensor that is monitoring network traffic then stronger restrictions and event logs can make this option even more difficult to attain.

The proposed solution will make it impossible for an adversary to setup an ICMP covert communication channel on a compromised machine since packets are scanned and erased by the kernel. The stateless model implemented in the kernel benefits from the fact that there is no way to turn off this functionality by simply terminating or modifying an application, which could easily be done on a compromised machine if packets were queued to a user-space intrusion detection application. The proposed stateless model of scanning and erasing the data fields can be implemented in the kernel used by hosts, sensors, gateways and routers so as to completely eliminate ICMP tunneling.

4.1   Results of the Proposed Solution

The icmp_mon scanning and erasing times were tested on ICMP ECHO request packets. The testing machine was a Dual Pentium III 450 MHz machine with 512 MB of RAM. Internally all network packets are time stamped upon arrival in the Linux kernel. The time from arrival up to when the icmp_mon routines are referred as the "Kernel Time", or specifically the time the packet has been traversing inside the kernels packet processing. The total time spent inside the icmp_mon routine, ignoring the overhead caused by the netfilter hooks will be referred to as the "erase/scan time" depending on the operation performed.

The first test was implemented in the kernel of a host machine. In the second test the proposed module was implemented in the kernel of a machine acting as a router. For each of these tests the time to process packets of fixed size in the kernel was compared with the scan and erase time. The tests on host machine and router were again repeated with the packets of variable sizes. All the tests were performed using the standard Unix "ping" command; it was typically run as follows "ping -c Count -s Size -f host", were the Count and Size were either fixed or varied depending on the test. The "-f" option was used to flood ping, the icmp_mon module would sum the processing times for a given number of packets (corresponding to the Count given to the ping command) then the mean time was calculated after the given number of packets had passed through. The gettimeofday() call was used to get the time, on the Intel platform the granularity available is microseconds.

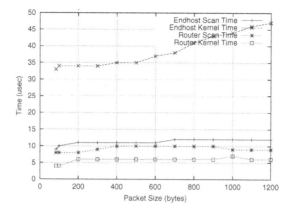

Fig. 1. Scanning vs. Kernel Time for Variable Size Packets

The graph shown in figure 1 presents the performance cost associated with the string scanning routines of the icmp_mon. The size of the packet was increased from 100 bytes to 1200 bytes and time to process 1000 packets of each size was measured and plotted in the graph shown in figure 1. This test was performed both for the router and for the end host. The simple words searched for were "passwd", "root", "tmp" ,"etc", "ls" , and "dir". They were never present in the ping packets thus the scans never raised any alarms. As per the graph for the router the scan time is more than the time to process packet. The machine is simply receiving the packets in one interface and sending them out another, which makes the kernel time incredibly small. In the case of the end host the time to process a packet increases with the packet size, however the processing time is small as compared to the kernel time. The scan time shows a marginal increase, however it remains constant when the size of packet is increases from 700 bytes to 1200 bytes.

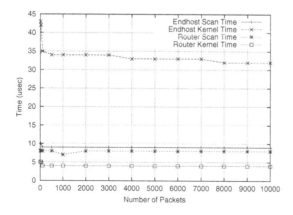

Fig. 2. Scanning vs. Kernel Time for Fixed Size Packets

The graph shown in figure 2 shows the time taken for scanning the ICMP payloads of fixed size of 84 bytes. For this test the number of packets was increased from 10 to 10000 and the scan time was plotted. A 2 microsecond increase was observered when the number of packets increased from 1000 to 10000. As the number of back to back packets increased (due to the ping flood) the kernel time per packet decrease. The kernel time goes down because the flood of packets allows the kernel routines to grab multiple packets back to back without returning to a different routine (thus loosing time due to context switching). When the machine is acting as a router the scan time is again more than the time to process a packet by the kernel. The scan time shows a marginal increase as the number of packet increases.

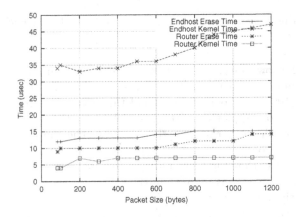

Fig. 3. Erase Time vs. Kernel Time for Variable Size Packets

The result showing in figure 3 gives the average time spent inside the kernel and the icmp_mon _erase routines when the patch is running on a router and on and end host. This test was performed by keeping the number of ICMP packet to 1000 packets for each size and increasing the size of packets from 84 bytes to 1200 bytes. As the packet size increases, the time to process packet inside the kernel for the end host increases. This increase is almost linear. Size has no effect on the processing time for the end routers. The time is contrasted against and increasing packet size, starting with 84 byte IP packets (54 unused/padded bytes inside the PING), the default "ping" packet size. The time spent increases marginally up to about 700 byte packets. As the size of the packet increases erase time increases. Erase time increases by around 5 microsecond in routers and around 3 microseconds for end host kernel when the size of packet is increased from 84 bytes to 1200 bytes.

The result shown in figure 4 shows the performance result of the erase time contrasted with the fixed packet size. As the number of back to back packets increased (due to the ping flood) the kernel time per packet shows a slight decrease but the erase time shows a very low variance. The decrease in the

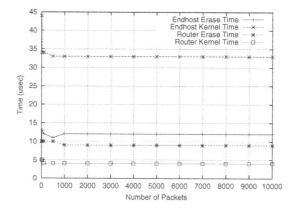

Fig. 4. Erasing Time vs. Kernel Time for Fixed Size Packets

kernel time is due to the loss in context switching. The increase in the time to erase 10000 packets as compared to 1000 packets is very small and can be considered constant. From these tests following conclusions can be made.

- In the case of routers the packets get the initial timestamp after it has been fully received by the driver. Then the kernel simply looks at the ip dst field and adds the packet buffer to the output queue, which is a simple pointer assignment. Thus the total kernel processing time is marginal, extremely small, a few micro seconds as compared to the scan and erase time. This means that the overhead for scanning/erasing is much higher in comparison.
- In the case of end hosts the scan and erase time is very small as compared to the total time to process the packet.
- For fixed size packets the scan and erase time remains constant or shows a very low variance as the number of packets increases.
- As the packet size increases from 84 bytes to 1200 bytes the scan and erase time increases. The worst case increase was observed to be 5 microseconds.

5   Conclusion and Future Work

ICMP tunneling can be used in an efficient way by malicious software. To prevent ICMP tunneling kernel modifications were proposed to enforce a fixed predefined payload policy for ICMP packets. If the proposed solution becomes an integral part of kernels that runs as host, gateways, and DMZ routers then it will be impossible to establish ICMP tunnels. Another way to remove ICMP tunneling could be to simply truncate the data field of ICMP. However truncation of the data field will require amendments in the RFC [6] [5] that supports data field for ICMP. Scanning and erasing of the ICMP data field is compliant with RFC and prevents ICMP tunneling irrespective of the type of firewall used.

The results show that simply marking out unused and potentially dangerous portions of ICMP packets is a straightforward task and requires little overhead on a modest system. Simple string scans are also not costly and can be done to test for unencrypted covert communication. This is highly recommended for the end hosts where it offers minimal overhead on the system. For routers it can be expensive. However, weighted against the potential security risks the marginal overhead can be worth the security benefits in some cases. Moreover if the proposed solution became an integral part of kernels in operating systems like Solaris, Windows, and Linux, which runs on host machines; then the routers will not have to examine all the ICMP packets that it comes across. The router could in this case adopt some sort of probabilistic scheme to check some ICMP packets and allow the other packets to pass through. This would reduce the load on the routers.

This work presents some of our initial steps to prevent ICMP tunneling. In this work covert channel due to the data carrying capability of echo_request/echo_reply was considered. Various others fields in TCP, UDP, IPv4, IPv6 and ICMP can be the potential candidate for the establishment of covert channel. Ongoing work explores the fields in every protocol and proposes the use of either stateless or stateful model for the removal of covert channel.

References

[1] CERT Advisory. Denial of service attack tools.
    http://www.cert.org/advisories/CA-1999-17.html.
[2] Backorifice SDK Documents.
    http://bo2k.sourceforge.net/indexnews.html.
[3] Root Exploit and Dos in the Linux Kernel.
    http://linux.oreillynet.com/pub/a/linux/2001/10/22/insecurities.html.
[4] ISS. Loki icmp tunneling back door.
    http://www.iss.net/securitycenter/static/1452.php.
[5] Postel J. Internet control mesage protocol – darpa internet program protocol specification. RFC 792, September 1981.
[6] Postel J. Internet protocol – darpa internet program protocol specification. RFC 791, September 1981.
[7] Phrack. Loki 2(the implementation).
    http://www.phrack.com/show.php?p=51&a=6.
[8] Phrack. Project loki.
    http://www.phrack.com/show.php?p=49&a=6.
[9] Guido Van Rooji. Real stateful tcp packet filtering. In 10th USENIX Secutrity Symposium, August 2001.
[10] Craig H. Rowland. Covert channels in the tcp/ip protocol suite.
    http://www.firstmonday.dk/issues/issue25/rowland.
[11] Sans. Icmp attacks illustrated.
    http://www.sans.org/rr/threats/ICMP_attacks.php.
[12] Sans. Intrusion detection faqs.
    http://www.sans.org/resources/dfaq/icmp_misuses.php.

On Fair E-cash Systems Based on Group Signature Schemes

Sébastien Canard and Jacques Traoré

France Telecom R&D
42, rue des Coutures, BP6243
14066 Caen Cedex, France
{sebastien.canard, jacques.traore}@francetelecom.com

Abstract. A fair electronic cash system is a system that allows customers to make payments anonymously. Moreover, under certain circumstances, a trusted authority can revoke the anonymity of suspicious transactions. Various fair e-cash systems using group signature schemes have been proposed [4,15,16,18]. Unfortunately, they do not realize coin tracing [4,15,18] (the possibility to trace the coins withdrawn by a customer). In this paper, we describe several failures in the solution of [16] and we present a secure and efficient fair e-cash system based on a group signature scheme. Our system ensures traceability of *double-spenders*, supports coin tracing and provides coins that are unforgeable and anonymous under standard assumptions.

1 Introduction

Many anonymous electronic cash systems have been proposed in the recent years. In these systems, there is no mechanism for the bank, the merchants or any other party to identify the users involved in a transaction. If desirable from a user's point of view, this unconditional anonymity could however be misused for illegal purposes, such as money laundering or perfect blackmailing.

Fair electronic cash systems have been suggested independently by [3] and [17] as a solution to prevent such fraudulent activities. The main feature of these systems is the existence of a trusted authority that can revoke, under specific circumstances, the anonymity of the coins.

Brickell et al. in [3] proposed the first fair off-line electronic cash system. Unfortunately, their scheme requires the participation of the trustee in the withdrawals of coins, which is undesirable in practice. Camenisch, Maurer and Stadler [5] and independently Frankel et al. [11] proposed fair e-cash schemes with an off-line (passive) authority: the participation of the trustee is only required in the set-up of the system and for anonymity revocation. The efficiency and the security (anonymity) of these schemes [3,5,11] have been later improved [12,14]. Unfortunately, the security for the bank (namely the unforgeability of the coins) relies, in these schemes, on non-standard assumptions.

R. Safavi-Naini and J. Seberry (Eds.): ACISP 2003, LNCS 2727, pp. 237–248, 2003.
© Springer-Verlag Berlin Heidelberg 2003

Group signature schemes have been introduced in 1991 by Chaum and van Heyst [6]. They allow members to sign a document on behalf of the group in such a way that the signatures remain anonymous and untraceable for everyone but a designated authority, who can recover the identity of the signer whenever needed (this procedure is called "signature opening"). Currently, the best group signature scheme is the one of Ateniese et al. [1].

In 1999, Traoré [18] proposed a solution that combine a group signature scheme and a blind signature scheme in order to design a privacy-protecting fair off-line electronic cash system. Unfortunately, his proposal does not realize coin tracing (the possibility to trace the coins withdrawn by a customer). In 2001, Maitland and Boyd [15] proposed a variant of this solution based on the group signature scheme of Ateniese et al. [1]. Very recently, Qiu et al. [16] designed a new electronic cash system, using again a combination of a group signature scheme and a blind signature scheme. However, their solution does not work for various reasons (owing to space limitations, the cryptanalysis of [16] will appear in the full paper). Camenisch and Lysyanskaya [4] proposed a fair electronic cash system where blind signatures are not used (named one-show credentials) but they don't achieve coin tracing.

In this paper, we investigate the same way of using a group signature scheme for designing a fair off-line electronic cash system as [4] do. In fact in [15], [16] and [18], each customer is a member of a group whereas in this paper, a group certificate corresponds to a coin delivered by the bank. This implies a relatively efficient solution which is completely secure and that does not need the use of a blind signature such as other proposals [15,16,18]. Our way of realizing tracing after a double-spending is also different from the solution of [4].

Our paper is organized as follows. In Section 2, we describe our solution and in Section 3, we analyse the security of our proposal.

2   A New Electronic Cash System

In this section, we describe a new fair off-line e-cash scheme based on the group signature scheme of Ateniese et al. [1]. Our fair e-cash scheme however differs from the one of Maitland and Boyd [15] which is based on the same group signature scheme: in their system, the group is formed from the customers that spend the electronic coins, whereas in our system the group is formed from the coins themselves. This difference will allow us, as we will see, to easily incorporate a coin tracing mechanism.

In the simplified model of fair electronic cash that we use, four types of parties are involved: a bank B, a trusted authority T, shops S and customers C. A fair e-cash system consists of five basic protocols, three of which are the same as in anonymous e-cash, namely a withdrawal protocol with which C withdraws electronic coins from B, a payment protocol with which C pays S with the coins he has withdrawn, and a deposit protocol with which S deposits the coins to B.

The two additional protocols are conducted between B and T, namely **owner tracing** and **coin tracing**. They work as follows:

- **Coin tracing protocol:** the bank provides the trusted authority with the view of a withdrawal protocol and asks for the information that allows it to identify the corresponding coin in the deposit phase.
- **Owner tracing protocol:** the bank provides the trusted authority with the view of a (suspect) payment and asks for the identity of the withdrawer of the coins used in this (suspect) payment.

The security of our scheme relies on the Strong-RSA (S-RSA) assumption (see [13]), and on the Decision Diffie-Hellman (DDH) assumption in groups of unknown order [2].

2.1 Setup

Let $\epsilon > 1$, k and l_p be security parameters (the parameter ϵ controls the tightness of the statistical zero-knowledgeness and the parameter l_p sets the size of the modulus to use). Let λ_1, λ_2, γ_1 and γ_2 denote lengths satisfying $\lambda_2 > 4l_p$, $\lambda_1 > \epsilon(\lambda_2 + k) + 2$, $\gamma_2 > \lambda_1 + 2$ and $\gamma_1 > \epsilon(\gamma_2 + k) + 2$. Let us define $\Lambda =]2^{\lambda_1} - 2^{\lambda_2}, 2^{\lambda_1} + 2^{\lambda_2}[$ and $\Gamma =]2^{\gamma_1} - 2^{\gamma_2}, 2^{\gamma_1} + 2^{\gamma_2}[$. Finally, let H be a collision-resistant hash function $H : \{0, 1\}^* \to \{0, 1\}^k$.

Bank's Setup Protocol (performed once by B):

- Select random secret l_p-bits primes p', q' such that $p = 2p' + 1$ and $q = 2q' + 1$ are primes. Set the modulus $n = pq$.
- Choose random generators[1] a, a_0, g, h, m of $QR(n)$ (the set of all quadratic residues modulo n).

T's Setup Protocol (performed once by T):

- Choose $y, Y \in_R \mathbb{Z}_{p'q'}^*$ and publish $z = g^y \pmod{n}$ and $Z = g^Y \pmod{n}$.

Finally, the public key of the system is $PK = (n, a, a_0, g, h, m, z, Z)$, the bank's private key is $SK_B = (p', q')$ and T's private one is $SK_T = (y, Y)$.

2.2 Withdrawal Protocol

For the sake of simplicity, we assume that there is only one coin denomination in the system (extension to multiple denominations will be described in the full paper). So all coins will have the same monetary value (d \$).
The withdrawal protocol[2] (Fig. 1) has some similarities with the **Join protocol** of Ateniese et al. [1]: each coin obtained by a customer can be seen as a (new) membership certificate of the group signature scheme of Ateniese et al. At the end

---

[1] It is assumed that the discrete log of these elements w.r.t. the others is unknown.
[2] In the sequel, $PK(\alpha : f(\alpha, \ldots))(M)$ will be a *signature of knowledge* on message M of a value α that verifies the predicate f. Signatures of knowledge are signatures derived from zero-knowledge proofs of knowledge using the Fiat-Shamir heuristic [10].

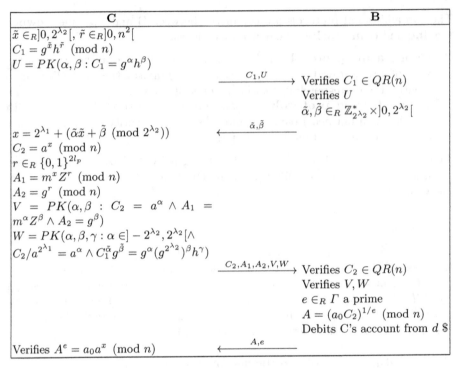

Fig. 1. The Withdrawal Protocol.

of the protocol, the customer C obtains a coin $(x, [A, e])$ s.t. $A^e = a_0 a^x \pmod n$. The value x is only known by C. The purpose of the pair (A_1, A_2), which is an El Gamal encryption [9] of the message m^x under T's private key, and the proof V is to ensure the possibility of "coin tracing". B stores a^x and (A_1, A_2) in the user's entry of the withdrawal database for possible later anonymity revocation.

2.3 Payment Protocol

During the payment protocol (Fig. 2), the payment transcript tr (where tr includes various information such as the identification number of the shop, the date and time of the transaction, etc.) is signed using the group (membership) certificate (A, e) and the secret key x (obtained during the withdrawal protocol). More precisely: the customer first chooses at random $w, w_1, w_2, w_3 \in_R I_{2l_p}$ (where $I_d = \pm\{0, 1\}^d$) and then computes the following equations:

$$T_1 = a^x z^w \pmod n \quad T_2 = g^w \pmod n \quad T_3 = A h^{w_1} \pmod n$$
$$T_4 = m^x \pmod n \quad T_5 = g^{w_1} h^{w_2} \pmod n \quad T_6 = g^e h^{w_3} \pmod n$$

Noting the fact that the equation of T_3 can be rewritten $a_0 = T_3^e/(a^x h^{ew_1})$ $\pmod n$ using $A^e = a_0 a^x \pmod n$. Then, putting the equation of T_5 to e, we

C	S
$r_1 \in_R I_{\epsilon(\gamma_2+k)}, \; r_2 \in_R I_{\epsilon(\lambda_2+k)}$	
$r_3, r_7, r_8 \in_R I_{\epsilon(\gamma_1+2l_p+k+1)}$	
$r_4, r_5, r_6, r_9 \in_R I_{\epsilon(2l_p+k)}$	
$d_1 = a^{r_2} z^{r_4} \pmod{n}$	
$d_2 = g^{r_4} \pmod{n}$	
$d_3 = T_3^{r_1}/(a^{r_2} h^{r_7}) \pmod{n}$	
$d_4 = m^{r_2} \pmod{n}$	
$d_5 = g^{r_5} h^{r_6} \pmod{n}$	
$d_6 = T_5^{r_1}/(g^{r_7} h^{r_8}) \pmod{n}$	
$d_7 = g^{r_1} h^{r_9} \pmod{n}$	

$$\xrightarrow{\;d_1,\dots,d_7\;} \quad c = H(T_1\|\dots\|T_6\|d_1\|\dots\|d_7\|tr)$$

$$\xleftarrow{\quad c \quad}$$

C	S
$s_1 = r_1 - c(e - 2^{\gamma_1})$	
$s_2 = r_2 - c(x - 2^{\lambda_1})$	
$s_3 = r_3 - cew$	
$s_4 = r_4 - cw$	
$s_5 = r_5 - cw_1$	
$s_6 = r_6 - cw_2$	
$s_7 = r_7 - cew_1$	
$s_8 = r_8 - cew_2$	
$s_9 = r_9 - cw_3 \quad \text{(all in } \mathbb{Z})$	

$$\xrightarrow{\;s_1,\dots,s_9\;} \quad \text{Verifies } c = H(T_1\|\dots\|T_6\|T_1^c a^{s_2-c2^{\lambda_1}} z^{s_4}\|$$
$$T_2^c g^{s_4}\|a_0^c T_3^{s_1-c2^{\gamma_1}}/(a^{s_2-c2^{\lambda_1}} h^{s_7})\|$$
$$T_4^c m^{s_2-c2^{\lambda_1}}\|T_5^c g^{s_5} h^{s_6}\|$$
$$T_5^{s_1-c2^{\gamma_1}}/(g^{s_7} h^{s_8})\|T_6^c g^{s_1-c2^{\gamma_1}} h^{s_9}\|tr)$$
$$\text{Verifies } s_1 \in I_{\epsilon(\gamma_2+k)+1}, \; s_2 \in I_{\epsilon(\lambda_2+k)+1}$$
$$\text{Verifies } s_3, s_7, s_8 \in I_{\epsilon(\gamma_1+2l_p+k+1)+1}$$
$$\text{Verifies } s_4, s_5, s_6, s_9 \in I_{\epsilon(2l_p+k)+1}$$

Fig. 2. The Payment Protocol.

obtain that $1 = T_5^e/(g^{ew_1} h^{ew_2}) \pmod{n}$. The payment protocol is then the following interactive signature of knowledge between C and S (see Fig. 2):

$$U = PK(\; \alpha, \beta, \gamma, \delta, \zeta, \eta, \theta, \iota, \kappa : T_1 = a^\beta z^\delta \wedge T_2 = g^\delta \wedge a_0 = T_3^\alpha/(a^\beta h^\theta) \wedge$$
$$T_4 = m^\beta \wedge T_5 = g^\zeta h^\eta \wedge 1 = T_5^\alpha/(g^\theta h^\iota) \wedge T_6 = g^\alpha h^\kappa).$$

2.4 Deposit and Tracing Protocols

To be credited of the value of this coin, the shop sends the transcript of the execution of the payment protocol to the bank, which verifies, exactly as the shop did, that the signature on tr is correct (namely the signature of knowledge U). If this is successful, the bank checks for double-spending[3] by searching if T_4

---

[3] i.e., using the same coin in two different transactions. In other words, the bank tries to determine whether the group certificate (A, e) and the secret key x, underlying this payment transaction, have already been used or not.

is already in its deposit database. If this value is not found, T_4 is stored in the deposit database and the payment is accepted as valid[4].

If T_4 has been previously used, the bank sends both transcripts to the trusted authority T. From these transcripts, T can retrieve $a^x = T_1/T_2^y \pmod{n}$. With a^x, the bank can identify the withdrawal session in which this value has been used and consequently can also identify the fraudulent customer.

Coin Tracing. T is given a withdrawal transcript. T decrypts the El Gamal ciphertext (A_1, A_2) to obtain the value m^x. This value can be put on a blacklist for recognizing it when it is spent.

Owner Tracing. T is given the values T_1 and T_2 observed in a payment. T decrypts this ciphertext to obtain the value a^x. With this value, the bank can identify a withdrawal session and consequently a customer C.

3   Security Analysis

We focus on the main security requirements of an electronic cash system: one-more unforgeability[5] and anonymity (the inability for anyone, except T, to match a transaction with a user).

3.1   Unforgeability

Theorem 1. *Under the S-RSA assumption, a probabilistic polynomial-time (PPT) adversary cannot, after initiating polynomially many withdrawal sessions, output, with non-negligible probability (in l_p), a coin $(x, [A, e])$ with $x \in \Lambda$ and $e \in \Gamma$ that is different from all the coins obtained in the withdrawal sessions (where the withdrawal sessions can be performed in an adaptive and arbitrary interleaving manner).*

Proof. Let $\mathcal{M}$ be an attacker who can adaptively run the withdrawal protocol so as to obtain the coins $(x_j, [A_j, e_j]), j = 1, \ldots, l$ with $x_j \in \Lambda$, $e_j \in \Gamma$ and $A_j = (a_0 a^{x_j})^{1/e_j} \pmod{n}$ and then can output $(\hat{x}, [\hat{A}, \hat{e}])$ with $\hat{x} \in \Lambda$, $\hat{e} \in \Gamma$, $\hat{A} = (a_0 a^{\hat{x}})^{1/\hat{e}} \pmod{n}$ and $(\hat{x}, \hat{e}) \neq (x_j, e_j)$ for all $1 \leq j \leq l$ with a non negligible probability.

Given a pair (n, v), we randomly repeat one of the two following algorithms with $\mathcal{M}$ and we hope to succeed in computing a pair $(u, d) \in \mathbb{Z}_n^* \times \mathbb{Z}_{>1}$ such that $u^d = v \pmod{n}$ from $\mathcal{M}$'s answers.

- First algorithm:
    1. Choose $x_1, \ldots, x_l \in_R \Lambda$ and $e_1, \ldots, e_l \in_R \Gamma$.
    2. Compute $a = v^{\prod_{1 \leq k \leq l} e_k} \pmod{n}$.
    3. Choose $r \in_R \Lambda$ and compute $a_0 = a^r \pmod{n}$.

---

[4] This technique has been first introduced in [18] and subsequently used by Camenisch and Lysyanskaya [4] for their one-show credentials scheme.

[5] which means that is must be infeasible to create more than l coins from l withdrawals.

4. $\forall 1 \leq i \leq l$, compute $A_i = v^{(x_i+r)} \prod_{k \neq i} e_k \pmod{n}$.

5. Choose $g, h, m \in_R QR(n)$ and $y, Y \in_R \{1, \ldots, n^2\}$ and compute $z = g^y$ $\pmod{n}$ and $Z = g^Y \pmod{n}$.

6. Run the withdrawal protocol l times with $\mathcal{M}$ and with $(n, a, a_0, g, h, m, z, Z)$ as input. At the i-th run, we receive C_1 and U from $\mathcal{M}$. Use the proof of knowledge U to extract $\tilde{x}_i$ and $\tilde{r}_i$ such that $C_1 = g^{\tilde{x}_i} h^{\tilde{r}_i}$ $\pmod{n}$ (rewinding $\mathcal{M}$ twice for a similar commitment). Choose $\tilde{\alpha}_i$ and $\tilde{\beta}_i$ such that the prepared x_i (see step 1.) is $x_i = 2^{\lambda_1} + (\tilde{\alpha}_i \tilde{x}_i + \tilde{\beta}_i \pmod{2^{\lambda_2}}))$ Then, send $\tilde{\alpha}_i$ and $\tilde{\beta}_i$ to $\mathcal{M}$. Follow the protocol and then send to $\mathcal{M}$ the couple $[A_i, e_i]$.

After the l withdrawals, $\mathcal{M}$ outputs $(\hat{x}, [\hat{A}, \hat{e}])$ with $\hat{x} \in \Lambda$, $\hat{e} \in \Gamma$, $\hat{A} = (a_0 a^{\hat{x}})^{1/\hat{e}} \pmod{n}$ and $(\hat{x}, \hat{e}) \neq (x_j, e_j)$ for all $1 \leq j \leq l$.

7. If there exists $1 \leq j \leq l$ such that $gcd(\hat{e}, e_j) \neq 1$, then output $\perp$ and quit. Else, let $\tilde{e} = (\hat{x} + r) \prod_{1 \leq k \leq l} e_k$ (and then $\hat{A}^{\hat{e}} = v^{\tilde{e}} \pmod{n}$). Since $gcd(\hat{e}, e_j) = 1$ for all $1 \leq j \leq l$, then $gcd(\hat{e}, \tilde{e}) = gcd(\hat{e}, (\hat{x} + r))$. Hence, by the Bezout's theorem, it exists $\alpha, \beta \in \mathbb{Z}$ such that $\alpha \hat{e} + \beta \tilde{e} = gcd(\hat{e}, (\hat{x}+r))$. Let $u = v^\alpha \hat{A}^\beta \pmod{n}$ and $d = \hat{e}/gcd(\hat{e}, (\hat{x} + r))$ $(\gamma_2 > \lambda_1 + 2 \Longrightarrow \hat{e} > (\hat{x}+r) \Longrightarrow d > 1)$ and then $u^d = v \pmod{n}$. Output (u, d).

This algorithm only succeeds if $\mathcal{M}$ outputs a coin $(\hat{x}, [\hat{A}, \hat{e}])$ such that $gcd(\hat{e}, e_j) = 1$ for all $1 \leq j \leq l$. The next algorithm can find a couple (u, d) if $gcd(\hat{e}, e_j) \neq 1$ for some $1 \leq j \leq l$ (since e_j is prime, $gcd(\hat{e}, e_j) \neq 1 \Longrightarrow gcd(\hat{e}, e_j) = e_j$).

- Second algorithm:

1. Choose $x_1, \ldots, x_l \in_R \Lambda$ and $e_1, \ldots, e_l \in_R \Gamma$.

2. Choose $j \in_R \{1, \ldots, l\}$ and compute $a = v^{\prod_{k \neq j} e_k} \pmod{n}$.

3. Choose $r \in_R \Lambda$ and compute $A_j = a^r \pmod{n}$ and $a_0 = A_j^{e_j}/a^{x_j}$ $\pmod{n}$.

4. $\forall 1 \leq i \leq l, i \neq j$, compute $A_i = v^{(x_i + e_j r - x_j)} \prod_{k \neq i, j} e_k \pmod{n}$.

5. Choose $g, h, m \in_R QR(n)$ and $y, Y \in_R \{1, \ldots, n^2\}$ and compute $z = g^y$ $\pmod{n}$ and $Z = g^Y \pmod{n}$.

6. Similar to the step 6. of the first algorithm.

7. If $gcd(\hat{e}, e_j) \neq e_j$, then output $\perp$ and quit. Else, $\exists t/\hat{e} = te_j$ and we can define $B = \hat{A}^t/A_j \pmod{n}$ if $\hat{x} \geq x_j$ and $B = A_j/\hat{A}^t \pmod{n}$ otherwise. Then $B = (a^{|\hat{x}-x_j|})^{1/e_j} = (v^{|\tilde{e}|})^{1/e_j} \pmod{n}$ with $\tilde{e} = (\hat{x} - x_j) \prod_{k \neq j} e_k$. Since $gcd(e_j, \prod_{k \neq j} e_k) = 1$, then $gcd(e_j, |\tilde{e}|) = gcd(e_j, |\hat{x} - x_j|)$. Hence, by the Bezout's theorem, it exists $\alpha, \beta \in \mathbb{Z}$ such that $\alpha e_j + \beta |\tilde{e}| = gcd(e_j, |\hat{x} - x_j|)$. Let $u = v^\alpha B^\beta \pmod{n}$ and $d = e_j/gcd(e_j, |\hat{x} - x_j|)$ $(\gamma_2 > \lambda_1 + 2 \Longrightarrow e_j >$ $|\hat{x} - x_j| \Longrightarrow d > 1)$ and then $u^d = v \pmod{n}$. Output (u, d).

Consequently, randomly running one of the two algorithms until the output is not $\perp$ permits an attacker getting access to the machine $\mathcal{M}$ to solve the S-RSA problem in expected running-time polynomial in l. As the S-RSA problem is assumed to be infeasible, we can conclude that no one can create more than l coins from l withdrawals (where l is polynomial in l_p). $\qquad \square$

We will now prove that if S *accepts* a payment, then this implies that C necessarily knows a coin $(x, [A, e])$, with $x \in \Lambda$ and $e \in \Gamma$ s.t. $A^e = a_0 a^x \pmod{n}$.

Theorem 2. *Under the S-RSA assumption, the interactive payment protocol is a proof of knowledge of a withdrawal coin* $(x, [A, e])$.

Proof. We have to show that a knowledge extractor is able to recover the coin $(x, [A, e])$ from two accepting signatures. Let $(c, s_1, \ldots, s_9, d_1, \ldots, d_7, T_1, \ldots, T_6)$ and $(\tilde{c}, \tilde{s}_1, \ldots, \tilde{s}_9, d_1, \ldots, d_7, T_1, \ldots, T_6)$ be these two accepting tuples. Using Lemma 1 (see below), we can show that for all $i = 1, \ldots, 9$, there exists $\theta_i \in \mathbb{Z}$ such that $s_i - \tilde{s}_i = \theta_i(\tilde{c} - c)$.

As $T_5^{\tilde{c}-c} = g^{s_5 - \tilde{s}_5} h^{s_6 - \tilde{s}_6} \pmod{n}$, it follows (since $\tilde{c} - c$ can be either even or odd) that there exists some v such that $T_5 = v g^{\theta_5} h^{\theta_6} \pmod{n}$ with $v^2 = 1$. Moreover, the value v must be either 1 or -1 as otherwise $\gcd(v \pm 1, n)$ is a non trivial factor of n. Using d_6 and the result above, it comes:

$$(T_5^{-2^{\gamma_1}})^{\tilde{c}-c} = T_5^{s_1 - \tilde{s}_1}/(g^{s_7 - \tilde{s}_7} h^{s_8 - \tilde{s}_8}) \pmod{n}$$

$$((v g^{\theta_5} h^{\theta_6})^{-2^{\gamma_1}})^{\tilde{c}-c} = (v g^{\theta_5} h^{\theta_6})^{s_1 - \tilde{s}_1}/(g^{s_7 - \tilde{s}_7} h^{s_8 - \tilde{s}_8}) \pmod{n}$$

$$1 = \tilde{v} v^{\theta_1 + 2^{\gamma_1}} g^{\theta_5(\theta_1 + 2^{\gamma_1}) - \theta_7} h^{\theta_6(\theta_1 + 2^{\gamma_1}) - \theta_8} \pmod{n}$$

where $\tilde{v}^2 = 1$. Since 1, g and h are in $QR(n)$ and $v = \pm 1$, it is necessary that $\tilde{v} v^{\theta_1 + 2^{\gamma_1}} = 1$ (since $-1 \notin QR(n)$) and, under the fact that the discrete logarithm of g in base h is unknown, that $\theta_5(\theta_1 + 2^{\gamma_1}) = \theta_7 \pmod{p'q'}$ (as g is of order $p'q'$).

From d_3, we obtain, using similar arguments as for T_5 and this last result, that:

$$(a_0 T_3^{-2^{\gamma_1}}/a^{-2^{\lambda_1}})^{\tilde{c}-c} = T_3^{s_1 - \tilde{s}_1}/(a^{s_2 - \tilde{s}_2} h^{s_7 - \tilde{s}_7}) \pmod{n}$$

$$a_0 T_3^{-2^{\gamma_1}}/a^{-2^{\lambda_1}} = u T_3^{\theta_1}/(a^{\theta_2} h^{\theta_7}) \pmod{n}$$

$$a_0 = u T_3^{\theta_1 + 2^{\gamma_1}} \left(\frac{1}{a}\right)^{\theta_2 + 2^{\lambda_1}} \left(\frac{1}{h^{\theta_5}}\right)^{\theta_1 + 2^{\gamma_1}} \pmod{n}$$

$$a_0 = u \left(\frac{T_3}{h^{\theta_5}}\right)^{\theta_1 + 2^{\gamma_1}} \left(\frac{1}{a}\right)^{\theta_2 + 2^{\lambda_1}} \pmod{n}$$

where u is such that $u^2 = 1$. Again, $u = \pm 1$ as otherwise $\gcd(u \pm 1, n)$ is a non trivial factor of n. Let us note $\pi_1 = \theta_1 + 2^{\gamma_1}$, $\pi_2 = \theta_2 + 2^{\lambda_1}$ and $s = 1$ if $\pi_1 > 0$ and -1 otherwise (and consequently $\pi_1 = s|\pi_1|$). Then we have:

$$A^{|\pi_1|} = a_0 a^{\pi_2} \pmod{n} \text{ with } A = \begin{cases} (\frac{u T_3}{h^{\theta_5}})^s & \text{if } \pi_1 \text{ is odd} \\ (\frac{T_3}{h^{\theta_5}})^s & \text{if } \pi_1 \text{ is even} \end{cases}$$

The case "π_1 even" implies that $(\frac{T_3}{h^{\theta_5}})^{\pi_1}$ is a quadratic residue modulo n: as a_0 and a are in $QR(n)$, it is then necessary that $u = 1$ since $-1 \notin QR(n)$ (and $QR(n)$ is a group).

Since $\pi_1 = \theta_1 + 2^{\gamma_1}$, $\theta_1 = \frac{s_1 - \tilde{s}_1}{\tilde{c} - c}$ and $s_1, \tilde{s}_1 \in I_{\epsilon(\gamma_2 + k) + 1}$, we have $s_1 - \tilde{s}_1 \in I_{\epsilon(\gamma_2 + k) + 2}$ and since the smallest value that $\tilde{c} - c$ can take is 1 the integer π_1 must lie in $[2^{\gamma_1} - 2^{\epsilon(\gamma_2 + k) + 2}, 2^{\gamma_1} + 2^{\epsilon(\gamma_2 + k) + 2}]$. Similarly, we can prove that π_2 must lie in $[2^{\lambda_1} - 2^{\epsilon(\lambda_2 + k) + 2}, 2^{\lambda_1} + 2^{\epsilon(\lambda_2 + k) + 2}]$ which is in accordance with what is expected with a signature of knowledge that proves that a discrete logarithm lies in an interval (see [1]).

Consequently, by putting $x = \pi_2$, $A = \left(\frac{T_3}{h^{\theta_5}}\right)^s$ and $e = |\pi_1|$, we obtain that $(x, [A, e])$ is a valid certificate such that $A^e = a_0 a^x \pmod{n}$ and hence, this is a valid proof of knowledge. □

Lemma 1. *Given two accepting payment protocols $(c, s_1, \ldots, s_9, d_1, \ldots, d_7, T_1, \ldots, T_6)$ and $(\tilde{c}, \tilde{s}_1, \ldots, \tilde{s}_9, d_1, \ldots, d_7, T_1, \ldots, T_6)$ it is necessary that, for all $i = 1, \ldots, 9$, there exists $\theta_i \in \mathbb{Z}$ such that $s_i - \tilde{s}_i = \theta_i(\tilde{c} - c)$.*

Proof. From the two representations of $d_2 = T_2^c g^{s_4} = T_2^{\tilde{c}} g^{\tilde{s}_4} \pmod{n}$ we can write that $g^{s_4 - \tilde{s}_4} = T_2^{\tilde{c} - c} \pmod{n}$. Let δ_4 be the greatest common divisor (gcd) of $s_4 - \tilde{s}_4$ and $\tilde{c} - c$. By the Bezout's theorem there exists $\alpha_4, \beta_4 \in \mathbb{Z}$ such that $\alpha_4(s_4 - \tilde{s}_4) + \beta_4(\tilde{c} - c) = \delta_4$. As a consequence, we can write g as $g = g^{(\alpha_4(s_4 - \tilde{s}_4) + \beta_4(\tilde{c} - c))/\delta_4} = (T_2^{\alpha_4} g^{\beta_4})^{\frac{\tilde{c} - c}{\delta_4}} \pmod{n}$. If $\tilde{c} - c \neq \delta_4$ we have found a $(\frac{\tilde{c} - c}{\delta_4})^{th}$ root of g, which contradicts the S-RSA assumption. Then, $\tilde{c} - c = \delta_4 = gcd(s_4 - \tilde{s}_4, \tilde{c} - c)$ and consequently:

$$\exists \theta_4 \in \mathbb{Z}/s_4 - \tilde{s}_4 = \theta_4(\tilde{c} - c).$$

From the two representations of $d_1 = (T_1 a^{-2^{\lambda_1}})^c a^{s_2} z^{s_4} = (T_1 a^{-2^{\lambda_1}})^{\tilde{c}} a^{\tilde{s}_2} z^{\tilde{s}_4} \pmod{n}$ we can write that $a^{s_2 - \tilde{s}_2} = (T_1 a^{-2^{\lambda_1}})^{\tilde{c} - c} z^{\tilde{s}_4 - s_4} = (T_1 a^{-2^{\lambda_1}} z^{-\theta_4})^{\tilde{c} - c} \pmod{n}$. Let $\delta_2 = gcd(s_2 - \tilde{s}_2, \tilde{c} - c)$ and $\alpha_2, \beta_2 \in \mathbb{Z}$ such that $\alpha_2(s_2 - \tilde{s}_2) + \beta_2(\tilde{c} - c) = \delta_2$. Hence, we can write a as $a = a^{(\alpha_2(s_2 - \tilde{s}_2) + \beta_2(\tilde{c} - c))/\delta_2} = ((T_1 a^{-2^{\lambda_1}} z^{-\theta_4})^{\alpha_2} a^{\beta_2})^{\frac{\tilde{c} - c}{\delta_2}} \pmod{n}$. If $\tilde{c} - c \neq \delta_2$ we have found a $(\frac{\tilde{c} - c}{\delta_2})^{th}$ root of g, which contradicts the S-RSA assumption. Then, $\tilde{c} - c = \delta_2 = gcd(s_2 - \tilde{s}_2, \tilde{c} - c)$ and consequently:

$$\exists \theta_2 \in \mathbb{Z}/s_2 - \tilde{s}_2 = \theta_2(\tilde{c} - c).$$

Then, using the two representations of $d_5 = T_5^c g^{s_5} h^{s_6} = T_5^{\tilde{c}} g^{\tilde{s}_5} h^{\tilde{s}_6} \pmod{n}$, we can write that $T_5^{\tilde{c} - c} = g^{s_5 - \tilde{s}_5} h^{s_6 - \tilde{s}_6} \pmod{n}$. We can show (see Lemma 2 below) that it is necessary that $\tilde{c} - c$ divides both $s_5 - \tilde{s}_5$ and $s_6 - \tilde{s}_6$. As a consequence:

$$\forall i \in \{5, 6\}, \exists \theta_i \in \mathbb{Z}/s_i - \tilde{s}_i = \theta_i(\tilde{c} - c).$$

We can do the same things for d_3, d_6 and d_7 to conclude that:

$$\forall i \in \{1, 3, 7, 8, 9\}, \exists \theta_i \in \mathbb{Z}/s_i - \tilde{s}_i = \theta_i(\tilde{c} - c). \qquad \square$$

Lemma 2. *Under the S-RSA assumption, given two representations of $d = T^c g^s h^t = T^{\tilde{c}} g^{\tilde{s}} h^{\tilde{t}} \pmod{n}$, it is necessary that $\tilde{c} - c$ divides both $s - \tilde{s}$ and $t - \tilde{t}$.*

Proof. In fact, if $\tilde{c} - c$ does not divide both $s - \tilde{s}$ and $t - \tilde{t}$ then, there are three cases. Suppose first that $\tilde{c} - c$ divides $s - \tilde{s}$ and not $t - \tilde{t}$. Then, there exists $\theta \in \mathbb{Z}$ such that $s - \tilde{s} = \theta(\tilde{c} - c)$. From d, we can write that $h^{t - \tilde{t}} = T^{\tilde{c} - c} g^{\tilde{s} - s} = (Tg^{-\theta})^{\tilde{c} - c}$. Let δ be the greatest common divisor of $t - \tilde{t}$ and $\tilde{c} - c$. By the Bezout's theorem there exists $\alpha, \beta \in \mathbb{Z}$ such that $\alpha(t - \tilde{t}) + \beta(\tilde{c} - c) = \delta$. As a consequence, we can write h as $h = h^{(\alpha(t - \tilde{t}) + \beta(\tilde{c} - c))/\delta} = ((Tg^{-\theta})^{\alpha} h^{\beta})^{\frac{\tilde{c} - c}{\delta}} \pmod{n}$. As $\tilde{c} - c \neq \delta$ ($\tilde{c} - c$ does not divide $t - \tilde{t}$) we have found a $(\frac{\tilde{c} - c}{\delta})^{th}$ root of h, which contradicts the S-RSA assumption.

Suppose then that $\tilde{c} - c$ divides $t - \tilde{t}$ and not $s - \tilde{s}$, we can do the same argument to contradict the S-RSA assumption. Finally, if $\tilde{c} - c$ does not divide $s - \tilde{s}$ nor $t - \tilde{t}$, it is possible to construct an algorithm that can also break the S-RSA assumption (see [7] for such an algorithm). □

We can now conclude from Theorem 1 and 2 that from l withdrawals with the bank, the customer can at most obtain l coins that a shop S will accept.

3.2 Anonymity

The following theorem proves that the bank cannot know who is involved during the payment protocol: the identity of the customer is kept secret even from the bank (except from the trusted authority for obvious reasons).

Theorem 3. *Under the DDH assumption and in the random oracle model, given a bank's view $W(C)$ of a withdrawal with a customer C and the view of a payment P, no PPT machine (apart from T) can decide whether the coin underlying the payment P comes from $W(C)$ or not with probability non-negligibly better than random guessing (in l_p).*

Proof. (sketch) Suppose we have a PPT machine $\mathcal{M}$ that can, on input $W(C)$ (a bank's view of withdrawal) and P (a payment transcript) decide, with probability non-negligibly better than random guessing, whether the coin used in P comes from $W(C)$. We will show that the bank can use this machine as an oracle to break the DDH assumption.

Let $n = pq$ be the product of two distinct safe primes of length l_p (where l_p is a security parameter). Let a be a random generator of $QR(n)$, m a random element of $QR(n)$, a^x a random element of $\langle a \rangle$ (the subgroup of $QR(n)$ generated by a) and $m^{x'}$ a random element of $\langle m \rangle$ (n, a, m, a^x and $m^{x'}$ will be the target instance of the DDH problem).

We will show that given $\mathcal{M}$, the bank can decide non-negligibly better than random guessing if $m^x = m^{x'} \pmod{n}$ [6]. We will first construct a (polynomial) converting algorithm $\mathcal{AL}$ which will transform the target instance of the DDH problem into a valid bank's view of a withdrawal and a correct payment transcript of our fair e-cash scheme.

Construction of $\mathcal{AL}$:

- Initialisation:
  The bank first chooses $r \in_R \Lambda$ and $e \in_R \Gamma$. B then computes $A = a^r \pmod{n}$ and $a_0 = A^e/a^x \pmod{n}$. Finally, B chooses two random generators g and h of $QR(n)$ and two random elements z and Z of $QR(n)$. The public key of the fair e-cash scheme becomes $PK = (n, a, a_0, g, h, m, z, Z)$ (where n, a and m are the values defined in the target instance of the DDH problem).

- Simulation of the withdrawal session:
  1. B chooses at random $\tilde{\alpha} \in \mathbb{Z}_{2^{\lambda_2}}^*$ and $\tilde{\beta} \in]0, 2^{\lambda_2}[$ and defines $C_2 = a^x \pmod{n}$. Note that for a given triplet $(x, \tilde{\alpha}, \tilde{\beta})$ (with $x \in \Lambda$), there always exists a $\tilde{x}$ such that $x = 2^{\lambda_1} + (\tilde{\alpha}\tilde{x} + \tilde{\beta} \pmod{2^{\lambda_2}})$ (since $\tilde{\alpha}$ is an inversible element of $\mathbb{Z}_{2^{\lambda_2}}$).
  2. B chooses $C_1 \in_R QR(n)$. Notice that $\forall \tilde{x} \in]0, 2^{\lambda_2}[, \exists \tilde{r} \in]0, n^2[$ such that $C_1 = g^{\tilde{x}} h^{\tilde{r}} \pmod{n}$.

---
[6] In fact, this is a straightforwardly equivalent formulation of the DDH problem.

3. B simulates the proof U which is possible in the random oracle model. For this purpose, B chooses $c \in_R I_k$, $s_1, s_2 \in_R I_{\epsilon(2l_p+k)+1}$, computes $t = C_1^c g^{s_1} h^{s_2} \pmod{n}$, defines $c = H(g\|h\|C_1\|t)$ and returns $U = (c, s_1, s_2)$ as the signature of knowledge.

4. B chooses two random values in $QR(n)$ and defines these values as A_1 and A_2 (recall that B does not know $m^x \pmod{n}$). Notice that the machine $\mathcal{M}$ will not be able to distinguish this random pair (A_1, A_2) from a "correct" El Gamal encryption of $m^x \pmod{n}$. Otherwise this would imply that $\mathcal{M}$ can break the El Gamal encryption in the sense of indistinguishability, i.e. break the DDH assumption (see [14] for example. A detailed proof of this fact will appear in the full paper). Notice then that the "correctness" of the ("wrong") ciphertext (A_1, A_2) (i.e., the proof V) can still be simulated in the random oracle model using standard techniques. The fact that the statement being "proved" is false is irrelevant since $\mathcal{M}$ will not be able to discern it.

5. B then simulates in the random oracle model, using standard techniques, the proof W.

$W(C) = (C_1, U, \tilde{\alpha}, \tilde{\beta}, C_2, V, W, A, e)$ is then a valid bank's view of a withdrawal protocol.

- Simulation of the payment:

  1. B chooses two random values in $QR(n)$ and defines these values as T_1 and T_2 (recall that B does not know $a^{x'} \pmod{n}$). See the remarks in step 4 of the simulation of the withdrawal session.

  2. B defines $T_4 = m^{x'} \pmod{n}$.

  3. B chooses $e' \in_R \Gamma$ and $w_3 \in_R I_{2l_p}$ and computes $T_6 = g^{e'} h^{w_3} \pmod{n}$. Notice that $\forall (x', e') \in \Lambda \times \Gamma, \exists A' \in QR(n)$ such that $A'^{e'} = a_0 a^{x'} \pmod{n}$. Notice also that $\forall T_3 \in QR(n), \exists w_1 \in I_{2l_p}$ such that $T_3 = A' h^{w_1} \pmod{n}$ (in our case, B does not know (and cannot compute) the value A', since B does not know x').

  4. B chooses at random $T_3 \in QR(n)$ and $T_5 \in QR(n)$. Notice that $\exists w_2 \in I_{2l_p}$ such that $T_5 = g^{w_1} h^{w_2} \pmod{n}$.

  5. B simulates U in the random oracle model, using standard techniques.

$P = (T_1, \ldots, T_6, U)$ is then a valid payment transcript.

$W(C)$ and P are then feed to $\mathcal{M}$ which returns a bit b (where $b = 0$ if P is linked to $W(C)$ and 1 otherwise). If $b = 0$, B concludes that $m^x = m^{x'} \pmod{n}$ and that $m^x \neq m^{x'} \pmod{n}$ otherwise.

We thus have constructed a polynomial-time algorithm which can break the DDH assumption. As this is assumed to be infeasible, we can conclude that no one but T can match a transaction with a user.   □

References

1. G. Ateniese, J. Camenisch, M. Joye, G. Tsudik. A Practical and Provably Secure Coalition-Resistant Group Signature Scheme. Crypto'2000, volume 1880 of LNCS, pages 255–270. Springer-Verlag, 2000.

2. D. Boneh. The Decision Diffie-Hellman Problem. 3rd Algorithmic Number Theory Symposium, volume 1423 of LNCS, pages 48–63. Springer-Verlag, 1998.

3. E. Brickell, P. Gemmel, D. Kravitz. Trustee-Based Tracing Extensions to Anonymous Cash and the Making of Anonymous Change. 6th ACM-SIAM, pages 457–466. ACM Press, 1995.

4. J. Camenisch, A. Lysyanskaya. An Efficient System for Non-transferable Anonymous Credentials with Optional Anonymity Revocation. Eurocrypt 2001, volume 2045 of LNCS, pages 93–118. Springer-Verlag, 2001.

5. J. Camenisch, U.M. Maurer, M. Stadler. Digital Payment Systems with Passive Anonymity-Revoking Trustees. Esorics'96, pages 33–43. Springer-Verlag, 1996.

6. D. Chaum, E. van Heyst. Group Signatures. Eurocrypt'91, volume 547 of LNCS, pages 257–265. Springer-Verlag, 1991.

7. I. Damgård, E. Fujisaki. A Statistically-Hiding Integer Commitment Scheme Based on Groups with Hidden Order. Asiacrypt 2002, volume 2501 of LNCS, pages 143–159. Springer-Verlag, 2002.

8. G. Davida, Y. Frankel, Y. Tsiounis, M. Yung. Anonymity Control in E-Cash Systems. Financial Crypto'97, volume 1318 of LNCS, pages 1–16. Springer-Verlag, 1997.

9. T. El Gamal. A Public Key Cryptosystem and a Signature Scheme Based on Discrete Logarithms, IEEE Trans. Inform. Theory, 31, pages 469–472. 1985.

10. A. Fiat, A. Shamir. How to Prove Yourself: Practical Solutions to Identification and Signature Problems. Crypto'86, volume 263 of LNCS, pages 186–194. Springer-Verlag, 1987.

11. Y. Frankel, Y. Tsiounis, M. Yung. Indirect Discourse Proofs: Achieving Efficient Fair Off-Line E-Cash. Asiacrypt'96, volume 1163 of LNCS, pages 286–300. Springer-Verlag, 1996.

12. Y. Frankel, Y. Tsiounis, M. Young. Fair Off-Line e-cash Made Easy, Asiacrypt'98, volume 1514 of LNCS, pages 257–270. Springer-Verlag, 1998.

13. E. Fujisaki, T. Okamoto. Statistical Zero-Knowledge Protocols Solution to Identification and Signature Problems. Crypto'97, volume 1294 of LNCS, pages 16–30. Springer-Verlag, 1997.

14. M. Gaud, J. Traoré. On the Anonymity of Fair Off-Line e-Cash Systems, Financial Crypto'03 (to appear).

15. G. Maitland, C. Boyd. Fair Electronic Cash Based on a Group Signature Scheme. ICICS 2001, volume 2229 of LNCS, pages 461–465. Springer-Verlag, 2001.

16. W. Qiu, K. Chen, D. Gu. A New Off-line Privacy Protecting E-Cash System with Revokable Anonymity. ISC 2002. 2002.

17. M. Stadler, J.M. Piveteau, J. Camenisch. Fair Blind Signatures, Eurocrypt'95, volume 921 of LNCS. pages 209–219. Springer-Verlag, 1995.

18. J. Traoré. Group Signatures and Their Relevance to Privacy-Protecting Off-Line Electronic Cash Systems. ACISP'99, volume 1587 of LNCS, pages 228–243. Springer-Verlag, 1999.

A Taxonomy of Single Sign-On Systems

Andreas Pashalidis* and Chris J. Mitchell

Royal Holloway, University of London,
Egham, Surrey, TW20 0EX, United Kingdom
{A.Pashalidis, C.Mitchell}@rhul.ac.uk
http://www.isg.rhul.ac.uk

Abstract. At present, network users have to manage one set of authentication credentials (usually a username/password pair) for every service with which they are registered. Single Sign-On (SSO) has been proposed as a solution to the usability, security and management implications of this situation. Under SSO, users authenticate themselves only once and are logged into the services they subsequently use without further manual interaction. Several architectures for SSO have been developed, each with different properties and underlying infrastructures. This paper presents a taxonomy of these approaches and puts some of the SSO schemes, services and products into that context. This enables decisions about the design and selection of future approaches to SSO to be made within a more structured context; it also reveals some important differences in the security properties that can be provided by various approaches.

1 Introduction

Network users typically maintain a set of authentication credentials (usually a username/password pair) with every Service Provider[1] (SP) they are registered with. The number of such SPs with which a typical user routinely interacts has grown beyond the point at which most users can memorize the required credentials. The most common solution is for users to use the same password with every SP with which they register[2] — a tradeoff between security and usability in favour of the latter.

A potential solution for this security issue is Single Sign-On (SSO), a technique whereby the user authenticates him/herself only once and is automatically logged into SPs as necessary, without necessarily requiring further manual interaction. SSO thereby increases the usability of the network as a whole and at the same time centralises the management of relevant system parameters.

---

* The author is sponsored by the State Scholarship Foundation of Greece.

[1] In the context of this paper a service provider is any entity that provides some kind of service or content to a user. Examples of SPs include web services, messenger services, FTP/web sites, and streaming media providers.

[2] There are even tools that 'synchronize' passwords, such as those at www.psynch.com and www.proginet.com/products/securpass/spsync.asp.

R. Safavi-Naini and J. Seberry (Eds.): ACISP 2003, LNCS 2727, pp. 249–264, 2003.
© Springer-Verlag Berlin Heidelberg 2003

Several different SSO architectures have emerged, each with different properties and underlying infrastructures. In this paper we identify four generic architectures for SSO systems and discuss their strengths and weaknesses. The remainder of the paper is organised as follows. Section 2 presents the taxonomy, and section 3 discusses the main properties of the architectures. Section 4 then presents a variety of SSO schemes in the context of the taxonomy, and section 5 concludes the paper.

2   A Taxonomy of SSO Systems

As mentioned above, SSO systems support automatic user authentication to SPs. As authentication implies identification, SSO systems have to incorporate the life cycle management of the identifiers by which a user is known to the SPs he/she is registered with. These identifiers can take various forms. We refer to them collectively as 'SSO identities'.

We distinguish between two main types of SSO systems. The first type, which we call 'pseudo-SSO', involves use of a component which achieves SSO simply by automatically executing whatever authentication mechanisms are in place at the different SPs. At the beginning of a session the user has to authenticate him/herself to this pseudo-SSO component: we call this step *primary authentication*. One key distinguishing feature of this SSO type is that, during an 'SSO session', a separate authentication occurs every time the user is logged into an SP. The pseudo-SSO component manages the SP-specific authentication credentials, which constitute the SSO identities in this case. Since these SSO identities are thus SP-specific, the SSO Identity/SP relationship can be said to be $n : 1$; that is, any given SSO identity corresponds to exactly one SP, and a user may, in principle, have multiple SSO identities for a single SP. This type of SSO scheme is illustrated in Figure 1.

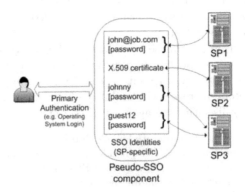

Fig. 1. Pseudo-SSO

Pseudo-SSO is fundamentally different from the second type of SSO system, which we call 'true SSO'. In a true SSO scheme the user authenticates to an entity called the *Authentication Service Provider* (ASP). The ASP is required to have an established relationship with all SPs to which SSO is to be achieved. This relationship requires a level of trust, and might typically be supported by a contractual arrangement. There would also typically need to be a supporting infrastructure to enable secure communications between ASPs and SPs. The key distinguishing feature of true SSO is that the only authentication process that involves the user occurs between the user and the ASP — SPs are notified of the authentication status of the user via so-called *authentication assertions*. These are statements that contain the user's SSO identity and his/her authentication status at the ASP. Note that the transport of these authentication assertions will itself need to be secured by a means specific to the SSO scheme in use. The exact form of SSO identities depends on the system design, but would typically be uniform throughout the whole system.

In contrast to pseudo-SSO, under true SSO the SSO identity/SP relationship can be $n : m$. That is, if supported by the scheme, not only can the user can potentially choose from a 'pool of identities' for any given SP, but the same SSO identity could, if the user wishes, be used with multiple SPs. This enables the assignment of specific *roles* to SSO identities (which then act as 'role pseudonyms' as defined in [19]). A true SSO scheme is depicted in Figure 2.

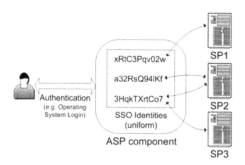

Fig. 2. True SSO

More generally, the information flows in an SSO system are shown in Figure 3. The user first authenticates to the ASP or pseudo-SSO component in step 1. Whenever a service is requested (step 2), the ASP or pseudo-SSO component automatically logs the user into the SP in step 3. Under true SSO this identity establishment phase involves the ASP (securely) conveying assertions about the user's authentication status to the SP, whilst in a pseudo-SSO scheme this step simply involves the pseudo-SSO component automatically performing the SP-specific (legacy) authentication mechanism on the user's behalf. Finally, assuming that step 3 is successfully completed, service provision proceeds in step 4.

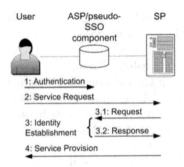

Fig. 3. Information flows in a generic SSO system

SSO architectures can be further categorised based on the location of the ASP/pseudo-SSO component; specifically, this component can either be local to the user platform, or offered as a service by an external entity, which we refer to as the 'SSO proxy'. We thus arrive at the following four main categories of SSO systems:

- Local pseudo-SSO systems,
- Proxy-based pseudo-SSO systems,
- Local true SSO systems, and
- Proxy-based true SSO systems.

We next consider each of these four types of scheme in a little more detail.

2.1   Local Pseudo-SSO Systems

In a local pseudo-SSO system, the pseudo-SSO component is resident within the user machine. This component maintains a (typically encrypted) database of the various authentication credentials for the different SPs. The user authenticates him/herself to the pseudo-SSO component at the beginning of a session. From that point on the component automatically executes SP-specific authentication protocols whenever needed, by supplying the (if necessary decrypted) authentication credentials. A key property of this SSO architecture is that the user machine needs access to cleartext versions of the long-term authentication credentials, and the user must therefore trust the machine not to compromise these credentials.

2.2   Proxy-Based Pseudo-SSO Systems

In a proxy-based pseudo-SSO architecture, the pseudo-SSO component resides on an external proxy server; as in the local case, this external server has access to the user's credentials, and hence must be trusted for this purpose by the user. Primary authentication occurs between the user and the proxy at the beginning of a session (and possibly thereafter if the proxy wishes to perform a re-authentication). Subsequent user authentication at SPs is redirected to, or intercepted by, the proxy, which automatically executes the SP-specific authentication protocol including supplying the requested credentials. A key property of this architecture is that the local machine never has access to the user's SP-specific credentials; authentication to SPs occurs directly between the proxy and the SPs.

2.3   Local True SSO Systems

As explained above, under true SSO the ASP authenticates the user, and subsequently conveys authentication assertions to relying SPs whenever necessary. When a trusted component within the user system takes the role of the ASP, the resulting architecture falls into the category of local true SSO systems. Of course a trust relationship between the local ASP, the relying SPs, and a supporting security infrastructure must exist. Since, in this setting, the ASP is under the physical control of the user, mechanisms must be in place that guarantee the integrity and trustworthiness of the ASP component itself.

2.4   Proxy-Based True SSO Systems

In a proxy-based true SSO architecture, an external server takes the role of the ASP. This external server acts as a broker between users and SPs; registered users can benefit from SSO at SPs that maintain a trust relationship with the ASP. It is worth noting that the ASP can trivially impersonate any registered user at every relying SP, simply by conveying an assertion. Therefore, both users and SPs have to trust the ASP for the purposes of SSO. Note also that this observation holds for the ASP in all (local or proxy-based) true SSO systems, as well as for the pseudo-SSO component in all pseudo-SSO systems.

3   Properties of SSO Schemes

This section presents some properties that distinguish the various types of SSO system. The four SSO categories are examined with respect to these properties. Examples of SSO implementations are also mentioned wherever appropriate.

3.1   Privacy Protection

Privacy protection is of particular importance in open environments [23]. With respect to SSO systems, privacy concerns arise if SSO identities contain personally identifying information, or if it is possible for an attacker (which could be one or more colluding SPs) to correlate distinct identities of the same user without his/her consent. Thus SSO identity pseudonymity, in the sense that they do not include any personally identifying information, and unlinkability are potentially desirable properties, where the latter implies the former [19].

Pseudo-SSO systems cannot guarantee the pseudonymity and therefore cannot guarantee the unlinkability of SSO identities, because the identities are SP-specific; some SPs may require users to log in using their e-mail addresses (as is the case with 'anonymous' FTP sites and some web sites), public key certificates, or their social security numbers. True SSO systems, on the other hand, can be designed such that SSO identities do not contain any personally identifying information and remain unlinkable even if SPs collude.

Of course, the success of privacy protection assumes that unlinkable means of payment exist (where users need to pay for services). Whilst many such schemes have been proposed, they have yet to make a major impact in the commercial environment.

3.2   Anonymous Network Access

Whether or not otherwise unlinkable SSO identities remain secure when an attacker has access to network address information depends on the wider context within which the SSO scheme is deployed. If, for example, the lower layer protocols do not provide anonymous network access, an attacker can easily compromise unlinkability by correlating SSO identities using information found in packet headers or traffic analysis [1]. Unfortunately, the user's network address (which *is* typically included in packet headers) also reveals the identity and geographical location of his/her network access provider. The provider can then help link the network address (and thereby SSO identities) back to the user's real identity.

These privacy issues are addressed by schemes that provide anonymous network access. Such schemes are typically implemented through an externally operated 'anonymising proxy'. All traffic between the user and the SPs is physically routed through that proxy, which replaces the user's real network address (and perhaps other identifying information) with its own. The achieved level of anonymity depends, of course, on the number of users in the system [19]. Examples of such anonymity services are the Anonymizer (`www.anonymizer.com`) and Freedom WebSecure[3] from zerøknowledge.

Such single-proxy schemes do not protect against traffic analysis, and all trust resides within the proxy operator. There exist more powerful schemes, such as those described in [4,7], that do protect against traffic analysis and ideally distribute the trust amongst disparate security domains. An example of such a system is JAP (`anon.inf.tu-dresden.de`).

Anonymising services can be employed in conjunction with SSO systems in order to increase the level of SSO identity unlinkability. In fact, SSO-proxies could be augmented with the functionality of an anonymising proxy. Of course all traffic would have to be physically routed through the proxy, but the user would not have to trust an additional entity. In the case of proxy-based pseudo-SSO, the architecture might be completely transparent to SPs: they would not even need to be aware of the proxy's existence.

---

[3] www.freedom.net/products/websecure

3.3   User Mobility

Proxy-based SSO architectures inherently support user mobility; users can authenticate themselves to the ASP/pseudo-SSO component from anywhere in the network (except, of course, if the authentication method itself imposes restrictions on this). We thus concentrate on how user mobility can be supported in local SSO schemes.

In local pseudo-SSO systems, user mobility can be supported if the credential database is held on an external server: initial authentication between user and server occurs once at the beginning of a session and credentials are then downloaded to the local machine as needed. The degree of trust in the server varies according to whether or not credentials are stored in an encrypted form. Novell's SecureLogin[4], Passlogix' V-GO (`www.passlogix.com/sso`) and Protocom's SecureLogin (`www.protocom.cc`) products are examples of local pseudo-SSO systems with support for user mobility. One can also regard automatic form-fillers as products with pseudo-SSO functionality. Examples include the automatic form completion functions of popular web browsers and Novell's DigitalMe (`www.digitalme.com`) service.

However, the local true SSO scheme described in [18] does not support cross-platform user mobility per se, as SSO identities are bound to the user platform itself (see section 4.5).

3.4   Use in an Untrusted Environment

Some scenarios require users to access SPs from untrusted or hostile environments, such as Internet cafés or public terminals. In this situation it is undesirable if the untrusted machine ever has access to authentication credentials that will allow it to later launch successful impersonation attacks.

In such scenarios proxy-based SSO schemes might prove useful. Of course, the initial authentication between user and proxy must have the property that observation of one authentication exchange does not enable subsequent impersonation of the user, as in, for example, a one-time password scheme or a suitable challenge/response protocol (see, for example, [16]). Building on this, and assuming that all network traffic between the user and the SPs is physically routed through it, the proxy may also provide an additional privacy protection service by 'stripping off' all personal data before it reaches the untrusted machine.

3.5   Deployment and Maintenance Costs

Generally speaking, it is far less costly to deploy pseudo-SSO schemes, because they do not require any common security infrastructure; moreover, existing SPs may not need to change at all. On the other hand, if any SP *does* change its user authentication mechanisms after deployment, this has to be reflected in the pseudo-SSO component. This increases the maintenance costs, especially in dynamically changing environments.

---

[4] www.novell.com/products/securelogin

The situation is reversed in true SSO-schemes. Deployment of true SSO systems requires a costly, system-wide security framework (such as a Public Key Infrastructure) to support SP-ASP secure communications, which might involve service level and liability transfer agreements. Once the infrastructure is in place, however, maintenance costs are likely to be small, since changes in the authentication interface occur only between the user and his/her chosen ASP(s).

3.6   Running Costs

The running costs of local SSO schemes are likely to be lower than those of proxy-based systems. This is because local SSO schemes do not require the continuous online presence of a server.

Proxy-based systems depend, of course, on the security and availability of the external proxy server. The server constitutes a single point of failure in the system, and must be protected against service denial attacks. Moreover additional communications costs might be incurred if all traffic is physically routed through the proxy. Further, in proxy-based true SSO systems, SPs may be charged by the ASP for the authentication service.

3.7   Trust Relationships

As explained in section 2.4, under both pseudo and true SSO, users and SPs need to trust the Pseudo-SSO component/ASP for the purposes of SSO. A local SSO system, such as the one described in [18], has the advantage that the user does not have to trust an externally operated entity, although the user will still need to trust the integrity of the software providing the SSO functionality.

It is important to note that, despite the universal need for user trust in the SSO component, there remain differences in the nature of the trust relationships involved in true and pseudo-SSO schemes. In the case of a true SSO scheme, the common security infrastructure allows for the trust relationships between the SPs and ASPs to be precisely described and regulated by policies, service level and liability transfer agreements, and other means outside the scope of SSO in the technical sense. Furthermore, if the user's authentication credentials are compromised, SSO can be disabled centrally.

Under pseudo-SSO the trust relationships are more diffuse. SPs may not even be aware that a SSO scheme is in place. Credential databases may be encrypted and replicated at several servers. The trust relationship between the user, any servers and the pseudo-SSO component depends on the implementation details of the scheme. The trust relationship between pseudo-SSO component and SPs may be different for each SP, and may change whenever individual SPs modify their authentication interfaces.

3.8   Conflict Resolution and Lawful Access

In the event of a dispute or lawful investigation, the operator of the proxy in a proxy-based (true or pseudo) SSO scheme may provide evidence of events, as a trusted third party, by keeping logs of authentications. The situation is likely to be better defined in a true SSO system, as in such systems there is necessarily a well-defined relationship between ASPs and SPs.

Local SSO schemes are much less likely to be useful in this sense, since evidence can either be deleted, e.g. if it might be embarrassing to the user, or modified. However, if the ASP in a local true SSO system incorporates physical protection measures, which enables it to be trusted by third parties (see, for example, [18]), then locally stored event logs may still possess evidential value.

3.9 Open versus Closed Environments

The issue of privacy protection (which includes anonymous network access and use in untrusted environments) is usually deemed to be of less importance in closed environments. Thus, the main focus for SSO for closed systems is likely to be the deployment, running and maintenance costs. Since these are less for pseudo-SSO systems, especially in relatively stable environments, 'enterprise' pseudo-SSO solutions promise a rapid and concrete return on investment. Architectures of such systems are examined in [6], and examples of real-world implementations include Computer Associates' eTrust Single Sign-On[5] and Evidian's AccessMaster (www.evidian.com/accessmaster).

However, the need for privacy protection in open environments may well outweigh the deployment cost of true SSO schemes. Thus it seems likely that true SSO systems will eventually be required in open environments such as the Internet. Some well-known proxy-based true SSO systems designed for open environments are discussed in the next section.

4 Some Examples of SSO Schemes

This section provides more detailed descriptions of certain SSO schemes. First note that the preponderance of existing discussed and deployed SSO schemes fall into two of the four categories discussed above, namely local pseudo-SSO and proxy-based true SSO schemes (examples of the former class have already been mentioned in section 3.3). Because of this, in this section we first discuss three important examples of the latter class. However, to show that other possibilities exist, we also briefly discuss two further examples, namely of a proxy-based pseudo-SSO scheme and a local true SSO scheme.

4.1 Kerberos

Although Kerberos is formally described as a 'network authentication system' [8, 22], one can regard it as a SSO scheme. A single security domain, or *realm*, consists of a set of users, an Authentication Server, a 'Ticket Granting Server' and a set of relying SPs. The Authentication Server and Ticket Granting Server

---

[5] www3.ca.com/Solutions/Product.asp?ID=166

can be combined into a single entity called the 'Kerberos server' which acts as the ASP. The security infrastructure of Kerberos relies solely on symmetric cryptography; every user and SP shares a long-term secret key with the ASP.

A simplified description of SSO under Kerberos follows. The protocol is executed whenever the uses wishes to log into an SP of the realm.

1. If the user already possesses a valid 'Ticket Granting Ticket' (TGT) from a previous protocol run, this step is skipped. Otherwise, the user requests a fresh TGT from the ASP. The ASP replies with a message that contains a fresh TGT, and a 'session key' which will be used to construct an 'authenticator', i.e. a data structure which is encrypted under a session key and contains elements that protect against replay attacks. This session key is encrypted under the long-term key the user shares with the ASP (or a key derived from it). The user decrypts the session key by supplying his/her long-term key.

2. The user sends a message to the ASP that contains the TGT, an authenticator (encrypted under the aforementioned session key), and the identifier of the SP he/she wishes to access. The ASP checks the validity of the received message. If not satisfied, (if, for example, the TGT has expired) authentication fails. Otherwise the user is now deemed authenticated at the ASP.

3. The ASP replies with a message that contains a 'Service Granting Ticket' (SGT) a data structure encrypted under the key shared by the ASP and the SP in question, and a second session key which is encrypted under the session key of step 1.

4. The user now constructs a message containing the SGT and an authenticator encrypted under the second session key. This message, if constructed correctly, demonstrates the user's ability to decrypt the second session key and can be regarded as an authentication assertion. The user sends it to the SP which decrypts it and, if valid, logs the user in.

The tickets (TGT and SGT) are encrypted data structures that contain (among other things) the user identifier and network address, the server identifier, corresponding session keys and expiration timestamps. SSO is achieved by the fact that the user does not need to reenter his/her long-term key as long as the TGT remains valid.

SSO among multiple realms is achieved by setting up the required relationships and symmetric keys between the involved Kerberos servers. There is no restriction as to the type (web, FTP, etc.) of SPs that may rely on Kerberos for user authentication as long as they follow the protocol.

Since the same user identifier is used with every SP, the SSO identity/SP relationship under Kerberos is $1 : n$. Thus, unlinkability of SSO identities is not an issue. It is interesting to observe that even distinct Kerberos accounts of a given user are still linkable as tickets bind them to the user's network address. Since the authentication mechanism is based on a long-term secret key, user mobility can be supported (if the key is derived from a password, for example) but it is not suitable for use in an untrusted environment.

4.2   The Liberty Alliance

The Liberty Alliance (`www.projectliberty.org`), a consortium of over 140 member companies, recently developed a set of open specifications for web-based SSO. In Liberty terminology [12], the ASP and the user are the 'Identity Provider' and 'Principal' respectively. The specifications use the Security Assertions Markup Language (SAML), a platform-independent framework for exchanging authentication and authorisation information[6]. Liberty is based on the notion of 'trust circles' which are formed by trusted ASPs and sets of relying SPs. The relationship between ASP and SPs has to be supported by contractual agreements outside the scope of the specifications.

According to the specifications, users first authenticate themselves to the ASP, which subsequently conveys authentication assertions to the relying SPs in order to facilitate SSO. The assertions contain 'name identifiers' that allow SPs to differentiate between users. For any given user, the ASP has to use a distinct identifier with each SP of the trust circle. Thus, under Liberty, the SSO identity/SP relationship is 1 : 1. Furthermore, name identifiers "must be constructed using pseudo-random values that have no discernible correspondence with the Principal's identifier (e.g. username) at the Identity Provider [ASP]" [15, p.12]; SSO identities are pseudonymous and, by themselves, unlinkable. Unlinkability, however, can be compromised, as SPs may be able to correlate SSO identities based on the users' network addresses. Use of an anonymous network access scheme (section 3.2) could help with this. Profile information that individual SPs may maintain (such as shopping habits, telephone numbers or credit card details) can also compromise unlinkability. For the time being, "the only protection is for Principals to be cautious when they choose service providers and understand their privacy policies" [14, p.70]. An independent assessment of the specifications with respect to privacy appears in [20].

The Liberty specifications are authentication method neutral; the details of the particular method employed are explicitly stated in the authentication assertions [13]. This means that, under a suitable user authentication mechanism, user mobility or even use in an untrusted environment can be supported.

The Liberty Protocols and Schema Specification [15] defines generic requirements for the protocols for conveying assertion requests and responses between parties. Concrete protocol bindings are only specified in the context of a Liberty *profile*. All currently specified profiles rely on the Secure Socket Layer (SSL) or the Transport Layer Security (TLS) [21] protocol in order to provide secure channels between parties. Hence, a Public Key Infrastructure (PKI) must be in place. A separate PKI may be required if a profile is used that requires assertions to be digitally signed. Authentication assertions sent from the ASP to the SP are routed through the user browser via web redirects; in the 'browser/POST' profile, for example, assertions are sent within an HTTP form while in the 'browser/artifact' profile an 'artifact' is encoded in the URL that the SP can later resolve into an assertion [14].

---

[6] www.oasis-open.org/committees/security

According to [10], the next version of Liberty will include a framework for permissions-based attribute sharing which will allow organisations of a given trust circle to be linked together, as opposed to operating independently. Thus, the specifications are targeted towards a more comprehensive treatment of Identity Management that extends beyond the provision of SSO.

4.3   Microsoft Passport

Microsoft Passport (www.passport.com) is a web-based SSO service offered by Microsoft since 1999. The passport server acts as the ASP. Users register with the ASP by supplying a valid e-mail address and a password (or, if they register from a mobile phone, their phone number and a Personal Identification Number). Additional profile information, such as address, date of birth and credit card details, may also be stored in their passport accounts. Every account is uniquely identified by a 64-bit number called the 'Passport User ID' (PUID). SPs that wish to offer SSO for registered passport users need to sign a contractual agreement with Microsoft (which involves a yearly provisioning fee of $10,000 [17]), implement a special component in their web server software, and share a secret key with the ASP. Since SSL/TLS channels are required between the user and the passport server (and optionally between user and SP), an appropriate PKI must also be in place.

SSO is achieved by the following protocol, which is executed whenever the user wishes to log into an SP.

1. The user's browser is redirected to the ASP.
2. The ASP tries to retrieve a 'Ticket Granting Cookie' (TGC) from the web browser's cookie cache. If one is found, if it decrypts successfully, and if it is valid, the user is deemed authenticated and the rest of this step is skipped. Otherwise, the ASP requests the user to authenticate him/herself. Assuming successful authentication, the ASP saves a fresh TGC in the browser's cookie cache. This cookie is encrypted under a 'master key' only known to the ASP. Its function is similar to the TGT of Kerberos; there is, however, no 'authenticator' in Passport — replaying a stolen TGC results in successful impersonation.
3. The ASP saves a set of cookies in the browser's cookie cache which includes the user's PUID and other profile information the user has consented to share at registration time. This cookie set is encrypted under the secret key shared between the ASP and the SP in question. Its functionality is similar to Kerberos' SGT and acts as an authentication assertion.
4. The user's browser is redirected back to the desired SP which reads and decrypts the aforementioned cookie set and, if satisfied, logs in the user.

SSO is achieved by the fact that, as long as the TGC remains valid, the user does not need to re-authenticate (in step 1) in subsequent protocol runs. As the authentication method is password-based, user mobility is supported, but it is not suitable for use in an untrusted environment. Passport, like Kerberos, uses a single SSO identity (the PUID) with every SP. The SSO identity/SP relationship is therefore $1 : n$ and unlinkability is not an issue.

According to [11], in the future Passport will be based on Kerberos.

4.4   An Outline of a Proxy-Based Pseudo-SSO Scheme

One alternative to the true SSO schemes described above would involve a proxy acting as a gateway to service providers. The user would first authenticate to the proxy, e.g. using a one-time password scheme. The user would connect to SPs via the proxy, which would transparently 'fill in' identifiers and passwords for specific SPs, using information from its credential database.

Such an approach would have several major advantages. It would enable access to services from an untrusted PC since SP-specific credentials would not reach the user PC (see section 3.3). Like other pseudo-SSO schemes it could be deployed transparently, i.e. without requiring individual SPs to make any changes to their authentication procedures. Moreover user mobility is supported. However, like other pseudo-SSO schemes, unlinkability of SSO identities cannot be guaranteed.

4.5   A Local True SSO Scheme Built upon TCPA

The final example scheme we consider is described in much greater detail in [18]. The Trusted Computing Platform Alliance (TCPA) is an industry consortium established to agree specifications for ways in which to include a trusted component within a computing platform. The scheme shows how to use a TCPA-compliant platform to establish a local true SSO system.

In this scheme a component within the user's platform, which we call the Authentication Service (AS), acts as the ASP; it authenticates the user and subsequently conveys assertions to SPs whenever necessary. The integrity of the user platform's software state (which includes the AS) is measured by a TCPA function called 'Integrity Metrics'. Any given SP reliably acquires these software metrics through an 'Integrity Challenge/Response' session, also specified by TCPA. This step requires a PKI to be in place. The SP then needs to verify that the given metrics represent a software configuration that is trusted for the purposes of SSO. This step includes verification of certificates supplied by the manufacturer(s) of software (including the AS) running on the user's platform.

The scheme uses TCPA-specified credentials, called 'Identity Credentials', as SSO identities. An Identity Credential is a certificate issued by a special authority and certifies that the specified platform conforms to the TCPA specifications (without, however, uniquely identifying the particular platform). Any given user can acquire an arbitrary number of such credentials for his/her platform. As these Identity Credentials act as SSO identities, SPs also need to verify them — a function which requires another PKI to be in place.

The scheme offers a $n : m$ relationship between SSO identities and SPs, allowing the assignment of roles to SSO identities. User mobility, however, is not supported per se, as SSO identities are bound to the user's platform.

5   Conclusions

We have presented an abstract taxonomy of SSO systems and have analysed the properties of the identified four main types of SSO scheme. The characteristics of these four types of scheme are summarised in Table 1. We have also presented some examples of SSO schemes in the light of the taxonomy. Unfortunately, (with the exception of the recently proposed scheme described in section 4.5) none of the true SSO schemes offers a $n : m$ SSO identity/SP relationship and therefore cannot be used to assign roles to SSO identities; a separate account has to be created at the ASP for every role. This is clearly a topic meriting further study.

Table 1. Properties of SSO systems.

	Local pseudo-SSO	Proxy-based pseudo-SSO	Local true-SSO	Proxy-based true SSO
Pseudonymity and Unlinkability	cannot be guaranteed	cannot be guaranteed	can be guaranteed	can be guaranteed
Anonymous Network Access	needs additional services	can be integrated	needs additional services	can be integrated
Support for User Mobility	needs additional services	under suitable authentication method	needs additional services	under suitable authentication method
Use in Untrusted Environment	not supported	under suitable authentication method	not supported	under suitable authentication method
Deployment Costs	low	low	high	high
Maintenance Costs	potentially high	potentially high	low	low
Running Costs	low	high	low	high
Trust Relationships	dynamically changing	dynamically changing	concrete and consistent	concrete and consistent

It is clear that each SSO architecture has its strengths and weaknesses, and one must carefully consider the environment before opting for a particular SSO solution. Generally speaking, pseudo-SSO schemes are probably more suitable for closed systems, where privacy protection is less of an issue. Identity Management in that context just refers to the management of the life cycle of the credentials the user maintains within the closed system. On the other hand, Identity Management in open environments like the Internet, may well need to incorporate privacy protection. SSO schemes, privacy protection services (such as the ones discussed in sections 3.2 and 3.4) and privacy-aware Identity Management schemes, such as the ones described in [2,5,9], could be integrated into a true SSO scheme. Indeed, it would appear that a precise indication of the achieved privacy level is possible only with the combined use of a suitable *true* SSO scheme. A practical scheme that could deliver such an indication would potentially be useful. Moreover, it would be interesting to see how anonymous credential systems, such as the one described in [3], could be combined with authentication method-neutral SSO (possibly along with anonymous network access).

References

1. Adam Back, Ulf Möller, and Anton Stiglic. Traffic analysis attacks and trade-offs in anonymity providing systems. In I. S. Moskowitz, editor, *Information Hiding, 4th International Workshop, IHW 2001*, volume 2137 of *Lecture Notes in Computer Science*, pages 245–257. Springer Verlag, Berlin, 2001.
2. Oliver Berthold and Marit Köhntopp. Identity management based on P3P. In H. Federrath, editor, *Designing Privacy Enhancing Technologies, International Workshop on Design Issues in Anonymity and Unobservability, July 2000*, number 2009 in Lecture Notes in Computer Science, pages 141–160. Springer-Verlag, Berlin, 2001.
3. Jan Camenisch and Els Van Herreweghen. Design and implementation of the idemix anonymous credential system. In *Proceedings of the 9th ACM Conference on Computer and Communications Security*, pages 21–30. ACM Press, New York, 2002.
4. David L. Chaum. Untraceable electronic mail, return addresses, and digital pseudonyms. *Communications of the ACM*, 24(2):84–90, 1981.
5. Sebastian Clauß and Marit Köhntopp. Identity management and its support of multilateral security. *Computer Networks*, 37:205–219, 2001.
6. Jan De Clercq. Single sign-on architectures. In George I. Davida, Yair Frankel, and Owen Rees, editors, *Infrastructure Security, International Conference, InfraSec 2002 Bristol, UK, October 1-3, 2002, Proceedings*, volume 2437 of *Lecture Notes in Computer Science*, pages 40–58. Springer Verlag, 2002.
7. David M. Goldschlag, Michael G. Reed, and Paul F. Syverson. Onion routing for anonymous and private internet connections. *Communications of the ACM*, 42(2):84–88, January 1999.
8. Internet Engineering Task Force. *RFC 1510: The Kerberos Network Authentication Service (V5)*, September 1993.
9. Uwe Jendricke and Daniela Gerd tom Markotten. Usability meets security — the Identity-Manager as your personal security assistant for the internet. In *Proceedings of the 16th Annual Computer Security Applications Conference (ACSAC 2000)*, pages 344–355. IEEE Computer Society, 2000.
10. Liberty Alliance. *The Liberty Alliance News Letter*, volume 1, issue 1 edition, November 2002.
11. Liberty Alliance. *Identity Systems and Liberty Specification version 1.1 Interoperability*, January 2003.
12. Liberty Alliance. *Liberty Architecture Glossary v.1.1*, January 2003.
13. Liberty Alliance. *Liberty Authentication Context Specification v.1.1*, January 2003.
14. Liberty Alliance. *Liberty Bindings and Profiles Specification v.1.1*, January 2003.

15. Liberty Alliance. *Liberty Protocols and Schemas Specification v.1.1*, January 2003.
16. A. J. Menezes, P. C. van Oorschot, and S. A. Vanstone. *Handbook of Applied Cryptography*. CRC Press, Boca Raton, 1997.
17. Microsoft. *Microsoft .NET Passport Review Guide*, November 2002.
18. Andreas Pashalidis and Chris J. Mitchell. Single sign-on using trusted platforms. Technical Report RHUL–MA–2003–3, Mathematics Department, Royal Holloway, University of London, March 2003.
19. Andreas Pfitzmann and Marit Köhntopp.   Anonymity, unobservability, and pseudonymity — a proposal for terminology. In H. Federrath, editor, *Designing Privacy Enhancing Technologies, International Workshop on Design Issues in Anonymity and Unobservability, July 2000*, number 2009 in Lecture Notes in Computer Science, pages 141–160. Springer-Verlag, Berlin, 2001.
20. Birgit Pfitzmann. Privacy in enterprise identity federation — Policies for Liberty single signon. In *Proceedings: 3rd Workshop on Privacy Enhancing Technologies (PET 2003), Dresden, March 2003*, Lecture Notes in Computer Science. Springer-Verlag, Berlin, to appear.
21. Eric Rescorla. *SSL and TLS*. Addison-Wesley, Reading, Massachusetts, 2001.
22. J. G. Steiner, B. Clifford Neuman, and J.I. Schiller. Kerberos: An authentication service for open network systems. In *Proceedings of the Winter 1988 Usenix Conference*, pages 191–201, February 1988.
23. World Wide Web Consortium. *The Platform for Privacy Preferences 1.0 (P3P 1.0) Specification*, April 2002.

Key Recovery Attacks on the RMAC, TMAC, and IACBC

Jaechul Sung[1], Deukjo Hong[2], and Sangjin Lee[2]

[1] Cryptographic Technology Team, Korea Information Security Agency(KISA),
78, Karag-Dong, Songpa-Gu, Seoul, KOREA
sjames@kisa.or.kr
[2] Center for Information Security Technologies(CIST), Korea University,
Anam-Dong 5-ga, Sungbuk-Gu, Seoul, KOREA
{hongdj, sangjin}@cist.korea.ac.kr

Abstract. The RMAC[6] is a variant of CBC-MAC, which resists birthday attacks and gives provably full security. The RMAC uses $2k$-bit keys and the size of the RMAC is $2n$, where n is the size of underlying block cipher. The TMAC[10] is the improved MAC scheme of XCBC[4] such that it requires $(k+n)$-bit keys while the XCBC requires $(k+2n)$-bit keys. In this paper, we introduce trivial key recovery attack on the RMAC with about 2^n computations, which is more realistic than the attacks in [9]. Also we give a new attack on the TMAC using about $2^{n/2+1}$ texts, which can recover an $(k+n)$-bit key. However this attack can not be applied to the XCBC. Furthermore we analyzed the IACBC mode[8], which gives confidentiality and message integrity.

Keywords: Message Authentication Codes, Modes of Operation, Key Recovery Attacks, CBC-MAC, RMAC, TMAC, XCBC, IACBC.

1 Introduction

Message Authentication Codes(MACs) based on block ciphers are used to provide data integrity and data authenticity. In a typical setting, a sender and a receiver share the secret key K. The sender sends a message M together with a MAC on M, denoted by $MAC_K(M)$. The receiver recomputes the MAC on M and checks whether result has the same value as the received MAC.

There are two main kinds of practical attack on MAC schemes. One is a forgery attack and the other is a key recovery attack. In order to be resistant against forgery, it must be computationally infeasible for someone who does not know the secret key to find an arbitrary new message and its corresponding MAC value. On the other hand, a key recovery attack can obtain the secret key used to generate one or more MACs. A successful key recovery attack enables the construction of arbitrary numbers of forgeries. In this paper we will consider key recovery attacks.

Among many existing methods to build MACs, the Cipher Block Chaining Message Authentication Codes(CBC-MAC) is widely used in practice [5]. The

R. Safavi-Naini and J. Seberry (Eds.): ACISP 2003, LNCS 2727, pp. 265–273, 2003.
© Springer-Verlag Berlin Heidelberg 2003

security of CBC-MAC for fixed message lengths was proved in [1]. However, when message can vary, the CBC-MAC is not secure. The simple way of forgery uses two message of one block each M and M' and queries their MACs m and m' respectively. Then it can forge the MAC of $M||(M' \oplus m)$, namely m'. Many variants have been suggested in order to improve the security of the CBC-MAC [4,6,10,13].

The RMAC[6] was suggested in order to protect MACs from birthday attacks. Many variants of the CBC-MAC except the RMAC is just to encrypt the plain CBC-MAC with another key [4,10,13]. These methods can be attacked by computing about $O(2^{n/2})$ texts to forge a new message. The RMAC uses an n-bit random value and appends this value to an n-bit MAC value which is computed with $2k$-bit key. So the MAC length of the RMAC is $2n$-bits, which implies that it is required about $O(2^n)$ texts to forge a new message. In [6], they also proved the security of the RMAC in information theoretical model.

T. Kohno introduce the security of the RMAC against forgery attacks [9]. He introduced a new forgery attack in the muliti-user(variable-key) attack model, which requires about $O(2^{n/2})$ users and about $O(2^{3n/4})$ messages per each user. Also he improved this attack with about $O(2^{n/2})$ users and about $O(2^{n/2})$ messages per each user. This attack requires about $O(2^n)$ messages in total [9]. In this paper we introduce trivial key recovery attack in a single-user(fixed-key) model using about $O(2^n)$ computations with only one messages if the key size k is equal to n. This trivial attack is more realistic than the attack of [9] since obtaining $O(2^n)$ messages and MAC pairs is more difficult than off-line key searching with $O(2^n)$ computations in general.

The EMAC, which was first suggested in [2], is obtained by encrypting the CBC-MAC value with another key. In [13] they proved that the EMAC is secure if the message length is a multiple of n, where n is its block length. To obtain the security for the arbitrary length we usually use the padding method 2 in [5], which appends the minimal 10^i to a message M as a padding so that the length is a multiple of n. This approach requires one more encryption if the size of message is a multiple of n. Also the EMAC needs two key scheduling for two keys. Three key constructions were suggested to improve the EMAC. In [4] they proposed the three different variants of the CBC-MAC, which is the ECBC, FCBC, and XCBC.

The XCBC requires $(k+2n)$-bit keys, where k is the key length of underlying block cipher and n is its block length. It uses different n-bit keys depending on the length of original message. If the length of message is already multiple of n, it uses one n-bit key K_2. Otherwise it uses another n-bit key K_3. Recently Kurosawa and Iwata proposed the TMAC, which improves the EMAC using only $(k+n)$-bit keys [10]. The TMAC attains the provable security of the TMAC as the EMAC do. In this paper we also introduce a new key recovery attack on the TMAC, which can not be applied to the XCBC though.

In general it is required two passes in order to achieve confidentiality and message integrity. The IACBC mode is a new mode of operation which assures confidentiality and message integrity . The cost of IACBC is not much more than the cost of CBC mode or CTR mode. Here we introduce a key recovery attack on the IACBC mode.

This paper is organized as follows. In Section 2 we give the descriptions of RMAC and TMAC . In Section 3 we propose the new key recovery attacks of RMAC and TMAC. In Section 4 we analyze the IACBC mode and summarize our conclusion in Section 5.

2   Preliminaries

The most popular MAC is by far the CBC-MAC. The CBC-MAC defines as follows. Let $M = m_1, \cdots, m_r$ be a message, where each block m_i is of size n bits. Let $E_K(x)$ denote the encryption of x using a key K with an n-bit block cipher E and $H_0 = 0$. The CBC-MAC of M is defined as $CBC - MAC_K(M) = H_r$, where

$$H_i = E_K(H_{i-1} \oplus m_i) , \; 1 \leq i \leq r.$$

2.1   RMAC

Now we describe the RMAC. The RMAC uses two different keys, say K_1 and K_2, and a random value R for each message. The RMAC can be seen as an extension of EMAC[4]. In this setting we assume that the each key size k is equal to n.

The RMAC encrypts with $K_2 \oplus R$, where R is an n-bit random value and it is a part of the MAC value. We can describe the RMAC as the following.

$$RMAC_{K_1,K_2}(M) = (E_{K_2 \oplus R}(CBC - MAC_{K_1}(M)), R).$$

In their proposal, they showed that the security is beyond the birthday paradox limit. Since the MAC size of the RMAC is twice than the other CBC-MAC variants, it is required about $O(2^n)$ messages to forge the RMAC with the birthday paradox.

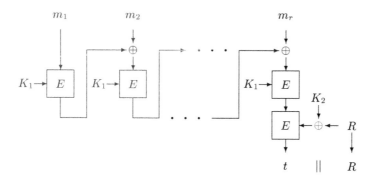

Fig. 1. The RMAC Algorithm

2.2   TMAC

The XCBC[4] is as same as the CBC-MAC except the last block transform. The XCBC uses three independent keys, say K_1, K_2, and K_3. Let K_1 be the key of the underlying block cipher and K_2 and K_3 be the n-bit keys for the last block transform.

Let us describe the XCBC. Let M be a message. If M is a multiple of n, then the XCBC computes exactly the same as the CBC-MAC, except for XORing an n-bit key K_2 before encrypting the last block. Otherwise, after minimal 10^i padding is appended to M so that the length is a multiple of n, then the XCBC computes exactly the same as the CBC-MAC, except for XORing another n-bit key K_3 before encrypting the last block.

The TMAC[10] is a refinement of the XCBC such that it requires $(k+n)$-bit keys while XCBC requires $(k+2n)$-bit keys. The $2n$-bit key pair (K_2, K_3) of the TMAC is obtained by only an n-bit key. In [10], they proposed the method to generate $2n$-bit keys from n-bit key using an almost universal hash function family. In their example, (K_2, K_3) can be obtained with $(H_{K_2}(Cst1), H_{K_2}(Cst2))$, where H is an AXU(Almost Xor Universal) hash function family and $Cst1$ and $Cst2$ are two different constants. As the proposed specification, they proposed $H_K(x) = K \cdot x$, $Cst1 = u$, and $Cst2 = 1$, where $\cdot$ denotes multiplication over $GF(2^n)$ and $u \in GF(2^n)$. For details, see the paper [10].

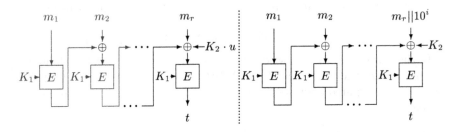

Fig. 2. The TMAC Algorithm

3   Key Recovery Attack on RMAC and TMAC

3.1   Key Recovery Attack on RMAC

E. Biham introduced the notion of a key-collision attack [3]. Using this notion T. Kohno introduced new forgery attacks on RMAC [9] in the multi-user(variable-key) attack model. These attacks are kinds of related-key attacks. Table 1 summarizes the resources for the attacks in [9]. The required resources of T. Kohno's attacks are more than $O(2^n)$ messages in total. This is too much to forge a new message.

Table 1. The required resources of the attacks in [9]

	Number of Users	Messages per User	Total Messages
Standard Attack I	1	2^n	2^n
Standard Attack II	$2^{n/2}$	$2^{3n/4}$	$2^{5n/4}$
Trade-Off Attack	$2^{n/2}$	$2^{n/2}$	2^n

Now we can consider a trivial key recovery attack with about $O(2^n)$ off-line computations using a few messages. Let $(M, (t, R))$ be a message and its corresponding MAC values. Then we have the following equations.

$$E_{K_2 \oplus R}(E_{K_1}(M)) = t.$$

Using the meet-in-the-middle-attack, we can find about 2^n pairs of (K_1, K_2). With another message, we can uniquely determine the right key. This attack only need a few(two or three in average) messages and about $O(2^n)$ off-line computations. This trivial attack is more realistic and efficient than the attacks in [9].

3.2   Key Recovery Attack on TMAC

The TMAC gives the provable security for arbitrary length messages as same as the XCBC does. The TMAC only uses $(k + n)$-bit key and only one key scheduling for the block encryption. If we consider the key size and the number of required encryptions among the existing CBC-MAC variants, the TMAC is the most optimized algorithm. However, in the course of reducing the key size from the XCBC, there exist some security gaps between the XCBC and TMAC.

Here we assume that the XCBC and TMAC take the full size. Then we have the following.

Lemma 1. *For the TMAC, there exists an attack which finds the n-bit key K_2, which requires chosen $2 \cdot 2^{n/2}$ messages with one block.*

Proof. Let $X = \{X^i \mid 1 \le i \le 2^{n/2}\}$ and $Y = \{Y^i \mid 1 \le i \le 2^{n/2}\}$, where X^i be an n-bit message and Y^i be an n-bit message after padding to Y'^i. If an attacker obtains the message-MAC pairs of X^i and Y^i respectively, there occurs the same MAC value between X and Y by the birthday paradox. Let X^i and Y^j be the messages which have the same MAC value. Then we have the following equation.

$$E_{K_1}(X^i \oplus H_{K_2}(Cst1)) = E_{K_1}(Y^j \oplus H_{K_2}(Cst2)).$$

Since E is a permutation, we have that $X^i \oplus H_{K_2}(Cst1) = Y^j \oplus H_{K_2}(Cst2)$. So we obtain the following equation.

$$H_{K_2}(Cst1) \oplus H_{K_2}(Cst2) = X^i \oplus Y^j. \tag{1}$$

As the specification of the TMAC, we have $K_2 \cdot (u+1) = X^i \oplus Y^j$. Therefore K_2 can be easily obtained.

For practical application of Lemma 1, we can set X^i is a random value whose last significant bit is zero and Y^i is a random values whose last significant bit is one. Then MAC values of the set X and Y are computed with $K_2 \cdot u$ and K_2 respectively. Lemma 1 can be applied for the TMAC using any XOR universal hash family H if K_2 can be easily obtained from the equation (1). However, the attack cannot be applied to the XCBC, since K_2 and K_3 are independent.

If we find the n-bit key K_2 using Lemma 1, then we can find K_1 by the exhaustive search attack. Therefore we can find two keys with about $O(2^n)$ computations of E using about $2^{n/2+1}$ messages if we assume that k is equal to n.

4   Key Recovery Attack on the IACBC Mode

C. S. Jutla proposed interesting encryption modes[12,8], IACBC and IAPM. The main feature distinguishing the two proposed modes from existing modes is that along with providing confidentiality of the message, they also provide message integrity. The cost of IACBC is not much more than the cost of CBC mode or CTR mode.

The IACBC(Integrity Aware Cipher Block Chaining) mode is similar to the CBC mode. It differs from the CBC mode in that the output is whitened with a pairwise independent random sequence. The IAPM mode is highly parallelizable. This mode removes the chaining from the above mode, and instead an input whitening with a pairwise independent sequence. Thus, it becomes similar to the ECB mode. The pairwise independent sequence can be generated with little overhead.

There are two different versions of the IACBC mode[12,8]. Here we will consider the proposed mode[12] which is appeared in NIST. Another version[8] of the mode in EUROCRYPT 2001 is slightly different from the proposed mode in NIST. Although these two mask generation algorithms are different, the main ideas of attack are quite similar. The mode in EUROCRYPT 2001 was analyzed by A. Joux et al.[7] independently with ours.

Now we analyze the practical security of the IACBC mode. Let n be the block size of the underlying block cipher. The IACBC mode requires two independent keys of length k. Let these keys be called K_0 and K_1. The message to be encrypted P is divided into blocks of length n each. Let these blocks be P_1, P_2, $\cdots$, P_{m-1}. As in the randomized CBC mode, a random initial vector r of length n bits is chosen. This random vector is expanded into $t = \lceil log(m+1) \rceil$ new random vectors, $W_i = E_{K_0}(r+i+1)$, $0 \le i \le t-1$.

The t random vectors are used to prepare $m(\le 2^t - 1)$ new pairwise independent random vectors $S_0, S_1, \cdots, S_{m-1}$. This can be done by taking all subsets of $W_0, W_1, \cdots, W_t$, and for each subset taking their xor-sum. The following is the method of generating subsets.

- $S_{-1} = 0$.
- for $i = 0$ to $m - 1$ do the followings.
    1. $j = i + 1$.
    2. $k = 0$.
    3. while$((j \& 1) == 0)$ do $k = k + 1$ and $j = j >> 1$.
    4. end while.
    5. if$((j \oplus 1) == 0)$ $W_k = E_{K_0}(r + k + 1)$.
    6. $S_i = S_{i-1} \oplus W_k$.
- end for.

After generating $S_0, S_1, \cdots, S_{m-1}$, the message $P_1, P_2, \cdots, P_{m-1}$ is encrypted with the key K_1. For details, see the Figure 3.

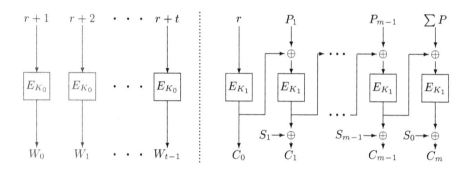

Fig. 3. The IACBC mode

The IACBC mode uses two independent keys, K_0 and K_1. Therefore the expecting security of the mode is about $2k$ bits. However we can cut down the security to the level of k bits.

Let us see the sequence $S_0, S_1, \cdots, S_{m-1}$. This sequence is generated by W_i's, which is generated by the key K_0. By the above sequence generating algorithm, we have the followings.

$$S_0 = W_0,$$
$$S_1 = W_0 \oplus W_1, \; S_2 = W_1,$$
$$S_3 = W_1 \oplus W_2, \; S_4 = W_0 \oplus W_1 \oplus W_2,$$
$$S_5 = W_0 \oplus W_2, \; S_6 = W_2, \cdots$$

The sequence $S_0, S_1, \cdots, S_{m-1}$ is pairwise independent. But, in this sequence, we can find relations of the sequence. For example, $S_0 \oplus S_1 \oplus S_2 = 0$, $S_1 \oplus S_2 \oplus S_3 \oplus S_4 = 0$, and so on. With these relations, we can attack the IACBC mode.

Assume an attacker obtains the ciphertext $(C_0, C_1, C_2, C_3, C_4, C_5)$ of a plaintext (P_1, P_2, P_3, P_4). Then we have the following equations.

$$S_1 = E_{K_1}(P_1 \oplus C_0) \oplus C_1$$
$$S_2 = E_{K_1}(E_{K_1}(P_1 \oplus C_0)) \oplus P_2) \oplus C_2$$
$$S_3 = E_{K_1}(E_{K_1}(E_{K_1}(P_1 \oplus C_0)) \oplus P_2) \oplus P_3) \oplus C_3$$
$$S_4 = E_{K_1}\left(E_{K_1}(E_{K_1}(E_{K_1}(P_1 \oplus C_0)) \oplus P_2) \oplus P_3) \oplus P_4\right) \oplus C_4$$

Since $S_1 \oplus S_2 \oplus S_3 \oplus S_4 = 0$, we have the following.

$$E_{K_1}(P_1 \oplus C_0) \oplus E_{K_1}(E_{K_1}(P_1 \oplus C_0)) \oplus P_2) \oplus E_{K_1}\left(E_{K_1}(E_{K_1}(P_1 \oplus C_0)) \oplus P_2) \oplus P_3\right)$$
$$\oplus E_{K_1}\left(E_{K_1}\left(E_{K_1}(E_{K_1}(P_1 \oplus C_0)) \oplus P_2) \oplus P_3\right) \oplus P_4\right) = C_1 \oplus C_2 \oplus C_3 \oplus C_4$$

The above equation does not contain K_0. So we can find K_1 by the exhaustive key search attack with 4 encryptions for each key. After finding K_1, we can find K_0 by the exhaustive key search.

Our attack needs 1 known plaintext/ciphertext pair which have 4 blocks and $5 \cdot 2^k$ encryption times. This means the IACBC attains the less security than that was expected.

5   Conclusion

A key recovery attack can obtain the secret key used to generate one or more MACs. In this paper we considered the trivial key recovery attack on RMAC, which is more realistic and efficient than the attacks in [9], and we suggested a new key recovery attack on TMAC. Also we analyzed the IACBC mode.

References

1. M. Bellare, J. Kilian, and P. Rogaway, *The Security of the Cipher Block Chaining Message Authentication Code*, Advanced in Cryptology – CRYPTO'94, LNCS 839, pp. 341–358, Springer-Verlag, 1994.
2. A. Berendschot, B. den Boer, J. P. Boly, A. Bosselaers, J. Brandt, D. Chaum, I. Damgård, M. Dichtl, W. Fumy, M. van der Ham, C. J. A. Jansen, P. Landrock, B. Preneel, G. Roelofsen, P. de Rooij, and J. Vandewalle, *Integrity Primitives for Secure Information System*, Final Report of RACE integrity primitives evaluation (RIPE-RACE 1040), RIPE Integrity Primitives, LNCS 1007, pp. 226, Springer-Verlag, 1995.
3. E. Biham, *How to Decrypt or Even Substitute DES-encrypted message in 2^{28} steps*, Information Proceeding Letters, vol. 84, Issue 3, 117–124, Elsevier Science, 15 November, 2002.

4. J. Black and P. Rogaway, *CBC-MACs for Arbitray-Length Messages : The Three Key Constructions*, Advanced in Cryptology – CRYPTO 2000, LNCS 1880, pp. 197–215, Springer-Verlag, 2000.
5. ISO/IEC 9797-1 *Information technology – Security techniques – Message Authentication Codes (MACs) – Part I : Mechanisms using a block cipher*, International Organization for Standardization, Geneve, Swizerland, 1999.
6. É. Jaulmes, A. Joux, and F. Valette, *On the Security of Randomized CBC-MAC beyond the Birthday Limit : A New Construction*, Fast Software Encryption 2002, LNCS 2365, pp. 237–251, Springer-Verlag, 2002.
7. A. Joux, G. Martinet, and F. Vallete, *Blockwise-Adaptive Attackers – Revisiting the (In)Security of Some Provably Secure Encryption Modes : CBC, GEM, IACBC*, Advances in Cryptology – CRYPTO 2002, LNCS 2442, pp. 17–30, Springer-Verlag, 2002.
8. C. S. Jutla, *Encryption Modes with Almost Free Message Integrity*, Advances in Cryptology – EUROCRYPT 2001, LNCS 2045, pp. 529–544, Springer-Verlag, 2001.
9. T. Kohno, *Key-Collision Attacks against RMAC*, The preliminary version published on eprint, October 21, 2002. Available at *http://eprint.iacr.org/2002/159/*.
10. K. Kurosawa and T. Iwata, *TMAC : Two-Key CBC MAC*, Topics in Cryptology - CT-RSA 2003(The Cryptographers Track at the RSA Conference 2003), LNCS 2612, pp. 33–49, Springer-Verlag, 2003. Also available at *http://csrc.nist.gov/encryption/modes*.
11. National Bureau of Standards, *DES modes of operation*, FIPS-Pub.46, National Bureau of Standards, U.S. Department of Commerce, Washington D.C., December 1980.
12. National Institute of Standards and Technology, *AES Mode of Operation Development Effort*, Available at *http://csrc.nist.gov/encryption/modes*.
13. E. Petrank and C. Rackofff, *CBC-MAC for Real Time Data Sources*, Journal of Cryptology, vol. 13, no.3, pp. 315–318, 2000.

Key Recovery Attacks on NTRU without Ciphertext Validation Routine

Daewan Han, Jin Hong, Jae Woo Han, and Daesung Kwon

National Security Research Institute
161 Gajeong-dong, Yuseong-gu, Daejeon, 305-350, Korea
{dwh,jinhong,jwhan,ds_kwon}@etri.re.kr

Abstract. NTRU is an efficient public-key cryptosystem proposed by Hoffstein, Pipher, and Silverman. Assuming access to a decryption oracle, we show ways to recover the private key of NTRU systems that do not include a ciphertext validating procedure. The strongest of our methods will employ just a single call to the oracle, and in all cases, the number of calls needed will be small enough to be realistic.

1 Introduction

NTRU cryptosystem([3]), introduced during the rump session of Crypto'96, is one of the most efficient public key cryptosystem now available. Because the encryption/decryption process of this system involves polynomials with small coefficients, it is quite fast compared to systems like RSA, ElGamal, or ECC. It also requires only a small amount of memory and hence is suitable for constrained environments like smart cards, PDAs, and mobile phones. The NTRU cryptosystem is currently being considered by standards bodies([1,7]).

In Crypto 2000, E. Jaulmes and A. Joux ([8]) showed that a chosen ciphertext attack on NTRU could succeed probabilistically. Reaction attacks([5]) were also presented on NTRU. To counter-measure these attacks, various padding schemes were proposed([4,6]). Later, P. Nguyen and D. Pointcheval([9]) showed that there were weakness in the padding schemes proposed by the NTRU company and suggested a method which is claimed to be IND-CCA.

In this paper, we show how to obtain the private key of the NTRU cryptosystem, assuming access to an Unconditionally Decrypting Oracle(UDO). We define a UDO to be an oracle that returns a decryption of any given ciphertext without checking its validity as a ciphertext. Access to a UDO could be realistic if, for some reason, the ciphertext validating procedure was incorrectly implemented. For example, when implementing NTRU-REACT ([9]), unlike other padding schemes, it is easy to leave out the ciphertext validation procedure. This situation could also be possible if the implementer just left it out with ill intentions.

Under the UDO assumption, we show ways to *deterministically* recover the private key of NTRU cryptosystem. The first of our methods applies to the original NTRU system as given in [3]. Let N be the NTRU parameter defining

R. Safavi-Naini and J. Seberry (Eds.): ACISP 2003, LNCS 2727, pp. 274–284, 2003.
© Springer-Verlag Berlin Heidelberg 2003

the working ring size. Using $\mathcal{O}(N^2)$ calls to the UDO, we can always recover the private key. We can also recover the private key, with probability of failure less than $1/2^{90}$, using less than $2N$ calls to the UDO.

We have found three more methods that apply to *optimized* NTRU ([4,1, 7]), but show only two methods in this paper for lack of space. The method not given in this paper is shown in the extended version of this paper[2]. To the best of our knowledge, the present work is the first in acknowledging attacks specific to the optimized version of NTRU. All three of the methods will recover the private key completely. Of the three, the last one we shall present(Section 5) is the strongest, using just a *single* UDO call. Thus, the NTRU cryptosystem should never be used without a proper padding scheme.

If the use of a UDO were possible on some (flawed) implementation of RSA-OAEP or the Cramer-Shoup scheme, we would no longer be sure of their IND-CCA2 property. But contrary to the NTRU situation presented by this work, nothing is known in the direction of key recovery attacks on the RSA or ElGamal primitive. This suggests that we should still be very careful in the use of NTRU cryptosystem.

2   Overview of the NTRU Cryptosystem

The NTRU cryptosystem has gone through some changes since its first appearance. To set the grounds of our discussion, we quickly present various parameters and encryption/decryption processes for three versions of it. The readers may refer to [3] and [1,4] for more information. The reference [11] is also helpful in understanding why the decryption process works.

Let N be an odd prime. We will be working over the ring $\mathcal{R} = \mathbf{Z}[x]/(x^N - 1)$. The ring $\mathcal{R}$ is identified with the set of integer polynomials of degree less than N. Multiplication in $\mathcal{R}$ is denoted by $*$.

The sets $\mathcal{L}_\mathbf{f}$, $\mathcal{L}_\mathbf{g}$, $\mathcal{L}_\mathbf{r}$, and $\mathcal{L}_\mathbf{m}$, to be fixed below for each version, are subsets of $\mathcal{R}$. Two parameters $\mathbf{p}$ and q are chosen so that they are relatively prime and the private key $\mathbf{f} \in \mathcal{L}_\mathbf{f}$ is taken so that it is invertible modulo q. The inverse will be denoted by $\mathbf{f}_q$, and using a random polynomial $\mathbf{g} \in \mathcal{L}_\mathbf{g}$ the public key is set to

$$\mathbf{h} \equiv \mathbf{p} * \mathbf{f}_q * \mathbf{g} \pmod{q}. \tag{1}$$

To encrypt a message $\mathbf{m} \in \mathcal{L}_\mathbf{m}$, we choose a random $\mathbf{r} \in \mathcal{L}_\mathbf{r}$ and compute

$$\mathbf{e} = \mathbf{r} * \mathbf{h} + \mathbf{m}. \tag{2}$$

The decryption process is more involved and explained below for each version of NTRU. Let us fix one notation before doing this. Given $m, n \in \mathbf{Z}$ and $t \in \mathbf{R}$, define $\mathrm{Mod}_n^t(m)$ to be the unique integer in the interval $(t - \frac{n}{2}, t + \frac{n}{2}]$ congruent to m modulo n. For a polynomial $f(x) \in \mathcal{R}$, we may similarly define $\mathrm{Mod}_n^t(f(x))$, by applying it to the coefficients.

2.1   Original Version

In the original version [3], the parameter **p** is fixed to be 3. When choosing a private key **f**, it is also required to have a modulo **p** = 3 inverse **f**$_p$. We define $\mathcal{L}(d_+, d_-)$ to be the set of polynomials in $\mathcal{R}$ with d_+ coefficients equal to 1, d_- coefficients equal to -1, and all other coefficients equal to 0. Table 1 lists the various parameters as originally given in [3]. The message space $\mathcal{L}_\mathbf{m}$ is set to all

Table 1. Parameters for original NTRU (**p** = 3)

	N	q	$\mathcal{L}_\mathbf{f}$	$\mathcal{L}_\mathbf{g}$	$\mathcal{L}_\mathbf{r}$
Case A	107	64	$\mathcal{L}(15, 14)$	$\mathcal{L}(12, 12)$	$\mathcal{L}(5, 5)$
Case B	167	128	$\mathcal{L}(61, 60)$	$\mathcal{L}(20, 20)$	$\mathcal{L}(18, 18)$
Case C	503	256	$\mathcal{L}(216, 215)$	$\mathcal{L}(72, 72)$	$\mathcal{L}(55, 55)$

polynomials in $\mathcal{R}$ with coefficients in $\{-1, 0, 1\}$.

To decrypt a ciphertext **e**, we go through the following process.

1. $\mathbf{a} \leftarrow \mathrm{Mod}_q^0(\mathbf{f} * \mathbf{e})$.
2. Return $\mathrm{Mod}_\mathbf{p}^0(\mathbf{f}_p * \mathbf{a})$.

We say that a *wrapping* has occurred during the decryption process if

$$\mathbf{a} \neq \mathbf{f} * \mathbf{e},$$

i.e., the Mod_q^0 operation has changed at least one coefficient. Notice that even though **e** is defined only up to modulo q, when we use **e** as an input to the decryption machine, an explicit representative of **e** will be used. Hence this equation makes sense as an equation in $\mathcal{R}$.

2.2   Binary-F Version

Set **p** = $x + 2$. The private key space $\mathcal{L}_\mathbf{f}$ is taken to be polynomials of the form

$$\mathbf{f} = 1 + \mathbf{p} * \mathbf{F}, \tag{3}$$

with **F** a binary polynomial having d_F-many nonzero coefficients.

The sets $\mathcal{L}_\mathbf{g}$ and $\mathcal{L}_\mathbf{r}$ are to contain binary polynomials with d_g and d_r coefficients equal to 1, respectively. The message space $\mathcal{L}_\mathbf{m}$ is the set of all binary polynomials in $\mathcal{R}$. Table 2 lists parameters as given in [1].

Given a ciphertext **e**, the decryption process goes through the following steps.

1. $I \leftarrow \mathrm{Mod}_q^{\frac{N}{2}}(\mathbf{e}(1) - \mathbf{r}(1) \cdot \mathbf{h}(1))$.
2. $\mathcal{A} \leftarrow \frac{1}{N}(\mathbf{p}(1) \cdot \mathbf{r}(1) \cdot \mathbf{g}(1) + I \cdot \mathbf{f}(1))$.
3. $\mathbf{a} \leftarrow \mathrm{Mod}_q^\mathcal{A}(\mathbf{f} * \mathbf{e})$.
4. Return $\mathrm{Mod}_\mathbf{p}(\mathbf{a})$.

Here, the $\mathrm{Mod}_\mathbf{p}$ operation chooses a representative of **a** in a binary polynomial form. We refer the readers to [4] for more detail.

As before, we say that a *wrapping* has occurred during decryption if $\mathbf{a} \neq \mathbf{f} * \mathbf{e}$.

2.3   Low Hamming Weight-F Version

This version of NTRU is identical to the previous binary-**F** version except that the polynomial **F** used in defining the private key **f** is of the form

$$\mathbf{F} = \mathbf{F}_1 * \mathbf{F}_2 + \mathbf{F}_3, \tag{4}$$

with each $\mathbf{F}_i$ a binary polynomial having d_{F_i}-many nonzero coefficients. The parameter values are given in Table 2. Notice that $d_F = d_{F_1} \cdot d_{F_2} + d_{F_3}$ in all cases. We shall call this the LHW-**F** case.

Table 2. Parameters for NTRU with $\mathbf{p} = x + 2$

N	q	d_F	d_{F_1}	d_{F_2}	d_{F_3}	d_g	d_r
251	128	72	8	8	8	72	72
347	128	64	7	8	8	173	64
503	256	420	20	20	20	251	170

When we want to refer to both the binary-**F** and LHW-**F** versions of NTRU at the same time, we shall use the phrase *optimized* NTRU.

Remark 1. Since $\mathbf{r}(1) = d_r$, $\mathbf{g}(1) = d_g$, and $\mathbf{f}(1) = 1 + 3 \cdot d_F$, the values I and $\mathcal{A}$ may be calculated from just **e** and public values.

Remark 2. The value I is calculated as

$$I = \mathrm{Mod}_q^{\frac{N}{2}} \left(\mathbf{f}_q(1) \cdot (\mathbf{a}(1) - \mathbf{p}(1) \cdot \mathbf{r}(1) \cdot \mathbf{g}(1)) \right)$$

in [11,7,1]. This may seem different from what is done in step 1. Furthermore, in this form, knowledge of the secrete information $\mathbf{f}_q$ also seems to be required. But both are calculating the same value $\mathbf{m}(1)$, assuming that it is close to $\frac{N}{2}$.

3   Adaptive Use of Wrapping Behavior

We shall work with the original NTRU setting (Section 2.1) in this section. While the arguments of this section may be modified and applied to other settings, it is better explained in the original setting and does not involve the use of special forms for the private key **f** that appears in other settings.

We show how to exploit the *wrapping* behavior of the modulo q reduction process done during decryption to recover the private key, using less than $2N$ calls to the decryption oracle.

3.1 Descriptive Argument

We assume that we have access to a decryption oracle and may distinguish whether or not a wrapping has occurred during the decryption process. For example, this could be possible, in some situations, through timing techniques. This could also be possible if we may obtain the decrypted message, since the decrypted output of ciphertext $\mathbf{e}$ is equal to $\mathrm{Mod}_p^0(\mathbf{e})$ if and only if no wrapping has occurred.

We first remark that any cyclic shift $\mathbf{f} * x^i$ of the private key $\mathbf{f}$ may work as a decryption key. The cyclic shift added to $\mathbf{a}$ during the first step of decryption is removed when $\mathbf{f}_p$ is applied in the second step.

Consider what would happen if we ran the ciphertext

$$\mathbf{e} = -\left(1 + x + x^2 - x^3 + (\frac{q}{2} - 4)x^4\right) \tag{5}$$

through the decryption oracle. Recall that the coefficients of $\mathbf{f}$ all belong to the set $\{-1, 0, 1\}$. Hence wrapping occur if and only if there exists some consecutive run of coefficients in $\mathbf{f}$ equal to the sequence $(1, 1, 1, -1, 1)$, in reverse order.

Suppose we do have wrapping for the above particular $\mathbf{e}$. We may then run

$$\mathbf{e}\pm = -\left(1 + x + x^2 - x^3 + x^4 \pm (\frac{q}{2} - 5)x^5\right) \tag{6}$$

through the decryption oracle. If either one brings a wrapping behavior, we may continue, knowing a longer consecutive sequence of coefficients from $\mathbf{f}$. If neither returns a wrapping behavior, we know neither $(1, 1, 1, -1, 1, 1)$ nor $(1, 1, 1, -1, 1, -1)$ is a consecutive run of coefficients from $\mathbf{f}$ (in reverse order). But we know the shorter subsequence $(1, 1, 1, -1, 1)$ is present in $\mathbf{f}$, so the sequence $(1, 1, 1, -1, 1, 0)$ must be present in $\mathbf{f}$. We may then use

$$\mathbf{e}0\pm = -\left(1 + x + x^2 - x^3 + x^4 \pm (\frac{q}{2} - 5)x^6\right)$$

to find the next coefficient of $\mathbf{f}$.

We can continue with this process until we know a consecutive sequence of coefficients from $\mathbf{f}$ that contains $\frac{q}{2}$-many ± 1's. So, for Case A of Table 1, this process obtains some cyclic shift of $\mathbf{f}$ completely.

To cope with the other two cases given in Table 1, let us go back and suppose that $\mathbf{e}$ given by (5) induces a wrapping so that $(1, 1, 1, -1, 1)$ appears as a consecutive run of coefficients in $\mathbf{f}$. Let us also assume that $\frac{q}{2} = 5$. Then we cannot use $\mathbf{e}\pm$ given by (6) since they are both just equal to $\mathbf{e}$. But, if we can assume that the probability of the subsequence $(1, 1, 1, -1)$ appearing in $\mathbf{f}$ *more than once* is negligible, we can use

$$\mathbf{e}'\pm = -\left(1 + x + x^2 - x^3 \pm x^5\right) \tag{7}$$

to find the next coefficient. The probability of some sequence of length n appearing in $\mathbf{f}$ more than once is at most $\frac{N}{3^n}$. So, in Case B, this will be at most

$167/3^{63} \sim 1/2^{92.47}$ and in Case C, this is at most $503/3^{127} \sim 1/2^{192.32}$, indeed, values that may be ignored in real world applications.

Hence, we can obtain a cyclic shift of $\mathbf{f}$, which in turn can be used later to find the plain text $\mathbf{m}$ corresponding to any given ciphertext $\mathbf{e}$.

We have shown a complete example of this approach in [2].

3.2   Algorithm

We summarize arguments of the previous subsection in an algorithm.

Algorithm 1

1. *Initialize secret key* $\mathbf{f} = \sum_{i=0}^{N-1} f_i x^i$, *input ciphertext* $\mathbf{e} = \sum_{i=0}^{N-1} e_i x^i$, *and integer* w *as follows.*
   a) $f_0 = 1$, $f_j = 0$ *for* $1 \leq j \leq N-1$
   b) $e_j = 0$ *for* $0 \leq j \leq N-1$
   c) $w = 1$
2. *For* i *from 1 to* $N-1$ *do the following:*
   a) *If* $w < q/2$, *then set* $e_{i-1} = -f_{i-1}$, *otherwise set* $e_{i-1} = 0$.
   b) *If* $w < q/2$, *then set* $e_i = -(\frac{q}{2} - w)$, *otherwise set* $e_i = -1$.
   c) *Run* $\mathbf{e}$ *through the decryption oracle.*
   d) *If wrapping has occurred, set* $f_i = 1$, $w = w + 1$, *and skip* (e)$\sim$(h).
   e) *Set* $e_i = -e_i$.
   f) *Run* $\mathbf{e}$ *through the decryption oracle.*
   g) *If wrapping has occurred, set* $f_i = -1$, $w = w + 1$, *and skip (h).*
   h) *Set* $f_i = 0$.
3. *Reverse the order of* f_i. *That is, set* $f_i = f_{N-1-i}$ *for* $i = 0, 1, \cdots, N-1$.
4. *Return* $\mathbf{f} = \sum_{i=0}^{N-1} f_i x^i$.

This algorithm obtains some cyclic shift of $\mathbf{f}$ using $2N - d_+ - 1$ calls to the decryption oracle. Probability of this algorithm returning a wrong value of $\mathbf{f}$ is at most $N/3^{\frac{q}{2}-1}$.

Remark 3. Using ideas present in this algorithm, it is possible construct an algorithm that returns a cyclic shift of $\mathbf{f}$ deterministically without failure. But the algorithm would use $\mathcal{O}(N^2)$ calls to the decryption oracle and become much more complex.

Remark 4. We have found another method that related to the one of this section which is applicable to both of the optimized NTRU versions. It uses pre-designed wrapping behavior and while it does use outputs of the decryption process, inputs to the UDO do not depend on previous outputs. It is presented in the extended version of this paper[2] due to lack of space.

4   Bypassing Wrapping (Using p_q)

In this section, we assume the private key is given by a binary-**F**(Section 2.2). We present a chosen-ciphertext attack which makes one query to the decryption machine and recovers the private key completely.

Let us denote the modulo q inverse of **p** by $\mathbf{p}_q$, so that

$$\mathbf{p}_q * \mathbf{p} \equiv 1 \quad (\bmod\ q).$$

If $q = 2^k$, we may specifically set

$$\mathbf{p}_q = \sum_{i=1}^{k} (-2)^{i-1} x^{N-i} \quad (\bmod\ q). \tag{8}$$

4.1   Simple Case

If we insert $\mathbf{p}_q$ into the decryption machine, it will calculate

$$
\begin{aligned}
\mathbf{a} &= \mathrm{Mod}_q^{\mathcal{A}(\mathbf{p}_q)}(\mathbf{f} * \mathbf{p}_q) \\
&= \mathrm{Mod}_q^{\mathcal{A}}\big((1 + \mathbf{p} * \mathbf{F}) * \mathbf{p}_q\big) \\
&= \mathrm{Mod}_q^{\mathcal{A}}(\mathbf{p}_q + \mathbf{F}).
\end{aligned}
$$

Since all the coefficients of **F** are either 0 or 1, with high probability, we will have

$$\mathbf{a} = \mathrm{Mod}_q^{\mathcal{A}}(\mathbf{p}_q) + \mathbf{F}. \tag{9}$$

Assume for the moment that this is true. Then, we have

$$\mathrm{Mod}_\mathbf{p}(\mathbf{a}) - \mathrm{Mod}_q^{\mathcal{A}}(\mathbf{p}_q) \equiv \mathbf{a} - \mathrm{Mod}_q^{\mathcal{A}}(\mathbf{p}_q) \equiv \mathbf{F} \quad (\bmod\ \mathbf{p}).$$

Notice that the first term on the left is the output of the decryption machine, and that the second term on the left may readily be computed. Hence we may obtain

$$\mathrm{Mod}_\mathbf{p}\big(\mathrm{Mod}_\mathbf{p}(\mathbf{a}) - \mathrm{Mod}_q^{\mathcal{A}}(\mathbf{p}_q)\big) = \mathrm{Mod}_\mathbf{p}(\mathbf{F}) = \mathbf{F}.$$

The second equality holds, since **F** is a binary polynomial. We have obtained the private key $\mathbf{f} = 1 + \mathbf{p} * \mathbf{F}$ with just one query.

It remains to justify equation (9). For parameters given in Table 2, we have calculated various values.

N	$\mathbf{f}(1)$	$\mathbf{f}_q(1)$	$\mathbf{r}(1)\mathbf{h}(1)$	$\mathbf{p}_q(1)$	$I(\mathbf{p}_q)$	$\mathcal{A}(\mathbf{p}_q)$
251	217	105	64	43	107	154.47
347	193	65	64	43	235	226.43
503	1261	229	242	171	185	718.28

Some of these values are defined only up to modulo q. Now, using equation (8) and this table, we list all coefficients (including the one corresponding to zero) of $\mathrm{Mod}_q^{\mathcal{A}}(\mathbf{p}_q)$ in the following table. We've also written down the lower and upper boundaries (LB,UB) of the *representative interval*. Last column contains the distance between UB and the coefficient maximum.

N	LB	coefficients	UB	headroom
251	91	129, 126, 132, 120, 144, 96, 192, 128	218	26
347	163	257, 254, 260, 248, 272, 224, 192, 256	290	18
503	591	769, 766, 772, 760, 784, 736, 832, 640, 768	846	14

So at least, for the parameter values given in Table 2, equation (9) is always satisfied.

4.2   Wrapping Case

Assumption of the previous subsection, namely, equation (9), fails if and only if

1. some coefficient c of $\mathrm{Mod}_q^{\mathcal{A}(\mathbf{P}_q)}(\mathbf{p}_q)$ satisfies $c \leq \mathcal{A}(\mathbf{p}_q) + \frac{q}{2} < c + 1$,
2. and the corresponding coefficient of $\mathbf{F}$ is equal to 1.

Since we know the exact polynomial $\mathrm{Mod}_q^{\mathcal{A}}(\mathbf{p}_q)$, we know which coefficients satisfy the first of the above conditions. Suppose some coefficient c_i of the x^i term in $\mathrm{Mod}_q^{\mathcal{A}}(\mathbf{p}_q)$ satisfies both conditions. Suppose further, for the moment, that such a coefficient is unique. Then

$$\mathbf{a} = \mathrm{Mod}_q^{\mathcal{A}}(\mathbf{p}_q + \mathbf{F})$$
$$= \mathrm{Mod}_q^{\mathcal{A}}(\mathbf{p}_q) - qx^i + \mathbf{F}.$$

And the output of the decryption machine satisfies

$$\mathrm{Mod}_\mathbf{p}(\mathbf{a}) \equiv \mathrm{Mod}_q^{\mathcal{A}}(\mathbf{p}_q) - qx^i + \mathbf{F} \pmod{\mathbf{p}}.$$

As before, we may obtain the private key by computing

$$\mathrm{Mod}_\mathbf{p}\left(\mathrm{Mod}_\mathbf{p}(\mathbf{a}) - \mathrm{Mod}_q^{\mathcal{A}}(\mathbf{p}_q) + qx^i\right) = \mathrm{Mod}_\mathbf{p}(\mathbf{F}) = \mathbf{F}.$$

In conclusion, if $\mathbf{p}_q$ contains t-many coefficients satisfying the above condition 1, with just one query to the decryption machine, we may find 2^t candidates for $\mathbf{F}$, one of which corresponds to the true private key $\mathbf{f} = 1 + \mathbf{p} * \mathbf{F}$.

Remark 5. If $q = 2^k$, we know from equation (8) that all of the coefficients of $\mathbf{p}_q$ are distinct modulo q. (Read next remark to see why this isn't strictly true.) Hence there can be at most one coefficient satisfying the first of the above two conditions.

Remark 6. In the $q = 2^k$ case, if it happens that some coefficient $c \equiv 0 \pmod{q}$ satisfies the first condition, application of this method is not feasible. But with some modifications we could use $-\mathbf{p}_q$ or even $2\mathbf{p}_q$ in a similar attack.

5   Uniform Wrapping (Using the Public Key h)

This section contains the simplest, and perhaps, the strongest of our attacks on un-padded NTRU. Using just one query to the decryption machine, we shall obtain completely, the binary polynomial $\mathbf{g}$ used in defining the public key, with probability $(q - 1)/q$. Since the public key is given by $\mathbf{h} = \mathbf{p} * \mathbf{f}_q * \mathbf{g}$, this is (almost) equivalent to having obtained the private key $\mathbf{f}$.

As before, let $\mathbf{p}_q$ be the modulo q inverse of $\mathbf{p}$. We run $\mathbf{e} = \mathbf{p}_q * \mathbf{h}$ through the decryption machine. The output of the machine will be

$$\mathrm{Mod}_\mathbf{p}\mathrm{Mod}_q^{\mathcal{A}}(\mathbf{f} * \mathbf{e}) = \mathrm{Mod}_\mathbf{p}\mathrm{Mod}_q^{\mathcal{A}}(\mathbf{f} * \mathbf{p}_q * \mathbf{p} * \mathbf{f}_q * \mathbf{g})$$

$$= \mathrm{Mod}_\mathbf{p}\mathrm{Mod}_q^{\mathcal{A}}(\mathbf{g}).$$

We shall use the notation

$$\mathrm{dc}(n, \mathcal{A}) = \frac{1}{q}(n - \mathrm{Mod}_q^{\mathcal{A}}(n)) \tag{10}$$

for any integer n and centering value $\mathcal{A}$. An equivalent definition would be

$$\mathrm{Mod}_q^{\mathcal{A}}(n) = n - q \cdot \mathrm{dc}(n, \mathcal{A}).$$

It measures how far n is from the *representative interval*. When the value $\mathcal{A}$ is clear from context, $\mathrm{dc}(n)$ will be used.

With probability $(q - 1)/q$, we can expect to have $\mathrm{dc}(0) = \mathrm{dc}(1)$. For the parameter values of Table 2, we may easily check that they are equal.

N	$I(\mathbf{p}_q * \mathbf{h})$	$\mathcal{A}(\mathbf{p}_q * \mathbf{h})$	LB	UB	$\mathrm{dc}(0)$	$\mathrm{dc}(1)$
251	72	124.21	61	188	-1	-1
347	173	191.95	128	255	-1	-1
503	149	628.03	501	756	-2	-2

Assume $\mathrm{dc}(0) = \mathrm{dc}(1)$ and let d denote this common value. Set

$$S(x) = 1 + x + \cdots + x^{N-1}.$$

Then, we may write

$$\mathrm{Mod}_q^{\mathcal{A}}(\mathbf{g}) = \mathbf{g} - d \cdot q \cdot S(x).$$

Hence

$$\mathrm{Mod}_\mathbf{p}\left(\mathrm{Mod}_q^{\mathcal{A}}(\mathbf{f} * \mathbf{e})\right) + d \cdot q \cdot S(x) \equiv \mathrm{Mod}_q^{\mathcal{A}}(\mathbf{g}) + d \cdot q \cdot S(x) \equiv \mathbf{g} \pmod{\mathbf{p}}$$

and we may obtain

$$\mathrm{Mod}_\mathbf{p}\left(\mathrm{Mod}_\mathbf{p}\left(\mathrm{Mod}_q^{\mathcal{A}}(\mathbf{f} * \mathbf{e})\right) + d \cdot q \cdot S(x)\right) = \mathbf{g}$$

from just one query to the decryption machine. The value

$$\mathbf{f} * \mathbf{h} \equiv \mathbf{f} * \mathbf{p} * \mathbf{f}_q * \mathbf{g} \equiv \mathbf{p} * \mathbf{g} \pmod{q}$$

is in our hands. Now, if $\mathbf{h}$ is invertible modulo q, or equivalently, if $\mathbf{g}$ is invertible modulo q, we can obtain $\mathbf{f}$ modulo q. We know the form of $\mathbf{f}$, so can find $\mathbf{f}$ exactly. Furthermore, the random binary polynomial $\mathbf{g}$ is invertible with a very high probability. Even if it is not, we still have the possibility of using a pseudo inverse of $\mathbf{h}$ to obtain $\mathbf{f}$.

Remark 7. In the case $dc(0) \neq dc(1)$, we may use $-\mathbf{p}_q * \mathbf{h}$ in a similar attack. Again, we have about $1/q$ chance of encountering the same problem.

Remark 8. Suppose $dc(0) \neq dc(1)$, or equivalently, $dc(0) + 1 = dc(1)$. We may write $\mathbf{g} = 0 \cdot \mathbf{g}_0 + 1 \cdot \mathbf{g}_1$ with $S(x) = \mathbf{g}_0 + \mathbf{g}_1$. Then

$$\mathrm{Mod}_\mathbf{p}\left(\mathrm{Mod}_q^\mathcal{A}(\mathbf{g})\right) + q \cdot dc(0) \cdot S(x)$$
$$\equiv \mathbf{g} - q \cdot dc(0) \cdot \mathbf{g}_0 - q \cdot dc(1) \cdot \mathbf{g}_1 + q \cdot dc(0) \cdot (\mathbf{g}_0 + \mathbf{g}_1) \quad (\mathrm{mod}\ \mathbf{p})$$
$$= 0 \cdot \mathbf{g}_0 + (1 - q) \cdot \mathbf{g}_1$$
$$= (1 - q) \cdot (0 \cdot \mathbf{g}_0 + 1 \cdot \mathbf{g}_1) = (1 - q) \cdot \mathbf{g}.$$

Hence, if $1 - q$ is invertible modulo $\mathbf{p}$ in $\mathcal{R}$, we may find $\mathbf{g}$. This is true for the values $N = 251$ with $q = 128$ and $N = 347$ with $q = 128$.

6   Conclusion

We've seen three chosen-ciphertext attacks applicable to un-padded versions of NTRU cryptosystem in this paper.

The first of these, given in Section 3, is an improvement to previous reaction attacks. It applies to the most general NTRU cryptosystem and uses less than $2N$ queries to the decryption oracle.

The approaches of the next two sections apply to optimized versions of NTRU. They uses just one query to the decryption machine to recover the private key completely, under realistic parameter values. These two methods depend on the private key being of the form $\mathbf{f} = 1 + \mathbf{p} * \mathbf{F}$. None of these two attacks on optimized NTRU are applicable to the original NTRU cryptosystem. By giving special forms for the private key, the key generation and decryption processes of NTRU cryptosystem became simpler. But at the same time, it has opened new ways of recovering the private key.

The number of decryption oracle use needed in approaches of this paper is small enough to be realistic. Hence NTRU should never be used without some form of padding, protecting it from chosen ciphertext attacks.

However, we believe any reasonable padding scheme will provide the optimized NTRU cryptosystem protection from our attacks. Of course, with explicit hash functions chosen to be used in the padding schemes, the story could be different. This part still remains to be considered.

References

1. Consortium for Efficient Embedded Security, Efficient embedded security standards #1: Implementation aspects of NTRUEncrypt and NTRUSign. Draft version 5. Available from http://www.ceesstandards.org.

2. Daewan Han, Jin Hong, Jae Woo Han, and Daesung Kwon, Key recovery attacks on NTRU without ciphertext validation routine. IACR ePrint 2002/188. Available from http://eprint.iacr.org.

3. Jeffrey Hoffstein, Jill Pipher, and Joseph H. Silverman, NTRU: A ring-based public key cryptosystem. In *Proc. of ANTS III*, LNCS 1423. Springer-Verlag, 1998.

4. Jeffrey Hoffstein and Joseph Silverman, Optimizations for NTRU. In *Public-Key Cryptogrphy and Computational Number Theory*. DeGruyter, 2002. Available from [10].

5. Jeffrey Hoffstein and Joseph H. Silverman, Reaction attacks against the NTRU public key cryptosystem. Techinal report #015, NTRU Cryptosystems. Available from [10].

6. Jeffrey Hoffstein and Joseph H. Silverman, Protecting NTRU Against Chosen Ciphertext and Reaction Attacks, Technical Report #016, NTRU Cryptosystems. Available from [10].

7. IEEE Standard P1363.1/D4, Standard specifications for public key cryptography : Techniques based on hard problems over lattices, IEEE. Available from http://grouper.ieee.org/group/1363.

8. Éliane Jaulmes and Antoine Joux, A chosen-ciphertext attack against NTRU. *Advances in Cryptology – CRYPTO 2000*, LNCS 1880. Springer-Verlag, 2000.

9. Phong Q. Nguyen and David Pointcheval, Analysis and improvements of NTRU encryption paddings. *Advances in Cryptology – CRYPTO 2002*, LNCS 2442. Springer-Verlag, 2002.

10. NTRU Cryptosystems, Technical reports. Available from http://www.ntru.com.

11. NTRU Cryptosystems, The NTRU public key cryptosystem – A tutorial. Available from http://www.ntru.com.

Permanent Fault Attack on the Parameters of RSA with CRT[*]

Sung-Ming Yen[1], SangJae Moon[2], and JaeCheol Ha[3]

[1] Laboratory of Cryptography and Information Security (LCIS)
Dept of Computer Science and Information Engineering
National Central University, Chung-Li, Taiwan 320, R.O.C.
yensm@csie.ncu.edu.tw
http://www.csie.ncu.edu.tw/~yensm/

[2] Mobile Network Security Technology Research Center (MSRC)
Kyungpook National University
Taegu, Korea 702-701
sjmoon@knu.ac.kr

[3] Dept of Computer and Information
Korea Nazarene University, Choong Nam, Korea 330-718
jcha@kornu.ac.kr

Abstract. Chinese remainder theorem has been widely employed to speedup the RSA computation. In this paper, one kind of permanent fault attack on RSA with CRT will be pointed out which exploits a permanent fault on the storage of either p or q. This proposed attack is generic and powerful which can be applicable to both the conventional RSA with CRT and Shamir's fault attack immune design of RSA with CRT. Two popular and one recently proposed CRT recombination algorithms which are necessary for the above two mentioned RSA with CRT will be carefully examined in this paper for their immunity against the proposed parameter permanent fault attack.

Keywords: Chinese remainder theorem (CRT), Computational fault, Cryptography, Factorization, Hardware fault cryptanalysis, Permanent fault, Physical cryptanalysis, Side channel attack.

1 Introduction

In order to provide a better support for data protection under strong cryptographic schemes (e.g., RSA [1] or ElGamal [2] systems), varieties of implementations based on tamper-proof devices (e.g., smart IC cards) are proposed. Due to this popular usage of tamper-resistance, much attention has recently been paid regarding the security issues of cryptosystems implemented on tamper-proof devices [3,4,5,6,7,8,9,10,11,12,13,14,15,16,17,18,19] from the view point of presence

[*] This research was supported by University IT Research Center Project.

R. Safavi-Naini and J. Seberry (Eds.): ACISP 2003, LNCS 2727, pp. 285–296, 2003.
© Springer-Verlag Berlin Heidelberg 2003

of hardware faults. Note that the fault attack by optical illumination [19] presented in CHES 2002 already made this category of physical attack be much more feasible and potential.

This category of cryptanalysis is called the *fault-based cryptanalysis*. In the fault-based cryptanalysis model, it is assumed that when an adversary has physical access to a tamper-proof device she may purposely induce a certain type of fault into the device. Based on a set of incorrect responses or outputs from the device, due to the presence of faults, the adversary can then extract the secrets embedded in the tamper-proof device. These attacks exploit the presence of many kinds of transient or permanent faults. These attacks are of very general nature and remain valid for a large variety of cryptosystems, e.g., the LUC public key cryptosystem [20] and elliptic curve cryptography (ECC).

In this paper, we focus our attention on public key cryptosystems in which their computation can be sped up using the Chinese remainder theorem (CRT) [21,22]. These cryptosystems may be vulnerable to the hardware fault cryptanalysis to reveal the secret key if the following three conditions are met: (1) the message m to sign (or to decrypt) is known or the correct signature on message m is available; (2) a random fault occurs during the computation of a residue number system; (3) the device outputs the faulty signature on message m. This kind of attacks was called the CRT-based hardware fault cryptanalysis [6,13, 14]. Our main objective is to emphasize the importance of a careful implementation of cryptosystems with CRT-based speedup. Suppose you are in a context involving trusted third parties (e.g., banks) where thousands of signatures being produced each day. If, for some reasons, a single signature is faulty, then the security of the whole system may be compromised. Leakage of the secret key can be avoided by making sure that either of the above three conditions will not be met.

Shamir developed a countermeasure [16,17] to disable the CRT-based hardware fault attack and this countermeasure becomes well known and widely employed. Only the general kind of computational fault has been considered in Shamir's countermeasure. However, in a real application, other kind of hardware faults may occur which can also lead to the CRT-based hardware fault attack as will be shown in this paper.

The previous countermeasure for RSA with CRT did not consider a potential and important fault attack, i.e., the *permanent fault* attack. In a permanent fault attack, some parameters of RSA with CRT countermeasure may be permanently corrupted by the attacker (by some means) or be damaged because of serious hardware malfunction or environmental factor. The main contribution of this paper is that we provide new and detailed result that considers this potential and important fault attack on using CRT speedup technique for both the conventional [21,22] and Shamir's approaches [16,17]. The analysis also covers the very important part of using RSA with CRT, i.e., the CRT recombination algorithm. Two popular [22, p.68;pp.612–613] and one recently proposed [23] CRT recombination algorithms will be carefully examined in this paper for their immunity against the proposed permanent fault attack.

The proposed CRT based attacks are nontrivial since the CRT speedup technique has already been widely employed for almost all popular implementations. Many application scenarios should especially be taken care of under this physical attack model. One of them is the attack on smart IC card since it is mostly easy to expose under a dangerous environment of physical attack. Another example is the attack on some large servers for the purpose of signature generation since a large amount of signatures may be generated within a short time. Banking servers or certification server are two typical examples of such attack targets.

2   Preliminary Background of CRT-Based Cryptanalysis

2.1   Chinese Remainder Theorem

Chinese remainder theorem [22] (CRT) tells that given a set of integers (moduli) $n_1, n_2, \ldots, n_k$ that are pairwise relatively prime, then the following system of simultaneous congruence

$$s \equiv s_1 \pmod{n_1}$$
$$s \equiv s_2 \pmod{n_2}$$
$$\vdots$$
$$s \equiv s_k \pmod{n_k}$$

has a unique solution modulo $n = \prod_{i=1}^{k} n_i$.

For the case of RSA secret computation, there are two moduli p and q and the unique integer solution s can be computed by the following two well known CRT recombination algorithms.

Given s_p and s_q, one of the possible CRT recombination computes

$$s = (s_p \cdot q \cdot (q^{-1} \bmod p) + s_q \cdot p \cdot (p^{-1} \bmod q)) \bmod n$$
$$= (s_p \cdot X_p + s_q \cdot X_q) \bmod n \tag{1}$$

where both X_p and X_q can be precomputed and stored in advance. The above method is often called Gauss's algorithm [22, p.68].

There is a well known improved CRT recombination, called Garner's algorithm [22, pp.612–613], which computes

$$s = s_q + ((s_p - s_q) \cdot (q^{-1} \bmod p) \bmod p) \cdot q. \tag{2}$$

This CRT-based method was proposed to speed up the RSA signature and decryption computation [21]. This CRT-based speedup for RSA computation has been widely adopted as an implementation standard with the performance of four times faster than a direct computation in terms of bit operations. The applications range from large servers to very tiny smart IC cards. For servers, there are huge amount and very frequent RSA computations to be performed. For smart IC cards, the card processors are often not powerful enough to perform complicated cryptographic computations, e.g., RSA signature and decryption. Therefore, the CRT speedup technique can provide substantial assistance.

2.2 The CRT-Based Cryptanalysis

Let p and q be two primes and $n = p \cdot q$. In the RSA cryptosystem, a message m is signed with a secret exponent d as $s = m^d \bmod n$. Using the CRT-based approach, the value of s can be evaluated more efficiently from computing both $s_p = m^d \bmod p$ and $s_q = m^d \bmod q$, then by using the Chinese remainder theorem to reconstruct s.

Suppose that an error (any random error) occurs during the computation of s_p ($\hat{s}_p$ denotes the erroneous result), but the computation of s_q is error free. Applying the CRT on both $\hat{s}_p$ and s_q will produce a faulty signature $\hat{s}$. The CRT-based hardware fault cryptanalysis [6,13,14] enables the factorization of n by computing

$$q = \gcd((\hat{s} - s) \bmod n, n). \tag{3}$$

or

$$q = \gcd((\hat{s}^e - m) \bmod n, n). \tag{4}$$

Notice that in the above computation $\gcd((\hat{s}^e - m) \bmod n, n) = \gcd(\hat{s}^e - m, n)$. Similarly, p can be derived from a faulty signature computed by applying the CRT on a faulty $\hat{s}_q$ and a correct s_p.

2.3 Shamir's Countermeasure

Shamir presented a simple countermeasure in the rump session of Eurocrypt '97 [16] and applied a patent [17] which is announced to be secure against the factorization attack. In Shamir's countermeasure, it is assumed that the smart IC card stores the prime numbers p and q, the secret exponent d, and a precomputed parameter $q^{-1} \bmod p$ (suppose that Garner's algorithm will be employed). For each RSA secret computation, a random prime r is chosen, then $p' = p \cdot r$ and $d'_p = d \bmod (p-1) \cdot (r-1)$ are computed. The intermediate value $s'_p = (m \bmod p')^{d'_p} \bmod p'$ is computed, then a partial signature $s_p = s'_p \bmod p$ is computed. A value of $s_q = s'_q \bmod q$ is also computed in a similar way where $s'_q = (m \bmod q')^{d'_q} \bmod q'$. The IC card checks whether

$$s'_p \equiv s'_q \pmod{r}. \tag{5}$$

If the above checking is correct, then both s_p and s_q are assumed to be error free and Garner's algorithm is employed to obtain the RSA signature as $s = s_q + ((s_p - s_q) \cdot (q^{-1} \bmod p) \bmod p) \cdot q$.

3 The Proposed Permanent Fault Attack on Parameters

Previous hardware fault attack on RSA with CRT did not consider a potential and important fault attack, i.e., the *permanent fault* attack on parameters. In this permanent fault attack, some parameters of the conventional version of RSA with CRT [21,22] or its enhanced version with countermeasure (e.g., Shamir's method

[16,17]) may be permanently corrupted by the attacker (by some means) or be damaged accidently because of serious hardware malfunction or environmental factor.

In the following, the conventional version of RSA with CRT speedup will be examined against this type of parameter permanent fault attack.

3.1   Immunity of RSA with CRT by Garner's Algorithm

Suppose that a permanent fault on p has occurred within a smart IC card and the stored faulty prime factor becomes $\hat{p}$. Accordingly, when signing a message the IC card produces an erroneous partial signature modulo $\hat{p}$ as $\hat{s}_p$.

If Garner's algorithm [22, pp.612–613] will be employed to recombine the two partial signatures, then the signature will be

$$\hat{s} = s_q + ((\hat{s}_p - s_q) \cdot (q^{-1} \bmod p) \bmod \hat{p}) \cdot q. \tag{6}$$

In this situation, the CRT-based factorization attack works by computing $\gcd(\hat{s}^e - m, n) = q$. This can be shown in the following Theorem 1. In the following discussions, it is assumed that the register used to store p (or q) has a bit length of $|p|$ (or $|q|$) (where $|p|$ means the bit length of p) and also $|p| = |q|$. This is reasonable in most practical implementations. Therefore, a faulty $\hat{p}$ will have at most the same bit length as p which implies that $p \nmid \hat{p}$. In some rare cases, if the register used to store

p has a bit length of $|p| + k$ for k to be a small integer, say two or three. The following Lemma 1 says that the probability of $p|\hat{p}$ (where $\hat{p} \neq p$, otherwise no error occurred) is extremely small if p is an extremely large integer as in all cryptography applications.

Lemma 1. *Suppose the register used to store p has a bit length of $|p| + k$, then the number of positive integers within $[1, 2^{|p|+k} - 1]$ which is divisible by p is at most $2^k - 1$. Therefore, the probability of a random integer $\hat{p}$ (other than p) within the range $[1, 2^{|p|+k} - 1]$ and also $p|\hat{p}$ is at most $\frac{2^k - 2}{2^{|p|+k} - 1}$ (≈ 0 for extremely large p).*

Theorem 1. *Given $\hat{s} = s_q + ((\hat{s}_p - s_q) \cdot (q^{-1} \bmod p) \bmod \hat{p}) \cdot q$ where $\hat{p}, \hat{s}_p$, and $\hat{s}$ are the permanently corrupted prime factor p, the erroneous partial signature modulo $\hat{p}$, and the recombined erroneous signature, respectively. It leads to the result that $\gcd(\hat{s}^e - m, n) = q$.*

Proof. From the given erroneous signature $\hat{s}$, we obtain $\hat{s} \not\equiv m^d \pmod{p}$ with extremely large probability and $\hat{s} \equiv m^d \pmod{q}$.

More precisely, for the case of $\hat{s} \bmod p$, it can be derived that $\hat{s} \bmod p = (s_q + T) \bmod p$ (where $T \in_R [0, p-1]$ and $T \not\equiv s_p - s_q \pmod{p}$) since

$$((\hat{s}_p - s_q) \cdot (q^{-1} \bmod p) \bmod \hat{p}) \cdot q \not\equiv \hat{s}_p - s_q \pmod{p}$$

with extremely large probability, except for the following cases:

(1) $p|\hat{p}$ which also leads to $\hat{s}_p \equiv s_p \pmod{p}$ (refer to Lemma 1 for the probability);

(2) the rare case of $\hat{s}_p - s_q = 0$.

Totally, the above statements lead to $\hat{s} \not\equiv m^d \pmod{p}$ with extremely large probability.

For the case of $\hat{s} \equiv m^d \pmod{q}$, it is evident since no storage fault on q or computational fault on s_q is assumed.

Therefore, $\hat{s}^e - m \not\equiv 0 \pmod{p}$ and $\hat{s}^e - m \equiv 0 \pmod{q}$ and this leads to the result of $p \nmid (\hat{s}^e - m)$ and $q|(\hat{s}^e - m)$. Evidently, this proves $\gcd(\hat{s}^e - m, n) = q$. □

On the other hand, if a permanent fault on q has occurred and the stored faulty prime factor becomes $\hat{q}$ and accordingly an erroneous partial signature modulo $\hat{q}$ will be computed as $\hat{s}_q$. Similarly, if Garner's algorithm will be employed to recombine the two partial signatures, then the signature will be

$$\hat{s} = \hat{s}_q + ((s_p - \hat{s}_q) \cdot (q^{-1} \bmod p) \bmod p) \cdot \hat{q}. \tag{7}$$

However, the CRT-based factorization attack does not work for this case which can be proven by the following Theorem 2.

Theorem 2. *Given* $\hat{s} = \hat{s}_q + ((s_p - \hat{s}_q) \cdot (q^{-1} \bmod p) \bmod p) \cdot \hat{q}$ *where* $\hat{q}$, $\hat{s}_q$, *and* $\hat{s}$ *are the permanently corrupted prime factor* q, *the erroneous partial signature modulo* $\hat{q}$, *and the recombined erroneous signature, respectively. It leads to the result that* $\gcd(\hat{s}^e - m, n) = 1$.

Proof. From the given erroneous signature $\hat{s}$, we obtain $\hat{s} \not\equiv m^d \pmod{p}$ and $\hat{s} \not\equiv m^d \pmod{q}$ with extremely large probability.

More precisely, for the case of $\hat{s} \bmod p$, it can be derived that $\hat{s} \bmod p = (\hat{s}_q + T) \bmod p$ (where $T \in_R [0, p-1]$ and $T \not\equiv s_p - \hat{s}_q \pmod{p}$) since $(q^{-1} \bmod p) \cdot \hat{q} \not\equiv 1 \pmod{p}$. This leads to $\hat{s} \not\equiv m^d \pmod{p}$.

For the case of $\hat{s} \bmod q$, it can be derived that $\hat{s} \bmod q = (\hat{s}_q + T) \bmod q$ (where $T \in_R [1, q-1]$) since

$$[((s_p - \hat{s}_q) \cdot (q^{-1} \bmod p) \bmod p) \cdot \hat{q}] \bmod q \neq 0$$

with extremely large probability, except for the following cases:

(1) $q|\hat{q}$ which also leads to $\hat{s}_q \equiv s_q \pmod{q}$ (refer to Lemma 1 for the probability where p is replaced by q);

(2) the rare case of $q|((s_p - \hat{s}_q) \cdot (q^{-1} \bmod p) \bmod p)$ which happens with probability of $1/p$ (≈ 0 for large p) if we assume reasonably $|p| = |q|$.

Totally, the above statements lead to $\hat{s} \not\equiv m^d \pmod{q}$ with extremely large probability.

Therefore, $\hat{s}^e - m \not\equiv 0 \pmod{p}$ and $\hat{s}^e - m \not\equiv 0 \pmod{q}$ and this leads to the result of $p \nmid (\hat{s}^e - m)$ and $q \nmid (\hat{s}^e - m)$. Evidently, this proves $\gcd(\hat{s}^e - m, n) = 1$. □

3.2   Immunity of RSA with CRT by Gauss's Algorithm

If Gauss's CRT recombination algorithm [22, p.68] will be employed and assume that a permanent storage fault on p has occurred (according an erroneous $\hat{s}_p$ is computed), then the obtained erroneous signature will become

$$\hat{s} = (\hat{s}_p \cdot q \cdot (q^{-1} \bmod p) + s_q \cdot p \cdot (p^{-1} \bmod q)) \bmod (\hat{p} \cdot q)$$
$$= (\hat{s}_p \cdot X_p + s_q \cdot X_q) \bmod (\hat{p} \cdot q) \tag{8}$$

where both X_p and X_q are precomputed and stored in advance. The following Theorem 3 proves that the CRT-based factorization attack works by computing $\gcd(\hat{s}^e - m, n) = q$.

Theorem 3. *Given $\hat{s} = (\hat{s}_p \cdot q \cdot (q^{-1} \bmod p) + s_q \cdot p \cdot (p^{-1} \bmod q)) \bmod (\hat{p} \cdot q)$ where $\hat{p}$, $\hat{s}_p$, and $\hat{s}$ are the permanently corrupted prime factor p, the erroneous partial signature modulo $\hat{p}$, and the recombined erroneous signature, respectively. It leads to the result that $\gcd(\hat{s}^e - m, n) = q$.*

Proof. From the given erroneous signature $\hat{s}$, we obtain $\hat{s} \not\equiv m^d$ (mod p) because $(p \cdot (p^{-1} \bmod q) \bmod (\hat{p} \cdot q)) \bmod p \neq 0$ and $(q \cdot (q^{-1} \bmod p) \bmod (\hat{p} \cdot q)) \bmod p \neq 1$ only except when $p | \hat{p}$ (refer to Lemma 1 for the probability).

On the other hand, $\hat{s} \equiv m^d$ (mod q) since $\hat{s} \bmod q = (\hat{s}_p \cdot q \cdot (q^{-1} \bmod p) + s_q \cdot p \cdot (p^{-1} \bmod q)) \bmod q = (s_q \cdot p \cdot (p^{-1} \bmod q)) \bmod q = s_q = m^d \bmod q$.

Therefore, $\hat{s}^e - m \not\equiv 0$ (mod p) and $\hat{s}^e - m \equiv 0$ (mod q) and this leads to the result of $p \nmid (\hat{s}^e - m)$ and $q | (\hat{s}^e - m)$. Evidently, this proves $\gcd(\hat{s}^e - m, n) = q$.   □

Notice that in some implementation of Gauss's CRT recombination algorithm, the modulus integer $n = p \cdot q$ in the Eq. 8 may be precomputed in advance and is stored for later usage. In this situation, it can be derived that $\hat{s} \bmod p = \hat{s}_p \neq m^d \bmod p$ (i.e., $\hat{s} \not\equiv m^d$ (mod p) only except when $p | \hat{p}$) and $\hat{s} \bmod q = s_q = m^d \bmod q$ (i.e., $\hat{s} \equiv m^d$ (mod q)). Therefore, the CRT-based attack still works.

Potential permanent fault attack on the parameter q is similar to the case of permanent fault attack on storage p.

3.3   Immunity of RSA with CRT by Enhanced Garner's Algorithm

In [23], an enhanced CRT recombination formula was suggested in order to avoid a possible CRT-based factorization attack due to the possible memory access fault or permanent fault on $q^{-1} \bmod p$ in the original Garner's algorithm. This enhanced Garner's algorithm is listed in the following

$$s = s_q + [(s_p - s_q) \cdot (q^{-1} \bmod p) \cdot q] \bmod n$$
$$= s_q + [(s_p - s_q) \cdot X] \bmod n \tag{9}$$

where $X = (q^{-1} \bmod p) \cdot q$ can be precomputed and stored in advance.

In the above enhanced Garner's algorithm, if a permanent fault on p has occurred and the signature is computed as

$$\hat{s} = s_q + [(\hat{s}_p - s_q) \cdot (q^{-1} \bmod p) \cdot q] \bmod n$$
$$= s_q + [(\hat{s}_p - s_q) \cdot (q^{-1} \bmod p) \cdot q] \bmod (\hat{p} \cdot q). \tag{10}$$

In this situation, the CRT-based factorization attack works by computing $\gcd(\hat{s}^e - m, n) = q$ no matter whether the approach of storing n directly or the approach of computing it when required in the Eq. 10 will be employed. This can be seen from the following Theorem 4.

Theorem 4. *Given* $\hat{s} = s_q + [(\hat{s}_p - s_q) \cdot (q^{-1} \bmod p) \cdot q] \bmod (\hat{p} \cdot q)$ *where* $\hat{p}$, $\hat{s}_p$, *and* $\hat{s}$ *are the permanently corrupted prime factor* p, *the erroneous partial signature modulo* $\hat{p}$, *and the recombined erroneous signature, respectively. It leads to the result that* $\gcd(\hat{s}^e - m, n) = q$.

Proof. It can be proven in a similar way as the Theorem 1 and Theorem 3. □

If the modulus integer $n = p \cdot q$ is precomputed and stored in advance, then it can be derived that $\hat{s} \bmod p = \hat{s}_p \neq m^d \bmod p$ and $\hat{s} \bmod q = s_q = m^d \bmod q$. Therefore, the CRT-based attack still works.

On the other hand, if a permanent fault on q has occurred and accordingly an erroneous partial signature modulo $\hat{q}$ is computed as $\hat{s}_q$, then the signature will be

$$\hat{s} = \hat{s}_q + [(s_p - \hat{s}_q) \cdot (q^{-1} \bmod p) \cdot q] \bmod n$$
$$= \hat{s}_q + [(s_p - \hat{s}_q) \cdot (q^{-1} \bmod p) \cdot q] \bmod (p \cdot \hat{q}). \tag{11}$$

Recall that $(q^{-1} \bmod p) \cdot q$ is precomputed and stored in advance.

It is different from the original Garner's algorithm[1] that in this situation the CRT-based factorization attack is applicable (refer to the following Theorem 5) no matter whether to store n directly or to compute it when required.

Theorem 5. *Given* $\hat{s} = \hat{s}_q + [(s_p - \hat{s}_q) \cdot (q^{-1} \bmod p) \cdot q] \bmod (p \cdot \hat{q})$ *where* $\hat{q}$, $\hat{s}_q$, *and* $\hat{s}$ *are the permanently corrupted prime factor* q, *the erroneous partial signature modulo* $\hat{q}$, *and the recombined erroneous signature, respectively. It leads to the result that* $\gcd(\hat{s}^e - m, n) = p$.

Proof. From the given erroneous signature $\hat{s}$, we obtain $\hat{s} \bmod p = s_p$ (or $\hat{s} \equiv m^d$ (mod p)) and $\hat{s} \not\equiv m^d$ (mod q) with extremely large probability.

More precisely, for the case of $\hat{s} \bmod p$, $\hat{s} \bmod p = s_p$ since $(q^{-1} \bmod p) \cdot q \equiv 1$ (mod p). For the case of $\hat{s} \bmod q$, it can be derived that $\hat{s} \not\equiv m^d$ (mod q) (except when $q | \hat{q}$) since $[(q^{-1} \bmod p) \cdot q \bmod (p \cdot \hat{q})] \bmod q \neq 0$.

Therefore, $\hat{s}^e - m \equiv 0$ (mod p) and $\hat{s}^e - m \not\equiv 0$ (mod q) and this leads to the result of $p | (\hat{s}^e - m)$ and $q \nmid (\hat{s}^e - m)$. Evidently, this proves $\gcd(\hat{s}^e - m, n) = p$. □

---

[1] Recall that the original Garner's algorithm will be secure against the attack under this situation (refer to Theorem 2).

Table 1. Immunity of some RSA with CRT against permanent parameter fault attack.

	CRT recombination algorithm		
	Gauss's [22, p.68]	Garner's [22, p.612]	modified Garner's [23]
fault on p	insecure	insecure	insecure
fault on q	insecure	secure	insecure

If the modulus $n = p \cdot q$ is precomputed and stored in advance, then it can be derived that $\hat{s} \bmod p = s_p = m^d \bmod p$ and $\hat{s} \bmod q = \hat{s}_q \neq m^d \bmod q$. Similar to the case of permanent fault on p, the CRT-based attack is still applicable when a permanent fault has occurred on q.

All the above permanent fault cryptanalysis on parameters p or q of the conventional RSA with CRT speedup is summarized in the Table 1 with consideration of three possible candidates of CRT recombination algorithms, i.e., [22, p.68;pp.612–613] and [23].

4   Parameter Permanent Fault Attack on Shamir's Countermeasure

Shamir developed a countermeasure [16,17] against the CRT-based hardware fault attack and this countermeasure becomes well known and widely employed. In Shamir's countermeasure, only the general kind of computational fault has been considered. However, it will be shown in the following that the permanent fault on stored parameter p or q enables the CRT-based factorization attack.

4.1   Cryptanalysis of Shamir's Countermeasure

Suppose that a permanent fault on the stored parameter p has occurred and the stored faulty prime factor becomes $\hat{p}$. Accordingly, when signing a message the IC card produces an erroneous partial signature modulo $\hat{p}$ as $\hat{s}_p$. The detailed process of Shamir's protected RSA with CRT under the usage of faulty parameter $\hat{p}$ is described in the following.

(1) The IC card selects a random prime r.
(2) The following two partial signatures with expanded moduli are computed:
$\hat{s}'_p = m^{d \bmod (\hat{p}-1)\cdot(r-1)} \bmod (\hat{p} \cdot r)$ and $s'_q = m^{d \bmod (q-1)\cdot(r-1)} \bmod (q \cdot r)$.
(3) The IC card checks whether $\hat{s}'_p \overset{?}{\equiv} s'_q \pmod{r}$. If this congruence relationship is verified correctly, then the process goes to step (4), otherwise the process stops.
(4) The IC card computes the two necessary partial signatures as: $\hat{s}_p = \hat{s}'_p \bmod \hat{p}$ and $s_q = s'_q \bmod q$.
(5) The two partial signatures are recombined by using a specific CRT recombination algorithm as $\hat{s} = CRT(\hat{s}_p, s_q)$.

It can be derived that

$$\hat{s}_p' \equiv m^{d \bmod (r-1)} \pmod{r}$$
$$\equiv s_q' \pmod{r}.$$

This shows that the checking in step (3) will not detect the permanent storage fault on the parameter p. Also, we notice that

$$\hat{s}_p = \hat{s}_p' \bmod \hat{p} = m^{d \bmod (\hat{p}-1)} \bmod \hat{p}$$
$$s_q = s_q' \bmod q = m^{d \bmod (q-1)} \bmod q.$$

The above explicitely proves that the immunity of Shamir's countermeasure against the proposed parameter (p or q) permanent fault attack is "equivalent" to the case of employing the conventional RSA with CRT speedup no matter which CRT recombination algorithm will be used. Therefore, we ignore all other details of analyzing Shamir's countermeasure against the proposed attack.

5   Feasibility of the Attack and a Possible Countermeasure

5.1   Feasibility of the Proposed Attack

Someone may argue that permanent fault attack using errors on flash memory[2] (or ROM memory) is controversial. However, this observation will not reduce the feasibility and potential of the proposed attack from the following point of view.

We notice that in a real scenario (at least in our proposed attack) a parameter permanent fault can be achieved by conducting a *temporary* memory access fault when a parameter (say p or q) is retrieved from flash memory or even from a hard disk (considering the case of server that we mentioned previously) into RAM or a CPU register for later usage. Recall that the access time of CPU register is much smaller than the access time of flash memory, so most programmers may leave some parameters within the CPU registers for quick access if register space is allowed.

In another word, we consider a *generalized* form of parameter permanent fault which assumes that the parameter will be faulty only within a single cycle of computing RSA with CRT. This so called parameter permanent fault will occur when the parameter is accessed and moved into another location within the smart IC card where errors are much easier to mount. Note that we do not assume any specific type of fault to occur as in many previous publications about hardware fault attacks which were considered impractical. In our proposed attack, any random fault on the parameter is sufficient. Evidently, the proposed permanent fault attack is still practical in this scenario.

---

[2] Almost all individual RSA private parameters inside a smart IC card will be stored within the area of flash memory but not ROM memory. ROM memory is used to store cryptographic functions.

5.2   Possible Countermeasure

A simple countermeasure against the proposed permanent storage fault on parameter p or q is suggested in the following. In this countermeasure, a parameter $n = p \cdot q$ will be precomputed in advance and is stored within the IC card no matter whether it will be used in the following CRT recombination algorithm[3].

The IC card checks whether $p \cdot q \stackrel{?}{=} n$ "after" completing the CRT recombination computation in order to detect any possible permanent fault on the prime factors p or q.

We notice that if the above simple checking/countermeasure (by storing the additional parameter n) will be employed to detect the parameter permanent fault, then the enhanced CRT recombination formula in [23] may be superior to the other two algorithms discussed previously. The advantage of this choice is twofold that the enhanced Garner's algorithm can withstand another parameter permanent fault (i.e., permanent fault on $q^{-1} \bmod p$) and the algorithm itself needs the parameter n.

6   Concluding Remarks

In this paper, we consider permanent fault attack by corrupting parameters p or q in the conventional approach of RSA with CRT speedup and the enhanced speedup approach by using Shamir's countermeasure. It is emphasized that when developing a secure RSA with CRT speedup in order to be against the CRT-based factorization attack by exploiting hardware fault, any possible kind of hardware fault should be considered. Previously, countermeasures were developed primarily in order to withstand computational fault or some kind of temporary faults. However, the proposed CRT-based factorization attack in this paper exploits the existence of permanent fault on the parameters p or q. This attack is applicable to the conventional speedup approach and Shamir's enhanced approach with countermeasure against computational fault.

References

1. R.L. Rivest, A. Shamir, and L. Adleman, "A method for obtaining digital signatures and public-key cryptosystem," *Commun. of ACM*, vol. 21, no. 2, pp. 120–126, 1978.
2. T. ElGamal, "A public key cryptosystem and a signature scheme based on discrete logarithms," *IEEE Trans. Inf. Theory*, vol. 31, no. 4, pp. 469–472, 1985.
3. R. Anderson and M. Kuhn, "Tamper resistance – a cautionary note," In *Proceedings of the 2nd USENIX Workshop on Electronic Commerce*, pp. 1–11, 1996.
4. R. Anderson and M. Kuhn, "Low cost attacks on tamper resistant devices," In *Preproceedings of the 1997 Security Protocols Workshop*, Paris, France, 7–9th April 1997.
5. Bellcore Press Release, "New threat model breaks crypto codes," Sept. 1996, available at URL <http://www.bellcore.com/PRESS/ADVSRY96/facts.html>.

---

[3] Notice that Garner's recombination algorithm does not need the parameter n.

6. D. Boneh, R.A. DeMillo, and R.J. Lipton, "On the importance of checking cryptographic protocols for faults," In *Advances in Cryptology – EUROCRYPT '97*, LNCS 1233, pp. 37–51, Springer-Verlag, 1997.
7. F. Bao, R.H. Deng, Y. Han, A. Jeng, A.D. Narasimbalu, and T. Ngair, "Breaking public key cryptosystems on tamper resistant devices in the presence of transient faults," In *Pre-proceedings of the 1997 Security Protocols Workshop*, Paris, France, 1997.
8. Y. Zheng and T. Matsumoto, "Breaking real-world implementations of cryptosystems by manipulating their random number generation," In *Pre-proceedings of the 1997 Symposium on Cryptography and Information Security*, Fukuoka, Japan, 29th January–1st February 1997. An earlier version was presented at the rump session of *ASIACRYPT '96*.
9. I. Peterson, "Chinks in digital armor – Exploiting faults to break smart-card cryptosystems," *Science News*, vol. 151, no. 5, pp. 78–79, 1997.
10. M. Joye, J.-J. Quisquater, F. Bao, and R.H. Deng, "RSA-type signatures in the presence of transient faults," In *Cryptography and Coding*, LNCS 1355, pp. 155–160, Springer-Verlag, 1997.
11. D.P. Maher, "Fault induction attacks, tamper resistance, and hostile reverse engineering in perspective," In *Financial Cryptography*, LNCS 1318, pp. 109–121, Springer-Verlag, Berlin, 1997.
12. E. Biham and A. Shamir, "Differential fault analysis of secret key cryptosystems," In *Advances in Cryptology – CRYPTO '97*, LNCS 1294, pp. 513–525, Springer-Verlag, Berlin, 1997.
13. A.K. Lenstra, "Memo on RSA signature generation in the presence of faults," September 1996.
14. M. Joye, A.K. Lenstra, and J.-J. Quisquater, "Chinese remaindering based cryptosystems in the presence of faults," *Journal of Cryptology*, vol. 12, no. 4, pp. 241–245, 1999.
15. M. Joye, F. Koeune, and J.-J. Quisquater, "Further results on Chinese remaindering," Tech. Report CG-1997/1, UCL Crypto Group, Louvain-la-Neuve, March 1997.
16. A. Shamir, "How to check modular exponentiation," presented at the rump session of *EUROCRYPT '97*, Konstanz, Germany, 11–15th May 1997.
17. A. Shamir, "Method and apparatus for protecting public key schemes from timing and fault attacks," United States Patent 5991415, November 23, 1999.
18. S.M. Yen and M. Joye, "Checking before output may not be enough against fault-based cryptanalysis," *IEEE Trans. on Computers*, vol. 49, no. 9, pp. 967–970, Sept. 2000.
19. S. Skorobogatov and R. Anderson, "Optical fault induction attacks," In *Pre-proceedings of Cryptographic Hardware and Embedded Systems – CHES 2002*, pp. 2–12, August 13–15, 2002, California, USA.
20. P.J. Smith and M.J.J. Lennon, "LUC: A new public key system," In *Ninth IFIP Symposium on Computer Security*, Elsevier Science Publishers, pp. 103–117, 1993.
21. J.-J. Quisquater and C. Couvreur, "Fast decipherment algorithm for RSA public-key cryptosystem," *Electronics Letters*, vol. 18, no. 21, pp. 905–907, 1982.
22. A.J. Menezes, P.C. van Oorschot, and S.A. Vanstone. *Handbook of applied cryptography*. CRC Press, 1997.
23. S.M. Yen, S.J. Kim, S.G. Lim, and S.J. Moon, "RSA speedup with residue number system immune against hardware fault cryptanalysis," In *Information Security and Cryptology – ICISC 2001*, LNCS 2288, pp. 397–413, Springer-Verlag, 2002.

Backdoor Attacks on Black-Box Ciphers Exploiting Low-Entropy Plaintexts

Adam Young[1] and Moti Yung[2]

[1] Cigital, Inc. ayoung@cigital.com
[2] Columbia University moti@cs.columbia.edu

Abstract. There has been much recent research in designing symmetric ciphers with backdoors that have either public designs or black-box designs. Current Digital Rights Management needs have resurrected the use of hidden ciphers (which were traditionally suggested by the government as black-box designs) in the form of obfuscated "white-box" algorithms. A recent backdoor proposal is the Monkey cipher which is intended to have a secret design and that can be implemented using any deterministic trapdoor one-way function. Monkey leaks information about its user's key to the designer. The primary drawback of Monkey is that it requires the designer (attacker) to obtain a sufficient number of ciphertexts all under the same symmetric key, such that each contains one *known plaintext* bit. In this paper a new design is proposed that eliminates the need for known plaintext *entirely*. Also, whereas Monkey reveals one plaintext bit of each ciphertext to the reverse-engineer (i.e., an entity that tries to learn the black-box device), our solution only leaks a bound on the message entropy to the reverse-engineer, while requiring that the designer obtain a sufficient number of ciphertexts that encrypt messages with a requisite level of redundancy. The information leakage method we use employs "data compression" as a basic tool for generating a hidden information channel. This highlights the need to only encrypt compressed strings when a block cipher with a secret design must be used.

Keywords: Symmetric ciphers, Digital Rights Management (DRM), kleptography, hidden ciphers, obfuscated ciphers, black-box ciphers, reverse-engineering, Huffman compression, subliminal channel, data compression, entropy.

1   Introduction

In the 1990's the US government proposed a secret block cipher called Skipjack [SKIP94] as part of the Clipper Initiative. This algorithm was later declassified and made publicly available. Also, the RC4 cipher was initially kept as a trade secret of RSA Data Security. Such ciphers were secret since their internal designs were kept secret and only their I/O and basic functionality (e.g., encryption/decryption) were disclosed. Kerckhoffs' principle states that the strength of a cryptosystem should reside entirely in the difficulty of determining the key

R. Safavi-Naini and J. Seberry (Eds.): ACISP 2003, LNCS 2727, pp. 297–311, 2003.
© Springer-Verlag Berlin Heidelberg 2003

from specific attacks, not from the secrecy of the algorithm. However, when a cipher is secret there is certainly an added level of protection in effect. This advantage arguably does not outweigh the disadvantage that such ciphers can conceal backdoors.

Even though the necessity for scrutiny is common knowledge, current DRM efforts and more recently the mobile phone industry have sought to utilize software obfuscation and hardware implementations [CEJO02]. Even though publicly known ciphers may be selected for use, the fact is that from the user's perspective, the underlying ciphers are concealed. In a recent paper [JBF02] a technique akin to differential fault analysis is used to attack a commercial software obfuscation package. Countermeasures are presented against this attack, including the possibility of using black-box designs prior to obfuscation. Such obfuscation techniques are intended to help solve the problem of software piracy and protect information content. The ultimate goal of obfuscation techniques is to effectively turn software, which is a "white-box" since its operation can be analyzed in its entirety, into a "black-box" which hides what it is actually computing. In this paper it is argued that obfuscating code can be quite dangerous, particularly in the case of obfuscating symmetric ciphers, since it may pave the way for backdoor attacks.

Rijmen and Preneel pursued a closely related approach that involved a cipher which can be made public [RP97], but which was subsequently cryptanalyzed [WBDY98]. The recovery ability in their algorithm is based on a specific trapdoor that allows the designer to break the encryption using linear cryptanalysis. Another attempt at embedding a backdoor in a public cipher was proposed [PG97] and later cryptanalyzed [Bi00,DKZ99]. Monkey is a "secret" symmetric cipher that contains a backdoor by design [YY98]. In order for Monkey to leak key information, the designer must obtain a sufficient number of ciphertexts under a given key k such that each contains a known-plaintext bit.

In this paper a "secret" symmetric cipher called Black Rugose[1] is described that uses 192 bit keys and has a 192 bit block size. When the cipher is given a suffiently redundant plaintext it activates a key leaking routine which causes the plaintext to be compressed and at the same time leaks a portion of the user's symmetric key within the resulting ciphertext. When the plaintext is not redundant enough it is encrypted normally. Recovery is successful provided that the designer obtains a sufficient amount of ciphertext corresponding to sufficiently redundant plaintexts. Also, whereas in Monkey the successful reverse-engineer is able to learn one plaintext bit from each encrypted message, in this cipher the reverse-engineer learns at most a bound on the entropy of the message. Black Rugose can be implemented using any deterministic trapdoor one-way function.

To substantiate this attack we remark that ciphers with 192 bit blocks and larger exist. For example, the RC5 cipher [Ri95] is a family of algorithms that vary in block size, rounds, and key length. The more recent Rijndael cipher

---

[1] The cipher is named after the *Black Rugose* trapdoor spider from Australia which attacks prey from a concealed trapdoor.

(which became a standard [AES01]) utilizes keys that are 128, 192, or 256 bits in length.

An important issue to stress is that due to the existence of this attack, the combination of data compression and hidden ciphers is risky. A safe approach to resolving this problem is to restrict the plaintext space to that of high-entropy strings. In the case that a message is smaller than the block size, it can be padded out pseudorandomly to fill the block. This would foil the subliminal channel that is "artificially" created. Hence, it may be prudent to consider a black-box cryptosystem with a K bit block size secure for large K only if the probability that it is given a highly redundant K bit plaintext is zero. This black-box scenario contradicts the standard ideology that a cipher is good provided that it is secure for any probability distribution over $\{0,1\}^K$.

2   General Design Approach

The following observations give rise to Black Rugose:

1. Often huge stretches of identical or nearly identical symbols appear in plaintexts (e.g., graphical, textual, program data, etc.).
2. The plaintext space $\{0,1\}^{192}$ is huge and the black-box devices will not be able to collectively encrypt every plaintext in any reasonable length of time.

Observation (1) suggests that such plaintext data can be compressed to "create" a subliminal channel [Si94] in the underlying cipher. Instead of encrypting the redundant plaintext normally, its compressed version plus the resulting Huffman tree [Hu52] is computed and stored efficiently, thereby making room for whatever else the designer wants to leak in the final ciphertext. The trick is to leak two pieces of information in this information channel. The first piece of information is a securely encoded piece of the users symmetric key. The second piece of information is a checksum that allows the designer to distinguish between normal encryptions and attacked encryptions. However, a problem may arise since an attacked encryption may end up appearing the same as a normal encryption. Observation (2) suggests that this form of collision should occur very infrequently since the number of ciphertexts will be so large in comparison to the already large number of checksum values. As will be shown in Section 6, there is a negligible chance that a given ciphertext will decrypt incorrectly due to collisions.

3   Definitions and Notation

Black Rugose is based on the following slightly modified operational definition of a "quasi-setup" [YY98].

Definition 1. *A **quasi-setup** is a black-box cryptosystem C with a specification known only to the designer, except after reverse-engineering, that satisfies the following:*

1. *The size of the input key, input plaintext, and output ciphertext is publicly known (and perhaps other extraneous and possibly erroneous information is given), and the key is supplied by the end-user.*

2. *If C is a symmetric cipher, then for efficiency, C does not use public-key operations in real-time (to avoid being recognized by time measurement). C pre-computes using the designer's secret public key E (and possibly other functions as well), contained within C.*

3. *The designer's private key D is not contained within C and is known only by the designer.*

4. *The output of C is secure based on the security of underlying block ciphers and other tools. At the same time it contains published bits (of the user's secret key) which can be derived efficiently by the designer, assuming that a sufficient number of ciphertexts are available that correspond to plaintexts with a requisite level of redundancy.*

5. *The fact that C leaks key bits is undetectable to everyone except the designer (attacker) and a successful reverse-engineer.*

6. *After the discovery of the specification of C (e.g., after reverse-engineering of the device), no one except the designer can determine past or future keys, though the successful reverse-engineer learns with overwhelming probability an upper bound on the entropy of a given plaintext when it is sufficiently redundant and a lower bound otherwise, given only the (past) ciphertext.*

The notation $|A|$ denotes the number of bits in the bit string A. For example, when $A = 00101$ it follows that $|A| = 5$. $A||B$ denotes the string resulting from the concatenation of bit string A with bit string B. Provided that $|A| = |B|$, $A \oplus B$ denotes the bitwise logical exclusive OR of A with B.

4   Tiny Huffman Tree Representations

Let $C = 0, 1, 2, ..., n-1$ be a set of characters. It is well known that any optimal prefix code on C can be represented by a sequence of $2n - 1 + n\lceil log_2 n \rceil$ bits [CLR99]. The encoding can be done by performing a pre-order traversal of the Huffman tree and writing down a binary 0 for each internal node and a binary 1 for each leaf. Since $n! \leq n^n$ it follows that the permutation of the left to write ordering of the leaves which correspond to the characters can be encoded in $n\lceil log_2 n \rceil > log_2(n!)$ bits. The ordering of these leaves can be stored using the Trotter-Johnson method of ranking and unranking permutations.

In Black Rugose the plaintext space is the set of strings $\{0, 1\}^{192}$. The compression algorithm that is used is Huffman compression using the eight symbols $000, 001, 010, ..., 111$. Hence, each input plaintext is broken down into 64 symbols, which are each three bits in length. Let HuffmanComp denote the Huffman compression algorithm, which outputs a Huffman tree T and a compression m_{comp} of message m. This is denoted by $(T, m_{comp}) = $ HuffmanComp(m). Let HuffmanDecomp denote the corresponding decompression algorithm. Hence, $(m, error) = $ HuffmanDecomp(T, m_{comp}) decompresses the compressed string.

The boolean value *error* is False if and only if decompression leads to an error (e.g., if the tree or compressed string has been altered).

The aforementioned bound tells us that at most $2 * 8 - 1 + 8 * 3 = 39$ bits are needed for storing the tree. However, since $2^{16} > 8! = 40320$ it follows that $2 * 8 - 1 + 16 = 31$ bits are actually needed. Clearly a more efficient encoding would be desirable.

It will now be shown how to represent such a tree in a mere 21 bits. It is well known that all Huffman trees are full binary trees [CLR99,HR94], where a full binary tree is defined as a tree where each vertex has zero or two children. The key observation here is that the left/right ordering of the nodes in the tree does not affect the efficiency of the compression at all. Only the distance from each leaf to the root affects the size of the compressed string. It follows that in order to store the structure of the full binary tree one need only consider the set of non-isomorphic rooted full binary trees. Recall that a rooted tree is a free tree in which one of the vertices is distinguished from the others and that a free tree is a connected, acyclic, and undirected graph.

The Wedderburn-Etherington numbers are the number of binary rooted trees (every node has out-degree 0 or 2) with n endpoints (and $2n-1$ nodes in all). The first few such numbers are $0, 1, 1, 1, 2, 3, 6, 11, 23, 46, 98, 207, 451, 983$. For more information, see [We22,Et37,Slo]. It follows that for a given Huffman tree with 8 symbols one need only reference one of 23 non-isomorphic binary rooted trees to store an equivalent Huffman tree. Let $T_0, T_1, ..., T_{22}$ be these trees represented using a standard array format. See [LR99,KK92,Pa89] for methods to compute these trees correctly.

Below the algorithm ShrinkTree is given which is specialized to the case of full rooted binary trees with eight leaves. This algorithm utilizes the function Treeisomorphism(T_1, T_2) which returns $(f, bool)$. The value *bool* is set to True if T_1 and T_2 are isomorphic and False otherwise. If they are isomorphic then an isomorphism is returned in f, otherwise f is set to the empty string [AHU74]. ShrinkTree also utilizes well known algorithms for permutation generation from algorithmic combinatorics [Tr62,Jo63,Ev73,KS99]. Let π be a permutation over $\{0, 1, 2, ..., n-1\}$ and let TrotJohnRank(π) denote the Trotter-Johnson ranking function. Hence, this function returns a rank $r \in \{0, 1, 2, ..., n! - 1\}$. Denote by TrotJohnUnrank(n, r) the unranking function which returns π.

ShrinkTree(T):
Input: full binary tree T in the standard array data structure
Output: value t which is an encoding of T
1. for $i = 0$ to 22 do:
2.   compute $(f, bool) = $ Treeisomorphism(T, T_i)
3.   if $bool = $ True the goto step 4
4. perform a pre-order traversal of T to obtain an ordering of
        the 8 symbols π corresponding to the leaves of T
5. compute $r = $ TrotJohnRank(π)
6. output i in binary concatenated with r in binary and halt

Observe that this algorithm iterates over Wedderburn-Etherington numbers and is therefore only efficient for the first several numbers in the sequence. We may assume that the Huffman compression algorithm assigns a binary zero to the edges connecting to the left-children and assigns a binary one to the edges connecting to the right-children.

GrowTree(t):
Input: value t which is an encoding of a full binary tree
Output: full binary tree T in the standard array data structure
1. set *upper* be the 5 most significant bits of t
2. set *lower* be the 16 least significant bits of t
3. Let i, r be the integers corresponding to *upper*, *lower* respectively
4. compute $\pi = $ TrotJohnUnrank$(8, r)$
5. perform a pre-order traversal of T_i and assign the 1st symbol in π to the 1st
   leaf visited, the 2nd symbols in π to the 2nd leaf visited, etc. to get tree T
6. output T and halt

It should be immediately apparent that the tree which is output by GrowTree is not always the same binary tree that was given to ShrinkTree. More specifically, it is not always the case that T will be equal to GrowTree(ShrinkTree(T)). The reason for this is that T is initially encoded using a tree T_i which is isomorphic to T but that may not be the same tree. In Appendix A a proof is given that the final tree which is output by GrowTree constitutes an optimal prefix code. Appendix B describes a method to encode Huffman trees even more efficiently.

5   Building Blocks for the Attack

Define PubKeyEncr(m, y) to be a deterministic public key encryption algorithm that takes a 192 bit plaintext m and a public key y as input. The output is a ciphertext c which in general is much larger than the input. Note that such ciphers can be implemented with small ciphertexts [SOMS95]. Denote by PubKeyDecr(c, x) the corresponding decryption algorithm which returns m. Here x is the private key corresponding to y. Let Z denote the bit length of the largest possible public key encryption c.

The backdoor that will be described cannot utilize a probabilistic public key cryptosystem since it is embedded within a device that has a public specification indicating the presence of a deterministic algorithm. This prevents the use of cryptosystems which are, e.g., semantically secure against known plaintext attacks. The notion of "security" for PubKeyEncr is therefore understood to mean the secrecy that is *argued* by the underlying trapdoor one-way function (e.g., in the case of RSA [RSA78] it is the eth roots problem, though we know the Jacobi symbol of the plaintext is leaked in each ciphertext).

Observe that the Diffie-Hellman key exchange is probabilistic and hence cannot be used directly to instantiate PubKeyEncr. Diffie-Hellman can be used to instantiate PubKeyEncr using the following heuristic. The key exchange exponent can be chosen pseudorandomly rather than truly at random using a pseudorandom function and a secret seed included within the black-box device. The other value that is supplied to the pseudorandom function can be set to be the symmetric key that is supplied to the encryption device (so that when this key is not known, the resulting function value is unknown). A portion of the Diffie-Hellman secret can then be used as a pad to XOR encrypt the plaintext. Efficiently encrypt a 192 bit plaintext, an elliptic curve cryptosystem defined over $GF(2^{155})$ can be used. The resulting ciphertext is then a 310-bit point over the curve concatenated with the 192-bit XOR encryption, resulting in an encryption that is 402 bits.

The designer chooses a keyed function $\mathsf{Pseudorand}_M(seed, input)$ that takes as input a large value for $seed$ (e.g., 160 bits) and a value $input$. This particular function invokes a pseudorandom function using seed and input and returns the M least significant bits of the result. For an explanation on how to construct pseudorandom functions, see [GGM86].

Let $\mathsf{SymKeyEncr}_i$ for $i = 1, 2, 3$ be deterministic symmetric encryption algorithms that utilize 192 bit symmetric keys. Let $\mathsf{SymKeyDecr}_i$ for $i = 1, 2, 3$ denote the corresponding decryption algorithms, respectively. For all messages m and all symmetric keys k it follows that,

$$m = \mathsf{SymKeyDecr}_i(\mathsf{SymKeyEncr}_i(m, k), k) \quad \text{for} \quad i = 1, 2, 3$$

In these ciphers the bit length of the ciphertext is always equal to the bit length of the plaintext. $\mathsf{SymKeyEncr}_1$ operates on plaintexts of length $128 - M$ in bits. $\mathsf{SymKeyEncr}_2$ and $\mathsf{SymKeyEncr}_3$ both operate on 192 bit plaintexts. These block private key cryptosystems may be instantiated using a pseudorandom invertible permutation generator, which will make them secure against chosen plaintext attacks [Lu96]. In practice symmetric ciphers are often designed using (much) more than four Feistel transformations based on Luby-Rackoff's construction [LR88,Kn98].

The algorithm $\mathsf{GetBitPos}(seed, input)$ is a Las-Vegas type algorithm that pseudorandomly (rather than randomly) chooses without replacement M symbols from the set $S = \{0, 1, 2, 3, ..., Z - 1\}$ and returns them as output. Hence, it outputs M distinct pseudorandomly chosen bit positions in a ciphertext string output by $\mathsf{PubKeyEncr}$. Observe that a pseudorandom string may be obtained by successively concatenating the output of a pseudorandom function applied to $seed$ and $(input || j)$ for $j = 0, 1, 2, 3, ...$ This pseudorandom string is used to generate the output as follows. Initially $\lceil log_2\binom{Z}{M} \rceil$ bits are taken from it to obtain a base-2 number r. If $r \geq \binom{Z}{M}$ then the next $\lceil log_2\binom{Z}{M} \rceil$ bits are considered and so on, thus making this a Las Vegas algorithm. If an r is found then the algorithm runs $\mathsf{KSubsetColexUnrank}$ using the rank r to obtain a pseudorandom subset [KS99].

6   Encryption, Decryption, and Recovery

The values $seed_1, seed_2, seed_3, k_1$, and the private key x corresponding to y are chosen uniformly at random by the designer. The values $seed_1, seed_2, seed_3$, the symmetric key k_1, and y are stored within the black-box device. The following is the encryption algorithm.

$RugoseEncrypt(m, k)$:
Input: 192 bit plaintext m, 192 bit symmetric key k
Output: 192 bit ciphertext c
1. compute $(T, m_{comp}) = \mathsf{HuffmanComp}(m)$
2. if $|m_{comp}| > 96$ then output $c = \mathsf{SymKeyEncr}_2(m, k)$ and halt
3. compute $t = \mathsf{ShrinkTree}(T)$
4. compute $w_3 = \mathsf{SymKeyEncr}_1(t||m_{comp}, k)$
6. compute $c_{pub} = \mathsf{PubKeyEncr}(k, y)$
7. compute $(p_1, p_2, ..., p_M) = \mathsf{GetBitPos}(seed_1, w_3)$
8. for $i = 1$ to M do:
         set u_i to be equal to the bit in bit position p_i of c_{pub}
9. set $B = (b_1||b_2||...||b_M)$
10. compute $pad = \mathsf{Pseudorand}_M(seed_2, w_3)$
11. compute $w_2 = B \oplus pad$
12. compute $w_1 = \mathsf{Pseudorand}_{64}(seed_3, w_2||w_3)$
13. output $c = \mathsf{SymKeyEncr}_3(w_1||w_2||w_3, k_1)$ and halt

To avoid timing analysis similar dummy computations can be performed even when the attack is not carried out (i.e., when $|m_{comp}| > 96$). Ideally, several public key ciphertexts will be cached in the event that a symmetric key is reused. A fingerprint of the symmetric key can also be cached to allow the correct cached ciphertext to be properly matched with the input symmetric key. This minimizes any real-time public key operations.

When $\mathsf{SymKeyEncr}_3$ employs Feistel transformations, the local differences in the bits of $w_1||w_2||w_3$ are spread uniformly over the final resulting ciphertext.

$RugoseDecrypt(c, k)$:
Input: 192 bit ciphertext c, 192 bit symmetric key k
Output: 192 bit plaintext m
1. compute $W = \mathsf{SymKeyDecr}_3(c, k_1)$
2. set $upper$ equal to the 64 uppermost bits of W
3. set $lower$ equal to the 128 lowermost bits of W
4. if $upper \neq \mathsf{Pseudorand}_{64}(seed_3, lower)$ then
5.   output $m = \mathsf{SymKeyDecr}_2(c, k)$ and halt
6. set str equal to W with the $64 + M$ most significant bits removed
7. compute $(t||m_{comp}) = \mathsf{SymKeyDecr}_1(str, k)$
8. compute $(T, error) = \mathsf{GrowTree}(t)$
9. if $error = \mathsf{True}$ then output $m = \mathsf{SymKeyDecr}_2(c, k)$ and halt
10. compute $(m, error) = \mathsf{HuffmanDecomp}(T, m_{comp})$
11. if $error = \mathsf{True}$ then output $m = \mathsf{SymKeyDecr}_2(c, k)$ and halt
12. output m and halt

It is possible that there exists a triple (m_1, m_2, k) such that m_1 compresses to 96 bits or below, m_2 does not compress to 96 bits or below, but that they encrypt under *RugoseEncrypt* using k to the same ciphertext c. In this case c always decrypts to m_1, and hence m_2 is unrecoverable. It is important to estimate this probability of occurrence. In analyzing this probably the simplifying assumption will be made that $\mathsf{Pseudorand}_{64}$ returns truly random 64 bit strings and that the 64 most significant bits of $\mathsf{SymKeyEncr}_2(m, k)$ are random.

Lemma 1. *Assuming that* $\mathsf{Pseudorand}_{64}$ *returns random 64 bit strings and that the 64 most significant bits of* $\mathsf{SymKeyEncr}_2(m, k)$ *are random, RugoseDecrypt fails to decrypt correctly with probability at most* $1/2^{64}$.

To see this note that clearly all strings which compress to 96 bits or less fail to decrypt with probability zero. It remains to consider those that compress to more than 96 bits. Let m_2 be any such string. Under the simplified assumptions it follows that $upper = \mathsf{Pseudorand}_{64}(seed_3, lower)$ with probability $1/2^{64}$. Hence, the encryption of m_2 decrypts incorrectly with probability at most $1/2^{64}$. Therefore, in all cases decryption fails with probability at most $1/2^{64}$.

The following algorithm is run by the malicious designer until the full symmetric key k is recovered. The designer needs to obtain a sufficient number of ciphertexts corresponding to redundant plaintexts encrypted using k. Note that the designer does not have to obtain consecutive or otherwise correlated messages to obtain a "cover" of the key due to the random choice of key bits in each message.

RugoseRecoverMBits(c):
Input: 192 bit ciphertext c
Output: bit positions $(p_1, p_2, ..., p_M)$, bit string V s.t. $|V| = M$,
             boolean result code in *error*
1. compute $W = \mathsf{SymKeyDecr}_3(c, k_1)$
2. set *upper* equal to the 64 uppermost bits of W
3. set *lower* equal to the 128 lowermost bits of W
4. if *upper* $\neq \mathsf{Pseudorand}_{64}(seed_3, lower)$ then
5.   output *error* = True and halt
6. set str_1 equal to the M most significant bits of *lower*
7. set str_2 equal to *lower* with the M most significant bits removed
8. compute $(p_1, p_2, ..., p_M) = \mathsf{GetBitPos}(seed_1, str_2)$
9. compute $pad = \mathsf{Pseudorand}_M(seed_2, str_2)$
10. compute $V = str_1 \oplus pad$ and set *error* = False
11. output $((p_1, p_2, ..., p_M), V, error)$ and halt

It remains to consider the expected number of ciphertexts needed to recover k. Suppose that Z is 402 (bit length of public key ciphertext c_{pub}), which results from applying the heuristic mentioned in Section 5. Also, assume that the ciphertexts that the attacker has are all distinct and that they are all encryptions under the same key k. Reconstructing c_{pub} amounts to collecting all 402 necessary ciphertext bits. If each bit were selected uniformly at random from the Z bit positions then $Z \log Z$ bits would need to be sampled on average. This results from analyzing the first moment of the Coupon Collector's Problem [Fe57]. In this particular case we have the advantage that M distinct bits are selected in each trial. So, an upper bound on the expected number of needed ciphertexts is $\frac{Z \log Z}{M}$. With $Z = 402$ and $M = 11$ this implies that on average 96 ciphertexts will be needed.

7   Security

In this section we review the security with respect to the reverse-engineer and the security against the user. In this, no specific definition for the security of a block cipher is used (fully specifying attacks and concrete analysis as e.g., in [KY00] is beyond the scope of this work). The general approach attempts to preserve within the overall design whatever notion of secrecy (resisting an adversary with given capabilities and a goal) the three SymKeyEncr algorithms have and rely on the strong security properties of the other building blocks. It is argued how the security amounts to breaking the secure building blocks, namely we only point at the reduction from attacking the design to attacking the design blocks.

Let $\mathcal{M} = \{0, 1\}^{192}$ denote the entire message space of Black Rugose. Clearly this can be partitioned into two disjoint message spaces $\mathcal{M}_{red}$ and $\mathcal{M}_{ent}$ where $\mathcal{M}_{red}$ consists of those redundant messages that compress to 96 bits or less and $\mathcal{M}_{ent}$ consists of the remaining plaintexts with high entropy. Thus, $\mathcal{M} = \mathcal{M}_{red} \cup \mathcal{M}_{ent}$. Due to the calculation of entropy and the "if" statement at the beginning of $RugoseEncrypt$ it is clear that $RugoseEncrypt$ in fact implements two separate symmetric encryption algorithms over two separate message spaces.

Suppose that a reverse-engineer succeeds in reverse-engineering the device. The attacker therefore knows all of the values in the device and the complete specification of the cipher. Thus, $SymKeyEncr_3$ may be ignored in this case. Let $\mathcal{C}_k = \{c_{k,1}, c_{k,2}, ..., c_{k,poly}\}$ be a set of Black Rugose ciphertexts found using symmetric key k, where $poly$ is some polynomial. Let $\mathcal{M}_k$ be the corresponding set of plaintexts. The following argument addresses what the reverse-engineer can compute based on $(\mathcal{C}_k, \mathcal{M}_k)$.

Claim 1. Given $(\mathcal{C}_k, \mathcal{M}_k)$ and a ciphertext c which encrypts m under key k, the reverse-engineer learns at most an upper or lower bound on the entropy of m.

From Lemma 1 it follows that with negligible probability $upper$ is equal to $\mathsf{Pseudorand}_{64}(seed_3, lower)$ when $m \in \mathcal{M}_{ent}$. Here $upper$ and $lower$ are as defined in $RugoseDecrypt$. It follows that with overwhelming probability the reverse-engineer learns which set $\mathcal{M}_{ent}$ or $\mathcal{M}_{red}$ contains m given c. Observe that these sets partition the set of strings $\{0, 1\}^{192}$ into those that compress using Huffman compression to more than 96 bits and those that compress to 96 bits or less, respectively. Hence, with overwhelming probability the reverse-engineer learns a lower bound on the entropy of m when $m \in \mathcal{M}_{ent}$ and an upper bound otherwise.

It may be assumed that the reverse-engineer obtains enough past ciphertexts to fully reconstruct the public key ciphertext c_{pub} of the symmetric key k. Hence, the ability for the reverse-engineer to learn anything more about m is dictated entirely by the definition of security of $SymKeyEncr_1$ and the definition of security of $\mathsf{SymKeyEncr}_2$ in conjunction with the fact that c_{pub} is known. Since all of these encryptions are strong encryptions it may be argued that secrecy is assured. $\diamond$

It remains to show the security with respect to the end-user.

Claim 2. If *Rugose* is a black-box cryptosystem with private specification then it constitutes a secure (in the sense of $\mathsf{SymKeyEncr}_i$) symmetric cipher.

Clearly the end-user learns no more than the reverse-engineer. Hence, from Claim 1 it follows that the end-user learns no more than a bound on the entropy of the input plaintext m. It is easy to see that determining this bound amounts to determining whether m is a member of $\mathcal{M}_{red}$ or $\mathcal{M}_{ent}$.

It will now be shown that the *Rugose* cryptosystem, which is the union of these two ciphers, produces ciphertexts that do not reveal which set contains m. Observe that the string which is concatenated with the ciphertext of $\mathsf{SymKeyEncr}_1$ during the encryption in *RugoseEncrypt* is pseudo-random with respect to the user who employs the black-box device. This follows from the fact that the output of $\mathsf{Pseudorand}_{64}$ is concatenated with a value that is one-time padded with the output of $\mathsf{Pseudorand}_M$. The final Feistel transformations in $\mathsf{SymKeyEncr}_3$ which are based on a pseudorandom function assures a strong inseparable encryption of the pseudorandom prefix and ciphertext from $\mathsf{SymKeyEncr}_1$ due to the properties of pseudorandom functions. The end-user must then distinguish between ciphertexts produced by $\mathsf{SymKeyEncr}_2$ and those produced by $\mathsf{SymKeyEncr}_3$, which have the same message space, to determine membership of m in $\mathcal{M}_{red}$ or $\mathcal{M}_{ent}$. Observe that the pseudorandom prefix in the plaintext given to $\mathsf{SymKeyEncr}_3$ is pseudorandom, thereby making $\mathsf{SymKeyEncr}_3$ produce pseudorandomized encryptions in *RugoseEncrypt*. Therefore, distinguishing between these two encryptions is intractable. $\diamond$

In the above arguments we informally used the well known fact that if the key of a pseudorandom function is not known to the end-user then the value of the function at a point cannot be approximated even in a very liberal sense even if the values of the function at polynomially many other points is also known [GGM86]. This implies, in particular, that when the key is not known the pseudorandom values used in the public key operation are not known as well and that distinguishing two such functions is intractable. It is this property of pseudorandom functions that makes this attack secure. Thus, the above shows that Black Rugose constitutes a quasi-setup as we defined.

References

[AES01]   Advanced Encryption Standard. FIPS 197, Federal Register, Dec. 6, 2001.

[AHU74]   A. Aho, J. Hopcroft, J. Ullman. The Design and Analysis of Computer Algorithms. Addison-Wesley, 1974, Theorem 3.3 and the following Corollary, pages 84–86.

[Bi00]   E. Biham. Cryptanalysis of Patarin's 2-Round Public Key System S Boxes (2R). In *Advances in Cryptology—Eurocrypt '00*, pages 408–416, 1999.

[CEJO02]   S. Chow, P. Eisen, H. Johnson, P. C. van Oorshot. A White-Box DES Implementation for DRM Applications. ACM Workshop on Digital Rights Management, 2002.

[CLR99]   T. Cormen, C. Leiserson, R. Rivest. Introduction to Algorithms. McGraw-Hill, 1999, Exercises 17.3-1 and 17.3-5, page 344.

[COS]   The Combinatorial Object Server, University of Victoria. Available on the WWW at http://www.theory.csc.uvic.ca/~cos/gen/tree.html.

[DKZ99]   Y. Ding-Feng, L. Kwok-Yan, D. Zong-Duo. Cryptanalysis of the "2R" schemes. In Advances in Cryptology—Crypto '99, pages 315–325, 1999.

[Et37]   I. M. H. Etherington. Non-associate powers and a functional equation. Math. Gaz. 21, 1937, pages 36–39, 153.

[Ev73]   S. Even. Algorithmic Combinatorics. New York, Macmillan, 1973.

[Fe57]   W. Feller. An Introduction to Probability Theory and its Applications. John Wiley & Sons, Inc., pages 210–212, 1957.

[GGM86]   O. Goldreich, S. Goldwasser, S. Micali. How to Construct Random Functions. J. of the ACM, 33(4), pages 210–217, 1986.

[HR94]   N. Hartsfield, G. Ringel. Pearls in Graph Theory. Academic Press, 1994, Exercise 7.3.2, page 148.

[Hu52]   D. A. Huffman. A method for the construction of minimum-redundancy codes. Proceedings of the IRE, v. 40, n. 9, Sept. 1952, pages 1098–1101.

[JBF02]   M. Jacob, D. Boneh, E. Felten. Attacking an obfuscated cipher by injecting faults. ACM Workshop on Digital Rights Management, 2002.

[Jo63]   S. M. Johnson. Generation of permutations by adjacent transpositions. Mathematics of Computation, v. 17, pages 282–285, 1963.

[KY00]   Jonathan Katz, Moti Yung. Complete characterization of security notions for probabilistic private-key encryption. STOC, pages 245–254, 2000.

[Kn98]   L. Knudsen. DEAL: A 128-bit block cipher. Technical Report 151, Department of Informatics,University of Bergen, Norway, Feb. 1998.

[KK92]   E. Kubicka, G. Kubicki. Constant Time Algorithm for Generating Binary Rooted Trees. Congressus Numerantium, 90, 1992, pages 57–64.

[KS99]   D. L. Kreher, D. R. Stinson. Combinatorial Algorithms - Generation, Enumeration, and Search. CRC Press, Algorithms 2.10, 2.17, 2.18, pages 47,57–61, 1999.

[LR88]   M. Luby, C. Rackoff. How to Construct Pseudorandom Permutations from Pseudorandom Functions. In SIAM J. on Computing, v. 17, 1988, pages 373–386.

[LR99]   G. Li, F. Ruskey. The Advantages of Forward Thinking in Generating Rooted and Free Trees. SODA '99.

[Lu96]   M. Luby. Pseudorandomness and Cryptographic Applications. Princeton Computer Science Notes, Princeton University Press, Lectures 13 & 14, pages 128–145, 1996.

[Pa89]   J. Pallo. Lexicographic generation of binary unordered trees. Pattern Recognition Letters, 10, 1989, pages 217–221.

[PG97]   J. Patarin, L. Goubin. Asymmetric Cryptography with S-Boxes. In Proceedings of ICICS '97, Springer, LNCS 1334, Nov. 1997, pages 369–380.

[Ri95]   R. L. Rivest. The RC5 encryption algorithm. In Proceedings of the 1994 K. U. Leuven Workshop on Cryptographic Algorithms, Springer-Verlag, 1995.

[RSA78]   R. Rivest, A. Shamir, L. Adleman. A Method for Obtaining Digital
            Signatures and Public-Key Cryptosystems. CACM, v. 21, n. 2, pages
            120–126, Feb. 1978.
[RP97]   V. Rijmen, B. Preneel, A Family of Trapdoor Ciphers. Fast Software
            Encryption, E. Biham Edition, pages 139–148, 1997.
[Si94]   G. J. Simmons. Subliminal Channels: past and present. *European Tra.
            on Telecommunications* v. 5, 1994, pages 459–473.
[SKIP94]   Digital Signature Standard. National Institute of Standards and Tech-
            nology, NIST FIPS PUB 186, US Dept. of Commerce, May '94 (declas-
            sified on WWW on June 23, 1998).
[Slo]   N. J. A. Sloane. Integer Sequence A001190 downloadable from AT&T
            Research at http://www.research.att.com/~njas/sequences/Seis.html.
[SOMS95]   R. Schroeppel, H. Orman, S. O'Malley, O. Spatscheck. Fast Key Ex-
            change with Elliptic Curve Systems. In *Advances in Cryptology—
            CRYPTO '95*, pages 43–56, 1995.
[Tr62]   H. F. Trotter. Algorithm 115, Communications of the ACM, v. 5, pages
            434–435, 1962.
[WBDY98]   H. Wu, F. Bao, R. Deng, Q. Ye. Cryptanalysis of Rijmen-Preneel
            Trapdoor Ciphers. In *Advances in Cryptology—Asiacrypt '98*, pages
            126–132, 1998.
[We22]   J. H. M. Wedderburn. The functional equation $g(x^2) = 2ax + [g(x)]^2$
            Ann. Math., 24, 1922-1923, pages 121–140.
[YY98]   A. Young, M. Yung. Monkey: Black-Box Symmetric Ciphers Designed
            for MONopolizing KEYs. In *Fast Software Encryption*, pages 122–133,
            1998.

A   Correctness of **ShrinkTree** and **GrowTree**

The following are the internal nodes to the 23 trees found using [LR99] expressed
using a parent array. When $Parent[i] = 0$, the vertex i is the root. For example,
in the first array vertex 1 is the root, the parent of vertex 2 is 1, the parent
of vertex 3 is 2, etc. It was found by generating rooted trees on-line with the
combinatorial object server [COS] with $n = 7$ and $m = 2$. To complete the
construction of the 23 trees it is necessary to (1) attach two leaves to each leaf in
the trees below, and (2) attach a single leaf to each internal vertex in the trees
below.

```
0 1 2 3 4 5 6    0 1 2 3 4 5 5    0 1 2 3 4 5 4    0 1 2 3 4 5 3    0 1 2 3 4 5 2
0 1 2 3 4 5 1    0 1 2 3 4 4 3    0 1 2 3 4 4 2    0 1 2 3 4 4 1    0 1 2 3 4 3 6
0 1 2 3 4 3 2    0 1 2 3 4 3 1    0 1 2 3 4 2 6    0 1 2 3 4 2 1    0 1 2 3 4 1 6
0 1 2 3 3 2 6    0 1 2 3 3 2 1    0 1 2 3 3 1 6    0 1 2 3 2 5 1    0 1 2 3 2 1 6
0 1 2 3 1 5 6    0 1 2 3 1 5 5    0 1 2 2 1 5 5
```

Let $G = (V, E)$ denote a graph with vertex set V and edge set E. When G is
a rooted tree, $depth(v)$ denotes the number of edges between $v \in V$ and the root
of G. Recall that two graphs G and $G' = (V', E')$ are isomorphic if there exists
a bijection $f : V \to V'$ such that $(u, v) \in E$ if and only if $(f(u), f(v)) \in E'$.

Lemma 2. *For all $n \in \mathbb{N}$, for all pairs of isomorphic rooted trees (G, G') such that $|V| = n$, and for all $v \in V$, $depth(v) = depth(f(v))$.*

Proof. Let the induction hypothesis be that this holds for some n. This trivially holds $n = 1, 2, 3$. Suppose that it holds for some $n > 3$. It will now be shown that it holds for $n + 1$. Add a vertex v to V and connect it by a single edge to any vertex u in V. Also, add a vertex v' to V' and connect it by a single edge to $f(u)$. By the induction hypothesis $depth(u) = depth(f(u))$. It follows that $depth(v) = depth(u) + 1 = depth(f(u)) + 1 = depth(v')$. ◇

Theorem 1. *The output of* GrowTree(ShrinkTree(T)) *constitutes a prefix code that is as optimal as T.*

Proof. It follows from the work of Wedderburn and Etherington that there are 23 non-isomorphic rooted binary trees with 8 leaves. Also, clearly ShrinkTree correctly encodes all 23 of these trees in $T_0, T_1, ..., T_{22}$ [LR99]. Since the input T is a full binary tree with 8 leaves it follows that it must be isomorphic to exactly one of $T_0, T_1, ..., T_{22}$. Clearly, upon reaching step 4 the correct isomorphic tree T_i is. Hence, it is clear that ShrinkTree encodes T into a tree represented as t which is isomorphic to T. Now, since TrotJohnUnrank is correct, GrowTree clearly expands t from its compact form into the standard array data structure for binary trees. Let T' denote this resulting binary tree. It remains to show that T' which is isomorphic to T constitutes a prefix code that is as optimal as T. Since f is a bijection, each leaf in T maps under f to one and only one leaf in T'. Hence, by Lemma 2 it follows that each symbol ψ in T has a prefix code that has the same bit length as ψ in T'. The prefix codes in T' are clearly unique since the tree is a full binary tree and the edges connecting to the left-children are assigned a binary zero and the edges connecting to the right-children are assigned a binary one. Since the prefix code corresponding to T is optimal it follows that the prefix code corresponding to T' is optimal. ◇

B   Even Smaller Huffman Trees

Consider the message $DABDDCBACCD$. Clearly

$$(A, B, C, D) = (000, 001, 01, 1)$$

is an optimal prefix code for this message. Observe that while there are 4! permutations over the symbols $\{A, B, C, D\}$, and hence 4! ways to order the leaves of the Huffman tree, only $\binom{4}{2,1,1}$ orderings of the symbols will ever be necessary for this particular rooted binary tree. This is because two leaves are at exactly the same depth from the root. Note that for this message $(A, B, C, D) = (001, 000, 01, 1)$ is another optimal prefix code, illustrating that the codes for the leaves A and B, which are at the same depth, are interchangeable. In general for each binary rooted tree there is a multinomial $\binom{n}{m_1, m_2, ..., m_t}$ which describes exactly how many orderings of the leaves are necessary to store an optimal code for the given tree. Here n is the number of leaves. We may order the values m_i where $1 \leq i \leq t$ such that m_1 is the number of leaves closest to the root where all m_1 are at the same depth, m_2 is the number of leaves that are the next closest where all m_2 have the same depth, and so on up to m_t which is the number of leaves furthest from the root that are all at the same depth. This was done for the 23 trees described in Appendix A and the resulting multinomials are given below.

$$\binom{8}{1,1,1,1,1,1,2} \quad \binom{8}{1,1,1,1,4} \quad \binom{8}{1,1,1,3,2} \quad \binom{8}{1,1,3,1,2} \quad \binom{8}{1,3,1,1,2}$$

$$\binom{8}{3,1,1,1,2} \quad \binom{8}{1,1,2,4} \quad \binom{8}{1,3,4} \quad \binom{8}{3,1,4} \quad \binom{8}{1,1,2,4}$$

$$\binom{8}{1,2,3,2} \quad \binom{8}{3,3,2} \quad \binom{8}{1,2,3,2} \quad \binom{8}{2,3,1,2} \quad \binom{8}{2,3,1,2}$$

$$\binom{8}{1,1,6} \quad \binom{8}{2,2,4} \quad \binom{8}{2,2,4} \quad \binom{8}{2,2,4} \quad \binom{8}{1,5,2}$$

$$\binom{8}{2,2,4} \quad \binom{8}{1,5,2} \quad \binom{8}{8}$$

The last value is unity since all of the leaves are at depth 3. Hence, any ordering of the leaves will yield prefix codes that are optimal. The sum of all of these multinomials is 46,873. We would thus like to establish ranking and unranking algorithms between these Huffman trees and $\{0, 1, 2, 3, ..., (46, 873) - 1\}$. This would permit the trees to be stored in 16 bits, since $2^{16} = 65, 536 > 46, 873$. Observe that,

$$\binom{n}{m_1,m_2,...,m_t} = \binom{n}{m_1} * \binom{n-m_1}{m_2} * ... * \binom{n-m_1-m_2-...-m_{t-2}}{m_{t-1}}$$

This suggests that the well known method for unranking binomial coefficients can be used successively in a method for unranking multinomials. It can be shown that this is possible by using a mixed-radix numbering system. Constructing the corresponding ranking function is also straightforward. Now that these individual combinatorial objects can be ranked, the entire object needs to be dealt with.

The way to handle this is as follows. If the Huffman tree is isomorphic to the first tree, then the ranking on the leaves of the first tree is returned as the rank of the Huffman tree combinatorial object. If the Huffman tree is isomorphic to the second tree then the rank that is returned is $\binom{8}{1,1,1,1,1,1,2}$ plus the ranking on the leaves of the second tree. If the Huffman tree is isomorphic to the third tree then the rank that is returned is $\binom{8}{1,1,1,1,1,1,2}$ plus $\binom{8}{1,1,1,1,4}$ plus the ranking on the leaves of the third tree, and so on. Which of the 23 non-isomorphic trees is needed is stored effectively in the offset created by successively adding these multinomials together. We defer a formal proof of this method to the full version of this paper.

Efficient ID-Based Blind Signature and Proxy Signature from Bilinear Pairings

Fangguo Zhang and Kwangjo Kim

International Research center for Information Security (IRIS)
Information and Communications University(ICU),
58-4 Hwaam-dong Yusong-ku, Taejon, 305-732 KOREA
{zhfg, kkj}@icu.ac.kr

Abstract. Blind signature and proxy signature are very important technologies in secure e-commerce. Identity-based (simply ID-based) public key cryptosystem can be a good alternative for certificate-based public key setting, especially when efficient key management and moderate security are required. In this paper, we propose a new ID-based blind signature scheme and an ID-based partial delegation proxy signature scheme with warrant based on the bilinear pairings. Also we analyze their security and efficiency. We claim that our new blind signature scheme is more efficient than Zhang and Kim's scheme [27] in Asiacrypt2002.

Keywords: Blind signature, Proxy signature, Bilinear pairings, ID-based cryptography.

1 Introduction

In a certificate-based public key system, before using the public key of a user, the participants must verify the certificate of the user at first. As a consequence, this system requires a large storage and computing time to store and verify each user's public key and the corresponding certificate. In 1984 Shamir [24] proposed ID-based encryption and signature schemes to simplify key management procedures in certificate-based public key setting. Since then, many ID-based encryption and signature schemes have been proposed. The main idea of ID-based cryptosystems is that the identity information of each user works as his/her public key, in other words, the user's public key can be calculated directly from his/her identity rather than being extracted from a certificate issued by a certificate authority (CA). ID-based public key setting can be a good alternative for certificate-based public key setting, especially when efficient key management and moderate security are required.

The bilinear pairings, namely the Weil pairing and the Tate pairing of algebraic curves, are important tools for study on algebraic geometry. Their usage in cryptography goes back to Victor Miller's [18] unpublished paper in 1986, and in particular the results of Menezes-Okamoto-Vanstone [17] and Frey-Rück [7]. However, most of the initial application was to attack elliptic curve or hyperelliptic curve cryptosystems (*i.e.*, using pairings to transform the ECDLP or HCDLP

R. Safavi-Naini and J. Seberry (Eds.): ACISP 2003, LNCS 2727, pp. 312–323, 2003.
© Springer-Verlag Berlin Heidelberg 2003

into a discrete logarithm problem (DLP) in the multiplicative group of a finite field). In the last couple of years, the bilinear pairings have been found various applications in cryptography, they can be used to realize some cryptographic primitives that were previously unknown or impractical [2,3,4,11,22]. More precisely, they are basic tools for construction of ID-based cryptographic schemes, many ID-based cryptographic schemes have been proposed using them. Examples are Boneh-Franklin's ID-based encryption scheme [3], Smart's ID-based authentication key agreement protocol [25], several ID-based signatures schemes [5,10,20, 22,27]. In this paper we concentrate ourselves to design ID-based blind signature and ID-based proxy signature scheme.

Blind signature firstly introduced by Chaum [6] in 1983 plays the central role in cryptographic protocols to provide the anonymity of users in e-cash or e-voting systems. Such signatures allow the user to obtain a signature of a message in a way that the signer learns neither the message nor the resulting signature. ID-based blind signature is attractive since one's public key is simply his/her identity. The first ID-based blind signature scheme was proposed by Zhang and Kim [27] in Asiacrypt2002. Their scheme is based on the bilinear pairings, but the security against the *generic parallel attack* to their ID-based blind signature scheme depends on the difficulty of ROS-problem [23]. In Crypto2002, Wagner [26] claimed that there is subexponential time to break ROS-problem. To be resistant against this attack, the size of q may need to be at least 1,600 bits long. In this paper, we propose a new ID-based blind signature scheme from the bilinear pairings and expect that the security against *generic parallel attack* to our new scheme doesn't depend on the difficulty of ROS-problem.

The concept of proxy signature was first introduced by Mambo, Usuda, and Okamoto in 1996 [16]. A proxy signature scheme consists of three entities: original signer, proxy signer and verifier. If an original signer wants to delegate the signing capability to a proxy signer, he/she uses the original signature key to create a proxy signature key, which will then be sent to the proxy signer. The proxy signer can use the proxy signature key to sign messages on behalf of the original signer. Proxy signatures can be verified using a modified verification equation such that the verifier can be convinced that the signature is generated by the authorized proxy entity of the original signer. There are three types of delegation, full delegation, partial delegation and delegation by warrant. After Mambo *et al.*'s first scheme was announced, many proxy signature schemes have been proposed such as [13,14,19,28]. In [13], S. Kim *et al.* gave a new type of delegation called partial delegation with warrant, which can be considered as the combination of partial delegation and delegation by warrant. In this paper, we will give an ID-based version of partial delegation with warrant proxy signature scheme.

The rest of the paper is organized as follows: The next section gives the definition of ID-based blind signature and proxy signature; Section 3 briefly explains the bilinear pairing and ID-based public key setting from pairings. Section 4 gives a detailed description of our ID-based blind signature scheme. In Section 5, an analysis about our ID-based blind signature scheme is presented. Section 6 and Section 7 give our ID-based partial delegation with warrant proxy signature scheme and its analysis, respectively. Section 8 concludes this paper.

2   ID-Based Blind Signature and Proxy Signature

An ID-based blind signature scheme is considered be the combination of a general blind signature scheme and an ID-based one, *i.e.*, it is a blind signature, but its public key for verification is just the signer's identity. It consists of the following four algorithms, **Setup, Extract, Blind signature issuing protocol**, and **Verification**. The security of an ID-based blind signature scheme consists of two requirements: the blindness property and the non-forgeability. We say *the blind signature scheme is secure* if it satisfies these two requirements. For detailed description of the definition of ID-based blind signature, the readers can refer to [27].

The ID-based proxy signature can be viewed as the combination of a general proxy signature and an ID-based signature. It consists of four participants: a Key Generation Center (KGC) or Trust Authority (TA), an original signer, a proxy signer, verifier, and the following five algorithms, **Setup, Extract, Generation of the proxy key, Proxy signature generation**, and **Verification**.

Like the general proxy signature, an ID-based proxy signature scheme should satisfy the following requirements [14,15,16]:

- **Distinguishability:** Proxy signatures are distinguishable from normal signatures by everyone.
- **Verifiability:** From the proxy signature, the verifier can be convinced of the original signer's agreement on the signed message.
- **Strong non-forgeability:** A designated proxy signer can create a valid proxy signature for the original signer. But the original signer and other third parties who are not designated as a proxy signer cannot create a valid proxy signature.
- **Strong identifiability:** Anyone can determine the identity of the corresponding proxy signer from the proxy signature.
- **Strong non-deniability:** Once a proxy signer creates a valid proxy signature of an original signer, he/she cannot repudiate the signature creation.
- **Prevention of misuse:** The proxy signer cannot use the proxy key for other purposes than generating a valid proxy signature. That is, he/she cannot sign messages that have not been authorized by the original signer.

3   ID-Based Public Key Setting with Pairing

In this section, we briefly describe the basic definition and properties of the bilinear pairing. We also present the ID-based public key setting based on pairing.

3.1   Bilinear Pairings

Let G_1 be a cyclic additive group generated by P, whose order is a prime q, and G_2 be a cyclic multiplicative group of the same order q. A bilinear pairing is a map $e : G_1 \times G_1 \to G_2$ with the following properties:

1. Bilinear: $e(aP, bQ) = e(P, Q)^{ab}$;
2. Non-degenerate: There exists $P, Q \in G_1$ such that $e(P, Q) \neq 1$;
3. Computable: There is an efficient algorithm to compute $e(P, Q)$ for all $P, Q \in G_1$.

Now we describe some mathematical problems in G_1.

- **Discrete Logarithm Problem (DLP):** Given two group elements P and Q, find an integer n, such that $Q = nP$ whenever such an integer exists.
- **Decision Diffie-Hellman Problem (DDHP):** For $a, b, c \in Z_q^*$, given P, aP, bP, cP, decide whether $c \equiv ab \bmod q$.
- **Computational Diffie-Hellman Problem (CDHP):** For $a, b \in Z_q^*$, given P, aP, bP, compute abP.

We assume through this paper that CDHP and DLP are intractable. When the DDHP is easy but the CDHP is hard on the group G, we call G a *Gap Diffie-Hellman (GDH) group*. Such groups can be found on supersingular elliptic curves or hyperelliptic curves over finite field, and the bilinear parings can be derived from the Weil or Tate pairing. We can refer to [3,5,10] for more details.

3.2 ID-Based Public Key Setting Using Pairings

In ID-based public key cryptosystem (IDPKC), everyone's public keys are pre-determined by information that uniquely identifies them, such as name, social security number, email address, *etc.*, rather than an arbitrary string. This concept was first proposed by Shamir [24]. Since then, many researchers devote their effort on ID-based cryptographic schemes. How to construct ID-based schemes using Weil or Tate pairings on supersingular elliptic curves or abelian varieties recently receives much research interest [3,5,9,10,20,22,25].

ID-based public key setting involves a KGC and users. The basic operations consists of **Setup** and **Private Key Extraction** (simply **Extract**). When we use bilinear pairings to construct IDPKC, **Setup** and **Extract** can be implemented as follows:

Let P be a generator of G_1. Remember that G_1 is an additive group of prime order q and the bilinear pairing is given by $e : G_1 \times G_1 \rightarrow G_2$. Define two cryptographic hash functions $H_1 : \{0, 1\}^* \rightarrow Z_q$ and $H_2 : \{0, 1\}^* \rightarrow G_1$.

- **Setup:** KGC chooses a random number $s \in Z_q^*$ and sets $P_{pub} = sP$. The center publishes system parameters $params = \{G_1, G_2, e, q, P, P_{pub}, H_1, H_2\}$, and keeps s as the *master-key*, which is known only by itself.
- **Extract:** A user submits his/her identity information ID to KGC. KGC computes the user's public key as $Q_{ID} = H_2(ID)$, and returns $S_{ID} = sQ_{ID}$ to the user as his/her private key.

4   New ID-Based Blind Signature Scheme

Recently, many ID-based signature schemes have been proposed using the bilinear pairings [5,10,20,22]. In these ID-based signature schemes, Cha-Cheon's scheme [5] is not only efficient but exhibits the provable security relative to CDHP. In this section, we propose a new ID-based blind signature scheme, which can be regarded as the blind version of Cha-Cheon's ID-based signature scheme.

Let G_1 be a GDH group of prime order q. The bilinear pairing is given as $e : G_1 \times G_1 \to G_2$.

[**Setup:**]

KGC publishes system parameters $params = \{G_1, G_2, e, q, P, P_{pub}, H_1, H_2\}$, and keeps s as the *master-key*, which is known only by itself.

[**Extract:**]

Given an identity ID, which implies the public key $Q_{ID} = H_2(ID)$, the private key $S_{ID} = sQ_{ID}$.

[**Blind signature issuing protocol:**]

Suppose that m is the message to be signed. Let $a \in_R$ denote the uniform random selection. The protocol is shown in Fig. 1.

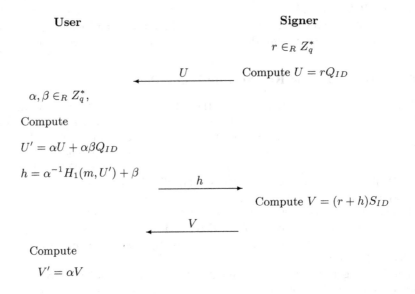

Fig. 1. The blind signature issuing protocol

- The signer randomly chooses a number $r \in_R Z_q^*$, computes $U = rQ_{ID}$, and sends U to the user as a commitment.
- (Blinding) The user randomly chooses $\alpha, \beta \in_R Z_q^*$ as blinding factors. He/She computes $U' = \alpha U + \alpha\beta Q_{ID}$ and $h = \alpha^{-1}H_1(m, U') + \beta$, sends h to the signer.
- (Signing) The signer sends back V, where $V = (r + h)S_{ID}$.
- (Unblinding) The user computes $V' = \alpha V$. He/She outputs $\{m, U', V'\}$.

Then (U', V') is the blind signature of the message m.

[**Verification:**]
Accept the signature if and only if

$$e(V', P) = e(U' + H_1(m, U')Q_{ID}, P_{pub}).$$

Our signature consists of two elements in G_1. In practice, the size of the element in G_1 (elliptic curve group or hyperelliptic curve Jacobians) can be reduced by a factor of 2 with compression techniques.

5   Analysis of the IDBSS

5.1   Correctness

The verification of the signature is justified by the following equations:

$$\begin{aligned}
&e(V', P)\\
&= e(\alpha V, P)\\
&= e((\alpha r + \alpha h)S_{ID}, P)\\
&= e((\alpha r + H_1(m, U') + \alpha\beta)Q_{ID}, P_{pub})\\
&= e((\alpha r + \alpha\beta)Q_{ID} + H_1(m, U')Q_{ID}, P_{pub})\\
&= e(U' + H_1(m, U')Q_{ID}, P_{pub})
\end{aligned}$$

5.2   Efficiency

We compare our blind signature scheme with the scheme in [27] from computation overhead and summarize the result in Table 1 (we ignore the operation of hash in all schemes). We denote Pa the pairing operation, Pm the point scalar multiplication on G_1, Ad the point addition on G_1, Mu the multiplication in Z_q, Div the division in Z_q and $MuG2$ the multiplication in G_2. From Table 1, it is

Table 1. Comparison of our blind scheme and the scheme in [27]

Schemes	Blind signature issuing	Verification
Proposed scheme	User : $3Pm + 1Ad + 1Mu + 1Div$ Signer : $2Pm$	$2Pa + 1Pm + 1Ad$
The scheme in[27]	User : $1Pa + 3Pm + 3Ad$ Signer : $3Pm + 1Ad$	$2Pa + 1Pm + 1MuG2$

easy to see that our scheme is more efficient than the scheme in [27]. We note that the computation of the pairing is the most time-consuming. Although there has been many papers discussing the complexity of pairings and how to speed up the pairing computation [1,8], the computation of the pairing still remains time-consuming. In the blind signature issuing protocol of our scheme, the user need not compute the pairing, but there is one pairing operation in [27] scheme.

The efficiency of the system is of paramount importance when the number of verifications is considerably large (*e.g.*, when a bank issues a large number of electronic coins and the customer wishes to verify the correctness of the coins). Our scheme is very efficient when we consider the batch verification. Assuming that $(U_1', V_1'), (U_2', V_2'), \cdots, (U_n', V_n')$ are ID-based blind signatures on messages $m_1, m_2, \cdots, m_n$ which issued by the signer with identity ID. The batch verification is then to test if the following equation holds:

$$e(\sum_{i=1}^{n} V_i', P) = e(\sum_{i=1}^{n} U_i' + (\sum_{i=1}^{n} H_1(m_i, U_i'))Q_{ID}, P_{pub}).$$

If we verify these signatures one by one, then we need $2nPa + nPm + nAd$, but at above batch verification, we only need $2Pa + 1Pm + 3(n-1)Ad$. Similar discussion can be applied to Cha-Cheon's ID-based signature scheme [5].

5.3   Security Proofs

Blindess Property. To prove the blindness we show that given a valid signature (m, U', V') and any view (U, h, V), there always exists a unique pair of blinding factors $\alpha, \beta \in Z_q^*$. Since the blinding factors $\alpha, \beta \in Z_q^*$ are chosen randomly, the blindness of the signature scheme naturally satisfy. We can find more formal definition about the blindness in [12,27].

Given a valid signature (m, U', V') and any view (U, h, V), then the following equations must hold for $\alpha, \beta \in Z_q^*$:

$$U' = \alpha U + \alpha\beta Q_{ID} \qquad (1)$$

$$h = \alpha^{-1} H_1(m, U') + \beta \pmod{q} \qquad (2)$$

$$V' = \alpha V \qquad (3)$$

It is obvious that $\alpha \in Z_q^*$ is existed uniquely from Eq (3) denoted by $log_V V'$. So we can get $\beta = h - (log_V V')^{-1} H_1(m, U')$ from Eq (2), and it is unique in Z_q. Next, we show that such α, β satisfy the first equation too. Obviously, due to the *non − degenerate* of the bilinear pairing, we have

$$U' = \alpha U + \alpha\beta Q_{ID} \Leftrightarrow e(U', P_{pub}) = e(\alpha U + \alpha\beta Q_{ID}, P_{pub})$$

So we only need to show that such α and β satisfy

$$e(U', P_{pub}) = e(\alpha U + \alpha\beta Q_{ID}, P_{pub}).$$

Notice that (m, U', V') is a valid signature, *i.e.*,

$$e(V', P) = e(U' + H_1(m, U')Q_{ID}, P_{pub}).$$

We have

$$
\begin{aligned}
&e(\alpha U + \alpha\beta Q_{ID}, P_{pub}) \\
&= e(log_V V'U + log_V V' \cdot (h - (log_V V')^{-1}H_1(m, U'))Q_{ID}, P_{pub}) \\
&= e(log_V V' \cdot rQ_{ID} + log_V V' \cdot hQ_{ID}, P_{pub})e(H_1(m, U')Q_{ID}, P_{pub})^{-1} \\
&= e(log_V V' \cdot (r + h)S_{ID}, P)e(V', P)^{-1}e(U', P_{pub}) \\
&= e((log_V V')V, P)e(V', P)^{-1}e(U', P_{pub}) \\
&= e(U', P_{pub})
\end{aligned}
$$

Thus the blinding factors always exist which lead to the same relation defined in the blind signature issuing protocol.

Non-forgeability. Assume that $\mathcal{A}$ is the adversary (he/she can be a user or any third party) holding the system parameters $params = \{G_1, G_2, e, q, P, P_{pub}, H_1, H_2\}$ and the identity public key Q_{ID} of the signer ID. $\mathcal{A}$ tries to forge a valid message-signature of the signer.

First, we assume that $\mathcal{A}$ performs the ID attack, *i.e.*, $\mathcal{A}$ queries **Extract** q_E ($q_E > 0$) times with (PARAMS, $ID_i \neq ID$) for $i = 1, \cdots, q_E$. **Extract** returns to $\mathcal{A}$ the q_E corresponding secret key S_{ID_i}. We assume that q_E is limited by a polynomial in k. If $\mathcal{A}$ can get a $(ID'_i, S_{ID'_i})$, such that $H_1(ID'_i) = H_1(ID) = Q_{ID}$, then he/she can forge a valid blind signature of the signer ID. But since H_1 is random oracle, **Extract** generates random numbers with uniform distributions. This means that $\mathcal{A}$ learns nothing from query results.

Next we assume that $\mathcal{A}$ had interacted with the signer ID, and let (U, h, V) be the view in the blind signature issuing phase. Since $V = (r + h)S_{ID}$, and $\mathcal{A}$ knows V, h, from V to get S_{ID}, $\mathcal{A}$ must know r, but r is chosen randomly by the signer. $\mathcal{A}$ knows $U = rQ_{ID}$, but from U to get r, this is DLP in G_1. We assume that DLP in G_1 is intractable, so $\mathcal{A}$ cannot get the private information of the signer at the blind signature issuing phase.

On the other hand, the signature and the verifying equation are same as Cha-Cheon's ID-based signature scheme. For any message m, if $\mathcal{A}$ can construct U' and V', such that $e(V', P) = e(U' + H_1(m, U')Q_{ID}, P_{pub})$, then $\mathcal{A}$ can forge a valid signature of Cha-Cheon's ID-based signature scheme on the message m. Due to Cha-Cheon's proof on their ID-based signature scheme (*i.e.*, Cha-Cheon's scheme is proven to be secure against existential forgery on adaptively chosen message and ID attacks, under the hardness assumption of CDHP and the random oracle model), we claim that this attack is impossible.

The most powerful attack on blind signature is *one-more signature forgery* introduced by Pointcheval and Stern in [21]. But at the moment we believe that their method can't be applied to our scheme, since multiple key components involve their blind signature scheme, while only one single private key is engaged in our scheme. Zhang and Kim proved that the security against the *generic parallel attack* to their ID-based blind signature scheme depends on the difficulty of ROS-problem. Since the signature of our ID-based blind signature scheme consists of two elements in G_1 (the signatures of Zhang-Kim's scheme in [27] and Schnorr scheme [23] are all consisted by one element in base group and one hash value), we believe that the security against *generic parallel attack* to our scheme doesn't depend on the difficulty of ROS-problem. We remain an open problem to find a formal proof against *one-more signature forgery* on our scheme.

6   ID-Based Proxy Signature Scheme from Pairings

Proxy signatures are very useful tools when one needs to delegate his/her signing capability to other party. In this section, we present an ID-based proxy signature scheme from pairings. Our ID-based proxy signature scheme is similar to Kim *et al.*'s scheme [13] which is based on certificate-based public key setting.

[**Setup:**]
KGC publishes system parameters $params = \{G_1, G_2, e, q, P, P_{pub}, H_1, H_2\}$, and keeps s as the *master-key*, which is known only by itself.

[**Extract:**]
Let Alice be the original signer with identity public key Q_A and private key S_A, and Bob be the proxy signer with identity public key Q_B and private key S_B.

[**Generation of the proxy key:**]
To delegate the signing capacity to proxy signer, the original signer Alice uses Hess's ID-based signature scheme [10] to make the signed warrant m_w. There is an explicit description of the delegation relation in the warrant m_w. If the following process is finished successfully, Bob gets a proxy key S_P.

- After computing $r_A = e(P, P)^k$, where $k \in_R Z_q^*$, $c_A = H_1(m_w \| r_A)$ and $U_A = c_A S_A + kP$, Alice sends (m_w, c_A, U_A) to a proxy signer Bob.
- Bob verifies the validity of the signature on m_w: Compute

$$r_A = e(U_A, P)e(Q_A, P_{pub})^{-c_A},$$

and accept this signature if and only if $c_A = H_1(m_w \| r_A)$. If the signature is valid, Bob computes the proxy key S_P as $S_P = c_A S_B + U_A$.

Of course, we can choose others ID-based signature schemes as the basic signature scheme, such as [5] [20] or [22].

[**Proxy signature generation:**]
Bob uses Hess's ID-based signature scheme [10] (takes the signing key as S_P) and obtains a signature (c_P, U_P) for any delegated message m. Here $c_P = H_1(m \| r_P)$, $U_P = c_P S_P + k_P P$, where $r_P = e(P, P)^{k_P}$, $k_P \in_R Z_q^*$. The valid proxy signature will be the tuple

$$< m, c_P, U_P, m_w, r_A >.$$

[**Verification:**]
A recipient can verify the validity of the proxy signature as follows: Compute

$$r_P = e(U_P, P)(e(Q_A + Q_B, P_{pub})^{H_1(m_w \| r_A)} \cdot r_A)^{-c_P}.$$

Accept the signature if and only if $c_P = H_1(m \| r_P)$.

7 Analysis of the Proposed Protocol

7.1 Correctness

The verification of the signature is justified by the following equations:

$$e(U_P, P)(e(Q_A + Q_B, P_{pub})^{H_1(m_w || r_A)} \cdot r_A)^{-c_P}$$
$$= e(U_P, P)(e(c_A \cdot (S_A + S_B), P) \cdot r_A)^{-c_P}$$
$$= e(U_P, P)(e(S_P - kP, P) \cdot r_A)^{-c_P}$$
$$= e(U_P, P)(e(S_P, P) \cdot e(-kP, P) \cdot r_A)^{-c_P}$$
$$= e(c_P S_P + k_P P, P)e(S_P, P)^{-c_P}$$
$$= e(k_P P, P)$$
$$= r_P$$

So, we have: $c_P = H_1(m || r_P)$.

7.2 Security

We will show that our ID-based proxy signature scheme satisfies all the requirements stated in Section 2.

- **Distinguishability:** This is obvious, because there is a warrant m_w in a valid proxy signature, at the same time, this warrant m_w and the public keys of the original signer and the proxy signer must occur in the verification equation of proxy signature.
- **Verifiability:** The valid proxy signature for message m will be the tuple $< m, c_P, U_P, m_w, r_A >$, and from the construction of (c_P, U_P, r_A) and the verification phase, the verifier can be convinced that the proxy signer has the original signer's signature on the warrant m_w. In general the warrant contains the identity information and the limit of the delegated signing capacity and so satisfies the verifiability.
- **Strong non-forgeability:** The third adversary who wants to forge the proxy signature of the message m' for the proxy signer Bob and the original signer Alice must have the original signer's signature on a warrant m_w, but cannot forge this signature, since the original signer Alice uses Hess's ID-based signature scheme: This signature scheme is proven to be secure against existential forgery on adaptive chosen-message attacks under the random oracle model assumption. On the other hand, the original signer cannot create a valid proxy signature. Since the proxy signature is obtained by the proxy signer using Hess's ID-based signature scheme [10] (take the signing key as the proxy key S_P), and the proxy key includes the private key S_B of the proxy signer.
- **Strong identifiability:** It contains the warrant m_w in a valid proxy signature, so anyone can determine the identity of the corresponding proxy signer from the warrant m_w.

- **Strong non-deniability:** As the identifiability, the valid proxy signature contains the warrant m_w, which must be verified in the verification phase, it cannot be modified by the proxy signer. Thus once a proxy signer creates a valid proxy signature of an original signer, he cannot repudiate the signature creation.
- **Prevention of misuse:** In our proxy signature scheme, using the warrant m_w, we had determined the limit of the delegated signing capacity in the warrant m_w, so the proxy signer cannot sign some messages that have not been authorized by the original signer.

Like the discussion in [15], our ID-based proxy signature scheme need not the secure channel for the delivery of the signed warrant. More precisely, the original signer Alice can send (m_w, c_A, U_A) to a proxy signer Bob through a public channel, in other word, any third adversary can get the original signer's signature on warrant m_w. Even this, the third adversary forges the proxy signature of the message m' for the proxy signer Bob and the original signer Alice, this is equivalent to forge a Hess's ID-based signature with some public key Q, here $e(c_A(Q_A + Q_B), P_{pub}) \cdot r_A = e(Q, P_{pub})$.

8   Conclusion

ID-based public key cryptosystem can be an alternative for certificate-based public key infrastructures. Blind signature and proxy signature are important in secure e-commerce. In this paper, we proposed a new ID-based blind signature scheme and an ID-based partial delegation proxy signature scheme with warrant. Both are based on the bilinear pairings. Also we analyze their security and efficiency. Our blind signature scheme is more efficient than Zhang and Kim's scheme in Asiacrypt2002, and the security against *generic parallel attack* doesn't depend on the difficulty of ROS-problem.

For a further work, we expect that we can find a security proof about our ID-based blind signature scheme against *one-more signature forgery*.

References

1. P.S.L.M. Barreto, H.Y. Kim, B.Lynn, and M.Scott, *Efficient algorithms for pairing-based cryptosystems*, Advances in Cryptology-Crypto 2002, LNCS 2442, pp.354–368, Springer-Verlag, 2002.
2. A. Boldyreva, *Efficient threshold signature, multisignature and blind signature schemes based on the Gap-Diffie-Hellman -group signature scheme*, Public Key Cryptography – PKC 2003, LNCS 2139, pp.31–46, Springer-Verlag, 2003.
3. D. Boneh and M. Franklin, *Identity-based encryption from the Weil pairing*, Advances in Cryptology-Crypto 2001, LNCS 2139, pp.213–229, Springer-Verlag, 2001.
4. D. Boneh, B. Lynn, and H. Shacham, *Short signatures from the Weil pairing*, In C. Boyd, editor, Advances in Cryptology-Asiacrypt 2001, LNCS 2248, pp.514–532, Springer-Verlag, 2001.
5. J.C. Cha and J.H. Cheon, *An identity-based signature from gap Diffie-Hellman groups*, Public Key Cryptography – PKC 2003, LNCS 2139, pp.18–30, Springer-Verlag, 2003.

6. D. Chaum, *Blind signatures for untraceable payments*, Advances in Cryptology-Crypto 82, Plenum, NY, pp.199–203, 1983.

7. G. Frey and H.Rück, *A remark concerning m-divisibility and the discrete logarithm in the divisor class group of curves*, Mathematics of Computation, 62, pp.865–874, 1994.

8. S. D. Galbraith, K. Harrison, and D. Soldera, *Implementing the Tate pairing*, ANTS 2002, LNCS 2369, pp.324–337, Springer-Verlag, 2002.

9. C. Gentry and A. Silverberg, *Hierarchical ID-based cryptography*, Proc. of Asiacrpt2002, LNCS 2501, pp. 548–566, Springer-Verlag, 2002.

10. F. Hess, *Efficient identity based signature schemes based on pairings*, SAC 2002, LNCS 2595, pp.310–324, Springer-Verlag, 2002.

11. A. Joux, *A one round protocol for tripartite Diffie-Hellman*, ANTS IV, LNCS 1838, pp.385–394, Springer-Verlag, 2000.

12. A. Juels, M. Luby and R. Ostrovsky, *Security of blind digital signatures*, Advances in Cryptology-Crypto 97, LNCS 1294, pp.150–164, Springer-Verlag, 1997.

13. S. Kim, S. Park, and D. Won, *Proxy signatures, revisited*, In Pro. of ICICS 97, LNCS 1334, Springer-Verlag, pp. 223–232, 1997.

14. B. Lee, H. Kim and K. Kim, *Secure mobile agent using strong non-designated proxy signature*, Proc. of ACISP2001, LNCS 2119, pp.474–486, Springer Verlag, 2001.

15. J.Y. Lee, J.H. Cheon and S. Kim, *An analysis of proxy signatures: Is a secure channel necessary?*, CT-RSA 2003, LNCS 2612, pp. 68–79, Springer-Verlag, 2003.

16. M. Mambo, K. Usuda, and E. Okamoto, *Proxy signature: Delegation of the power to sign messages*, In IEICE Trans. Fundamentals, Vol. E79-A, No. 9, Sep., pp. 1338–1353, 1996.

17. A. Menezes, T. Okamoto, and S. Vanstone, *Reducing elliptic curve logarithms to logarithms in a finite field*, IEEE Transaction on Information Theory, Vol.39, pp.1639–1646, 1993.

18. V. Miller, *Short programs for functions on curves*, unpublished manuscript, 1986.

19. T. Okamoto, M. Tada and E. Okamoto, *Extended proxy signatures for smart cards*, ISW'99, LNCS 1729, Springer-Verlag, pp. 247–258, 1999.

20. K.G. Paterson, *ID-based signatures from pairings on elliptic curves*, Electron. Lett., Vol.38, No.18, pp.1025–1026, 2002.

21. D. Pointcheval and J. Stern, *Security arguments for digital signatures and blind signatures*, Journal of Cryptology, Vol.13, No.3, pp.361–396, 2000.

22. R. Sakai, K. Ohgishi, M. Kasahara, *Cryptosystems based on pairing*, SCIS 2000-C20, Jan. 2000, Okinawa, Japan.

23. C. P. Schnorr, *Security of blind discrete log signatures against interactive attacks*, ICICS 2001, LNCS 2229, pp. 1–12, Springer-Verlag, 2001.

24. A. Shamir, *Identity-based cryptosystems and signature schemes*, Advances in Cryptology-Crypto 84, LNCS 196, pp.47–53, Springer-Verlag, 1984.

25. N.P. Smart, *An identity based authenticated key agreement protocol based on the Weil pairing*, Electron. Lett., Vol.38, No.13, pp.630–632, 2002.

26. D. Wagner, *A generalized birthday problem*, Advances in Cryptology-Crypto 2002, LNCS 2442, pp.288–303, Springer-Verlag, 2002.

27. F. Zhang and K. Kim, *ID-based blind signature and ring signature from pairings*, Proc. of Asiacrpt2002, LNCS 2501, pp. 533–547, Springer-Verlag, 2002.

28. K. Zhang, *Threshold proxy signature schemes*. 1997 Information Security Workshop, Japan, Sep., 1997, pp.191–197.

Digital Signature Schemes with Restriction on Signing Capability

Jung Yeon Hwang, Hyun-Jeong Kim, Dong Hoon Lee, and JongIn Lim

Center for Information and Security Technologies(CIST),
Korea University, Seoul, Korea,
{videmot, khj}@cist.korea.ac.kr,
{donghlee, jilim}@korea.ac.kr

Abstract. In some practical circumstances, the ability of a signer should be restricted. In group signature schemes, a group member may be allowed to generate signatures up to a certain number of times according to his/her position in the group. In proxy signature schemes, an original signer may want to allow a proxy signer to generate a certain number of signatures on behalf of the original signer. In the paper, we discuss signature schemes, called *c-times signature schemes*, that restrict the signing ability of a signer up to c times for pre-defined value c at set-up. We formally define the notion and the security model of c-times signature schemes. In fact, c-times signature schemes can be classified into two types according to restriction features: one with an explicit limitation, called a c-times signature scheme, and the other with an implicit limitation, called an implicit c-times signature scheme. We present two instances of implicit c-times signature schemes and then give proofs of the security. For one instance we suggest ^cS which is a composition of a signature scheme S based on the discrete logarithm and Feldman's VSS. For the other we present ^cDSA based on DSA. Our basic approach can be applied to signature schemes such as HVZK based signature schemes.

1   Introduction

BACKGROUND. The notion of a digital signature is one of the most fundamental and useful inventions of modern cryptography. Since a public key cryptosystem based on a trapdoor function model is introduced in the Diffe-Hellman paper [6], various signature schemes have been suggested to meet various needs in practical circumstances. A signature scheme allows a user, who has previously generated a secret key and the corresponding public key (which is made public), to generate a digital signature for a message. While anybody who knows the signer's public key can verify signatures, forging the signer's signature (i.e., generating valid signatures for messages not previously signed by the signer) is computationally infeasible without knowledge of the secret key.

Digital signature schemes can be classified into two types according to the ability of the signer. The first type, of which the first realization is the

R. Safavi-Naini and J. Seberry (Eds.): ACISP 2003, LNCS 2727, pp. 324–335, 2003.
© Springer-Verlag Berlin Heidelberg 2003

RSA system [18], is a signature scheme without any restriction on generating signatures. The second type is a signature scheme with a limitation on the number of signatures to be created. The examples of this type are one-time signature schemes based on a general one-way function [1,12]. One-time signature schemes are digital signature mechanisms which can be used to sign, at most, one message; otherwise, signatures can be forged.

We call a signature scheme with restriction on the signing ability a c-times signature scheme. This quantumized signing capability is applicable for various situations as follows. A company organized in a hierarchical structure (e.g., board of directors, supervisors and executives) may require that a member of the company generates signatures up to a certain number of times according to his/her position in the company. In group signature schemes [5], a member in a higher level is considered to have more representatibility for the group, and hence should be given more signing capability than members in a lower level. For another example we can use the quantumized capability to solve the delegation issue. A proxy signature scheme [14] is a signature scheme in which an original signer delegates his/her signing capability to a proxy signer and the proxy signer creates a signature on behalf of the original signer. An original signer may want to control the proxy signer by delegating the restricted signing capability.

The c-times signature schemes can be used for the temporary restriction of signing ability while the based ordinary signature system is maintained. Temporarily converting an ordinary signature scheme into a c-times signature scheme might be necessary when the board (or court) wants to restrict the ordinary signer who is suspected of illegal behavior. After the signer is proven to be innocent, he can be allowed to reuse the previous signature scheme by removing the restriction. The c-times signature schemes can be applicable to various situations which need the value of rarity or restriction.

Besides constant times signature schemes based on a general one-way function, we investigate schemes based on trapdoor one-way functions such as the DSA system. We are motivated by the diversity of the assumptions such as the integer factoring problem or the discrete logarithm problem on which the securities of the schemes are based.

OUR RESULTS. The purpose of this paper is to discuss the concept of constant-times signature schemes. The paper first classifies c-times signature schemes according to restriction features. One type has an explicit c-times property, called c-times signature scheme where generating more than c valid signatures is not possible, and the other has an implicit property, called *implicit* c-times signature scheme where generating more than c valid signatures is possible, but a signature is forgeable with more than c valid signatures. The latter includes one-time related signature schemes.

In the security model of c-times signature schemes we need a new attack model. An adversary of this scheme is allowed to use c or less valid signatures. For examples, in the known message attack (KMA) signatures less than the pre-determined number c are available to the adversary. Also in the (adaptive) chosen message attack (CMA), the adversary gets (adaptive) access to signing oracle at most c times. This aspect is quite different from the usual attack model in ordinary signature schemes.

In addition, we present two instances of implicit c-times signature schemes. These instances reveal the private key if the signer generates $c + 1$ or more signatures. One instance is based on the discrete logarithm(DL) and the Feldman's verifiable $(c + 1, c + 1)$-secret sharing scheme [9] where a public key could be reused as a public parameter in Feldman's VSS scheme. The other is based on the DSA. This scheme precomputes the commitment part of a DSA signature, which is attached to the public key. The basic approach can be applied to other signature schemes such as HVZK(honest verifier zero knowledge) based signature schemes. We show that both schemes satisfy the security goals defined in the paper.

RELATED WORK. An explicit c-times signature scheme was appeared in [7] without formal treatment where a credential center is used to insure the bounded life-span aspects. We formalized the notion of an explicit c-times signature scheme. The implicit c-times signing has been extensively dealt with in one-time related signatures in [1,12], which are based on a general one-way function. Our implicit scheme seems to be the first treatment of restricted signing capability not based on a general one-way function, but it reflects existing work.

For the application of restriction, there have been approach based on exposure of identity. Electronic cash schemes in [3,16] require that users are limited to pay only once and double-spending results in exposure of identity.

2   Definitions

In this section we review definitions. We refer to [10] for a part of the following signature definitions in detail.

NOTATION. Let $\{0,1\}^*$ denote the set of infinite binary strings and $\{0,1\}^n$ the set of binary strings of length n. A real-valued function $\epsilon(n)$ is *negligible* if for every $c > 0$, there exists $n_c > 0$ such that $\epsilon(n) < 1/n^c$ for all $n > n_c$. The notation $u \xleftarrow{R} S$ denotes that u is selected randomly from set S.

2.1   Signature Schemes

As usual a signature scheme is described via polynomial-time key generation, signing and verification algorithms.

- The randomized key generation algorithm KG is a polynomial-time algorithm which takes input 1^κ for the security parameter κ and outputs a pair of keys (sk, pk). sk is the signing key of the signer, which is kept secret, and pk is the verification key which is made public.

- The randomized signing algorithm Sig is a polynomial-time algorithm which takes as input the secret key sk and a message m from the associate message space $\mathcal{M}$, internally flips some coins and outputs a signature σ; $\sigma \leftarrow \mathsf{Sig}_{sk}(m)$.
- The deterministic verification algorithm Ver is a polynomial-time algorithm, which takes as input the signature σ, its corresponding message m and the public key pk, and returns either 1 or 0. With output value 1, we say that σ is a valid signature of a message m.

The security of signature schemes addresses two issues : attack models and security goals. Security goals are what we want to achieve against breaking a signature scheme. For the kinds of "breaks" we consider a scheme secure against *Existential Forgery*. This means any PPT (probabilistic polynomial time) adversary $\mathcal{F}$ should have a negligible probability of generating a valid signature of a new message which may be nonsensical or random. This security goal is existential unforgeability, denoted by EUF. Attack models are about what are the capabilities of adversary. In the known message attack, $\mathcal{F}$ is given access to signatures of messages, which are known to him but are not chosen by him. In the (adaptive) chosen message attack, the adversary $\mathcal{F}$ is given (adaptive) oracle access to the signing algorithm. The resulting security notion is denoted by EUF-ATK where ATK means attack model. The advantage $\mathbf{Adv}_{S,\mathcal{F}}^{EUF-ATK}$ in breaking S is defined as the probability that $\mathcal{F}$ outputs a valid signature for a new message under ATK model. The scheme S is said to be EUF-secure against the adversary under ATK model if $\mathbf{Adv}_{S,\mathcal{F}}^{EUF-ATK}(\cdot)$ is negligible for every forger $\mathcal{F}$ with polynomial running time in the security parameter κ.

2.2   Verifiable (t, n)-Secret Sharing

A secret sharing scheme is a protocol between a dealer who wants to share a secret and a group of n players who receive shares of the secret. In this scheme only certain subgroups of them can later reconstruct the secret. Verifiable Secret Sharing(VSS) was proposed first in [4] to overcome the problem of dishonest dealers. In a VSS scheme shareholders can verify the validity of their shares.

VERIFIABLE (t, n)-SECRET SHARING SCHEME. Let U be the set of shareholders, $\{P_1, ..., P_n\}$. Suppose Γ_t is an access structure defined by $\Gamma_t := \{A \mid A \in 2^{\{1,...,t\}} \wedge |A| \geq t\}$. For a given secret value sec a verifiable (t, n)-secret sharing scheme $(1 \leq t \leq n)$ consists of four algorithms : (t, n)-VSS=(PG, Share, Verify, Recover). The randomized PG takes as input 1^ℓ and the secret value sec where ℓ is the security parameter, and outputs public parameter $\leftarrow pp$. The randomized secret sharing algorithm Share takes as input the secret value sec and a random number u, internally flips some coins and outputs a share. The dealer executes the sharing algorithm n-times and outputs $\{s_1, ..., s_n\}$: for $1 \leq i \leq n$, $u \overset{R}{\leftarrow} \{0,1\}^*$, $s_i \leftarrow \mathsf{Share}(sec, u)$. $\mathsf{Share}(sec, \cdot)$ is denoted by $\mathsf{Share}_{sec}(\cdot)$. Then the dealer sends each share s_i secretly to P_i $(1 \leq i \leq n)$. The deterministic algorithm Verify which takes as input a share s_i and the public parameter pp, returns **true** or **false**. The deterministic algorithm Recover which takes as input an access instance $\{s_i \mid i \in A\}$, returns the secret value sec. We say that a (t,n)-VSS has the correctness and verifiability properties.

(Correctness) $\forall i\ (1 \leq i \leq n),\ u_i \overset{R}{\leftarrow} \{0,1\}^*, s_i \leftarrow \mathsf{Share}(sec, u_i) \Rightarrow \forall i \in A,\ \mathsf{Verify}(s_i, pp) = \mathbf{true}$,
(Verifiability) $\forall A \in \Gamma_t$: $\forall i \in A,\ \mathsf{Verify}(s_i, pp) = \mathbf{true} \Rightarrow \mathsf{Recover}(\{s_i \mid i \in A\}) = sec$.

SECURITY. For all $A' \notin \Gamma_t$ it should be computationally infeasible to calculate sec from $\{s_i \mid i \in A'\}$. That is, only those coalitions of participants defined by the access structure A are allowed to recover the original secret. This security goal is denoted by UREC. We suppose that a PPT adversary $\mathcal{A}$ who on input public parameter pp and $t-1$ is allowed to ask sharing oracle $Share_{sec}(\cdot)$ adaptively up to $t-1$ queries. Namely, $\mathcal{A}$ can get at most $t-1$ valid shares. This adversary model is denoted by $\mathcal{A}^{Share_{sec}(\cdot)}(pp, t-1)$. We define an experiment of running the adversary $\mathcal{A}$ in an attack on a (t,n)-VSS as follows.

Experiment $\mathbf{Exp}^{UREC}_{(t,n)\text{-VSS},\mathcal{A}}$

    Let $pp \overset{R}{\leftarrow} \mathsf{PG}(1^\ell, sec)$.   Let $s' \leftarrow \mathcal{A}^{Share_{sec}(\cdot)}(pp, t-1)$
    If $s' = sec$ then return 1; otherwise return 0

The advantage of $\mathcal{A}$ in breaking (t,n)-VSS is the function $\mathbf{Adv}^{UREC}_{(t,n)-\text{VSS},\mathcal{A}}$ defined as $\mathbf{Adv}^{UREC}_{(t,n)-\text{VSS},\mathcal{A}} = \Pr[\mathbf{Exp}^{UREC}_{(t,n)-\text{VSS},\mathcal{A}}=1]$ where the probability is over all the random choices made in the experiment. We say that a (t,n)-VSS is secure if the function $\mathbf{Adv}^{UREC}_{(t,n)-\text{VSS},\mathcal{A}}$ is negligible for any adversary $\mathcal{A}$ whose running time is polynomial in the security parameter ℓ.

3 Signature Schemes with Restriction on Signing Capability

3.1 The Concept

First we consider how to restrict the signing capability of a signer. In fact this feature is a negative (or maximum) threshold in the sense that as the number of times of signing increases, the life of the scheme decreases. The specific number of times (say c) is a deadline. Naturally, to achieve the goal we can approach in two directions according to the limitation feature as follows; one depends on the scheme itself and the other on a signer. In the first approach, after c times of signing, the signature scheme itself becomes not available, i.e. the signing key cannot be used to make any more valid signatures. We call the schemes with this property explicit c-times signature schemes. The second approach uses "penalty" for a signer who has signed excessively even though a signature scheme itself cannot prohibit a signer from signing more than c-times. This is a sort of implicit limitation feature which deters a signer from generating $c + 1$ or more signatures. But in schemes with implicit limitation even a (malicious) signer creates the $(c+i)$-th signature which passes the verification. Therefore the role of the penalty is important. We call the schemes with this property *implicitly limited c-times signature schemes*.

Based on the discussion above, we can classify signature scheme with respect to signing capability from one-time to unlimited (or polynomial times on the security parameter) capability. Implicitly limited signature schemes play a role as a bridge between c-times signature schemes and unlimited (or polynomial times) signature schemes. In fact, any ordinary signature schemes can be transformed into implicitly limited c-times signature schemes by just putting penalties on signers. We consider these schemes in the next section.

3.2   c-Times Signature Scheme

We formalize the notion of c-times signature schemes as follows.

Definition 1. *(c-times signature scheme)*

A c-times signature scheme is a three-tuple $^cS = (^cKG, ^cSig, ^cVer)$.

- *The randomized key generation algorithm* ^cKG *is a polynomial-time algorithm which takes input* 1^κ *for the security parameter* κ *and outputs a pair of keys (sk, pk). sk is the signing key of the signer, which is kept secret, and pk is the verification key which is made public.*
- *The randomized signing algorithm* ^cSig *is a polynomial-time algorithm which takes as input the secret key sk and an i-th message* m_i *from the associate message space* $\mathcal{M}$, *internally flips some coins, check the counter and outputs a signature* $^c\sigma_i$; $^c\sigma_i \leftarrow ^cSig_{sk}(m_i)$ *if* $i \leq c$ *and* $^c\sigma_i = \perp$ *otherwise.*
- *The deterministic verification algorithm* ^cVer *is a polynomial-time algorithm, which takes as input the signature* $^c\sigma_i$, *its corresponding message* m_i *and the public key pk, and returns either 1 or 0. In the former case we say that* $^c\sigma_i$ *is a valid signature of a message* m_i.

Definition 2. *(Corretness of c-times signature scheme) We say that the c-times signature scheme* ^cS *is correct if* $\forall (sk, pk) \in \{^cKG(1^\kappa)\}$, $\{(^c\sigma_i, m_i) | 1 \leq i \leq c$, $^c\sigma_i \leftarrow ^cSig_{sk}(m_i), 1 \leftarrow ^cVer(pk, m_i, ^c\sigma_i)$, $m_i \in \mathcal{M}\}$, $^c\sigma' \leftarrow ^cSig_{sk}(m')$ *and* $^c\sigma' \notin \{^c\sigma_1, ..., ^c\sigma_c\} \Rightarrow 0 \leftarrow ^cVer(pk, m', ^c\sigma')$ *with overwhelming probability.*

SECURITY. In contrast to the attack model of an ordinary signature scheme the attack model of a c-times signature scheme should be required the restriction of the amount of information an adversary can have and the number of queries an adversary can ask to a signer. For examples, in the (adaptive) chosen message attack(CMA), the adversary gets (adaptive) access to a signing oracle at most c times. Thus we need a new attack model for a c-times signature scheme, i.e. the restricted attack model. This attack model is denoted by ^cATK. It is easy to see that ATK secure scheme implies ^cATK secure scheme where ATK means KMA or CMA. For the security goal we consider the strong existential unforgeability denoted by sEUF since the restriction is imposed on the number of signatures, not messages, in c-times signature schemes.

We formally define an experiment of running the adversary $\mathcal{F}$ in an attack on c-times signature scheme ${}^cS = (KG, Sig, Ver)$ as follows. The public key and index c are provided as an input to $\mathcal{F}$. $\mathcal{F}^{Sig_{sk}(\cdot)}(pk, c)$ is an adversary that has an access to signing oracle $Sig_{sk}(\cdot)$ at most c-times.

> Experiment $\mathbf{Exp}_{{}^cS, \mathcal{F}}^{sEUF-{}^cCMA}$
>
> Let $(pk, sk) \xleftarrow{R} KG.$ Let $(m, \sigma) \leftarrow \mathcal{F}^{Sig_{sk}(\cdot)}(pk, c).$
> If $Ver_{pk}(m, \sigma) = 1$ and σ was not returned to $\mathcal{F}$ by its oracle,
> then return 1; otherwise return 0

The advantage of $\mathcal{F}$ in its attack on ${}^cS$ is the function $\mathbf{Adv}_{{}^cS, \mathcal{F}}^{sEUF-{}^cCMA}$ defined as $\mathbf{Adv}_{{}^cS, \mathcal{F}}^{sEUF-{}^cCMA}(k) = \Pr[\mathbf{Exp}_{{}^cS, \mathcal{F}}^{sEUF-{}^cCMA}=1]$ where the probability is over all the random choices made in the experiment. We say that a c-times signature scheme ${}^cS$ is secure in the sense of sEUF-${}^cCMA$ if the function $\mathbf{Adv}_{{}^cS, \mathcal{F}}^{sEUF-{}^cCMA}(\cdot)$ is negligible for any adversary $\mathcal{F}$ whose running time is polynomial in the security parameter κ.

3.3   Implementation

A (explicit) c-times signature scheme can be easily implemented by using a trust third party (TTP). TTP plays a role of a sort of a counter. For example, whenever a signature σ of a signer is generated, TTP generates another signature σ^T and two signatures σ and σ^T is verified in the verification. After c signature generations, TTP stops generating a signature σ^T for the signer and so the signer cannot generate any valid signature.

4   Implicitly Limited c-Times Signature Scheme

In this section we consider the second type, i.e. implicitly limited c-times signature scheme.

4.1   Implicit c-Times Signature Scheme

To restrict the signer more strictly we need severer penalty for excessive signing. Then, what will be the worst penalty for the illegality? Maybe that is to make no decision of penalty but adversaries (or anyone) is given chances of judgement. Namely, after violation of c-times rule, the security of the signature scheme is broken and anyone can make a forgery of a signature. It is obvious that the forgery of a signature or the disclosure of the secret key of the signer causes serious problems for the signer. Since the signer should take responsibility for the illegal act, the self-breaking property prohibits the signer from violating the c-times rule.

Thus, to ensure the restriction on the number of times the signature scheme should have a legal forgery property which breaks the security of the system if the restriction is violated. We call these schemes *implicit c-times signature* schemes. With public signature views which consist of t signatures $(t > c)$, their corresponding messages and the public key as inputs, a forgery algorithm can legally forge a signature.

We formalize the notion of implicit c-times property as follows.

Definition 3. *(Legal forgery property)* *We say that S=(KG, Sig, Ver) is an implicit c-times signature scheme(denoted by ^cS) if there exists a PPT $Forge_{c+1}$ such that $\forall (sk, pk) \in \{KG(1^\kappa)\}$, $(m', \sigma') \leftarrow Forge_{c+1} (\{\sigma_i, m_i | 1 \leq i \leq c+1, \sigma_i \leftarrow Sig_{sk}(m_i), 1 \leftarrow Ver(pk, m_i, \sigma_i), m_i \in \mathcal{M}\}, pk) \Rightarrow \sigma' \notin \{\sigma_1, ..., \sigma_{c+1}\}$ and $1 \leftarrow Ver(pk, m', \sigma')$ with overwhelming probability.*

We note that the above property requires that the legitimate signer cannot circumvent Forge() function since Forge() is dependent on valid signatures.

The security definition of an implicit c-times signature scheme is the same as that of the c-times signature scheme in section 3 since in the implicit case after the break of the security by the violation of c-times rule the attack is already meaningless.

Remark 1. In the situation where there is a legal limit on the number of signatures, the excessive signatures themselves are the evidence that the limit has been exceeded. With an authority monitoring the limitation, we can use forward-secure schemes [2] with c intervals, and demand (by policy) that the signer produces only one signature per interval. The authority only needs to find two signatures within an interval, rather than $c+1$ signatures, to prove that the limit has been exceeded.

5   Instances of Implicit c-Times Signature Scheme

As well known examples we can take one-time signature schemes. These one-time signature schemes are based on general one-way functions. In this section we describe instances of an implicit c-times signature scheme based on the discrete logarithm or HVZK. These schemes have a *"total break"*, namely, the exposure of the private key as penalty.

5.1   Construction from Signature Scheme Which Is Based on Discrete-Logarithm

We can simply use a verifiable $(c+1, c+1)$-secret sharing scheme to construct an implicit c-times signature scheme. Whenever a signature is generated one share of the secret key is simultaneously generated as a part of a c-times signature. After c-times of signing the secret key is revealed by $c + 1$ shares. However we need caution to compose VSS and a signature scheme. In this subsection we construct implicit c-times signature schemes from DL-based signature schemes in groups of prime order. In these schemes system parameters are set up as follows. Let p be a κ-bit prime number and q a ℓ-bit prime divisor of $p-1$. The triple (p, q, g) is public where g is a generator of order q in $\mathbb{Z}_p^*$. A secret key is a randomly chosen value sk where $1 \leqslant x \leqslant q$ and its corresponding public verification key is $y = g^{sk} \bmod p$.

The presented scheme is a composition of a DL-based signature scheme S and Feldman's $(c+1,c+1)$-VSS [9]. A signature algorithm generates a signature $(\sigma, f(w))$ on a message m where σ is a normal signature of S and $f(w)$ is a part of a share which is calculated by a polynomial $f(x)$ of degree c with $w = h(m, \sigma)$ where h is a hash function. In fact, h should take the role of the random function. $(w = h(m, \sigma), f(w))$ is a share that means "one-time". A legal forgery algorithm is a pair (Lagrange interpolation formula, Signature generation algorithm).

THE SCHEME. Suppose we are given a DL-based signature scheme S=(KG, Sig, Ver). An implicit c-times signature scheme ^cS=(^cKG, ^cSig, ^cVer) can be constructed as follows.

- *Key generation algorithm.* Given input 1^ℓ, the key generation algorithm ^cKG first generates a DL-based triple parameter (p, q, g). Next it runs KG on input 1^ℓ to generate a key pair $(sk, y = g^{sk})$ for the underlying signature scheme S. Then it generates a polynomial $f(z)$ of degree c over $\mathbb{Z}_q$ with x as its constant coefficient. Namely it selects uniformly coefficients $(a_1, ..., a_c)$ in $\mathbb{Z}_q^c$ for $f(z)$, and computes $b_i = g^{a_i} \ (mod \ p) \ (1 \leqslant i \leqslant c)$. It outputs $PK = (y, (g^{a_1}, ..., g^{a_c}), (p, q, g))$ as the public key and $SK = (sk, (a_1, ..., a_c))$ as the secret key.
- *Signing algorithm.* The signing algorithm ^cSig, on input the secret key SK and a message $m \in \{0, 1\}^*$, computes $\sigma = Sig_{sk}(m)$ and $f(w) = sk + a_1 w + a_2 w^2 + \cdots + a_c w^c \ (mod \ q)$ where $w = h(m, \sigma)$ and $h : \{0, 1\}^* \to \{0, 1\}^\ell$ is a public hash function. Then it outputs a signature, $^c\sigma=(\sigma, f(w))$.
- *Verification algorithm.* The verification algorithm ^cVer on input PK, m and $^c\sigma$, outputs 1 if Ver(m, σ, y)=1 and $g^{f(w)} = yb_1^w b_2^{w^2} \cdots b_c^{w^c} \bmod p$, 0 otherwise.
- *Legal forgery property.* For given $c + 1$ signature values and their corresponding messages, the secret value of the signer is calculated by using the Lagrange interpolation formula. For given $(\{^c\sigma_i, m_i | 1 \leq i \leq c + 1, \ ^c\sigma_i \leftarrow {}^cSig_x(m_i), \ 1 \leftarrow {}^cVer(pk, m_i, {}^c\sigma_i), \ m_i \in \mathcal{M}\}, PK)$ where $^c\sigma_i = (\sigma_i, f(w_i))$, $w_i = h(m_i, \sigma_i)$ and $f(x) = \sum_{i=1}^{c+1} f(w_i) \prod_{j=1, j\neq i}^{c+1} \frac{x - w_j}{w_i - w_j} \ (mod \ q)$.
  Forge$_{c+1}(\{^c\sigma_i, m_i\}_{i=1}^{c+1}, pk) \rightarrow (m', (Sig_{f(0)}(m'), f(h(m', \sigma))))$ where $m' \notin \{m_i \ | 1 \leq i \leq c + 1\}$.

The expensive part of ^cS is the computation of the modular exponentiations in the verification step. This can be more efficiently computed by using the simultaneous exponentiation approach [13].

SECURITY. Even though we assume the underlying signature scheme and Feldman's (t,n)-VSS are secure respectively, we should consider how the security of the underlying signature scheme and Feldman's (t,n)-VSS influence the composed scheme. In fact, the security of the sharing part is obvious from the perfect security of the VSS scheme when public key is already given [17].

However, the usage of a signature scheme might compromise the total security of the scheme presented above. But it is also possible to amplify the security from underlying signature scheme S since the independent Feldman's (t,n)-VSS technique is required to generate a signature of ^cS. Thus the security should be considered for each concrete underlying signature scheme.

Next we prove the secuity of ^cS in which a base signature scheme is the ElGamal-type signature scheme. It is well known that the ElGamal scheme is subject to existential forgery. But we can show that ^cS based on the ElGamal scheme is secure. To show ^cS scheme is correct, we need to prove that the secret shared is indeed the correct secret key sk and then a signer cannot circumvent Forge() function. First we note that the signer generates not only a signature of S but also a share of the private key of the signer. And in the scheme ^cS the verification key y of S is again used to validate a share of the signing key sk of S. Thus the signer cannot generate an independent share of a random value, instead of the private key x. Furthermore we know that in an event $(h(m_1, \sigma_1), f(h(m_1, \sigma_1))) = (h(m_2, \sigma_2), f(h(m_2, \sigma_2))), \Leftrightarrow h(m_1, \sigma_1) = h(m_2, \sigma_2)$ Lagrange interpolation formula is not available. Since h is random, in fact collision-resistant, the probability that the event above occurs is the probability of the natural collision which is at most $c(c-1)/2q$ by the birthday problem and negligible. Hence the signer cannot generate the same share on different messages and their signatures of S.

The next theorem shows that ^cS satisfies the security notion defined in Section 3. We show that with c or less signatures of ^cS, no information about secret values are leaked (perfect secrecy) in the information theoretic sense and an adversary gets no advantage in generating a valid share, i.e. a part of a signature of ^cS, except just guessing. Thus any adversary cannot generate a valid signature $^c\sigma'$ on a message m' in the (adaptive) ^cCMA attack. $\mathcal{F}$ can existentially forges a signatue of ^cS with negligible probability. Hence ^cS scheme is $sEUF$-^cCMA secure.

Theorem 1. *If S is ElGamal-type signature scheme, such as Schnorr scheme, then the above construction is a secure implicit c-times signature scheme.*

The theorem is proved by using Vandermonde matrix under assumption of hardness of DL problem in random oracle model. For space limitation we omit the proof.

Remark 2. Whenever the "c-times" rule is applied new access instance for the same secret key is generated. Hence the multiple usages of "c-times" cannot compromise the security of ^cS.

Remark 3. A similar method to achieve self-delegation is used in [11] where a share of a primary key is calculated to ensure the validation of the secondary key by using Feldman's VSS. However, in contrast to [11] which is non-distributed setting we generate one share for every signature and distribute it as a part of a signature.

5.2 ^{c}DSA Based on DSA

In this subsection we present an implicit c-times signature scheme ^cDSA based on the DSA. We first review the DSA briefly.

DIGITAL SIGNATURE ALGORITHM. The Digital Signature Algorithm(DSA) [20] is a signature scheme based on the ElGamal signature scheme [8] which was adopted as the US standard digital signature algorithm.

- *Key generation algorithm.* This algorithm outputs a public key $pk = (y, (p, q, g))$ and a secret key $sk = x$, where (p, q, g) is a DL-based parameter. x is random $(1 \leqslant x \leqslant q)$ and the signing key. $y = g^x \bmod p$ is the verification key.
- *Signing algorithm.* Let h be a hash function and m be a message to be signed. The signer picks a random number $k \in \mathbb{Z}_q^*$, and caculates $r = (g^k \bmod p) \bmod q$ and $s = k^{-1}(h(m) + xr) \bmod q$. Then the pair (r, s) is a signature on m.
- *Verification algorithm.* A signature (r, s) of a message m can be publicly verified by checking if $r = (g^{h(m)s^{-1}} y^{rs^{-1}} \bmod p) \bmod q$.

To construct ^cDSA we can use the characteristic of DSA as follows; If the signer computes more than one signature with a pair $(k, r = g^k)$ the signer's private key is compromised. Thus the signer precomputes c pairs (k_i, r_i) $(1 \leq i \leq c)$ where $r_i = g^{k_i} \pmod{p} \pmod{q}$ and attaches $CP = \{r_i = g^{k_i} | (1 \leq i \leq c)\}$ to the signer's public key y. $CK = (k_1, ..., k_c)$ is kept secret. When the signer wants to sign a message she uses k_j sequentially. In this case the public key and secret key of ^cDSA are $pk = \{y, (g^{k_1}, ..., g^{k_c})\}$ and $sk = \{x, (k_1, ..., k_c)\}$. Similarly, this approach can be applied to other HVZK based signature schemes or GQ signature scheme. Refer to [15] for the precomputation of (k_i, r_i) pairs.

SECURITY. Without the modification of DSA we construct ^cDSA by just pre-computing the "r" part of a DSA signature and then making a part of the public key. Hence the security of ^cDSA straightforwardly follows that of DSA.

Remark 4. The presented scheme ^cDSA can be used for temporary restriction while DSA is maintained. Whenever the "c-times" rule is applied a new $CP' = \{r_i' = g^{k_i'} | (1 \leq i \leq c)\}$ for the same secret key of DSA is set and CP' is attached to the public key of DSA. Therefore the multiple usages of "c-times" rule cannot compromise the security of DSA.

6   Concluding Remark

We need to study (explicit) c-time signature schemes without any trust party. In such schemes a (static) private or public key could vary depending on c to make a $(c + i)$-th signature invalid in such schemes. Also in (implicit) c-times signature schemes, it would be worth finding a different scheme which avoids the linear expansion of the public key.

References

1. D. Bleichenbacher and U.M. mauer, *Directed acyclic graphs, one-way functions and digital signatures*, CRYPTO'94, Y. Desmedt(ed.),LNCS 839, Springer-Verlag, pp. 75–82,1994.
2. M. Bellare and S. Miner, *A Forward-Secure Digital Signature Scheme*, Michael Weiner(ed.), CRYPTO'99 Proceedings, LNCS 1666, Springer, 1999, pp. 431–448.
3. S. Brands, *Untraceable Off-Line Cash in Wallets with Observers* , Douglas R. Stinson(ed.), CRYPTO'93 Proceedings, LNCS 773, Springer, 1993, pp. 302–318.
4. B. Chor, S. Goldwasser, S. Micali, and B. Awerbuch, *Verifiable secret sharing and achieving simultaneity in the presence of faults*, In Proceedings of 26th IEEE Symposium on the Foundations of Computer Science(FOCS), pp. 383–395, 1985.
5. D. Chum, *Group Signatures*, EUROCRYPTO '91, Springer-Verlag, pp257–265,1991.
6. W. Diffe and M.E. Hellman, *New Directions in Cryptgraphy*, In IEEE Transactions on Information Theory, volume IT-22, no. 6, pp. 644–654, November 1976.
7. O. Delos and J-J. Quisquater, *An Identity-Based Signature Scheme with Bounded Life-Span*, Y. G. Desmedt(ed.), CRYPTO'94 Proceedings, LNCS 839, Springer, 1994, pp. 83–94.
8. T. ElGamal, *A public key cryptosystem and a signature scheme based on discrete logarithms*, IEEE Trans. Info. Theory, IT31, 1985.
9. P. Feldman, *A Practical Scheme for Non-Interactive Verifiable Secret Sharing*, In Proc. 28th IEEE Symp. on Foundations of Comp. Science, pp. 427–437, 1987.
10. S. Goldwasser, S. Micali and R. Rivest. *A digital signature scheme secure against adaptive chosen-message attacks*, SIAM Journal of Computing, Vol. 17, No.2, April 1988, pp.281–308.
11. O. Goldreich, B. Pfitzmann, and R. L. Rivest, *Self-delegation with Controlled Propagation -or- What If You Lose Your Laptop*, Hugo Krawczyk(ed.),CRYPTO'98 Proceedings, LNCS 1462, Springer, 1998, pp. 153–168.
12. L. Lamport, *Constructing digital signaturs from a one-way function*, Technical Report SRI Intl. CSL 98, 1979
13. B. Moller, *Algorithms for multi-exponentiation*, In SAC2001, pp. 165–180. Springer-Verlag, 2001. LNCS No. 2259
14. M.Mambo, K. Usuda, and E. Okamoto, *Proxy Signatures*, Proceedings of the 1995 Symposium on Cryptography and Information Security, Inuyama, Japan, 24–27 Jan 1995 ppB1.1.1–17
15. D. Naccache, D. M'RAIHI, Serge Vaudenay and Dan Raphaeli, *Can D.S.A be Improved? Complexity Trade-Offs with the Digital Signature Standard.*, A. D. Santis(ed.),Eurocrypt'94 Proceedings, LNCS 950, Springer, 1995, pp. 77–85.
16. T. Okamoto and K. Ohta, *Universal Electronic Cash*, J. Feigenbaum (ed.), CRYPTO'91 Proceedings, LNCS 576, Springer, 1991, pp. 324–337.
17. T.P. Pedersen, *Distributed Provers with Applications and their Applications to Undeniable Signatures*, Donald W. Davies(ed.),Eurocrypt'91 Proceedings, LNCS 547, Springer, 1991, pp. 221–242.
18. R.L. Rivest, A. Shamir, and L. Adleman, *A method for obtaining digital signatures and public-key cryptosystem*, communications of the ACM, vol. 21,no. 2, pp. 120–126, 1978.
19. A. Shamir, *How to Share a Secret*, Communications of the ACM, 22:612–613,1979.
20. *National Institute for Standard and Technology*, Digital Signature Standard(DSS) Technical Report 169, August 30 1991.

On the Exact Security of Multi-signature Schemes Based on RSA

Kei Kawauchi[1] and Mitsuru Tada[2]

[1] Graduate School of Science and Technology, Chiba University,
1-33 Yayoi-cho, Inage, Chiba 263-8522, Japan.
kei-k@graduate.chiba-u.jp
[2] Institute of Media and Information Technology, Chiba University,
1-33 Yayoi-cho, Inage, Chiba 263-8522, Japan.
mt@math.s.chiba-u.ac.jp

Abstract. Up to present, we have yet seen no multi-signature schemes based on RSA secure against active attacks proposed. We have examined the possibility of simulation of signatures in the MM scheme [7] in order to investigate whether that scheme has the security against active attacks. The MM scheme cannot be shown secure against active attacks. We have constructed the RSA-based multi-signature scheme in order to overcome the problem that the MM scheme has. The proposed scheme provides the security against adaptive chosen message insider attack targeting one signer, and can keep tighter reduction rate.

1 Introduction

Recently, the digital document has grown to exchange actively. When we intend to authorize the contents of a document, digital signature schemes realized the digital seal are effectual expedient. On one hand, when plural signers jointly sign an identical message efficiently, multi-signature schemes are effectual expedient. If we apply *Batch verification*, then plural single-signatures can be verified efficiently. However since the modular must be restricted to be common, we can say that multi-signature schemes are still effectual expedient. Up to present various multi-signature schemes have already been proposed, but nevertheless we see only a few schemes secure against active attacks. Moreover, all the multi-signature schemes proved to be secure against active attacks are based on DLP. We can see [6,9,11] as representative examples. On the other hand, we have seen no multi-signature scheme based on RSA proved to be secure against active attacks. The RSA algorithm is occupied in most cryptographical technology, and widely employed in the world, since the numerical formula is simple, the implementation is relatively easy from the fact that the signature generation (decrypt) algorithm and the verification (encrypt) algorithm are symmetric and the keys are also symmetric. Therefore it seem to be a worthwhile work to construct a *secure* multi-signature scheme based on RSA.

We can classify the multi-signature scheme based on RSA into two types. In the first one, a common modular is used among signers as seen in [5]. In

R. Safavi-Naini and J. Seberry (Eds.): ACISP 2003, LNCS 2727, pp. 336–349, 2003.
© Springer-Verlag Berlin Heidelberg 2003

the other one, each signer uses a distinct modular as seen in [7,8]. The former type has a defect that participating signers have to register the key in advance since the modular is common, but it has a merit that the computational cost for verification is independent of the number of the signers. The latter type has the opposite properties those the former one has. In this paper, we deal with the latter one, that is, schemes in which signers have distinct moduli and we argue the security of such schemes. As a consequence, we can point out the following two:

1. We have examined the possibility of simulation of signatures in the RSA-based multi-signature scheme given by [7], in order to investigate whether that scheme has the security against active attacks. Then we have concluded that the scheme is hardly possible to prove the security not only against active attacks by A_1 (See section 2.3, for the definition.), but also against active attacks by A_a (Also see section 2.3.) which is a weaker model than A_1, since signatures in that scheme cannot be simulated by a probabilistic polynomial time Turing machine (PPTM). Table 1 summarizes the security consideration.

Table 1. Comparison between schemes

	Against A_a	Against A_1
The scheme [7]	Unshown	Unshown
Proposed scheme	Secure	Secure

2. We have constructed an RSA-based multi-signature scheme, in which each signer P_i uses two hash functions G_i and H_i, and in which a signer puts the signature by the previous signer into the argument of hash function H_i. The proposed scheme provides the security against adaptive chosen message insider attack by A_1, and can keep tighter reduction rate.

2   Definitions

In a multi-signature scheme where n signers participate, each signer P_i publishes a public-key pk_i, while keeping a secret-key sk_i, and the coalition of all signers $P := \{P_1, \ldots, P_n\}$ proves the validity of a message m authenticated by them.

Definition 1 (Multi-signature scheme). *A multi-signature scheme* (Gen, MSig, Ver) *is defined by the following:*

Key Generation Algorithm: Gen *is a probabilistic algorithm which given* 1^{K_i} *by each signer* P_i, *where* K_i *is the security parameter, produces a pair of matching public-key and secret-key* (pk_i, sk_i).

Multi-signature Generation Algorithm: MSig *takes a message m to be signed, P_{i-1}'s signature $\sigma_{i-1}(\sigma_0 = 1)$ and (pk_i, sk_i), and returns a multi-signature $\sigma_i = \text{MSig}_{sk_i, pk_i}(m, \sigma_{i-1})$. The multi-signing algorithm may be probabilistic[1].*

Verification Algorithm: *The verification algorithm* Ver *takes a message m, a candidate multi-signature σ_n and the public-keys $\boldsymbol{pk} := \{pk_1, \ldots, pk_n\}$. It returns 1 if the multi-signature is valid, and 0 otherwise. Note that the verification algorithm is deterministic.*

2.1   Exact Security

Here we use the definitions given by [1,2] which take the presence of ideal hash functions into account, and give an exact security analysis [2] for multi-signature schemes based on RSA.

2.2   Quantifying the Security of RSA

Definition 2. *A probabilistic Turing machine (inverter) $\mathcal{I}$ is said to break an inverting RSA with (τ^*, ϵ^*), if and only if $\mathcal{I}$ can compute an x such that $\eta = x^e \bmod N_i$ for given N_i being a composite of two primes, $e \in \mathbb{Z}^*_{\lambda(N_i)}$ and $\eta \in_R \mathbb{Z}_{N_i}$ with a success probability greater than $\epsilon^*(K_i)$ within processing time $\tau^*(K_i)$ for all security parameter $K_i \in \mathbb{N}$. The probability is taken over the coin flips of $\mathcal{I}$.*

Definition 3. *RSA is said to be (τ^*, ϵ^*)-secure, if there is no inverter $\mathcal{I}$ which (τ^*, ϵ^*)-breaks RSA.*

2.3   Quantifying the Security of Multi-signature Schemes

In [7], the security consideration is argued under the following attack model: The adversary $\mathcal{A}$ colludes the signers $\mathcal{P} \backslash \{P_i\}$, where P_i is targeted by $\mathcal{A}$. $\mathcal{A}$ obtains the secret information $\boldsymbol{sk} \backslash \{sk_i\}$ ($\boldsymbol{sk} := \{sk_1, \ldots, sk_n\}$) from $\mathcal{P} \backslash \{P_i\}$, all public information, a message m and a valid partial signature. By using these information, $\mathcal{A}$ tries to forge P_i's signature. Accordingly, considered is the only passive attacks in the security proof. In this paper, we consider the security consideration against the following two active attack models.

The first one is introduced by [9], the adversary $\mathcal{A}_a$ can execute an *adaptive chosen-message insider attack* (CMIA).

Definition 4 (Adversary $\mathcal{A}_a$). *An adversary $\mathcal{A}_a$ executes the following step q_s times, where q_s is the number of signature queries:*

---

[1] It is possible for each P_i to check the validity of σ_{i-1} before generating her signature σ_i.

Step: *First $\mathcal{A}_a$ chooses a message $m_j \in \mathbb{N}$, where $j \in [1, q_s]$, and a signer $P_{i_j} \in \mathcal{P}$. By colluding with $\mathcal{P} \backslash \{P_i\}$, $\mathcal{A}_a$ generates a multi-signature σ_{i_j-1} by $\{P_1, \ldots, P_{i_j-1}\}$, sends m_j and σ_{i_j-1} to P_i, asks P_{i_j} to sign m_j, and obtains the multi-signature σ_{i_j} by $\{P_1, \ldots, P_{i_j}\}$.*

After q_s-time iteration, $\mathcal{A}_a$ outputs a forgery which is a message/signature pair (m^*, σ_n^*), but the message m^* has a restriction that signature of m^* has never been requested by $\mathcal{A}_a$.

The second attack model is stronger than that by [9]. It is, so to speak, the attack model adapted in [7].

Definition 5 (Adversary $\mathcal{A}_1$). *The adversary model $\mathcal{A}_a$ is almost the same with the first one except for that every i_j is fixed (Denote it by i.) and that the rest $\mathcal{P} \backslash \{P_i\}$ share the secret-keys with the adversary $\mathcal{A}_1$. It is only sk_i that is a secret-key $\mathcal{A}_1$ does not know.*

In this attack model, only the hash oracle H_i is assumed to be a random oracle. No hash functions except for H_i are assumed to be random oracle functions.[2]

Here we define the forgery by $\mathcal{A}_a$ as follows.

Definition 6 (CMIA by $\mathcal{A}_a$). *A probabilistic Turing machine(adversary) $\mathcal{A}_a$ is said to $(\tau_1, \ldots, \tau_n, q_s, q_{hash_1}, \ldots, q_{hash_n}, \epsilon_1, \ldots, \epsilon_n)$-break the multi-signature scheme (Gen, MSig, Ver), if after at most $q_{hash_1}(K_1)$, ..., $q_{hash_n}(K_n)$ queries to the hash oracles $hash_1, \ldots, hash_n$ and $q_s(K_n)$ signature queries, it outputs a forgery in time at most $\sum_{i=1}^{n} \tau_i(K_i)$ with a success probability at least $\prod_{i=1}^{n} \epsilon_i(K_i)$ for all $K_i \in \mathbb{N}$.*

Next, we define the forgery by $\mathcal{A}_1$ as follows.

Definition 7 (CMIA by $\mathcal{A}_1$). *A probabilistic Turing machine(adversary) $\mathcal{A}_1$ is said to $(\tau_i, q_s, q_{hash_i}, \epsilon_i)$-break the multi-signature scheme (Gen, MSig, Ver), if after at most $q_{hash_i}(K_i)$ queries to the hash oracle $hash_i$ and $q_s(K_i)$ signature queries and $\tau_i(K_i)$ processing time, it outputs a forgery in time at most $\tau_i(K_i)$ with a success probability at least $\epsilon_i(K_i)$ for all $K_i \in \mathbb{N}$.*

Here we can see that if a multi-signature scheme is secure against CMIA by $\mathcal{A}_1$, then the multi-signature scheme is secure against CMIA by $\mathcal{A}_a$. This is proven trivially. Hence, we define the security of multi-signature schemes as follows.

Definition 8. *A multi-signature scheme (Gen, MSig, Ver) is said to be $(\tau_i, q_s, q_{hash_i}, \epsilon_i)$-secure, if there is no adversary $\mathcal{A}_1$ which $(\tau_i, q_s, q_{hash_i}, \epsilon_i)$-breaks the scheme.*

3   The Problem on the MM Scheme [7]

As we can seen in [7], the multi-signature scheme given by [7][3] has not been proven secure against active attacks. Hence we try the simulation of signatures

---

[2] In [6,12] every hash function is assumed to be a random oracle function.
[3] Hereafter, we call the multi-signature scheme based on RSA [7] *the MM scheme*.

in the MM scheme, in order to investigate whether the MM scheme has the resistance against active attacks. Consequently the MM scheme does not seem to be proven to provide the security not only against $\mathcal{A}_1$, but also against $\mathcal{A}_a$ unfortunately. Under the attack by $\mathcal{A}_1$ and $\mathcal{A}_a$, we are faced with a problem in the process of simulation in the security proof. We show the MM scheme as follows. In this paper, we restrict the message to the fixed message for simplicity, though it has the property of *message flexibility* [7].

3.1   The MM Scheme [7]

Key-generation step: Each signer P_i has the RSA-key generator $\mathcal{RSA}$, which on input 1^{K_i}, randomly selects two distinct $K_i/2$-bit primes p_i and q_i, and calculates the modulus $N_i = p_i \cdot q_i$. It randomly picks an encryption exponent $e_i \in \mathbb{Z}^*_{\lambda(N_i)}$, and calculates the corresponding decryption exponent d_i such that $e_i \cdot d_i \equiv 1 \, (\mathrm{mod}\,\lambda(N_i))$, where $\lambda(N_i) = \mathrm{LCM}(p_i - 1, q_i - 1)$. The each generator returns (N_i, e_i, d_i). Also each P_i has an appropriate hash function $h_i : \{0,1\}^* \to \{0,1\}^{K_i}$.

Signature generation step: Suppose that a set of signers $\mathcal{P}$ generates a multi-signature for a message m. The first signer P_1 computes the hash value $y_1 = h_1(ID_1, m)$ and $\sigma_1 = y_1^{d_1} \bmod N_1$, where ID_1 is P_1's identification information. Then P_1 sends (m, ID_1, σ_1) as a signature for m to P_2. For each $i \in [2, n]$, the following is executed.

- P_i receives $(m, ID_1, \dots, ID_{i-1}, \sigma_{i-1})$ from P_{i-1}.
  P_i computes $y_i = h_i(ID_i, m)$ and $\rho_i = \sigma_{i-1} \oplus y_i$, where $\oplus$ denotes the bitwise Xor operation. Finally P_i computes $\sigma_i = \rho_i^{d_i} \bmod N_i$, and sends $(m, ID_1, \dots, ID_i, \sigma_i)$ to P_{i+1}, where P_{n+1} is the verifier.

Verification step: Suppose that the verifier V receives $(m, ID_1, \dots, ID_n, \sigma_n)$ as a multi-signature for a message m. For each $i = n$ to $i = 2$, the following is executed by the verifier.

- V computes $\rho_i = \sigma_i^{e_i} \bmod N_i$ and $y_i = h_i(ID_i, m)$, and calculates $\sigma_{i-1} = \rho_i \oplus y_i$.

Finally V obtains σ_1, and checks the following equations : $\sigma_1^{e_1} \bmod N_1 = h_1(ID_1, m)$. If it holds, then the multi-signature is regarded as a valid one, and as an invalid one, otherwise.

The security proof of the multi-signature scheme against active attacks is based on the following strategy: Under the assumption of the random oracle model [1], if there exists an adversary $\mathcal{A}_a$ which can break the multi-signature scheme, then we can construct an inverter $\mathcal{I}_n$ using $\mathcal{A}_a$, and the $\mathcal{I}_n$ can invert n pieces of RSA problems. In the same way, if there exists an adversary $\mathcal{A}_1$ which can break the multi-signature scheme, then we can construct an inverter $\mathcal{I}$ using $\mathcal{A}_1$, and the $\mathcal{I}$ can invert one RSA problem.

3.2   Argument

Consequently we can see that signatures in the MM scheme cannot be simulated when we try to prove the security against $\mathcal{A}_a$, also $\mathcal{A}_1$. That means it is impossible to simulate individually the signing-oracle Σ_{sk_i} by $\mathcal{I}$. As we can see in the following theorem, assuming that the signing oracle Σ_{sk_i}.

Theorem 1. *If there exists a* PPTM $\mathcal{I}$ *which can simulate the signing oracle* Σ_{sk_i} *in the model* CMIA *for the MM scheme, then we can construct* PPTM $\mathcal{M}$ *which can invert the RSA by using* $\mathcal{I}$ *as an oracle.*

Proof. The $\mathcal{M}$ receives (N_i, e_i, η) as its input where (N_i, e_i) is the public-key and η is chosen at random in $\mathbb{Z}_{N_i}$. $\mathcal{M}$ tries to find an x such that $\eta = x^{e_i} \bmod N_i$. $\mathcal{M}$ is allowed to make h_i hash oracle queries and signing queries to Σ_{sk_i}. When $\mathcal{M}$ makes an h_i hash query for an arbitrary m, $\mathcal{I}$ returns some value y. When $\mathcal{M}$ makes a signing query for m and $y \oplus \eta$ as σ_{i-1}, $\mathcal{I}$ can return σ_i as the multi-signature for m. Eventually, $\mathcal{M}$ can compute the inverting RSA for η, since $\mathcal{M}$ has only to output σ_i as the x such that $\eta = x^{e_i} \bmod N_i$. Note $\sigma_i^{e_i} = \sigma_{i-1} \oplus y = (y \oplus \eta) \oplus y = \eta$, so the x indeed satisfies $x^{e_i} = \eta \bmod N_i$ as desired. Therefore this theorem is now proven.   □

Why has this attack developed? Because the MM scheme has the property of *order flexibility*. As a result, the inverter $\mathcal{I}$ cannot guess the previous signer in the simulation.

3.3   The Revision of the MM Scheme to Solve the Problem

We can also prevent from this attack in the following three solutions.

1. Omit the property of *order flexibility*. The signing order is determined in advance.
2. The signature generation step is modified so that P_i checks the validity of σ_{i-1} before σ_i generated. The signature generation cost must be much increased.
3. The hash function h_i is modified to include $ID_1, \ldots, ID_i, m$ not only ID_i, m.

Consequently we can see that the revised MM scheme which is adopted the solution 3 has resistance against $\mathcal{A}_1$. The following theorem summarizes the exact security of the revised MM scheme in random oracle model.

Theorem 2 (Security for the revised MM scheme against $\mathcal{A}_1$). *Suppose the i-th inverting RSA is $(\tau^*(K_i), \epsilon^*(K_i))$-secure. Then the revised MM scheme is $(\tau_{mm_i}, q_s, q_{h_i}, \epsilon_{mm_i})$-secure, where*

$$\epsilon^*(K_i) \geq \frac{\epsilon_{mm_i}}{q_s}\left(1 - \frac{1}{q_s + 1}\right)^{q_s + 1},$$
$$\tau^*(K_i) \leq \tau_{mm_i} + (q_s + q_{h_i} + 1) \cdot T_{exp}(K_i),$$

for $1 \leq i \leq n$, and $T_{exp}(K_i)$ denotes the time complexity for modular exponentiation $\bmod N_i$.

Proof. (Sketch) The revised MM scheme is the multi-signature version of RSA-FDH scheme [3], we obey the strategy of the security proof in [3]. Our overall strategy for the proof is as follows: We apply the Game introduced by [10,13] to evaluate the security. We define a sequence $Game_0$, $Game_1$, $\ldots$, $Game_5$ of modified attack games starting from the actual game. Each of the games operates on the same underlying probability space. In particular, the public-key and secret-key of the cryptosystem, the coin tosses of $\mathcal{A}_1$, the values of the random oracle h_i take on identical values across the games. We start from the actual situation $Game_0$, in which $\mathcal{A}_1$ can access the real signing oracle Σ_{sk_i}, and construct $\mathcal{I}$ using the output of $\mathcal{A}_1$, with gradually altering the situation around $\mathcal{A}_1$, and with simulating Σ_{sk_i}. $\mathcal{I}$ receives a part of its input a list of query-answer pairs corresponding to calls to the random oracle h_i, which we denote by h_i-List.

When the simulation of $h_1, \ldots, h_n$, the random oracle h_i is simulated by $\mathcal{I}$ as a general rule. When the adversary $\mathcal{A}_1$ makes an h_i oracle query for m_ℓ, the inverter $\mathcal{I}$ returns $y_{i_\ell} \in_R \mathbb{Z}_{N_i}$ where $\ell \in [1, q_s + q_{h_i}]$. $\mathcal{I}$ registers $(m_\ell, \sigma_{i-1}, y_{i_\ell})$ with the h_i-List. Here, in spite of the no input of h_i includes the previous signer's signature σ_{i-1}, why $\mathcal{I}$ register the σ_{i-1}? Because the hash function h_i is modified to include $ID_1, \ldots, ID_i, m$ not only ID_i, m. Thus, P_i can recognize that who the previous signer is, $\mathcal{I}$ too. From this reason, $\mathcal{I}$ can register the σ_{i-1} corresponding m_ℓ with the h_i-List. $\square$

Theorem 2 relates the security of the revised MM scheme based on RSA against $\mathcal{A}_1$, with the security of the RSA inversion, the reduction rate is much looser than that for the proposed scheme.

4   Proposed Multi-signature Scheme Based on RSA

Here we present the proposed scheme. This scheme is secure not only against $\mathcal{A}_a$ but also against $\mathcal{A}_1$. In the proposed scheme, each P_i uses two hash functions G_i and H_i, and the input of H_i includes the previous signer's signature σ_{i-1} in order to overcome the problem that the MM scheme has. The first one, H_i, called the compressor, maps as $H_i : \{0,1\}^* \to \{0,1\}^{k_2}$ and the other one, G_i, called the generator, maps as $G_i : \{0,1\}^{k_2} \to \{0,1\}^{K_{i-1}+k_1}$, where $K_i = 1 + K_{i-1} + k_1 + k_2$, $K_0 = k_0$. Use of two hash functions makes the proposed scheme preserve the efficiency and better security guarantee than that of the revised MM scheme.

In this paper, we omit ID_i from the input of the hash function for simplicity. However the proposed scheme satisfies the security against $\mathcal{A}_1$ is different from the revised MM scheme. We give the proposed scheme in the following. Refer to Figure 1 for a picture.

Key-generation step: P_i has $\mathcal{RSA}$, which on input 1^{K_i}, randomly selects two distinct $K_i/2$-bit primes p_i and q_i, and calculates the modulus $N_i = p_i \cdot q_i$. It randomly picks up an encryption exponent $e_i \in \mathbb{Z}^*_{\lambda(N_i)}$. Here, P_i must select $K_i = 1 + K_{i-1} + k_1 + k_2$, $K_0 = k_0$.

Signature generation step: Suppose that $\mathcal{P}$ generates a multi-signature for a message m. P_1 picks up an $r_1 \in_R \{0,1\}^{k_1}$ to compute $\omega_1 = H_1(m, r_1)$.

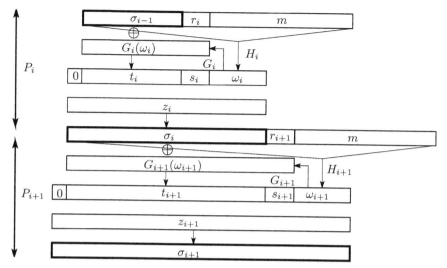

Fig. 1. Proposed scheme

Also P_1 computes $\sigma_1 = z_1^{d_1} \bmod N_1$, where $z_1 = 0 \parallel t_1 \parallel s_1 \parallel \omega_1$, $(t_1 \parallel s_1) = (0^{k_0} \parallel r_1) \oplus G_1(\omega_1)$. Then P_i sends (m, σ_1) as a signature for m to P_2.
For each $i \in [2, n]$, the following is executed.

- P_i receives (m, σ_{i-1}) from P_{i-1}. P_i may check whether the partial multi-signature σ_{i-1} for a message m is a valid or not[4]. P_i picks up an $r_i \in_R \{0,1\}^{k_1}$ to compute $\omega_i = H_i(m, r_i, \sigma_{i-1})$. Also P_i computes $\sigma_i = z_i^{d_i} \bmod N_i$, where $z_i = 0 \parallel t_i \parallel s_i \parallel \omega_i$, $(t_i \parallel s_i) = (\sigma_{i-1} \parallel r_i) \oplus G_i(\omega_i)$. Then P_i sends (m, σ_i) as a signature on m to P_{i+1}, where P_{n+1} is the verifier.

Verification step: Suppose that the verifier V receives (m, σ_n) as a multi-signature for a message m. For each $i = n$ to $i = 2$, the following is executed by the verifier.

- First, V computes $z_i = \sigma_i^{e_i} \bmod N_i$, breaks up z_i as $b_i \parallel t_i \parallel s_i \parallel \omega_i$. (That is, let b_i be the first bit of z_i, t_i the next K_{i-1} bits, s_i the next k_1 bits, and ω_i the remaining k_2 bits.) And V calculates $(\alpha_i \parallel \beta_i) = (t_i \parallel s_i) \oplus G_i(\omega_i)$. If $b_i = 0$ and $\omega_i = H_i(m, \beta_i, \alpha_i)$, then V computes $\alpha_i = \sigma_{i-1}$ and goes on the step.

Finally V obtains σ_1, computes $z_1 = \sigma_1^{e_1} \bmod N_1$, breaks up z_1 as $b_1 \parallel t_1 \parallel s_1 \parallel \omega_1$, and calculates $(\alpha_1 \parallel \beta_1) = (t_1 \parallel s_1) \oplus G_1(\omega_1)$. If $b_1 = 0$, $\omega_1 = H_1(m, \beta_1, \alpha_1)$ and $\alpha_1 = 0^{k_0}$, then V returns 1 else return 0.

Notice that the input of H_i consists of a message m, a random seed r_i and the previous signer's signature σ_{i-1}. Therefore ID_i is omitted from the input of the hash function. The hash function H_i which on input σ_i made the proposed scheme independent of ID_i for the security. The proposed scheme has the fol-

---

[4] If P_i checks the validity and if σ_{i-1} appears invalid, P_i must not go on the signature generation, and halts.

lowing two features. *the order flexibility* and *the message and order verifiability* [7]. It can probably be added the property of *the message flexibility*, but in this paper, we focus only on the security proof.

5   Security Consideration

The following theorem shows the security of the proposed scheme. The proposed scheme has much better reduction rate than that the MM scheme has. In the proposed scheme, the input of H_i includes the previous signer's signature σ_{i-1} and hence we can prove the security against $\mathcal{A}_1$.

Theorem 3 (Security for the proposed scheme against $\mathcal{A}_1$). *Suppose the i-th inverting RSA is $(\tau^*(K_i), \epsilon^*(K_i))$-secure. Then the proposed multi-signature scheme is $(\tau_i, q_s, q_{G_i}, q_{H_i}, \epsilon_i)$-secure, where*

$$\epsilon^*(K_i) \geq \epsilon_i - \frac{1}{2^{k_2}} - (q_s + q_{H_i}) \cdot \left(\frac{1}{2^L} + \frac{q_{G_i} + q_{H_i} + q_s}{2^{k_2}} \right) - q_s \cdot \frac{q_{H_i}}{2^{k_1}},$$

$$\tau^*(K_i) \leq \tau_i + L(q_s + q_{H_i}) \cdot T_{exp}(K_i),$$

for $1 \leq i \leq n$, and $T_{exp}(K_i)$ denotes the time complexity for modular exponentiation mod N_i.

Proof. The strategy of the proof is the same with that Theorem 2. We include the proof in Appendix A.   □

From Theorem 3, we can show that the security of the proposed multi-signature scheme by n signers is reduced the complexity of inverting RSA.

Here, we try to evaluate the size k_1 and k_2. Taking $q_s = 2^{30}$, $q_{H_i} = 2^{60}$, $q_{G_i} = 2^{60}$ and $\epsilon^* = 2^{-60}$ as in [2], we obtain that k_1, k_2 must satisfy $k_1 > 121$ and $k_2 > 183$, respectively.

6   Efficiency Consideration

We evaluate the computational amount for verification (CompVer) in the proposed scheme with the required number of modular-N_1 multiplications as its measure, and also with the total size of a signature. Assuming the condition that n signers participated, we compare the verification costs and the total sizes of signatures for the scheme in which each signer applies RSA-PSS [2] and a multi-signature by $\mathcal{P}$ is the sequence of n signatures by the n signers, those for the MM scheme[5], and those for the proposed scheme. We can evaluate that when the security parameter for P_i is K_i, the computational cost for one exponentiation under the modulo N_i is $\left(\frac{3}{2}|\lambda(N_i)| - 1\right) \frac{|N_i^2|}{|N_1|^2} \mathsf{costM}(K_1)$ $(|\lambda(N_i)| = K_i - 1)$, where $\mathsf{costM}(K_1)$ denotes the computational cost for one multiplication mod N_1. Table 2 summarizes the efficiency consideration. Hereafter, we discuss the effi-

---

[5] According to [7], the security parameter is defined $K_i = 10 + K_{i-1}$.

Table 2. Comparison among schemes

	Total size of signatures	CompVer ($\times$ costM(K_1))
n pieces of RSA-PSS	Kn	$\mathcal{O}(n)$
MM scheme	$10(n-1) + K_1$	$\frac{750}{2K_1^2} \cdot n^4 + \mathcal{O}(n^3)$
Proposed scheme	$(k_1 + k_2 + 1)(n-1) + K_1$	$\frac{3}{8K_1^2}(1 + k_1 + k_2)^3 n^4 + \mathcal{O}(n^3)$

ciency giving the concrete sizes for k_1 and k_2. We obtain the sizes $k_1 = 122$ and $k_2 = 184$ from the discussion in the previous section. Assuming that $K_1 = 1024$, the signature size in the proposed scheme is increased by only $1 + k_1 + k_2 < \frac{3K_1}{10}$, and is in proportion to the increase of the signers. Therefore, the proposed scheme is satisfied the condition multi-signature schemes are required, since the total signature size is less than $K_1 n$. Moreover, RSA-PSS has *the tightest* security proof in [4], and in the proof, we can see that k_1 can be as small as $\log_2 q_s$, where q_s is the number of signature queries made by $\mathcal{A}_1$. Thereby we can evaluate k_1 to be about 30. We can see that the security proof [4] can be adapted also for the proposed scheme, and hence we can decrease the signature size. However, we find that the computational amount for verification is increased by $\mathcal{O}(n^4)$. This problem happens not only in the proposed scheme but also in the MM scheme. This problem is the common property in the multi-signature scheme based on RSA which different moduli are used among the signers. In such multi-signature schemes based on RSA, the security parameter for each signer must be larger than that for the previous signer. As a result, we can estimate the computational amount for verification to be increased by $\mathcal{O}(n^4)$ in the multi-signature scheme based on RSA, since the verification has to be executed in the way like peeling away the out layers of an onion. This is one of the typical difference between multi-signature schemes based on RSA and ones based on DLP.

7 Conclusion

In this paper, we have examined the possibility of simulation of signatures in the MM scheme in order to investigate whether that scheme has the security against active attacks. Then we have concluded that the MM scheme is hardly possible to prove the security not only against $\mathcal{A}_1$, but also against $\mathcal{A}_a$, since signatures in that scheme cannot be simulated by a PPTM, if RSA inversion is intractable. After that, we have constructed an RSA-based multi-signature scheme, in which each signer P_i uses two hash functions G_i and H_i, and in which a signer puts the signature by the previous signer into the argument of hash function H_i. The proposed scheme provides the security against $\mathcal{A}_1$, and can keep tighter reduction rate.

Acknowledgments. We would like to thank Prof. Kazuo Ohta and Mr. Yuichi Komano. They gave us the invaluable advice about the security analysis. We wish to thank anonymous reviewers for useful comments.

References

1. M. Bellare and P. Rogaway: *"Random oracles are practical: A paradigm for designing efficient protocols"*, Proceedings of the 1st Conference on Computer and Communications Security, 1993.
2. M. Bellare and P. Rogaway: *"The Exact Security of Digital Signatures – How to Sign with RSA and Rabin"*, Proceedings of Eurocrypt'96, LNCS vol.1070, pp.399–416, Springer-Verlag, 1996.
3. J.S. Coron: *"On the Exact Security of Full Domain Hash"*, Proceedings of Crypto'00, LNCS vol.1880, pp.229–235, Springer-Verlag, 2000.
4. J.S. Coron: *"Optimal Security Proofs for PSS and Other Signature Schemes"*, Proceedings of Eurocrypt'02, LNCS vol.2332, pp.272–287, Springer-Verlag, 2002.
5. H. Doi, M. Mambo and E. Okamoto: *"RSA-based Multisignature Scheme for Various Group Structures"*, Transactions of IPSJ, vol.41, no.08, pp.2080–2091, 2000.
6. S. Micali, K. Ohta and L. Reyzin: *"Accountable-Subgroup Multisignatures"*, Proceedings of the Eighth ACM Conference on Computer and Communications Security '01, pp.245–254, 2001.
7. S. Mitomi and A. Miyaji: *"A multisignature scheme with message flexibility, order flexibility and order verifiability"*, Proceedings of ACISP'00, LNCS vol.1841, pp.298–312, Springer-Verlag, 2000.
8. T. Okamoto: *"A Digital Multisignature Scheme Using Bijective Public-Key Cryptosystems"*, ACM Transactions on Computer Systems, vol.6, no.8, pp.432–441, 1988.
9. K. Ohta and T. Okamoto: *"Multi-Signature Schemes Secure against Active Insider Attacks"*, IEICE transactions of fundamentals, vol.E82-A, no.1, pp.22–31, 1999.
10. K. Ohta: *Private communication*, The lecture note in the class of cryptographic theory for undergraduate students at The University of Electro-Communications, 2002.
11. M. Tada: *"An Order-Specified Multisignature Scheme Secure against Active Insider Attacks"*, Proceedings of ACISP'02, LNCS vol.2384, pp.328–345, Springer-Verlag, 2002.
12. M. Tada: *"Intended multisignature schemes and trivially constructed multisignature schemes"*, Proceedings of The Computer Security Symposium 2002, IPSJ, pp.291–296, 2002.
13. V. Shoup: *"OAEP Reconsidered"*, Journal of Cryptology, vol.15 no.4, pp.223–249, Springer-Verlag, 2002.

A   The Security for the Proposed Scheme against $\mathcal{A}_1$

Theorem 3 (Security for the proposed scheme against $\mathcal{A}_1$). *Suppose the i-th inverting RSA is $(\tau^*(K_i), \epsilon^*(K_i))$-secure. Then the proposed multi-signature scheme is $(\tau_i, q_s, q_{G_i}, q_{H_i}, \epsilon_i)$-secure, where*

$$\epsilon^*(K_i) \geqq \epsilon_i - \frac{1}{2^{k_2}} - (q_s + q_{H_i}) \cdot \left(\frac{1}{2^L} + \frac{q_{G_i} + q_{H_i} + q_s}{2^{k_2}} \right) - q_s \cdot \frac{q_{H_i}}{2^{k_1}},$$

$$\tau^*(K_i) \leqq \tau_i + L(q_s + q_{H_i}) \cdot T_{exp}(K_i),$$

for $1 \leq i \leq n$, and $T_{exp}(K_i)$ denotes the time complexity for modular exponentiation mod N_i.

Proof. Our overall strategy for the proof is as follows: We apply the Game introduced by [10,13] to evaluate the security. We define a sequence Game_0, Game_1, ..., Game_6 of modified attack games starting from the actual game.

Game_0: Let Game_0 be the original attack game. $\mathcal{I}$ generates $\mathcal{P}$'s pairs of keys $(\boldsymbol{sk}, \boldsymbol{pk})$ to follow the regular key generation protocol. Here, $\mathcal{A}_1$ can know the untargeted signers' secret-keys $\boldsymbol{sk} \backslash \{sk_i\}$. $\mathcal{I}$ starts running $\mathcal{A}_1$ on input $\boldsymbol{pk}$. $\mathcal{A}_1$ will make oracle queries (each signing queries, H_i queries, G_i queries). Then $\mathcal{I}$ answers the signing query from $\mathcal{A}_1$ using sk_i which $\mathcal{I}$ has. We denoted by S_0 the event $\mathsf{Ver}(\boldsymbol{pk}_{[1,i]}, m^*, \sigma_i^*) = 1$ and use similar notations $S_1, \ldots, S_6$ in $\mathsf{Game}_1, \ldots, \mathsf{Game}_6$. We have $\Pr[S_0] = \epsilon_i$, according to the success probability of $\mathcal{A}_1$'s forgery.

Game_1: The random oracle G_i is simulated by $\mathcal{I}$ as a general rule. When the adversary $\mathcal{A}_1$ makes a G_i oracle query for w_{i_ℓ}, the inverter $\mathcal{I}$ returns $\zeta_{i_\ell} \in_R \{0,1\}^{K_{i-1}+k_1}$ as $G_i(w_{i_\ell})$. $\mathcal{I}$ registers $(w_{i_\ell}, \zeta_{i_\ell})$ with the G_i-List prepared beforehand, where $\ell \in [1, q_{G_i} + q_{H_i} + q_s]$. The G_i's distribution of probability are exactly the same by this simulation (by the assumption of G_i to be a random oracle). Thus we have $\Pr[S_1] = \Pr[S_0]$.

Game_2: The random oracle H_i is simulated by $\mathcal{I}$. $\mathcal{A}_1$ generates a partial multi-signature σ_{i-1} for an arbitrary message m_ℓ using the secret information $\boldsymbol{sk}_{[1,i-1]}$ from the untargeted signers. $\mathcal{I}$ replies to the new arbitrary query $(m_\ell, r_{i_\ell}, \sigma_{i-1})$ from $\mathcal{A}_1$ with a hash value w_{i_ℓ}. Here w_{i_ℓ} is produced by $\mathcal{I}$ as follows: $\mathcal{I}$ selects $u_{i_\ell} \in_R \mathbb{Z}_{N_i}$, computes $z_{i_\ell} = \eta \cdot u_{i_\ell}^{e_i} \bmod N_i$ by $\eta \in_R \mathbb{Z}_{N_i}$ previously obtained. Then $\mathcal{I}$ generates a random u_{i_ℓ} until the first bit of z_{i_ℓ} is 0, but if that has never been 0 after L-time trial then $\mathcal{I}$ aborts. If $\mathcal{I}$ finds u_{i_ℓ} such that the first bit is 0, $\mathcal{I}$ breaks up z_{i_ℓ} as $z_{i_\ell} = 0 \parallel t_{i_\ell} \parallel s_{i_\ell} \parallel w_{i_\ell}$. And it registers $(w_{i_\ell}, (t_{i_\ell} \oplus \sigma_{i-1}) \parallel (s_{i_\ell} \oplus r_{i_\ell}))$ with the G_i-List, $(1, m_\ell, r_{i_\ell}, \sigma_{i-1}, u_{i_\ell}, w_{i_\ell})$ with the H_i-List, respectively. The $\mathcal{I}$ aborts if w_{i_ℓ} has already appeared in Game_1. Eventually, $\mathcal{I}$ sets $G_i(w_{i_\ell}) := (t_{i_\ell} \oplus \sigma_{i-1}) \parallel (s_{i_\ell} \oplus r_{i_\ell})$ and $H_i(m_\ell, r_{i_\ell}, \sigma_{i-1}) := w_{i_\ell}$. Thus there are at most q_{H_i} H_i hash queries in H_i-List. In the Game_2, the simulation of $\mathcal{I}$ shall fail,
  - In case that the first bit of z_{i_ℓ} cannot be 0 after L-time probing of z_{i_ℓ};
  - In case that the collision occurs in G_i-List.
Thus the success probability is changed as follows:

$$|\Pr[S_2] - \Pr[S_1]| \leq q_{H_i} \cdot \left(\frac{1}{2^L} + \frac{q_{G_i} + q_{H_i} + q_s}{2^{k_2}} \right).$$

Game_3: We change Game_2 into the following. If $\mathcal{A}_1$ makes an H_i oracle queries for $m_\ell \parallel r_\ell \parallel \sigma_{i-1}$ which means $(1, m_\ell, r_{i_\ell}, \sigma_{i-1}, \star, \star)$, then it aborts. Thus there are at most q_{H_i} H_i hash queries of the form $(1, m_\ell, r_{i_\ell}, \sigma_{i-1}, \star, \star)$ in H_i-List. Therefore the success probability is changed as follows:

$$|\Pr[S_3] - \Pr[S_2]| \leq q_s \cdot \frac{q_{H_i}}{2^{k_1}}.$$

Game₄: We change the simulation of H_i into the following. $\mathcal{I}$ replies to a new arbitrary query $(m_\ell, r'_{i_\ell}, \sigma_{i-1})$ from Σ_{sk_i} with the hash value ω'_i. Here ω'_{i_ℓ} is produced by $\mathcal{I}$ as follows: $\mathcal{I}$ selects $u_{i_\ell} \in_R \mathbb{Z}_{N_i}$, and computes $z'_{i_\ell} = u_{i_\ell}^{e_i} \bmod N_i$. Then $\mathcal{I}$ generates a random u_{i_ℓ} until the first bit of z_{i_ℓ} is 0, but if that has never been 0 after L-time trial, then $\mathcal{I}$ aborts. If $\mathcal{I}$ finds u_{i_ℓ} such that the first bit is 0, $\mathcal{I}$ breaks up z'_{i_ℓ} as $z'_{i_\ell} = 0 \parallel t'_{i_\ell} \parallel s'_{i_\ell} \parallel \omega'_{i_\ell}$. And it registers $(\omega'_{i_\ell}, (t'_{i_\ell} \oplus \sigma_{i-1}) \parallel (s'_{i_\ell} \oplus r'_{i_\ell}))$ with the G_i-List, $(0, m_\ell, r'_{i_\ell}, \sigma_{i-1}, u_{i_\ell}, \omega'_{i_\ell})$ with the H_i-List, respectively. $\mathcal{I}$ aborts if ω'_{i_ℓ} has already appeared in Game₁ or Game₂. Eventually, $\mathcal{I}$ sets $G_i(\omega'_{i_\ell}) := (t'_{i_\ell} \oplus \sigma_{i-1}) \parallel (s'_{i_\ell} \oplus r'_{i_\ell})$ and $H_i(m_\ell, r'_{i_\ell}, \sigma_{i-1}) := \omega'_{i_\ell}$. Owing to the bijectivity of the RSA function, $\mathcal{A}_1$ can not distinguish z_i from z'_i, and similarly the reply of H_i, ω_i from ω'_i. Thus there are at most q_s H_i hash queries from Σ_{sk_i} in H_i-List.

Unlike in Game₃, $\mathcal{I}$ shall fail also,
- In case that the first bit of z'_{i_ℓ} cannot be 0 after L-time probing of z'_{i_ℓ};
- In case that the collision occurs in G_i-List.

Thus the success probability is changed as follows:

$$|\Pr[S_4] - \Pr[S_3]| \leqq q_s \cdot \left(\frac{1}{2^L} + \frac{q_{G_i} + q_{H_i} + q_s}{2^{k_2}} \right).$$

Game₅: A signing oracle Σ_{sk_i} is simulated by $\mathcal{I}$. Since we give the restriction to Game₃, $(1, m_\ell, r_{i_\ell}, \sigma_{i-1}, \star, \star) \in H_i$-List cannot be produced for the arbitrary signing query $(m_\ell, r_{i_\ell}, \sigma_{i-1})$ from $\mathcal{A}_1$. Accordingly, z'_{i_ℓ} is defined by $u_{i_\ell}^{e_i} \bmod N_i$, so $\mathcal{I}$ returns u_{i_ℓ} as a multi-signature for $(m_\ell, r'_{i_\ell}, \sigma_{i-1})$. The simulation of Σ_{pk_i} is always succeeded by $\mathcal{I}$. Thus we have $\Pr[S_5] = \Pr[S_4]$.

Game₆: The $\mathcal{I}$ receives (N_i, e_i, η) as its input from the outside where N_i, e_i is the public-key pk_i and η is chosen at random in $\mathbb{Z}_{N_i}$ such that $\eta = x^{e_i} \bmod N_i$. And $\mathcal{I}$ starts running $\mathcal{A}_1$ on inputs $\boldsymbol{pk}$ including this pk_i. $\mathcal{A}_1$ will make oracle queries (each signing queries, H_i queries and G_i queries). Then $\mathcal{I}$ answers the signing query and the hash query from $\mathcal{A}_1$ using the pk_i and the η which $\mathcal{I}$ receives from the outside. But $\mathcal{A}_1$ cannot distinguish the pk_i which is generated from $\mathcal{RSA}(1^{K_i})$ by $\mathcal{I}$ from the one which are given to the $\mathcal{I}$ from the outside. Thus we have $\Pr[S_6] = \Pr[S_5]$.

As the pair of (m^*, σ_i^*) which is the output by $\mathcal{A}_1$ in Game₆ satisfies the verification formula, if we set with $\sigma_i^{*e_i} \bmod N_i = 0 \parallel t_i^* \parallel s_i^* \parallel \omega_i^*$ and $(\alpha_i^* \parallel \beta_i^*) = (t_i^* \parallel s_i^*) \oplus G_i(\omega_i^*)$, then it will be set to $\omega_i^* = H_i(m^*, \beta_i^*, \alpha_i^*)$ and $\alpha_i^* = \sigma_{i-1}^*, \beta_i^* = r_i^*$.

Finally, $\mathcal{A}_1$ generates a forged multi-signature σ_n^* for some message m^* from σ_i^* which have been output by $\mathcal{A}_1$ and the secret information $\boldsymbol{sk}_{[i+1,n]}$, and outputs.

With the following, we evaluate the success probability that m^* is found in H_i-List by $\mathcal{A}_1$. AskH$_i$ denotes the event that $(m^*, r_i^*, \sigma_{i-1}^*)$ has been asked to H_i by $\mathcal{A}_1$.

- In case of AskH$_i$ is not satisfied: The hash value of $H_i(m^*, r_i^*, \sigma_{i-1}^*)$ is not asked by $\mathcal{A}_1$, namely undefined. Accordingly, if there was no H_i oracle query for $(m^*, r_i^*, \sigma_{i-1}^*)$ before, the probability that $H_i(m^*, r_i^*, \sigma_{i-1}^*) = \omega_i^*$ is at most 2^{-k_2}.[6] Namely, we have $\Pr[S_6 | \neg\mathsf{AskH}_i] \leq 2^{-k_2}$.

- In case of AskH_i is satisfied: Since we give the restriction to Game_3 it is impossible to ask H_i about $(m^*, r_i^*, \sigma_{i-1}^*)$ by Σ_{sk_i}. Then $\mathcal{I}$ can succeed in outputting $\eta^{d_i} \bmod N_i$ owing to $H_i(m^*, r_i^*, \sigma_{i-1}^*) = \omega_i^*$, $G_i(\omega_i^*) = (t_i^* \oplus \sigma_{i-1}^*) \parallel (s_i^* \oplus r_i^*)$ and $\eta \cdot u_i^{*e_i} = 0 \parallel s_i^* \parallel t_i^* \parallel \omega_i^* = \sigma_i^{*e_i} \bmod N_i$. Consequently $\mathcal{I}$ can solve the i-th inverting RSA. We have $\Pr[S_6 \wedge \mathsf{AskH}_i] \leq \mathsf{Succ}^{\mathsf{rsa}_i}(\tau^*, K_i)$.

Here τ^* denotes the time complexity for Game_6. τ^* consists of the time for executing $\mathcal{A}_1$, $\mathcal{I}$'s simulation and $L(q_s + q_{H_i})$ times required time for exponentiation $\bmod N_i$. Thus we have $\tau^*(K_i) \leq \tau_i + L(q_s + q_{H_i}) \cdot T_{exp}(K_i)$. From what is mentioned above, $\Pr[S_6] \leq \mathsf{Succ}^{\mathsf{rsa}_i}(\tau^*, K_i) + \frac{1}{2^{k_2}}$.

Finally, we can obtain

$$\epsilon_i = \Pr[S_0] = \Pr[S_1]$$

$$\leq \Pr[S_2] + q_{H_i} \cdot \left(\frac{1}{2^L} + \frac{q_{G_i} + q_{H_i} + q_s}{2^{k_2}} \right)$$

$$\leq \Pr[S_3] + q_{H_i} \cdot \left(\frac{1}{2^L} + \frac{q_{G_i} + q_{H_i} + q_s}{2^{k_2}} \right) + q_s \cdot \frac{q_{H_i}}{2^{k_1}}$$

$$\leq \Pr[S_4] + q_{H_i} \cdot \left(\frac{1}{2^L} + \frac{q_{G_i} + q_{H_i} + q_s}{2^{k_2}} \right) + q_s \cdot \frac{q_{H_i}}{2^{k_1}} + q_s \cdot \left(\frac{1}{2^L} + \frac{q_{G_i} + q_{H_i} + q_s}{2^{k_2}} \right)$$

$$\leq \mathsf{Succ}^{\mathsf{rsa}_i}(\tau^*, K_i) + \frac{1}{2^{k_2}} + (q_s + q_{H_i}) \cdot \left(\frac{1}{2^L} + \frac{q_{G_i} + q_{H_i} + q_s}{2^{k_2}} \right) + q_s \cdot \frac{q_{H_i}}{2^{k_1}}$$

$$\leq \epsilon^* + \frac{1}{2^{k_2}} + (q_s + q_{H_i}) \cdot \left(\frac{1}{2^L} + \frac{q_{G_i} + q_{H_i} + q_s}{2^{k_2}} \right) + q_s \cdot \frac{q_{H_i}}{2^{k_1}}.$$

The Theorem 3 is now proven.   □

---

[6] This probability is made a lucky shot by $\mathcal{A}_1$.

A Length-Flexible Threshold Cryptosystem with Applications

Ivan Damgård and Mads Jurik

Aarhus University, Dept. of Computer Science, **BRICS**[*]

Abstract. We propose a public-key cryptosystem which is derived from the Paillier cryptosystem. The scheme inherits the attractive homomorphic properties of Paillier encryption. In addition, we achieve two new properties: First, all users can use the same modulus when generating key pairs, this allows more efficient proofs of relations between different encryptions. Second, we can construct a threshold decryption protocol for our scheme that is length-flexible, i.e., it can handle efficiently messages of arbitrary length, even though the public key and the secret key shares held by decryption servers are of fixed size. We show how to apply this cryptosystem to build a self-tallying election scheme with perfect ballot secrecy, and to build a length-flexible mix-net which is universally verifiable, where the size of keys and ciphertexts do not depend on the number of mix servers, and is robust against a corrupt minority.

Keywords: length-flexible, length-invariant, mix-net, group decryption, self-tallying, election, perfect ballot secrecy.

1 Introduction

1.1 Background

In [4], Paillier proposed a public-key cryptosystem which, like RSA, uses computations with a composite modulus, but has some very attractive properties making it potentially interesting for applications such as electronic voting and mix-nets: it is additively homomorphic and decryption is efficient for all ciphertexts: there is no need to solve discrete logarithms, as with additive homomorphic schemes derived from El-Gamal encryption.

In [9] the system was generalized to handle arbitrary size messages (with the same modulus) and a threshold decryption protocol was proposed. Unfortunately, this protocol can only handle efficiently messages of length smaller than a threshold set at key generation time, for longer messages a cumbersome multiparty computation protocol is needed.

Another unsatisfactory property is that the secret key is essentially the factorization of the modulus, so different users cannot use the same modulus. This

---

[*] Basic Research in Computer Science, Centre of the Danish National Research Foundation.

R. Safavi-Naini and J. Seberry (Eds.): ACISP 2003, LNCS 2727, pp. 350–364, 2003.
© Springer-Verlag Berlin Heidelberg 2003

means that natural tasks such as proving in zero-knowledge that two ciphertexts (from different public keys) contain the same message become difficult and seem to require generic solutions.

One possible application of homomorphic encryption is to build mix-nets. These are protocols used to provide anonymity for senders by collecting encrypted messages from several users and have a collection of servers process these, such that the plaintext messages are output in randomly permuted order. A useful property for mix-nets is length-flexibility, which means that the mix-net is able to handle messages of arbitrary size. More precisely, what we mean by this is the following: although all messages submitted to a single run of the mix-net must have the same length in order not to break the anonymity, this common length can be decided freely for each run of the mix-net, without having to change any public-key information. This is especially useful for providing anonymity for e.g. E-mails. One way to achieve length-flexibility is to use hybrid mix-nets. These mix-nets use a public key construction to create keys for a symmetric cipher that is used for encrypting the bulk of the messages.

Two length-flexible hybrid mix-nets have been proposed. Ohkubo and Abe in [5] proposed a scheme in which verification of server behavior relies on a generic method by Desmedt and Kurosawa [6]. This results in a system that is robust when at most the square root of the number of mix servers are corrupt. After this Juels and Jakobsson suggested in [11] that verification can be added by using message authentication codes (MACs), which are appended to the plaintext for each layer of encryption. This allows tolerating more corruptions at the expense of efficiency - for instance, the length of the ciphertexts now depends on the number of mix servers as opposed to [5], and each server has to store more secret material. Although the system is verifiable, it is not universally verifiable, which means that external observers cannot verify that everything was done correctly.

In [3] (with some minor pitfall corrected in [8]), Abe introduced verifiable mix-nets using a network of binary switching gates, which is based on the permutation networks of Waksman [1]. This mix-network is robust with up to half of the mix servers being controlled by an active and malicious adversary. One approach to make this length-flexible would be to exchange El-Gamal with a verifiable length-flexible encryption scheme. The cryptosystem in [9] however does not support efficient and length-flexible threshold decryption.

Another application area for homomorphic encryption is electronic voting. In [14] Kiayias and Yung introduced a new paradigm for electronic voting, namely protocols that are self-tallying, dispute-free and have perfect ballot secrecy (STDFPBS for short). This paradigm is suitable for, e.g. boardroom elections where a (small) group of users want a maximally secure vote without help from external authorities. The main property is perfect ballot secrecy, which means that for *any* coalition of voters (even a majority) the only information they can compute is what follows from the result and their own votes, namely the tally of honest users' votes. This is the best we can hope for, and is the type of privacy that is actually achieved by paper based elections. Self-tallying means that as soon as all votes have been cast, no further interaction is needed to compute the result, it can be efficiently computed by just looking at all ballots, which can be done, even by a (casual) third party. Dispute-freeness means that no disputes between players can arise, because all faults are detected in public.

In [14], it is argued that STDFPBS elections cannot be achieved efficiently by traditional methods. For instance, large scale solutions are typically not of this type because they assume that some set of authorities are available to help with the election. The authorities typically share a secret key that can be reconstructed by a majority. In a small scale scenario we could let each voter play the role of an authority himself, but this would not give perfect ballot secrecy because a corrupt majority would know how *every* single voter voted. If we try to repair this by setting the threshold of the secret sharing scheme to be the total number of voters, then even a single fault will mean that the secret key is lost, and an expensive key generation phase would be needed.

In [14] STDFPBS elections are achieved for a yes/no vote by using constructs based on discrete log modulo a prime. This results in a tallying phase that needs to find a discrete log, which requires $O(\sqrt{u})$ work when there are u voters. It also implies that generalization to multi-way elections either results in larger ballots or much worse complexity for the tallying phase. Given earlier work on electronic voting, it is natural to speculate that this could be solved simply by using Paillier encryption instead. However as noted in [14], this does not work, we would lose some essential properties of the scheme.

1.2   Our Contribution

In this paper, we suggest a new public-key cryptosystem. It is a further development of the scheme from [9], it is as efficient up to a constant factor and inherits the homomorphic property. It is semantically secure based on the Paillier and composite DDH assumptions, or - at a moderate loss of efficiency - based only on the Paillier assumption. It is also related to a Paillier-based scheme presented in [12], but is more efficient and is also length-flexible.

We achieve two new properties. First, our scheme allow several users to use the same modulus. This allows efficient zero-knowledge proofs for relations between ciphertexts created under different public keys. We apply this to construct STDFPBS elections, where the tallying phase reveals the result with a small number of additions, instead of $O(\sqrt{u})$ multiplications as in [14]. This also shows that STDFPBS elections with all the essential properties can be based on Paillier encryption, thus solving a problem left open in [14]. Finally, it implies a natural and efficient generalization to multi-way elections.

Second, we propose a threshold decryption protocol where keys can be set up so that messages of arbitrary length can be handled efficiently with the same (fixed size) keys. In addition, the computational work done by each server does not depend on the message length, only the cost of a final public post-processing is message dependent. We also give efficient zero-knowledge protocols for proving various claims on encrypted values.

We combine these with ideas from [3,5] to construct a mix-net that has several desirable properties at the same time: 1) **Length-flexible:** the public key does not limit the size of plaintexts that can be encrypted and mixed efficiently. 2) **Length-invariant:** lengths of keys and ciphertexts do not depend on the number of mix servers. 3) **Provably secure:** provable secure in the random oracle model under the Decisional Composite Residuosity Assumption and composite DDH 4) **Universally verifiable:** anyone can verify the correctness of the output from the mix-net. 5) **Strong correctness:** messages submitted by malicious users cannot be changed once they have been submitted. 6) **Order flexible:** mix servers do not need to be invoked in a certain order. This improves resilience to temporary server unavailability. We note that all this is achieved by using public key encryption everywhere, which in the passive adversary case makes it less efficient than the Hybrid mix-nets that uses symmetric key crypto to encrypt the messages.

2   Preliminaries

The systems in this paper use a modified version of the Damgård-Jurik generalization [9] of the Paillier cryptosystem [4]. The security of this encryption scheme depends on the Decisional Composite Residuosity Assumption first introduced by Paillier.

Conjecture 1 (The Decisional Composite Residuosity Assumption (DCRA)) *Let $\mathcal{A}$ be any probabilistic polynomial time algorithm, and assume $\mathcal{A}$ gets n, x as input. Here $n = pq$ is an admissible RSA modulus of length k bits, and x is either random in $\mathbb{Z}_{n^2}^*$ or it is a random n'th power in $\mathbb{Z}_{n^2}^*$. $\mathcal{A}$ outputs a bit b. Let $p_0(\mathcal{A}, k)$ be the probability that $b = 1$ if x is random in $\mathbb{Z}_{n^2}^*$, and $p_1(\mathcal{A}, k)$ the probability that $b = 1$ if x is a random n'th power. Then $|p_0(\mathcal{A}, k) - p_1(\mathcal{A}, k)|$ is negligible in k.*

The encryption is extended with some discrete logarithm constructions, so the DDH assumption is also needed in a slightly modified version to capture the group.

Conjecture 2 (The Decisional Diffie-Hellman (composite DDH)) *Let $\mathcal{A}$ be any probabilistic polynomial time algorithm, and assume $\mathcal{A}$ gets $(n, g, g^a \bmod n, g^b \bmod n, y)$ as input. Here $n = pq$ is an admissible RSA modulus of length k bits, g is a element of Q_n the group of squares in $\mathbb{Z}_n^*$. The values a and b are chosen uniformly random in $\mathbb{Z}_{\phi(n)/4}$ and the value y is either random in Q_n or satisfies $y = g^{ab} \bmod n$. $\mathcal{A}$ outputs a bit b. Let $p_0(\mathcal{A}, k)$ be the probability that $b = 1$ if y is random in Q_n, and $p_1(\mathcal{A}, k)$ the probability that $b = 1$ if $y = g^{ab} \bmod n$. Then $|p_0(\mathcal{A}, k) - p_1(\mathcal{A}, k)|$ is negligible in k.*

Note that the number $\phi(n)/4$ is not publicly known, so we cannot choose an exponent r with the uniform distribution over $\mathbb{Z}_{\phi(n)/4}$. Throughout this paper we will pick the random values from the group $\mathbb{Z}_N$, where N is a sufficiently large value. A discussion of how to choose N can be seen in [15].

In the Damgård and Jurik paper [9] an algorithm for calculating the discrete logarithm with respect to the element $(n+1)$ is described. In this paper we will use L_s to denote an application of this function, that satisfies:

$$L_s((n+1)^m \bmod n^{s+1}) = m \bmod n^s$$

computing this function requires work $O(s^4 k^2) = O(s^2 |n^s|^2)$

3   A Proof Friendly Cryptosystem

We propose a cryptosystem that can handle efficient zero knowledge proofs:

Key Generation: Choose an RSA modulus $n = pq$ of length k bits, with $p = 2p' + 1$ and $q = 2q' + 1$ where p, q, p', q' are primes. Select an element $g \in Q_n$, the group of all squares of $\mathbb{Z}_n^*$, and $\alpha \in \mathbb{Z}_\tau$, where $\tau = p'q' = |Q_n|$. Pick the secret value $a_0 = \alpha \in \mathbb{Z}_\tau$ and some random coefficients $a_i \in \mathbb{Z}_\tau$ for $1 \leq i \leq t$, where $t \geq w/2$ is the threshold of the system with w servers. The polynomial $f(x) = \sum_{0 \leq i \leq t} a_i x^i$ is created and the secret shares are calculated as $\alpha_i = f(i)$. The public value is $h = g^\alpha \bmod n$, and the values for verification are $h_i = g^{\alpha_i} \bmod n$. The public key is (n, g, h), the verification values $(h_1, ..., h_w)$, and the private key of server i is α_i.

Encryption: Given a plaintext $m \in \mathbb{Z}^+$, choose an integer $s > 0$, such that $m \in \mathbb{Z}_{n^s}$, and pick a random $r \in \mathbb{Z}_N$ and $b_0, b_1 \in \{0, 1\}$. The ciphertext is then

$$E^\pm(m, r, b_0, b_1) = ((-1)^{b_0} g^r \bmod n, (-1)^{b_1} (h^{4\Delta^2 r})^{n^s} (n+1)^m \bmod n^{s+1})$$

Threshold Decryption: Given a ciphertext $c = (G, H) = E^\pm(m, r, b_0, b_1)$, it is only decrypted if the Jacobi symbol of G and H is 1. Each server then computes:

$$d_i = G^{2\Delta\alpha_i} \bmod n$$

and a proof that $\log_g(h_i) = \log_{G^{4\Delta}}(d_i^2)$. The proof used for this is shown in section 3.2. The d_i values, from the set S of servers with legal proofs, are combined using Lagrange interpolation to create the exponent $4\Delta^2\alpha$:

$$d = \prod d_i^{2\lambda_i^S} = G^{4\Delta^2\alpha} = h^{4\Delta^2 r} \bmod n \quad \text{where } \lambda_i^S = \prod_{j \in S \setminus \{i\}} \Delta \frac{j}{j - i}$$

The reason for the factor Δ is to ensure $\lambda_i^S \in \mathbb{Z}$. To make sure that we work in Q_n we have to square H, and so we can remove $h^{4\Delta^2 r}$ by computing

$$H' = H^2 d^{-2n^s} = (n+1)^{2m} \bmod n^{s+1}$$

and the plaintext is found as $m = L_s(H')/2 \bmod n^s$.

This cryptosystem is additivly homomorphic under pairwise multiplication:

$$E^{\pm}(m_0, r_0, b_{00}, b_{01})E^{\pm}(m_1, r_1, b_{10}, b_{11}) =$$
$$E^{\pm}(m_0 + m_1 \bmod n^s, r_0 + r_1 \bmod \tau, b_{00} \oplus b_{10}, b_{01} \oplus b_{11})$$

In section 3.2 three protocols are shown: 1) a proof that something is a legal encryption, 2) a proof that something is a legal encryption of some publicly known plaintext, and 3) the threshold decryption proof. In the final version [15] some techniques for improving the complexity of most computations from $O(s^3 k^3)$ to $O(s^2 k^3)$ are shown along with some simplified cryptosystems.

3.1   Security of the Threshold Cryptosystems

Due to its homomorphic properties, our basic cryptosystem cannot be chosen ciphertext secure, so we cannot hope to prove that the threshold version is chosen ciphertext secure either. However, we can show a result saying essentially that as long as the adversary does not control the ciphertexts being decrypted, the threshold decryption releases no information other than the plaintext.

Definition 1. *A chosen plaintext threshold adversary $\mathcal{A}$ runs in probabilistic polynomial time and can statically and actively corrupt $t < w/2$ of the servers. In addition, for any efficiently samplable distribution $\mathcal{D}$, he may request that a message m be chosen according to $\mathcal{D}$ and then to see a random ciphertext containing m be decrypted using the threshold decryption protocol. A threshold public-key cryptosystem is secure against such an adversary if his view can be simulated in probabilistic polynomial time given only the public key.*

Now the following theorem can be proven.

Lemma 1. *The threshold cryptosystem is semantically secure under Conjectures 1 and 2. They are also secure against any chosen plaintext threshold adversary as defined above.*

The proof and a more formal definition of semantic security are shown in [15] along with a proof that if we simplify the system by setting $E(m, r) = E^{\pm}(m, r, 0, 0)$ we still have a semantically secure cryptosystem (but then, the protocols from section 3.2 will not work).

3.2   Proofs for the Proof Friendly Variant

Proof of Legal Encryption. The purpose of the proof is to prove that given (G, H) there exist an $r \in \mathbb{Z}_N$ and an $m \in \mathbb{Z}_{n^s}$ such that $G = \pm g^r \bmod n$ and $H = \pm h^{4\Delta^2 r}(n+1)^m$.

Protocol for legal encryption
Input: $n, g, h, c = (G, H)$
Private input for P: $r \in \mathbb{Z}_N$ and $m \in \mathbb{Z}_{n^s}$, such that $c = E^{\pm}(m, r, b_0, b_1)$ for some b_0 and b_1.

1. P chooses at random r' in $\{0, ..., 2^{|N|+2k_2}\}$ and $m' \in \mathbb{Z}_{n^s}$, where k_2 is a secondary security parameter (e.g. 160 bits). P sends $c' = (G', H') = E^{\pm}(m', r', 0, 0)$ to V.
2. V chooses e, a random k_2 bit number, and sends e to P.
3. P sends $\hat{r} = r' + er$ and $\hat{m} = m' + em \bmod n^s$ to V. V checks that G, H, G', H' are prime to n, have Jacobi symbol 1 and that the equation $E^{\pm}(2\hat{m}, 2\hat{r}, 0, 0) = (G'^2 G^{2e} \bmod n, H'^2 H^{2e} \bmod n^{s+1}) = c'^2 c^{2e}$, hold and accepts if and only if this is the case.

The protocol above can be proven to be sound and complete honest verifier zero-knowledge. This is enough for the election protocol in section 5, since it will only be used in an non-interactive setting using the Fiat-Shamir Heuristic and hash function $\mathcal{H}$ to generate the challenge $e = \mathcal{H}(G, H, G', H')$.

Proof of Legal Encryption of Certain Plaintext. The protocol for legal encryptions, can be altered to a protocol for proving that something is a legal encryption of a certain plaintext m. This can be done by fixing $m' = 0$ which means that the message $\hat{m} = em$ doesn't have to be sent in the third step. This is also sound and complete honest verifier zero-knowledge, since c' have to be an encryption of 0 or there is at most one e such that P can satisfy the test.

Decryption Proof. To make the decryption share, the server calculated the value

$$d_i = G^{2\Delta\alpha_i} \bmod n$$

The server needs to prove that this was indeed what it submitted, but we have to allow a possible factor of -1, so we accept that $d_i = \pm G^{2\Delta\alpha_i}$, which is why the value d_i^2 is used in the Lagrange interpolation. What needs to be proven is that

$$\alpha_i = \log_g(h_i) = \log_{G^{4\Delta}}(d_i^2) \bmod p'q'$$

This can be done using a proof identical to that of Shoup RSA Threshold signatures [7].

Proof: Given a hash function $\mathcal{H}$ that outputs a k_2 bit hash, pick a random $r \in \{0, ..., 2^{|n|+2k_2} - 1\}$ and calculate

$$\hat{g} = g^r \bmod n, \hat{G} = G^{4\Delta r} \bmod n, c = \mathcal{H}(g, G^{4\Delta}, h_i, d_i^2, \hat{g}, \hat{G}), z = \alpha_i c + r$$

The proof is the pair (c, z).
Verification: For a proof to be accepted the following equation has to hold

$$c = \mathcal{H}(g, G^{4\Delta}, h_i, d_i^2, h_i^{-c} g^z \bmod n, d_i^{-2c} G^{4\Delta z} \bmod n)$$

This proof of correctness is sound and statistical zero-knowledge under the random oracle model. This is proven in Shoups paper on Practical Threshold signatures [7] and is therefore omitted here.

4   Verifiable Length-Flexible Mix-Net

4.1   The Mix-Net Model

A mix-net is a network of servers that receive a number of encryptions, perform a random permutation of these, and output the plaintexts of the encryptions. This is done in such a way, that unless all servers (or most in some schemes) cooperate no one can link the input encryptions to the output plaintexts.

Note that for any single mix of messages, the inputs for the servers must be of the same length, since otherwise one could match the sizes of the inputs and outputs to find some information on the permutation. For practical applications this means, that a fixed upper bound will have to be decided for each mix, and all input messages for that mix have to be of the chosen size. This bound can chosen freely for each mix, however.

4.2   Adversaries

An adversary in [5] is defined by $(t_u, t_s)^{**}$, where the $*$ is either A for an active adversary or P for a passive adversary. The thresholds t_u and t_s are the maximal number of users and servers respectively, that can be controlled by the adversary. For example $(t_u, t_s)^{AP}$-adversary means that the adversary can read and change any value for up to t_u users and view any value inside t_s servers. A passive adversary only observes the values passing a server or user, but does not try to induce values into the process. An active adversary can attack the protocol by changing any value or refuse to supply results in any part of the protocol. The adversary is assumed to be non-adaptive, meaning that the users and servers being controlled by the adversary are decided in advance.

The mix-net in this paper is safe against these adversaries of increasing strength (u is the number of users and w the number of servers):

- $(u - 2, w - 1)^{PP}$-adversary
- $(u - 2, w - 1)^{AP}$-adversary
- $(u - 2, \lfloor (w - 1)/2 \rfloor)^{AA}$-adversary

Compared to the length-flexible mix-net in [5], the 2 first adversaries are the same, but the last one is improved from $(u - 2, O(\sqrt{w}))^{AA}$ to $(u - 2, \lfloor (w - 1)/2 \rfloor)^{AA}$.

4.3   Security of the Mix-Net

We will use a strong version of correctness, so even if users are working together with servers, they will not be able to change the message once the mix has started.

Definition 2 (Strong Correctness). *Given x encrypted messages as input, where y of the encryptions are malformed. The mix-net will output a permutation of the $x - y$ messages with correct decryptions, and discard all y malformed encryptions.*

Definition 3 (Anonymity). *Given an $(t_u, t_s)^{**}$-adversary, and a mix of x messages. Then the adversary should be unable to link any of the $x - t_u$ messages with any of the $x - t_u$ uncorrupted users who sent them.*

Definition 4 (Universal Verifiability). *Given the public view of the protocol being all the information written to the bulletin board, there exist a poly-time algorithm V that accepts only if the output of the protocol is correct, and otherwise outputs reject.*

Definition 5 (Robustness). *Given an $(t_u, t_s)^{*A}$-adversary the protocol should always output a correct result.*

The mix-network presented can be shown to satisfy these definitions under the different adversaries.

Theorem 1. *The basic mix-network provides strong correctness and anonymity (and robustness) against an $(u - 2, w - 1)^{*P}$-adversary, where u is the number of users and w the number of servers.*

Theorem 2. *The mix-network with threshold decryption provides strong correctness, anonymity, universal verifiability and robustness against an $(u-2, \lfloor (w-1)/2 \rfloor)^{*A}$-adversary, where u is the number of users and w the number of servers.*

Proofs for these theorems can be seen in [15].

4.4 The System

It is assumed that all communication in the protocol goes through a bulletin board, that anyone can access to verify the result. This means that the public key, and all outputs and proofs from the mix servers are written to this bulletin board. Using this, the mix-network can be built from the threshold cryptosystem in the following way:

Key Generation: A trusted third party (TTP) generates $n = pq$ (as above) and $g \in Q_n$. Depending on the model the server picks the secrets the following way.

- **Passive adversary model:** For each mix server ($0 < i \leq w$) the TTP picks a random value $\alpha_i \in \mathbb{Z}_\tau$ and sets $\alpha = \sum_{0 < i \leq w} \alpha_i \bmod \tau$. The public value is computed as $h = g^\alpha \bmod n$. The public key posted is (n, g, h) and the private key of server i is α_i.
- **Active adversary model:** Here, the key generation takes place exactly as described above for the threshold cryptosystem. The private key α_i is given to the i'th server in a secure way. The public key (n, g, h) and the verification values $(h_1, ..., h_w)$ are posted to the bulletin board.

Encryption: The s have to be fixed for each mix, so given a $m \in \mathbb{Z}_{n^s}$, random values $r \in \mathbb{Z}_N, b_0, b_1 \in \{0, 1\}$ are chosen. The ciphertext posted on the bulletin board is $E^\pm(m, r, b_0, b_1)$.

Mixing phase: Before the mixing begins any ciphertext (G, H), where either G or H has Jacobi symbol -1 will be discarded as being incorrect. If an illegal ciphertext with Jacobi symbol 1 have been submitted it will be caught during decryption. Next set $I = \{1, ..., w\}$. While $I \neq \emptyset$ pick an $i \in I$ and let the i'th server make its mix permutation on the last correct output posted on the bulletin board:

- **Passive adversary model:** Since the adversary is passive, the mix server just do a random permutation and output a re-encryption for each of the ciphertexts (G, H) using the random values b_0, b_1, r:

$$(G', H') = (G, H)E^{\pm}(0, r, b_0, b_1)$$

- **Active adversary model:** Here verification is needed to satisfy the universal verifiability, correctness and robustness of the system. To do this, the server picks a random permutation and creates a network of binary gates using the Waksman construction [1]. This network consists of $O(u \log(u))$ binary gates and can create any permutation of the inputs. For each binary gate a bit B is defined (and $\bar{B} = 1 - B$), determining if the gate should pass the encryptions straight through the gate or switch them, depending on the complete permutation of the mix. Each gate also has 2 ciphertexts (G_0, H_0) and (G_1, H_1) as input. The server chooses 6 random values: $x_0, x_1 \in \mathbb{Z}_N$ and $b_{00}, b_{01}, b_{10}, b_{11} \in \{0, 1\}$, and sets the 2 output ciphertexts for the gate to

$$(G'_B, H'_B) = (G_0, H_0)E^{\pm}(0, x_0, b_{00}, b_{10})$$
$$(G'_{\bar{B}}, H'_{\bar{B}}) = (G_1, H_1)E^{\pm}(0, x_1, b_{01}, b_{11})$$

To prove this is done correctly the server needs to prove that the B, satisfying the 2 equations above, really exist. This can be done by showing that the difference between (G'_B, H'_B) and (G_0, H_0) is a legal encryption of 0 (and likewise for $(G'_{\bar{B}}, H'_{\bar{B}})$ and (G_1, H_1)) for some $B \in \{0, 1\}$. This can be done by using 4 concurrent runs of the legal encryption of the message 0 protocol using the technique from [2]. These proofs are posted to the bullitin board along with the outputs and intermediate encryptions. Outputs from servers with incorrect proofs are simply ignored

When the mix is over or if the server refuses to output a mix, the server is removed from the set $I := I \backslash \{i\}$.

Decryption: After the mixing has been performed the decryption of each of the output ciphertexts (G, H) needs to be performed. The removal of the h^r part is different depending on the model and is achieved the following way

- **Passive adversary model:** The servers perform a decryption by each calculating their decryption part $d_i = G^{\alpha_i} \mod n$. These values are removed from the encryption

$$H' = (H(\prod_{0 < i \leq w} d_i)^{-n^s})^2 = (n + 1)^{2m} \mod n^{s+1}$$

- **Active adversary model:** The servers check that at least $t+1$ servers have performed a legal mix, in which case at least 1 of them is honest, and it is safe to decrypt the encryptions. The value H' is computed as in the proof friendly threshold decryption in section 3.

In both the passive and active model the value H' has the form $(n+1)^{2m}$ if the input was a correct encryption. If it was not a correct encryption it will have a power of h remaining: $H' = (h^r)^{n^s}(n+1)^{2m}$. This is the case if and only if $n \nmid H' - 1$ (since $n|(n+1)^{2m} - 1$) and the decryption is aborted in this case. Otherwise the message is decrypted as $m = L_s(H')/2 \bmod n^s$.

The order of the mix servers can be chosen arbitrarily, which means that if server i is unavailable when it is supposed to mix, the server $i+1$ can do its mix. When server i gets back again it can perform its mix on the last output.

In the final version [15] a method is shown, that optimizes all computations except the last public exponentiation, from using $O(s^3k^3)$ time to only $O(s^2k^3)$.

5   Self-Tallying Elections with Perfect Ballot Secrecy

In this section it will be shown how to make a more efficient self-tallying elections with perfect ballot secrecy based on the cryptosystem introduced in this paper. Note that for all practical purposes $s = 1$ will be sufficient for this application. This will only be a brief walk-through of the technical details, so for a more in-depth explanation the reader is referred to [14].

The system uses the bulletin board model and it is assumed that a safe prime product n and a generator $g \in Q_n$ is setup in advance[1].

The modulus n can be generated once and for all. One option is to let a trusted third party do this. Note that since the factorization of n is never needed, not even in shared form, a trusted party solution can be quite acceptable, for instance one could use a secure hardware box that is destroyed after n has been generated.

Another option is to use a distributed protocol such as [13] or a generic multiparty computation. To ensure perfect ballot secrecy, all values in these protocols have to be shared such that no subset can get the secret. This comes at the expense of possibly having to restart the key generation if faults occur, but this cost cannot be avoided if we need to handle dishonest majorities and is consistent with the way corrective fault tolerance is defined in [14].

The element g can be generated by jointly generating some random value $x \in \mathbb{Z}_n^*$ and then defining g as $g = x^2$ which will be in Q_n.

The bulletin board also participates in the protocol to ensure that none of the actual voters will know the result before they vote. With a self-tallying scheme, this type of fairness cannot be achieved without such trust (see [14]). One may think of the bulletin board as a party that must vote 0 (so it will not influence the result), and is trusted to submit its vote only after all players have voted.

---

[1] Accepting some extra conjectures, the techniques of [10] can be employed in order to use any RSA modulus n where $\phi(n)/4$ is prime to Δ

The bulletin board however does not have to participate in every step of the protocol. It will only participate in: 1) the registration phase, where it registers its public key, 2) the error correction of the ballot casting, where it has some encrypted values it needs to reveal, and 3) the post ballot casting step, where it reveals its 0 vote, thereby enabling everyone to calculate the result.

5.1   Setup Phase

The setup phase consists of two tasks. First the voter registration and then the initialization of the voting system itself. In the registration phase voters, that want to participate in the election, register on the bulletin board. After all voters are registered, the voters need to setup the values to be used in the protocol. Since voters can be malicious in this part of the protocol there is an error correction step to correct any problems encountered.

Voter Registration. Voter i chooses the private key α_i at random in $\mathbb{Z}_N$ and computes the value $h_i = g^{\alpha_i} \bmod n$. The voter registers by posting the public key $pk_i = (g, h_i)$ on the bulletin board. Let R be the set of all registered voters and for simplicity let's assume that $R = \{1, 2, ..., u\}$. To ensure fairness the bulletin board also generates a public key pk_0 and posts it on the bulletin board (we set $R_0 = R \cup \{0\}$).

Initialization. Each voter $i \in R$ picks random values $s_{ij} \in \mathbb{Z}_{n^s}$ for each $j \in R$ and random $r_{ij} \in \mathbb{Z}_N$ for each $j \in R_0$. The value s_{i0} is set to $-\sum_{j \in R} s_{ij} \bmod n^s$, which ensures that $\sum_{j \in R_0} s_{ij} = 0 \bmod n^s$.
   The voter i publishes the encryptions

$$c_{ij} = (G_{ij}, H_{ij}) = E^{\pm}_{pk_j}(s_{ij}, r_{ij})$$

for all $j \in R_0$ along with a proof, that these are indeed legal encryptions and the sum of the plaintexts is 0 modulo n^s.
   To prove these are legal encryptions, the proof from section 3.2 is used. To prove that the sum of the plaintexts in the encryptions $(G_{i0}, H_{i0}), ..., (G_{iu}, H_{iu})$ is 0, it is enough to look at the product $H_{i0} \cdots H_{0u}$. The resulting value is

$$H_{i0} \cdots H_{iu} = (h_0^{r_{i0}} \cdots h_u^{r_{iu}})^{n^s} (n+1)^{s_{i0}+\cdots+s_{iu}}$$

which is an n^s'th power iff $\sum_{j \in R_0} s_{ij} = 0 \bmod n^s$. The protocol for n^s'th powers from [9] can be used to prove this, since the voter knows an n^s'th root of this number, namely $h_0^{r_{i0}} \cdots h_u^{r_{iu}}$.

Error Correction of the Initialization. Let Q_1 be the set of voters that either doesn't supply all the encryptions or supply invalid proofs. Any values submitted by voters in Q_1 are simply ignored. The values that the honest voters created for the voters in Q_1 will remain unused, which is a problem since the numbers should sum to 0. To correct this, the honest voters open all encryptions assigned to voters in Q_1.

More formally for all $i \in R\backslash Q_1$ the voter i releases the values s_{ij}, r_{ij} for all $j \in Q_1$. Since these values are uniquely determined by the encryption, this step can be verified by checking that $c_{ij} = E_{pk_j}^{\pm}(s_{ij}, r_{ij})$. Should a voter refuse to publish this information they are simply added to Q_1 and their values are revealed.

5.2   Ballot Casting

Ballot Casting. Each voter $j \in R\backslash Q_1$ retrieves the encryptions $c_{ij} \ \forall i \in R\backslash Q_1$ and combines them:

$$c_j = \prod_{\forall i \in R\backslash Q_1} c_{ij} = E_{pk_j}^{\pm}\Big(\sum_{\forall i \in R\backslash Q_1} s_{ij}, r \Big)$$

for some value of r. Voter j decrypts c_j using the private key α_j to get $t_j = \sum_{\forall i \in R\backslash Q_1} s_{ij}$.

Voter j then submits the values $d_j = E_{pk_j}^{\pm}(v_j, r_j)$ and $x_j = v_j + t_j$, where v_j is the value representing the candidate voter j votes for, say 0 or 1 for a yes/no election; the value $r_j \in \mathbb{Z}_N$ is chosen at random. The easiest way to understand this is to note that if we ignore the error correction (i.e., assume that no faults occur), then the t_j's will be a set of random numbers that sum to 0. So if we can ensure that x_j was formed by adding an allowable value of v_j to t_j, then $res = \sum_j x_j$ will be the election result, i.e., the sum of the v_j 's. Moreover, the randomness of the t_j ensures that given the x_j's, all possible sets of v_j's summing to res are equally likely.

To prove that d_j is a legal encryption of an allowable value of v_j, the proof from section 3.3 can be used to ensure that it is a correct encryption, and the proof of a legal vote value in [9] (which is logarithmic in the number of candidates) can be used on the second value in the encryption to prove that a legal v_j have been encrypted. To prove that d_j is an encryption of the same v_j, that was used to make x_j, the voter proves that

$$d_j c_j E_{pk_j}^{\pm}(x_j, 0)^{-1} = E_{pk_j}^{\pm}(0, r')$$

for some given r' using the n^s'th power proof from [9], and sends this proof to the bulletin board. This time the required n^s'th root can be computed as: $h_j^{r_j} \cdot (\prod G_{ij}^{4\Delta^2 \alpha_j}) \cdot 1$. This holds iff the same v_j is used in d_j and x_j since

$$d_j c_j (E_{pk_j}^{\pm}(v_j + t_j, 0))^{-1} = E_{pk_j}^{\pm}(v_j + t_j - (v_j + t_j), r') = E_{pk_j}^{\pm}(0, r')$$

Error Correction of Ballot Casting. Let Q_2 be the set of voters disqualified during the ballot casting. Again there are some values that will not be used by the voters in Q_2, and these are simply published on the bulletin board as in the error correction of the initialization.

However this time the values created by voters in Q_2 have been used by the honest voters (for any $i \in Q_2$ the value of s_{ii} is only know by i, and all honest voters j have used s_{ij}). To correct this the values have to be published, but the secret values r_{ij} are unknown to j. So for all $i \in Q_2$ each $j \in R_0 \backslash (Q_1 \cup Q_2)$ (voters and bulletin board) decrypts and reveals the plaintext of c_{ij}, which is s_{ij} and proves that

$$c_{ij} E_{pk_j}^{\pm}(s_{ij}, 0)^{-1} = E_{pk_j}^{\pm}(0, r)$$

using the n^s'th power proof from [9]. This time the required n^s'th root is: $G_{ij}^{4\Delta^2 \alpha_j}$.
1. Should anyone refuse to participate in the error correction they're simply added to Q_2 and their values published as before.

Now let $Q_{bad} = Q_1 \cup Q_2$ denote all voters that have been removed in the error correction steps, and let $R_{good} = R \backslash Q_{bad}$ be the voters that completed the whole protocol honestly.

Post Ballot Casting. When the ballot phase is over, and all parties have either submitted their vote or been removed using the error correction, the bulletin board computes

$$c_0 = \prod_{\forall i \in R \backslash Q_{bad}} c_{i0} = E_{pk_0}^{\pm} \left(\sum_{\forall i \in R \backslash Q_{bad}} s_{i0}, r \right)$$

for some r and gets the plaintext $t_0 = \sum_{\forall i \in R \backslash Q_{bad}} s_{i0}$ by decrypting c_0. The bulletin board then posts t_0 along with a proof that $c_0 E_{pk_0}^{\pm}(t_0, 0)^{-1}$ is a n^s'th power according to the proof in [9] (the value is calculated as $(\prod G_{i0}^{4\Delta^2 \alpha_0}) \cdot 1$).

5.3   Tallying

At this point the result can be computed as:

$$\sum_{j \in R_{good}} v_i = t_0 + \sum_{j \in R_{good}} x_j + \sum_{i \in R_{good}, j \in Q_{bad}} s_{ij} - \sum_{i \in Q_2, j \in R_{good} \cup \{0\}} s_{ij} \bmod n^s$$

The first sum is all the x_j values that have been posted on the bulletin board according to protocol. The values in the second sum are the values of the disqualified voters that where revealed in the error correction of the initialization and the first value revealed in the error correction of the ballot casting. The third sum is the sum of the second values revealed in the error correction of the ballot casting.

For lack of space, we do not give formal definitions and proofs of security here. However, perfect ballot secrecy follows since first, we can ignore those encryptions that remain unopened, due to the semantic security. What remains are the public numbers: x_i's, and the numbers revealed during error correction. One then observes that for any corrupted subset and given result, all possible sets of votes from honest players leading to the given result are equally likely. The correctness can be verified from the above formula.

5.4 Efficiency Comparison to Scheme from [14]

The work of the 2 schemes are comparable in all steps of the protocol except in the tallying phase. Here the protocol of [14] needs to do an exhaustive search in a space of size $2u$, which can be optimized to $O(\sqrt{u})$ multiplications. However, the protocol above obtains the result of the election by simply adding the values posted to the bulletin board.

Our scheme generalizes to multi-candidate elections in exactly the same way as [9]. In particular, the tallying phase remains at the same number of additions. For the scheme from [14], the search for the result would take $\Omega((\sqrt{u})^l)$ multiplications for l candidates.

References

1. A. Waksman: *A permutation network*, Journal of the ACM 15(1), January 1968, pp. 159–163.
2. R. Cramer, I. Damgård and B. Schoenmakers: *Proofs of Partial Knowledge and Simplified Design of Witness Hiding Protocols*, Proceedings of Crypto '94, Springer Verlag LNCS 839, pp. 174–187.
3. M. Abe: *Mix-networks on Permutation Networks*, Proceedings of AsiaCrypt '99, Springer Verlag LNCS 1716, pp. 258–273.
4. P. Paillier: *Public-Key Cryptosystems based on Composite Degree Residue Classes*, Proceedings of EuroCrypt '99, Springer Verlag LNCS 1592, pp. 223–238.
5. M. Abe and M. Ohkubo: *A Length-Invariant Hybrid Mix*, Proceedings of AsiaCrypt 2000, Springer Verlag LNCS 1976, pp. 178–191.
6. Y. Desmedt and K. Kurosawa: *How to break a practical MIX and design a new one*, Proceedings of EuroCrypt 2000, Springer Verlag LNCS 1807, pp. 557–572.
7. V. Shoup: *Practical Threshold Signatures*, Proceedings of EuroCrypt 2000, Springer Verlag LNCS 1807, pp. 207–220.
8. M. Abe and F. Hoshino: *Remarks on Mix-network Based on Permutation Networks*, Proceedings of PKC 2001, Springer Verlag LNCS 1992, pp. 317–324.
9. I. Damgård and M. Jurik: *A Generalisation, a Simplification and some Applications of Paillier's Probabilistic Public-Key System*, Proceedings of PKC 2001, Springer Verlag LNCS 1992, pp. 119–136.
10. I. Damgård and M. Koprowski: *Practical Threshold RSA Signatures Without a Trusted Dealer*, Proceedings of EuroCrypt 2001, Springer Verlag LNCS 2045, pp. 152–165.
11. M. Jakobsson and A. Juels, *An optimally robust hybrid mix network*, Annual ACM Symposium on Principles of Distributed Computing 2001, pp 284–292.
12. R. Cramer and V. Shoup: *Universal Hash Proofs and a Paradigm for Adaptive Chosen Ciphertext Secure Public-Key Encryption*, Proceedings of EuroCrypt 2002, Springer Verlag LNCS 2332, pp. 45–64.
13. J. Algesheimer, J. Camenisch and V. Shoup: *Efficient Computation Modulo a Shared Secret with Application to the Generation of Shared Safe-Prime Products* Proceedings of Crypto 2002, Springer Verlag LNCS 2442, pp. 417–432.
14. A. Kiayias and M. Yung: *Self-Tallying Elections and Perfect Ballot Secrecy*, Proceedings of Public Key Cryptography 2002, Springer Verlag LNCS 2274, pp. 141–158.
15. I. Damgård, and M. Jurik: *A Length-Flexible Threshold Cryptosystem with Applications*, BRICS report series, record 03/16, http://www.brics.dk/RS/03/16/

Separating Encryption and Key Issuance in Digital Rights Management Systems*

Goichiro Hanaoka[1], Kazuto Ogawa[2], Itsuro Murota[2], Go Ohtake[2],
Keigo Majima[2], Kimiyuki Oyamada[2], Seiichi Gohshi[2], Seiichi Namba[2], and
Hideki Imai[1]

[1] Information & Systems, Institute of Industrial Science, University of Tokyo
4-6-1 Komaba, Meguro-ku, Tokyo 153-8508, Japan.
hanaoka@imailab.iis.u-tokyo.ac.jp, imai@iis.u-tokyo.ac.jp
[2] Science & Technical Research Laboratories, Japan Broadcasting Corporation,
1-10-11, Kinuta, Setagaya-ku, Tokyo 157-8510, Japan.

Abstract. Secure distribution of digital goods is now a significantly important issue for protecting publishers' copyrights. In this paper, we study a useful primitive for constructing a secure and efficient *digital rights management system* (DRM) where a server which encrypts digital content and one which issues the corresponding decryption key works independently, and existing schemes lack this property. We first argue the desired property necessary of an encryption scheme for constructing an efficient DRM, and formally define an encryption scheme as *split encryption scheme* containing such property. Also, we show that an efficient split encryption scheme can be constructed from any identity-based scheme. However, since currently there is no identity-based encryption scheme which is based on well-known computational assumption and/or provable security without the random oracle, by reasonably tuning the system parameter, we show another construction of split encryption which is secure against chosen ciphertext attacks in the standard model assuming that the *decision Diffie-Hellman* problem is hard to solve.

1 Introduction

MOTIVATION. Recently, digital media has become extremely popular, and consumers can get digital goods from the Internet at all times and in no time. Consequently, secure distribution of digital goods is now a significantly important issue for protecting publishers' copyrights. In response, several *data distribution systems with digital rights management* (DRM) have been proposed and established by some commercial organizations, e.g. [11,10]. Such a data distribution system allows a content publisher to package his digital content by encrypting it with a key. In order to utilize the packaged data, the consumer needs to obtain a "license" that contains a decryption key. The license, which is separated from the content, enables the content publisher to determine the consumer's usage

---

* The first author is supported by a Research Fellowship from Japan Society for the Promotion of Science (JSPS).

R. Safavi-Naini and J. Seberry (Eds.): ACISP 2003, LNCS 2727, pp. 365–376, 2003.
© Springer-Verlag Berlin Heidelberg 2003

of that content. The license can be issued at different points in the consumer transaction, depending on the content owner's business model.

For flexibly implementing the DRM, it is desired that functions for packaging contents and issuing licenses are to be split. In other words, a package server who encrypts a content and a license server that issues a license, should work independently, so to avoid concentration of tasks that weigh heavily on one center server. However, it is not too easy to satisfy this requirement for several reasons. In this paper, we study this problem for separating a package server and a license server and propose efficient solutions for it.

BRIEF REVIEW OF DRM. A typical and basic construction of DRM is as follows. In a DRM, there are mainly four kinds of players: *consumers, content publishers, package servers* and *license servers*. When a content publisher intends to distribute a digital content to consumers, she first asks a package server to package the content. Next, the package server encrypts the content according to the usage of the content which is determined by the content publisher. When consumer wants to utilize the content, he will have to purchase "digital right" from on-line shop and obtain a particular digital data which can later be determined as an evidence that the content has been bought by right means. Finally, the consumer transmits the digital data to the license server, and if the digital data is valid, the license server issues the license which corresponds to the digital data. The main problem of DRM is that it is not easy to independently set up a package server and a license server. Namely, a package server's encryption key which is used for encrypting a content must be corresponded to a license server's decryption key which will be needed for recovering the content. Therefore, in a straightforward manner, these two servers have to cooperate with each other in order to generate the two keys. For this fact, the flexibility in implementing DRM is considerably lost.

EXAMPLES OF DRM KEY GENERATION. Here, we give examples of key generation methods in existing DRMs. In [11], in the initial phase, a package server and a license server share a secret **seed**, which is called *license seed*, and generate their key (for symmetric encryption) by using the secret. More specifically, for a digital content m whose identifier is ID_m, the package server's encryption key is generated as $h(\mathsf{seed}\|\mathsf{ID}_m)$, where h is an appropriate hash function, for example [13], and "$\|$" means concatenation. In the same manner, the license server generates the decryption key. In this method, the two servers need to securely establish **seed** in advance, and furthermore, not only the license server but also the package server, who does not issue a license, must safely keep **seed**. In another DRM which is provided by [10], for each time when a package server encrypts a digital content, the package server transmits his encryption key (for symmetric encryption) to a license server via a secure channel, for example, by using public key cryptography. This method allows the package server to delete the encryption key, hence, contrarily to the above DRM, the package server does not have to safely keep a secret. However, it should be noticed that this scheme requires more communication cost in comparison to [11] since for every packaging, the package server and the license server need to establish a cryptographic communication between them. Anyway, also in this method, it is considered that the package server does not independently work to the license server. Together, we can see that both these schemes do not sufficiently achieve separation of a package server and a license server.

A SIMPLE SOLUTION. A simple (but inefficient) solution of this problem is as follows. In the initial phase, a license server generates a set of key pairs of public key cryptography, such that any possible identifier of a content uniquely maps to an element of this set, and broadcasts all of the public keys (and the mapping). When package server intends to encrypt a content m whose identifier is ID_m, he picks the public key which corresponds to ID_m and encrypts m by using the public key. For a consumer's request, the license server issues a license which contains the private key which corresponds to ID_m. In this method, a package server and a license server do not have to share a secret in priori nor need to make a (cryptographic) communication for every packaging, consequently, allowing flexibility for constructing DRM. However, this scheme is quite inefficient for some reasons. That is, since the license server needs to prepare a huge number of key pairs, therefore, costs for key management become enormous.

REQUIREMENTS. Here, in view of the above discussions, we illustrate requirements for a practical implementation of DRM as follows: (i) A package server can encrypt a content without any communication with a license server (the license server may publish public parameters). (ii) The license server can issue a decryption key to a valid consumer without any communication with the package server. (iii) By using the decryption key, the valid consumer can correctly recover the content. (iv) Letting $|\mathcal{ID}|$ be the cardinality of the set of all possible identifiers of contents, $\log |\mathcal{ID}| \geq O(\mathsf{poly}(k))$, where k is a security parameter of the system. In addition to these requirements, we further consider the following requirement: (v) The encryption scheme is semantically secure against chosen ciphertext attacks [12,2]. More specifically, an adversary tries a modified IND-CCA Game [12,2], and an encryption scheme is considered secure if the probability that adversary wins the game is $1/2 + neg$, where neg is a negligible value. In our modified IND-CCA Game, an adversary may give a pair of a content identifier and a ciphertext to a decryption oracle which has the license server's secret, and obtain a plaintext which is computed from the ciphertext and the decryption key which corresponds to the content identifier. Furthermore, the adversary is also allowed to access a key issue oracle which issues decryption keys that the adversary requests. Under such environment, the adversary chooses a content identifier which is not asked for by the key issue oracle, and tries the IND-CCA Game for the content identifier. See Section 2 for details.

OUR RESULTS. In this paper, we first define an encryption scheme for DRM as *split encryption scheme*. Next, a comparison of split encryption scheme to an *identity-based encryption scheme* [4] is investigated, and it is shown that an efficient split encryption scheme can be constructed from any identity-based scheme which is semantically secure against chosen ciphertext attacks. More precisely, we show an equivalence result which implies that a split encryption scheme for some system parameter setting and an identity-based encryption scheme have the same primitives for different uses. Since currently there is no identity-based encryption scheme which is based on a well-known computational assumption and/or provably secure in the standard model (i.e. without the random oracle model), by reasonably tuning a system parameter, we show another construction of split encryption which is secure against chosen ciphertext attacks in the standard model assuming that the *decision Diffie-Hellman* problem is hard to solve.

2   Definition and Building Block

2.1   Definitions

We now formalize a model for an encryption scheme for a practical DRM. Since, as already mentioned above, an important requirement for such encryption is that a package server and a license server are to be *split*, we call the encryption scheme *split encryption scheme* (SENC).

Definition 1 A *split encryption scheme* (SENC) is a 4-tuple of polynomial-time algorithms (MKG, ENC, DKG, DEC) whose functionality is as follows: MKG: The *master key generation algorithm* MKG takes input security parameter k and returns (mst, pub), where mst is the license server's private key, and pub is the license server's public parameter. ENC: For a given content identifier i and its corresponding content m, the package server applies the *encryption algorithm* ENC to i, m and pub to obtain a ciphertext c. We may assume that the content identifier of m could be uniquely obtained from m, and therefore in such a case, the content identifier might be omitted from the inputs of ENC. DKG: For a given content identifier $i \in \mathcal{ID}$, the license server applies the *decryption key generation algorithm* DKG to i and mst to obtain the decryption key d_i which corresponds to i, where $\mathcal{ID}$ is the set of all possible content identifiers such that $\log |\mathcal{ID}| \geq O(\mathrm{poly}(k))$ (possibly, $\mathcal{ID} = \{0,1\}^*$). DEC: For a given content identifier i and a ciphertext c, the user applies the *decryption algorithm* DEC to c and d_i to obtain either m or the special symbol $\perp$ indicating failure. We require that if c was computed as $c = \mathsf{ENC}(i, m, pub)$, then, $\mathsf{DEC}(c, d_i) = m$.

In order to prove security of SENC, applying the standard IND-CCA Game [12,2] is not sufficient since an adversary can also obtain a certain number of decryption keys from the license server. Therefore, we introduce a modified IND-CCA Game in which an adversary is allowed to access the key issue oracle. More formally, we give the adversary access to the following three types of oracles: The first one is a *key issue oracle* KI$(\cdot, mst)$ which on input $i \in \mathcal{ID}$ returns its corresponding decryption key $d_i := \mathsf{DKG}(i, mst)$. The second is a *left-or-right oracle* LR$(\cdot, \cdot, \cdot, pub, b)$ [1] that with a given $i \in \mathcal{ID}$ and equal length messages m_0, m_1 returns a *challenge ciphertext* $c := \mathsf{ENC}(i, m_b, pub)$ where $b \in \{0,1\}$. This models encryption requests by the adversary for content identifiers and message pairs of his choice. Finally, adversary is allowed to access to a *decryption oracle* D$(\cdot, \cdot, mst)$ which on input $i \in \mathcal{ID}$ and ciphertext c, returns $\mathsf{DEC}(c, d_i)$.

This models a chosen ciphertext attack. The adversary may query these oracles adaptively, in any order he wants, subject to the restriction that he makes only one query to the left-or-right oracle. We may also set up another restriction on the number of accesses to the key issue oracle. Let $i \in \mathcal{ID}$ be the content identifier of this query, and let c denote the challenge ciphertext returned by the left-or-right oracle in response to this query. The adversary succeeds by guessing the value b, and a scheme is secure if any probabilistic polynomial time adversary has success negligibly close to $1/2$. We formally define chosen ciphertext security of SENC as follows:

Definition 2 Let SENC = (MKG, ENC, DKG, DEC) be a split encryption scheme. Define adversary A's succeeding probability in the above modified IND-CCA game as:

$$\mathsf{Succ}_{A,\mathsf{SENC}} := \Pr[(mst, pub) \leftarrow \mathsf{MKG}(k); b \in_R \{0,1\};$$
$$(i, b') \leftarrow A^{\mathsf{KI}(\cdot, mst), \mathsf{LR}(\cdot, \cdot, \cdot, pub, b), \mathsf{D}(\cdot, \cdot, mst)} : b' = b],$$

where i is never asked to $\mathsf{KI}(\cdot, mst)$, and A is not allowed to query $\mathsf{D}(i, c, mst)$ if c was returned by the left-or-right oracle $\mathsf{LR}(\cdot, \cdot, \cdot, pub, b)$. Then, SENC is called a *t-secure split encryption scheme* (*t*-SENC) if for any probabilistic polynomial time adversary A who submits at most t requests to $\mathsf{KI}(\cdot, mst)$, $|\mathsf{Succ}_{A,\mathsf{SENC}} - 1/2|$ is negligible.

2.2   Efficiency Parameters

It is clear that the simple solution in the previous section does not satisfy requirement for SENC since its MKG will not halts within polynomial steps. Namely, by assigning a key pair for each of $\mathcal{ID}$, the license server needs to generate exponentially many number of key pairs. Moreover, this scheme is completely impractical since this method requires extremely large size of storage both for the license server's private key mst and the public parameter pub. Therefore, our motivation of this work is to construct efficient SENCs whose required memory size is sufficiently small enough to implement a practical system. For evaluating efficiency of a SENC, we introduce the following parameters:

Definition 3 The two basic efficiency parameters of a SENC are (i) the size of the license server's private key $|mst|$, (ii) the size of the public parameter $|pub|$.

2.3   A Building Block: Identity-Based Encryption

One of our constructions of SENC is based on *identity-based encryption* (IBE) [14,4]. IBE is a class of public key encryption which allows a recipient's unique identity to be utilized as his public key. As an example, assume that a recipient's e-mail address is used as his identifier, a sender simply encrypts a message with the public key string "recipient@xxx.xxx" which is sent to the recipient at "recipient@xxx.xxx". It should be noticed that in IBE there must be a trusted authority who must generate a decryption key and distribute it to the corresponding owner. IBE can be formally defined as follows:

Definition 4 An *identity-based encryption scheme* is a 4-tuple of polynomial-time algorithms (IMKG, IDKG, IENC, IDEC) whose functionality is as follows: IMKG: The *master key generation algorithm* IMKG takes input security parameter k and returns $(imst, ipub)$, where $imst$ is a trusted center's secret, and $ipub$ is his public parameter. IDKG: For a given user's identity $i \in \mathcal{USER}$, the trusted center applies the *decryption key generation algorithm* IDKG to u and $imst$ to obtain the user u's decryption key d_u which will be given to u, where $\mathcal{USER}$ is the set of all possible users' identities such that $\log |\mathcal{USER}| \geq O(\mathrm{poly}(k))$ (possibly, $\mathcal{USER} = \{0,1\}^*$). IENC: For a given recipient u and a plaintext m, a sender applies the *encryption algorithm* IENC to u, m and $ipub$ to obtain a ciphertext c which will be sent to u. IDEC: For a given ciphertext c which was transmitted to user u, u applies the *decryption algorithm* IDEC to c and d_u to obtain either m or the special symbol $\perp$ indicating failure. We require that if c was computed as $c = \mathrm{IENC}(u, m, ipub)$, then, $\mathrm{IDEC}(c, d_u) = m$.

Security of IBE is well-defined in [4], and a semantically secure identity-based encryption scheme is also presented in [4]. Semantic security of IBE against chosen ciphertext atatcks (CCA) can be defined as follows: An adversary is allowed to access to the following three types of oracles: The first one is a *key generation oracle* KG$(\cdot, imst)$ which on input $u \in \mathcal{USER}$, returns user u's decryption key $d_u := \mathrm{IDKG}(u, mst)$. The second is a *left-or-right oracle* LR$(\cdot, \cdot, \cdot, ipub, b)$ which given $u \in \mathcal{USER}$ and equal length messages m_0, m_1 returns a *challenge ciphertext* $c := \mathrm{IENC}(u, m_b, ipub)$ where $b \in \{0, 1\}$. This models encryption requests by the adversary for users' identities and message pairs of his choice. Finally, the adversary is allowed to access the *decryption oracle* D$(\cdot, \cdot, imst)$ which on input $u \in \mathcal{USER}$ and a ciphertext c, returns $\mathrm{IDEC}(c, d_u)$. This models a chosen ciphertext attack. The adversary may query these oracles adaptively, in any order he wants, subject to the restriction that he makes only one query to the left-or-right oracle. The adversary succeeds by guessing the value b, and a scheme is secure if any probabilistic polynomial time adversary has success negligibly close to $1/2$. The formal definition is given in [4].

3   An Efficient Construction from IBE

In this section, we present an efficient construction of SENC by using IBE. Interestingly, $(|\mathcal{ID}| - 1)$-SENC can be constructed from any IBE which is semantically secure against CCA, assuming that $|\mathcal{ID}| \leq |\mathcal{USER}|$, and a semantically secure IBE against CCA can also be constructed from any $(|\mathcal{ID}| - 1)$-SENC, assuming that $|\mathcal{USER}| \leq |\mathcal{ID}|$. This implies that $(|\mathcal{ID}| - 1)$-SENC is equivalent to semantically secure IBE against CCA. In other words, these are the same primitive for different uses.

3.1   An Equivalence Result

Now, we show the above equivalence result.

IBE $\Rightarrow$ SENC: Let (IMKG, IDKG, IENC, IDEC) be an IBE. Then, letting f :

Table 1. Comparison of proposed schemes, where $|mst|$ and $|pub|$ denote the size of the license server's private key and that of the public parameter, respectively, and $|\mathcal{ID}|$, $|d|$, $|e|$, $|imst|$, $|ipub|$, $|d_{CS}|$ and $|e_{CS}|$ are sizes of $\mathcal{ID}$, a decryption key of a conventional public key encryption, an encryption key of a conventional public key encryption, a trusted center's secret in IBE, a public parameter in IBE, a decryption key in Cramer-Shoup encryption and an encryption key in Cramer-Shoup encryption, respectively. Note that $\log|\mathcal{ID}| = O(\mathsf{poly}(k))$, $|d| \simeq |imst|$, $|e| \simeq |ipub|$, $|d_{CS}| \simeq 2 \cdot |d|$ and $|e_{CS}| \simeq 2.5 \cdot |e|$ when using ElGamal encryption [7] and Boneh-Franklin IBE [4] as the underlying (standard) public key encryption and identity-based encryption, respectively.

	simple solution	IBE-based scheme	DDH-based scheme
$|mst|$	$|\mathcal{ID}| \cdot |d|$	$|imst|$	$|d_{CS}| + 6t|q|$
$|pub|$	$|\mathcal{ID}| \cdot |e|$	$|ipub|$	$|e_{CS}| + 3t|p|$

$\mathcal{ID} \rightarrow \mathcal{USER}$ be an injective mapping, a SENC $(\mathsf{MKG}, \mathsf{ENC}, \mathsf{DKG}, \mathsf{DEC})$ such that $|\mathcal{ID}| \leq |\mathcal{USER}|$ can be constructed from the underlying IBE as follows. MKG: run $\mathsf{IMKG}(k) = (imst, ipub)$, and output $(imst, ipub)$ as (mst, pub). ENC: run $\mathsf{IENC}(f(i), m, pub) = c$ for plaintext m, and output c as a ciphertext. DKG: run $\mathsf{IDKG}(f(i), mst) = d_{f(i)}$, and out put $d_{f(i)}$ as d_i. DEC: run $\mathsf{IDEC}(c, d_i)$, and output m or $\perp$.

SENC $\Rightarrow$ IBE: Let $(\mathsf{MKG}, \mathsf{ENC}, \mathsf{DKG}, \mathsf{DEC})$ be a SENC. Then, letting $g : \mathcal{USER} \rightarrow \mathcal{ID}$ be an injective mapping, an IBE $(\mathsf{IMKG}, \mathsf{IDKG}, \mathsf{IENC}, \mathsf{IDEC})$ such that $|\mathcal{USER}| \leq |\mathcal{ID}|$ can be constructed from the SENC as follows. IMKG: run $\mathsf{MKG}(k) = (mst, pub)$, and output (mst, pub) as $(imst, ipub)$. IDKG: run $\mathsf{DKG}(g(u), mst) = d_{g(u)}$, and out put $d_{g(u)}$ as d_u. IENC: run $\mathsf{ENC}(g(u), m, ipub) = c$, and output c as a ciphertext. IDEC: run $\mathsf{DEC}(c, d_u)$, and output m or $\perp$.

From security definitions of SENC and IBE (see section 2.1 and 2.3, respectively), if an IBE is semantically secure against CCA, a SENC from the IBE is a $(|\mathcal{ID}| - 1)$-SENC, and that if a SENC is a $(|\mathcal{ID}| - 1)$-SENC, an IBE from the SENC is semantically secure against CCA. This fact can be formally addressed as follows:

Theorem 1 *A SENC Π converted from an IBE Π' by the above method is a $(|\mathcal{ID}| - 1)$-SENC if Π' is semantically secure against CCA and $|\mathcal{ID}| \leq |\mathcal{USER}|$.*

Theorem 2 *An IBE Π' converted from a $(|\mathcal{ID}| - 1)$-SENC Π by the above method is semantically secure against CCA if $|\mathcal{USER}| \leq |\mathcal{ID}|$.*

3.2   Performance

As discussed above, a $(|\mathcal{ID}| - 1)$-SENC can be produced from a semantically secure IBE against CCA. We now evaluate the performance of the SENC generated from IBE. Specifically, the size of the license server's private key and that of the public parameter are estimated as $|imst|$ and $|ipub|$, where $|imst|$

and $|ipub|$ are the size of $imst$ and $ipub$ of the underlying IBE. It should be noticed that comparing this scheme with the simple solution (see section 2.2), sicne $|imst| \simeq |d|$ and $|ipub| \simeq |e|$ for appropriate IBE and public key encryption (e.g. [4] and [7]), both the size of the license server's private key and that of the public parameter can be considerably reduced. Note also that $\log |\mathcal{ID}| = O(\text{poly}(k))$. In the followings, we call the above scheme *IBE-based scheme*. Table 1 illustrates a comparison of the above scheme with other schemes.

Although by applying IBE, a secure SENC can be efficiently constructed, for such a construction we have some restrictions which can not be ignored. Namely, at the present time there exists only one fully functional IBE, i.e. [4], and we do not have any other choices for selecting underlying IBE for constructing a secure SENC. Furthermore, we note that the security of [4] is proven in the random oracle model under a specific assumption which is called the *bilinear Diffie-Hellman assumption*. This implies that it is difficult to construct a secure SENC in the standard model and/or based on a well-known assumption.

3.3   An Extension

As a useful extension of IBE, *hierarchical identity-based encryption* (HIBE) [9, 8] is proposed, recently. In HIBE, it is possible to hierarchically set up multiple trusted authorities, and therefore, tasks for issuing decryption keys can be distributed while remaining secure and efficient. By applying HIBE, we can similarly extend SENC for relaxing a license server's tasks, that is, the root license server, who is fully trusted, generates its children license servers' keys, and in a similar manner, each license server generates its children's keys. (Each license server in the lowest level issues licenses (i.e. decryption keys) which he is expected to generate.) We note that due to the property of HIBE, even if a license server's key is exposed, only its descendants' keys are compromised while other keys are remained secure. Especially, even if a license server in the lowest level is violated, and its key is revealed, only the licenses of which the license server allowed to publish are compromised.

4   SENC without the Random Oracle

As described so far, a $(|\mathcal{ID}| - 1)$-SENC can be constructed from only the semantically secure IBE against CCA since these primitives are equivalent. Furthermore, the only one existing semantically secure IBE against CCA is based on the random oracle model with a very specific assumption. This means that in order to construct a secure SENC based on a well-known assumption in the standard model (i.e. without the random oracle), it is necessary to relax the requirement and therefore abandon the realization of a $(|\mathcal{ID}| - 1)$-SENC (unless another semantically secure IBE based on a well-known assumption in the standard model is proposed). Here, we consider a t-SENC for significantly smaller t compared to $(|\mathcal{ID}| - 1)$. More specifically, we let $t = O(\text{poly}(k))$. In such a scheme, the number of requests that an adversary is allowed to submit to the license server is assumed to be restricted. It should be noticed that this restriction is reasonable in a practical situation. Namely, in a practical on-line contents distribution system, an adversary needs to pay per a request for the issuing of a license (i.e. a decryption key), and hence, it will not be able to submit requests many times. In the rest of this section, we show a secure construction of SENC for such system parameter setting. Our basic concept is as follows: In order to remove the random oracle assumption, we extend Cramer-Shoup encryption [5], which is a practical IND-CCA scheme in the standard model, to be a t-SENC. Furthermore, Cramer-Shoup encryption is based on the decision Diffie-Hellman problem (DDH) [3], which is well-known to be hard, therefore, our scheme can also be proven secure under a well-known assumption, i.e. DDH. We note that DDH is equivalent to the semantic security of ElGamal encryption [7] under chosen plaintext attacks. Letting G be a group of large prime order q, an algorithm that solves DDH is a statistical test that can effectively distinguish the following two distributions: $\mathcal{R}$ of random $\langle g_1, g_2, v_1, v_2 \rangle \in G^4$; $\mathcal{D}$ of $\langle g_1, g_2, v_1, v_2 \rangle \in G^4$, where g_1, g_2 are random, and $v_1 = g_1^r$ and $v_2 = g_2^r$ for random $r \in Z_q$.

4.1 Proposed Scheme

In our t-SENC, for given security parameter k, MKG chooses a generator g_1 of group G with order q, such that $\log q = O(\mathsf{poly}(k))$, and calculates $g_2 := g_1^w$ for some w which is uniformly chosen at ramdom from Z_q^*. MKG further picks $\{f_i\}_{1 \leq i \leq 6}$ over Z_q uniformly at random, where $f_i(\lambda) := \sum_{j=0}^{t} a_{i,j} \lambda^j$ for $i = 1, \cdots, 6$, and also calculates $\{u_{i,j} | u_{i,j} = g_1^{a_{i,j}} g_2^{a_{i+1,j}}$ for $i = 1, 3, 5, \ 0 \leq j \leq t\}$. In addition, H is chosen from a family of *collision-resistant hash functions*, such that it is infeasible to find two distinct inputs m_0 and m_1 which satisfy $\mathsf{H}(m_0) = \mathsf{H}(m_1)$. Then, MKG outputs a license server's private key $\langle g_1, g_2, G, \mathsf{H}, \{f_i\}_{1 \leq i \leq 6} \rangle$ and its corresponding public parameter $\langle g_1, g_2, G, \mathsf{H}, \{u_{i,j}\}_{i=1,3,5, \ 0 \leq j \leq t} \rangle$.

For content identifier $\ell \in \mathcal{ID}$, where $\mathcal{ID} := Z_q$, and its corresponding content $m \in G$ (m may also be a session key for a content), ENC computes $\alpha := g_1^r$, $\beta := g_2^r$ and $\gamma := m \cdot (\prod_{j=0}^{t} u_{5,j}^{\ell^j})^r$ for r which is uniformly chosen at random from Z_q. ENC also calculates $\kappa := \mathsf{H}(\ell, \alpha, \beta, \gamma)$ and $\delta := (\prod_{j=0}^{t} u_{1,j}^{\ell^j})^r (\prod_{j=0}^{t} u_{3,j}^{\ell^j})^{r\kappa}$. Then, $c := \langle \alpha, \beta, \gamma, \delta \rangle$ is output as the ciphertext.

In order to generate a decryption key for content identifier ℓ, DKG computes and outputs $\{f_i(\ell)\}_{1 \leq i \leq 6}$ as the decryption key.

For a ciphertext $c' := \langle \alpha', \beta', \gamma', \delta' \rangle$ and a decryption key $\{f_i(\ell)\}_{1 \leq i \leq 6}$ for content identifier ℓ, DEC calculates $\kappa' := \mathsf{H}(\ell, \alpha', \beta', \gamma')$ and tests if $\delta' = \alpha'^{f_1(\ell) + f_3(\ell)\kappa'} \cdot \beta'^{f_2(\ell) + f_4(\ell)\kappa'}$. If this is not the case, DEC outputs $\perp$ and halts, otherwise, computes $m' = \gamma' / (\alpha'^{f_5(\ell)} \cdot \beta'^{f_6(\ell)})$ as the plaintext which corresponds to c'.

4.2 Proof of Security

In this subsection, we show a proof of security of our proposed scheme. More precisely, we address the following theorem:

Theorem 3 *The proposed scheme in the previous subsection is a t-SENC for any t, such that $t = O(\text{poly}(k))$, assuming DDH is hard to solve.*

Proof. The proof of the above theorem is similar to [5] except that in our attack model, an adversary can access to the key issuance oracle to adaptively obtain at most t decryption keys.

Let A be the adversary for Π such that $|\text{Succ}_{A,\Pi} - 1/2|$ is non-negligible. We now demonstrate to construct another adversary A' that can also solve the DDH with non-negligible probability by using A. In the initial stage, a tuple $\langle g_1, g_2, v_1, v_2 \rangle$ which is from either $\mathcal{R}$ or $\mathcal{D}$ is given to A'. Then, A' picks $\{f_i\}_{1 \leq i \leq 6}$ over Z_q uniformly at random, where $f_i(\lambda) := \sum_{j=0}^{t} a_{i,j} \lambda^j$ for $i = 1, \cdots, 6$, and also calculates $\{u_{i,j} | u_{i,j} = g_1^{a_{i,j}} g_2^{a_{i+1,j}}$ for $i = 1, 3, 5, \ 0 \leq j \leq t\}$. In addition, H is chosen from a family of collision-resistant hash functions. Then, A' calculates $\langle g_1, g_2, G, \mathsf{H}, \{u_{i,j}\}_{i=1,3,5, \ 0 \leq j \leq t} \rangle$ and hands it to A as a public parameter of Π. A' simulates the key issuance oracle $\mathsf{KI}(\cdot, mst)$ query ℓ for A by computing $\{f_i(\ell)\}_{1 \leq i \leq 6}$, and it will be returned to A. In order to simulate the decryption oracle $\mathsf{D}(\cdot, \cdot, mst)$ for query ℓ and $c := \langle \alpha, \beta, \gamma, \delta \rangle$, A' computes $\gamma/(\alpha^{f_5(\ell)} \cdot \beta^{f_6(\ell)})$ and returns it to A if $\delta = \alpha^{f_1(\ell) + f_3(\ell)\kappa} \cdot \beta^{f_2(\ell) + f_4(\ell)\kappa}$ holds, where $\kappa := \mathsf{H}(\ell, \alpha, \beta, \gamma)$, otherwise A' returns $\bot$. When A outputs the left-or-right oracle $\mathsf{LR}(\cdot, \cdot, \cdot, pub, b)$ query ℓ', m_0, m_1 for A, A' computes $c' := \langle v_1, v_2, \gamma', \delta' \rangle$, where $\gamma' := m_b \cdot v_1^{f_5(\ell')} \cdot v_2^{f_6(\ell')}$, $\delta' := v_1^{f_1(\ell') + f_3(\ell')\kappa'} v_2^{f_2(\ell') + f_4(\ell')\kappa'}$ and $\kappa' := \mathsf{H}(\ell', v_1, v_2, \gamma')$. Then, from Lemma 1 and 2, Theorem 3 can be proven. □

Lemma 1 *When the simulator's input comes from $\mathcal{D}$, the joint distribution of the adversary's view and the hidden bit b is indistinguishable from that in the actual attack.*

The proof of the lemma is straightforward. More precisely, when $\langle g_1, g_2, v_1, v_2 \rangle$ comes from $\mathcal{D}$, it is clear that the outputs of the left-or-right oracle, the decryption oracle and the left-or-right oracle have the identical distribution to those in the actual attack.

Lemma 2 *When the simulator's input comes from $\mathcal{R}$, the distribution of the hidden bit b is essentially independent from the adversary's view.*

The proof of the lemma will appear in the full version of this paper.

4.3   Performance

The most remarkable property of the above scheme is that its security can be proven based on the "well-known" DDH assumption without the random oracle (In the followings, we call this scheme *DDH-based scheme*). Namely, the underlying mathematical problem of the DDH-based scheme is considered more reasonable than that of the proposed scheme in the previous section, i.e. the IBE-based scheme. However, it should be noted that in the DDH-based scheme, the number of queries that an adversary is allowed to submit to the key issue oracle is restricted, and therefore, security of the DDH-based scheme is addressed in a weaker attack model in comparison to the IBE-based scheme. Actually, this is a crucial result since as we showed in an earlier part of this paper, there is no way to construct a SENC without using IBE when addressing the strongest attack model. Hence, one should utilize the DDH-based scheme if he mostly cares about the strength of the underlying mathematical problem, else, it is preferred to use the IBE-based scheme.

Next, we estimate the efficiency parameters of the DDH-based scheme. In the DDH-based scheme, the size of the license server's private key and that of the public parameter are estimated to be $|d_{CS}| + 6t|q|$ and $|e_{CS}| + 3t|p|$, where $|d_{CS}|$ and $|e_{CS}|$ are the sizes of a decryption key and an encryption key in Cramer-Shoup encryption, respectively, and $|q|$ and $|p|$ are the sizes of q and p of the underlying IBE, assuming that $G \subset Z_p$. It should be noticed that in a practical parameter setting, $|d_{CS}|$ and $|e_{CS}|$ are determined almost the same as $2 \cdot |imst|$ and $2.5 \cdot |ipub|$, respectively, and hence, the IBE-based scheme is superior to the DDH-based scheme in terms of required memory sizes. However, also note that the efficiency parameters of the DDH-based scheme is still significantly smaller than that of the simple solution (see section 2.2). Table 1 illustrates a comparison of the DDH-based scheme with other schemes.

4.4   Relation with Key Insulated Encryption

We note that the construction of the DDH-based scheme is similar to that of *key insulated public key encryption* (KIPE) [6] which deals with the key exposure problem. Actually, this is crucial since both SENC and KIPE can be regarded as relaxed versions of IBE, and hence, these can be similar with each other. This implies that further improvement of KIPE could also be adapted to SENC to enhance its performance.

5   Another Relaxed SENC

In the previous section, we considered a relaxed version of SENC in which an adversary is limited to access the key exposure oracle. In this section, we further explore another relaxation of SENC for a flexible construction of a DRM.

In the relaxed setting, we assume that issuance of a license by the license server is always performed after the user obtains (a part of) the corresponding encrypted content. Actually, this relaxation sacrifices one of main advantages of SENC, and therefore, users are enforced to access the package server before they apply to get licenses. However, although restrictive, this setting can provides flexibility for choosing underlying encryption schemes. Namely, in the relaxed setting, the license server, the package server and users can carry out the following procedures: The license server first chooses an arbitrary public encryption scheme (with appropriate security) and generates a key pair (pk, sk) of the encryption scheme, where pk and sk are the public key and the private key, respectively. The public key pk will be the public parameter of the system.

Second, the package server picks a random session key s and encrypts a content m and s by using s and pk, respectively, where the content is enciphered by appropriate symmetric key encryption $E_{sym}(s, \cdot)$, and s is enciphered by the underlying public key encryption $E_{pub}(pk, \cdot)$. Also, the package server generates his signature for $\langle \ell, E_{pub}(pk, s) \rangle$, where ℓ is the identifier of the content, and puts the ciphertext $\langle E_{sym}(s, m), E_{pub}(pk, s) \rangle$ and the signature on a public directory. Third, a user who intends to play the content downloads $E_{pub}(pk, s)$ (or the whole ciphertext) and the signature. And, he submits $\langle \ell, E_{pub}(pk, s) \rangle$ and the signature to the license server. Next, the license server verifies validity of the user's request, and if valid, he issues s, which is recovered from $E_{pub}(pk, s)$ and sk, to the user. Note that the license server also verifies the signature in order to determine the relationship between ℓ and $E_{pub}(pk, s)$. Finally, the user downloads $E_{sym}(s, m)$ and decrypt it by using s. The user may skip downloading $E_{sym}(s, m)$ if he has already obtained it in a former phase.

References

1. M. Bellare, A. Desai, E. Jokipii and P. Rogaway, "A concrete security treatment of symmetric encryption," Proc. of 38th IEEE Symposium on Foundations of Computer Science (FOCS), pp.394–403, 1997.
2. M. Bellare, A. Desai, D. Pointcheval and P. Rogaway, "Relations among notions of security for public-key encryption schemes," Proc. of CRYPTO'98, pp.26–45, 1998.
3. D. Boneh, "The decision Diffie-Hellman problem," Proc. of ANTS III, pp. 48–63, 1998.
4. D. Boneh and M. Franklin, "Identity-based encryption from the Weil pairing," Proc. of CRYPTO 2001, pp.213–229, 2001.
5. R. Cramer and V. Shoup, "A practical public key cryptosystem provably secure against adaptive chosen ciphertext attack," Proc. of CRYPTO'98, pp.13–25, 1998.
6. Y. Dodis, J. Katz, S. Xu and M. Yung, "Key-insulated public key cryptosystems," Proc. of Eurocrypt 2002, pp.65–82, 2002.
7. T. ElGamal, "A public key cryptosystem and a signature scheme based on discrete logarithms," IEEE Trans. on Inform. Theory, IT-31, 4, pp.469–472, 1985.
8. C. Gentry and A. Silverberg, "Hierarchical ID-based cryptography," Proc. of Asiacrypt 2002, pp.548–566, 2002.
9. J. Horwitz and B. Lynn, "Toward hierarchical identity-based encryption," Proc. of Eurocrypt 2002, pp.466–481, 2002.
10. http://www.intertrust.com/
11. http://www.microsoft.com/windows/windowsmedia/drm.asp
12. C. Rackoff and D.R. Simon, "Non-interactive zero-knowledge proof of knowledge and chosen ciphertext attack," Proc. of CRYPTO'91, pp.433–444, 1992.
13. NIST, "Secure hash standard," FIPS PUB 180-1, Department of Commerce, Washington D.C., 1995.
14. A. Shamir, "Identity-based cryptosystems and signature schemes," Proc. of CRYPTO'84, pp.47–53, 1985.
15. http://www.xrml.com/

An Efficient Revocation Scheme with Minimal Message Length for Stateless Receivers[*]

Yong Ho Hwang, Chong Hee Kim, and Pil Joong Lee

Department of Electronic and Electrical Engineering,
Pohang University of Science & Technology (POSTECH),
San 31 Hyoja-dong, Nam-gu, Pohang, Kyoungbuk, 790-784, Rep. of Korea
{yhhwang, chhkim}@oberon.postech.ac.kr, pjl@postech.ac.kr

Abstract. We deal with the revocation scheme such that the revoked receivers should not be able to obtain available information when a center broadcasts data to all receivers. We propose a new revocation scheme with minimal message length for stateless receivers, where the receivers do not update their state from session to session. The proposed scheme requires storage of $\frac{1}{2} \log^2 n - \frac{1}{2} \log n + 2$ keys at the receiver and a message length of at most $r+1$. The main contribution of the proposed scheme is to reduce the message length. Namely, the proposed scheme minimizes the number of subsets which the non-revoked receivers are partitioned.

1 Introduction

Broadcast encryption schemes enable a center to deliver available information to a large group of users so that only legitimate users can decrypt the data. They can be applied to pay-TV systems, multicast communications, the distribution of copyrighted materials, and audio streaming. The center in these applications should efficiently broadcast information to a dynamically changing group of users. Such schemes have many variants. One interesting variant is a revocation scheme for stateless receivers. A stateless receiver is not capable of recording the past history of transmissions and changing its state accordingly. Therefore, each legitimate user can decrypt the transmission with an initial collection of keys while a coalition of revoked users cannot decrypt the transmission. Stateless receivers are important in cases where the receiver is not constantly on-line. For example, suppose that a user with a media player on on-line service has not used it for a few days. If his player is not a stateless receiver, then he should receive the past history of transmissions to take the on-line service again. However, he needs only the current transmission in the case of a stateless receiver.

In this paper, we propose a very efficient revocation scheme for stateless receivers. One of our main cntributions is a new subset algorithm which minimizes

---

[*] This research was supported by University IT Research Center Project, the Brain Korea 21 Project, and Com2MaC-KOSEF.

R. Safavi-Naini and J. Seberry (Eds.): ACISP 2003, LNCS 2727, pp. 377–386, 2003.
© Springer-Verlag Berlin Heidelberg 2003

the number of groups of legitimate receivers. The proposed scheme is substantially better than any previously known algorithm on the message length over the stateless receiver scenario.

The organization of this paper is as follows. We introduce related works and summary of our results in the remainder of this section. In section 2, we describe the proposed scheme in detail. We compare our scheme with other revocation schemes for stateless receivers in section 3 and summarize our results in section 4.

1.1   Related Works

The basic definition and paradigms of broadcast encryption were first introduced by Fiat and Naor [2] in 1994 and have received much attention since then. They proposed an r-resilient method which is resistant to a collusion of up to r revoked receivers. The scheme requires storage of $O(r \log r \log n)$ keys at each receiver and broadcast of $O(r^2 \log^2 r \log n)$ messages when n is the total number of receivers in the system. This method is difficult to be applied to a practical system because of too high complexity.

The efficient multicast method using a logical-tree-hierarchy (LKH) was independently suggested by Wallner et al. [6] and Wong et al. [7]. These schemes require to store $\log n + 1$ keys at each receiver and to transmit $2r \log n$ ciphertexts. In addition, each receiver is required to perform at most $\log n$ decryption.

In 2001, Naor et al. [5] introduced revocation schemes for stateless receivers. They proposed two schemes, the CS (Complete Subtree) scheme and the SD (Subset Difference) scheme. The main disadvantage of the CS scheme is that the non-revoked receivers are partitioned into a number of subsets that are too large. The SD scheme reduced a number of subsets, whereas it required more keys at each receiver. The SD scheme requires the storage of $\frac{1}{2} \log^2 n + \frac{1}{2} \log n + 1$ keys and message length of at most $2r-1$, while the CS scheme requires the storage of $\log n + 1$ keys at each receiver and a message length of at most $r \log \frac{n}{r}$. There is a tradeoff between the CS scheme and the SD scheme. Although the SD scheme needs more storage than the CS scheme, the SD scheme is the most efficient scheme among previously proposed schemes with respect to message length.

Halevy and Shamir proposed the LSD (Layered Subset Difference) scheme in 2002 [3]. They improved and generalized the SD scheme. The LSD scheme is a stateless broadcast encryption scheme with $O(\log^{1+\epsilon} n)$ keys and $O(r)$ message length. The LSD scheme reduces the number of keys by using the notion of "layer". However, there is a tradeoff between storage and message length. If the storage of keys is reduced, the message length increases. Therefore, the LSD scheme is not more efficient than SD scheme with respect to message length.

Asano [1] proposed efficient schemes with respect to the number of keys stored at each receiver. His scheme requires the storage of one key and a message length of at most $r(\frac{\log \frac{n}{r}}{\log a} + 1)$. This scheme uses an a-ary tree and the security of the scheme is based on Integer Factoring Problem (IFP) as RSA. However, this scheme has a disadvantage that the center generates and broadcasts $(2^a - 2)\frac{n-1}{a-1} + 1$ primes.

In this paper, we propose an efficient scheme with respect to message length compared with previously proposed schemes for stateless receivers. Our scheme uses a binary-tree and is based on IFP as Asano's scheme [1].

1.2   Summary of Our Results

The main improvement of our scheme is to reduce message length. Namely, our scheme minimizes the number of subsets whose the non-revoked receivers are partitioned. The proposed subset algorithm reduces the number of subsets to at best half that of SD, which is the most efficient scheme among previously proposed schemes with respect to message length. The storage of keys of the proposed scheme is also similar to that of the SD scheme. Our scheme requires the storage of $\frac{1}{2}\log^2 n - \frac{1}{2}\log n + 2$ keys and at most $r+1$ messages. We compare our scheme with previously revocation schemes for stateless receivers [5,3,1], in detail in section 4.

2   The Proposed Method

We propose a new revocation method for stateless receivers in this section. The proposed method is very efficient with respect to the message size broadcasted by the center for stateless receivers. The center imagines a rooted full binary tree with n leaves (assume that n is a power of 2) and assigns each receiver to each leaf of the tree. Each node is named $v_i (1 \le i \le 2n-1)$. Let N represent the set of all receivers and R be the revoked set, N/R be the set of the remaining receivers when r receivers are revoked. We denote by $ST(R)$ the Steiner Tree induced by R and the root, i.e. the minimal subtree of the full binary tree that connects all the leaves in R ($ST(R)$ is unique)[5].

2.1   The Framework

Let $S_1, S_2, \cdots, S_w$ be the subsets of N. Each subset S_j is assigned a long-lived key L_j. Each receiver u of subset S_j should be able to deduce L_j from its secret information. Given R, the remaining receivers N/R are partitioned into disjoint subsets $S_{i_1}, \cdots, S_{i_m}$ so that $N/R = \bigcup_{j=1}^{m} S_{i_j}$. The center chooses a session key K and encrypt it m times with $L_{i_1}, \cdots, L_{i_m}$. Finally, the center broadcasts the ciphertext as follows:

$$< [i_1, \cdots, i_m, E_{L_{i_1}}(K), \cdots, E_{L_{i_m}}(K)], F_K(M) >$$

Here i_j is information about the members of S_{i_j}, E_L is an encryption scheme to deliver the session key to receivers and F_K is a scheme to encrypt the message itself. The $E_L : \{0,1\}^l \to \{0,1\}^l$ is a block cipher and the $F_K : \{0,1\}^* \to \{0,1\}^*$ is a stream cipher generated by K because F_K should be a fast method and should not expand the plaintext. We define message length (or the number of ciphertexts) as the length of the header that is attached to $F_K(M)$. It is the number of subsets which partition N/R.

When the user u receives a broadcast message, he finds i_j such that $u \in S_{i_j}$. Each receiver of subset S_j obtain K by computing $D_{L_j}(E_{L_j}(K))$ using L_j deduced from its secret information. Then u decrypts $F_K(M)$ and outputs M.

2.2   The Subset Algorithm

For a set R of revoked receivers, the following algorithm finds a collection of disjoint subsets $S_{i_1}, \cdots, S_{i_m}$ which partitions N/R. The method builds the subsets collection iteratively, maintaining a tree T which is a subtree of $ST(R)$ with the property that any $u \in N/R$ that is below a leaf of T has been covered. We start by making T equal to $ST(R)$.

Step A. Iteratively remove nodes from T (while adding subsets to the collection) until T consists of one leaf only.

1. If the leaf of T is only one, then
   a) If the leaf of T is the root of $ST(R)$, then conclude the algorithm
   b) Go to Step B.
2. Find two leaves v_i and v_j in T such that the least-common-ancestor v_r of v_i and v_j does not contain any other leaf of T in its subtree. Let v_l and v_k be the two children of v_r such that v_i is a descendant of v_l and v_j is a descendant of v_k.
3. If $v_l \neq v_i$ or $v_k \neq v_j$ then add the subset $S_{r,(i,j)}$ to the collection.
4. Remove from T all the descendants of v_r and make it a leaf.

Step B. Let v_i be the leaf of T and v_r be the the root of $ST(R)$. (Let v_j be the a child of v_r such that v_j is not an ancestor of v_i in the rooted full binary tree)

1. If v_i is a child of v_r (namely v_i and v_j are sibling) then add the subset $S_{j,(0,0)}$ to the collection
2. Else add the subset $S_{r,(i,j)}$ and $S_{j,(0,0)}$ to the collection.
   (the subset $S_{j,(0,0)}$ is the set composed of all descendants of v_j which has no revoked node)

A subset S is represented by three nodes (v_r, v_i, v_j) such that v_r is the least-common-ancestor of v_i and v_j. We denote such subset by $S_{r,(i,j)}$. Figure 1 depicts $S_{r,(i,j)}$.

Our subset algorithm is similar to that of the SD method [5]. However, the subset $S_{r,(i,j)}$ of Figure 1 separates $S_{l,i}$ and $S_{k,j}$ in case of the SD method. Therefore, the proposed algorithm reduces the number of subsets to at best half that of SD. Theorem 1 shows that our subset algorithm contains at most $(r+1)$ subsets for any set of r revocations.

Theorem 1 *Given any set of revoked receivers R, the proposed subset algorithm partitions N/R into at most $r+1$ disjoint subsets.*

Proof. Every iteration of Step A increases the number of subsets by at most one (in Step A.3) and reduces the number of leaves by one (in Step A.4) until T consists of only a single leaf. Starting with r receivers, the process generates at most $r-1$ subsets. If the number of the leaf of T is only one then the algorithm terminates (in Step A.1.a) or goes to Step B (in Step A.1.b). An operation of Step B increases the number of subsets by at most two (in Step B.2). Therefore, the proposed subset algorithm generates at most $r+1$ subsets. Moreover, every

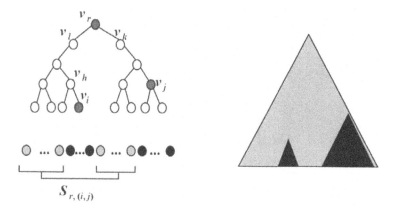

Fig. 1. The subset contains all marked(non-black) leaves.

non-revoked user u is in exactly one subset, the one defined by the first chain of nodes of outdegree 1 in $ST(R)$ that is encountered while moving from u towards the root. This encounter must hit a non-empty chain, since the path from u to the root cannot join $ST(R)$ in an outdegree 2 node, since this implies that $u \in R$ □

2.3   The Key Assignment

The security of the proposed algorithm is based on Integer Factoring Problem. The center chooses two large primes p, q and publishes M $(= pq)$. Two primes p, q are not published. The center gives the secret information to each receiver u_k $(1 \leq k \leq n)$. Each receiver can deduce the long-term key $L_{r,(i,j)}$ of the subset $S_{r,(i,j)}$ from the received secret information where v_r is an ancestor of itself and v_i, v_j are not an ancestor of itself. Naturally, the descendents of v_i and v_j cannot compute $L_{r,(i,j)}$.

We use the following indexing process: Consider the subset $S_{r,(i,j)}$. The center assigns $K_r(\in Z_M^*)$ to the root v_r of the subtree T_r. Let v_l and v_k be the two children of v_r and let $I_{r,(i,j)}$ be the index of $S_{r,(i,j)}$. Here v_i is a descendant of v_l and v_j is a descendant of v_k. The key $L_{r,(i,j)}$ assigned to $S_{r,(i,j)}$ is $H(I_{r,(i,j)})$, where $H() : \{0,1\}^* \to \{0,1\}^l$ is a one-way hash function. Figure 2 shows the method of the computing $I_{r,(i,j)}$.

The center generates and publishes $4(\log n - 1)$ primes, $Left_{1L}$, $Left_{1R}$, $Right_{1L}$, $Right_{1R}$, $\cdots$, $Left_{(\log n - 1)L}$, $Left_{(\log n - 1)R}$, $Right_{(\log n - 1)L}$, $Right_{(\log n - 1)L}$ (such that $\gcd(label_{iR(orL)}, \phi(M)) = 1$ where label is $Left$ or $Right$, $1 \leq i \leq \log n - 1$ [7]). No one can compute the inverse of $label_{iR(orL)}$ except the center. The index $I_{r,(i,j)}$ in Figure 2 is computed as follows;

$$I_{r,(i,j)} = K_r^l \bmod M (\text{where } l = Left_{1R}Right_{1R}Right_{2R})$$

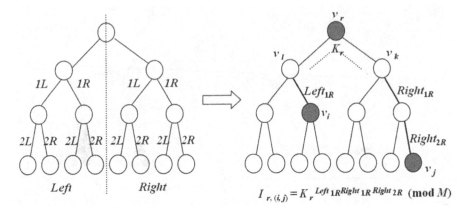

$$I_{r,(i,j)} = K_r^{Left_{1R}Right_{1R}Right_{2R}} \pmod{M}$$

Fig. 2. The Key assignment method(Left : label assignment, Right : the method of the computing index)

For convenience, we will omit "*mod M*" in the remainder of this paper where it is clear from the context.

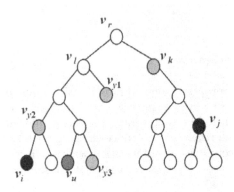

Fig. 3. An example of the key assignment in T_r

Figure 3 shows an example of the key assignment in T_r with depth 4. The center provides secret information, $I_{r,(y1,k)}, I_{r,(y2,k)}, I_{r,(y3,k)}$, to the receiver v_u over a secure channel. Here, v_{y1}, v_{y2} and v_{y3} are descendants of v_l and are sibling of ancestors of v_u. Then v_u can compute $I_{r,(i,j)}$ $(=I_{r,(y2,k)}^{Left_{3L}Right_{1R}Right_{2R}})$ from his secret information when two nodes v_i and v_j are revoked. While v_u cannot compute $I_{r,(a,j)}$ where a is an ancestor of itself. To compute $I_{r,(a,j)}$ from $I_{r,(y1,k)}, I_{r,(y2,k)}$, and $I_{r,(y3,k)}$, he must know the inverse of $Left_{1R}, Left_{2L}$, or $Left_{3R}$. However, he cannot compute the inverse of $Left_{1R}, Left_{2L}$, or $Left_{3R}$ because our scheme is based on IFP.

Regarding the total number of keys stored by receiver u, each tree T_r of depth d that contains u contributes $d-1$ keys (plus one key for the group key of child of root for Step B and one key for the case where exists no revocation). Thus, the total is

$$2 + \sum_{d=1}^{\log n}(d-1) = 2 + \frac{(\log n + 1)\log n}{2} - \log n = \tfrac{1}{2}\log^2 n - \tfrac{1}{2}\log n + 2.$$

2.4   The Complete Scheme

To state the complete scheme, we show an example of our scheme for $n=16$ in Figure 4. A process of the proposed scheme is as follows.

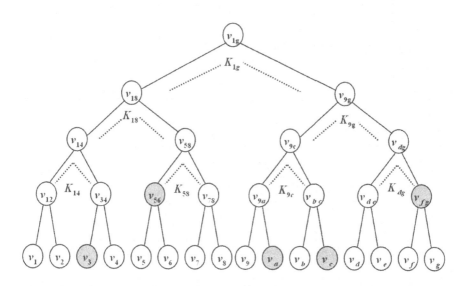

Fig. 4. An example of our scheme for $n=16$

Setup(The center) The center makes a rooted full binary tree with 16 leaves and assigns each receiver to each leaf of the tree.

1. Select large prime p, q and publish $M(=pq)$.
2. Randomly choose $K_i \in Z_M^*(1 \le i \le 7)$ and $L_{1g,(0,0)}, L_{18,(0,0)}, L_{9g,(0,0)}$
3. Choose and broadcast 12 primes $(\gcd(label_{iR(orL)}, \phi(M)) = 1)$:
   $Left_{1L}, Left_{1R}, Right_{1L}, Right_{1R}, \cdots, Left_{3L}, Left_{3R}, Right_{3L}, Right_{3R}$
4. Give the secret information to each receiver over a secure channel. The secret information in each receiver is as follows. (key size : $8 = (\tfrac{1}{2})4^2 - (\tfrac{1}{2})4 + 2$)

$$u_1 : K_{1g}^{Left_1R}, K_{1g}^{Left_1L Left_2R}, K_{1g}^{Left_1L Left_2L Left_3R},$$
$$K_{18}^{Left_1R}, K_{18}^{Left_1L Left_2R}, K_{14}^{Left_1R}, L_{9g,(0,0)}, L_{1g,(0,0)}$$

$$u_2 : K_{1g}^{Left_1R}, K_{1g}^{Left_1L Left_2R}, K_{1g}^{Left_1L Left_2L Left_3L},$$
$$K_{18}^{Left_1R}, K_{18}^{Left_1L Left_2L}, K_{14}^{Left_1L}, L_{18,(0,0)}, L_{1g,(0,0)}$$

$$u_3 : K_{1g}^{Left_1R}, K_{1g}^{Left_1L Left_2R}, K_{1g}^{Left_1L Left_2L Left_3R},$$
$$K_{18}^{Left_1L}, K_{18}^{Left_1R Left_2R}, K_{14}^{Right_1R}, L_{18,(0,0)}, L_{1g,(0,0)}$$

$$\cdots$$
$$\cdots$$

$$u_g : K_{1g}^{Right_1L}, K_{1g}^{Right_1R Right_2L}, K_{1g}^{Right_1R Right_2R Right_3L},$$
$$K_{9g}^{Right_1L}, K_{9g}^{Right_1R Right_2L}, K_{fg}^{Right_1L}, L_{18,(0,0)}, L_{1g,(0,0)}$$

Encryption(The center) Assume that 7 receivers, $v_3, v_5, v_6, v_a, v_c, v_f, v_g$ are revoked in Figure 4.

1. Find a collection of disjoint subsets (using the subset algorithm of section 2.2)
   A collection of Subsets : $\{S_{18,(3,56)}, S_{9c,(a,c)}, S_{9g,(9c,fg)}\}$
2. Compute the long-term key $L_{r,(i,j)}$ of the subset $S_{r,(i,j)}$
   $L_{18,(3,56)} = H(I_{18,(3,56)})$ where $I_{18,(3,56)} = K_{18}^{Left_1R Left_2L Right_1L}$
   $L_{9c,(a,c)} = H(I_{9c,(a,c)})$ where $I_{9c,(a,c)} = K_{9c}^{Left_1R Right_1R}$
   $L_{9g,(9c,fg)} = H(I_{9g,(9c,fg)})$ where $I_{9g,(9c,fg)} = K_{9g}^{Right_1R}$
3. Choose a session key K and broadcasts the ciphertext as follows.
   $< [i_1, i_2, i_3, E_{L_{18,(3,56)}}(K), E_{L_{9c,(a,c)}}(K), E_{L_{9g,(9c,fg)}}(K)], F_K(M) >$
   where i_1, i_2 and i_3 are information of $\{18, (3,56)\}, \{9c, (a,c)\}, \{9g, (9c, fg)\}$.

Decryption(The receiver) Each receiver receives a broadcast message $< [i_1, i_2, i_3, C_1(K), C_2(K), C_3(K)], F_K(M) >$. We consider the receiver, u_1.

1. Find i such that $u \in S_i$(Here $i=18,(3,56)$)
2. Compute the long-term key $L_{18,(3,56)}$ of the subset $S_{18,(3,56)}$ from secret information as follows.
   $l = Left_{2L} Right_{1L}$
   $I_{18,(3,56)} = (K_{18}^{Left_1R})^l$
   $L_{18,(3,56)} = H(I_{18,(3,56)})$
3. Decrypt $C_1(K)$ using the $L_{18,(3,56)}$
4. Obtain M from $F_K(M)$ using K.

In this example, u_3 cannot compute $I_{18,(3,56)}$ from $K_{18}^{Left_1L}$ or $K_{18}^{Left_1R Left_2R}$ because he cannot compute an inverse of $Left_{1L}$ or $Left_{2R}$.

2.5   The Security of the Proposed Scheme

To discuss the security of the proposed method, we first state the notion of revocation-scheme security. The adversary has broken the system means that the adversary can obtain something about the subset key or the encrypted message when all revoked users have provided their secret information. Asano [1] showed the security of his scheme under the assumption related to RSA cryptosystem. The proposed system is also based on an Integer Factoring Problem as RSA cryptosystem. Therefore, the security of the proposed system also follows from that of Asano [1]. In addition, if the encryption primitives E_L and F_K satisfy the following requirements, then the proposed revocation scheme is secure under the above definition. E_L is required to be semantically secure against chosen-ciphertext attacks and F_K to be chosen-plaintext attacks since E_L uses long-lived keys whereas F_K uses short-lived ones.

3   Comparison

We compare the proposed scheme with other schemes [5,3,1]. The LSD scheme [3] improved the SD scheme [5] with respect to the storage of the receiver. However, the SD scheme is more efficient than the LSD scheme with respect to message length. Therefore, we compare our scheme with the CS/SD scheme in detail because our original contribution concerns message length. We also compare our scheme with Asano's schemes [1] because it is based on IFP (or RSA cryptosystem) as our scheme. Table 1 shows the comparison with other schemes. (Though Asano's schemes use the a-ary tree, we assume that his schemes use a binary tree for a fair comparison with other schemes.)

Table 1. Comparison with other schemes

	Message length	Storage of keys at receiver	Prime generator	Modular Exponentiations
Asano 1	$r(\log \frac{n}{r} + 1)$	1	$2(n-1)+1$	1
Asano 2	$r(\log \frac{n}{r} + 1)$	$\log n$	1	1
CS	$r\log \frac{n}{r}$	$\log n$	-	-
SD	$2r-1$	$\frac{1}{2}\log^2 n + \frac{1}{2}\log n + 1$	-	-
Our scheme	$r+1$	$\frac{1}{2}\log^2 n - \frac{1}{2}\log n + 2$	$4(\log n - 1)$	1

The proposed scheme has about half the message length of the SD. For example, in Figure 4 the message length of CS is 6, SD is 5, and Asano 1(or 2) is 6, but the proposed scheme is only 3. The storage of keys of the proposed scheme is similar to that of the SD scheme. Therefore, our scheme is more efficient than the SD scheme.

The message length of Asano's schemes [1] is not efficient rather than that of the CS scheme. In addition, Asano 2 [1] also has no advantage in the storage of keys than the CS. The Asano 1 [1] has minimal storage of keys. However, Asano states that receivers of Asano 1 need a total storage of $(\log n(\log n + \log\log n + 3))$ which includes keys and primes [1]. The center of Asano 1 also generates and broadcasts $2(n-1)+1$ primes. The proposed scheme requires the total storage of $\frac{1}{2}\log^2 n + (7/2)\log n - 2$ because each receiver additionally needs a storage of $4(\log n - 1)$ primes. Therefore, the proposed scheme is more efficient not only in message length but also in the total storage at the receiver compared with Asano 1 [1].

The Asano 1 reduces the message length to $r(\frac{\log\frac{n}{r}}{\log a}+1)$ when it uses an a-ary tree. However, the center of Asano 1 has to generate and broadcast $(2^a-2)\frac{n-1}{a-1}+1$ primes and the receiver needs the storage of $(\frac{2^{a-1}-1}{\log a})\log n(\log n + \log\log n + 3)$. While the message length reduces in proportion to $\frac{1}{\log a}$, the required storage increases in proportion to 2^a. Therefore, the larger the a, the more the system requires many primes and large storage.

4   Conclusions

We proposed a new revocation scheme for stateless receivers. We use a technique which makes two subsets of the SD scheme into one subset in order to reduce the message length. Therefore, our scheme reduces the message length of the SD scheme by (about) half. In addition, our scheme and the SD scheme require the storage of $O(\frac{1}{2}\log^2 n)$. The proposed scheme has a better performance in a practical system because the transmitted data from the center is reduced.

References

1. T. Asano, A Revocation Scheme with Minimal Storage at Receivers, *Advances in Cryptology – ASIACRYPT '02*, pp.433–450, 2002.
2. A. Fiat and M. Naor, Broadcast Encryption, *Advances in Cryptology – CRYPTO '93*, pp.480–491,1994.
3. D. Halevy and A. Shamir, The LSD Broadcast Encryption Scheme, *Advances in Cryptology – CRYPTO '02*, pp.47–60, 2002.
4. A. Menezes, P.van Oorschot and S. Vanstone, Handbook of applied cryptography, *CRC Press, Inc.*, 1997.
5. D. Naor, M. Naor and J. Lotspiech, Revocation and Tracing Schemes for Stateless Receivers, *Advances in Cryptology – CRYPTO '01*, pp.41–62, 2001
6. D. M. Wallner, E. J. Harder and R.C. Agee, Key Management for Multicast: Issues and Architectures, *IETF Network Working Group, Request for Comments 2627*, June, 1999.
   http://ftp.ietf.org/rfc/rfc2627.txt
7. C. K. Wong, M. Gouda and S. Lam, Secure Group Communications Using Key Graphs, *Proceedings of ACM SIGCOMM '98*, pp.68–79, 1998.

Parallel Authentication and Public-Key Encryption

Josef Pieprzyk[1] and David Pointcheval[2]

[1] Centre for Advanced Computing – Algorithms and Cryptography
Department of Computing, Macquarie University
Sydney, NSW 2109, AUSTRALIA
josef@ics.mq.edu.au
[2] École Normale Supérieure – Laboratoire d'informatique
45, rue d'Ulm, 75230 Paris Cedex 05, FRANCE
David.Pointcheval@ens.fr – www.di.ens.fr/users/pointche

Abstract. A parallel authentication and public-key encryption is introduced and exemplified on joint encryption and signing which compares favorably with sequential Encrypt-then-Sign ($\mathcal{EtS}$) or Sign-then-Encrypt ($\mathcal{StE}$) schemes as far as both efficiency and security are concerned. A security model for signcryption, and thus joint encryption and signing, has been recently defined which considers possible attacks and security goals. Such a scheme is considered secure if the encryption part guarantees indistinguishability and the signature part prevents existential forgeries, for outsider but also insider adversaries. We propose two schemes of parallel signcryption, which are efficient alternative to Commit-then-Sign-and-Encrypt ($\mathcal{CtE\&S}$). They are both provably secure in the random oracle model. The first one, called *generic parallel encrypt and sign*, is secure if the encryption scheme is semantically secure against chosen-ciphertext attacks and the signature scheme prevents existential forgeries against random-message attacks. The second scheme, called *optimal parallel encrypt and sign*, applies random oracles similar to the OAEP technique in order to achieve security using encryption and signature components with very weak security requirements — encryption is expected to be one-way under chosen-plaintext attacks while signature needs to be secure against universal forgeries under random-plaintext attack, that is actually the case for both the plain-RSA encryption and signature under the usual RSA assumption. Both proposals are generic in the sense that any suitable encryption and signature schemes (*i.e.* which simply achieve required security) can be used. Furthermore they allow both parallel encryption and signing, as well as parallel decryption and verification. Properties of parallel encrypt and sign schemes are considered and a new security standard for parallel signcryption is proposed.

Keywords: Signcryption, authentication, privacy, parallelization.

1 Introduction

The need for fast cryptographic transformations has never been so urgent as today when new multimedia applications such as distance learning, video on

R. Safavi-Naini and J. Seberry (Eds.): ACISP 2003, LNCS 2727, pp. 387–401, 2003.
© Springer-Verlag Berlin Heidelberg 2003

demand and TV channels delivery via Internet, interactive e-Commerce, etc. rely on secure transfer of large volumes of data. Typically data in transit needs to be cryptographically protected to provide either confidentiality and/or authenticity. As modern multimedia applications are run in real time, there are stringent requirements imposed on delay introduced by cryptography.

To speed up cryptographic transformations, we may apply two basic approaches. Firstly, we may design faster (symmetric or asymmetric) cryptographic algorithms. This option is not available most of the time. Once an algorithm becomes the standard or has been incorporated in hardware, users will be stuck with it for some time. Besides, the speed is typically determined by the number of rounds (in private key case) or by the size of the message (in public-key case). In the second approach, we can implement a parallel cryptographic system. Note that block ciphers (such as DES) have several operation modes from which some are sequential (like CBC and CFB) and some are parallel (like ECB and OFB).

The main idea is to take a large message block, divide it into blocks of the size determined by the applied cryptographic algorithm (in case of DES, the block size would be 64 bits) and apply the chaining using less expensive operations before the chained blocks are subject to cryptographic operation performed in parallel.

Consider what kind of cryptographic operations make sense for parallel execution. Encryption can be sped up by putting parallel encryption threads. For public-key cryptography, the chaining can be done by using hashing (hashing is much faster than public-key encryption). In the case of private-key cryptography, the chaining must be based on operations much faster than hashing (and encryption) such as bit-wise XOR.

The situation with digital signature looks differently. If the signer is a single person, then generation of parallel signatures (for the same message) is not very useful – one signature normally is enough. A plausible application of parallel signatures with a single signer is the case when the message is long lived and whose authenticity must be asserted even if one or more signature algorithms have been broken. More realistic application is when the same message is being signed by many co-signers in parallel as this is often required in group-oriented cryptography.

The most interesting case is, however, joint parallel encryption and signing. The scheme produces strings that can be seen from two different angles as designated verifier signatures or signed ciphertexts which can be verified by unique receiver. The parallel encryption and signing was introduced by [1]. Independently, the concept has been developed by the authors in this work. The both works can be seen as generalizations of the signcryption concept introduced by Zheng [17].

The work is structured as follows. Section 2 puts forward arguments for parallel encryption and signature, a.k.a. signcryption, and contrasts the approach with the previous ones. The security model for signcryption is presented in Section 3. The generic and optimal schemes for parallel signcryption are defined and analyzed in Sections 4 and 5, respectively. Section 6 concludes the work.

2   The Concept of Parallel Signing and Public-Key Encryption

The encryption and signature algorithms are two basic cryptographic tools providing privacy and authenticity, respectively. However, in many applications it is desired to achieve both privacy and authenticity. Among many examples, we can mention transport of session keys between nodes of a network whose secrecy and authenticity is absolutely imperative to ensure secure data handling during sessions. Negotiations between two parties (businesses, institutions, countries, etc) typically have to be conducted in such a way that both the confidentiality and authenticity are guaranteed. The lack of confidentiality can be exploited by competitors. On the other hand, the lack of authenticity undermines the credibility of the negotiation process.

Both security goals are relatively easy to achieve if the cryptographic operations are performed using symmetric primitives. Note that in this setting, the fact that both parties share the same cryptographic key, means that everything not generated by one party had to be originated by the other one. In the public-key setting, cryptosystem can be applied either for privacy or authenticity. Clearly, when both goals have to be achieved, two cryptosystems have to be used in either Sign-then-Encrypt ($\mathcal{S}t\mathcal{E}$) or Encrypt-then-Sign ($\mathcal{E}t\mathcal{S}$) configuration [3]. Note that both configurations are inherently sequential.

Encryption and authentication are inseparable with conventional cryptography. The discovery of the public-key cryptography [7] divorced these two nicely coupled security goals and enabled party to choose either confidentiality (public-key encryption schemes) or authentication (signature schemes). Now in many applications, one would like to get both confidentiality and authentication but using public-key cryptography. Note that the come back to the conventional cryptography remains an unattractive option. Indeed, once the public-key cryptography is properly implemented with a secure and reliable public-key infrastructure (PKI), every single pair of parties may establish a secure communication (with confidentiality or/and authenticity) using the certificates of their public keys. Note also that within a single pair of parties, each party is uniquely identifiable by the public key of the receiver and the public key of the sender. Moreover, a signed ciphertext generated during communication between two parties can be explicitly attributed to a single sender whereas with symmetric cryptography this is not the case. Cryptograms are attributed implicitly — if I did not send this message, the other party did. However, it does not provide the important non-repudiation property. Furthermore, authentication fails when the secret key is shared by more than two parties.

Authenticated encryption has been studied by many authors mainly in the context of secret-key cryptography and message authentication code that is a symmetric-key equivalent to signature (see [3,4]). Zheng [17] considered the problem in the context of public-key cryptography, with signcryption. The main problem considered in the paper [17] was how to design encryption and signature so that their concatenation maximizes savings of computing resources. A security model of parallel signcryption was defined recently in the work [1].

Our goal is to achieve the lower bound in terms of time necessary to perform authenticated encryption, and decryption as well, or

$$\text{time(parallel encrypt \& sign)} \approx \max\{\text{time(encrypt),time(sign)}\}$$
$$\text{and time(parallel decrypt \& verify)} \approx \max\{\text{time(decrypt),time(verify)}\}$$

At best, one would expect that parallel encryption and sign will consume roughly the same time as the most time-consuming operation (either signing or encryption, for the joint encryption and signing, and either verifying or decrypting, for the joint decryption and verifying).

A hybrid approach called the envelop method can be used for authenticated encryption. Public key encryption and signature are used independently to generate cryptograms of both a secret key (which has been chosen at random by the sender) and a signature of a message. This method can concurrently encrypt and sign. The encryption is used for a secret key that is decrypted by the receiver. The secret key can be applied to encrypt a message using a symmetric encryption. This method can be simplified by independent encryption and signing (perhaps performed in parallel) of the same message. Note that in this case, weaknesses of encryption and signature schemes are likely to be preserved. In contrast, we show how to combine encryption and signature schemes so that they strengthen each other while they can still be run in parallel.

The Commit-then-Encrypt-and-Sign ($\mathcal{CtE\&S}$) can also be used to solve our problem [1], but it still requires strongly secure encryption and signature primitive to provide secure signcryption.

3   Model of Security

3.1   Signature Schemes

Description. A digital signature scheme SIGN consists of three algorithms [10]:

- GenSig, the *key generation algorithm* which, on input 1^k, where k is the security parameter, outputs a pair (pk, sk) of matching public and private keys;
- Sig, the *signing algorithm* which receives a message m and the private key sk, and outputs a signature $\sigma = \text{Sig}_{sk}(m)$;
- Ver, the *verification algorithm* which receives a candidate signature σ, a message m, and a public key pk, and returns an answer $\text{Ver}_{pk}(m, \sigma)$ as to whether or not σ is a valid signature of m with respect to pk.

Security Notions. Attacks against signature schemes can be classified according to the goals of the adversary and to the resources that it can use. The goals are diverse and include:

- Disclosing the private key of the signer. This is the most drastic attack. It is termed the *total break*.

- Constructing an efficient algorithm that is able to sign any message with a significant probability of success. This is called the *universal forgery*. When the scheme prevents this kind of forgery it is said to be *Non Universally Forgeable* (NUF).
- Providing a single message/signature pair. This is called the *existential forgery*. When the scheme prevents this kind of forgery it is said to be *Non Existentially Forgeable* (NEF).

In terms of resources, we focus on two specific attacks against signature schemes: the *no-message attacks* and the *known-message attacks*. In the first scenario, the attacker only knows the public key pk of the signer. In the second, the attacker has access to a list of valid message/signature pairs. But this list may contain messages randomly and uniformly chosen, the attack is thus termed the *random-message attack* (RMA). Finally, the messages may be chosen, adaptively, by the adversary himself, we thus talk about the *chosen-message attack* (CMA).

In known-message attacks, one should point out that we consider a forgery of any valid signature that is not in the above list. This is the strongest security level, *a.k.a.* non-malleability [16].

3.2   Public-Key Encryption

Description. A public-key encryption scheme ENCRYPT is defined by three algorithms:

- GenEnc, the *key generation algorithm* which, on input 1^k, where k is the security parameter, produces a pair $(\mathsf{pk}, \mathsf{sk})$ of public and private keys;
- Enc, the *encryption algorithm* which, on input a plaintext m and a public key pk, outputs a ciphertext c;
- Dec, the *decryption algorithm* which, on input a ciphertext c and a private key sk, outputs the associated plaintext m (or $\perp$, if c is an invalid ciphertext).

Security Notions. The simplest security notion is *one-wayness* (OW): with public data only, an attacker cannot recover the whole plaintext m of a given ciphertext c. We denote by $\mathsf{Succ}^{\mathsf{ow}}_{\mathsf{Encrypt}}(t)$ the maximum probability of success that an adversary can invert the encryption of a random plaintext in time t.

A stronger security notion has also been defined. It is the so-called *semantic security* (*a.k.a. indistinguishability of encryptions* [9], IND). If an attacker has some information about the plaintext, the view of the ciphertext should not leak any additional information. This security notion more formally considers the advantage an adversary can gain when trying to guess, between two messages, which one has been encrypted. In other words, an adversary is seen as a 2-stage Turing machine (A_1, A_2), and the advantage $\mathsf{Adv}^{\mathsf{ind}}_{\mathsf{Encrypt}}(\mathcal{A})$ should be negligible for any adversary, where

$$\mathsf{Adv}^{\mathsf{ind}}_{\mathsf{Encrypt}}(\mathcal{A}) = 2 \times \Pr\left[\begin{array}{l} (\mathsf{pk}, \mathsf{sk}) \leftarrow \mathsf{Gen}(1^k), (m_0, m_1, s) \leftarrow A_1(\mathsf{pk}), \\ b \in \{0,1\}, c = \mathsf{Enc}_{\mathsf{pk}}(m_b) : A_2(m_0, m_1, s, c) = b \end{array} \right] - 1.$$

On the other hand, an attacker can use many kinds of attacks, depending on the information available to him. First, in the public-key setting, the adversary can encrypt any plaintext of his choice with the public key: this basic scenario is called the *chosen-plaintext attack*, and denoted by CPA. Extended scenarios allow the adversary a restricted or unrestricted access to various oracles. The main and strongest one is the decryption oracle which can be accessed adaptively in the *chosen-ciphertext* scenario, denoted CCA. There is the natural restriction that any query to this oracle should be different from the challenge ciphertext.

3.3   Joint Encryption and Signing: Signcryption

The following security model has been recently suggested and analyzed [1].

Description. A signcryption scheme SIGNCRYPT is defined by three algorithms:

- Gen, the *key generation* algorithm which, for a security parameter k, outputs a pair of keys (SDK, VEK). SDK is the user's sign/decrypt key, which is kept secret, and VEK is the user's verify/encrypt key, which is made public.
- SigEnc, the *encryption and signing* algorithm which, for a message m, the public key of the receiver VEK_R and the private key of the sender SDK_S, produces a *signed–ciphertext* $c = \mathsf{SigEnc}_{\mathsf{SDK}_S,\mathsf{VEK}_R}(m)$.
- VerDec, the *decryption and verifying* algorithm which, for a *signed–ciphertext* c, the private key SDK_R of the receiver and the public key VEK_S of the sender, recovers the message $m = \mathsf{VerDec}_{\mathsf{VEK}_S,\mathsf{SDK}_R}(c)$. If this algorithm fails either to recover the message or to verify authenticity, it returns $\perp$.

Security Notions. For the security notions of a signcryption, one can combine the classical ones for signature [10] and encryption [2], under adaptive attacks. With an access to the public information, $\mathsf{PUB} = (\mathsf{VEK}_S, \mathsf{VEK}_R)$, and oracle access to the functionalities of both S and R (i.e. access to the *signcryption* and the *de-signcryption* oracles), the adversary should be able to break:

- authenticity (NEF) — come up with a valid *signed–ciphertext* of a new message, and thus provide an *existential forgery*;
- privacy (IND) — break the *indistinguishability* of *signed–ciphertexts*.

One should note that the adversary may be one of S or R themselves. But then, S may want to break the privacy, or R may want to break authenticity. If the signcryption scheme prevents existential forgeries and guarantees indistinguishability, in the above attack scenario, called *adaptive attacks* (AdA), we say the scheme is *secure*.

Definition 1. *A signcryption scheme is **secure** if it achieves* IND/NEF *under adaptive attacks.*

Some Notations. Denote by $\mathsf{Succ}^{\mathsf{nef-ada}}_{\mathsf{SignCrypt}}(\mathcal{A})$ the probability of success of an adversary in forging a new valid *signed–ciphertext*. Similarly, denote by $\mathsf{Adv}^{\mathsf{ind-ada}}_{\mathsf{SignCrypt}}(\mathcal{A})$ the advantage of an adversary in distinguishing *signed–cipher-texts*. Finally, denote $\mathsf{Win}^{\mathsf{secure}}_{\Pi}(\mathcal{A})$ as the maximum of these two values.

Let $\mathsf{Succ}^{\mathsf{nef-ada}}_{\mathsf{SignCrypt}}(t, q_1, q_2)$, $\mathsf{Adv}^{\mathsf{ind-ada}}_{\mathsf{SignCrypt}}(t, q_1, q_2)$ and $\mathsf{Win}^{\mathsf{secure}}_{\mathsf{SignCrypt}}(t, q_1, q_2)$ be the respective probabilities for an adaptive adversary whose running time is bounded by t, while asking at most q_1 queries to the signcryption oracle and q_2 queries to the de-signcryption oracle.

4   Generic Parallel Signcryption

A trivial implementation of parallel signcryption could be as simple as encrypt and sign (with message recovery to allow parallel decryption and verification) the same message in parallel. This, of course, does not work as the signature reveals the message. Another classical solution could be the well-known *envelope technique* that first defines a secret session key. This key is encrypted under the public key encryption and is used, in parallel, to encrypt, under a symmetric encryption, the message and a signature on it. If one assumes that the symmetric encryption has a negligible cost (some may disagree with), then this allows parallel encryption and signing. The recipient first decrypts the session key, and then extracts the message and the signature. Only when all that operations have been completed, one can verify the signature. Therefore, decryption and verification cannot be done in parallel.

The Commit-then-Encrypt-and-Sign $(\mathcal{C}t\mathcal{E}\&\mathcal{S})$ [1] is a little bit better. Indeed, it first commits the message m, getting c the actual committed value, and d the decommitment. Then one encrypts d in e and signs c in s. The *signed–ciphertext* (e, c, s) can be de-signcrypted by first verifying (c, s) and decrypting e into d. The decommitment d finally helps to recover m. But the decommitment may not be as efficient as required.

Our idea exemplifies this technique, but with an efficient commitment scheme, in the random oracle model: given a message, we design a (2,2) Shamir secret sharing scheme [14] for which the secret is the message. Next, one of the shares is encrypted, the other is authenticated (in parallel). The perfectness of Shamir secret sharing guarantees that the knowledge of one of the shares provides no information (in the information-theoretical sense) about the secret.

4.1   Description

The building blocks are:

- an encryption scheme $\textsc{Encrypt} = (\mathsf{GenEnc}, \mathsf{Enc}, \mathsf{Dec})$,
- a signature scheme $\textsc{Sign} = (\mathsf{GenSig}, \mathsf{Sig}, \mathsf{Ver})$,
- a large k-bit prime p which defines the field $\mathbb{Z}_p$,
- a hash function $h : \mathbb{Z}_p \to \mathbb{Z}_p$ (assumed to behave like a random oracle [5]),
- k_1 and k_2, two security parameters such that $k = k_1 + k_2$.

Key Generation: Gen(1^k) = GenSig $\times$ GenEnc(1^k)
One first gets $(\mathsf{sk}_1, \mathsf{pk}_1) \leftarrow \mathsf{GenSig}(1^k)$ and $(\mathsf{sk}_2, \mathsf{pk}_2) \leftarrow \mathsf{GenEnc}(1^k)$. Then, one defines $\mathsf{SDK} = (\mathsf{sk}_1, \mathsf{sk}_2)$ and $\mathsf{VEK} = (\mathsf{pk}_1, \mathsf{pk}_2)$.

Encrypt and Sign Algorithm: $\mathsf{SigEnc}_{\mathsf{SDK}_S, \mathsf{VEK}_R}(m)$

1. Let $m \in \{0,1\}^{k_1}$ be the message to be encrypted and signed. Choose a random integer $r \in \{0,1\}^{k_2}$ such that $(m\|r) \in \mathbb{Z}_p$ and compute $a = h(m\|r)$.
2. Form an instance of $(2,2)$ Shamir secret sharing scheme over $\mathbb{Z}_p$ with the polynomial $F(x) = (m\|r) + ax \bmod p$. Define two shares $s_1 = F(1)$ and $s_2 = F(2)$.
3. Calculate (in parallel) $c_1 = \mathsf{Enc}_{\mathsf{pk}_R}(s_1)$ and $c_2 = \mathsf{Sig}_{\mathsf{sk}_S}(s_2)$. The *signed–ciphertext* (c_1, c_2) is then dispatched to the receiver R.

Decrypt and Verify Algorithm: $\mathsf{VerDec}_{\mathsf{VEK}_S, \mathsf{SDK}_R}(c_1, c_2)$

1. Perform decryption and signature verification in parallel so, $t_1 = \mathsf{Dec}_{\mathsf{sk}_R}(c_1)$ and $t_2 = \mathsf{Ver}_{\mathsf{pk}_S}(c_2)$. Note that both the decryption Dec and verification Ver algorithms return integers in $\mathbb{Z}_p$, unless some failure occurs. Indeed, it is possible that Dec returns $\perp$ if it decides that the cryptogram is invalid. Similarly, Ver returns a message (signature with message recovery), or $\perp$ if the signature is invalid. In case of one failure, the decryption and verifying algorithm VerDec returns $\perp$ and stops.
2. Knowing two points $(1, t_1)$ and $(2, t_2)$, use the Lagrange interpolation and find the polynomial $\bar{F}(x) = a_0 + a_1 x \bmod p$.
3. Check whether $a_1 = h(a_0)$. If the check holds, the algorithm extracts m from a_0 (note that $a_0 = (m\|r)$) and returns m. Otherwise, the algorithm outputs $\perp$.

4.2   Security of Generic Scheme

Theorem 1. *If the encryption scheme is* IND-CCA *and the signature scheme is* NEF-RMA, *then the generic parallel signcryption scheme is secure (*IND/NEF-AdA*).*

More precisely, one can claim the following result:

Lemma 1. *Let us consider an* AdA *adversary $\mathcal{A}$ against* IND *and* NEF *of the generic parallel signcryption, with a running time bounded by t, while asking q_h queries to the random oracle h, and q_1 and q_2 queries to the signcryption and designcryption oracles respectively. Then, the winning probability of this adversary is bounded by*

$$2 \times \mathsf{Adv}^{\mathsf{ind-cca}}_{\mathsf{Encrypt}}(t', q_2) + 6 \times \mathsf{Succ}^{\mathsf{nef-rma}}_{\mathsf{Sign}}(t', q_1) + (5 + 2q_1) \times \frac{q_h + q_1 + q_2}{2^{k_2}},$$

with $t' \leq t + (q_1 + q_2)(\tau + \mathcal{O}(1))$, where τ denotes the maximal running time of the encryption, decryption, signing and verification algorithms.

The proof can be found in the full version of the paper [11].

4.3   Properties

From the efficiency point of view, this generic scheme is almost optimal since only one hash value and two additions are required before the parallel encryption and signature processes. The reverse process reaches the same kind of optimality.

However, the security requirements of the basic schemes, the encryption scheme ENCRYPT and the signature scheme SIGN, are very strong. Indeed, the encryption scheme is required to be semantically secure against chosen-ciphertext attack and the signature scheme must already prevent existential forgeries.

5   Optimal Parallel Signcryption

Adding a kind of OAEP technique [6], we can improve the generic scheme, in the sense that we can weaken the security requirements of the basic primitives. The new proposal just requires the encryption scheme to be deterministic and one-way against chosen-plaintext attack, which is a very weak security requirement (even the plain-RSA [12] achieves it under the RSA assumption). The signature scheme is required to prevent universal forgeries under random-message attack (the plain-RSA signature also achieves this security level).

5.1   Description

The building blocks are:

- an encryption scheme $\text{ENCRYPT} = (\text{GenEnc}, \text{Enc}, \text{Dec})$,
- a signature scheme $\text{SIGN} = (\text{GenSig}, \text{Sig}, \text{Ver})$,
- a large k-bit prime p which defines the field $\mathbb{Z}_p$,
- k_1 and k_2, two security parameters such that $k = k_1 + k_2$.
- hash functions (assumed to behave like random oracles [5]),

$$f : \{0,1\}^k \to \{0,1\}^k, g : \{0,1\}^k \to \{0,1\}^k \text{ and } h : \{0,1\}^{k+k_1} \to \{0,1\}^{k_2}.$$

Key Generation: $\text{Gen}(1^k) = \text{GenSig} \times \text{GenEnc}(1^k)$
One first gets $(\text{sk}_1, \text{pk}_1) \leftarrow \text{GenSig}(1^k)$ and $(\text{sk}_2, \text{pk}_2) \leftarrow \text{GenEnc}(1^k)$. Then, one defines $\text{SDK} = (\text{sk}_1, \text{sk}_2)$ and $\text{VEK} = (\text{pk}_1, \text{pk}_2)$.

Encrypt and Sign Algorithm: $\text{SigEnc}_{\text{SDK}_S, \text{VEK}_R}(m)$

1. Let $m \in \mathbb{Z}_p$ be the message to be encrypted and signed. Choose a random integer $r \in \{0,1\}^{k_1}$ and compute $a = h(m\|r)$.
2. Form an instance of a $(2,2)$ Shamir secret sharing scheme over $\mathbb{Z}_p$ with the polynomial $F(x) = (a\|r) + mx \bmod p$. Define two shares $s_1 = F(1)$ and $s_2 = F(2)$.
3. Compute the transform $r_1 = s_1 \oplus f(s_2)$ and $r_2 = s_2 \oplus g(r_1)$.
4. Calculate (in parallel) $c_1 = \text{Enc}_{\text{pk}_R}(r_1)$ and $c_2 = \text{Sig}_{\text{sk}_S}(r_2)$. The signed–ciphertext (c_1, c_2) is then dispatched to the receiver R.

Decrypt and Verify Algorithm: $\mathsf{VerDec}_{\mathsf{VEK}_S,\mathsf{SDK}_R}(c_1, c_2)$

1. Perform decryption and signature verification in parallel so, $u_1 = \mathsf{Dec}_{\mathsf{sk}_R}(c_1)$ and $u_2 = \mathsf{Ver}_{\mathsf{pk}_S}(c_2)$. Note that both the decryption Dec and verification Ver algorithms return integers in $\mathbb{Z}_p$, unless some failure occurs. Indeed, it is possible that Dec returns $\bot$ if it decides that the cryptogram is invalid. Similarly, Ver returns a message (signature with message recovery), or $\bot$ if the signature is invalid. In case of one failure, the decryption and verifying algorithm VerDec returns $\bot$ and stops.
2. Compute the inversion $t_2 = u_2 \oplus g(u_1)$ and $t_1 = u_1 \oplus f(t_2)$.
3. Knowing two points $(1, t_1)$ and $(2, t_2)$, use the Lagrange interpolation and find the polynomial $\hat{F}(x) = a_0 + a_1 x \bmod p$.
4. Extract r from a_0 and check whether $h(a_1\|r)\|r = a_0$. If the check holds, the algorithm returns a_1, to be m. Otherwise, the algorithm outputs $\bot$.

5.2   Security Analysis

Theorem 2. *If the encryption scheme is deterministic and OW-CPA, and the signature scheme is NUF-RMA, then the optimal parallel signcryption scheme is secure (IND/NEF-AdA).*

About this theorem, one can claim a more precise result:

Lemma 2. *Let us consider an AdA adversary $\mathcal{A}$ against IND and NEF of the optimal parallel signcryption scheme, with a running time bounded by t, while asking q queries to the random oracles, and q_1 and q_2 queries to the signcryption and de-signcryption oracles, respectively. Then the winning probability of this adversary is bounded by*

$$\mathsf{Succ}^{\mathsf{ow-cpa}}_{\mathsf{Encrypt}}(t) + Q \times \mathsf{Succ}^{\mathsf{nuf-rma}}_{\mathsf{Sign}}(t', Q) + \frac{1}{2^{k_2}} \times (1 + 4Q^2 + 3q_2 + q_1) + \frac{q}{2^{k_1}},$$

with $t' \le t + Q(\tau + \mathcal{O}(1))$, where τ denotes the maximal running time of the encryption, decryption, signing and verification algorithms, and $Q = q + q_1 + q_2$.

Proof. The proof is similar to the proof of the Lemma 1. It is therefore also divided into two parts. In the first one, we are going to show that the scheme meets IND-AdA, but under the assumption that it meets NEF-AdA. The second part deals with NEF, and shows that it actually meets NEF-AdA.

In the proof, when one calls to f, g, or h, if the query has already been asked, or the answer has already been defined by the simulation, the same answer is returned, otherwise a random value in the according range is given. Of course, one has to be careful when one defines an answer of a random oracle:

– this answer must not have already been defined
– the answer must be uniformly distributed

Furthermore, we denote by q_F, q_G and q_H the number of answers defined for f, g and h, respectively. We will see at the end of the simulation the relations with q_f, q_g and q_h, the number of queries directly asked by the adversary (thus $q = q_f + q_g + q_h$).

Indistinguishability: IND. Let us assume that after q_1 queries to oracle SigEnc and q_2 queries to oracle VerDec, after having chosen a pair of message m_0 and m_1, and received a *signed–ciphertext* (c_1, c_2) of either m_0 or m_1, say m_b, an adversary $\mathcal{A}$ outputs a bit d which is equal to b with advantage ε: $\Pr[d = b] = (1 + \varepsilon)/2$.

Let us first remark that because of the randomness of the random oracles f and g, to get any information about the bit b (and thus about the encrypted and signed message), an adversary must have got some information about s_1 or s_2 from either the *signed–ciphertext*, or from the plaintext and the random tape.

The former case is only possible if the adversary asks for r_1 to the oracle g (otherwise it has no information about s_2, and s_1 neither). This event is denoted AskG. The latter case means that the adversary asked either $h(m_0\|r)$ or $h(m_1\|r)$. This event is denoted AskR. Consequently,

$$
\begin{aligned}
\mathsf{Adv}^{\mathrm{ind-ada}}_{\mathsf{SignCrypt}}(\mathcal{A}) &= 2\Pr[d = b] - 1 \\
&= 2\Pr[d = b \wedge (\mathsf{AskG} \vee \mathsf{AskR})] + 2\Pr[d = b \wedge \neg(\mathsf{AskG} \vee \neg\mathsf{AskR})] - 1 \\
&\leq 2\Pr[\mathsf{AskG} \vee \mathsf{AskR}] + \Pr[\neg(\mathsf{AskG} \vee \mathsf{AskR})] - 1 = \Pr[\mathsf{AskG} \vee \mathsf{AskR}] \\
&\leq \Pr[\mathsf{AskG}] + \Pr[\mathsf{AskR} \mid \neg\mathsf{AskG}] \leq \Pr[\mathsf{AskG}] + \frac{q_h}{2^{k_1}}
\end{aligned}
$$

Therefore, r_1 the plaintext of c_1 necessarily appears in the queries asked to g. For each query asked to g, one runs the deterministic encryption algorithm and therefore can find the plaintext of a given c_1: we may use this adversary $\mathcal{A}$ to break OW-CPA of the encryption scheme (GenEnc, Enc, Dec). To achieve this aim, we design a simulator $\mathcal{B}$ which is given the private/public keys $(\mathsf{sk}_S, \mathsf{pk}_S)$ for the signature scheme, but is just further given the public key pk_R of the encryption scheme.

- $\mathcal{B}$ is given a ciphertext c (of a random message) to decrypt under the encryption scheme ENCRYPT, and then runs $\mathcal{A}$.
- When $\mathcal{B}$ receives the pair of messages m_0 and m_1 from $\mathcal{A}$, it defines c (the challenge ciphertext to decrypt) as c_1, and randomly chooses $r_2 = t_2$, that it can sign using the private key of the signature scheme, to produce c_2. It therefore sends the pair (c_1, c_2) as a *signed–ciphertext* of m_b (for some bit b). Finally, the adversary $\mathcal{A}$ follows in its attack.
- Any call by $\mathcal{A}$ to the oracle SigEnc can be simply answered by $\mathcal{B}$ using the private key of the signature scheme, and the public key of the encryption scheme. It makes one more call to each of the random oracles f, g and h.
- Before simulating the oracle VerDec, let us explain how one deals with h-queries. Indeed, a list Λ_h is managed. For any query $h(m\|r)$, one anticipates the signcryption:

$$
H = h(m\|r) \quad a_0 = H\|r \quad t_1 = a_0 + m \bmod p \quad t_2 = a_0 + 2m \bmod p.
$$

  Then, $u_1 = t_1 \oplus f(t_2)$ and $u_2 = t_2 \oplus g(u_1)$ (using the simulations of f and g). Eventually, one stores $(m, r, H, u_1, u_2, t_1, t_2)$ in Λ_h.
- Any call by $\mathcal{A}$ to the oracle VerDec can be simulated using the queries-answers of the random oracles. Indeed, to a query (c'_1, c'_2), one first gets u'_2

from c_2', thanks to the public key of the signature scheme ($u_2' = \mathsf{Ver}_{\mathsf{pk}_R}(c_2')$). Then, one looks up into Λ_h for tuples $(m, r, H, u_1, u_2', t_1, t_2)$. Then, one checks whether one of the u_1 is really encrypted in c_1', thanks to the deterministic property of the encryption. If no tuple is found, the simulator outputs $\perp$, considering it is a wrong *signed–ciphertext*. Otherwise, the simulator returns m, to be the plaintext.

For all the *signed–ciphertexts* correctly constructed (with $s_2' = t_2'$ asked to f, $r_1' = u_1'$ asked to g and $(m'\|r')$ asked to h), the simulation gets back the message. But the adversary may produce a valid *signed–ciphertext* without asking $h(m'\|r')$ required by the above simulation. In that sole case, the simulation may not be perfect.

First, let us assume that $(m'\|r')$ has not been asked to h. Then, either $(m'\|r') \neq (m\|r)$ (the pair involved in the challenge *signed–ciphertext*) then H is totally random. The probability for $H\|r'$ to match with a_0' is less than 2^{-k_2}. Or $(m'\|r') = (m\|r)$. Since all the process to produce r_1' and r_2' is deterministic, $r_1' = r_1$ and $r_2' = r_2$, the same as in the challenge *signed–ciphertext*. The encryption is deterministic, then $c_1' = c_1$. Therefore, either the adversary produced a new *signed–ciphertext*, which is bounded by $\mathsf{Succ}_{\mathsf{SignCrypt}}^{\mathsf{nef-ada}}(\mathcal{A})$, or the simulation of the sign-crypt oracle signed twice the value t_2 involved in the challenge *signed–ciphertext*, which is upper-bounded by $q_1/2^{k_2}$, because of the randomness of r Therefore, the probability that some $(m'\|r')$ is equal to $(m\|r)$ is upper-bounded by $\mathsf{Succ}_{\mathsf{SignCrypt}}^{\mathsf{nef-ada}}(\mathcal{A}) + q_1/2^{k_2}$. As a consequence, $(m'\|r')$ has been likely asked to h, otherwise the simulation just fails with probability less than 2^{-k_2}.

Then, the simulator can extract t_1' and t_2'. But because of the randomness of H, the probability for t_2' to be equal to t_2 (the one involved in the challenge *signed–ciphertext*) is less than $q_H/2^{-k_2}$. If it is not the case, and t_2' not asked to f, then the probability for the resulting u_1' to be in the list of the queries asked to g (explicitly or implicitly) is less than $(q_G + 1)/2^k$. If it is not the case, the probability for u_2' to match with u_2 (the one involved in the challenge *signed–ciphertext*) is less than 2^{-k}.

Therefore, the probability that the simulation is not correctly decrypted (provided that no signature forgery occurs and there is no double signatures on r_2) is less than

$$2^{-k_2} + q_H \cdot 2^{-k_2} + (q_G + 1) \cdot 2^{-k} + 2^{-k} = \frac{q_H + 1}{2^{k_2}} + \frac{q_G + 2}{2^k} \leq \frac{q_G + q_H + 3}{2^{k_2}}.$$

And thus, the simulations are all perfect with the probability greater than

$$1 - \frac{q_2 \cdot (q_G + q_H + 3) + q_1}{2^{k_2}} - \mathsf{Succ}_{\mathsf{SignCrypt}}^{\mathsf{nef-ada}}(\mathcal{A}).$$

If all the decryption simulations are correct (no occurrence of the event BadD), we have seen that with a good probability the plaintext c_1, and thus of c, appears in the queries asked to g, which is immediately detected thanks to the deterministic property of the encryption scheme so

$$\Pr[\mathsf{AskG}\,|\,\neg\mathsf{BadD}] \geq \Pr[\mathsf{AskG}] - \Pr[\mathsf{BadD}]$$

$$\geq \mathsf{Adv}_{\mathsf{SignCrypt}}^{\mathsf{ind-ada}}(\mathcal{A}) - \frac{q_h}{2^{k_1}} - \frac{q_2 \cdot (q_G + q_H + 3) + q_1}{2^{k_2}} - \mathsf{Succ}_{\mathsf{SignCrypt}}^{\mathsf{nef-ada}}(\mathcal{A}).$$

The expression upper-bounds the advantage of $\mathcal{A}$ in IND-AdA by

$$\mathsf{Succ}_{\mathsf{Encrypt}}^{\mathsf{ow-cpa}}(t') + \frac{q_h}{2^{k_1}} + \frac{q_2 \cdot (q_G + q_H + 3) + q_1}{2^{k_2}} + \mathsf{Succ}_{\mathsf{SignCrypt}}^{\mathsf{nef-ada}}(\mathcal{A}),$$

where $q_F \leq q_f + q_H$, $q_G \leq q_g + q_H$, and $q_H \leq q_h + q_1$.

Non Existential Forgery: NEF. Let us assume that after q_1 queries to oracle SigEnc and q_2 queries to oracle VerDec, an adversary $\mathcal{A}$ outputs (or asks to VerDec) a new *signed–ciphertext* (c_1, c_2) which is valid with probability ε. We will use this adversary to perform a universal forgery, as thus produces a new signature on a designated random message (under a known random-message attack) against the signature scheme SIGN.

To achieve this aim, we design a simulator $\mathcal{B}$ which has access to a list of message-signature pairs, produced by the signing oracle (the messages are assumed to have been randomly drawn in $\mathbb{Z}_p$, but not chosen by the adversary). Note that a valid *signed–ciphertext* must satisfy the equality $h(m\|r)\|r = a_0$. Therefore, the probability to output such a valid *signed–ciphertext* without asking $h(m\|r)$ is smaller than 2^{-k_2}: with probability greater than $\varepsilon - 2^{-k_2}$, this query $(m\|r)$ has been asked to h.

The simulator $\mathcal{B}$ is given the private/public keys $(\mathsf{sk}_R, \mathsf{pk}_R)$ for the encryption scheme, but is just given the public key pk_S of the signature scheme. It is furthermore given a list of q_H message-signature (M, S), in which we assume that the message on which one has to produce a new signature is randomly located, say M_i.

- For any new query $(m\|r)$ asked to h (by the adversary, or by our simulations of SigEnc and VerDec), a new valid message-signature pair (M, S) is taken from the list. Then, one chooses a random ρ, defines $h(m\|r) \leftarrow \rho$ and sets

$$s_1 \leftarrow \rho\|r + m \bmod p \quad s_2 \leftarrow \rho\|r + 2m \bmod p \quad r_1 \leftarrow s_1 \oplus f(s_2).$$

One eventually defines $g(r_1) \leftarrow s_2 \oplus M$, which is a random value, since M is randomly distributed. It may fail if $g(r_1)$ has already been defined. But because of the random choice of ρ this may just occurs with probability less than $q_G/2^{k_2}$. Remark that the comments above would be wrong if the value $h(m\|r)$ would not be a new random value, but a value already defined by the simulation. But one can remark that no answer for h is defined by a simulator in the proof, but all using this simulation.
- Any query m by $\mathcal{A}$ to the oracle SigEnc can be simulated, thanks to above simulation of h. Indeed, one simply chooses a random r, asks for $h(m\|r)$. Then the signature S involved in the pair (M, S) used for the h simulation is a signature c_2 of $r_2 = M$. Using the public key pk_R of the encryption scheme, one can encrypt r_1 to obtain c_1. The pair (c_1, c_2) is a valid *signed–ciphertext* of m.

– Any call by $\mathcal{A}$ to the oracle VerDec can be simulated using the private key sk_R of the encryption scheme and the public key pk_S of the signature scheme.

Finally, the adversary $\mathcal{A}$ produces a new *signed–ciphertext* (c_1, c_2) which is valid with probability greater than ε, unless the above simulation of h failed (such a failure happens with probability upper bounded by $q_H q_G / 2^{k_2}$).

Furthermore, this *signed–ciphertext* is involved in one of the h-queries, but with probability $1/2^{k_2}$. With probability $1/q_H$, this *signed–ciphertext* is involved in the i-th query to the h-oracle: c_2 is a valid signature of M_i. But either this is a new signature, or it was already involved in a *signed–ciphertext* (c'_1, c'_2) produced by SigEnc. But in this latter case, since $c_2 = c'_2$, necessarily $c_1 \neq c'_1$. But because of the determinism of the encryption scheme, it means that $u_1 \neq u'_1$, and then the redundancy may hold but with probability less than $q_G q_H / 2^{k_2}$.

Finally, the probability for $\mathcal{B}$ to produce a new valid signature of M_i is greater than

$$\frac{1}{q_H} \times \left(\varepsilon - \frac{2 q_G q_H + 1}{2^{k_2}} \right).$$

Furthermore, one can easily see that $q_F = q_f + q_H$ and $q_G = q_g + q_H$, where $q_H \leq q_h + q_1 + q_2$. $\square$

6   Conclusion

We have introduced parallel signcryption schemes which are superior to well-studied sequential Sign-then-Encrypt or Encrypt-then-Sign schemes, or any other combination, in term of their efficiency, since they allow parallel signature and encryption as well as parallel decryption and verification.

The optimal scheme is especially attractive as it is secure using a weak encryption (i.e., one-way under chosen-plaintext attack) and a weak signature scheme (i.e., signature is required to be secure against universal forgeries under random-message attack).

It has been shown that the OAEP technique which was applied for encryption [6] (with other recent studies [15,8]) can also be used for parallel signcryption. The OAEP technique was incorporated into RSA Security standards for encryption (for details see the description of PKCS#1 v2.1 [13].) Parallel signcryption is potentially a candidate for the third missing standard for parallel authenticated encryption.

The message redundancy of the parallel signcryption scheme can be measured as the ratio of the *signed–ciphertext* length to the message length. It is easy to see that both schemes considered expand the length of *signed–ciphertext* by the factor of more than 2. It is an interesting question whether the redundancy can be reduced while leaving security conclusions intact.

Acknowledgement. The work was partially supported by Australian Research Council grants A00103078 and DP0345366.

References

1. J. H. An, Y. Dodis, and T. Rabin. On the Security of Joint Signatures and Encryption. In *Eurocrypt '02*, LNCS 2332, pages 83–107. Springer-Verlag, Berlin, 2002.
2. M. Bellare, A. Desai, D. Pointcheval, and P. Rogaway. Relations among Notions of Security for Public-Key Encryption Schemes. In *Crypto '98*, LNCS 1462, pages 26–45. Springer-Verlag, Berlin, 1998.
3. M. Bellare and C. Namprempre. Authenticated Encryption: Notions and Constructions. In *Asiacrypt '00*, LNCS 1976. Springer-Verlag, Berlin, 2000.
4. M. Bellare and P. Rogaway. Encode-Then-Encipher Encryption: How to Exploit Nonces or Redundancies in Plaintexts for Efficient Cryptography. In *Asiacrypt '00*, LNCS 1976. Springer-Verlag, Berlin, 2000.
5. M. Bellare and P. Rogaway. Random Oracles Are Practical: a Paradigm for Designing Efficient Protocols. In *Proc. of the 1st CCS*, pages 62–73. ACM Press, New York, 1993.
6. M. Bellare and P. Rogaway. Optimal Asymmetric Encryption – How to Encrypt with RSA. In *Eurocrypt '94*, LNCS 950, pages 92–111. Springer-Verlag, Berlin, 1995.
7. W. Diffie and M. E. Hellman. New Directions in Cryptography. *IEEE Transactions on Information Theory*, IT–22(6):644–654, November 1976.
8. E. Fujisaki, T. Okamoto, D. Pointcheval, and J. Stern. RSA–OAEP is Secure under the RSA Assumption. In *Crypto '01*, LNCS 2139, pages 260–274. Springer-Verlag, Berlin, 2001.
9. S. Goldwasser and S. Micali. Probabilistic Encryption. *Journal of Computer and System Sciences*, 28:270–299, 1984.
10. S. Goldwasser, S. Micali, and R. Rivest. A Digital Signature Scheme Secure Against Adaptive Chosen-Message Attacks. *SIAM Journal of Computing*, 17(2):281–308, April 1988.
11. J. Pieprzyk and D. Pointcheval. Parallel Authentication and Public-Key Encryption. In *ACISP '03*, LNCS. Springer-Verlag, Berlin, 2003.
Full version available from http://www.di.ens.fr/users/pointche/.
12. R. Rivest, A. Shamir, and L. Adleman. A Method for Obtaining Digital Signatures and Public Key Cryptosystems. *Communications of the ACM*, 21(2):120–126, February 1978.
13. RSA Data Security, Inc. Public Key Cryptography Standards – PKCS. Available from http://www.rsa.com/rsalabs/pubs/PKCS/.
14. A. Shamir. How to Share a Secret. *Communications of the ACM*, 22:612–613, November 1979.
15. V. Shoup. OAEP Reconsidered. In *Crypto '01*, LNCS 2139, pages 239–259. Springer-Verlag, Berlin, 2001.
16. J. Malone-Lee, D. Pointcheval, N. Smart, and J. Stern. Flaws in Applying Proof Methodologies to Signature Schemes. In *Crypto '02*, LNCS 2442, pages 93–110. Springer-Verlag, Berlin, 2002.
17. Y. Zheng. Signcryption or How to Achieve Cost(Signature & Encryption) << Cost(Signature) + Cost(Encryption). In *Crypto '97*, LNCS 1294. Springer-Verlag, Berlin, 1997.

Is Cross-Platform Security Possible?

Li Gong

Sun Microsystems
li.gong@sun.com

Today in any IT system installation of a non-negligible size, heterogeneity is a given. From hardware platforms, to operating systems, to networking protocols, to applications, one is bound to discover a variety of technologies for every layer of the system stack. Heterogeneity has its advantages: it fosters innovation, competition, and it even has the potential to improve security and reliability in that one may hope that the same error or security hole does not exist in all of the different designs.

Heterogeneity also brings a number of problems for implementing security requirements. For example, system administrators with different knowledge and skills are needed to manage different systems. In addition, these different systems may offer vastly different sets of security properties so that interoperability becomes difficult if not impractical.

The most important problem, though, is how to provide security support for application developers. In other words, when developing an application that must run on a number of different platforms (think about web services, for example), how does the developer ensure that the required security properties can be correctly implemented and deployed across the different platforms.

The primitive way to deal with heterogeneity is to find out the collection of the target deployment platforms a priori and design a solution that works on this set of platforms. However, a solution obtained this way does not apply to a new environment. It also needs to change, usually with great difficulty, when a new target platform is added into the mix. What is desirable is a systematic approach to cross-platform security.

This talk takes a look at a number of common or "popular" approaches to the cross-platform security problem. We argue that most approaches do not actually work, for various reasons. We further argue that a couple of most technically promising solutions are fraught with commercial competition complexities that they are unlikely to see the light of day. Is cross-platform security possible?

R. Safavi-Naini and J. Seberry (Eds.): ACISP 2003, LNCS 2727, p. 402, 2003.
© Springer-Verlag Berlin Heidelberg 2003

A Novel Use of RBAC to Protect Privacy in Distributed Health Care Information Systems[*]

Jason Reid[1], Ian Cheong[2], Matthew Henricksen[1], and Jason Smith[1]

[1] Queensland University of Technology, Information Security Research Centre,
GPO Box 2434, Brisbane, Queensland 4001, Australia
{jf.reid,m.henricksen,j4.smith}@qut.edu.au
[2] {ian.cheong}@acm.org

Abstract. This paper examines the access control requirements of distributed health care information networks. Since the electronic sharing of an individual's personal health information requires their informed consent, health care information networks need an access control framework that can capture and enforce individual access policies tailored to the specific circumstances of each consumer. Role Based Access Control (RBAC) is examined as a candidate access control framework. While it is well suited to the task in many regards, we identify a number of shortcomings, particularly in the range of access policy expression types that it can support. For efficiency and comprehensibility, access policies that grant access to a broad range of entities whilst explicitly denying it to subgroups of those entities need to be supported in health information networks. We argue that RBAC does not support policies of this type with sufficient flexibility and propose a novel adaptation of RBAC principles to address this shortcoming. We also describe a prototype distributed medical information system that embodies the improved RBAC model.

1   Introduction

A fundamental concept underpinning the delivery of health care services is the notion that personal information shared with a clinician in the context of treatment is confidential. This means that the clinician must have the consent of the consumer to share information about the consumer with a third party[1]. In practice, it is becoming far more challenging to ensure that all confidential health information disclosures have been consented to, particularly as health service providers adopt electronic systems based on internet technologies to facilitate

---

[*] This research was funded and supported by the Commonwealth of Australia – Department of Health and Ageing.

[1] In practice there are a number of important exceptions to the requirement for express consent, e.g., consent can be implied by circumstances or deemed unnecessary by legislation. For more information on consent requirements in health care see [4,5].

R. Safavi-Naini and J. Seberry (Eds.): ACISP 2003, LNCS 2727, pp. 403–415, 2003.
© Springer-Verlag Berlin Heidelberg 2003

information exchange. Electronic health information networks[2] and electronic health records improve the ability of service providers to exchange personal health information and coordinate service delivery between clinical teams that cross organisational and geographic boundaries. As a direct consequence, an individual's personal health information is potentially available to larger numbers of people, significantly increasing the risk that the information will be accessed for purposes for which the consumer has not given their consent. A key challenge that attends the adoption of electronic health information networks is therefore to ensure that the principle of consent is meaningfully respected and enforced in electronic contexts. To achieve this a health information network needs to be capable of recording and enforcing *individual* access policies where the consumer defines the policy details.

1.1   Privacy in Health Care

Unauthorised disclosure of health information can have serious consequences including refusal of prospective employment, difficulties in obtaining or continuing insurance contracts and loans, ostracisation from family and community groups and personal embarrassment [15]. Once information has been disclosed, the damage cannot be *undone* so, to earn consumer trust it is important that unauthorised disclosure is prevented, not merely detected after the fact through audit processes. Broad consumer support for electronic health records will be predicated on a justifiable and well founded trust that the system will protect their highly sensitive health information in accordance with the consent that they are entitled to give or withhold. This includes accommodating the needs of consumers with especially demanding privacy requirements, e.g. persons receiving treatment for sensitive conditions (HIV/AIDS, addiction, psychiatric illness etc.), health care professionals receiving treatment and celebrities. If health information networks are to be adopted and supported by consumers, their privacy concerns must be addressed.

1.2   Overview of the Paper

Section 2 examines access control requirements in distributed health care information systems, focusing on the types of access policy expression that need to be supported. Section 3 describes the basic concepts underlying Role Based Access Control (RBAC) and highlights why it is well suited for health care information systems. Section 4 reviews related work. In Section 5 a shortcoming of RBAC is presented that limits its ability to support the required types of

---

[2] An electronic health information network aims to connect a broad range of organisations involved in delivering health related services. The network is used to collect, store and exchange personal health information. Examples include the national HealthConnect network currently under development in Australia (http://www.health.gov.au/healthconnect/)and the National Health Service Network in the United Kingdom (http://www.nhsia.nhs.uk/).

access policy expression that are discussed in Section 2. A novel modification to RBAC is introduced in Section 6 that addresses the identified problems. Section 7 describes a prototype distributed medical information system based on the proposed access control framework.

2   Access Policy Requirements for Health Care

In consent-based information sharing, consumers themselves are able to define the policies that control third party access to their personal health information. This represents a significant departure from the traditional approach where organisations established the access policy. The change is necessary because health care organisations are internetworking their systems, increasing the potential for unauthorised access. Since there is a myriad of individual scenarios, circumstances and relationships, the access control framework must be flexible and highly expressive, to ensure that a consumer's access policy can be recorded and enforced in a manner that mirrors their understanding of who they want to have access and who they don't want to have access. This will typically involve granting *qualified* consent to groups or roles, e.g. access is allowed for General Practitioners except Dr X, who is the consumer's father in law. To achieve these goals efficiently, the access control framework needs to support policy expressions of the following form [4,5]:

- a broadly expressed or *general* consent (possibly) qualified by one or more *explicit* denials e.g., all clinicians except Doctor X; and,
- a broadly expressed or *general* denial (possibly) qualified by one or more *explicit* consents e.g., no clinician except Doctor X.

Expressions formulated as *general denial with explicit consent* are required when the consumer wants access to be tightly restricted e.g., for information relating to sensitive conditions. In such cases, it will be more efficient to explicitly name the individuals or groups to be granted access rather than listing those that should not.

Support for expressions of the alternate form, *general consent qualified by explicit denial* are particularly important for efficiency and comprehensibility. To minimise system management effort, individual access policies will commonly be based on defaults appropriate to the clinical context that reflect acceptable current practice. This default policy will be expressed as a broadly expressed consent that grants access to appropriate roles. Individual consumers may wish to modify this default consent with a qualification that removes access from particular groups or named individuals, in recognition of their specific circumstances.

Explicit denial is also necessary to ensure that a consumer's access policy is reliably enforced over time (where that policy involves denying access). Since explicit denial is more than just the absence of a positive access right it must be removed for it to be overridden. To illustrate the importance of this feature, consider a scenario where a consumer wishes to exclude a particular Doctor, (Dr X) from access to their records. The consumer has also given consent for Doctors at Acme Clinic to access their records. If Doctor X subsequently comes to work at Acme Clinic, explicit denial ensures that he will not be given access to the consumer's records despite the fact that he holds the role of Doctor at Acme Clinic, to which consent has been granted.

To construct complex policy expressions with a minimum number of statements, and support the qualification of default policies to meet individual needs, the nesting of different expression types is desirable. Within a hierarchy of clinical roles, nesting would allow access policy statements such as: allow all clinicians (general consent), except for nurses (explicit denial), except for nurses at Acme Clinic (explicit consent), except for the nurse Alice at Acme Clinic who is the consumer's mother in law (explicit denial). We believe that policy expressions of this form are a practical requirement for efficient and manageable consent-based health information sharing.

3   An Overview of Role Based Access Control

Role Based Access Control (RBAC) is a mechanism for access control that decouples users from privileges by the inter-positioning of roles [8,9,11]. Users are assigned to roles and roles are authorised to access objects with privileges. This decoupling lends a greater degree of scalability to systems in which access must be regulated. A role can reflect the responsibilities of a position or job description in the context of an organization e.g. Doctor or Nurse. When an individual is assigned the responsibility to perform a particular job, a security administrator puts them in the appropriate role. They can exercise the privileges associated with the role because they are recognised as holding the role.

Unlike traditional Access Control List (ACL) based approaches, RBAC does not allow users to be directly associated with privileges as all privileges are held by roles. This layer of indirection between users and privileges that is introduced by the concept of roles is a defining feature of RBAC. It is the primary distinction that motivates the common claim that RBAC is more manageable than ACL based approaches in large scale systems with many users.

The primary motivation for RBAC lies in reducing the complexity and effort required to manage authorisation data in large scale systems [8]. It has been designed for environments where Discretionary Access Control (DAC) is inappropriate because end users do not *own* the information they are allowed to access and therefore should not have the discretion to grant access to others. It is particularly well suited to environments where access rights are based on competency or recognition of a professional qualification. Since this describes key aspects of the health care environment, it is hardly surprising that role-based approaches have found considerable support in health care settings [1,3,6].

Roles facilitate efficient assignment and removal of privileges and importantly, analysis of privilege authorisation to users. Role/privilege associations typically change less frequently than user/privilege associations because work flow processes, (which define the set of privileges required by a role) are relatively stable whereas user/task assignments are not - individual user's job responsibilities change as they move between departments, change jobs etc. [7]. RBAC severs the user/privilege association through the interpositioning of roles, resulting in reduced management overhead. User membership of roles can be easily granted or revoked, thereby conferring or removing a potentially rich set of privileges in one simple step.

In systems implementing RBAC, the consistency of privilege allocation, (who can access what) can be audited efficiently, thereby reducing undetected configuration errors, a key advantage in the highly distributed environments encountered in health care. This is a key difference to traditional ACL based approaches utilising groups. Groups bring together users but they do not bring together privileges as roles do. This makes the analysis of privilege assignments difficult in ACL based systems since every object must be examined to ascertain the privileges of a user or group. In RBAC systems, only the roles need to be reviewed as all privileges are held through their assignment to roles. This distinction has an important consequence in terms of the ease with which a consumer can change or revoke their consent for information disclosure. When all privileges are held through roles, this is a significantly easier operation as privileges are centralised.

RBAC systems adhere to the principle of general denial with explicit consent. Only users that are assigned to roles are permitted to access objects for which the roles have positive privileges. Through static constraints, users can be prevented from joining roles for which they are not qualified (prerequisite constraints) or combinations of roles that are inappropriate (static separation of duty) [11]. Where selective role activation is permitted, dynamic constraints allow users to belong to multiple roles but enforce that only a subset of those roles may be active at a time (dynamic separation of duty) [16].

The use of inheritance allows roles to implicitly acquire the privileges and constraints of roles beneath them in the inheritance hierarchy. For the sake of consistency, it is usually not appropriate to impose constraints upon roles within the same path (from root to leaf) on a hierarchy (for example, a member of a role is automatically the member of its descendant, so a static constraint forbidding joint membership of both does not permit consistency). In Section 5 we argue that as a result of the inheritance of constraints, RBAC does not efficiently support access policy statements in the form of general consent qualified by explicit denial or the nesting of explicit denials and consents that successively qualify each other in a role hierarchy. Policy expressions of this form are a practical requirement for consent based health information sharing.

4   Related Work

4.1   RBAC in Health Care

RBAC has received considerable attention in the context of health care, particularly in the hospital environment, e.g. [3,6,14]. However, the practical implications of implementing access policies based on individual consumer consent are not directly addressed. Access policies are determined at an organisational or departmental level and the ability to support individual exceptions to default policies is not a supported feature.

The OASIS project [12] has examined the application of RBAC principles to distributed health care information networks. In [1] the authors recognise that the standard RBAC framework is not suitable when individual exceptions to default access policies need to be supported. Their approach to addressing this problem involves storing exceptions to the default policy with the affected records themselves. This is not entirely consistent with the role based approach which stipulates that *all* permissions are held by roles, (since the exceptions are effectively negative permissions). Our proposal differs in that it enables individually tailored policies that are based on defaults through the ability to explicitly grant *and* deny authorisation for a set of privileges, (a consumer-centric role) *without* resorting to storing overriding access policy with records, an approach which we believe violates the simplicity of the role based metaphor. Since all access policy remains centrally located in the role definition, update or revocation of consent (e.g. when an consumer's circumstances change) can be carried out more easily.

In [13] the authors describe an authorisation model developed for the distributed health care environment of the U.K. National Health Service. Access privileges can be both granted and denied through the use of positive or negative confidentiality permissions. The model describes four different confidentiality permission types that have a fixed hierarchical precedence. Higher order confidentiality permissions types can override lower order types. The model addresses similar issues to our proposal. However our model differs in that negation of the privilege set of a role can be effected for any other role(s) within a role hierarchy rather than being limited to using four fixed precedence confidentiality permissions types. We believe this produces a more general and flexible solution.

4.2 Negative Privileges and Explicit Denial of Authorisation

The RBAC model that NIST has proposed for standardisation does not support explicit denial except in a limited way through the use of constraints [10].

Packet filtering firewalls implement positive and negative authorisation through allow and deny rules where the ordering of the rules is crucial. Since the order determines the effect of the rules, firewall rule sets can be notoriously difficult to to configure and comprehend [2]. In our modified RBAC proposal, the role hierarchy effectively determines the rule order so misconfiguration due to incorrect ordering is not possible.

4.3 Contribution

The main contribution of this work is to propose a modified RBAC model in which a set of privileges held by a role can be allowed or denied to other roles without using traditional RBAC constraints concepts such as static and dynamic separation of duty. While this necessitates a more complex authorisation algorithm, the model allows highly flexible policy expressions and supports policies that can be based on defaults for efficiency but can be qualified to implement individual exceptions, a key requirement for health care information systems.

5   Implementing Explicit Denial in RBAC

RBAC does not efficiently support policy expressions in the form of a broadly expressed consent qualified by explicit denials since it implements a model where anything that is not explicitly allowed is *implicitly* denied. The mechanism of constraints is used in standard RBAC to deny the exercising of the privileges of a role that would otherwise be allowed. However, constraints do not provide an elegant solution when nesting of the policy expression types is required. This is due to the fact that constraints are also inherited in a role-based hierarchy supporting inheritance. Since an inherited role *is* also an instance of its parent role, i.e. a nurse *is* a clinician, constraints applying to clinician must also apply to nurse for them to be consistently applied.

Consider the the example access policy from Section 2. A static constraint that denied the nurses role will not be effective in implementing the policy because the role of nurses at Acme Clinic inherits the role of nurse, so it also inherits the constraint. As a consequence, nurses at Acme Clinic would be denied. There is no way to turn the constraint off for roles higher up the hierarchy on the same path, whilst maintaining consistency.

6   The Proposed Model

In our proposed health care model and prototype implementation an individual's access policy and the personal information it relates to are recorded and enforced through a consumer-centric role that we will refer to as a *care team role*[3]. Figure 1 illustrates the important components of a care team role. Authorisation (who can activate the role and exercise its privileges) for a care team role is determined by the contents of the role's allowed and denied lists. These two lists contain roles drawn from the affiliation and competency role hierarchies (discussed in Section 6.1). Specifically denied roles override equal or more general roles (i.e., equivalent or lower in a hierarchy) in the allowed list. This permits nested expressions as in the example given in Section 2. Figure 1 shows the allowed and denied roles that implement the example policy.

The support for nested expressions allows complex consents to be expressed in an intuitive and efficient way, without sacrificing the granularity of that expression. Denying access to an exception, (e.g. all clinicians *except* nurses) is more efficient than explicitly naming all the clinical roles that are not nurses. It also mirrors the way that people think about access policies, i.e, they commonly know who they want to exclude or include.

---

[3] The description *care team role* is used since the role defines the entities that will have access to the individual's records. Entities requiring access are generally involved in the consumer's care and are therefore part of a care team for the consumer. Care team roles are always associated with a single consumer. A consumer will have multiple care team roles if subsets of their health information require different access policies. A care team role controls access to the records whose identifiers are listed in the permission set of the role.

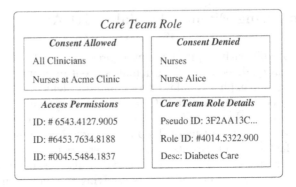

Fig. 1. Care Team Role - a consumer-centric role

6.1   Role Hierarchies

In our proposed design, a consumer's consent instructions are expressed by means of allowing and denying hierarchically related roles that employ a range of different classifications and granularity. More generally, the model allows any number of role hierarchies to be used. Hierarchies with different roots can be joined, allowing multi-dimensional structures that support complex (multiple) inheritance. The prototype provides a convenient method of expression to identify entities using two principle role-based hierarchies:

- *the clinical competency hierarchy* - this hierarchy is used to recognise and identify registered clinicians. The hierarchy includes a special role for each individual registered clinician, e.g. Registered Nurse: Barry Roberts. Individual roles of *the user acting as them self* are used to implement explicit acceptance or denial of individuals. Note that any node in the hierarchy can be specifically allowed or denied;
- *the affiliation hierarchy* - this hierarchy allows provider organisations to recognise individuals as members of clinical (e.g. Psychologist @ Acme Health Care) and administrative organisational roles.

6.2   Explanation of the Model

In simple terms, our proposed model implements an *anti-RBAC* that represents general consent with explicit denial. This *anti-RBAC* is unified with *standard RBAC* which implements general denial with explicit consent via a new authorisation algorithm. This permits a flexible and expressive revised model which retains RBAC's elegance without the need for constraints.

Figure 2 shows the modified relationship between roles and permissions. A care team role encapsulates a consent allowed role (from *standard RBAC*) and a consent denied role (from *anti-RBAC*). The denied role is associated with a negative permission and the allowed role is associated with a positive permission. Care teams are populated, as in the usual way, by inheritance. Each role can inherit from any number of subsidiary roles, (e.g. Dr X inherits from Doctors) and each role or its descendants can be associated with either consent allowed or consent denied.

The example in Figure 2 shows general consent for all Doctors qualified by explicit denial for Dr X. The user Doctor X assumes the role of the *user acting as them self*[4] - i.e. the role Doctor X, as shown in Figure 2, and inherits permissions from *Care Team #6667 Consent Denied*. Under normal RBAC rules, he also inherits the permissions from *Care Team #6667 Consent Allowed* via the Doctors role, but the new algorithm states that the first permission inherited down the path of a hierarchy is the one that takes precedence or *sticks*. Therefore, Doctor X is denied.

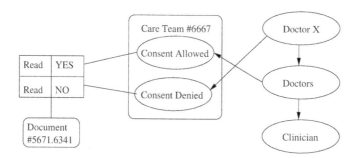

Fig. 2. Consent for Doctors qualified by explicit denial of Dr X

Authorisation Algorithm. This section presents the authorisation algorithm for the proposed scheme. Any node in a hierarchy has access rights that are explicitly allowed, explicitly denied or ambiguous. The case for explicit allowance or denial is simple - that node is accorded that access role without relying upon other nodes in the hierarchy.

An ambiguous node inherits permission from its children. If any of its immediate children have explicit denial, then the ambiguity of the node resolves also to denial. If this is not the case, then ambiguous children must first be resolved into either allowance or denial, and any emerging denial also passes to the ambiguous parent. The ambiguity of the parent translates to allowance only if none of the children have denial. Ambiguous nodes in the hierarchy can not be resolved if all of their children (immediate and remote) are also ambiguous. In this case, the model of implicit denial decrees that ambiguous leaves can resolve automatically to denial.

---

[4] In our proposed health information scheme users always make access requests through the role of the user acting as them self. This is enforced by the system to ensure that explicit allowance or denial of individuals cannot be bypassed through selective role activation.

This is formalised in the following algorithm, which resolves the access rights of the role labeled *start*[5]

1. Consider role *start*. Go to step 2.
2. Does this role have explicit denial?
   - if yes, then halt algorithm with *access denied*
   - if no, go to step 3.
3. Does this role have explicit allow?
   - if yes, then if this role is *start*, halt algorithm with *access allowed*
   - if yes, but this role is not *start*
     • if no more siblings, go to step 5, otherwise
     • resume at step 2 with next sibling and *access allowed*
   - if no, go to step 4.
4. For each child 'x' of this role,
   - set role to child 'x'
   - go to step 2.
5. Has an *access allowed* been received?
   - if yes and role is *start*, halt algorithm with *access allowed*
   - if no and role is *start*, halt algorithm with *access denied*
   - otherwise set role to parent's next sibling and resume at step 2 with any received *access allowed*

An Example of a Nested Allow and Deny Policy. Figure 3 illustrates the example that we introduced in Section 2. Doctors are allowed to access the document by virtue of the inheritance of *Care Team #6667 Consent Allowed* through the clinicians role. Nurses at City Clinic obtain the first permission through the Nurses role, which happens to be the negative permission associated with *Care Team #6667 Consent Denied*. Nurses at Acme Clinic obtain the positive permission associated with *Care Team #6667 Consent Allowed*, except for the Mother-in-law Nurse, Alice who directly obtains *Care Team #6667 Consent Denied*.

7   Prototype Implementation

We have developed a prototype distributed health information system that implements the proposed access control model to establish the model's viability and practicality. The prototype was successfully tested against a broad set of sample case scenarios to ensure that access policies reflecting realistic and challenging situations could be represented and enforced[6].

---

[5] In the context of the prototype, the *start* role is the role of the user acting as them self i.e., the individualised role of the user requesting access.
[6] Details of some of the sample case scenarios that were used to validate the model can be accessed at http://www.health.gov.au/hsdd/primcare/it/pdf/testcase.pdf.

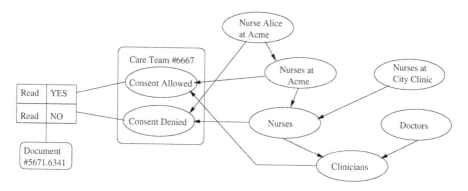

Fig. 3. Nested consent and denial

7.1 Prototype Architecture

The prototype consists of a directory server, a document server and a client application. The directory server is a logically centralised LDAP[7] directory that is used by the document server to retrieve information about the roles that individuals hold and the details of the role hierarchies. While it is logically centralised, its actual deployment and management can be distributed. This is important because the data contained in the directory needs to be kept up to date by different organisations.

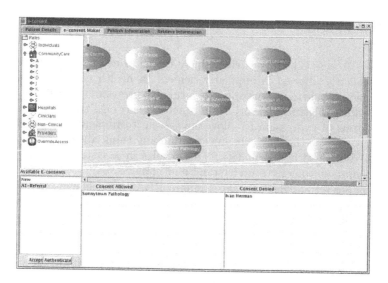

Fig. 4. Client Application - configuring access policy in a care team role

---

[7] Lightweight Directory Access Protocol (LDAP) is an internet protocol for accessing directory services.

In the prototype, the document server is responsible for storing and mediating access to protected health information. Our proposed RBAC access control logic is implemented in the document server. The design supports retrieval of individual documents or all the data that a requester is authorised to see for a particular consumer. All interactions with the document server are authenticated. The client application is used for consent administration, document publishing and document retrieval. Care team roles are created and modified with a simple drag and drop interface that allows clinical and organisational roles to be added to the consent allowed and denied lists. This is illustrated in Figure 4. The role hierarchies are graphically displayed, with allowed roles in green and implicitly or explicitly denied roles in red.

Documents are published to the document server by associating care team roles with the document elements and approving the transfer. The consent allowed and denied lists display as each individual section of a document is selected. This makes it easy for the consumer and clinician to understand how access will be controlled. Different sections or elements of the same record, message, or document, (the data) may have different levels of sensitivity and therefore, different consent conditions will be applicable. This is supported in our design because these different elements can each reference a separate care team role. This assumes that the underlying data format is structured in a way that permits the unique identification of data elements, as is the case with medical record standards such as HL7[8]. This does not imply that HL7 based systems are a prerequisite for the proposed model. The required structure can be added to information extracted from legacy systems at the time it is retrieved.

8   Conclusions

Role-based Access Control systems adhere to the principle where anything that is not explicitly allowed is implicitly denied. In health care, it is often more efficient and reliable to use the opposite form of expression, where denied access is explicitly stated. Distributed health information networks require a combination of both forms of expression to allow the system to implement access policy in a way that mirrors the way consumers commonly think about who should have access to their health information. This results in a system that is easier for clinicians and consumers to understand and manage.

This paper has indentified that standard RBAC models don't support a policy expression in the form of a general consent with explicit denial with adequate flexibility for distributed health information networks. We have presented an adaptation of RBAC that supports general consent with explicit denial. The proposed model also permits allow and deny policies to successively qualify each other in a role hierarchy supporting inheritance. This results in an access control framework that exhibits great flexibility and efficiency in the range of access policies that it can support. This model has been implemented in a prototype distributed health information system.

---

[8] http://www.hl7.org/

References

1. J. Bacon, M. Lloyd, and K. Moody. Translating role-based access control policy within context. In *Policy 2001, Workshop on Policies for Distributed Systems and Networks*, pages 107–120. Springer-Verlag, 2001.
2. Y. Bartal, A. J. Mayer, K. Nissim, and A. Wool. Firmato: A novel firewall management toolkit. In *IEEE Symposium on Security and Privacy*, pages 17–31, 1999.
3. R. Chandramouli. A framework for multiple authorization types in a healthcare application system. In *17th Annual Computer Security Applications Conference (ACSAC)*, December 2001.
4. R. Clarke. e-Consent: a critical element of trust in e-business. In *15th Bled Electronic Commerce Conference. e-Reality: Constructing the e-Economy – Research Volume*, 2002.
5. E. Coeira. "e-Consent" Consumer Consent in Electronic Health Data Exchange. downloaded from http://www.health.gov.au/hsdd/primcare/it/pdf/coiera.pdf on 3 February 2003.
6. I. Denley and S. Weston Smith. Privacy in clinical information systems in secondary care. *British Medical Journal*, 318:1328–1331, May 1999.
7. D. Ferraiolo, J. Barkley, and D. Kuhn. A role-based access control model and reference implementation within a corporate intranet. *ACM Transactions on Information and System Security*, 2(1):34–64, February 1999.
8. D. Ferraiolo, J. Cugini and R. Kuhn. Role based access control (RBAC): Features and motivations. In *Annual Computer Security Applications Conference*. IEEE Computer Society Press, 1995.
9. D. Ferraiolo and R. Kuhn. Role-based access controls. In *15th NIST-NCSC National Computer Security Conference*, pages 554–563, 1992.
10. D. Ferraiolo, R. Sandhu, S. Gavrila, D. Kuhn, and R. Chandramouli. Proposed NIST standard for role-based access control. *ACM Transactions on Information and System Security (TISSEC)*, 4(3):224–274, 2001.
11. L. Giuri and P. Iglio. A formal model for role-based access control with constraints. In *9th IEEE Computer Security Foundations Workshop*, pages 136–145, 1996.
12. R.J. Hayton, J.M. Bacon, and K. Moody. Access control in an open distributed environment. In *19th IEEE Computer Society Symposium on Research in Security and Privacy*, pages 3–14.
13. J. J. Longstaff, M. A. Lockyer, and M. G. Thick. A model of accountability, confidentiality and override for healthcare and other applications. In *5th ACM workshop on Role-based access control*, pages 71–76. ACM Press, 2000.
14. I. Mavridis, G. Pangalos, and M. Khair. eMEDAC: Role-based access control supporting discretionary and mandatory features. In *13th IFIP WG 11.3 Working Conference on Database Security*, 1999.
15. T. Rindfleisch. Privacy, information technology, and health care. *Communications of the ACM*, 40(8):93–100, August 1997.
16. R. Simon and M. E. Zurko. Separation of duty in role-based environments. In *IEEE Computer Security Foundations Workshop*, pages 183–194, 1997.

Cryptanalysis of a New Cellular Automata Cryptosystem

Feng Bao

Institute for Infocomm Research
21 Heng Mui Keng Terrace, Singapore 119613
baofeng@i2r.a-star.edu.sg

Abstract. Cellular automata provide discrete deterministic mathematical models for physical, biological and computational systems. Despite their simple construction, cellular automata are shown to be capable of complicated behaviour, and to generate complex and random patterns. There have been constant efforts to exploit cellular automata for cryptography since the very beginning of the research on cellular automata. Unfortunately, most of the previous cryptosystems based on cellular automata are either insecure or inefficient. [8] is the latest effort in cellular automata cryptosystems (CACs) design, where the affine cellular automata are combined with non-affine transformations. It is claimed that the weakness in some of the previous CACs due to affine property is removed. In this paper we show that the new CAC is still insecure. It can be broken by a chosen-plaintext attack. The attack is very efficient, requiring only hundreds of chosen plaintexts and a small computation amount. We also consider the possibility of modifying the new CAC. Our results show, however, that it is not easy to secure the scheme by minor modifications. The cryptanalysis in this paper enforces the opinion once more that the security must be very carefully analyzed in designing the cryptosystems based on some mathematical systems. We should not blindly trust the pseudo randomness brought by the available mathematical systems. The designing techniques developed by cryptographic community are always optimal.

1 Introduction

1.1 Cellular Automata

Cellular automata were introduced by von Neumann and Ulam as simple models to study biological processes such as self-reproduction. Any system with many identical discrete elements undergoing deterministic local interactions may be modelled as a cellular automaton. Many complex systems may be broken down into identical components, each obeying simple laws. The huge number of components that make up the whole system act together to yield very complex behavior.

A cellular automaton (CA) consists of a number of cells, which evolve by a simple local rule. The value of each cell in the next stage is determined by the values of the cell and its neighbor cells in the current stage under the local rule.

R. Safavi-Naini and J. Seberry (Eds.): ACISP 2003, LNCS 2727, pp. 416–427, 2003.
© Springer-Verlag Berlin Heidelberg 2003

A one-dimensional CA has n cells linked in a line (non-circle CA) or in a circle (circle CA). Denote the value in the i-th cell at the t-th stage by $v_i[t]$. The local function f_i is a deterministic function to determine the next-stage value of the i-th cell,

$$v_i[t+1] = f_i(v_{i-1}[t], v_i[t], v_{i+1}[t]).$$

The first and the last cells are only affected by their one-side neighbor in non-circle CA. For circle CA, we take $v_n[t]$ for $v_0[t]$ and $v_1[t]$ for $v_{n+1}[t]$. If f_i's are identical for all $i = 1, 2, \cdots, n$, the CA is called *homogeneous* CA; otherwise, it is called *non-homogeneous* CA. If all f_i's are linear functions, the CA is called *linear* CA; otherwise, it is called *non-linear* CA. Let GF be a field and all $v_i[t] \in GF$. A CA is called an affine CA if

$$f_i(v_{i-1}[t], v_i[t], v_{i+1}[t]) = w_{i-1} \cdot v_{i-1}[t] + w_i \cdot v_i[t] + w_{i+1} \cdot v_{i+1}[t] + u_i$$

where $w_{i-1}, w_i, w_{i+1}, u_i \in GF$, $\cdot$ is the multiplication and $+$ is the addition of GF.

An example of two-dimensional CA is that the cells are arranged in a grid. Therefore, each cell is determined by its eight neighbor cells and itself in evolving. Two-dimensional CA may have other topologies as well, such as in hexagon, where each cell depends on its six neighbors and itself.

Cellular automata are examples of mathematical systems constructed from many identical components, each simple, but together capable of complex behaviour. This feature of simple-local-rule leading to complex-global-behaviour attracted many researchers in 80's. Interested reader is referred to [2], [5], [7], [9], [10] and the references therein.

1.2   Cellular Automata Cryptosystems

Cellular automata have been considered for the application in cryptography ever since they appeared. There are two reasons for the constant efforts. One is that cellular automata is a simple model that can generate pseudo-random patterns. The other is that cellular automata can be efficiently implemented by hardware.

However, the pseudo-randomness (by Komogorov complexity theory, it cannot be true randomness due to the simple local rules) is mainly estimated in statistical tests, which may not be enough for cryptosystems. The random sequences generated by a cellular automaton may be qualified for the random sources in some simulations, but need more careful cryptanalyses for cryptosystems. Although the (pseudo) random generators, such as in [10], [11], are efficient by hardware, they are not efficient as well by software. The random generators presented in [10], [11] are less secure than the random generators designed by conventional cryptographic techniques for the same efficiency (in key size, computational and space complexity etc).

In [4], non-homogeneous cellular automata are proposed for public key cryptosystems. But there are only the description of the general principle and some small-size examples given in the paper. There are no recommended key sizes and key generation procedures. Therefore, it is difficult to conduct cryptanalysis to the system although the small-size examples are apparently insecure. However, the security of CA public key cryptosystem in [4] is questionable since there is no cryptanalysis but a simple claim that the security is based on the NP hard problem of solving simultaneous boolean quadratic equations. It is well known that NP-hardness does not necessarily guarantee the cryptographic security.

Both block cipher and stream cipher CACs were proposed in [6]. But they were broken in [1] due to the affine property of the used CAs. In [3], another CA-based block cipher was proposed. Unfortunately it is also unable to get rid off affine property and hence fails to achieve the claimed security. The latest CAC is proposed in [8], where an affine CA is mixed with non-affine transformations to make a block cipher. Although the cipher may resist the previous attacks to affine CA based ciphers, it is still insecure against some other attacks. In this paper we show that the new CAC can be broken by a chosen-plaintext attack.

The common annoying feature of the cryptosystems based on some mathematical models, e.g., those based on chaos systems, is that only the principle is given. There lack details, such as recommended key sizes and key generation steps etc, therefore it is not possible for others to implement the ciphers. The new CAC is much better than those cryptosystems in explicitly specifying the block size 128 bits and key size 128 bits, while the encryption/decryption consists of four transformations. However, there are still many parts omitted, such as how to derive the secret CAs from the secret key, how to drive the "control bits" from the secret key and how to derive the rotate number etc. Our attack succeeds without needing those details. Instead of finding the secret key, we can find those secret CAs, control bits and rotate number etc, directly from a chosen-plaintext attack. That is, instead of targeting at the secret key, we target at the components generated from the secret key. Our attack is very efficient in the sense that we only need hundreds of chosen plaintexts and a small computation amount equivalent to thousands of encryptions/decryptions.

We also consider possible minor modifications that do not thoroughly change the structure of the new CAC. Our results show that it is almost impossible to repair the cipher with minor modifications. The design is a complete failure.

The rest of the paper is organized as follows. In Section 2, we describe the new CAC. In Section 3 we present the attack. In Section 4 we discuss the possible modifications that still fail to secure the cipher. Section 5 concludes the paper.

2   Description of the New CAC

The new CAC presented in [8] is based on one-dimensional 16-cell $GF(2^8)$ cellular automata, where the value of each cell is from $GF(2^8)$ and the local function $f_i, i = 1, 2, \cdots, 16$ is a function over $GF(2^8)$. There are two automata being used in the CAC. One is called *Minor* CA, the other called *Major* CA. The Minor CA is used to transform a secret key K into a secret state S_N, which controls the four transforms of the CAC, namely $\mathbf{T}_1$, $\mathbf{T}_2$, $\mathbf{T}_3$ and $\mathbf{T}_4$.

The CAC is a block cipher with both key size and block size 128-bit as described and explained as follows.

Role of Minor CA. – The Minor CA is a linear 16-cell $GF(2^8)$ CA. The secret key K is taken as the initial state of the minor CA. Run the Minor CA a fixed number of clock cycles (d). Denote the obtained state by S_N.

$\mathbf{T}_1$ – **Rotate**: Derive a number δ from S_N. Rotate each byte of the input (plaintext) $\mathcal{T}$ by δ steps (bits). The result $\mathcal{T}_1$ is the input to the major CA. (In the decryption, each byte is rotated back.)

$\mathbf{T}_2$ – **Major CA**: The Major CA is generated by an efficient synthesis algorithm from S_N (the synthesis algorithm is not provided in [8]). The Major CA is an affine CA, which has circles of equal length 32. That is, for any initial state, the Major CA goes back after running 32 clock cycles. S_N also determines a number $1 < \Delta < 32$. $\mathbf{T}_2$ takes the $\mathcal{T}_1$ as input and runs Δ clock cycles. The result $\mathcal{T}_2$ is input to $\mathbf{T}_3$. (In the decryption, the Major CA is run $32 - \Delta$ clock cycles.)

$\mathbf{T}_3$ – **Non-Affine Transform**: A non-affine transform is achieved by selective use of *Control Major Not* (CMN) gate. The CMN gate is controlled by 3 control bits c_1, c_2, c_3, in formula

$$y = x \oplus \{(c_1 \cdot c_2) \oplus (c_2 \cdot c_3) \oplus (c_3 \cdot c_1)\}$$

The S_N determines 2 sets of control bits and 5 fixed bit positions of $\mathcal{T}_2$ from 1 to 128, say $1 \leq p_1, p_2, p_3, p_4, p_5 \leq 128$. The five fixed bits of $\mathcal{T}_2$ at positions p_1, p_2, p_3, p_4, p_5 determine whether $\mathcal{T}_2$ should go through the CMN gate. If there are more than two 1's among the five fixed bits (*Majority Evaluation Function, MEF for short*), all other bits (non-fixed bits) of $\mathcal{T}_2$ go through CMN gate with the two sets of control bits alternately. Otherwise $\mathcal{T}_2$ remains as it is. (Since the five bits at positions p_1, p_2, p_3, p_4, p_5 do not go through the CMN gate, $\mathbf{T}_3$ is invertible for decryption.)

$\mathbf{T}_4$ – **Key Mixing**: Denote the output of $\mathbf{T}_3$ by $\mathcal{T}_3$. The output of $\mathbf{T}_4$ is denoted by $\mathcal{T}_{encr}$, $\mathcal{T}_{encr} = \mathcal{T}_3 \oplus S_N$.

The following encryption algorithm is quoted from [8].

Algorithm 1 Encryption
Input: input file to be encrypted
K=key
Output: encrypted file
begin
    Step 1. *Divide the file into 128 bits tokens $(\mathcal{T})$.*
    Step 2. *Load intial seed of Minor CA $S_0 = K$*
    For each token $\mathcal{T}$ begin loop
        Step 3. *Run the Minor CA for d time steps and obtain S_N*
        Step 4. *Obtain δ from S_N. Rotate $\mathcal{T}$ by δ steps and obtain $\mathcal{T}_1$*
        Step 5a. *Randomly synthesize Major CA using S_N as seed*
        Step 5b. *Obtain Δ from S_N*
        Step 5c. *Run Major CA for Δ steps with $\mathcal{T}_1$ as seed to obtain $\mathcal{T}_2$*
        if $\mathcal{T}_2$ satisfies MEF
            Step 6a *Obtain the two sets of control bits for CMN gate*

Step 6b *Apply CMN gate to non-fixed bits of T_2 by control bits*
alternately
Step 6c *Assign the result to T_3*
end if
Step 7. *XOR T_3 with S_N to get T_{encr}*
Step 8. *write T_{encr} in output file*
Go to Step 3 *until the input file is exhausted*
end

The decryption algorithm is just the inverse procedure of the encryption algorithm and is omitted here.

It is claimed in [8] that the software implementation of the CAC is faster than that of AES but slower than the optimized code of AES. Table 1 shows the experiment results provided in [8]. The experiments are claimed to be implemented on P-III 633 MHz processor. The optimized software code of the CAC is being developed for commercial application and is expected to be faster than the optimized AES.

Table 1. Comparison of time of software version of CAC and AES.

Input file size (in MB)	CAC Reference code (in second)	AES Reference code (in second)	AES Optimized code (in second)
1.00	2.70	10.00	0.87
2.00	5.00	25.20	0.89
3.00	7.00	36.40	1.90
4.24	9.80	42.36	2.25
5.14	11.00	56.78	2.79
6.108	11.30	59.34	3.20
7.125	16.00	79.86	3.40
8.00	17.91	87.10	3.90
9.76	23.30	116.67	4.0
10.30	23.70	121.53	5.11
11.40	27.40	136.40	5.20
12.00	27.90	140.21	5.40

The advantage of CAC is actually at the hardware implementation. [8] also gives the analysis of the hardware design with 0.25μMOS technology. The expected pipelined speed is 128Gb/sec.

3   Chosen-Plaintext Attack

The CAC presented in [8] lacks the details on how to derive δ and Δ from S_N, how to construct the Minor CA and the Majority CA, and how to drive the control bits and the 5 fixed bit positions for MEF. Hence we cannot target at finding the secret key K. We cannot even find the S_N (the reason will be explained later). Instead, we can find δ, the function of the Major CA running Δ steps, control bits etc, so that we can construct the transforms that are equivalent to $E_K()$ and $D_K()$ of the CAC with a chosen-plaintext attack.

3.1   An Equivalent Transform of the CAC

Before we start to describe our attack, we first present a transform that is equivalent to the CAC. In CAC, the Majority CA is an affine CA. That means the local function for the i-th cell can be expressed as

$$f_i(v_{i-1}, v_i, v_{i+1}) = w_{i-1} \cdot v_{i-1} + w_i \cdot v_i + w_{i+1} \cdot v_{i+1} + u_i$$

where $w_{i-1}, w_i, w_{i+1}, u_i \in GF(2^8)$, $\cdot$ is the multiplication and $+$ is the addition of $GF(2^8)$. Running the Major CA Δ steps is equivalent to Δ iterations of the local function, which lead to another affine function. The function relies on not only three cells but also the other cells. Formally, the i-th cell is determined by all the $(i - \Delta)$-th, $\cdots$, $(i + \Delta)$-th cells after Δ steps.

We denote the i-th byte of $\mathcal{T}_1$ by $\mathcal{T}_1(i)$ and the i-th byte of $\mathcal{T}_2$ by $\mathcal{T}_2(i)$, $i = 1, 2, \cdots, 16$. We have

$$\mathcal{T}_2(i) = \sum_{j=1}^{16} W_j(i) \cdot \mathcal{T}_1(j) + U(i)$$

for some $W_1(i), W_2(i), \cdots, W_{16}(i), U(i) \in GF(2^8)$. If $\Delta \geq 16$, every cell affects every cell. Otherwise some cells are not affected by all the cells. For example, we must have $W_{16}(1) = 0$ if $\Delta < 15$ (if we assume the Major CA is not circle CA). However, we do not care about what is the value of Δ in our attack and whether the Major CA is circle or not. We just find all the $W_j(i)$ in the above equation.

It is not possible to find $U(i)$'s. This is because $\mathcal{T}_2$ will be xored with S_N, no matter whether it goes through CMN or not. Since the $+$ in $GF(2^8)$ is xor, $U(i)$ will be xored with $S_N(i)$ finally. We can find $U(i) \oplus S_N(i)$ in our attack. But it is impossible to separate $U(i)$ and $S_N(i)$ from the $U(i) \oplus S_N(i)$. This is the reason why we say S_N cannot be found (unless there is detailed description on how to construct the Major CA from S_N).

Denote the i-th bit of $\mathcal{T}_2$ by $b_i(\mathcal{T}_2)$. The CAC (encryption) transform is as follows.

Transform 1 ($E_K()$ of CAC with key K)
   $\mathbf{T}_1$: obtain $\mathcal{T}_1$ by rotating each byte of $\mathcal{T}$, $\mathcal{T}(i)$, δ steps.
   $\mathbf{T}_2$: obtain $\mathcal{T}_2$ by setting

$$\mathcal{T}_2(i) = \sum_{j=1}^{16} W_j(i) \cdot \mathcal{T}_1(j) + U(i)$$

for secret $W_j(i), U(i) \in GF(2^8)$ derived from S_N.

T$_3$: obtain $\mathcal{T}_3$ by setting

$$\mathcal{T}_3 = \begin{cases} \mathcal{T}_2 \oplus \mathcal{T}_{CMN} & \text{if } \sum_{j=1}^{5} b_{p_j}(\mathcal{T}_2) > 2 \\ \mathcal{T}_2 & \text{if } \sum_{j=1}^{5} b_{p_j}(\mathcal{T}_2) \leq 2 \end{cases}$$

where $\mathcal{T}_{CMN}$ denotes the 128-bit configuration from CMN gate.

T$_4$: obtain $\mathcal{T}_4$ by setting $\mathcal{T}_4 = \mathcal{T}_3 \oplus S_N$.

We construct the equivalent transform as follows.

Transform 2 ($E_K()$ of CAC with key K)

T$'_1$: obtain $\mathcal{T}_1$ by rotating each byte of $\mathcal{T}$, $\mathcal{T}(i)$, δ steps.

T$'_2$: obtain $\mathcal{T}_2$ by setting

$$\mathcal{T}_2(i) = \sum_{j=1}^{16} W_j(i) \cdot \mathcal{T}_1(j) \tag{1}$$

for secret $W_j(i) \in GF(2^8)$ derived from S_N.

T$'_3$: obtain $\mathcal{T}_3$ by setting

$$\mathcal{T}_{encr} = \begin{cases} \mathcal{T}_2 \oplus C_1 & \text{if } b_{p_1}(\mathcal{T}_2)b_{p_2}(\mathcal{T}_2) \cdots b_{p_5}(\mathcal{T}_2) \in \mathcal{S} \subset \{0,1\}^5 \\ \mathcal{T}_2 \oplus C_2 & \text{if } b_{p_1}(\mathcal{T}_2)b_{p_2}(\mathcal{T}_2) \cdots b_{p_5}(\mathcal{T}_2) \in \{0,1\}^5 - \mathcal{S} \end{cases} \tag{2}$$

Here $C_1 = U \oplus S_N \oplus \mathcal{T}_{CMN}$ ($U = U(1)U(2) \cdots U(16)$) and $C_2 = U \oplus S_N$. Hence $C_1 = C_2 \oplus \mathcal{T}_{CMN}$. The set
$\mathcal{S} = \{x \in \{0,1\}^5 | x \oplus b_{p_1}(U)b_{p_2}(U) \cdots b_{p_5}(U)$ has more than two 1's\}.

It is not difficult to see that **Transform 1** equals **Transform 2**. In the next subsection, we break **Transform 2** by chosen-plaintext attack. We target at finding out C_1, C_2, δ, $W_i(j)$'s and the control bits.

3.2   Description of the Attack

Finding C_1, C_2 and $\mathcal{T}_{CMN}$

Randomly choose plaintexts A_1 and A_2 from $\{0,1\}^{128}$. Encrypt A_1, A_2 and $A_1 \oplus A_2$ and denote the three ciphertexts by B_1, B_2 and B_3. It is easy to see from **Transform 2** that $B_1 \oplus B_2 \oplus B_3 = C_1$ or C_2. The probability is 50% since $|\mathcal{S}| = 16$ (i.e., $\mathcal{S}$ divides $\{0,1\}^5$ evenly). By repeating above several times we can find both C_1 and C_2 (The probability of not obtaining both C_1 and C_2 goes exponentially low in the number of trials). But at this stage we do not know which one is C_1 and which one is C_2. It does not matter. We know that they are the C_1 and C_2 in equation (2). Also we find $\mathcal{T}_{CMN}$, which equals $C_1 \oplus C_2$.

Finding δ and $W_i(j)$'s

Randomly choose $a \in GF(2^8)$ and plaintext pairs (A_1, A_2) such that $A_1(i) = A_2(i)$ for $i = 2, 3, \cdots, 16$ and $A_1(1) + A_2(1) = a$, where $A_1(i)$ denotes the i-th byte of A_1 and $+$ denotes the addition of $GF(2^8)$ (that is $\oplus$ of $\{0,1\}^{16}$). Denote the ciphertext of A_1 and A_2 by B_1 and B_2. From (2) we have $B_1(j) + B_2(j) =$

$W_1(j) \cdot R_\delta(a)$ or $\mathcal{T}_{CMN}(j) + W_1(j) \cdot R_\delta(a)$, where $R_\delta(a)$ denotes the result of rotating a by δ steps and $j = 1, 2, \cdots, 16$. For same a we choose several pairs and compute the corresponding

$$\frac{B_1(j) + B_2(j)}{R_\delta(a)} \tag{3}$$

The result is either $W_1(j)$ or $W_1(j) + \mathcal{T}_{CMN}(j)/R_\delta(a)$. We choose pairs until we obtain both values.

If we repeat the above procedure for a different a, say $a' \neq a$, the two values of (3) are $W_1(j)$ and $W_1(j) + \mathcal{T}_{CMN}(j)/R_\delta(a')$. That is, there is a common value of (3) for a and a'. That common value is $W_1(j)$.

The above argument is based on the assumption that δ is already known. The problem is we still do not know δ yet. The following observation allows us to find δ.

Observation The value δ can only be from 1 to 7. We can guess δ to be $i = 1, 2, \cdots, 7$. The value of (3) can be expressed by

$$\frac{B_1(j) + B_2(j)}{R_i(a)} = W_1(j)\frac{R_\delta(a)}{R_i(a)} \text{ or } W_1(j)\frac{R_\delta(a)}{R_i(a)} + \frac{\mathcal{T}_{CMN}(j)}{R_i(a)} \tag{4}$$

For a', it is

$$\frac{B_1(j) + B_2(j)}{R_i(a')} = W_1(j)\frac{R_\delta(a')}{R_i(a')} \text{ or } W_1(j)\frac{R_\delta(a')}{R_i(a')} + \frac{\mathcal{T}_{CMN}(j)}{R_i(a')} \tag{5}$$

Unless $i = \delta$, $\frac{R_\delta(a)}{R_i(a)}$ may not equal $\frac{R_\delta(a')}{R_i(a')}$ for different a, a' (Appendix A). Therefore, when $i \neq \delta$ the two values of (4) may not have common value with the two values of (5). While for $i = \delta$, there must be a common value between (4) and (5). That is, we can exclude i when we find non-intersection of (4) and (5). The attack procedure is as follows.

Step 1 Randomly choose $r \in \{0, 1\}^{120}$. Encrypt $a\|r$ for all the 256 $a \in GF(2^8)$. Denote the ciphertext of $a\|r$ by B_a.

Step 2 For each $b \in GF(2^8)$, consider the 256 pairs $(B_a, B_{a \oplus b})$ for $a \in GF(2^8)$. Compute

$$S(i, b) = \{\frac{B_a(1) + B_{a \oplus b}(1)}{R_i(b)} \mid i = 1, 2, \cdots, 7; \ a \in GF(2^8)\} \tag{6}$$

For each i, the set in (6) has to two values.

Step 3 Construct a 7×256 table as bellow

Step 4 Observe the 7 rows of the table. The i whose corresponding row has a common value in all the 256 cells is the δ we are looking for. And the common value is $W_1(1)$

Table 2. Here b is an element of $GF(2^8)$, denoted by 0 to 255.

	$b=0$	$b=1$	$\cdots$	$b=255$
$i=1$	$S(1,0)$	$S(1,1)$	$\cdots$	$S(1,255)$
$i=2$	$S(2,0)$	$S(2,1)$	$\cdots$	$S(2,255)$
$\vdots$	$\vdots$	$\vdots$	$\vdots$	$\vdots$
$i=7$	$S(7,0)$	$S(7,1)$	$\cdots$	$S(7,255)$

Step 5 Once δ is fixed, we can find $W_1(j)$, $j = 2, 3, \cdots, 16$, by looking for the common value of

$$\{\frac{B_a(j) + B_{a\oplus b}(j)}{R_\delta(b)} \mid a \in GF(2^8)\} \tag{7}$$

and

$$\{\frac{B_a(j) + B_{a\oplus b'}(j)}{R_\delta(b')} \mid a \in GF(2^8)\} \tag{8}$$

for $b \neq b'$.

(After δ is fixed, we do not need 256 chosen plaintext-ciphertext pairs to find out $W_i(j)$ for each $i = 2, 3, \cdots, 16$. We use the method of equation (3).)

Step 6 For each $i = 2, 3, \cdots, 16$, we do the following

Step 6.1 Randomly choose plaintext pairs (A_1, A_2) such that $A_1(j) = A_2(j)$ for $j \neq i$ and $A_1(i) + A_2(i) = a$ for a randomly fixed $a \in GF(2^8)$. Denote the two ciphertexts by B_1 and B_2. Compute

$$\frac{B_1(j) + B_2(j)}{R_\delta(a)}, \ j = 1, 2, \cdots, 16 \tag{9}$$

Step 6.2 Repeat Step 6.1 until (9) leads to two values for each j (It is not difficult to see that for every j the second value comes at the same time).

Step 6.3 Randomly choose plaintext-ciphertext pairs (A_1, A_2) such that $A_1(j) = A_2(j)$ for $j \neq i$ and $A_1(i) + A_2(i) = a'$ for a randomly fixed $a' \neq a$. Denote the two ciphertexts by B_1 and B_2. Compute

$$\frac{B_1(j) + B_2(j)}{R_\delta(a')} \tag{10}$$

Step 6.4 Repeat Step 6.3 until the value of (10) equals one of the two values of (9) for each j (this also happens simultaneously for all j's). The common value for each j is $W_i(j)$

After we find all the $W_i(j)$'s and δ, we can claim the encryption scheme is already broken. Although we have not considered the control bits, we can decrypt any ciphertext in 50% probability. Let B be a given ciphertext. We apply the reverse transform of formula (1) to $B \oplus C_1$ and $B \oplus C_2$, and rotate each byte δ steps back (it is easy to see that (1) is invertible). One of the two results must be the plaintext.

Correctness of the Attack. The following fact guarantees Step 1 to Step 4 of the attack effective. For any $\delta, i \in \{1, 2, \cdots, 7\}$ and $\delta \neq i$, there exist $a, a' \in GF(2^8)$ such that

$$\frac{R_\delta(a)}{R_i(a)} \neq \frac{R_\delta(a')}{R_i(a')}$$

Control bits and fixed bit positions $p_1, \cdots, p_5$

As stated before, we have $\mathcal{T}_{CMN} = C_1 \oplus C_2$. Hence it is not necessary to find control bits. Having the configuration of the CMN is enough.

We suppose that $\mathcal{T}_{CMN}$ is not all-zero, otherwise it is too easy to break the scheme. If both the two sets of control bits lead to 1, the fixed bit positions $p_1, \cdots, p_5$ can be easily found out. In this case $\mathcal{T}_{CMN}$ is all-one except 5 zeros. That 5 zeros identify the $p_1, \cdots, p_5$.

If the CMN gate leads to an alternate 0-1 xor, we have $\mathcal{T}_{CMN}$ to be a configuration of alternate 0-1 with 5 more 0's embeded in. In such situation we cannot identify the $p_1, \cdots, p_5$ exactly, but we can find the small district they fall in. For example, if $\mathcal{T}_{CMN} = \cdots 0101001010 \cdots$ we know that some p_i must be at one of the two neighboring 0's. But we cannot know which one. If $\mathcal{T}_{CMN} = \cdots 01010001010 \cdots$ we know that some two p_i's must be at two of the three neighboring 0's. Again we cannot know which two.

If the major CA synthesis algorithm is published, it very likely that S_N can be found out from $W_i(j)$'s. In that case, $p_1, \cdots, p_5$ and the controls bits can be derived from S_N.

Number of chosen plaintext-ciphertext pairs required

To find C_1 and C_2, we need $3m$ paintext-ciphertext pairs so that the failure probability is as small as $1/2^m$. We need 256 plaintext-ciphertext pairs To find $W_1(j)$'s, meanwhile we find δ. After δ is known, we need fewer plaintext-ciphertext pairs to find $W_i(j)$'s for $i = 2, 3, \cdots, 16$. For each i, we need only 30 pairs so that the successful probability reaches $1 - 1/2^{10}$. We say 30 instead of 40 because we can optimize Step 6 by sharing a plaintext between Step 6.1 and Step 6.3. Therefore, we need $256 + 16 \times 30$ (for $m = 10$) pairs to break the CAC scheme with large probability. Actually there are more optimized methods for choosing plaintexts so that the attack is more efficient.

4   Discussion on Modifications

We discuss the possible minor modifications to the CAC and show that it is hard to secure the scheme unless there is a thorough change.

Different δ for different byte

In the CAC, the rotate number δ is identical for all the bytes of the plaintext. It is obviously a design weakness. It is easy to drive 16 δ's from S_N, one for each byte. S_N has sufficient number of bits to provide such information.

But that modification is useless in securing the scheme. We can repeat the Step 1 to Step 5 of our attack to each byte. The number of required chosen plaintext-ciphertext pairs is increased to 256×16. The scheme is still broken.

Add a permutation of bytes to plaintext

A permutation (including rotation) of $\mathcal{T}$ in byte unit does not affect the attack. This is because each byte of $\mathcal{T}_2$ depends on all the bytes of $\mathcal{T}$. Adding a permutation will change the value of $W_i(j)$ but the attack still works the same way.

Increase number of control bits

There are only two sets of control bits for CMN gate and applied to $\mathcal{T}_2$ alternately. That leads a regular configuration $\mathcal{T}_{CMN}$. It is possible for S_N to provide more sets of control bits. But it does not help since we can find $\mathcal{T}_{CMN}$ easily no matter how complex it is.

A further improvement is to have more $\mathcal{T}_{CMN}$'s. The bits at the fixed bit positions decide which one to use. However, it will not help in securing the scheme either. The attack to those $W_i(j)$ still works. The scheme can be broken completely if the Major CA synthesis algorithm is known, which is supposed to be known.

Using non-affine Major CA

This discussion is a bit far away from the proposed CAC, which is based on the affine Major CA. But suppose the Major CA is replaced by non-affine CA, the scheme is still hardly secure. But we need a different attack since there are no $W_i(j)$'s any more.

Let the Major CA be a non-affine CA. It should be homogeneous and circle. This is because the Major CA must have the property that every state comes back after 32 running steps. On that assumption we can provide another chosen plaintext-ciphertext attack that breaks the system. The central idea of the attack is as follows.

Choose plaintexts such that they have bytes all zero's and all one's. In this case the rotating operation is absorbed. But we still have 2^{16} possible plaintexts for choosing. Due to the homogeneous and circle property of the Major CA, the output of $\mathbf{T}_2$ is rotate-related with the plaintext. More formally, $R_e(\mathbf{T}_2\mathbf{T}_1(\mathcal{T})) = \mathbf{T}_2\mathbf{T}_1(R_e(\mathcal{T}))$, where $R_e(X)$ denotes the result of rotating X by e cells. The output of $\mathbf{T}_2$ will go through CMN gate with 50%. With a probability of 50% we can get a $\mathcal{T}$ such that either neither $\mathbf{T}_2\mathbf{T}_1(\mathcal{T})$ nor $\mathbf{T}_2\mathbf{T}_1(R_e(\mathcal{T}))$ go through CMN gate, or both of them go through CMN gate. In that case, we can obtain $S_N \oplus R_e(S_N)$. With some more such information (by a set of $\mathcal{T}$'s) we can get S_N by brute force. Then we check whether the S_N obtained is correct. If not, we try again with another set of $\mathcal{T}$'s.

The inherent weakness

The inherent weakness of the new CAC is that it is actually like a one-round block cipher. The scheme cannot be secured if the whole encryption procedure is repeated by a small number of times. It is possible that the scheme is secured by repeating the encryption sufficient many times (with more careful key schedule).

But designing secure block cipher is never a big issue if the efficiency can be ignored. The challenge is to design a block cipher both secure and efficient. AES was selected in that criterion.

5 Conclusion

In this paper we break the latest effort on cellular automata cryptosystem. Our analysis shows that the design is a complete failure. We can break it without knowing some details. We deem that the scheme is more vulnerable if all the details are known, where we can directly target at S_N and check its correctness.

It enforces the idea that we should not blindly trust the pseudo randomness brought by mathematical systems. Careful cryptanalyses must be conducted by cryptographic community before the application. Many cryptosystems are invented by exploiting chaos systems or some other mathematical systems, and pushed to the market by companies. But the cryptanalysis is seldom seen. In most cases, it is due to the lack of details of the design. Companies tend to hide the details as their intelligent property. That is dangerous to the users of their cryptosystems.

References

1. S. Blackburn, S. Merphy, and K. Paterson, "Comments on 'theory and applications of cellular automata in cryptography'", IEEE Transactions on Computers, Vol. 46, No. 5, pp. 637–638, May 1997.
2. M. Creutz, "Deterministic Ising dynamics", Annals of Physics Vol. 167, No. 62, 1986.
3. N. Ganguly, A. Das, B. Sikdar, and P. Chaudhuri, "Cellular automota model for cryptosystem", Cellular Automata Conference, Yokoham University, Japan, 2000.
4. P. Guan, "Cellular automata public key cryptosystem", Complex System Vol. 1, pp. 51–57, 1987.
5. S. Kirkpatrick et al., "Global optimization by simulated annealing", Science Vol. 220, No. 671, 1986.
6. S. Nandi, B. Kar, and P. Chaudhuri, "Theory and applications of cellular automata in cryptography", IEEE Transactions on Computers, Vol. 43, No. 12, pp. 1346–1357, Dec 1994.
7. Y. Pomeau, "Invariant in cellular automata", Journal of Physics A17 (1984) L415.
8. S. Sen, C. Shaw, R. Chowdhuri, N. Ganguly, and P. Chaudhuri, "Cellualr automata based cryptosystem (CAC)", Proceedings of the 4th International Conference on Information and Communications Security (ICICS02), LNCS 2513, pp. 303–314, Dec 2002.
9. S. Wolfram, "Cellular automata as models of complexity", Nature Vol. 311, No. 419, 1984.
10. S. Wolfram, "Cryptography with cellular automata", Proceedings of Advances in Cryptology-Crypto'85, Lecture Notes in Computer Science 218, pp. 429–432, 1986.
11. S. Wolfram, "Origins of randomness in physical systems", Phys. Rev. Lett. Vol. 55, No. 449, 1985.
12. S. Wolfram, "Random sequence generation by cellular automata", Advances in Applied Mathematics Vol. 7, No. 123, 1986.

A CCA2 Secure Key Encapsulation Scheme Based on 3rd Order Shift Registers

Chik How Tan, Xun Yi, and Chee Kheong Siew

Centre for Information Security
School of Electrical and Electronic Engineering
Nanyang Technological University
Nanyang Avenue, Singapore 639798
{echikhow, exyi, ecksiew}@ntu.edu.sg

Abstract. In 1998, Cramer and Shoup proposed the first practical and provable cryptosystem against adaptive chosen ciphertext attack under the standard assumption in the standard model, that is, decisional Diffie-Hellman assumption. Recently, Lucks extended the Cramer-Shoup cryptosystem to a group of quadratic residues modulo a composite number and showed that the scheme is provably secure in the standard model. In this paper, we extend Lucks' key encapsulation scheme to a third order linear feedback shift register and is based on a new assunmption which is called shift register based decisional Diffie-Hellman assumptions (SR-DDH). The proposed scheme is provably secure against adaptive chosen ciphertext attack based on the hardness of shift register based decisional Diffie-Hellman assumption in the standard model and not in random oracle model. Furthermore, the size of public key and ciphertext are shorter than Cramer-Shoup cryptosystem and the computational complexity is also more efficient than Cramer-Shoup cryptosystem and Lucks scheme.

Keywords: Public key cryptosystem, shift registers, adaptive chosen-ciphertext attack

1 Introduction

The semantic security, was first introduced by Goldwasser and Micali [15] in 1984, is a formal approach of defining cryptosystem security. The semantic security means that an adversary is not able to obtain any partial information about a message given its corresponding ciphertext. This notion of security only guarantees the secrecy under the passive attack, that is, an adversary can only eavesdrop and cannot mount an active attack. The first active attack was introduced by Naor and Yung [23] in 1990; which is called non-adaptive chosen ciphertext attack (CCA1) and is sometime referred to a lunch-time attack. It means that an adversary allows making any query to the decryption oracle and obtaining partial information of the corresponding ciphertext before obtaining the target ciphertext. The most powerful attack on a cryptosystem is an adaptive chosen ciphertext attack (CCA2) which was introduced by Rackoff and Simon [24] in

R. Safavi-Naini and J. Seberry (Eds.): ACISP 2003, LNCS 2727, pp. 428–442, 2003.
© Springer-Verlag Berlin Heidelberg 2003

1991. This attack allows adversary to make any query to the decryption oracle as many times as possible even if an adversary obtains the target ciphertext and partial information about the corresponding ciphertext through its interaction with the decryption oracle. In 1998, Tsiounis and Yung [30] showed that the semantic security of the ElGamal encryption scheme [14] is essentially equivalent to the hardness of the decisional Diffie-Hellman, but the ElGamal encryption scheme is vulnerable to CCA2. This shows that semantic security is not a sufficient criterion for defining cryptosystem security. As CCA2 is the most powerful attack on a cryptosystem, it is generally accepted that any secured cryptosystem should be against CCA2. In 1991, Dolev, Dwork and Naor [12] introduced another notion of defining cryptosystem security, called non-malleability, which turns out to be equivalent to CCA2 and was proved by Bellare et al. [5] in 1998.

Although Rackoff and Simon [24] and Dolev et al. [12] proposed provably secure cryptosystems against adaptive chosen ciphertext attack under the standard assumptions in the standard model, both schemes are impractical. Since then, there were many practical cryptosystems proposed against CCA2. For example, Zheng-Seberry scheme [31], OAEP by Bellare and Rogaway [4], Tsiounis-Yung scheme [30], Baek-Lee-Kim scheme [2], Schnorr-Jakobsson scheme [25], Kurosawa-Ogata-Matsuo-Makishima scheme [18], Buchmann-Sakurai-Tagagi scheme [7], etc. Most of these cryptosystems were provably secure against CCA2 in the random oracle model [3]. The Random Oracle Model is an ideal model of computation such that a cryptographic hash function is usually modeled as a black box. In 1998, Canetti, Goldreich and Halevi [8] proved that the security proof in the Random Oracle model do not always imply the security of an actual scheme in the "real world". Hence, the random oracle model is still a heuristic proof as it does not rule out all the possible attacks. Therefore, a natural goal is to design a secure cryptosystem against CCA2 and proven secure under well-defined intractability assumptions.

Provably secure public key cryptosystems

The first practical and provably secured cryptosystem against CCA2 under the standard assumption in the standard model was proposed by Cramer and Shoup [10] in 1998. The scheme is a variant and enhanced security of ElGamal encryption scheme against CCA2. In 1999, R. Canetti and S. Goldwasser [9] constructed a threshold public key cryptosystem based on the idea of Cramer and Shoup [10] and proved that their scheme is secure against CCA2 in the standard model. In 2001, Müller [22] constructed a William based public key encryption and is provably secure against CCA2 based on the factorization problem. In the same year, Abdalla et al. [1] proved that the DHIES scheme is secured against CCA2 in the standard model based on the non-standard assumption, that is, hash Diffie-Hellman assumption. In 2002, Cramer and Shoup [11] generalised and extended the ideas of [10] to obtain a new and quite practical encryption schemes that are secure against CCA2 under two different standard assumptions, that is, Paillier's decision composite residuosity assumption and the classical quadratic residuosity assumption. The schemes in [11] are provably secure against CCA2 in the standard model. In 2002, Lucks [20] extended Cramer-Shoup cryptosystem to a group of quadratic residues modulo a composite number and is provably secure against CCA2 in the standard model. The scheme proposed by Lucks, called key encapsulation scheme, is slightly different from a public key encryption scheme. A key encapsulation scheme uses public key encryption technique to encrypt a secret key which is used to encrypt the actual message. The key encapsulation scheme shares the same security requirement as public key encryption scheme, which means, if a key encapsulation scheme is secure against CCA2, then its corresponding public key encryption scheme is also secure against CCA2.

Related works and our contribution

In 1999, Brouwer *et al.* [6] proposed a trace function for Diffie-Hellman key exchange to reduce the number of bits transmitted to 2/3 of the original Diffie-Hellman key exchange. In the same year, Gong and Harn [16] proposed a new public key cryptosystem based on a third order linear feedback shift registers over $GF(p)$. In 2000, Lenstra and Verheul [19] proposed a ElGamal-like public key cryptosystem, called XTR, which used a trace function in $GF(p^6)$ over $GF(p^2)$. In fact, XTR can be viewed as a third order linear feedback shift registers over $GF(p^2)$ with a special type of feedback function. In 2001, Tan *et al.* [26,27] proposed a signature scheme based on a third order shift register over $GF(p^e)$. The authors showed that the security of their scheme is based on the hardness of shift register based discrete logarithm problem in an extension fields $GF(p^{3e})$. Although public key cryptosystems were proposed over a third order linear feedback shift register, no security proof was given. Furthermore, the extension of Cramer-Shoup encryption to other algebraic groups structure is non-trivial, it is because some cryptographic properties in a group may be lost. For example, Joux and Nguyen [17] showed that there exists some groups in which the decisional Diffie-Hellman problem is easy, but the computational Diffie-Hellman problem is hard. A group in super-singular elliptic curve has this property. Recently, Tan *et al.* [29] showed that the decisional Diffie-Hellman problem in shift register (SR-DDH) is as hard as the decisional Diffie-Hellman problem of a subgroup in a finite field. Hence, it is possible to extend Cramer-Shoup encryption to shift register based structure. In this paper, we extend the idea of Cramer-Shoup encryption and Lucks scheme to a third order linear feedback shift register by constructing a key encapsulation scheme. A key encapsulation scheme is a hybrid encryption scheme which uses public key encryption technique to encrypt a secret key and the encryption algorithm with input of the secret key is a symmetric key cryptosystem. We prove that the proposed key encapsulation scheme is secured against CCA2 in the standard model provided that the SR-DDH is hard and the hash function is a collision resistant one-way hash function. The idea of the proof is borrowed from Cramer-Shoup, but the proof is non-trivial as the algebraic structure is different from a multiplicative group over a prime number. This is shown in the proof of the main Theorem. Furthermore, the proposed key encapsulation scheme is more efficient than Cramer-Shoup scheme and Lucks scheme.

Organization of paper

The paper is organised as follows: The cryptographic properties and the analogue of Diffie-Hellman assumptions of a third order linear feedback shift register over $GF(p^e)$ are given in section two. In section three, we construct a new key encapsulation scheme based on a third order linear feedback shift register and discuss its computational complexity. Section four gives a detail proof of this scheme secure against CCA2 under the hardness of shift register based decisional Diffie-Hellman assumption (SR-DDH) in the standard model. Finally, we conclude that the proposed key encapsulation scheme is a practical and provably secure scheme suitable for applications.

2   Preliminaries

In this section, we describe some definitions and properties of the linear feedback shift register. These will be used for the later construction of key encapsulation scheme.

Let p be an odd prime and e be a positive integer. Let $GF(p^e)$ be a finite field. We define an order of a polynomial $f(x)$ as the smallest positive integer n such that $f(x)|x^n - 1$. Let $f(x) = x^3 - ax^2 + bx - 1$, $a, b \in GF(p^e)$ be an irreducible polynomial over $GF(p^e)$ of prime order q such that q divides $p^{3e} - 1$ and does not divide $p^l - 1$ for $l|3e$ and $1 \leq l < 3e$. A sequence $\mathbf{s} = \{s_k\}$ generated by the polynomial $f(x)$ of degree 3 is called a third order linear feedback shift register (LFSR) sequence over $GF(p^e)$ and an elements of $\mathbf{s}$ satisfy

$$s_k = as_{k-1} - bs_{k-2} + s_{k-3}, \ k \geq 3.$$

with the initial values $s_0 = 3$, $s_1 = a$ and $s_2 = a^2 - 2b$.

In order to distinguish the sequence $\{s_k\}$ generated by $f(x) = x^3 - ax^2 + bx - 1$, we denote s_k by $s_k(a, b)$. Assume that $\alpha_1, \alpha_2, \alpha_3$ are all roots of $f(x)$ in the extension field of $f(x)$ over $GF(p^e)$, then according to Newton's formula, the elements of $\mathbf{s}$ can be represented by the symmetric k-th power sum of the roots as $s_k = \alpha_1^k + \alpha_2^k + \alpha_3^k$. Let k be any positive integer and $S_k = [s_k, s_{k+1}, s_{k+2}]$ be a vector over $GF(p^e)$, then s_k can also be obtained through matrix representation as $S_k^T = A^k S_0^T$, where S_0^T is a transpose of a vector $S_0 = [s_0, s_1, s_2]$ and

$$A = \begin{pmatrix} 0 & 1 & 0 \\ 0 & 0 & 1 \\ 1 & -b & a \end{pmatrix},$$

where A^k can be computed as follows: As any $x^k \bmod f(x)$, for $k > 2$, can be expressed as $x^k = c_2^{(k)} x^2 + c_1^{(k)} x + c_0^{(k)} \bmod f(x)$, where $c_i^{(k)}$ are in $GF(p^e)$ for $0 \leq i \leq 2$, then there is a one-to-one correspondence for matrix A^k such as:

$$A^k = c_2^{(k)} A^2 + c_1^{(k)} A + c_0^{(k)} I \bmod f(x),$$

where I is an identity matrix. We denote the element of $x^k \bmod f(x)$ as $C^{(k)} = (c_0^{(k)}, c_1^{(k)}, c_2^{(k)})$.

For any positive integer k, we define $f_k(x)$ as follows:

$$f_k(x) = (x - \alpha_1^k)(x - \alpha_2^k)(x - \alpha_3^k) = x^3 - \sum_{i=1}^{3} \alpha_i^k x^2 + (\sum_{i \neq j}^{3,3} \alpha_i^k \alpha_j^k)x - \prod_{i=1}^{3} \alpha_i^k.$$

Then, we have $f_k(x) = x^3 - s_k x^2 + s_{-k} x - 1$.[1]

Now, we list the following important properties extracted from paper [27] for constructing key encapsulation scheme, the detailed proof can be found in the paper.

Theorem 1. [27] *Let $f(x) = x^3 - ax^2 + bx - 1$ be an irreducible polynomial over $GF(p^e)$ of prime order q where q divides $p^{3e} - 1$ and does not divide $p^l - 1$ for $l|3e$ and $1 \leq l < 3e$. Let $\mathbf{s}$ be the sequence generated by $f(x)$. Then,*
(a) *For any integer k and $f_k(x) = x^3 - s_k x^2 + s_{-k} x - 1$,*
   (i) *The order of $f_k(x)$ is q,*
   (ii) *$f_k(x)$ is irreducible iff $f(x)$ is irreducible,*
(b) *For any positive integers k and d,*

$$s_k(s_d(a,b), s_{-d}(a,b)) = s_{kd}(a,b) = s_d(s_k(a,b), s_{-k}(a,b)).$$

For the simplicity of describing a shift register based key encapsulation scheme, we introduce the following notation:

$$s_r^{(y)} := s_{yr} \quad \text{and} \quad S_r^{(y)} := (s_r^{(y)}, s_{-r}^{(y)}).$$

Then, from Theorem 1(b), we have $s_k^{(d)} = s_d^{(k)} = s_{dk}$. Now, we define an addition-like of sequences as $s_y \uplus s_z := s_{y+z}$.

Lemma 1. *With the above notation and definitions, we have*
(a) $s_1^{(y)} \uplus s_1^{(z)} = s_1^{(y+z)}$.
(b) $s_r^{(y)} \uplus s_r^{(z)} = s_{yr} \uplus s_{zr}$.
(c) $s_r^{(y)} \uplus s_r^{(z)} = s_r^{(y+z)}$.

Shift Register Based Diffie-Hellman Assumptions

In the original Diffie-Hellman assumptions, it is defined in a finite cyclic group $\mathcal{G}$ with a generator g, we state the three assumptions as follows:

Discrete Logarithm Assumption (DL): Given a generator g of $\mathcal{G}$ and a, it is assumed difficult to find an integer x such that $a = g^x$ holds.

Computational Diffie-Hellman Assumption (CDH): Given a generator g of $\mathcal{G}$ and a pair (g^w, g^y), it is assumed difficult to compute g^{wy}.

Decisional Diffie-Hellman Assumption (DDH): Given a generator g of $\mathcal{G}$ and a triple (g^w, g^y, g^z), it is assumed difficult to decide whether $z = wy$ or not.

---

[1] From the above notation, $C^{(k)}, C^{(kp^e)}, C^{(kp^{2e})}$ are the roots of $f_k(x)$.

From the original Diffie-Hellman assumptions, one can define a similar concept of shift register based Diffie-Hellman assumptions, which is defined in the sequences of a third order linear feedback shift register with a generator (s_1, s_{-1}).

Shift Register Based Discrete Logarithm Assumption (SR-DL): Given a generator (s_1, s_{-1}) and (s_k, s_{-k}), it is assumed difficult to find an integer k such that $s_k = s_k(s_1, s_{-1})$ and $s_{-k} = s_{-k}(s_1, s_{-1})$ hold.

Shift Register Based Computational Diffie-Hellman Assumption (SR-CDH): Given a generator $S_1^{(1)}$ and a pair $(S_1^{(w)}, S_1^{(y)})$, it is assumed difficult to compute $S_1^{(wy)}$.

Shift Register Based Decisional Diffie-Hellman Assumption (SR-DDH): Given a generator $S_1^{(1)}$ and a triple $(S_1^{(w)}, S_1^{(y)}, S_1^{(z)})$, it is assumed difficult to decide whether $z = wy$ or not.

We define distributions D and R as follows:

$$D = \{(S_1^{(1)}, S_1^{(w)}, S_1^{(y)}, S_1^{(z)}) \quad \text{if } z = wy\},$$
$$R = \{(S_1^{(1)}, S_1^{(w)}, S_1^{(y)}, S_1^{(z)}) \quad \text{if } z \neq wy\}.$$

For the shift register based decisional Diffie-Hellman assumption, we assume that it is infeasible to distinguish between the distribution D and the distribution R. "Difficult to find/compute/decide" or "infeasible to distinguish" means that the probability of a probabilistic polynomial time algorithm A for solving an assumption is negligible. "Negligible" means that for all constant c, there exists a security parameter $k_{c,A}$ such that for all $k > k_{c,A}$, the probability is at most $\frac{1}{k^c}$.

In the following theorem, we list the result from [27,29] the relationship between the shift register based Diffie-Hellman assumptions and the Diffie-Hellman assumptions:

Theorem 2. [27,29] *In a q-subgroup of $GF(p^{3e})$, the following equivalences hold:*
(i)   *SR-DL is equivalent to DL in $GF(p^{3e})$.*
(ii)   *SR-CDH is equivalent to CDH in $GF(p^{3e})$.*
(iii)   *SR-DDH is equivalent to DDH in $GF(p^{3e})$.*

3   Shift Register Based Key Encapsulation Mechanism

The advantage of a symmetric encryption is a message working on a whole space and normally running faster than public key encryption, while the advantage of a public key encryption is the provision of key agreement/exchange. In order to benefit from these advantages, a hybrid encryption scheme is introduced. Such a scheme uses public key encryption techniques to encrypt a key and then use it to encrypt the actual message. One of the techniques is *key encapsulation mechanism*. In this section, we propose a new key encapsulation scheme based on shift register and its construction is discussed in the following subsection.

Key Encapsulation Mechanism

A key encapsulation mechanism is like a public key encryption scheme, except that the encryption algorithm is to generate the encryption of a random key K which is used to encrypt an actual message, and not a ciphertext. A key encapsulation mechanism (KEM) can be seen as the *secret-key part* of a hybrid cryptosystem. A KEM consists of three algorithms, that is, key generation algorithm, key encapsulation algorithm and key decapsulation algorithm, which are described as follows:

- The key generation algorithm GEN is a randomized algorithm that returns a pair of keys (pk, sk) where pk is a public key and sk is a secret key; we write $(pk, sk) \longleftarrow$ GEN.
- The key encapsulation algorithm KE is a randomized algorithm that takes the public key pk and returns a pair (C, K), where C is a ciphertext and K is a encapsulated key; we write $(C, K) \longleftarrow$ KE(pk).
- The key decapsulation algorithm KD is a deterministic algorithm that takes the secret key sk and a ciphertext C to compute K', write $K' \longleftarrow$ KD(sk, C); and to reject invalid ciphertext.

A KEM is *sound* if $K = K'$ for any public-secret key pair (pk, sk) where $(C, K) =$KE(pk) and $K' =$KD(sk, C).

Shift Register Based Key Encapsulation Scheme (SR-KES)

Now, we describe a shift register based key encapsulation scheme which is based on a third order linear feedback shift register. The construction is described as follows:

KEY GENERATION: Let H be a collision resistant one-way hash function, p an odd prime number and e a positive integer. Let $f(x) = x^3 - ax^2 + bx - 1$ be an irreducible polynomial over $GF(p^e)$ of prime order q such that $q \equiv 1 \mod 3$, q divides $p^{3e} - 1$ and q does not divide $p^l - 1$ where $l|3e$ and $1 \le l < 3e$. Choose random numbers $v, w_1, w_2, y_1, y_2, z \in Z_q^*$ and compute the following:

$$s_{\pm 1}^{(v)} = s_{\pm v}, \quad s_{\pm 1}^{(z)} = s_{\pm z}, \quad C^{(w_1+vw_2)} = (c_0^{(w_1+vw_2)}, c_1^{(w_1+vw_2)}, c_2^{(w_1+vw_2)})$$

and $C^{(y_1+vy_2)} = (c_0^{(y_1+vy_2)}, c_1^{(y_1+vy_2)}, c_2^{(y_1+vy_2)})$, where $C^{(w_1+vw_2)}$ and $C^{(y_1+vy_2)}$ are the coefficients of $x^{w_1+vw_2} \mod f(x)$ and $x^{y_1+vy_2} \mod f(x)$ respectively. Then, the public key is $(S_1^{(1)}, S_1^{(v)}, C^{(w_1+vw_2)}, C^{(y_1+vy_2)}, S_1^{(z)}, H)$ and the private key is (w_1, w_2, y_1, y_2, z).

KEY ENCAPSULATION: Choose a random $r \in Z_q^*$ and compute

$$U_1 = (s_r, s_{-r}), \quad U_2 = (s_r^{(v)}, s_{-r}^{(v)}), \quad \lambda = H(U_1, U_2), \quad K = (s_r^{(z)}, s_{-r}^{(z)}),$$
$$d_+ = s_r^{(w_1+vw_2)} \uplus s_{r\lambda}^{(y_1+vy_2)} \quad \text{and} \quad d_- = s_{-r}^{(w_1+vw_2)} \uplus s_{-r\lambda}^{(y_1+vy_2)}.$$

Then, the ciphertext is $(U_1, U_2, d_\pm)$.

KEY DECAPSULATION: Given a ciphertext $(U_1, U_2, d_\pm)$. Let the order pairs of U_1 and U_2 be (u_{11}, u_{12}) and (u_{21}, u_{22}) respectively. The decapsulation algorithm first computes $\lambda = H(U_1, U_2)$ and checks $d_\pm = s_{\pm(w_1+y_1\lambda)}(u_{11}, u_{12}) \uplus s_{\pm(w_2+y_2\lambda)}(u_{21}, u_{22})$.

If they are not equal, then the key decapsulation algorithm outputs "reject"; otherwise, it outputs $K = (k_1, k_2)$ where $k_1 = s_z(u_{11}, u_{12})$ and $k_2 = s_{-z}(u_{11}, u_{12})$.

From the construction of SR-KES, it is easy to obtain the size of public/secret key and ciphertext and the number of exponentiations in key generation, key encapsulation and key decapsulation. Let $n = \log_2 p^{3e}$ and consider the same security parameter in Cramer-Shoup scheme and Lucks scheme. The results are compared with Cramer-Shoup scheme [10] and Lucks scheme [20]; and listed in the following table:

Table 1.

	Cramer-Shoup Sch.	Lucks Sch.	Proposed Sch.
Public size	$5n$	$5n$	$4n$
Secret size	$5n$	$5n$	$5 \log_2 q$
ciphertext size	$4n$	$3n$	$2n$
no. of exp. in key generation	5	5	4
no. of exp. in encapsulation	5	5	5
no. of exp. in decapsulation	3	3	3

Note - Exponentiation in [10] and [20] are referred to $g_1^k \bmod P$ and $g_2^k \bmod N$ where P and N are prime and composite number of size n bits respectively; g_1 and g_2 are generators in the respective groups, while exponentiation in the proposed scheme is referred to s_k for an exponent k.

In [28], the authors showed that the computation of s_k takes $13.24 \log_2 k$ p-bit modulo multiplication with precomputation. If one takes $\log_2 p^6 = 1024 = \log_2 P$, then the computation of s_k takes $\frac{13.24}{36} \log_2 k$ 1024-bit modulo multiplication, while $g^k \bmod P$ which takes $\frac{1}{2} \log_2 k$ 1024-bit modulo multiplication with precomputation. Therefore, the computation of s_k is faster than the usual exponentiation. Hence, the overall computational complexity of the proposed scheme is faster than Cramer-Shoup Scheme and Lucks scheme.

4   Security Proof in the Standard Model

ADAPTIVE CHOSEN CIPHERTEXT ATTACK (CCA2)

Consider the following game played by a challenger C and an adversary A.

Key Set Up. C takes a security parameter and runs the key generation algorithm to obtain a public key pk and private key sk. It gives pk to A and keeps sk secret.

Phase 1. In this phase, A adaptively interacts with C for a number of times specified by A. In each query, A sends a chosen $query$ σ to C. C runs the key decapsulation algorithm on input of the secret key sk and the query σ, and outputs the result of the query to A. The interaction is adaptive in the sense that the next query may depend on the previous queries.

Target Selection. $\mathcal{C}$ runs the key encapsulation algorithm to obtain a ciphertext C and the encapsulated key K. $\mathcal{C}$ selects a random $\delta \in \{0, 1\}$. $\mathcal{C}$ outputs σ^* to $\mathcal{A}$, where $\sigma^* = (C, K)$ if $\delta = 0$, otherwise, $\sigma^* = (C, K')$ where K' is a random value.

Phase 2. This phase is same as Phase 1, the only difference is that the key decapsulation algorithm of $\mathcal{C}$ only responds to queries σ that are different from the target ciphertext σ^*.

Guessing. $\mathcal{A}$ outputs a bit $\delta' \in \{0, 1\}$. It wins if $\delta' = \delta$.

We define the advantage of an adversary $\mathcal{A}$ to be $\mathbf{Adv}(\mathcal{A}) = |\Pr(\delta' = \delta) - \frac{1}{2}|$. A key encapsulation scheme is said secure against adaptive chosen ciphertext attack, if no polynomial time bounded adversary has non-negligible advantage in the game described above.

Theorem 3. *The proposed key encapsulation scheme (SR-KES) is secure against adaptive chosen ciphertext attack assuming (1) the hash function H is a collision resistant one-way function, and (2) the shift register based decisional Diffie-Hellman assumption (SR-DDH) is hard in a q-subgroup of $GF(p^{3e})$.*

We prove the above theorem by contradiction, that is, assuming that an adversary is able to break the SR-KES scheme, then it implies that there exists a polynomial time algorithm to solve shift register based decisional Diffie-Hellman assumption (SR-DDH). This contradicts the assumption that SR-DDH is intractable. To prove the theorem, we first construct a simulator as follows:

A SIMULATOR FOR SR-KEM

Given an input $(S_1^{(1)}, S_1^{(v)}, U_1, U_2)$ to the simulator. The simulator runs the following algorithms:

• **Key Generation Algorithm.** The key generation algorithm chooses $w_1, w_2, y_1, y_2, z_1, z_2 \in Z_q^*$ and computes $W = C^{(w_1 + vw_2)}$,[2] $Y = C^{(y_1 + vy_2)}$[3] and $Z = (s_{z_1} \uplus s_{z_2}^{(v)}, s_{-z_1} \uplus s_{-z_2}^{(v)})$. Then the public key is $(S_1^{(1)}, S_1^{(v)}, W, Y, Z)$ and the secret key is $(w_1, w_2, y_1, y_2, z_1, z_2)$.

• **Key Encapsulation Algorithm.** Let the order pairs of U_1 and U_2 be (u_{11}, u_{12}) and (u_{21}, u_{22}) respectively. The key encapsulation algorithm computes λ, $d_\pm$ and $K = (k_1, k_2)$ as follows:

$$\lambda = H(U_1, U_2), \quad d_\pm = s_{\pm(w_1 + y_1\lambda)}(u_{11}, u_{12}) \uplus s_{\pm(w_2 + y_2\lambda)}(u_{21}, u_{22}),$$

$$k_1 = s_{z_1}(u_{11}, u_{12}) \uplus s_{z_2}(u_{21}, u_{22}), \quad k_2 = s_{-z_1}(u_{11}, u_{12}) \uplus s_{-z_2}(u_{21}, u_{22}).$$

Then, the ciphertext is $(U_1, U_2, d_\pm)$ and the encapsulated key is $K = (k_1, k_2)$.

---

[2] Given $S_1^{(v)}$, one can easily find its corresponding polynomial, say $f_v(x)$; and obtain its roots in $GF(p^{3e})$, say a root representation, $C^{(v)} = (c_2^{(v)}, c_1^{(v)}, c_0^{(v)})$. Then $C^{(vw_2)}$ can be computed by taking the exponentiation of $C^{(v)}$ by w_2. Similarly, one can obtain $C^{(w_1)} = (c_2^{(w_1)}, c_1^{(w_1)}, c_0^{(w_1)})$. Hence W is obtained by multiplying $C^{(w_1)}$ and $C^{(vw_2)}$ modulo $f(x)$.

[3] The computation of Y is similar to 2.

- **Key Decapsulation Algorithm.** Given a $(U'_1, U'_2, d'_\pm)$ query, let the order pairs of U'_1 and U'_2 be (u'_{11}, u'_{12}) and (u'_{21}, u'_{22}) respectively. The key decapsulation algorithm first computes $\lambda' = H(U'_1, U'_2)$, $d''_\pm$ and $K' = (k'_1, k'_2)$ as follows:

$$d''_\pm = s_{\pm(w_1 + y_1 \lambda')}(u'_{11}, u'_{12}) \uplus s_{\pm(w_2 + y_2 \lambda')}(u'_{21}, u'_{22}),$$

$$k'_1 = s_{z_1}(u'_{11}, u'_{12}) \uplus s_{z_2}(u'_{21}, u'_{22}) \quad \text{and} \quad k'_2 = s_{-z_1}(u'_{11}, u'_{12}) \uplus s_{-z_2}(u'_{21}, u'_{22}).$$

If $d''_\pm = d'_\pm$, then output K', otherwise reject.

With the above constructed simulator, we first prove the following three lemmas which will be used to prove Theorem 3:

Lemma 2. *If a tuple $(S_1^{(1)}, S_1^{(v)}, U_1, U_2)$ input to the simulator is from the distribution D, then an adversary cannot distinguish the behaviour of the simulator from the actual key encapsulation scheme.*

Proof : Let the order pairs of U_1 and U_2 be (u_{11}, u_{12}) and (u_{21}, u_{22}) respectively. Given a tuple $(S_1^{(1)}, S_1^{(v)}, U_1, U_2)$ from the distribution D, then there exists a r such that $u_{11} = s_r(s_1, s_{-1})$, $u_{12} = s_{-r}(s_1, s_{-1})$, $u_{21} = s_r(s_1^{(v)}, s_{-1}^{(v)})$ and $u_{22} = s_{-r}(s_1^{(v)}, s_{-1}^{(v)})$. We will show that the simulator's responses are statistically indistinguishable from the actual key encapsulation scheme in the following two cases; that is, the key encapsulation query and key decapsulation query.
(i) In key encapsulation query, the simulator computes $\lambda = H(U_1, U_2)$, K and $d_\pm$ as follows:

$$
\begin{aligned}
K &= (s_{z_1}(u_{11}, u_{12}) \uplus s_{z_2}(u_{21}, u_{22}), s_{-z_1}(u_{11}, u_{12}) \uplus s_{-z_2}(u_{21}, u_{22})) \\
&= (s_{z_1}(s_r, s_{-r}) \uplus s_{z_2}(s_r^{(v)}, s_{-r}^{(v)}), s_{-z_1}(s_r, s_{-r}) \uplus s_{-z_2}(s_r^{(v)}, s_{-r}^{(v)})) \\
&= (s_r^{(z_1 + vz_2)}, s_{-r}^{(z_1 + vz_2)}) \quad \text{by Lemma 1} \\
&= (s_r(z_{11}, z_{12}), s_{-r}(z_{11}, z_{12})) \quad \text{where } Z = (z_{11}, z_{12}), \\
d_\pm &= s_{\pm(w_1 + y_1 \lambda)}(u_{11}, u_{12}) \uplus s_{\pm(w_2 + y_2 \lambda)}(u_{21}, u_{22}) \\
&= s_{\pm(w_1 + y_1 \lambda)}(s_r, s_{-r}) \uplus s_{\pm(w_2 + y_2 \lambda)}(s_r^{(v)}, s_{-r}^{(v)}) \\
&= s_{\pm r}^{(w_1 + vw_2)} \uplus s_{\pm r \lambda}^{(y_1 + vy_2)} \quad \text{by Theorem 1(b) and Lemma 1(b)} \\
&= s_{\pm r}(w_{11}, w_{12}) \uplus s_{\pm r \lambda}(y_{11}, y_{12})
\end{aligned}
$$

where $W = (w_{11}, w_{12})$ and $Y = (y_{11}, y_{12})$.[4] From the above computation of K and $d_\pm$, the distribution of the simulator response is identical to the distribution of the actual key encapsulation scheme with the response $(U_1, U_2, d_\pm)$ and the encapsulated key K if the selected random δ equals to 0, otherwise, output random $\overline{K}$.

---

[4] As W and Y are the elements in $GF(p^{3e})$, one can compute $W^{p^{ie}}$ and $Y^{p^{ie}}$ for $i = 1, 2$ and obtain its corresponding polynomials $f^{(W)}(x)$ and $f^{(Y)}(x)$ respectively. Then, w_{11}, w_{12} and y_{11}, y_{12} are the coefficients of polynomials $f^{(W)}(x)$ and $f^{(Y)}(x)$ respectively.

(ii) In key decapsulation query, given a $(U_1', U_2', d_\pm')$ query, let the order pairs of U_1' and U_2' be (u_{11}', u_{12}') and (u_{21}', u_{22}') respectively. We consider two types of queries, that is, a valid and an invalid query, as follows:

(a) If $(U_1', U_2', d_\pm')$ is a valid query, then there exists t such that $u_{11}' = s_t(s_1, s_{-1})$, $u_{12}' = s_{-t}(s_1, s_{-1})$, $u_{21}' = s_t(s_1^{(v)}, s_{-1}^{(v)})$ and $u_{22}' = s_{-t}(s_1^{(v)}, s_{-1}^{(v)})$. The key decapsulation oracle computes $\lambda' = H(U_1', U_2')$ and $d_\pm''$ as follows:

$$d_\pm'' = s_{\pm(w_1 + y_1 \lambda')}(u_{11}', u_{12}') \uplus s_{\pm(w_2 + y_2 \lambda')}(u_{21}', u_{22}')$$
$$= s_{\pm t(w_1 + vw_2)} \uplus s_{\pm t \lambda'(y_1 + vy_2)} \qquad \text{by Lemma 1(b)}.$$

If $d_\pm' \neq d_\pm''$, then both the simulator and the actual key encapsulation scheme will reject $(U_1', U_2', d_\pm')$ or else output K' computed as follows:

$$K' = (s_{z_1}(u_{11}', u_{12}') \uplus s_{z_2}(u_{21}', u_{22}'), s_{-z_1}(u_{11}', u_{12}') \uplus s_{-z_2}(u_{21}', u_{22}'))$$
$$= (s_t(z_{11}, z_{12}), s_{-t}(z_{11}, z_{12})) \quad \text{where } Z = (z_{11}, z_{12}).$$

Hence, both the simulator and the actual key encapsulation scheme output the same encapsulated key K'.

(b) If $(U_1', U_2', d_\pm')$ is an invalid query, then there exists $r_1' \neq r_2'$ such that $u_{11}' = s_{r_1'}(s_1, s_{-1})$, $u_{12}' = s_{-r_1'}(s_1, s_{-1})$, $u_{21}' = s_{r_2'}(s_1^{(v)}, s_{-1}^{(v)})$ and $u_{22}' = s_{-r_2'}(s_1^{(v)}, s_{-1}^{(v)})$. To answer the query, the key decapsulation oracle computes

$$d_\pm'' = s_{\pm(w_1 + y_1 \lambda')}(u_{11}', u_{12}') \uplus s_{\pm(w_2 + y_2 \lambda')}(u_{21}', u_{22}')$$
$$= s_{\pm(w_1 + y_1 \lambda')}(s_{r_1'}, s_{-r_1'}) \uplus s_{\pm(w_2 + y_2 \lambda')}(s_{r_2'}^{(v)}, s_{-r_2'}^{(v)})$$
$$= s_{\pm(w_1 r_1' + vw_2 r_2' + y_1 \lambda' r_1' + vy_2 \lambda' r_2')} \qquad \text{by Theorem 1(b) and Lemma 1(a)}.$$

To reject an invalid ciphertext $(U_1', U_2', d_\pm')$ depends on the quadruple (w_1, w_2, y_1, y_2). Let $\log_s C^{(w)} = \log_s S_1^{(w)} = \min_{0 \leq i \leq 2}\{wp^{ie} \bmod q\}$.[5] Without loss of generality, we write $\log_s C^{(w)} = \log_s S_1^{(w)} = w$. From the given public key $C^{(w_1 + vw_2)}$ and $C^{(y_1 + vy_2)}$, and the computed value $d_\pm''$, we have the following equations:

$$\log_s C^{(w_1 + vw_2)} = w_1 + vw_2 \tag{1}$$
$$\log_s C^{(y_1 + vy_2)} = y_1 + vy_2 \tag{2}$$
$$\log_s d_\pm = w_1 r + vw_2 r + y_1 \lambda r + vy_2 \lambda r \tag{3}$$
$$\log_s d_\pm'' = w_1 r_1' + vw_2 r_2' + y_1 \lambda' r_1' + vy_2 \lambda' r_2' \tag{4}$$

Let $\bar{a} = \log_s C^{(w_1 + vw_2)}$, $\bar{b} = \log_s C^{(y_1 + vy_2)}$ and $\bar{d} = \log_s d_\pm''$. Since equation (3) is dependent on equation (1) and (2) as $\log_s d_\pm = r\bar{a} + \lambda r\bar{b} = r(\bar{a} + \lambda\bar{b})$, there is no information leak on (w_1, w_2, y_1, y_2) and there is still q^2 possibilities for the quadruple (w_1, w_2, y_1, y_2). From equation (1), (2) and (4), we have $\bar{d} = r_1'(\bar{a} + \bar{b}\lambda') + v(r_2' - r_1')(w_2 + y_2\lambda')$. Therefore, each time an invalid ciphertext is rejected, it eliminates at most $3q$ of the q^2 possible quadruples (w_1, w_2, y_1, y_2). This follows

---

[5] As $S_1^{(w)}$ and $C^{(w)}$ represent the same polynomial $f_w(x)$, $\log_s$ is a coset leader and is well-defined.

that the oracle rejects the first invalid ciphertext submitted by the adversary with probability $1 - 3/q$. For the subsequent i-th query, the simulator rejects the invalid i-th ciphertext submitted by the adversary with the probability of at least $1 - 3/(q - 3(i - 1))$ for $i = 1, 2, \cdots, n$ for the n queries. Hence, the key decapsulation oracle rejects all invalid ciphertexts, except with negligible probability at most $3 \sum_i^n \frac{1}{q-3(i-1)}$.

Lemma 3. *If a tuple $(S_1^{(1)}, S_1^{(v)}, U_1, U_2)$ input to the simulator is from the distribution R, then the simulator rejects all invalid ciphertexts with overwhelming probability.*

Proof : Given a $(S_1^{(1)}, S_1^{(v)}, U_1, U_2)$ from the distribution R, let the order pairs of U_1 and U_2 be (u_{11}, u_{12}) and (u_{21}, u_{22}) respectively, then there exists $r_1 \neq r_2$ such that $u_{11} = s_{r_1}(s_1, s_{-1})$, $u_{12} = s_{-r_1}(s_1, s_{-1})$, $u_{21} = s_{r_2}(s_1^{(v)}, s_{-1}^{(v)})$ and $u_{22} = s_{-r_2}(s_1^{(v)}, s_{-1}^{(v)})$. We have $\lambda = H(U_1, U_2)$ and

$$
\begin{aligned}
K &= (s_{z_1}(u_{11}, u_{12}) \uplus s_{z_2}(u_{21}, u_{22}), s_{-z_1}(u_{11}, u_{12}) \uplus s_{-z_2}(u_{21}, u_{22})) \\
&= (s_{r_1 z_1 + r_2 v z_2}, s_{-(r_1 z_1 + r_2 v z_2)}) \quad (5) \\
d_{\pm} &= s_{\pm(w_1 + y_1 \lambda)}(u_{11}, u_{12}) \uplus s_{\pm(w_2 + y_2 \lambda)}(u_{21}, u_{22}) \\
&= s_{\pm(w_1 r_1 + v w_2 r_2 + y_1 \lambda r_1 + v y_2 \lambda r_2)}. \quad (6)
\end{aligned}
$$

Now, given a $(U_1', U_2', d_{\pm}')$ in key decapsulation query and let the order pairs of U_1' and U_2' be (u_{11}', u_{12}') and (u_{21}', u_{22}') respectively, the simulator computes $\lambda' = H(U_1', U_2')$. If $(U_1', U_2', d_{\pm}')$ is an invalid query, then there exists $r_1' \neq r_2'$ such that $u_{11}' = s_{r_1'}(s_1, s_{-1})$, $u_{12}' = s_{-r_1'}(s_1, s_{-1})$, $u_{21}' = s_{r_2'}(s_1^{(v)}, s_{-1}^{(v)})$ and $u_{22}' = s_{-r_2'}(s_1^{(v)}, s_{-1}^{(v)})$, and compute $d_{\pm}''$ as follows:

$$
\begin{aligned}
d_{\pm}'' &= s_{\pm(w_1 + y_1 \lambda')}(u_{11}', u_{12}') \uplus s_{\pm(w_2 + y_2 \lambda')}(u_{21}', u_{22}') \\
&= s_{\pm(w_1 r_1' + v w_2 r_2' + y_1 \lambda' r_1' + v y_2 \lambda' r_2')} \quad (7)
\end{aligned}
$$

Now, we consider the following three cases:
(a) $(U_1', U_2') = (U_1, U_2)$: In this case, the hash values must be the same, but $d_{\pm}' \neq d_{\pm}$. This implies that the key decapsulation oracle rejects the ciphertext.
(b) $(U_1', U_2') \neq (U_1, U_2)$ and $\lambda = \lambda'$: This is a collision for the target (U_1, U_2), which contradicts the assumption that H is a collision resistant one way hash function.
(c) $(U_1', U_2') \neq (U_1, U_2)$ and $\lambda \neq \lambda'$: The query is rejected if $d_{\pm}'' \neq d_{\pm}'$, but equations (1), (2), (6) and (7) are linearly independent as their determinant is non-zero and computed as follows:

$$
\det \begin{pmatrix} 1 & v & 0 & 0 \\ 0 & 0 & 1 & v \\ r_1 & v r_2 & \lambda r_1 & v \lambda r_2 \\ r_1' & v r_2' & \lambda' r_1' & v \lambda' r_2' \end{pmatrix} = v^2(\lambda' - \lambda)(r_2 - r_1)(r_1' - r_2') \neq 0.
$$

Hence, the key decapsulation oracle rejects all invalid queries except with negligible probability.

Lemma 4. *If a tuple $(S_1^{(1)}, S_1^{(v)}, U_1, U_2)$ input to the simulator is from the distribution R and K (the encapsulated key) is the response of the key encapsulation queries, then an adversary cannot distinguish K from a uniformly distributed random value.*

Proof : Since $Z = (s_{z_1} \uplus s_{z_2}^{(v)}, s_{-z_1} \uplus s_{-z_2}^{(v)}) = (s_{z_1+vz_2}, s_{-(z_1+vz_2)})$, then the public key provides a linear equation $\log_s Z = z_1 + vz_2$ and $p^{ie} \log_s Z$ where $i = 1, 2$. Given a key decapsulation query of $(U_1', U_2', d_\pm')$, let the order pairs of U_1' and U_2' be (u_{11}', u_{12}') and (u_{21}', u_{22}') respectively. We want to show that if the simulator rejects all invalid queries, then the adversary is infeasible to distinguish K from a randomly distributed value.

If $(U_1', U_2', d_\pm')$ is a valid key decapsulation query, then there exists t such that $u_{11}' = s_t(s_1, s_{-1})$, $u_{12}' = s_{-t}(s_1, s_{-1})$, $u_{21}' = s_t(s_1^{(v)}, s_{-1}^{(v)})$ and $u_{22}' = s_{-t}(s_1^{(v)}, s_{-1}^{(v)})$. Then $\log_s K' = t(z_1 + vz_2) = t \log_s Z$ and $tp^{ie} \log_s Z$, for $i = 1, 2$, which is a linear equation. This implies that there is no leak of the information of z_1, z_2. Now, considering the key K produced by the simulator's key encapsulation oracle on input $(S_1^{(1)}, S_1^{(v)}, U_1, U_2)$ and from equation (5), we have $\log_s K = r_1 z_1 + r_2 v z_2$ which is linearly independent of $\log_s Z = z_1 + v z_2$ as

$$\det \begin{pmatrix} 1 & v \\ r_1 & vr_2 \end{pmatrix} = v(r_1 - r_2) \neq 0.$$

Therefore, there is no information leak about K with a given public key Z.

Proof (Proof of Theorem 3): From Lemma 2, if the input to the simulator is from the distribution D, then an adversary will have a non-negligible advantage in distinguishing an actual encapsulated key from a random one. From Lemma 3 and 4, if the input to the simulator is from the distribution R, then the adversary is not able to distinguish an actual encapsulated key from the random one. If an adversary is able to break the key encapsulation scheme, then the adversary is able to distinguish an actual encapsulated key from the random one. Hence, the adversary is able to distinguish the distribution D from the distribution R. This contradicts the SR-DDH assumption.

5   Conclusion

In this paper, we proposed a new key encapsulation scheme based on a third order linear feedback shift register over $GF(p^{3e})$ and showed that this scheme is secure against adaptive chosen ciphertext attack (CCA2) under shift register based decisional Diffie-Hellman assumption (SR-DDH) in the standard model. Furthermore, this scheme is more efficient as compared to Cramer-Shoup [10] and Lucks scheme [20] in term of key sizes and computational complexity. Hence, the proposed scheme is an efficient and provably secure key encapsulation scheme. Furthermore, the idea of this construction might be able to extend to other schemes, for example, threshold encryption scheme, etc.

References

[1] M. Abdalla, M. Bellare and P. Rogaway. The Oracle Diffie-Hellman Assumptions and an Analysis of DHIES, *Topics in Cryptology - CT-RSA 2001*, Lecture Notes in Computer Science Vol. 2020, Springer-Verlag, (2001) 143–158.

[2] J. Baek, B. Lee and K. Kim. Secure length-saving ElGamal encryption under the computational Diffie-Hellman assumption, *Information Security and Privacy-ACISP'00*, Lecture Notes in Computer Science, Vol. 1841, Springer-Verlag, (2000) 49–58.

[3] M. Bellare and P. Rogaway. Random oracles are practical: a paradigm for designing efficient protocols, *First ACM Conference on Computer and Communications Security*, ACM press, (1993) 62–73.

[4] M. Bellare and P. Rogaway. Optimal asymmetric encryption, *Advances in Cryptology - Eurocrypt'94*, Lecture Notes in Computer Science Vol. 950, Springer-Verlag, (1995) 92–111.

[5] M. Bellare, A. Desai, D. Pointcheval and P. Rogaway. Relations among notions of security proofs and improvements, *Advances in Cryptology - Crypto'98*, Lecture Notes in Computer Science Vol. 1462, Springer-Verlag, (1998) 26–45.

[6] A. E. Brouwer, R. Pellikaan and E. R. Verheul. Doing more with fewer bits, *Advances in Cryptology - Asiacrypt'99*, Lecture Notes in Computer Science Vol. 1716, Springer-Verlag, (1999) 321–332.

[7] J. Buchmann, K. Sakurai, T. Takagi. An IND-CCA2 Public-Key Cryptosystem with Fast Decryption, *Information Security and Cryptology - ICISC 2001*, Lecture Notes in Computer Science Vol. 2288, Springer-Verlag, (2002) 51–71.

[8] R. Canetti, O. Goldreich and S. Halevi. The random oracle methodology, revisited, *The 30th Annual ACM Symposium on Theory of Computing - STOC'98*, ACM press, (1998) 209–218.

[9] R. Canetti and S. Goldwasser. An efficient threshold public key cryptosystem secure against adaptive chosen ciphertext attack, *Advances in Cryptology - Eurocrypt'99*, Lecture Notes in Computer Science Vol. 1592, Springer-Verlag, (1999) 90–106.

[10] R. Cramer and V. Shoup. A practical public key cryptosystem provably secure against adaptive chosen ciphertext attack, *Advances in Cryptology - Crypto'98*, Lecture Notes in Computer Science Vol. 1462, Springer-Verlag, (1998) 13–25.

[11] R. Cramer and V. Shoup. Universal hash proofs and paradigm for adaptive chosen ciphertext secure public-key encryption, *Advances in Cryptology - Eurocrypt'02*, Lecture Notes in Computer Science Vol. 2332, Springer-Verlag, (2002) 46–64.

[12] D. Dolev, C. Dwork and M. Naor. Non-malleable cryptography, *The 23rd Annual ACM Symposium on Theory of Computing - STOC'91*, ACM press, (1991) 542–552.

[13] D. Dolev, C. Dwork and M. Naor. Non-malleable cryptography, *SIAM J. Computing*, vol.30, no.2, (2000) 391–437.

[14] T. ElGamal, A public key cryptosystem and a signature scheme based on discrete logarithms, *IEEE Transaction on Information Theory*, vol. 31, no.4, (1985) 469–472.

[15] S. Goldwasser and S. Micali. Probabilistic encryption, *J. Computer and System Sciences*, vol. 28, (1984) 270–299.

[16] G. Gong and L. Harn. Public key cryptosystems based on cubic finite field extensions, *IEEE Transaction on Information Theory*, vol.45, no.7, (1999) 2601–2605.

[17] A. Joux and K. Nguyen. Separating decision Diffie-Hellman from Diffie-Hellman in cryptographic groups, available from eprint.iacr.org.

[18] K. Kurosawa, W. Ogata, T. Matsuo and S. Makishima. IND-CCA public key schemes equivalent to factoring $n = pq$, *Public Key Cryptography – PKC 2001*, Lecture Notes in Computer Science, Vol. 1992, Springer-Verlag, (2001) 36–47.

[19] A. K. Lenstra and E. R. Verheul. The XTR public key System, *Advances in Cryptology – Crypto'00*, Lecture Notes in Computer Science Vol. 1880, Springer-Verlag, (2000) 1–19.

[20] S. Lucks. A variant of the Cramer-Shoup cryptosystem for groups of unknown order, *Advances in Cryptology – Asiacrypt'02*, Lecture Notes in Computer Science Vol. 2501, Springer-Verlag, (2002) 27–45.

[21] U. M. Maurer and S. Wolf. The relationship between breaking the Diffie-Hellman Protocol and Computing Discrete Logarithms, *SIAM J. Computing*, vol.28, no.5, (1999) 1689–1721.

[22] S. Müller. On the security of a William based public key encryption scheme, *Public Key Cryptography – PKC'01*, Lecture Notes in Computer Science Vol. 1992, Springer-Verlag, (2001) 1–18.

[23] M. Naor and M. Yung. Public-key cryptosystems provably secure against chosen ciphertext attacks, *The 22nd Annual ACM Symposium on Theory of Computing – STOC'90*, ACM press, (1990) 427–437.

[24] C. Rackoff and D. Simon. Non-interactive zero-knowledge proof of knowledge and chosen ciphertext attack, *Advances in Cryptology – Crypto'91*, Lecture Notes in Computer Science Vol. 576, Springer-Verlag, (1991) 46–64.

[25] C. P. Schnorr and M. Jakobsson. Security of signed ElGamal encryption, *Advances in Cryptology–Asiacrypt'00*, Lecture Notes in Computer Science, Vol. 1976, Springer-Verlag, (2000) 73–89.

[26] C. H. Tan, X. Yi and C. K. Siew. Signature schemes based on 3rd order shift registers, *Information Security and Privacy-ACISP'01*, Lecture Notes in Computer Science, Vol. 2119, Springer-Verlag, (2001) 445–459.

[27] C. H. Tan, X. Yi and C. K. Siew. New signature schemes based on 3rd order shift registers, *IEICE Transaction on Fundamentals*, vol.E85-A, no.1, Jan, (2002) 102–109.

[28] C. H. Tan, X. Yi and C. K. Siew. Computation of signature schemes based on 3rd order shift registers, *The International Conference on Fundamentals, Electronics, Communications and Computer Sciences*, Tokyo, Japan, 2002.

[29] C. H. Tan, X. Yi and C. K. Siew. On Diffie-Hellman Problems in 3rd Order Shift Register, to be published in *IEICE Transaction on Fundamentals*.

[30] Y. Tsiounis and M. Yung. On the security of ElGamal based encryption, *Public Key Cryptography 1998 – PKC'98*, Lecture Notes in Computer Science Vol. 1431, Springer-Verlag, (1998) 117–134.

[31] Y. Zheng and J. Seberry. Practical approaches to attaining security against adaptively chosen ciphertext attacks, *Advances in Cryptology–Crypto'92*, Lecture Notes in Computer Science, Vol. 740, Springer-Verlag, (1992) 292–304.

Clock-Controlled Shrinking Generator of Feedback Shift Registers

Ali Kanso

Department of Mathematics
King Fahd University of Petroleum and Minerals
PO Box 2440, Hail, KSA
akanso@hotmail.com

Abstract. A system related to the shrinking generator that is made up of two feedback shift registers in which one (FSR $\mathbb{A}$) controls the clocking of the other (FSR $\mathbb{B}$) is introduced. It is established that if FSR $\mathbb{A}$ generates an m-sequence of period $(2^m - 1)$ and FSR $\mathbb{B}$ generates a de Bruijn sequence of period 2^n, then the output sequence of the system has period $P = 2^{m+n-1}$, linear complexity L bounded from below by 2^{m+n-2}, good statistical properties, and it is secure against correlation attacks. All these properties make it a suitable crypto-generator for stream cipher applications.

1 Introduction

Keystream sequence generators that produce sequences with large periods, high linear complexities and good statistical properties are very useful as building blocks for stream cipher applications. The use of clock-controlled generators in keystream generators appears to be a good way of achieving sequences with these properties [1].

In this paper, a clock-controlled generator composed of two feedback shift registers (FSRs) [2], FSR $\mathbb{A}$ and FSR $\mathbb{B}$ is introduced; The first is clocked normally, but the second is clocked by one plus the integer value represented in selected w fixed stages of the first register. FSRs $\mathbb{A}$ and $\mathbb{B}$ are called the control and generating registers of the system respectively. The output bits of the system are produced by shrinking the output of FSR $\mathbb{B}$ under the control of FSR $\mathbb{A}$ as follows: At any time t, the output of FSR $\mathbb{B}$ is taken if the current output of FSR $\mathbb{A}$ is 1; Otherwise it is discarded.

Suppose that the control register $\mathbb{A}$ has m stages and characteristic feedback function R. Similarly, suppose that the generating register $\mathbb{B}$ has n stages and characteristic feedback function T. Let $\underline{A}_0 = A_0(0), ..., A_{m-1}(0)$ and $\underline{B}_0 = B_0(0), ..., B_{n-1}(0)$ be the initial states of $\mathbb{A}$ and $\mathbb{B}$ respectively.

The initial state of the system at time $t = 0$ is given by: $\underline{S}_0 = (\underline{A}_0, \underline{B}_0)$.

Define a function F that acts on the state of $\mathbb{A}$ at a given time t to determine the number of times $\mathbb{B}$ is clocked such that: At any time t,

$$F(\underline{A}_t) = (1 + 2^0 A_{i_0}(t) + 2^1 A_{i_1}(t) + ... + 2^{w-1} A_{i_{w-1}}(t)), \qquad (1)$$

for $w < m$, and distinct integres $i_0, i_1, ..., i_{w-1} \in \{0, 1, ..., m-1\}$.

If no stages are selected (i.e. $w = 0$), define $F(\underline{A}_t) = 1$.

R. Safavi-Naini and J. Seberry (Eds.): ACISP 2003, LNCS 2727, pp. 443–451, 2003.
© Springer-Verlag Berlin Heidelberg 2003

Define the cumulative function of $\mathbb{A}$ to be $G_A : \{0, 1, 2, ...\} \rightarrow \{0, 1, 2, ...\}$ where:

$$G_A(t) = \sum_{i=0}^{t-1} F(\underline{A}_i) \tag{2}$$

for $t > 0$, and $G_A(0) = 0$.

The state of the system at time t is given by: $\underline{S}_t = (\underline{A}_t, \underline{B}_{G_A(t)})$.

At any time t, the output of the system is the content of the 0th stage of FSR $\mathbb{B}$ [i.e. $B_0(G_A(t))$] if $A_0(t)$ is 1; Otherwise there is no output.

The system may also be described in terms of the two output sequences (A_t) and (B_t) of the feedback shift registers $\mathbb{A}$ and $\mathbb{B}$ respectively.

Acting on their own, suppose that FSR $\mathbb{A}$ and FSR $\mathbb{B}$ produce output sequences $(A_t) = A_0, A_1, ...$ and $(B_t) = B_0, B_1, ...$ respectively. The sequences (A_t) and (B_t) are called the control sequence and the generating sequence of the system respectively and referred to as component sequences.

Define a function $G_e : \{0, 1, 2, ...\} \rightarrow \{0, 1, 2, ...\}$ as follows: Let $t\prime \geq 0$ and suppose that $A_{t\prime} = 1$. Let t be the total number of ones in $A_0, A_1, ..., A_{t\prime}$ then $G_e(t-1) = G_A(t\prime)$.

The output sequence (Z_t) of the system whose control sequence and generating sequence are (A_t) and (B_t) respectively is given by: $Z_t = B_{G_e(t)}$.

2   Properties of the Output Sequence $(\mathbf{Z_t})$

Suppose that $\mathbb{A}$ is an m-stage linear feedback shift register with initial state $\underline{A}_0$ and characteristic feedback function R (associated with a primitive polynomial $f(x)$ of degree m). Then the output sequence (A_t) of $\mathbb{A}$ is an m-sequence and it has period $M = (2^m - 1)$ [see 2]. Suppose that $\mathbb{B}$ is an η-stage (i.e. $n = \eta$) non-linear feedback shift register with initial state $\underline{B}_0$ and characteristic feedback function T defined as follows: At time t,

$$T(B_0(t), B_1(t), ..., B_{\eta-1}(t)) = T'(B_0(t), B_1(t), ..., B_{\eta-1}(t)) \oplus \prod_{j=1}^{\eta-1}(1 \oplus B_j(t)),$$
$$\tag{3}$$

where T' is the feedback function associated with a primitive polynomial $g(x)$ of degree η. Then the output sequence (B_t) of $\mathbb{B}$ is a de Bruijn sequence of span η and it has period $N = 2^\eta$ [see 2]. The effect of the above formula is to insert an extra $'0'$ to the end of each subsequence of $(\eta - 1)$ zeroes occuring in the m-sequence of period $(2^\eta - 1)$ generated using the primitive η-stage LFSR of initial state $\underline{B}_0$ and characteristic feedback function T' (associated with the primitive polynomial $g(x)$ of degree η). We will call the family of de Bruijn sequences generated in the above way special de Bruijn sequences.

Let (Z_t) be the output sequence of the system whose component sequences are (A_t) and (B_t).

In a full period $M = (2^m - 1)$ of (A_t) every non-zero subsequence of length $j \leq m$ occurs 2^{m-j} times, and the all-zero subsequence of length $k < m$ occurs $(2^{m-k} - 1)$ times [2]. Thus, after clocking $\mathbb{A}$ M times, $\mathbb{B}$ is clocked $G_A(M) = (2^{m-w} - 1)(1) + 2^{m-w}(2 + 3 + ... + 2^w) = 2^{m-w}(1 + 2 + 3 + ... + 2^w) - 1 = 2^{m-w}(2^w(2^w + 1)/2) - 1 = (2^{m-1}(2^w + 1) - 1)$ times.

Similarly, in a full period $N = 2^\eta$ of (B_t) every subsequence of length $j \leq \eta$ occurs $2^{\eta-j}$ times [2].

Let M_1 be the total number of ones in a full period $M = (2^m - 1)$ of (A_t). [i.e. $M_1 = 2^{m-1}$]

The following lemmas show that the output sequence (Z_t) has period $P = 2^{m+\eta-1}$, and linear complexity L bounded from below by $2^{m+\eta-2}$. Finally, it is shown that the collection of the output sequences of the system has good statistical properties.

2.1   Period and Linear Complexity of (Z_t)

After $M(lcm(G_A(M), N)/G_A(M))$ clock pulses have been applied to $\mathbb{A}$, $lcm(G_A(M), N)$ clock pulses will have been applied to $\mathbb{B}$. Then both $\mathbb{A}$ and $\mathbb{B}$ return to their initial states $\underline{A_0}$ and $\underline{B_0}$. Hence the state sequence of the generator is periodic with period dividing $M(lcm(G_A(M), N)/G_A(M)) = MN/gcd(G_A(M), N)$.

The system produces an output whenever the 0th stage of $\mathbb{A}$ contains a 1. Therefore, after $lcm(G_A(M), N)$ clock pulses have been applied to $\mathbb{B}$ the system produces $M_1 N/gcd(G_A(M), N)$ output bits. Hence, the period P_Z of the sequence (Z_t) is a divisor of $M_1 N/gcd(G_A(M), N)$.

The following two lemmas, that are generalizations of the results of Coppersmith et al on the Shrinking Generator SG [3], can be applied to the output sequence of this system.

Lemma 1. *If the length m of $\mathbb{A}$ satisfies $m < 2^{\eta-w}$ (i.e. $w < \eta - \log_2 m$) [where w is the number of selected fixed stages], and $gcd(G_A(M), N) = 1$, then the period P_Z of the sequence (Z_t) is equal to $M_1 N = 2^{m+\eta-1}$.*

Proof. Recall that $Z_i = B_{G_e(i)}$.

Fact 1: Recall that in a full period of (A_t) the number of ones is M_1, so when considering a full period of (A_t) there are M_1 outputs Z_i and the sequence (B_t) advances $G_A(M)$ places, so $(\forall j \geq 0)$

$$Z_{i+jM_1} = B_{G_e(i)+jG_A(M)}. \tag{4}$$

Fact 2: Let k, k' be any pair of indices. If $\forall j$: $B_{k+jG_A(M)} = B_{k'+jG_A(M)}$, then N divides $(k - k')$.

Proof of fact 2: Define a sequence (C_t) where $C_t = B_{tG_A(M)}$ $\forall t \geq 0$. The sequence (C_t) is a decimation of (B_t) by $G_A(M)$. As $gcd(G_A(M), N) = 1$ and (B_t) has period N, then the sequence (C_t) also has period N.

Now if $B_{k+jG_A(M)} = B_{k'+jG_A(M)}$ $\forall j \geq 0$, then the translates (C_{t+h}) and $(C_{t+h'})$ are equal where $k = hG_A(M)(mod\ N)$ and $k' = h'G_A(M)(mod\ N)$. Hence N divides $(h - h')$ so that N divides $(h - h')G_A(M)$ i.e. N divides $(k - k')$.

We now proceed with the main proof.

Let P_Z be the period of the sequence (Z_t). By the argument given above P_Z must divide $M_1 N / gcd(G_A(M), N) = M_1 N$.

Now we proceed to show that $M_1 N$ divides P_Z.

By definition, $Z_i = Z_{i+P_Z}$. In particular, $\forall \, i, j : Z_{i+jM_1} = Z_{i+P_Z+jM_1}$.

Using (eqn 4), we get $\forall \, i, j : B_{G_e(i)+jG_A(M)} = B_{G_e(i+P_z)+jG_A(M)}$.

Using (fact 2), we have $\forall \, i$:

$$N \; divides \; G_e(i + P_Z) - G_e(i). \tag{5}$$

Our next step is to show that (eqn 5) is possible only if M_1 divides P_Z. We rewrite (eqn 5) as follows: $\forall \, i, \exists \, j_i$:

$$G_e(i + P_Z) = G_e(i) + j_i N. \tag{6}$$

Putting $(i + 1)$ instead of (i) in (eqn 6) we get:

$$G_e(i + 1 + P_Z) = G_e(i + 1) + j_{i+1} N. \tag{7}$$

Subtracting (eqn 6) from (eqn 7) we get: $\forall \, i$:

$$G_e(i + P_Z + 1) - G_e(i + P_Z) = G_e(i + 1) - G_e(i) + (j_{i+1} - j_i)N. \tag{8}$$

Notice that, $G_e(i + 1) - G_e(i) \leq m2^w$ since we can not have more than $(m - 1)$ consecutive zeroes in the m-stage LFSR $\mathbb{A}$.

If $j_{i+1} - j_i$ were different than zero, it would imply that $N \leq m2^w$, which is impossible assuming $m < N2^{-w}$. Therefore, we get $(j_{i+1} - j_i = 0)$, and then $\forall \, i : G_e(i + 1 + P_Z) - G_e(i + P_Z) = G_e(i + 1) - G_e(i)$.

The latter implies that the translate of (A_t) starting at $A_{i\prime}$ [where $G_e(i) = G_A(i\prime)$, and $A_{i\prime} = 1$] is identical to the translate starting at $A_{(i+P_Z)\prime}$. This means that M divides $((i + P_Z)\prime - i\prime)$, or equivalently, that the number of elements in the sequence (A_t) between $A_{i\prime}$ and $A_{(i+P_Z)\prime}$ is a multiple of its period. But then the number of ones in this segment is a multiple of M_1. On the other hand, the number of ones is exactly P_Z, thus proving that M_1 divides P_Z.

Let h be such that:

$$P_Z = hM_1. \tag{9}$$

We have $\forall \, j$:

$$B_{G_e(0)} = Z_0 = Z_{jP_Z} = Z_{jhM_1} = B_{G_e(0)+jhG_A(M)}. \tag{10}$$

The last equality follows from (eqn 4). We get that $\forall \, j$:

$$B_{G_e(0)} = B_{G_e(0)+jhG_A(M)}. \tag{11}$$

This implies that N divides $hG_A(M)$, and since $gcd(G_A(M), N) = 1$, then N divides h. From (eqn 9) we get $M_1 N$ divides P_Z.

Hence, the period P_Z of (Z_t) is equal to $M_1 N = 2^{m+\eta-1}$.

Definition 1. *The linear complexity L of a periodic sequence (Z_t) is equal to the degree of its minimal polynomial. The minimal polynomial is defined as the characteristic feedback polynomial of the shortest LFSR that can generate the sequence (Z_t).*

Lemma 2. *If the length m of $\mathbb{A}$ satisfies $m < 2^{\eta-w}$ (i.e. $w < \eta - \log_2 m$), and $gcd(G_A(M), N) = 1$, then the sequence (Z_t) has linear complexity L such that: $L > 2^{m+\eta-2}$.*

Proof. Let $Q(x)$ denote the minimal polynomial of the sequence (Z_t). From the previous lemma the period of (Z_t) is $P_Z = 2^{m+\eta-1}$. Hence over $GF(2)$, $(x^{P_Z} - 1)$ can be written as $(x^{P_Z} - 1) = (x - 1)^{P_Z}$. Thus, the condition $Q(x)$ divides $(x^{P_Z} - 1)$ implies that $Q(x)$ is of the form $Q(x) = (x - 1)^L$ where L is the linear complexity of the sequence (Z_t). We claim that $L > 2^{m+\eta-2}$.

Assume $L \leq 2^{m+\eta-2}$. Then $Q(x) = (x - 1)^L$ would divide $(x - 1)^{2^{m+\eta-2}} = (x^{2^{m+\eta-2}} - 1)$, but then the period of (Z_t) is at most $2^{m+\eta-2}$ [see 4] contradicting lemma 1.

Therefore, the linear complexity L of (Z_t) satisfies: $L > 2^{m+\eta-2}$.

2.2   The Statistical Properties of (Z_t)

In this section, the number of ones and zeroes in a full period $P_Z = 2^{m+\eta-1}$ of the sequence (Z_t) are established. It is also discussed that if one chooses w to be sufficiently less than η, then the collection of the output sequences of the system in which the generating register $\mathbb{B}$ generates the family of special de Bruijn sequences (introduced earlier) has good statistical properties.

The appearance of ones and zeroes in the output sequence (Z_t):
In a full period $M = (2^m - 1)$ of (A_t) the number of ones that appears in the 0th stage of $\mathbb{A}$ is 2^{m-1}. Similarly, in a full period $N = 2^\eta$ of (B_t) the number of ones and zeroes that appears in the 0th stage of $\mathbb{B}$ is $2^{\eta-1}$. If the period of (Z_t) attains its maximum value $P_Z = 2^{m+\eta-1}$, then it is obvious that the number of ones and zeroes in a full period of (Z_t) is $2^{m+\eta-2}$.

It is shown in [5] that the collection of the output sequences of the system whose generating register is the η-stage feedback shift register $\mathbb{B}$ with initial state $\underline{B_0}$ chosen with uniform probability over all initial states of length η and feedback function T where the corresponding feedback function T' is associated with a primitive polynomial $g(x)$ chosen with uniform probability among all primitive polynomials of degree η has good statistical properties.

Next, consider some sample spaces that are used in the following theorem.
Let U_1^A be the sample space of all primitive feedback polynomials of degree m.
Let U_2^A be the sample space of all (non-zero) initial states of length m.
Let V_1^B be the sample space of all primitive feedback polynomials of degree η.
Let V_2^B be the sample space of all initial states of length η.
Define the sample spaces U^A and V^B such that:

$U^A = U_1^A \times U_2^A = \{(f(x), \underline{A_0}) | f(x) \in U_1^A, \underline{A_0} \in U_2^A\}$, and $V^B = V_1^B \times V_2^B = \{(g(x), \underline{B_0}) | g(x) \in V_1^B, \underline{B_0} \in V_2^B\}$.

The following theorem established in [5] states that the distribution of patterns in the collection of output sequences is almost uniform.

Theorem 1. *Let (Z_t) denote the output sequence of a system whose control register $\mathbb{A}$ has initial state $\underline{A_0}$ and characteristic feedback function R associated with the primitive polynomial $f(x)$, and whose generating register $\mathbb{B}$ has initial state $\underline{B_0}$ and characteristic feedback function T where the corresponding feedback function T' is associated with the primitive polynomial $g(x)$. Let the distribution on V^B be uniform [i.e. $P(g(x), \underline{B_0}) = 1/|V^B|$, $\forall (g(x), \underline{B_0}) \in V^B$]. Let k be a positive integer satisfying $(m(k-1)2^w) < 2^\eta$ i.e. $k < (2^{\eta-w}/m + 1)$. Let t_0 be a positive integer and let R_k be the Z_2^k-valued random variable on $U^A \times V^B$ that maps the elementary event $(f(x), \underline{A_0}, g(x), \underline{B_0})$ to the k consecutive output bits of (Z_t) beginning at t_0 i.e. $R_k(f(x), \underline{A_0}, g(x), \underline{B_0}) = Z_{t_0}, Z_{t_0+1}, ..., Z_{t_0+k-1}$. Let θ be any binary pattern of k bits. The probability that $R_k = \theta$ is in the range $2^{-k} \pm 2\,[(m(k-1)2^w) + 1]/2^\eta$.*

From the above theorem, any pattern of length k occurs with probability in the range $2^{-k} \pm 2[(m(k-1))2^w + 1]/2^\eta$ among any of the $|U^A| \times |V^B|$ k-tuples consisting of a specified set of k consecutive output bits of the system satisfying the conditions of theorem 1.

Clearly, the smaller the number of fixed stages w compared to η is, the better the above result is. This does not mean that it is suggested to take w to be very small, for example $w = 0$ or 1. For more security, it is better to irregularly clock the generating register $\mathbb{B}$ by large values, so that the gap between the bits selected from the output of $\mathbb{B}$ is large.

In the next section, some correlation attacks on the system are considered.

3   Attacks

A suitable stream cipher should be resistant against a "known-plaintext" attack. In a known-plaintext attack the cryptanalyst is given a plaintext and the corresponding cipher-text (in another word, the cryptanalyst is given a keystream), and the task is to reproduce the keystream somehow.

The most important general attacks on LFSR-based stream ciphers are correlation attacks. Basically, if a cryptanalyst can in some way detect a correlation between the known output sequence and the output of one individual LFSR, this can be used in a divide and conquer attack on the individual LFSR [6, 7, 8, 9].

The output sequence of the system is an irregular decimation of its generating sequence. Thus, one would not expect a strong correlation to be obtained efficiently, especially, if the primitive characteristic feedback polynomials associated with the feedback functions are of high hamming weight [8], and the selected w fixed stages $i_0, i_1, \ldots, i_{w-1}$ of the control register which are used to determine the number of clocks of the generating register are considered as part of the secret key [i.e. w and $i_0, i_1, ..., i_{w-1}$ are kept secret for distinct $i_0, i_1, ..., i_{w-1} \in \{0, 1, 2, ..., m-1\}$].

The following attack allows a cryptanalyst to reconstruct the initial states of the system in a running time upper bounded by: $O(\Phi 2^m \eta^3)$, where:

$$\Phi = \sum_{w=1}^{m} \frac{m!}{(m-w)!} \tag{12}$$

provided that the characteristic feedback functions of $\mathbb{A}$ and $\mathbb{B}$ are known. In this attack, a cryptanalyst can exhaustively search for the initial state of $\mathbb{A}$; each such state can be expanded to a prefix of the control sequence (A_t) using the feedback function of $\mathbb{A}$. Suppose that the sequence (A_t) is expanded until its ηth 1 is produced. From this prefix, and from the knowledge of a corresponding η-long prefix of the output sequence (Z_t), one can derive the value of η non-consecutive bits of the generating sequence (B_t). Since the feedback function of $\mathbb{B}$ is known, then the initial state of $\mathbb{B}$ can be revealed given these non-consecutive η-bits by solving a system of linear equations. But first one has to exhaustively search for the selected w fixed stages of $\mathbb{A}$ in order to reveal the location of the η non-consecutive bits in the sequence (B_t), so he/she can solve the system of linear equations.

If the number of the selected fixed stages w is known, but the selected stages $i_0, i_1, ..., i_{w-1}$ are kept secret, then (eqn 12) becomes:

$$\Phi = \frac{m!}{(m-w)!}. \tag{13}$$

Therefore, the complexity of the attack is $O(\Phi 2^m \eta^3)$.

If the feedback functions of $\mathbb{A}$ and $\mathbb{B}$ are kept secret, the attack takes $O(\Phi 2^{2m} m \eta)$ steps.

There is also another attack that can be applied to the system through the linear complexity, but this attack requires $(2^{m+\eta-1})$ consecutive bits of the output sequence (i.e. it requires a complete period of the output sequence).

For $m \cong 64$ and $\eta \cong 64$, the system appears to be secure against the correlation attacks introduced in [6, 7, 8, 9, 10, 11, 12, 13, 14, 15, 16].

For maximum security, the system should be used with secret w fixed stages, secret feedback functions, and w, m and η should satisfy $w < (\eta - \log_2 m)$ and $(2^{m-1}(2^w + 1) - 1, 2^\eta) = 1$. Subject to these constraints, if $m \cong l$ and $\eta \cong l$, the system has a security level approximately equal to $\Phi 2^{2l}$.

4   Related Work

Interesting examples of existing FSR-based constructions for comparison with the system are the Shrinking Generator SG of Coppersmith et al [3] and some of the clock-controlled generators introduced in [1], in particular the Binary Rate

Multiplier BRM of Chambers and Jenning [17]. The SG and the BRM have similar proven properties as this system.

The BRM is built up from two FSRs $\mathbb{A}$ and $\mathbb{B}$, and it works the same way as this system. The only difference is that the output of $\mathbb{B}$ under the control of $\mathbb{A}$ is taken to be the output of the BRM regardless of the current output of $\mathbb{A}$. One advantage of the BRM is that it generates an output bit each time $\mathbb{A}$ is clocked. On the other hand, the omission of bits that is important in FSR-based constructions is significantly more superior for this system than the BRM. For the BRM one of any 2^w consecutive bits originally output by $\mathbb{B}$ appears in the output sequence of the BRM, whereas for this system one of any $m2^w$ consecutive bits originally output by $\mathbb{B}$ appears in the output sequence of the system.

Also, if k bits from the control sequence are required to determine the original locations of k bits in the generating sequence of a BRM, then $2k$ bits of the control register (on average) are required to determine the locations of k bits in the generating sequence of the system.

The SG is a special case of the system; it is actually a system with no stages selected (i.e. $w = 0$). Although this system is slower than the SG, its advantage is that it provides more security [see 3]. Moreover, for the SG in order to produce a new sequence, one has to at least choose another initial state or another characteristic feedback function, whereas for this system in order to produce a new sequence, it suffices to choose another w fixed stages satisfying the conditions $w < \eta - \log_2 m$, and $(2^{m-1}(2^w + 1) - 1, 2^\eta) = 1$.

Conclusion 1 *From the theoretical results established, it is concluded that the system generates sequences with large periods, high linear complexities, good statistical properties, and they are secure against correlation attacks. Furthermore, using the same initial states and the same characteristic feedback functions, the system produces a new sequence each time different w fixed stages are selected. These characteristics and properties enhance its use as a suitable crypto-generator for stream cipher applications.*

References

1. D. Gollmann, and W. Chambers, "Clock-Controlled Shift Register: A Review" IEEE J. Sel. Ar. Comm. vol. 7, No. 4, May 1989, pp. 525–533.
2. S. W. Golomb, "Shift Register Sequences", Aegean Park Press, 1982.
3. D. Coppersmith, H. Krawczyk, and Y. Mansour, "The Shrinking Generator", Proceedings of Crypto 93, Springer-Verlag, 1994, pp 22–39.
4. R. Lidl, and H. Niederreiter, " Introduction to Finite Fields and Their Applications", UK: Cambridge University Press, 1986.
5. A. Kanso, "Clock-Controlled Generators", PhD thesis, University of London 1999, pp. 161.
6. J. Golic, and M. Mihaljevic, "A Generalized Correlation Attack on a Class of Stream Ciphers Based on the Levenstein Distance", Journal of Cryptology, 3, 1991, pp. 201–212.
7. J. Golic, "Towards Fast Correlation Attacks on Irregularly Clocked Shift Registers", Lecture Notes in Computer Science 921 (EuroCrypt 95), 1995, pp. 248–262.

8. W. Meir, and O. Staffelbach, "Fast Correlation Attacks on Certain Stream Ciphers", Journal of Cryptology, 1, 1989, pp. 159–176.
9. T. Siegenthaler, "Correlation-Immunity of Non-linear Combining Functions for Cryptographic Applications", IEEE Trans On Information Theory, 30, 1984, pp.776–780.
10. J. Golic, "On the Security of Shift Register Based Keystream Generators", R. Anderson, Editor, Fast Software Encryption, Cambridge Security Workshop (LNCS 809), Springer-Verlag, 1994, pp. 90–100.
11. T. Johansson, "Reduced Complexity Correlation Attacks on Two Clock-Controlled Generators", Advances of Cryptology (AsiaCrypt 98), Lecture Notes in Computer Science, vol. 1514, 1998, pp. 342–356.
12. M. Mihaljevic, "An Approach to the Initial State Reconstruction of a Clock-Controlled Shift Register Based on a Novel Distance Measure", Advances in Cryptology (AusCrypt 92), Lecture Notes in Computer Science, vol. 178, 1993, pp. 349–356
13. J. Golic, and L. O.Connor, "Embedding Probabilistic Correlation Attacks on Clock-Controlled Shift Registers", Advances in Cryptology (EuroCrypt 94), Lecture Notes in Computer Science, vol. 950, 1995, pp. 230–243.
14. L. Simpson, J. Golic, and E. Dawson, "A Probabilistic Correlation Attack on the Shrinking Generator", ACISP 1998, pp. 147–158.
15. T. Johansson, F.Jonsson, "Improved Fast Correlation Attacks on Certain Stream Ciphers via Convolutional Codes", Advances in Cryptography (EuroCrypt 99), Lecture Notes in Computer Science, vol. 1592, Springer-Verlag, 1999, pp. 347–362.
16. T. Johansson, F.Jonsson, "Fast Correlation Attacks Through Reconstruction of Linear Polynomials", Advances in Cryptology (Crypto 2000), Lecture Notes in Computer Science, vol. 1880, Springer-Verlag, 2000, pp. 300–315.
17. W. Chambers, and S. Jennings, "Linear Equivalence of Certain BRM Shift Register Sequences", Electronics Letters, vol. 20, November 1984, pp.1018–1019.

EPA: An Efficient Password-Based Protocol for Authenticated Key Exchange*

Yong Ho Hwang, Dae Hyun Yum, and Pil Joong Lee

Department of Electronic and Electrical Engineering,
Pohang University of Science & Technology (POSTECH),
San 31 Hyoja-dong, Nam-gu, Pohang, Kyoungbuk, 790-784, Rep. of Korea
yhhwang@oberon.postech.ac.kr, {dhyum, pjl}@postech.ac.kr

Abstract. A password-based protocol for authenticated key exchange must provide security against attacks using low entropy of a memorable password. We propose a new password-based protocol for authenticated key exchange, EPA (Efficient Password-based protocol for Authenticated key exchange), which has smaller computational and communicational workloads than previously proposed protocols with the same security requirements. EPA is an asymmetric model in which each client has a password and the server has a password file. While the server's password file is compromised, the client's password is not directly exposed. However, if the adversary mounts an additional dictionary attack, he can obtain the client's password. By using a modified amplified password file, we construct EPA+, which is secure against dictionary attack and server impersonation even if the server's password file is compromised.

1 Introduction

Electronic commerce has become an indispensable element of Internet communication. Cryptosystems are gaining a considerable attention because they can provide security services like authentication, confidentiality, and integrity. However, users are reluctant to adopt cryptosystems, since cryptographic keys are too long to be memorized and require cumbersome tamper-resistant storage. Hence, cryptographers developed a protocol that affords a reasonable level of security, with memorable passwords instead of long cryptographic keys. This is called a password-based protocol for authenticated key exchange (AKE) or a password-authenticated key exchange. In this protocol, a short password is memorized without unwieldy secure storage and they agree on a session key to be used for protecting their information over insecure channels.

After EKE [3] was introduced in 1992, many password-based protocols followed. However, the password-based protocol for AKE may be vulnerable to dictionary attack because a memorable password has low entropy. Therefore, it is important that key exchange steps in password-based protocol for AKE are

---

* This research was supported by University IT Research Center Project, the Brain Korea 21 Project, and Com2MaC-KOSEF.

R. Safavi-Naini and J. Seberry (Eds.): ACISP 2003, LNCS 2727, pp. 452–463, 2003.
© Springer-Verlag Berlin Heidelberg 2003

securely designed against dictionary attack and password-guessing attack. In addition, the client's password should not be exposed directly when the server's password file is compromised, i.e. the password-based protocol for AKE has to provide resilience to server compromise. Hence, recently proposed protocols are mostly based on an asymmetric model, in which each client has a password and the server has a password file that contains a verifier derived from the password. Securely designed asymmetric models, even if the server's password file is compromised, need additional dictionary attacks. In this paper, we limit our discussion to password-based protocols for AKE that are resilient to server compromise.

Authentication steps as well as key exchange steps are required in the password-based protocol to be secure against man-in-the-middle attack and other impersonation attacks. B-SPEKE[7], AMP[9] and SRP[18] separate key exchange steps and authentication steps. The first two passes are used for key exchange steps and the second two passes are used for authentication steps. Thus, they need four passes in total. On the other hand, the PAK protocols [4, 10,11] require only three passes. Even though they require only three passes, they need a complex mechanism compared with other four-pass protocols.

In this paper, we propose EPA (Efficient Password-based protocol for Authenticated key exchange), a new password-based protocol for AKE, which is resilient to server compromise. EPA is based on an asymmetric model and is secure against off-line dictionary attack. In addition, EPA provides perfect forward secrecy. To reduce the number of passes, EPA uses two generators, g and f, of a prime-order subgroup. EPA has only three passes with no more exponentiations compared with other protocols. Therefore, EPA can be executed faster than other previously proposed password-based protocols for AKE.

Password-based protocols resilient to server compromise do not expose the client's password directly when the server's password file is compromised. However, attackers can obtain the client's password from the server's password file with an additional dictionary attack. To solve this problem, AMP introduced an amplified password file [9]. Even if the server's amplified password file is compromised, AMP is secure against additional dictionary attack and server impersonation. We propose EPA+ which uses a modified amplified password file. The modified amplified password file of EPA+ is more efficient than the original amplified password file of AMP.

2   Design Principles

Until now, many password-based protocols for AKE have been proposed. However, no password-based protocol can fit all system environments. There are some tradeoffs among the password-based protocols. Therefore, in this section, we wish to clarify the design principles behind EPA.

Explicit authentication: In some password-based protocols, the involved parties are implicitly authenticated, meaning that if one of the communication parties is not who he/she claims to be, he/she simply will not be able to obtain the session key of the honest party. When we design a password-based protocol with implicit authentication, we can construct a very efficient password-based protocol with only two passes. However, we will design a password-based protocol with explicit authentication, where a party can explicitly confirm the identity of the communicating party.

Security against off-line dictionary attack: Generally, the password space from which passwords are chosen is so small that an attacker can mount an off-line dictionary attack where the attacker enumerates all possible candidates for the password. Hence, the password-based protocol has to be designed for security against an off-line dictionary attack. Note that an on-line dictionary attack can be easily detected and thwarted by counting access failures.

Security against Denning-Sacco attack: The Dennig-Sacco attack [5] is the case where an attacker compromises an old session key and tries to find the password or other session keys. We will design a password-based protocol that retains its security even if an old session key is compromised.

Perfect forward secrecy: The most dangerous situation is where a client's password is disclosed by some means. In this case, it is desirable that the effect of the disclosed password should be minimized. The proper security measure is perfect forward secrecy: the disclosed password does not reveal prior recorded conversation, i.e. the old session keys are not revealed by the disclosed password. Our password-based protocol will provide perfect forward secrecy.

Resilience to server compromise: The server has a password file that stores a verifier to verify a client's secret password. Even though a client keeps his/her password securely, the threat of server compromise still exists. In the case of server compromise, we cannot prevent an attacker from disguising himself/herself as a legitimate server. However, we can prevent the attacker from disguising himself/herself as a legitimate client. Firstly, it should be infeasible for an attacker to obtain the client's password directly from the server's password file. We call this condition "resilience to server compromise," and most of the previously proposed password-based protocols provide resilience to server compromise. Additionally, if we adopt an (modified) amplified password file, we can devise a password-based protocol where the attacker cannot obtain the client's password from the server's password file even with an additional dictionary attack.

Small computational and communicational workloads: Many password-based protocols that are resilient to server compromise have been proposed and they have different computational and communicational workloads. Some protocols require four communicational passes and a small number of exponentiations.

By contrast, some protocols require three communicational passes and a large number of exponentiations. We will design a three-pass password-based protocol with a small number of exponentiations. To accomplish this, we use two generators, g and f, of a prime-order subgroup. Our password-based protocol requires small communicational and computational workloads. Hence, our protocol shows a better performance in most environments.

3   Description of EPA

3.1   Preliminaries

EPA involves two entities, *Alice* and *Bob*. We refer to *Alice* as the client and *Bob* as the server. *Alice* has a memorable password π and *Bob* has a verifier π_b, in his password file, which is derived from *Alice*'s password π. How π_b is determined from π is explained in Section 3.2. The security parameter k, which can be thought of as the bit size of the hash funcation output, should be a long enough to prevent a brute-force attack. Let $\{0,1\}^*$ denote the set of finite binary strings of arbitrary length and $\{0,1\}^n$ the set of strings of length n. For convenience, we will omit "*mod p*" in the remainder of this paper where it is clear from the context.

NUMERICAL ASSUMPTIONS: We consider the multiplicative group Z_p^* and actually use its prime-order subgroup. The subgroup $G_{p,q}$ of prime order q is generated by either g or f, where $p = qr + 1$. The generators g and f must be selected so that their discrete logarithmic relation cannot be found. The prime q must be sufficiently large to resist Pohlig-Hellman decomposition and the various index-calculus methods [13,15,16]. We assume the hardness of the Decision Diffie-Hellman problem (DDH). The DDH problem is as follows: given $u_1 = g^a$, $u_2 = g^b$, $u_3 \in G_{p,q}$, determine if $u_3 = g^{ab}$. We assume that there is no polynomial time adversary who distinguishes g^{ab} from a random u_3 with non-negligible advantage over a random guess. The DDH assumption implies that the Discrete Logarithm Problem (DLP) and the Computational Diffie-Hellman problem (CDH) are also hard problems. We assume that all numerical operations of the protocol are performed on the prime-order cyclic subgroup $G_{p,q}$ where it is hard to solve DDH [13].

We summarize the notations used in this paper:

Alice	a client, or the name of the client
Bob	a server, or the name of the server
π	the client's password
π_b	the server's verifier that is derived from π
g, f	generators of a prime-order subgroup
p	a large prime
q	the size of a prime-order subgroup of Z_p^*
k	the security parameter

$$K_{A(or\,B)} \qquad Alice(Bob)\text{'s master key}$$

$K_{A(or\,B)}$	$Alice(Bob)$'s master key
K	a session key
$h(\cdot)$	a collision-resistant one-way hash function
$|a|$	the bit length of a
$\|$	concatenation
$\alpha \in_R Z_q$	random selection of an element from Z_q

We define $h_1(x) = h(00\|x\|00)$, $h_2(x) = h(01\|x\|01)$, $h_3(x) = h(01\|x\|10)$, $h_4(x) = h(10\|x\|10)$ and $h_5(x) = h(11\|x\|11)$ where $h : \{0,1\}^* \to \{0,1\}^k$, by following the construction given in Bellare and Rogaway's work [1]. We will consider these hash functions as a random oracle.

3.2 Setup of EPA

Before any transaction occurs, *Alice* and *Bob* share the domain parameters p, q, g and f. *Alice* chooses a memorable password π and *Bob* keeps *Alice*'s identity id with the verifier $\pi_b = (V_1, V_2)$ where

$$V_1 = f^{v_1}, \; v_1 = h_1(id, \pi),$$
$$V_2 = g^{v_2}, \; v_2 = h_2(id, \pi).$$

3.3 Complete EPA

When Alice and Bob want to agree on a session key to be used for protecting their information over insecure channels, they execute the protocol in Figure 1.

$$
\begin{array}{lcr}
Alice\ (id, \pi) & & Bob\ (id, V_1, V_2) \\[4pt]
v_1 = h_1(id, \pi),\ v_2 = h_2(id, \pi) & & \\
x \in_R Z_q & id, X & y \in_R Z_q \\
X = g^x f^{v_1} & \longrightarrow & X' = \frac{X}{V_1} \\
& & Y = (X'V_2)^y \\
& Y, H_B & K_B = (X')^y \\
w = x(x + v_2)^{-1} \bmod q & \longleftarrow & H_B = h_3(K_B\|X) \\
K_A = Y^w & & \\
H'_B = h_3(K_A\|X) & & \\
\text{Test } H'_B \stackrel{?}{=} H_B & H_A & \\
H_A = h_4(Y\|K_A) & \longrightarrow & H'_A = h_4(Y\|K_B) \\
K = h_5(id, K_A) & & \text{Test } H'_A \stackrel{?}{=} H_A \\
& & K = h_5(id, K_B)
\end{array}
$$

Fig. 1. Complete EPA

1. *Alice* computes $v_1 = h_1(id, \pi)$, $v_2 = h_2(id, \pi)$. She chooses a random number $x \in_R Z_q$ where $x \neq -v_2 \bmod q$. After *Alice* computes $X = g^x f^{v_1}$, she sends (id, X) to *Bob*.

2. After *Bob* receives (id, X), he chooses a random number $y \in_R Z_q$ and then computes $X' = \frac{X}{V_1} = g^x$, $Y = (X'V_2)^y = g^{(x+v_2)y}$. The master key from which the session key is derived can be obtained by $K_B = (X')^y = g^{xy}$. After *Bob* computes $H_B = h_3(K_B \| X)$, he sends (Y, H_B) to *Alice*.

3. After *Alice* receives (Y, H_B), she computes $w = x(x + v_2)^{-1} \bmod q$ and the master key $K_A = Y^w = g^{xy}$. *Alice* compares $H'_B = h_3(K_A \| X)$ with H_B. If H'_B is equal to H_B, *Alice* regards *Bob* as a valid server who knows π_b and accepts the master key K_A. *Alice* computes $H_A = h_4(Y \| K_A)$ and the session key $K = h_5(id, K_A)$. *Alice* sends H_A to *Bob*.

4. After *Bob* receives H_A, he computes $H'_A = h_4(Y \| K_B)$. *Bob* compares H'_A with H_A. If H'_A is equal to H_A, *Bob* regards *Alice* as a valid user who knows π and accepts the master key K_B. *Bob* computes the session key $K = h_5(id, K_B)$.

In EPA, *Alice* computes g^x, where x is randomly chosen by herself and *Bob* computes g^y, where y is randomly chosen by himself. After *Alice* and *Bob* exchange g^x and g^y, they obtain the master key g^{xy}. This is based on the Diffie-Hellman key exchange. If the above steps are successfully finished, *Alice* and *Bob* have the same session key $K = h_5(id, g^{xy})$ which is derived from the agreed master key. We will discuss the security of EPA in Section 4.1 and the performance of EPA in Section 4.2.

4   Analysis of EPA

4.1   Security of EPA

To date, many password-based protocols have been proposed. However, only a few protocols provide the proof for security in the concrete model. EKE2 was proved secure in the random oracle and ideal block cipher model under the DDH assumption [2]. A more elegant model was used in PAK-Z [11], which is based on the random oracle model without the ideal block cipher assumption.

In this section, we discuss the security of EPA. We provide the security of EPA in the random oracle model under the DDH assumption.

Theorem 1 *EPA is a secure password based authenticated key exchange protocol in the explicit-authentication model.*

Proof sketch. To prove the security of EPA, we adopt the model in [4,17] that is based on the multi-party simulatability tradition. Refer to [4] for the details of the model. The security is defined using an ideal system and a real system. A proof of security would show that anything an adversary can do in the real system can also be done in the ideal system where an ideal world adversary cannot break the security by definition. The requirement of security includes completeness and simulatability. Completeness means that for any real world adversary that faithfully delivers messages between two user instances, both user instances accept. The completeness requirement for EPA follows directly by inspection. Simulatability means that for every efficient real world adversary A there exists an efficient ideal world adversary A^* such that the transcripts of two adversaries are computationally indistinguishable. To demonstrate simulatability, we construct a simulator for a real system. The transcript of an adversary attacking the simulator will be computationally indistinguishable from the transcript of an adversary attacking the real system. To create an ideal world adversary A^* by running the real world adversary A against a simulated real world, the simulator need to respond to the real world adversary's queries without knowing the actual passwords. If the adversary A requests random oracle calls that take the password as an argument, the simulator use random values as responses. This is also valid for the adversary's direct random oracle queries. To simulate random oracles, the simulator should return the same value to the queries of the same input. Otherwise, the adversary can distinguish a simulated environment from the real world. The simulator will try to detect guesses on the password by examining the adversary's random oracle queries and this information will be used to break the DDH assumption. The simulated environment from the real world will work unless the simulator needs to perform disallowed test instance password operations in the ideal world. There are two cases of such violations.

Case 1: The query is made for an instance that performs a start session operation.

Case 2: Multiple queries are made for each user instance.

We show that if the adversary can perform either disallowed operation with non-negligible probability, we can break the DDH assumption with non-negligible probability.

Case 1: Assume that the offending query is made within T queries where T is polynomial and bounded by the adversary's running time. Let $u_1 = g^a$, $u_2 = g^b$, $u_3 \in G_{p,q}$ be a DDH challenge. The simulator chooses a random number i in $[0, T]$. On the i-th deliver message query to initiate a protocol between users Alice and Bob, set $X = u_1 f^{v_1}$ where v_1 is an output of random oracle h_1. This implies that Alice chooses a random x as a even though the simulator does not know the value of a. When a Bob instance replies to $X = u_1 f^{v_1}$, set $Y = u_3 u_2^{v_2}$ where v_2 is an output of random oracle h_2. This implies that Bob chooses a random y as b even though the simulator does not know the value of b. If the adversary makes a query to h_3, h_4 or h_5 with $X = u_1 f^{v_1}$, $Y = u_3 u_2^{v_2}$ and $K_A = K_B = u_3$, guess that the DDH challenge is a true DH instance, i.e., $u_3 = g^{ab}$. Otherwise, the simulator flips a coin to decide whether u_3 is equal to g^{ab} or not. Let ϵ be the probability of the adversary's breaking the ideal world rule. Since the probability of $u_3 = g^{ab}$ is equal to that of random u_3 in the DDH challenge, we can break the DDH assumption with the probability $\frac{1}{2} + \frac{\epsilon}{4T} \left(\frac{1}{2}(\frac{1}{2}(1-\frac{\epsilon}{T}) + \frac{\epsilon}{T}) + \frac{1}{2}(\frac{1}{2}) \right)$ which is non-negligible.

Case 2: To simplify the discussion, we assume that v_1 and v_2 are calculated from one random oracle. For example, v_1 is the upper half of $h^*(id, \pi)$ and v_2 the lower half of $h^*(id, \pi)$ where the output length of h^* is the sum of the output length of h_1 and h_2. Let $u_1 = g^a$, $u_2 = g^b$, $u_3 \in G_{p,q}$ be a DDH challenge. When the offending query is made within T queries, the simulator chooses a random number i in $[0, T]$. Each time $h^*(id, \pi)$ is queried for some π, flip a coin to decide whether to include a factor of u_1 in the return value. For the first message to a Bob instance with partner Alice, set $Y = u_3 u_2^{v_2}$. The master key values K_A, K_B used in any pair of h_3, h_4 or h_5 queries for the same X, Y and two different password guesses π_1, π_2 can be tested against the u_3 value if exactly one of $h^*(id, \pi_1)$ and $h^*(id, \pi_2)$ included a factor of u_1 in its calculation. If any of these pairs tests positively of the u_2 value, guess that the DDH challenge is a true DH instance. Let ϵ be the probability of the adversary's breaking the ideal world rule. Since the probability of $u_3 = g^{ab}$ is equal to that of random u_3 in the DDH challenge, we can break the DDH assumption with the probability $\frac{1}{2} + \frac{\epsilon}{4T} \left(\frac{1}{2}(\frac{1}{2}(1 - \frac{\epsilon}{T}) + \frac{\epsilon}{T}) + \frac{1}{2}(\frac{1}{2}) \right)$ which is non-negligible. □

Theorem 2 *EPA is secure against Denning-Sacco attack.*

The proof sketch is omitted due to page limits. The basic structure of the proof is similar to that of Theorem 1.

There are two kinds of key agreement protocols that satisfy forward secrecy[14]. The first type is based on the Diffie-Hellman key agreement and the second type is based on the confidentiality of a random nonce. EPA belongs to the first type since *Alice* chooses a random number x and *Bob* chooses another random number y to construct a session key g^{xy}. Even though the password is compromised, the Diffie-Hellman key agreement still holds since x and y are not exposed.

4.2   Performance of EPA

We compare EPA with other password-based protocols submitted to IEEE P1363.2 (Password-based Techniques) [20]. Protocols, which implement Diffie-Hellman key agreement, exchange g^x and g^y to compute $(g^x)^y$ and $(g^y)^x$. Hence, each party transmits a large data block of size $|p|$ and needs at least 2 exponentiations. Thus, complete password-based protocols for authenticated key exchange need to deliver two large blocks of size $|p|$ and require at least four exponentiations. In addition, they need more data transmission and computation for key confirmation and authentication.

AMP [9], SRP [18] and B-SPEKE [7] are four-pass protocols for password-based authenticated key exchange, but PAK-Z[11] is a three-pass protocol. AMP requires the smallest exponentiations and PAK-Z requires the smallest computational passes among the previously proposed protocols.

To construct the protocol with three passes, PAK-Z defines a new hash function over the subgroup of $G_{p,q}$. However the newly defined hash function in

PAK-Z requires additional exponentiations. In addition, PAK-Z requires more complex authentication-mechanism. By contrast, EPA implements a three-pass protocol without additional exponentiations by using two generators, g and f.

In EPA, each party performs approximately two exponentiations and the exchanged data size is only $2|p| + 2k$. Table 1 compares various password-based protocols based on asymmetric model [7,9,18,11].

Table 1. Comparison of various password-based protocols

Protocol	Passes	Exponentiations			Exchaged data size
		Client	Server	Total	
B-SPEKE	4	3	4	7	$3|p| + 2k$
SRP	4	3	3	6	$2|p| + 2k + |q|$
AMP	4	2	2.4(3)	4.4(5)	$2|p| + 2k$
PAK-Z	3	4-6	2	6-8	$2|p| + 3k$
EPA	3	2.2(3)	2	4.2(5)	$2|p| + 2k$

To compare the computational workload, we consider the number of exponentiations that consume the most execution time. As for the calculation of $g_1^{e_1} g_2^{e_2}$, we do not need to compute $g_1^{e_1}$ and $g_2^{e_2}$ separately. On average, $g_1^{e_1} g_2^{e_2}$ and $g_1^{e_1} g_2^{e_2} g_2^{e_3}$ need to perform only 20% and 40% more multiplications than $g_1^{e_1}$ [6,12,19]. In table 1, we use this counting method for the number of exponentiations. Note that the numbers in parentheses count $g_1^{e_1} g_2^{e_2}$ as two exponentiations.

From Table 1, we can see that EPA has the smallest computational and communicational workloads. The only drawback of EPA is the consumption of storage for V_2, since EPA uses two generators g and f.

5   EPA+: EPA with Modified Amplified Password File

In the password-based protocols presented in Section 4.2, the server keeps the verifier π_b that stores one-way function output of the client's password. However, if the server's password file is compromised, an adversary can mount an off-line dictionary attack and obtain the client's password. Only AMP [9] does not allow an attacker to obtain the client's password even if he mounts an additional dictionary attack with the compromised server's password file. To support this condition, AMP introduced an amplified password file.

The basic idea of the amplified password file is simple. When the server stores a verifier, the server selects a salt value s and computes the amplified password file from s and other values. After the server stores the amplified password file in the ordinary server system, the salt value s should be stored in a secure storage device such as a smart card. Then, even if the amplified password file is compromised, AMP does not allow additional dictionary attack and server impersonation. For example, if the password file stores $g^{h(\pi)}$, then the amplified password file stores $(V_1, V_2) = (\tau, g^{(s+\tau)^{-1}h(\pi)})$ where τ is a random number and s is the salt value in the secure storage device. When $g^{h(\pi)}$ needs to be used in the protocol, the server computes $g^{h(\pi)}$ using s and the verifier (V_1, V_2) in the amplified password file as follows:

$$i = s + \tau$$
$$g^{h(\pi)} = V_2^i$$

However, if we adopt the amplified password file of AMP without modification, the complete password-based protocol requires an additional exponentiation. Hence, we introduce a modified amplified password file which eliminates the additional exponentiation and unnecessary random number τ. After the server selects the salt value s, he computes g^s. The modified amplified password file stores $g^{s^{-1}h(\pi)}$ in the ordinary server system and g^s is stored in a secure storage device. By storing g^s instead of s, we change an exponentiation into a multiplication. Now, we construct EPA+ which uses a modified amplified password file to provide against attack with the compromised server's password file.

Setup of EPA+: Before any transaction occurs, *Alice* and *Bob* share the domain parameters, p, q, g and f. *Bob* randomly chooses a private salt value $s \in_R Z_q$ and keeps *Alice*'s identity id with the verifier $\pi_b = (V_1, V_2)$ where

$$V_1 = f^{v_1 - s}, v_1 = h_1(id, \pi),$$
$$V_2 = g^{v_2 - s}, v_2 = h_2(id, \pi).$$

Bob stores $(U_1, U_2) = (f^s, g^s)$ in a secure storage device, such as a smart card.

Complete EPA+: When *Alice* and *Bob* want to agree on a session key to be used for protecting their information over insecure channels, they execute the protocol in Figure 2. If all steps are successfully finished, *Alice* and *Bob* share the session key $K = h_5(id, g^{xy})$.

Security of EPA+: The security of EPA+ can be deduced from the security of EPA. The security against attack with the compromised server's password file can be easily shown because (U_1, U_2) are stored in a secure storage device. In addition, the client's password is not exposed directly, even if (V_1, V_2) and (U_1, U_2) are all revealed.

Performance of EPA+: Since we adopted a modified amplified password file, EPA+ does not need additional exponentiation. However, the server in EPA+ stores (f^s, g^s) instead of s and this requires more storage. If we implement EPA+ over an elliptic curve and use compressed coordinate expression, this storage requirement can be somewhat relaxed. The computational and communicational workloads of EPA+ are similar to those of EPA.

$$\text{Alice } (id, \pi) \qquad\qquad\qquad \text{Bob } (id, V_1, V_2)$$

$$v_1 = h_1(id, \pi),\ v_2 = h_2(id, \pi)$$
$$x \in_R Z_q \qquad\qquad id, X$$
$$X = g^x f^{v_1} \qquad\qquad \longrightarrow \qquad \text{Fetch } (U_1, U_2)$$
$$y \in_R Z_q$$
$$X' = \frac{X}{V_1 U_1} = g^x$$
$$V = V_2 U_2$$
$$Y = (X'V)^y = g^{(x+v_2)y}$$
$$\qquad\qquad\qquad\qquad Y, H_B \qquad\qquad K_B = (X')^y = g^{xy}$$
$$w = x(x + v_2)^{-1} \bmod q \qquad \longleftarrow \qquad H_B = h_3(K_B \| X)$$
$$K_A = Y^w = g^{xy}$$
$$H'_B = h_3(K_A \| X)$$
$$\text{Test } H'_B \overset{?}{=} H_B \qquad\qquad H_A$$
$$H_A = h_4(Y \| K_A) \qquad\qquad \longrightarrow \qquad H'_A = h_4(Y \| K_B)$$
$$K = h_5(id, K_A) \qquad\qquad\qquad \text{Test } H'_A \overset{?}{=} H_A$$
$$K = h_5(id, K_B)$$

Fig. 2. Complete EPA+

6   Concluding Remarks

In this paper, we proposed EPA, a new password-based protocol for AKE[1]. We also introduced a modified amplified password file and constructed EPA+ for the security against attack with the compromised servier's password file. Since EPA and EPA+ require a small number of exponentiations, three communicational passes and a small amount of exchanged data, they show a better performance in most environments.

References

1. M. Bellare and P. Rogaway, Entity authentication and key distribution, *Crypto'93*, pages 232–249, 1993.
2. M. Bellare D. Pointcheval, and P. Rogaway, Authenticated Key Exchange Secure Against Dictionary Attacks, *Eurocrypt 2000*, pages 139–155, 2000.

---

[1] Preliminary version of this paper was written in Aug, 2002. In parallel with this work, K. Kobara and H. Imai constructed a password based key exchange protocol based on two generators of a prime-order subgroup [8]. Even though performances of EPA and [8] look comparable, this misperception stems from the different counting methods between the two works. If the counting method of this paper is used for [8], the computational cost is 2.4(3-4) exponentiations for the server and 2.4(3-4) exponentiations for the client. Therefore, EPA is more efficient than [8]. Since the security proof of [8] is based on the standard model, the work of K. Kobara and H. Imai is of indepedent value.

3. S. Bellovin and M. Merritt, Encrypted Key Exchange: Password-based protocols secure against dictionary attacks, *Proceedings of IEEE Security and Privacy*, pages 72–84, 1992.
4. V. Boyko, P. MacKenzie, and S. Patel, Provably secure password authenticated key exchange using Diffie-Helman, *Eurocrypt 2000*, pages 156–171, 2000.
5. D. Denning and G. Sacco, Timestamps in key distribution protocols, *Communications of the ACM*, vol 24, no 8, pages 533–536, 1981.
6. V. S. Dimitrov, G. A. Jullien, and W. C. Miller, Complexity and fast algorithms for multi-exponentiations, *IEEE Transactions on Computers*, vol 49, no 2, pages 141–147, 2000.
7. D. Jablon, Extended password key exchange protocols immune to dictionary attack, *In WETICE'97 Workshop on Enterprise Security*, 1997.
8. K. Kobara and H. Imai, Pretty-Simple Password-Authenticated Key-Exchange Under Standard Assumptions, *Cryptology ePrint Archive*, Report 2003/038, 2003.
9. T. Kwon, Authentication and key agreement via memorable password, *Proceedings of the ISOC NDSS Symposium*, 2001.
10. P. MacKenzie, More efficient password-authenticated key exchange, *Progress in Cryptology – CT-RSA 2001*, pages 361–377, 2001.
11. P. MacKenzie, The PAK suit: Protocols for Password-Authenticated Key Exchange, *http://grouper.ieee.org/groups/1363/passwdPK/contributions.html#Mac02*, April, 2002.
12. B. Moeller, Algorithm for multi-exponentiation, *In Selected Areas in Cryptography, SAC 2001*, pages 165–180, 2001.
13. P. van Oorschot and M. Wiener, On Diffie-Hellman key agreement with short exponents, *Eurocrypt'96*, pages 332–343, 1994.
14. D. G. Park, C. Boyd, and S. J. Moon, Forward Secrecy and Its Application to Futher Mobile Communications Security, *Public Key Cryptography, PKC 2000*, pages 433–445, 2000.
15. S. Pohlig and M. Hellman, An improved algorithm for computing logarithms over GF(p) and its cryptographic significance, *IEEE Transactions on Information Theory*, vol 24, no 1, pages 106–110, 1978.
16. J. Pollard, Monte Carlo methods for index computation mod p, *Math. of computation*, pages 918–924, 1978.
17. V. Shoup, On formal models for secure key exchange, *IBM Research Report RZ 3120*, April, 1999.
18. T. Wu, Secure remote password protocol, *Proceedings of the ISOC NDSS Symposium*, pages 99–111, 1998.
19. S. M. Yen, C. S. Laih, and A. K. Lenstra, Multi-exponentiation (cryptographic protocols), *Computers and Digital Techniques, IEEE Proceedings*, vol 141, no 6, pages 325–326, 1994.
20. IEEE P1363.2 : Standard Specifications for Password-Based Public Key Cryptography Techniques, Draft D7, December 20, 2002. *http://grouper.ieee.org/group/1363/*.

Constructing General Dynamic Group Key Distribution Schemes with Decentralized User Join*

Vanesa Daza, Javier Herranz, and Germán Sáez

Dept. Matemàtica Aplicada IV, Universitat Politècnica de Catalunya
C. Jordi Girona, 1-3, Mòdul C3, Campus Nord, 08034-Barcelona, Spain
{vdaza,jherranz,german}@mat.upc.es

Abstract. In a dynamic group key distribution scheme, members of a group themselves generate private common keys with the help of a group controller in an initialization phase. The system must enable the revocation and the addition of members to the group in the successive periods of time. If the addition of new members can also be performed by the existing members themselves, then the scheme is said to have decentralized user join.

In this work we construct a general family of dynamic group key distribution schemes with decentralized user join by using linear secret sharing schemes as a tool. This allows to obtain new schemes with more flexible characteristics than the previous threshold-based constructions.

1 Introduction

A *group key distribution scheme* is a randomized protocol for the dissemination of group keys among the different groups in such a way that no participant outside the group obtains any useful information about the group key.

Different approaches to group key distribution protocols have been considered so far depending on how the group keys are generated and distributed. On the one hand, the use of a single entity to generate and distribute them. This entity is usually known as *group controller*. Obviously, this proposal presents the main drawbacks of the use of a single key distributor: for instance, it must be constantly available and it could become a communication bottleneck. On the other hand, another approach uses the group controller only in the initialization phase. After that, the existing members of the group take charge of the management of the system. This model is also known as *decentralized* group key distribution. Note that a decentralized system runs even if some members of the group fail.

Usually, the life of the underlying communication systems is divided in sessions. The set of members of the group may change in every session. Group key

---

* This work was partially supported by Spanish *Ministerio de Ciencia y Tecnología* under project TIC 2000-1044.

R. Safavi-Naini and J. Seberry (Eds.): ACISP 2003, LNCS 2727, pp. 464–475, 2003.
© Springer-Verlag Berlin Heidelberg 2003

distribution schemes fitting this model are commonly called *dynamic*. We distinguish two types of group membership operations the protocol must support. The *addition operation* allows to admit new members to the group. A first approach to perform this operation consists of the establishment of an initialization process for new members as it has been carried out in the initialization phase. This operation must be executed by the group controller. However, as we have mentioned before, it is interesting to consider the situation where the figure of the group controller is avoided. The notion of *sponsorship* is a solution for these cases. A member of the group allows a new member to enter in the group for the following session or any session initialized by this sponsor. In case a new user receives enough sponsorships, he becomes a full member of the group from this session on.

The other operation that the system must support is the *revocation* of users. At a certain point a subgroup of users may be disallowed for continuing in the group and therefore a new group key should be generated. This operation can be performed by any of the non-revoked users in such a way that those revoked users are not able to compute the new key.

Of course, the security of group key management itself is of paramount importance; for example, as we have just mentioned, a revoked group of users must not be able to compute a new key. Roughly speaking, we require the resulting scheme to be secure in front of an adversary who corrupts some users and uses this information to obtain the group key corresponding to a session in which neither of the corrupted users belong to the group.

The literature on group key distribution is quite sparse. First works of Berkovits [2] and Just *et al.* [10] studied the problem focused on the information theoretic model. Nevertheless, this model does not fit in a dynamic setting, because of the large amount of bits that need to be secret. To overcome this problem, keyed one way hash functions were used in [9]. In [14], group key distribution was related with another primitive, computational secret sharing schemes. Efficient schemes with low computational storage cost were considered in [4,13]. In relation to decentralized group key distribution protocols, first work was due to Caronni *et al.* [5].

Independently, Anzai *et al.* [1] and Naor and Pinkas [15] used Shamir's secret sharing scheme to design efficient protocols for the revocation of some users. The idea is to broadcast some values related to the revoked users in such a way that only the non-revoked users can combine these values with their secret information to compute the following group key. The protocol in [15] must be performed by the group controller, whereas the proposal in [1] is decentralized. Kurnio *et al.* follow in [12,11] the line opened by [1] to provide dynamic group key distribution schemes where the operation of adding new users to the group can be performed without the presence of the group controller: the existing members of the group sponsor the new users.

In this paper we construct a new family of dynamic group key distribution schemes, following the ideas of [12]. Instead of using as a tool the threshold scheme that they use, we consider a linear secret sharing scheme. This allows us to construct more flexible dynamic group key distribution schemes with decentralized user join, where by flexible we mean that our general protocol can be applied in many different situations. We show some of these situations and we point out how to make a good choice for some cases. As a particular case of our general construction, we obtain schemes with the same properties than the schemes of [12,11]. We discuss the efficiency of our protocols with regard to those in [12,11].

Organization of the paper: in Section 2 we deal with secret sharing schemes, explaining some specific access structures and secret sharing schemes that will appear in the paper. In Section 3 we construct a family of dynamic group key distribution schemes, following the ideas of [12] but considering any possible linear secret sharing scheme instead of a threshold one, as they do. We remark some parameters of the obtained group key distribution schemes. In Section 4 we give some examples of group key distribution schemes, obtained from our construction, with some desired features which cannot be achieved by the threshold-based schemes of [12,11].

2   Secret Sharing Schemes

Secret sharing schemes play an important role in distributed cryptography. In these schemes, a secret value is shared among a set $\mathcal{P} = \{1, \ldots, n\}$ of n players in such a way that only qualified subsets of players can reconstruct the secret from their shares. The family of qualified subsets is the *access structure*, denoted by Γ. This family $\Gamma \subset 2^{\mathcal{P}}$ must be *monotone increasing*, that is, if $A_1 \in \Gamma$ and $A_1 \subset A_2 \subset \mathcal{P}$, then $A_2 \in \Gamma$. The family of authorized subsets Γ is determined by the collection of minimal authorized subsets Γ_0. The family of non-authorized subsets $\overline{\Gamma} = 2^{\mathcal{P}} - \Gamma$ is *monotone decreasing*, that is, if $A_1 \in \overline{\Gamma}$ and $A_2 \subset A_1$, then $A_2 \in \overline{\Gamma}$. The family of non-authorized subsets $\overline{\Gamma}$ is determined by the collection of maximal non-authorized subsets $\overline{\Gamma}_0$.

A special participant called *dealer*, which is not in $\mathcal{P}$, computes the shares for a given secret and distributes them to the participants in $\mathcal{P}$. The length of every share is at least the length of the secret. The best situation is the one where the length of every share is equal to the length of the secret. Secret sharing schemes with this property are called *ideal*. An access structure realized by an ideal secret sharing scheme is called *ideal access structure*.

Probably, the most used monotone access structures are $(t, n)-threshold$ access structures, defined by $\Gamma = \{A \subset \mathcal{P} : |A| \geq t\}$, for some threshold t in a set $\mathcal{P}$ of n participants. *Shamir's secret sharing scheme* [18] realizes $(t, n)-$threshold access structures by means of polynomial interpolation.

The *vector space secret sharing scheme* was introduced by Brickell [3]. Let us suppose that the dealer is D and that there is a public map

$$\psi : \mathcal{P} \cup \{D\} \longrightarrow \mathbb{Z}_q^{\ell}$$

where q is a prime number and ℓ is a positive integer. This map induces the monotone increasing access structure Γ defined as follows: $A \in \Gamma$ if and only if the vector $\psi(D)$ can be expressed as a linear combination of the vectors in the set $\psi(A) = \{\psi(i) \,|\, i \in A\}$. An access structure Γ is said to be a *vector space access structure* if it can be defined in the above way. If Γ is a vector space access structure, we can construct an ideal secret sharing scheme for Γ with set of secrets $\mathbb{Z}_q$ (see [3] for a proof). For a secret value $k \in \mathbb{Z}_q$, the dealer takes at random an element $v \in \mathbb{Z}_q^\ell$, such that $k = v \cdot \psi(D)$. The share of a participant $i \in \mathcal{P}$ is $s_i = v \cdot \psi(i)$. Let B be an authorized subset, $B \in \Gamma$; then, $\psi(D) = \sum_{i \in B} \lambda_i^B \psi(i)$, for some $\lambda_i^B \in \mathbb{Z}_q$. In order to recover the secret, the players of B compute

$$\sum_{i \in B} \lambda_i^B s_i \;=\; \sum_{i \in B} \lambda_i^B v \cdot \psi(i) \;=\; v \cdot \sum_{i \in B} \lambda_i^B \psi(i) \;=\; v \cdot \psi(D) \;=\; k \mod q$$

A scheme constructed in this way is called a *vector space secret sharing scheme*. Shamir's (t, n)–threshold scheme [18] can be seen as a vector space secret sharing scheme, if $q > n$, by choosing $\psi(D) = (1, 0, \ldots, 0) \in \mathbb{Z}_q^t$ as the vector of the dealer and $\psi(i) = (1, i, \ldots, i^{t-1}) \in \mathbb{Z}_q^t$ for $i \in \mathcal{P}$ (with $q > n$).

Vector space secret sharing schemes are a particular ideal case of *linear secret sharing schemes*, which are essentially equal to vector space ones we have just explained, but where every participant can be associated with more than one vector. Simmons, Jackson and Martin [19] proved that any access structure Γ can be realized by a linear secret sharing scheme.

3   A New Family of Dynamic Group Key Distribution Schemes

Kurnio *et al.* presented in [12] and [11] some dynamic group key distribution schemes following some ideas of the proposal of Anzai *et al.* [1]. In this section we construct a new family of group key distribution schemes inspired by the scheme of Kurnio *et al.* [12], but considering linear secret sharing schemes instead of Shamir secret sharing scheme. Finally we discuss some parameters and properties of the resulting schemes.

3.1   The Construction

We suppose that the set of users is $\mathcal{U} = \{1, \ldots, n\}$, where some of the users may be dummy, not real users. The life of the system is divided in sessions $s = 1, \ldots, T$. The subset of users that belong to the group in session s is denoted by $\mathcal{U}_s$. Let p, q, g be public parameters of the scheme, where p and q are large primes with $q | p - 1$ and g is an element with order q in $\mathbb{Z}_p^*$. Let us consider a linear secret sharing scheme realizing some access structure Γ over the set $\mathcal{U}$. For simplicity, suppose that there exists a public map

$$\psi : \mathcal{U} \cup \{D\} \longrightarrow \mathbb{Z}_q^\ell$$

which defines Γ as a vector space access structure. But the construction that we present here can be extended in a natural way to work with a linear secret sharing scheme in which a participant is associated with more than one vector.

Now we describe the different phases of the generalized group key distribution scheme.

System initialization. This phase of the scheme is performed by the group controller. Let $\mathcal{U}_1 \subset \mathcal{U}$ be the group of users for the first period of time. The group controller selects randomly a value $K_1 \in \langle g \rangle$ such that $K_1 \neq 0 \bmod q$, and a symmetrical $\ell \times \ell$ matrix $A = A^\top$. He gives to every user $i \in \mathcal{U}_1$ his secret information $k_i = A \cdot \psi(i) \in \mathbb{Z}_q^\ell$ and the first key K_1. Observe that $\psi(j)^\top \cdot k_i = \psi(j)^\top \cdot A \cdot \psi(i) = (\psi(j)^\top \cdot A \cdot \psi(i))^\top = \psi(i)^\top \cdot A^\top \cdot \psi(j) = \psi(i)^\top \cdot A \cdot \psi(j) = \psi(i)^\top \cdot k_j$. Note that if we use a linear secret sharing scheme in which a participant i is associated with $m_i \geq 1$ vectors, then his secret information k_i consists of m_i vectors.

Revocation of a subset of users. With this operation, some users of a group are disallowed to obtain the group key for the following session. At the end of session s, the revocation of a subset of users $R \subset \mathcal{U}$ with $R \notin \Gamma$ is performed by a user $z \in \mathcal{U}_s$ not in R in such a way that the new key K_{s+1} can only be computed by users in $\mathcal{U}_{s+1} = \mathcal{U}_s - R$. User z executes the protocol *generate_key(z, R)*. This protocol is as follows:

1. Choose at random $r \in \mathbb{Z}_q$ and compute $G = g^r \bmod p$. If $G^{\psi(D)^\top \cdot k_z} \bmod p$ is null modulus q (this happens with low probability), choose another random $r \in \mathbb{Z}_q$.
2. Choose a subset of users $I \subset \mathcal{U} - \mathcal{U}_s$ with minimum cardinality such that $I \cup R \in \overline{\Gamma}_0$. Compute $G_j = G^{\psi(j)^\top \cdot k_z} \bmod p$ for $j \in I \cup R$.
3. Broadcast the message $\mathcal{M} = \{z, G, G_j \| j : j \in I \cup R\}$.

The resulting key is $K_{s+1} = G^{\psi(D)^\top \cdot k_z} \bmod p$. Observe that any user $i \notin R$ who has his own private information k_i can compute the key K_{s+1} because he knows $G_j = G^{\psi(j)^\top \cdot k_z}$ for $j \in I \cup R \cup \{i\}$ (using the fact that $G_i = G^{\psi(i)^\top \cdot k_z} = G^{\psi(z)^\top \cdot k_i}$). In effect, since $B = I \cup R \cup \{i\} \in \Gamma$, then $\psi(D) = \sum_{j \in B} \lambda_j \psi(j)$, for some $\lambda_j \in \mathbb{Z}_q$. Then:

$$\prod_{j \in B} G_j^{\lambda_j} = G^{\sum_{j \in B} \lambda_j \psi(j)^\top \cdot k_z} = G^{\left(\sum_{j \in B} \lambda_j \psi(j)^\top\right) \cdot k_z} = G^{\psi(D)^\top \cdot k_z} = K_{s+1} \bmod p .$$

A user i who does not know his k_i or who is in R, cannot compute the key K_{s+1} because he only knows the values broadcast in the message $\mathcal{M}$, corresponding to an unauthorized subset of the secret sharing scheme.

If a user must be permanently revoked, he must be included in the set of revoked users in all sessions. The protocol *generate_key* can also be used to refresh the key of a group, in case that the composition of the group does not change.

Sponsored addition of users for one session. This operation allows a user in a group to sponsor new users in such a way that they obtain the key of the group only for the following session and the sessions in which the same sponsor generates the common key. A secure unicast channel between the sponsor and every sponsored user is necessary.

The sponsored addition of a set of users $C \subset \mathcal{U} - \mathcal{U}_s$ by a user $z \in \mathcal{U}_s$ defines a new key K_{s+1} that can only be computed by users in $\mathcal{U}_{s+1} = \mathcal{U}_s \cup C$. All users in $\mathcal{U}_s$ change their own private information in the following way: $k_i^* = K_s k_i \bmod q \in \mathbb{Z}_q^\ell$ (remember that $K_s \neq 0 \bmod q$). The sponsor z gives privately the value $k_{c,z} = \psi(c)^\top \cdot k_z^* \in \mathbb{Z}_q$ to every user $c \in C$. Then, he executes the protocol *generate_key(z, R)* with input the subset of users R that must remain revoked in session $s + 1$.

The new group key is $K_{s+1} = G^{\psi(D) \cdot k_z^*} \bmod p$. We can observe that any user $i \in \mathcal{U}_{s+1} = (\mathcal{U}_s \cup C) - R$ can compute the key K_{s+1} because he knows $G_j = G^{\psi(j) \cdot k_z^*}$ for $j \in I \cup R \cup \{i\}$ where $I \cup R \cup \{i\} \in \Gamma$, taking into account that every new user $c \in C$ knows $G_c = G^{\psi(c)^\top \cdot k_z^*} = G^{k_{c,z}}$. Furthermore, users outside $\mathcal{U}_{s+1}$ cannot compute the value of the key because they only know the values broadcast in the message $\mathcal{M}$, corresponding to an unauthorized subset.

Sponsored full addition of users. If a new user receives enough sponsorships, the addition becomes a full addition. More concretely, when a user c is sponsored by all users of a subset from the family

$$\Gamma' = \{B \subset \mathcal{U} : \langle \{\psi(i)\}_{i \in B} \rangle = \mathbb{Z}_q^\ell\}$$

then he becomes a full user of the group because the knowledge of $k_{c,z} = \psi(c)^\top \cdot k_z^* = \psi(z)^\top \cdot k_c^*$, for $z \in B$, with $B \in \Gamma'$, determines uniquely the vector k_c^*. In effect, let e_i be the i-th vector of the canonical basis and write e_i as $e_i = \sum_{z \in B} \lambda_{i,z} \psi(z)$. Then the i-th component of the vector $k_c^* = K_s(A \cdot \psi(c)) \bmod q$ can be computed by user c as follows:

$$e_i^\top \cdot k_c^* = \left(\sum_{z \in B} \lambda_{i,z} \psi(z)^\top \right) \cdot k_c^* = \sum_{z \in B} \lambda_{i,z} K_s(\psi(z)^\top A \psi(c)) =$$

$$= \sum_{z \in B} \lambda_{i,z} K_s(\psi(c)^\top A \psi(z)) = \sum_{z \in B} \lambda_{i,z} \psi(c)^\top \cdot k_z^* = \sum_{z \in B} \lambda_{i,z} k_{c,z}$$

Every added user c has the same capabilities than the rest of members of the group from time period $s + 1$ on, and he cannot obtain any information about the group keys of the previous periods of time. Note that this protocol runs correctly because we require $K_s \neq 0 \bmod q$ in the generation of the group keys, for all period $s = 1, \ldots, T$.

Then, a user z in the set $\mathcal{U}_s \cup C$ executes the protocol *generate_key(z, R)* with input the subset of users R that must remain revoked in session $s + 1$ to establish the new key. In this way the revocation and the addition of users can be performed in the same step, and the resulting key could be computed only by those users in $\mathcal{U}_{s+1} = (\mathcal{U}_s \cup C) - R$.

It is important to remark that the family Γ' is a monotone increasing family included in Γ. The construction of Simmons, Jackson and Martin [19] produces a linear secret sharing scheme for a given structure Γ, satisfying $\Gamma' = \Gamma$. Another case in which $\Gamma' = \Gamma$ is when Γ is a threshold structure and Shamir secret sharing scheme is used to realize it.

Observe that user c will be fully added to the group if the necessary sponsorships are performed in consecutive sessions, not necessarily in the same one.

3.2 Parameters of the Resulting Schemes

In order to compare the efficiency of different dynamic group key distribution schemes, we consider the following parameters: L_{sec} the length of the private information that every user must keep secret, $\mathcal{R}_s$ the family of revocable subsets in session s and $L_{rev}(R)$ for $R \in \mathcal{R}_s$ the length of the information that must be broadcast to revoke a subset R. We also introduce parameters related to the sponsored addition of users. In the sponsored addition we should consider the family $\mathcal{S}$ of subsets of users who can perform a sponsored full addition. This family $\mathcal{S}$ is monotone increasing. In this operation, the sponsored user receives L'_{sec} bits of private information from every sponsor, and needs $L_{sponsor}(B)$ bits from a subset $B \in \mathcal{S}$ of sponsors in order to become a full user.

The parameters corresponding to the group key distribution schemes generated using the construction of Section 3.1 with a vector space secret sharing scheme are the following: $L_{sec} = \ell \log q$ bits, the family of revocable subsets is $\mathcal{R}_s = \{R : \text{there exists } I \subset \mathcal{U} \backslash \mathcal{U}_s \text{ with } I \cup R \in \overline{\Gamma}_0\}$ and $L_{rev}(R) = m(R) \log p$ bits with $m(R) = \min\{|I| + |R| : I \subset \mathcal{U} \backslash \mathcal{U}_s \text{ with } I \cup R \in \overline{\Gamma}_0\}$. In the sponsored addition $\mathcal{S} = \Gamma'$. The user receives $L'_{sec} = \log q$ bits from every sponsor and needs $L_{sponsor}(B) = |B| \log q$ bits from a subset $B \in \Gamma'$ of sponsors to become a full user of the group.

A group key distribution scheme very similar to the one of Kurnio $et~al.$ [12] is obtained as a particular scheme of this family, by considering $d = t - 1$ and the map ψ defined by $\psi(i) = (1, i, i^2, \ldots, i^{t-1})$ and $\psi(D) = (1, 0, \ldots, 0)$, that defines the Shamir secret sharing scheme [18] in $\mathcal{U}$. The parameters of this group key distribution scheme are the following: $L_{sec} = t \log q$, $\mathcal{R}_s = \{R \subset \mathcal{U}_s : |R| < t\}$, $L_{rev} = (t-1) \log p$, $L'_{sec} = \log q$ and $L_{sponsor}(B) = t \log q$ for any subset $B \in \Gamma'$ of sponsors because in this case $\mathcal{S} = \Gamma' = \Gamma = \{B : |B| \geq t\}$.

Kurnio $et~al.$ [11] extend the basic threshold scheme, in order to allow some $privileged$ subsets with less than t users to sponsor the full addition of new users. This means that in their extended scheme the subsets of sponsors are those in $\mathcal{S} = \{B : |B| \geq t\} \cup \{\text{privileged subsets}\}$. Other parameters of the extended scheme change with respect to their basic scheme: now the revocable subsets are those with less than t users and such that they do not contain any privileged subset. Furthermore, the length of the information that every user must keep secret increases (maybe meaningfully), depending on the size of the cumulative scheme [19] which realizes the structure of privileged subsets.

Security Analysis. The correctness and the level of security of the group key distribution schemes constructed in Section 3.1 are the same that in the Kurnio *et al.* scheme [12], and can be proved using similar techniques (we skip here the details for lack of space). The protocols satisfy the following security requirements, based on the Decisional Diffie-Hellman assumption:

Backward security: an adversary who corrupts a subset $B \notin \Gamma$ of users sponsored in session s cannot obtain any useful information about the group keys of the preceeding sessions.

Forward security: an adversary who corrupts a subset $B \notin \Gamma$ of users revoked in session s cannot obtain any useful information about the group keys of the following sessions.

4   Specific Schemes with Improved Parameters

Depending on the situation where a group key distribution scheme must be implemented, some parameters of the scheme will be more important than others.

We can improve some of the parameters of the schemes of Kurnio *et al.* [12, 11] by considering our general construction using linear secret sharing schemes realizing other access structures on the set $\mathcal{U}$, different from the threshold ones. As an illustration, we present two specific cases. Other schemes with distinct properties could be constructed in a similar way.

4.1   Improved Revocation of Users

In the schemes of Kurnio *et al.*, we have that $L_{rev} = (t-1)\log p$. That is, every time a subset of at most $t-1$ users is revoked, $t-1$ exponentiations must be done by one non-revoked user, and he must broadcast a message with $t-1$ values.

Suppose that we want to implement a group key distribution scheme in a context in which most of the revocations consists of revoking a small number of users (less than J, for some positive integer $J \leq t-1$), although we want to have the possibility to revoke up to $t-1$ users in some special circumstances. This situation would correspond for example to an interactive game in which the two or three worst players of a session (probably a short period of time) are penalized by rejecting them from the game the following session. If some players do not participate in the game during a session (this is assumed to happen rarely, and with at most $t-1$ players in the same session), then they are also rejected during the following session.

If we implement the scheme of Kurnio *et al.* in such a situation, then at the end of every session some user must compute $t-1$ exponentiations and broadcast $t-1$ values, despite only two or three users must be revoked.

However, if we consider a secret sharing scheme realizing a specific bipartite access structure defined in the set of users, this allows to improve the efficiency of these revocations of few users. Bipartite access structures were first presented in [16]. In such a structure Γ, there is a partition of the set of participants, $\mathcal{U} = X \cup Y$, such that all participants in the same class play an equivalent role in the structure. We associate any subset $A \subset \mathcal{U}$ with the point of non-negative integers $\pi(A) = (x(A), y(A)) \in \mathbb{Z}^+ \times \mathbb{Z}^+$, where $x(A) = |A \cap X|$, $y(A) = |A \cap Y|$. A bipartite access structure Γ is determined by the region

$$\pi(\Gamma) = \{\pi(A) \mid A \in \Gamma\} \subset \mathbb{Z}^+ \times \mathbb{Z}^+.$$

Let us come back to our previous situation. Let m be the total number of possible real users. We consider a set $\mathcal{U} = X \cup Y$, where $X = \{1, \ldots, m, m + 1, \ldots, m + t - J - 1\}$ contains the m possible real users and $t - J - 1$ dummy users, and $Y = \{m + t - J, \ldots, m + t - 1\}$ is formed by J dummy users. So, the set $\mathcal{U}$ contains $n = m + t - 1$ users. Let us consider the following bipartite access structure Γ defined in $\mathcal{U} = X \cup Y$:

$$\Gamma = \{A \subset X \cup Y \mid |A| \geq J+1 \text{ and } |A \cap Y| \geq 1\} \cup \{A \subset X \cup Y \mid |A \cap X| \geq t\},$$

which corresponds to the following region:

$$\pi(\Gamma) = \{(x, y) \in \mathbb{Z}^+ \times \mathbb{Z}^+ \mid (x \geq t) \text{ or } (x + y \geq J + 1 \text{ and } y \geq 1)\}.$$

If a subset of $\omega \leq J - 1$ users has to be revoked, then a non-revoked user must compute J exponentiations and broadcast J values: ω values related to the revoked users, and $J - \omega$ values related to dummy users in Y. Otherwise, if a subset of $\omega \geq J$ users is revoked, with $\omega \leq t - 1$, then a non-revoked user must compute $t - 1$ exponentiations and broadcast $t - 1$ values: ω values related to the revoked users, in addition to $t - 1 - \omega$ values related to dummy users in X.

Note that if we put $J = t-1$, we obtain a scheme very similar to the threshold one of Kurnio *et al.*[12]. With lower values of J, the revocation phase can be performed in a more efficient way.

This bipartite access structure Γ can not be realized by a vector space secret sharing scheme (except in the threshold case $J = t - 1$, see [16] for the details), but by a linear one in which each participant is associated with two vectors instead of one. Therefore, each operation will have twice the cost of the same operation in the threshold case. In particular, the parameters of this scheme related to the revocation phase are: $L_{rev}(R) = 2J \log p$, if $|R| < J$, and $L_{rev}(R) = 2(t - 1) \log p$, if $J \leq |R| < t$. If efficiency in the revocation of small subsets has priority, this scheme makes perfect sense. The following picture shows an example of this situation, with $t = 16$ and $J = 6$.

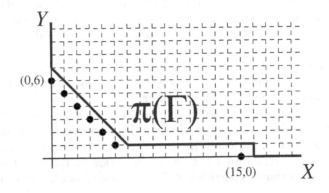

The region $\pi(\Gamma)$, delimited by thick lines, contains the points corresponding to the authorized subsets of the structure. The points corresponding to those subsets in $\overline{\Gamma}_0$, for example the one formed by 6 dummy users in Y, are marked with a circle.

In this example, if a subset of three users has to be revoked, a non-revoked user must compute and broadcast three values related to the three revoked users and three values related to three dummy users in Y. In this way, the broadcast information corresponds to a subset in $\overline{\Gamma}_0$ (symbolized by the point $(3,3)$ in the picture), and each non-revoked user can use the broadcast information and his private information to compute the new group key.

4.2 Considering Any Possible Family of Sponsor Subsets

In the threshold schemes proposed by Kurnio *et al.* any subset of t users is able to sponsor the join of a new user. In [11] the authors extend their basic threshold scheme in order to allow some other *privileged subsets* with less than t users to sponsor the join of a new user. This is done by performing an extra sharing of the secret information, in such a way that the privileged subsets will be able to recover it from their partial shares.

But let us consider a situation where a dynamic group key distribution scheme is implemented, and where the most important point is that of the subsets authorized to sponsor a new user. Imagine the following example: a new member of a club is accepted if some authorized subset of members of the club agrees. Maybe a subset is authorized if it contains the president of the club and one of the vice-presidents, or if it contains three of the vice-presidents, or if it contains two of the vice-presidents and at least five plain members of the club, etc. But any subset formed only by plain members is not authorized to sponsor new members. So the threshold (either basic [12] or extended [11]) solutions are not useful in such a situation. However, our general construction can be used.

The solution for this cases, in which the *family of sponsor subsets* authorized to join new users is the most important point of the scheme, is the following: let $\mathcal{U}$ be the set of users, and let $\mathcal{S} \subset 2^{\mathcal{U}}$ be the desired family of sponsor subsets. Then we must find an assignment of vectors $\psi : \mathcal{U} \cup \{D\} \longrightarrow \mathbb{Z}_q^\ell$ such that $\Gamma' = \mathcal{S}$, where Γ' is defined as in Section 3.1: $B \in \Gamma' \Longleftrightarrow \langle \{\psi(i)\}_{i \in B} \rangle = \mathbb{Z}_q^\ell$.

An appropriate assignment of vectors ψ satisfying this condition always exists. For example, the linear secret sharing scheme proposed by Simmons, Jackson and Martin in [19] provides such an assignment for any possible structure $\mathcal{S}$. This construction is not very efficient in general (in the sense that any user can be associated with a large number of vectors). But sometimes this is not the best solution, and it could be possible to find a more efficient assignment which satisfies also the desired condition.

Once an appropriate assignment ψ has been found, then we must construct the group key distribution scheme that results of using ψ in our general method explained in Section 3.1. In this way, only those subsets of users in $\Gamma' = \mathcal{S}$ will be authorized to sponsor the join of new users, as desired.

5   Conclusions and Comments

In this work we have shown how to construct a family of dynamic group key distribution schemes [1,12,11] by using general linear secret sharing schemes as a tool instead of the threshold one considered in the previous works. This leads to a flexible method to construct new schemes with some features that cannot be achieved with the threshold-based constructions. We illustrate this fact with two examples of situations in which our method is used to provide dynamic group key distribution schemes with some specific properties.

It is possible to add some properties (proactivity, verifiability, etc.) to the resulting group key distribution schemes by using in our construction linear secret sharing schemes with these properties. As an example we can consider the design of a dynamic group key distribution scheme without a centralized group controller, even in the initialization phase. This can be achieved using a variation of the standard joint generation of secrets without a trusted dealer (see [6,8]). The only modification regarding to our construction in Section 3.1 is that the initialization phase of the scheme is performed jointly by the group $\mathcal{U}_1 \subset \mathcal{U}$. Every $i \in \mathcal{U}_1$ selects at random a symmetrical $\ell \times \ell$ matrix $A_i = A_i^\top$ and gives secretly the vector $k_{ij} = A_i \cdot \psi(j) \in \mathbb{Z}_q^\ell$ to every user $j \in \mathcal{U}_1$. After that, every user j can compute his secret information $k_j = \sum_{i \in \mathcal{U}_1} k_{ij} \in \mathbb{Z}_q^\ell$ that corresponds to the distribution with a centralized group controller which uses as random matrix $A = \sum_{i \in \mathcal{U}_1} A_i$. The first key $K_1 \in \mathbb{Z}_p^*$ must be established by a user z in the set $\mathcal{U}_1$ executing the protocol $generate\_key(z, \emptyset)$.

This protocol requires secure channels between every pair of users in $\mathcal{U}_1$. If these channels are not available in the initialization phase, the joint generation can be executed by using publicly verifiable schemes [17,7].

On the other hand, if we consider a group key distribution scheme in which sponsored addition of users is not needed, then we can use a centralized full addition where users of a subset $C \subset \mathcal{U} - \mathcal{U}_s$ are accepted to enter in the group in session $s + 1$, without obtaining any information about the keys of the previous sessions. This can be performed in the following way: the group controller sends privately to every user $c \in C$ the value $k_c^* = K_s k_c \mod q \in \mathbb{Z}_q^\ell$, where $k_c = A \cdot \psi(c) \in \mathbb{Z}_q^\ell$. Every user i in the set $\mathcal{U}_s$ updates his secret share k_i to $k_i^* = K_s k_i \mod q \in \mathbb{Z}_q^\ell$. Then, as in the additions of Section 3.1, a user establishes the new key following the same steps and with the same capabilities for added users.

Note that in this situation where the sponsored join of users is not necessary, we could use a dynamic group key distribution scheme with centralized user join. For example, the threshold scheme by Anzai et al. [1], which can be extended to more general schemes using the same techniques that we have used in Section 3, is more efficient than the schemes of Kurnio et al. [12,11], because the private information that every user must keep secret decreases. Another difference is that in the scheme of Anzai et al. the group controller must publish some information in the initialization phase.

References

1. J. Anzai, N. Matsuzaki and T. Matsumoto. A quick group key distribution scheme with "Entity Revocation". *Advances in Cryptology-Asiacrypt'99*, LNCS **1716**, Springer-Verlag, pp. 333–347 (1999).

2. S. Berkovits. How to broadcast a secret. *Advances in Cryptology-Eurocrypt'91*, LNCS **547**, Springer-Verlag, pp. 536–541 (1991).

3. E.F. Brickell. Some ideal secret sharing schemes. *Journal of Combinatorial Mathematics and Combinatorial Computing*, **9**, pp. 105–113 (1989).

4. R. Canetti, T. Malkin and K. Nissim. Efficient communication-storage trade-offs for multicast encryption. *Advances in Cryptology-Eurocrypt'99*, LNCS **1592**, Springer-Verlag, pp. 469–479 (1998).

5. G. Caronni, B. Plattner, D. Sun, M. Wandvogel and N. Weiler. The VersaKey framework: versatile group key management. *IEEE Journal on Selected Areas in Communications*, **17** (9), (1999).

6. P. Feldman. A practical scheme for non-interactive verifiable secret sharing. *Proceedings of FOCS'87*, IEEE Press, pp. 427–437 (1987).

7. P.A. Fouque and J. Stern. One round threshold discrete-log key generation without private channels. *Proceedings of PKC'01*, LNCS **1992**, Springer-Verlag, pp. 190–206 (2001).

8. R. Gennaro, S. Jarecki, H. Krawczyk and T. Rabin. Secure distributed key generation for discrete-log based cryptosystems. *Advances in Cryptology-Eurocrypt'99*, LNCS **1592**, Springer-Verlag, pp. 295–310 (1999).

9. L. Gong. New protocols for third party based authentication and secure broadcast. *Proceedings of 2nd ACM Conference CCS*, pp. 176–183 (1994).

10. M. Just, E. Kranakis, D. Krizanc and P. van Oorschot. On key distribution via true broadcasting. *Proceedings of 2nd ACM Conference CCS*, pp. 81–88 (1994).

11. H. Kurnio, L. McAven, R. Safavi-Naini and H. Wang. A dynamic group key distribution scheme with flexible user join. *Proceedings of ICISC'02*, LNCS **2587**, Springer-Verlag, pp. 478–496 (2002).

12. H. Kurnio, R. Safavi-Naini and H. Wang. A group key distribution scheme with decentralised user join. *Proceedings of SCN'02*, LNCS **2576**, Springer-Verlag, pp. 146–163 (2002).

13. D.A. McGrew and A.T. Sherman. Key establishment in large dynamic groups using one-way function trees. Manuscript (1998).

14. A. Mayer and M. Yung. Generalized secret sharing and group-key distribution using short keys. *Proceedings of IEEE Conference on Compression and Complexity of Sequences*, pp. 30–44 (1997).

15. M. Naor, B. Pinkas. Efficient trace and revoked schemes. *Proceedings of Financial Cryptography'00*, LNCS **1962**, Springer-Verlag, pp. 1–20 (2000).

16. C. Padró and G. Sáez. Secret sharing schemes with bipartite access structure. *IEEE Transactions on Information Theory*, **46** (7), pp. 2596–2604 (2000).

17. B. Schoenmakers. A simple publicly verifiable secret sharing scheme and its applications to electronic voting. *Advances in Cryptology-Crypto'99*, LNCS **1666**, Springer-Verlag, pp. 148–164 (1999).

18. A. Shamir. How to share a secret. *Communications of the ACM*, **22**, pp. 612–613 (1979).

19. G.J. Simmons, W. Jackson and K. Martin. The geometry of secret sharing schemes. *Bulletin of the ICA* **1**, pp. 71–88 (1991).

Robust Software Tokens – Yet Another Method for Securing User's Digital Identity

Taekyoung Kwon

Sejong University, Seoul 143-747, Korea
tkwon@sejong.ac.kr

Abstract. This paper presents a robust software token that was developed to protect user's digital identity by simple software-only techniques. This work is closely related to Hoover and Kausik's software smart cards, and MacKenzie and Reiter's networked cryptographic devices, in the fact that user's private key is protected by postulating a remote server rather than tamper-resistance. The robust software token is aimed to be richer than the related schemes in terms of security, efficiency and flexibility. A two-party RSA scheme was carefully applied for the purpose, in a way of considering practical construction rather than theoretical framework.

1 Introduction

A public key infrastructure (PKI) appeared so promisingly, for example, for ensuring user's digital identity in a distributed environment. However, key management is still the issue both for public and private keys. Confidentiality should be assured for private keys while authenticity and validity are necessary for public keys[3]. A key roaming capability is another requisite for them[17,6,13]. In order for securing the private keys, a stable and portable container is required since those keys are not favorable to human memory. A *software token* which is stored in a user-controlled device, is widely accepted in general as a temporary alternative to the tamper-resistant device. However, such a password-encrypted token is susceptible to adversarial search in a small space of passwords[19]. Lately the networked methods were introduced, which could complicate the task of adversaries by postulating a remote server and its co-operation[11,15], in spite that they respectively assumed different models and had some weaknesses[12].

The goal of this paper is to present a new *robust software token*, which is "robust" in the sense that no party can influence the output of the token co-operating with its remote server, beyond the influence exerted by one's own input. The robustness must be assured even if the token is captured in an hostile environment. We design the robust software token and its various protocols to be richer than the related schemes in terms of security, efficiency, and flexibility. In Section 2 we will discuss the basic terms. Then we propose the method for generating the robust software token in Section 3. The robust software token protocols are proposed in Section 4 and Section 5, respectively. We analyze the proposed method in Section 6 and conclude this paper in Section 7.

R. Safavi-Naini and J. Seberry (Eds.): ACISP 2003, LNCS 2727, pp. 476–487, 2003.
© Springer-Verlag Berlin Heidelberg 2003

2   Preliminaries

2.1   Basic Notation

We define security parameters: $\kappa = 160$ and $\lambda = 1024$. Let us borrow some notation from [15]. So dvc and svr denote a user-controlled device and a trusted server, respectively. Also rst denotes the robust software token while vrf a verifier, π a password, pk_{svr} server's authentic public key, and sk_{svr} its corresponding private key. For RSA, e and d denote respectively encryption and decryption exponents satisfying $e, d \in Z^*_{\phi(N)}$ and $ed \equiv 1(\mod \phi(N))$, where N is a product of two distinct odd primes, satisfying $2^{\lambda-1} \leq N < 2^{\lambda}$, and $\phi(N)$ is the Euler totient function[20]. Additional notation is declared in each part of this paper.

2.2   Related Terms

Open PKI. An open PKI is a PKI where each certificate serves to establish authenticity in a potentially unbounded number of applications[3].
Closed PKI. A closed PKI is a PKI which has an influential issuer and clear contractual relationships among the issuer, certificate applicants, and verifiers[3]. In other words, it is the notion of private operation of the PKI framework.
Two-Party RSA. Since Boyd introduced a multiparty RSA signature[4], a great amount of related work has been done[1,2,7,9,10,18,21]. The two-party RSA is the case that an RSA private key is split into two shares[1].
HK Model. Hoover and Kausik presented a pioneer study applying cryptographic camouflage to software tokens[11]. The idea was to make a private key unidentifiable by encrypting a random-looking part only. However, they had to encrypt user's public key and could not import the existing digital identity, for security reasons. Also impersonation was not considered carefully[12]. The HK model is a closed PKI model in which a client is a certificate applicant and a server is a verifier. So, two-factor authentication was most applicable[11].
MR Model. MacKenzie and Reiter presented the networked cryptographic devices along with a security proof[15]. They used the two-party RSA scheme in an additive manner, namely by splitting d into $d_1 + d_2$ of which one is a Ganensan's exponent[8], and allowed interesting features including key disable functions. However, adversarial replays or impersonation attempts could make a server busy without any detection[12]. It seems hard to obtain the untrusted server on the contrary to the original assumption[15]. The MR model is an open PKI model in which a server assists a client to perform a private key operation.

3   Robust Software Tokens

The robust software token is yet another method for securing user's digital identity in a user-controlled environment where the software token can be captured. The basic notion is given simply from two-party RSA derivation, $m^{dd_1} \to (m^{dd_1})^{e_1} \to m^d$ where mod N is omitted. Let us summarize our scheme

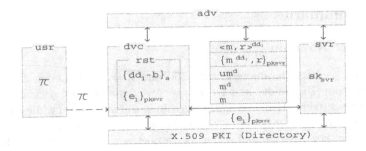

Fig. 1. Basic Concept

briefly with Figure 1 before describing the details: (i) rst holds user's private key d, which was camouflaged[1] and encrypted under a password derived key a. (ii) dvc stores rst in its local memory and communicates with svr. (iii) A user controls dvc and relies on its output in hand. (S)he types the password π into dvc so as to run rst. (iv) svr does not maintain and cannot acquire any sensitive information about a user, but rather relies on PKIs. (v) An adversary has a dictionary of passwords and controls the whole network, meaning that (s)he can control the inputs to dvc and svr, and hear all of their outputs. However, (S)he cannot succeed in factoring N. Our scheme must consider the followings.

1. (Intrinsic Adversary) The adversary controls the whole network for the adversarial goals such as *chosen signature generation* or *private key recovery*. The protocol messages are summarized as $< m, r >^{dd_1}$, $\{m^{dd_1}, r\}_{pk_{svr}}$, um^d, m^d, m, and $\{e_1\}_{pk_{svr}}$, while they should not allow such goals.
2. (Partial Compromise) The adversary who compromised either one of dvc and svr, should not gain more advantage than the intrinsic adversary.
3. (Dictionary Attack) The adversary must compromise svr as well as dvc, i.e., obtain rst and sk_{svr} together, in order to attempt the dictionary attack.
4. (Compatibility) Security must hold in the HK model and the MR model simultaneously. For example, a digital signature generated in the HK model should not degrade overall security in the MR model, and vice versa.

3.1 Robust Software Token Generation

The following rst-*generation* procedure can be performed *off line*. So, even dvc as well as an authorized party could perform it without communicating with svr.

Stage 0. For initialization, a new RSA key pair must be generated or an existing key pair must be imported for a user. Then the values must be given, such as $< e, N >$, $< d, N >$, $\phi(N)$, π, and pk_{svr}. Note that $\phi(N)$ is necessary for algebraic conversion to two-party RSA, as it was in the related work[11,15,1]. Also the public key is presumed to be certified by a certificate authority (CA)[11,15].

---

[1] Our camouflage method is different from that of Hoover and Kausik[11]. For example, our scheme does not encrypt user's public key e, but rather encrypts its friend e_1.

Stage 1. The following must be computed in this stage:

$e_1 \leftarrow_R Z^*_{\phi(N)}$

$d_1 \leftarrow e_1^{-1} \bmod \ \phi(N)$

$a \leftarrow k(\pi)$

$b \leftarrow_R \{0,1\}^1$

$c \leftarrow (dd_1 \bmod \phi(N)) - b$

$x \leftarrow E_a(R(c))$

$y \leftarrow \mathcal{E}_{pk_{svr}}(e_1)$

A new *friend exponent* e_1 is chosen at random, satisfying $1 \leq e_1 < \phi(N)$ and $\gcd(e_1, \phi(N)) = 1$. Its modular inverse d_1 is called a *camouflage exponent*. Their lengths will be discussed in the following section. A symmetric cipher key a is derived from π by a key derivation function $k()$, for example, PBKDF of PKCS#5[19]. Subsequently one bit integer b is chosen at random. Then d is multiplied by d_1 in $Z^*_{\phi(N)}$, and b is subtracted from the product. The random-looking[2] value c is encrypted under a. A function $R()$ runs random padding[11]. The private key can be camouflaged in that sense. Finally the friend exponent e_1 is encrypted under pk_{svr} so that only svr can obtain e_1 afterward. $E_i()$ denotes symmetric key encryption while $\mathcal{E}_i()$ asymmetric key encryption for each key i.

Stage 2. Our scheme provides various protocols in the MR model (See Section 5). For the purpose, this stage adds some extension to the previous computation:

$u \leftarrow_R Z^*_N$

$v \leftarrow u^{-d} \bmod \ N$

$y \leftarrow \mathcal{E}_{pk_{svr}}(e_1, u)$

A random number u is chosen, satisfying $1 \leq u < N$ and $\gcd(u, N) = 1$. Small u can be chosen for further efficiency. Then the value v is computed from u and d. The value u must be included in the value y when encrypting it above.

Finally all values such as $e, d, N, \phi(N), \pi, e_1, d_1, a, b, c, x, y, u, v$, and pk_{svr}, must be erased from the generating device, while rst is given to the user. Note that rst is composed of the basic values, $< x, y, N >$, the X.509 certificate $\mathcal{C}$, and the extensive values such as u, v, and pk_{svr}. Then rst is stored in dvc by software-only methods. Note that the pure private key, $< d, N, (p, q) >$, can be stored in a tamper-resistant device, so as to be used for the same public key.

3.2   Discussion on Camouflage Parameters

In general it is desirable to choose a private exponent d being roughly the same size as N while we prefer to use a low public exponent e such as $2^{16}+1$[16,22]. Let us discuss informally the length of camouflage parameters including e_1 and d_1. The friend exponent e_1 was encrypted so as to be read by svr only. It was treated as like a private exponent. So, the length of e_1 must be set to resist exhaustive search, since an adversary can derive M^d from M^{dd_1} if e_1 is so short as to find. Also e_1 must resist Wiener's attack for the case that dd_1 is compromised under

---

[2] Two random odd integers were multiplied in $Z^*_{\phi(N)}$ and subtracted by one bit.

a guessed password. Both for security and efficiency, we recommend 2κ bits for e_1, satisfying $e_1 > \sqrt[3]{N}$. Similarly it must be avoided that $d_1 < \sqrt[4]{N}$ for the opposite case. Fortunately it is unlikely that small d_1 will be generated from e_1 of length 2κ[16]. Also it could be obtained that dd_1 is greater than $\sqrt{N}$ due to the length of ee_1 such as $2\kappa + 17$.

Strictly speaking, the value c resides in $Z_{\phi(N)}$ rather than $Z^*_{\phi(N)}$ because b was one bit integer and subtracted from the $\phi(N)$-modular product, dd_1, of the values that are relatively prime to $\phi(N)$. Notice that $dd_1(\text{mod } \phi(N))$ must be an odd integer in $Z^*_{\phi(N)}$. As a result, the least significant bit and the most significant bit of c, respectively, can be 0 or 1 equally likely. This is due to the modular multiplication dd_1 and the normal integer subtraction $-b$. The remaining bits are random as well. So, it might be secure to encrypt the value c with the password-derived key a in a way of cryptographic camouflage[11].

4   Robust Software Tokens in the HK Model

We can devise two kinds of protocols respectively for *two-factor authentication* and *closed digital signature* in the HK Model.

4.1   Two-Factor Authentication

In the HK model, a limited number of servers should verify a closed signature using user's authentic public key. Though the original HK method encrypted the public key[11], our method can be released from such restriction. Figure 2 depicts the two-factor authentication protocol for using rst in the HK model.

Protocol Setup. A user knows π and has rst, i.e., storing rst in stable storage of dvc. Also svr may retain sk_{svr} in its storage device securely.

Protocol Run. An application may invoke rst, so that dvc sends an initiating signal to svr and the user types π on dvc. Upon receiving a random challenge $\mathcal{G}$ from svr, dvc derives a from π and recovers c by decrypting x. Here dvc must add 1 to c if it is even, meaning that dd_1 is recovered and denoted by c. Subsequently dvc computes $m = h(\text{svr}, h(\mathcal{G}))$ and selects a random number r of κ bits. $h()$ denotes a strong one-way hash function. Then dvc concatenates m and r, and signs M with c, actually dd_1. Find this signature form, $< m, r >^{dd_1}$, in Figure 1. Finally dvc sends $< \mathcal{C}, y, s >$ to svr. Then svr acquires the value e from $\mathcal{C}$ in an authentic manner and the value e_1 by decrypting y. Note that $\mathcal{C}$ is optional for the case that user's public key was certified by a CA. The value s is raised to e_1 and subsequently to e in Z_N, meaning $(M^{dd_1})^{ee_1} \mod N$. Finally svr obtains m_1 and verifies the signature with m_2 such that $m_2 = h(\text{svr}, h(\mathcal{G}))$. If they match, svr authenticates the user.

Discussion. The reasons for signing $h(\text{svr}, h(\mathcal{G}))$ are: (1) to prevent an adversary who masquerades svr, from getting a chosen message signed, and (2) to keep s from being re-used illegally, for example, in the outside of svr's PKI domain. The random number r was included in the signature so as to keep an adversary from obtaining the chosen ciphertext s. That means, the adversary cannot acquire the same signature for a message even with a correct guess on c.

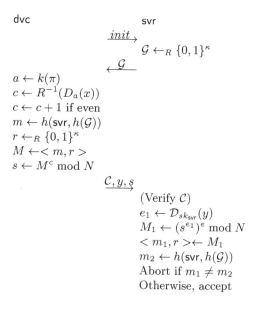

Fig. 2. Two-factor Authentication Protocol

4.2   Closed Signature

It is trivial to derive an arbitrary signature generation protocol in the HK model. Simply dvc signs an arbitrary message m instead of $\mathcal{G}$ while only svr can verify it. Note that dvc must generate a signature in a form of $h(h(m), \mathsf{svr})$ for the same reasons above. Also signing with a timestamp may work against replays.

5   Robust Software Tokens in the MR Model

In this section, we extend the MR model to devise three kinds of rst protocols for generating an RSA signature. The first will generate a signature simply by entrusting the signature completion to svr, so that it will be called an *entrusted open signature protocol*. The second will generate a signature with svr's assistance, as it did in the original MR scheme[3]. It means that svr assists the signature generation only and is not able to obtain a complete signature in the midst of the protocol run though the message could be understandable. So, we call it an *assisted open signature protocol*. The third is similar to the second

---

[3] It was a misconception to assume the untrusted server in the original MR scheme where the server was not able to detect impersonation or replay of an adversary[15, 12]. Our assisted signature schemes could allow the untrusted server under postulating a PKI support (See Figure 4 and 5). In spite of the improvement, we recommend the server be trusted because it is unlikely to assume that the untrusted server would not deny the service.

dvc   svr   vrf

$m \leftarrow \{0,1\}^*$

$a \leftarrow k(\pi)$

$c \leftarrow R^{-1}(D_a(x))$

$c \leftarrow c + 1$ if even

$M \leftarrow h(m)$

$s_0 \leftarrow M^c \bmod N$

$r \leftarrow_R \{0,1\}^\kappa$

$s_1 \leftarrow \mathcal{E}_{pk_{svr}}(s_0, r, \mathsf{vrf}, t)$

$\xrightarrow{\;\mathcal{C}, y, s_1, m\;}$ Verify $\mathcal{C}$

$e_1 \leftarrow \mathcal{D}_{sk_{svr}}(y)$

$< s_0, r, \mathsf{vrf}, t > \leftarrow \mathcal{D}_{sk_{svr}}(s_1)$

$s \leftarrow (s_0)^{e_1} \bmod N$

$h_1(m) \leftarrow s^e \bmod N$

Abort if $h(m) \neq h_1(m)$

Record(optional)

$\xleftarrow{\;\text{report(ack)}\;}$

Record(optional) $\xrightarrow{\;\mathcal{C}, s, m\;}$ Verify $\mathcal{C}$

$h_2(m) \leftarrow s^e \bmod N$

Abort if $h(m) \neq h_2(m)$

Otherwise, accept

Fig. 3. Entrusted Open Signature Protocol

except that svr is not able to understand a message when assisting the signature generation. In that sense, we call it a *blind-assisted open signature protocol*.

Common Requirements. (1) The open signature protocols must generate a signature that can be verified by user's authentic public key $< e, N >$ in the open PKI. (2) Also svr must not be able to acquire any information about user's sensitive data such as a password or a private key in the protocol run. (3) Finally svr must be able to authenticate a user so as to discourage on-line attacks in the protocol run. Specific requirements will be added in the following sections. The main difference stems from the degree of user's trusts on svr[4] in each protocol.

Common Protocol Setup. In addition to the previous protocol setup, a verifier vrf is able to access and verify user's certificate $\mathcal{C}$.

5.1   Entrusted Open Signature

This protocol is the most simple and efficient one for using rst in the MR model. See Figure 3. The basic notion is that svr is trusted, so as to complete user's open signature and transmit the signature to vrf on behalf. When we set vrf = dvc in s_1, svr may return the complete signature to dvc. Also vrf can be set as a list of many verifiers. Possible application may include the signed e-mail delivery.

Protocol Run. Given the inputs such as π, vrf and m where m means a message, dvc should derive a from π and decrypt x to obtain the value c. Also dvc should add one if it is even. The hash value $h(m)$ is derived and signed with

---

[4] If svr is compromised, the service denial is unavoidable. This is the shared weakness of all the related work that exploits network connectivity[11,15].

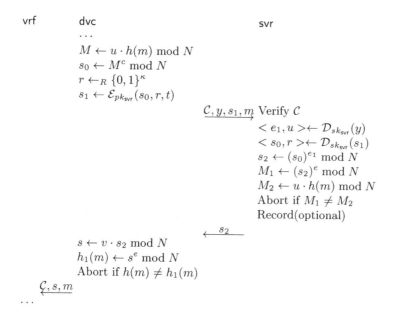

Fig. 4. Assisted Open Signature Protocol

c. The random number r is chosen at length κ, and concatenated with s_0 and vrf. Then $<s_0, r, \text{vrf}, t>$ is encrypted with pk_{svr}. A timestamp t is optional for resisting possible replays on s_1. Subsequently dvc sends $<\mathcal{C}, y, s_1, m>$ to svr. Then svr decrypts y and s_1 so as to acquire e_1 and s_0, respectively. Here svr can generate a complete signature s by using e_1 and s_0, and verify it with user's public key $<e, N>$. If s is a valid signature, svr on behalf of dvc, transmits it to vrf and reports the result. Note that svr and dvc can log the record to meet the requirement of non-repudiation. Finally vrf verifies user's signature with $\mathcal{C}$.

Discussion. The reason for encrypting s_0 and r under pk_{svr} is to keep an adversary, acquired rst and s_1, from running dictionary attacks. A common encoding rule can be used for signing $h(m)$. A timestamp t is necessary only if retransmission of s needs to be prevented, because replaying s_1 cannot change s.

5.2 Assisted Open Signature

Figure 4 depicts the assisted open signature protocol for rst. From now on, $\cdots$ should be considered as legacy steps (see Figure 3). In addition to the common requirements, this protocol must meet the followings requirements as well: (1) dvc must complete the signature generation, and (2) svr should not acquire a complete signature in the midst of the protocol run. The protocol setup is enhanced that svr is not allowed to complete the signature generation.

Protocol Run. Again dvc derives a from π and decrypts x to obtain the odd integer c. The hash value $h(m)$ is derived and the random number r is cho-

vrf   dvc   svr

···

$w \leftarrow_R \{0,1\}^\kappa$
$M \leftarrow w^e \cdot h(m) \bmod N$
$s_0 \leftarrow M^c \bmod N$
$r \leftarrow_R \{0,1\}^\kappa$
$s_1 \leftarrow \mathcal{E}_{pk_{svr}}(s_0, r, t)$

$\xrightarrow{\quad \mathcal{C}, y, s_1, M \quad}$ Verify $\mathcal{C}$

$e_1 \leftarrow \mathcal{D}_{sk_{svr}}(y)$
$< s_0, r > \leftarrow \mathcal{D}_{sk_{svr}}(s_1)$
$s_2 \leftarrow (s_0)^{e_1} \bmod N$
$M_1 \leftarrow (s_2)^e \bmod N$
Abort if $M_1 \neq M$
Record(optional)

$\xleftarrow{\quad s_2 \quad}$

$s \leftarrow w^{-1} \cdot s_2 \bmod N$
$h_1(m) \leftarrow s^e \bmod N$
Abort if $h(m) \neq h_1(m)$

$\xleftarrow{\quad \mathcal{C}, s, m \quad}$

···

Fig. 5. Blind-Assisted Open Signature Protocol

sen. Then $h(m)$ is multiplied by u in Z_N, and the result is signed with c. Here $< s_0, r, t >$ is encrypted under pk_{svr}. The timestamp t is also optional. Subsequently dvc sends $< \mathcal{C}, y, s_1, m >$ to svr. Then svr decrypts y and s_1 to obtain e_1, u and s_0. The value M_1 is obtained by raising s_0 to e_1 and then e in Z_N, while the value M_2 by multiplying u and $h(m)$ in Z_N. If M_1 and M_2 match, svr sends s_2 to dvc. Also svr can log the record for satisfying non-repudiation. Upon receiving s_2, dvc multiplies it by v in Z_N and verifies the result using $< e, N >$. If s is a valid signature, dvc could transmit it to vrf which would verify it.

Discussion. All discussion held on the entrusted signature also applies in this case. In addition, the reason for signing $u \cdot h(m)$ is to keep svr from completing the signature generation or obtaining s before dvc finishes the protocol run. Note that s is not derivable from s_2 without v or d.

5.3   Blind-Assisted Open Signature

A blind signature scheme, first introduced by Chaum, allows a user to get a message signed by another party without revealing any information about the message [5]. We can apply this technique to the assisted open signature protocol, so as to keep svr from understanding the message. Figure 5 depicts the blind-assisted open signature protocol in that sense. An additional requirement is that svr should not acquire any information about a message when assisting the signature generation. So, the protocol setup is enhanced again that svr is not allowed to read the original message.

Protocol Run. Similarly dvc derives a from π and decrypts x to obtain the odd integer c. The hash value $h(m)$ is derived from a message m while the random number w is chosen at length κ, satisfying $\gcd(w, N) = 1$. Then w is raised to e and multiplied by $h(m)$ in Z_N. The product M is signed with c. Note that we can replace $h(m)$ with m in all open signature protocols. The random number r is chosen at length κ. Here $< s_0, r >$ is encrypted under pk_{svr}. The timestamp t is also optional. Subsequently dvc sends $< \mathcal{C}, y, s_1, M >$ to svr. Then svr decrypts y and s_1 so as to obtain e_1 and s_0, respectively. The value M_1 is acquired by raising s_0 to e_1 and then e in Z_N. If M and M_1 match, svr sends s_2 to dvc. Also svr can log the record for satisfying non-repudiation. Upon receiving s_2, dvc multiplies it by w^{-1} in Z_N and verifies the result using user's public key, $< e, N >$. If s is a valid signature, dvc transmits it to vrf. Finally vrf can verify user's signature by obtaining $< e, N >$ from $\mathcal{C}$.

Discussion. All discussion held on the entrusted signature applies in this case as well. In addition, the reason for signing $w^e \cdot h(m)$ is to keep svr from understanding $h(m)$ in a notion of the blind signature. This protocol can derive a RSA decryption protocol using rst in that sense.

6   Analysis and Comparison

6.1   Security

Security of the proposed scheme was informally discussed in Section 3.2 and each discussion part in Section 4 and 5. Notice that rst retained user's components in the form of $< E_a(R(dd_1 - b)), N, u, v, \mathcal{E}_{pk_{\mathsf{svr}}}(e_1, u) >$, satisfying the notion of cryptographic camouflage. The most significant bit and the least significant bit of "$dd_1(\bmod \phi(N)) - b$" are not predictable, while the remaining bits are random as well. The friend exponent e_1 is encrypted under pk_{svr} and handled carefully with d_1. As for each protocol run, we were able to see that the flexible goals were respectively attained. Let us stop discussing security due to the strict page restriction in this paper. For more details of the security both with formal and informal discussions, readers are referred to the longer version of this paper[14].

6.2   Efficiency

If the RSA exponent is chosen at random, RSA encryption using the repeated square-and-multiply algorithm will take λ modular squarings and expected $\frac{\lambda}{2}$ modular multiplications[16]. From this simple view, we can evaluate the computational performance of software token methods. See Table 1. Define a new parameter $\sigma = 16$, and assume $e = pk_{\mathsf{svr}} = 2^{16} + 1$. The costs for certificate verification $(\sigma + 1)$ were involved in HK schemes and all of our schemes. All RSA moduli are assumed λ bits for simplicity. Also we have implemented three assisted signature protocols and found the similar result to Table 1[14].

Table 1. Performance Evaluation of Software Token Methods

Number of Multiplications	*Client* (dvc)	*Server* (svr)
HK Scheme-1[11]	1.5λ	$2.25\lambda + (\sigma + 1)$
HK Scheme -2[11]	$1.5(\sigma + 1)\lambda$	$1.5\lambda + (1.5\kappa + \sigma + 1)$
RST (Two-factor Auth.)	1.5λ	$1.5\lambda + (3\kappa + 2\sigma + 2)$
MR Scheme[15]	$1.5\lambda + (3\sigma + 4)$	9λ
Augmented MR Scheme[12]	$1.5\lambda + (3\sigma + 4)$	$10.5\lambda + \sigma + 1$
RST (Entrusted)	$1.5\lambda + (2\sigma + 2)$	$4.5\lambda + (3\kappa + 2\sigma + 2)$
RST (Assisted)	$1.5\lambda + (3\sigma + 5)$	$4.5\lambda + (3\kappa + 2\sigma + 3)$
RST (Blind-Assisted)	$1.5\lambda + (4\sigma + 6)$	$4.5\lambda + (3\kappa + 2\sigma + 2)$

7   Conclusion

In this paper, we introduced a simple method called the robust software token in order to protect user's digital identity by software-only techniques. Authentication and various types of signature generation are possible applications for this scheme under postulating a PKI support to user-controlled environments. A networked device, which holds the robust software token, could be more promising for ubiquitous computing environment. We considered security, efficiency, and flexibility while designing the software token in the way to improve various features of the invaluable predecessors such as the software smart cards[11] and the networked cryptographic devices[15]. The robust software token can be used flexibly in the MR model as well as the HK model, without ignoring security and efficiency. It is so *robust* that only the legitimate party can generate or update it even off-line while it must be used on-line afterwards. A discretionary control of the legitimate party can be made to the degree of server assistance. In order for describing the schemes, practical construction was more considered than theoretical framework in this paper. More details can be found at [14].

Acknowledgement. I would like to thank anonymous referees for their helpful comments.

References

1. M. Bellare and R. Sandhu, "The security of practical two-party RSA signature schemes," Manuscript, 2001.
2. D. Boneh and M. Franklin, "Efficient generation of shared RSA keys," *Advances in Cryptology – Crypto'97*, Lecture Notes in Computer Science, Vol. 1294, Springer-Verlag, pp.425–439, 1997.
3. S. Brands, *Rethinking public key infrastructures and digital certificates*, The MIT Press, p.11 and pp.219–224, 2000.
4. C. Boyd, "Digital multisignatures," *Cryptography and Coding*, Oxford University Press, pp.241–246, 1989.

5. D. Chaum, "Blind signatures for untraceable payments, " *Advances in Cryptology – Crypto'82*, Lecture Notes in Computer Science, Vol. 1440, Springer-Verlag, pp.199–203, 1983.
6. W. Ford and B. Kaliski, "Server-assisted generation of a strong secret from a password," In Proceedings of the *International Workshops on the Enabling Technologies: Infrastructure for Collaborative Enterprise*, IEEE, June 2000
7. Y. Frankel, P. MacKenzie, and M. Yung, "Robust efficient distributed RSA key generation," In Proceedings of the *ACM Symposium on Theory of Computing*, pp.663–672, 1998.
8. R. Ganesan, "Yaksha: Augmenting Kerberos with public key cryptography," In Proceedings of the *ISOC Network and Distributed System Security Symposium*, February 1995.
9. R. Gennaro, S. Jarecki, H. Krawczyk, and T. Rabin, "Robust and efficient sharing of RSA functions," *Advances in Cryptology – Crypto'96*, Lecture Notes in Computer Science, Vol. 1109, Springer-Verlag, pp.157–172, 1996.
10. N. Gilboa, "Two party RSA key generation," *Advances in Cryptology – Crypto'99*, Lecture Notes in Computer Science, Vol. 1666, Springer-Verlag, pp.116–129, 1999.
11. D. Hoover, B. Kausik, "Software smart cards via cryptographic camouflage," In Proceedings of the *IEEE Symposium on Security and Privacy*, 1999.
12. T. Kwon, "On the difficulty of protecting private keys in software," *Information Security – ISC 2002*, Lecture Notes in Computer Science, Vol. 2433, Springer-Verlag, September 2002. A revised version can be found at http://dasan.sejong.ac.kr/~tkwon/research/difficulty.pdf.
13. T. Kwon, "Virtual Software Tokens – A practical way to secure PKI roaming," *Infrastructure Security – InfraSec 2002*, Lecture Notes in Computer Science, Vol. 2437, Springer-Verlag, October 2002.
14. T. Kwon, "Robust Software Tokens – Yet another method for securing user's digital identity," A full version can be found at http://dasan.sejong.ac.kr/~tkwon/research/rst.pdf.
15. P. MacKenzie and M. Reiter, "Networked cryptographic devices resilient to capture," In Proceedings of the *IEEE Symposium on Security and Privacy*, 2001, a full and updated version is DIMACS Technical Report 2001–19, May 2001.
16. A. Menezes, P. van Oorschot, and S. Vanstone, *Handbook of Applied Cryptography*, CRC Press, pp.287–291, pp.312–315, 1997.
17. R. Perlman and C. Kaufman, "Secure password-based protocol for downloading a private key," In Proceedings of the *ISOC Network and Distributed System Security Symposium*, February 1999.
18. G. Poupard and J. Stern, "Generation of shared RSA keys by two parties," *Advances in Cryptology – Asiacrypt'98*, Lecture Notes in Computer Science, Vol. 1514, Springer-Verlag, pp.11–24, 1998.
19. PKCS #5, "Password-based encryption standard," *RSA Laboratories Technical Note*, Version 2.0, 1999.
20. R. Rivest, A. Shamir, and L. Adleman, "A method for obtaining digital signatures and public-key cryptosystems," *Communications of the ACM*, vol.21, pp.120–126, 1978.
21. V. Shoup, "Practical Threshold Signatures," *Advances in Cryptology – Eurocrypt'00*, Lecture Notes in Computer Science, Vol. 1807, Springer-Verlag, pp.207–220, 2000.
22. M. Wiener, "Cryptanalysis of short RSA secret exponents," *IEEE Transactions on Information Theory*, vol.36, no.3, May 1990.

Public-Key Cryptosystems Based on Class Semigroups of Imaginary Quadratic Non-maximal Orders

Hwankoo Kim[1,3] and SangJae Moon[2,3]

[1] Information Security Major, Division of Computer Science & Engineering, Hoseo University, Asan 336-795, Korea.
`hkkim@office.hoseo.ac.kr`
[2] School of Electronic and Electrical Eng., Kyungpook National University, Taegu 702-701, Korea.
`sjmoon@knu.ac.kr`
[3] Mobile Network Security Technology Research Center, Kyungpook National University, Taegu 702-701, Korea.

Abstract. In this paper we propose a key-exchange system and a public-key encryption scheme based on the class semigroups of imaginary quadratic non-maximal orders, the former is analogous to the Diffie-Hellman's key-exchange system and the latter is similar to the ElGamal's encryption scheme, whose security is based on the difficulty of the discrete logarithm problem of that class semigroup.

1   Introduction

The security of many cryptographic systems has been based on the difficulty of several number theoretic problems [7,17,23]. Prominent examples are the factoring problem for integers [22,21] and the discrete logarithm problem (DLP) in the multiplicative group of a finite field [20], in the class group of an order of a quadratic field [4], in the group of points on an elliptic curve over a finite field [14], in the Jacobian of a hyperelliptic curve over a finite field [15], and others. There is, however, no guarantee that these problems will remain difficult to solve in the future. On the contrary, as the experience with the factoring problem and some DLPs shows, unexpected breakthroughs are always possible. Therefore, it is important to design cryptographic schemes in such a way that the underlying mathematical problem can easily be replaced with another one.

The ideal class group of an imaginary quadratic maximal order has received attention in the context of key exchange protocols, cryptosystems, and even an identification scheme. However, in [16,10], a sub-exponential running time (and space) algorithm for computing class groups of imaginary quadratic maximal orders in number fields was invented by J. L. Hafner and K. S. McCurley and it was shown how to use this algorithm and the index-calculus method to calculate discrete logarithms. The improved algorithms for computing class groups to simplify the index-calculus algorithm in class groups were presented in [1,12].

R. Safavi-Naini and J. Seberry (Eds.): ACISP 2003, LNCS 2727, pp. 488–497, 2003.
© Springer-Verlag Berlin Heidelberg 2003

Therefore, in order to protect these cryptosystems from attacks by index-calculus algorithms, much larger discriminants are required than any square-root algorithm or the $(p-1)$-algorithm [2]. Real quadratic orders have also been proposed for use in these contexts. They have the distinction of being the first discrete logarithm-based systems to make use of a structure which is not a group, that is, the infrastructure of the principal class. On the other hand, Buchmann and Paulus proposed a one way function based on ideal arithmetic in arbitrary number fields in [3] and Meyer *et al* first implemented cryptographic protocols based on algebraic number fields in [18].

This paper is organized as follows: In Section 2 we will recall the necessary basics concerning quadratic orders in this work. In Section 3 we will propose a key-exchange system and a public-key encryption scheme based on the class semigroups of imaginary quadratic non-maximal orders, the former is analogous to the Diffie-Hellman's key-exchange system and the latter is similar to the ElGamal's encryption scheme, whose security is based on the difficulty of the discrete logarithm problem of that class semigroup. In Section 4 and 5 we will consider the security and efficiency of our cryptosystems respectively. We conclude this work in Section 6 by sketching future works.

2   Quadratic Orders

There are plenty of cryptographic primitives using quadratic fields and several public-key cryptosystems have been proposed [2,4,16,18,21]. We briefly review the class (semi-)group of a quadratic order. A more complete treatment may be found in [19,5].

Let $D_1 < 0$ be a square-free integer and let $\Delta_1 = \frac{4D_1}{r_1}$, where $r_1 = 2$ if $D_1 \equiv 1$ (mod 4) and $r_1 = 1$ otherwise. The value Δ_1 is congruent to either 1 or 0 modulo 4 and is called a *fundamental discriminant* with *fundamental radicand* D_1. If we set $\mathfrak{K} = \mathbb{Q}(\sqrt{D_1})$, i.e. the adjunction of a root of the irreducible polynomial $x^2 - D_1$ to $\mathbb{Q}$(the set of all rational numbers), then $\mathfrak{K}$ is called a *a quadratic field of discriminant* Δ_1. If $\alpha \in \mathfrak{K}$, we denote by $\overline{\alpha}$ the *conjugate* of α, by $\mathsf{Tr}(\alpha)$ the value of $\alpha + \overline{\alpha}$, i.e., the *trace* of α, and by $\mathsf{N}(\alpha)$, the value of $\alpha\overline{\alpha}(\geq 0)$, i.e., the *norm* of α. Note that $|\alpha|^2 = \alpha\overline{\alpha} = \mathsf{N}(\alpha)$. We call $\omega_{\Delta_1} = \frac{r_1-1+\sqrt{D_1}}{r_1}$ the *principal surd*.

Let $\Delta_1 < 0$ be a fundamental discriminant and set $\Delta_f = \Delta_1 f^2$ for some positive integer f. If $g = \gcd(r_1, f)$ and $r = \frac{r_1}{g}$, then $\Delta_f = \frac{4D_f}{r}$ is called a *discriminant* with *associated radicand* $D_f = (\frac{f}{g})^2 D_1$ (and underlying fundamental discriminant Δ_1 having fundamental radicand D_1).

If $\alpha, \beta \in \mathfrak{K}$, we denote by $[\alpha, \beta]$ the set $\alpha\mathbb{Z} + \beta\mathbb{Z}$, where $\mathbb{Z}$ is the set of all rational integers. Set $\omega_{\Delta_f} = f\omega_{\Delta_1} + h$, where $h \in \mathbb{Z}$, called the *principal surd associated with the discriminant* Δ_f. Then $\Delta_f = (\omega_{\Delta_f} - \overline{\omega_{\Delta_f}})$ and

$$\mathcal{O}_{\Delta_f} = [1, f\omega_{\Delta_1}] = [1, \omega_{\Delta_f}]$$

is called an *order* in $\mathfrak{K} = \mathbb{Q}(\sqrt{D_1})$ having *conductor* f and associated discriminant Δ_f with radicand D_f. It is a one-dimensional Noetherian (integral) domain.

When $f = 1$, $\mathcal{O}_{\Delta_f}$ is the ring of integers $\mathcal{O}_{\Delta_1}$ of $\mathfrak{K}$ called a *maximal order*. If Δ_f is not a fundamental discriminant, then $\mathcal{O}_{\Delta_f} \subset \mathcal{O}_{\Delta_1}$ and $\mathcal{O}_{\Delta_f}$ has finite index f in $\mathcal{O}_{\Delta_1}$. Moreover, we have $\mathcal{O}_{\Delta_f} = \mathbb{Z} + f\mathcal{O}_{\Delta_1}$. The order $\mathcal{O}_{\Delta_f}$ is called the *non-maximal order* with *conductor* f.

A subset $\mathfrak{a}$ of $\mathcal{O}_{\Delta_f}$ is an (integral) ideal of $\mathcal{O}_{\Delta_f}$ if $\alpha + \beta \in \mathfrak{a}$ whenever $\alpha, \beta \in \mathfrak{a}$, and $\alpha\gamma \in \mathfrak{a}$ whenever $\alpha \in \mathfrak{a}, \gamma \in \mathcal{O}_{\Delta_f}$. Every ideal $\mathfrak{a}$ of $\mathcal{O}_{\Delta_f}$ is given by

$$\mathfrak{a} = [a, b + c\omega_{\Delta_f}], \tag{1}$$

where $a, b, c \in \mathbb{Z}$, and $a > 0, c > 0$. Further, from the definition of an ideal it is easy to show that $c|a, c|b$, and $ac|N(b + c\omega_{\Delta_f})$. Also, if $\mathfrak{a} = [a, b + c\omega_{\Delta_f}]$, where $a, b, c \in \mathbb{Z}, c|a, c|b$, and $ac|N(b + c\omega_{\Delta_f})$, then $\mathfrak{a}$ is an ideal of $\mathcal{O}_{\Delta_f}$. For a given ideal $\mathfrak{a}$ the value of a in (1) is unique. We denote this by $L(\mathfrak{a})$; it is the least positive rational integer in $\mathfrak{a}$. The norm of an ideal $\mathfrak{a}$ is defined by $N(\mathfrak{a}) = ac$. For two given ideals $\mathfrak{a}, \mathfrak{b}$, we can define their product $\mathfrak{a}\mathfrak{b}$ (see, for example, [4,5]). The computation of a representation of $\mathfrak{a}\mathfrak{b}$ needs $O((\log(\max\{N(\mathfrak{a}), N(\mathfrak{b})\}))^2)$ bit operations. We say that a fractional ideal $\mathfrak{a}$ is *invertible* if there is a fractional ideal $\mathfrak{b}$ such that $\mathfrak{a}\mathfrak{b} = \mathcal{O}_{\Delta_f}$.

We describe the class semigroup of $\mathcal{O}_{\Delta_f}$. We denote by $\mathcal{F}_{\Delta_f}$ the set of all nonzero fractional ideals of $\mathcal{O}_{\Delta_f}$. Two ideals $\mathfrak{a}$ and $\mathfrak{b}$ are called *equivalent* if there is an $\alpha \in \mathfrak{K}$ such that $\mathfrak{a} = \alpha\mathfrak{b}$. Denote this equivalence relation by $\mathfrak{a} \sim \mathfrak{b}$. We also denote the equivalence class containing an ideal $\mathfrak{a}$ by $[\mathfrak{a}]$. For an element $\gamma \in \mathfrak{K}$ the ideal $\gamma\mathcal{O}_{\Delta_f}$ is called a *principal* ideal. The principal ideals $\mathcal{P}_{\Delta_f}$ form a subgroup of $\mathcal{F}_{\Delta_f}$. The quotient semigroup $\mathcal{F}_{\Delta_f}/\mathcal{P}_{\Delta_f}$ is called the *class semigroup* of $\mathcal{O}_{\Delta_f}$; denote it by $Cls(\Delta_f)$. It is well-known that $Cls(\Delta_f)$ is a *finite* commutative semigroup with identity $[\mathcal{O}_{\Delta_f}]$.

Definition 1. *[19, Definition 1.2.1] If $\mathfrak{a}$ is an $\mathcal{O}_{\Delta_f}$-ideal with $L(\mathfrak{a}) = N(\mathfrak{a})$, i.e., $c = 1$, then $\mathfrak{a}$ is called primitive, which means that $\mathfrak{a}$ has no rational integer factors other than ± 1. (When $\mathfrak{a}$ is primitive then $N(\mathfrak{a}) = L(\mathfrak{a}) = |\mathcal{O}_{\Delta_f} : \mathfrak{a}|$, the index of $\mathfrak{a}$ in $\mathcal{O}_{\Delta_f}$.)*

Definition 2. *[19, Definition 1.4.1] Let $\mathcal{O}_{\Delta_f}$ be an order and let $\mathfrak{a}$ be an $\mathcal{O}_{\Delta_f}$-ideal. Then $\mathfrak{a}$ is said to be reduced if it is primitive and does not contain any nonzero element α such that both $|\alpha| < N(\mathfrak{a})$ and $|\overline{\alpha}| < N(\mathfrak{a})$. (Note that when $\Delta_f < 0$, this means that there is no $\alpha \in \mathfrak{a}$ such that $|\alpha| < N(\mathfrak{a})$, where $|\alpha|^2 = \alpha\overline{\alpha} = N(\alpha)$.)*

Theorem 1. *(cf. [19, Theorem 1.4.2]) Let $\mathcal{O}_{\Delta_f}$ be an order.*

(a) If $\mathfrak{a}$ is any primitive ideal of $\mathcal{O}_{\Delta_f}$, then there exists some $\alpha \in \mathfrak{a}$ such that $\mathfrak{a} = [N(\mathfrak{a}), \alpha]$ and $Tr(\alpha) \leq N(\mathfrak{a})$. Furthermore, $|Tr(\alpha)|$ is unique (i.e., if $\mathfrak{a} = [N(\mathfrak{a}), \alpha] = [N(\mathfrak{a}), \beta]$ and $Tr(\alpha) \leq N(\mathfrak{a})$ and $Tr(\beta) \leq N(\mathfrak{a})$, then $Tr(\alpha) = Tr(\beta)$).

(b) If $\mathfrak{a}$ is any primitive ideal of $\mathcal{O}_{\Delta_f}$ and $\mathfrak{a} = [N(\mathfrak{a}), \alpha]$ with $Tr(\alpha) \leq N(\mathfrak{a})$, then $\mathfrak{a}$ is a reduced ideal if and only if $|\alpha| \geq N(\mathfrak{a})$.

(c) If $\mathfrak{a}$ is a reduced ideal of $\mathcal{O}_{\Delta_f}$, then $N(\mathfrak{a}) < \sqrt{\frac{|\Delta_f|}{3}}$.

(d) If $\mathfrak{a}$ is a primitive ideal of $\mathcal{O}_{\Delta_f}$ and $N(\mathfrak{a}) < \sqrt{\frac{|\Delta_f|}{4}}$, then $\mathfrak{a}$ is a reduced ideal.

The following algorithm and theorem show that given a primitive ideal $\mathfrak{a}$, we can compute a reduced ideal $\mathfrak{r}$ such that $\mathfrak{r} \sim \mathfrak{a}$.

We first note from [4, pp. 110] that if $\mathfrak{a} = [L(\mathfrak{a}), \alpha]$ is a primitive ideal of $\mathcal{O}_{\Delta_f}$, then so is $\mathfrak{b} = [\frac{N(\alpha)}{L(\mathfrak{a})}, -\overline{\alpha}]$. Further,

$$(\overline{\alpha})\mathfrak{a} = (L(\mathfrak{a}))\mathfrak{b};$$

hence, $\mathfrak{a} \sim \mathfrak{b}$.

Algorithm 2 *(cf. [4, Algorithm 3.1])*

1. For a given primitive ideal $\mathfrak{a} = \mathfrak{a}_1 = [L(\mathfrak{a}), \alpha]$ of $\mathcal{O}_{\Delta_f}$, put $Q_0 = rL(\mathfrak{a})(> 0)$, put $P_0 = r\alpha - \sqrt{D_f} \in \mathbb{Z}$. The value of r here is that defined at the beginning of Section 2.
2. Compute

$$
\begin{cases}
q_i = Ne(\dfrac{P_i}{Q_i}), \\[2mm]
P_{i+1} = q_i Q_i - P_i, \\[2mm]
Q_{i+1} = \dfrac{(P_{i+1})^2 - D_f}{Q_i},
\end{cases}
\tag{2}
$$

where by $Ne(\gamma)$ we denoted an integer such that $|\gamma - Ne(\gamma)| \leq \frac{1}{2}$. *(Unique unless $|\cdot| = \frac{1}{2}$.)*
3.

$$\mathfrak{a}_{i+1} = [\frac{Q_i}{r}, \frac{P_i + \sqrt{D_f}}{r}]$$

is a reduced ideal of $\mathcal{O}_{\Delta_f}$ when

$$Q_{i+1} \geq Q_i.$$

Theorem 3. *(cf. [4, Theorem 3.2])* If $\mathfrak{a}$ is given as in Algorithm 2, then we get $Q_{i+1} \geq Q_i$ for some $i \leq 2 + \lceil \frac{1}{2} \log_2 \frac{3Q_0}{5\sqrt{|D_f|}} \rceil$.

An efficient algorithm for multiplication of ideals is given in [4, pp. 113], that is, it was shown that, given an ideal $\mathfrak{a}$ and a positive integer x, to compute the reduced ideal $\mathfrak{s}$ such that $\mathfrak{s} \sim \mathfrak{a}^x$ requires the performance of $O(\log x \log |D_1|)$ elementary operations. Fortunately, it can be applied to ideals in any order.

The following theorem shows that two distinct reduced ideals have the same greatest common divisor if they are in the same class.

Theorem 4. *[24, pp. 387]* Let $[a_1, b_1 + \omega_{\Delta_f}]$ and $[a_2, b_2 + \omega_{\Delta_f}]$ be two primitive ideals of $\mathcal{O}_{\Delta_f}$. Then $[a_1, b_1 + \omega_{\Delta_f}] \sim [a_2, b_2 + \omega_{\Delta_f}]$ if and only if $\gcd(a_1, \frac{N(b_1 + \omega_{\Delta_f})}{a_1}, Tr(b_1 + \omega_{\Delta_f})) = \gcd(a_2, \frac{N(b_2 + \omega_{\Delta_f})}{a_2}, Tr(b_2 + \omega_{\Delta_f}))$.

Note that $[a_1, b_1 + \omega_{\Delta_f}]$ is invertible if $\gcd(a_1, \frac{N(b_1 + \omega_{\Delta_f})}{a_1}, Tr(b_1 + \omega_{\Delta_f})) = 1$.

3   Public-Key Cryptosystems

The utilization of imaginary quadratic class groups in cryptography is due to Buchmann and Williams [4], who proposed a key agreement protocol analogue to [8] based on class groups of imaginary quadratic fields, i.e., the class group of a maximal order. Since then, many cryptosystems based on class groups of imaginary quadratic orders(IQC) have been proposed. The security of IQC is based on the difficulty of computing discrete logarithm in class groups of imaginary quadratic orders(Cl-DLP). The following problem is a generalization of the Cl-DLP.

Discrete Logarithm Problem in Class Semigroups. Given ideals $\mathfrak{a}$ and $\mathfrak{b}$ of $Cls(\Delta_f)$, compute $x \in \mathbb{N}$ such that

$$[\mathfrak{b}] = [\mathfrak{a}]^x \qquad (\text{i.e., } \mathfrak{b} \sim \mathfrak{a}^x),$$

if such an x exists.

3.1   Analogue of Diffie-Hellman's Key-Exchange System

Buchmann and Williams proposed a key exchange protocol analogous to [8] based on the class group of a *maximal* order. We can now modify a method similar to that of [4] for a secret key exchange based on the class semigroup of a *non-maximal* order. Two users Alice and Bob select a value D_f such that $|D_f|$ is sufficiently large($\approx 10^{200}$) and a non-invertible ideal $\mathfrak{a}$ in $\mathcal{O}_{\Delta_f}$. The value of D_f and the ideal $\mathfrak{a}$ can be made public.

1. Alice selects at random an integer x and computes a reduced ideal $\mathfrak{b}$ such that
$$\mathfrak{b} \sim \mathfrak{a}^x.$$
   Alice sends $\mathfrak{b}$ to Bob.
2. Bob selects at random an integer y and computes a reduced ideal $\mathfrak{c}$ such that
$$\mathfrak{c} \sim \mathfrak{a}^y.$$
   Bob sends $\mathfrak{c}$ to Alice.
3. Alice computes a reduced ideal $\mathfrak{l}_1 \sim \mathfrak{c}^x$; Bob computes a reduced ideal $\mathfrak{l}_2 \sim \mathfrak{b}^y$.

   Note that $\mathfrak{l}_1 \sim \mathfrak{c}^x \sim (\mathfrak{a}^y)^x = (\mathfrak{a}^x)^y \sim \mathfrak{b}^y \sim \mathfrak{l}_2$. Thus if $\mathfrak{l}_1 = [L(\mathfrak{l}_1), \alpha_1]$ and $\mathfrak{l}_2 = [L(\mathfrak{l}_2), \alpha_2]$, then by Theorem 4, Alice and Bob can use

$$\gcd(L(\mathfrak{l}_1), \frac{N(\alpha_1)}{L(\mathfrak{l}_1)}, \mathsf{Tr}(\alpha_1)) = \gcd(L(\mathfrak{l}_2), \frac{N(\alpha_2)}{L(\mathfrak{l}_2)}, \mathsf{Tr}(\alpha_2))$$

as their secret key.

   Also note that our key-exchange system works on a cyclic subsemigroup of the class semigroup, while Buchmann-Williams' key-exchange system([4]) works on a cyclic subgroup of the class group.

3.2   Analogue of ElGamal's Public-Key Encryption Scheme

In [4], Buchmann and Williams converted the idea of a key-exchange system into a public-key cryptosystem in a manner similar to that proposed by ElGamal [9]. We can now set up a method similar to that of [4] for a public-key cryptosystem based on the *class semigroup* of a *non-maximal* order. Two entities (usually Alice and Bob) select a radicand $D_f < 0$ of an imaginary quadratic number field $\mathfrak{K}$ of discriminant Δ_f, and a non-invertible $\mathcal{O}_{\Delta_f}$-ideal $\mathfrak{a}$. Both D_f and $\mathfrak{a}$ can be made public. Suppose that Alice wants to send a secure message m to Bob.

1. Alice selects at random an $x \in \mathbb{Z}$ and computes a reduced $\mathcal{O}_{\Delta_f}$-ideal $\mathfrak{b}$ such that $\mathfrak{b} \sim \mathfrak{a}^x$. Then Alice sends $\mathfrak{b}$ to Bob.
2. Bob selects at random a $y \in \mathbb{Z}$ and computes a reduced $\mathcal{O}_{\Delta_f}$-ideal $\mathfrak{c}$ such that $\mathfrak{c} \sim \mathfrak{a}^y$. Then Bob sends $\mathfrak{b}$ to Alice.
3. Alice computes a reduced ideal $\mathfrak{k}_1 \sim \mathfrak{c}^x$, and Bob computes a reduced ideal $\mathfrak{k}_2 \sim \mathfrak{b}^y$.
4. Alice sends the first block $E < \gcd(\mathsf{L}(\mathfrak{k}_1), \frac{\mathsf{N}(\alpha)}{\mathsf{L}(\mathfrak{k}_1)}, \mathsf{Tr}(\alpha))$ of the message m in the form of the encrypted $\mathcal{O}_{\Delta_f}$-ideal $(E + \gcd(\mathsf{L}(\mathfrak{k}_1), \frac{\mathsf{N}(\alpha)}{\mathsf{L}(\mathfrak{k}_1)}, \mathsf{Tr}(\alpha)), \mathfrak{b})$, the ciphertext.
5. To find E, Bob must determine $\gcd(\mathsf{L}(\mathfrak{k}_1), \frac{\mathsf{N}(\alpha)}{\mathsf{L}(\mathfrak{k}_1)}, \mathsf{Tr}(\alpha))$. Since Bob has $\mathfrak{b} \sim \mathfrak{a}^x$ and y, then $\mathfrak{k}_2 \sim \mathfrak{b}^y \sim (\mathfrak{a}^x)^y \sim \mathfrak{c}^x \sim \mathfrak{k}_1$.
6. To send subsequent blocks of m, Alice repeats each of the above steps, but must choose a new $x \in \mathbb{Z}$ for each block she sends.

Note that the above idea can also be converted into a digital signature, which is a variant of DSA, in a way similar to that proposed by Buchmann and Hamdy [2]. More details of a digital signature and implementation of our cryptosystems will be published somewhere later.

4   Security Considerations

In order to guarantee the security of our cryptosystems, it is necessary that the order of $Cls(\Delta_f)$ (i.e., the number of elements in $Cls(\Delta_f)$) be sufficiently large. For, let $\mathcal{O}_{\Delta_f}$ be the nonmaximal order having conductor f, which is contained in the maximal order $\mathcal{O}_{\Delta_1}$ of an imaginary quadratic field and let $Cl(\Delta_f)$ be the ideal class group (For definitions, see [6, pp. 136]). Then from [6, Theorem 7.24], $|Cl(\Delta_f)|$ is always an integer multiple of $|Cl(\Delta_1)|$, and so for any $\varepsilon > 0$, $|Cls(\Delta_f)| > |\Delta_1|^{\frac{1}{2}-\varepsilon}$ for all sufficiently large Δ_1 by [4, pp.114]. We can also deduce from the above result and Theorem 4 that $\gcd(\mathsf{L}(\mathfrak{k}), \frac{\mathsf{N}(\alpha)}{\mathsf{L}(\mathfrak{k})}, \mathsf{Tr}(\alpha))$ may be sufficiently large for some primitive ideal $\mathfrak{k} = [\mathsf{L}(\mathfrak{k}), \alpha]$.

The security of our cryptosystems is based on the difficulty of computing discrete logarithm in class semigroups of imaginary quadratic non-maximal orders. Since the class semigroup depends only on the discriminant, the discriminant is the main cryptographic parameter. In [11] all known strategies to compute discrete logarithms and the selection of the cryptographic parameter in class groups have been investigated. The main idea behind their algorithms is as follows: First, compute the structure of the class group $Cl(\Delta_1)$ as a direct product of cyclic groups,

$$Cl(\Delta_1) \cong \prod_{i=1}^{l} C(m_i), \tag{3}$$

together with generators $\mathfrak{g}_i$ of each cyclic subgroup (order of $\mathfrak{g}_i$ in $Cl(\Delta_1)$ is m_i). Then compute the representations

$$\mathfrak{a} \sim \prod_{i=1}^{l} \mathfrak{g}^{a_i} \quad \text{and} \quad \mathfrak{b} \sim \prod_{i=1}^{l} \mathfrak{g}^{b_i} \tag{4}$$

of $\mathfrak{a}$ and $\mathfrak{b}$ over the generators. If Cl-DLP is solvable, then there exists $x \in \mathbb{Z}_{\geq 0}$ such that

$$\prod_{i=1}^{l} \mathfrak{g}^{a_i} \sim \prod_{i=1}^{l} \mathfrak{g}^{x b_i}, \tag{5}$$

and x can be found by solving the system of simultaneous congruences

$$a_i \equiv x b_i \pmod{m_i}, \quad 1 \leq i \leq l, \tag{6}$$

using the generalized Chinese remainder theorem. If the above congruence cannot be solved, then there is no solution to CL-DLP.

Note that the above idea can not be applied to the class semigroups of non-maximal orders in general. For, first, there is no efficient algorithm to compute the structure of the class semigroup of a non-maximal order. Second, unique factorization can fail for non-invertible ideals. Also note that unique factorization can fail even for proper ideals of non-maximal orders [6, pp. 136 or Exercise 7.9]. However, there are some classes of non-maximal orders, in which it is easy to compute their class groups, via reductions to discrete logarithm computations in multiplicative groups of finite fields, for example, the class of totally non-maximal orders [11,13], i.e., non-maximal orders with $|Cl(\Delta_1)| = 1$, where $\Delta_f = f^2 \Delta_1$ is a discriminant of the non-maximal order. In the case of class semigroups, we do not know if there are such classes. To the best of our knowledge, there is no efficient algorithm to compute our DLP.

5   Efficiency Aspects

In [2], the first realistic benchmarks for IQ cryptosystems are presented, where the cryptographic parameter has been chosen of such a size that solving the Cl-DLP is about as hard as solving the integer factoring problem for integers of certain size. Their result is that IQ cryptosystems appear to be practical. Since IQ arithmetic is essentially the same as the computation of binary quadratic forms [5, Section 5.2] and since our arithmetic is the same as the IQ arithmetic from the results of the previous section, the efficiency of our schemes is similar to that of schemes in [2, Section 5]. Since the efficiency of the arithmetic of cryptography based on the class groups of imaginary quadratic orders received comparably little attention in the past, it is reasonable to expect significant improvements in the future [2]. These improvements will make our cryptosystems together with IQ cryptosystems even more competitive with traditional cryptosystems.

6   Conclusion and Further Works

In this work we proposed a key-exchange system and a public-key encryption scheme based on the class semigroups of imaginary quadratic non-maximal orders, the former is analogous to the Diffie-Hellman's key-exchange system and the latter is similar to the ElGamal's encryption scheme, whose security is based on the difficulty of the discrete logarithm problem of that class semigroup. We analyze the security and efficiency of our cryptosystems by comparing them with those of cryptosystems based on the class groups of imaginary quadratic maximal orders. We think that our proposed cryptosystems in non-maximal imaginary quadratic orders provide a comparable level of security using substantially smaller keys. Thus it remains to consider more precisely the efficiency and performance of our cryptosystems for parameter sizes, which provide comparable security.

Acknowledgements. We would like to thank the anonymous referees for their helpful comments. This work was supported by the Korea Research Foundation Grant (KRF-2002-003-D00273) and partially by University IT Research Center Project.

References

1. Buchmann, J., Düllmann, S.: On the computation of discrete logarithm in class groups, in *Advances in Cryptology – CRYPTO '90*, LNCS 537, Springer-Velag, Berlin, 1991, pp. 134–139.
2. Buchmann, J., Hamdy, S.: A survey on IQ cryptography. Technical Report No. TI-4/01, Darmstadt University of Technology, 2001.
3. Buchmann, J., Paulus, S.: A one way function based on ideal arithmetic in number fields, in *Advances in Cryptology – CRYPTO '97*, LNCS 1294, Springer-Velag, Berlin, 1997, pp. 385–394.
4. Buchmann, J., Willams, H. C.: A key-exchange system based on imaginary quadratic fields. J. Cryptology **1** (1988) 107–118.
5. Cohen, H.: A course in Computational Algebraic Number Theory, Springer, Berlin, 1995.
6. Cox, D.: Primes of the Form $x^2 + ny^2$, Wiley, New York, 1989.
7. Delfs, H., Knebel, H.: Introduction to Cryptography: Principles and Applications, Springer-Verlag, Berlin, 2002.

8. Diffie, W., Hellman, M.: New directions in cryptography. IEEE Trans. Inform. Theory **22** (1976) 472–492.

9. ElGamal T.: A Public key cryptosystem and a signature scheme based on discrete logarithms. IEEE Trans. Inform. Theory **31** (1985), 469–472.

10. Hafner, J. L., McCurley, K. S.: A rigorous subexponential algorithm for computation of class group. J. Amer. Math. Soc. **2** (1989) 837–850.

11. Hamdy, S., Möller, B.: Security of cryptosystems based on class groups of imaginary quadratic orders, in *Advances in Cryptology – ASIACRYPT 2000*, LNCS 1976, Springer-Velag, Berlin, 2000, pp. 234–247.

12. Jacobson Jr., M. J.: Computing discrete logarithms in quadratic orders. J. Cryptology **13** (2000) 473–492.

13. Hühnlein, D., Takagi, T.: Reducing logarithms in totally non-maximal imaginary quadratic orders to logarithms in finite fields, in *Advances in Cryptology – ASIACRYPT '99*, LNCS 1716, Springer-Verlag, Berlin, 1999, pp. 219–231.

14. Koblitz, N.: Elliptic curve cryptosystems. Math. Comp. **48** (1987) 203–209.

15. Koblitz, N.: Hyperelliptic cryptosystems. J. Cryptology **1** (1989) 139–150.

16. McCurley, K. S.: Cryptographic key distribution and computation in class groups, in R. A. Mollin, editor, *Number Theory and Applications*, Kluwer Academic Publishers, 1989, pp. 459–479.

17. Menezes, A. J., Oorschot, P. C., Vanstone, S. A.: Handbook of Applied Cryptography, CRC Press, Boca Raton, 1997.

18. Meyer, A., Neis, S., Pfahler, T.: First implementation of cryptographic protocols based on algebraic number fields, in *Information Security and Privacy*, LNCS 2119, Springer-Velag, Berlin, 2001, pp. 84–103.

19. Mollin, R. A.: Quadratics, CRC Press, Boca Raton, 1996.

20. Odlyzko, A. M.: Discrete logarithms in finite fields and their cryptographic significance, *Advances in Cryptology – EUROCRYPT '84*, LNCS 209, Springer-Velag, Berlin, 1985, pp. 224–314.

21. Paulus, S., Takaki, T.: A new public-key cryptosystem over a quadratic order with quadratic decryption time. J. Cryptology **13** (2000) 263–272.

22. Rivest, R. L., Shamir, A., Adelman, L.: A method for abtaining digital signatures and public key cryptosystems. Communications of the ACM **21** (1978) 120–126.

23. Stinson, D. R.: Cryptography: Theory and Practice, CRC Press, Boca Raton, 2002.

24. Zanardo, P.: The class semigroup of orders in number fields. Math. Proc. Camb. Phil. Soc. **115** (1994) 379–391.

Appendix

The following proofs of Algorithm 2 and Theorem 3, which are included here for easy reference, can be obtained by modifying the proofs of [4, Algorithm 3.1] and [4, Theorem 3.2].

Proof of Algorithm 2. By (2), we have

$$\mathfrak{a}_{j+1} = [\frac{Q_j}{r}, \frac{P_j + \sqrt{D_f}}{r}] = [\frac{Q_j}{r}, \frac{-P_{j+1} + \sqrt{D_f}}{r}].$$

Thus, by the remark proceeding this algorithm and the formulas of (2), we see that if $\mathfrak{a}_{j+1}$ is an ideal, then so is $\mathfrak{a}_{j+2}$ and $\mathfrak{a}_{j+2} \sim \mathfrak{a}_{j+1}$. Further, if $\alpha_{i+1} = \frac{-P_{i+1}+\sqrt{D_f}}{r}$, then $|\mathrm{Tr}(\alpha_{i+1})| = |\frac{2P_{i+1}}{r}| = \frac{2|q_i Q_i - P_i|}{r} = 2Q_i \frac{|q_i - \frac{P_i}{Q_i}|}{r} \leq \frac{Q_i}{r} = \mathsf{L}(\mathfrak{a}_{i+1})$. It follows from Theorem 1(b) that $\mathfrak{a}_{i+1}$ is reduced when $\mathrm{N}(\alpha_{i+1}) \geq (\mathsf{L}(\mathfrak{a}_{i+1}))^2$, that is, when $Q_{i+1} \geq Q_i$. Note that $Q_i > 0$ for all $i = 0, 1, \ldots$.

Proof of Theorem 3. We first note that

$$0 < Q_{j+1} \leq \frac{(\frac{Q_j}{2})^2 + |D_f|}{Q_j} = \frac{Q_j}{4} + \frac{|D_f|}{Q_j}.$$

If we define $\rho_j = \frac{Q_j}{\sqrt{|D_f|}}$, then

$$\rho_{j+1} \leq \frac{\rho_j}{4} + \frac{1}{\rho_j}. \tag{7}$$

Also let $K_j = \frac{5 \cdot 4^j + 1}{3}$. Then it is easy to show that for $j > 1$,

$$\frac{K_j}{4} + \frac{1}{K_{j-1}} < K_{j-1}. \tag{8}$$

Now if $2 < \rho_j < K_1 = 7$, then by (1) it is clear that

$$\rho_{i+1} < \begin{cases} K_0 = 2 & \text{when} \quad \rho_i > 4, \\ \frac{3}{2} & \text{when} \quad \rho_i \leq 4. \end{cases}$$

Thus, by using (3) and (4) we see that $\rho_{i+1} \leq K_{j-1}$ when $2 < \rho_i < K_j$ $(j > 0)$. It follows that if $\rho_0 < K_m$, then $\rho_t < K_0 = 2$ for some $t \leq m$. Setting $m = [\frac{1}{2} \log_2 \frac{3\rho_0}{5}] + 1$, we have $K_m > \rho_0 + \frac{1}{3} > \rho_0$; thus, for some $i \leq 1 + [\frac{1}{2} \log_2 \frac{3Q_0}{5\sqrt{|D_f|}}]$, we have $Q_i < 2\sqrt{|D_f|}$.

From now on we suppose that $Q_i < 2\sqrt{|D_f|}$. If $Q_{i+1} \geq Q_i$, then $\mathfrak{a}_{i+1}$ is reduced. If $Q_{i+1} < Q_i$, then $\mathfrak{a}_{i+1}$ is not a reduced ideal, and so there must be some nonzero $\gamma \in \mathfrak{a}_{i+1}$ such that $|\gamma|$ is minimal and $|\gamma| < \frac{Q_i}{r}$. Further, by Theorem 1(d), we have $\frac{Q_i}{r} > \frac{\sqrt{\Delta_f}}{2}$. Since $r^2 |\gamma|^2 = (xQ_i + yP_i)^2 + |D_f|y^2$ $(x, y \in \mathbb{Z})$, we must have $|y| = 1$. If $M = \min\{|xQ_i \pm P_i| : x \in \mathbb{Z}\}$, then $r^2 |\gamma|^2 = M^2 + D_f$, where $M = |P_{i+1}| = |q_i Q_i - P_i| \leq \frac{Q_i}{2}$; hence we can put $\gamma = \frac{-P_{i+1}+\sqrt{D_f}}{r}$. Since $\mathfrak{a}_{i+1} = [\frac{Q_i}{r}, \gamma]$, we must have a reduced ideal $\mathfrak{a}_{i+2} = [\frac{Q_i}{r}, \frac{P_{i+1}+\sqrt{D_f}}{r}]$ of $\mathcal{O}_{\Delta_f}$. For if $\mathfrak{a}_{i+2}$ is not reduced, then there exists some $\beta \in \mathfrak{a}_{i+2}$ such that $\mathrm{N}(\beta) < \mathsf{L}(\mathfrak{a}_{i+2})^2 = (\frac{\mathrm{N}(\gamma)}{\mathsf{L}(\mathfrak{a}_{i+1})})^2$. Since $\beta \in \mathfrak{a}_{i+2}$, by the previous remark we also have $\mathsf{L}(\mathfrak{a}_{i+1})\beta = \overline{\gamma}\lambda$ for some $\lambda \in \mathfrak{a}_{i+1}$. Since $\mathrm{N}(\beta) = \frac{\mathrm{N}(\gamma)\mathrm{N}(\lambda)}{\mathsf{L}(\mathfrak{a}_{i+1})^2}$, we get $\mathrm{N}(\lambda) < \mathrm{N}(\gamma)$, which, by the choice of γ, is impossible. Since $\mathfrak{a}_{i+1}$ is a reduced ideal, we also have $Q_{i+2} \geq Q_{i+1}$. The theorem now follows from our earlier bound on i.

New Constructions for Resilient and Highly Nonlinear Boolean Functions

Khoongming Khoo[1] and Guang Gong[2]

[1] Department of Combinatorics and Optimization,
kkhoo@math.uwaterloo.ca
[2] Department of Electrical and Computer Engineering,
University of Waterloo, Waterloo, Ontario N2L 3G1, Canada.
ggong@calliope.uwaterloo.ca

Abstract. We explore three applications of geometric sequences in constructing cryptographic Boolean functions. First, we construct 1-resilient functions of n Boolean variables with nonlinearity $2^{n-1} - 2^{(n-1)/2}$, n odd. The Hadamard transform of these functions is 3-valued, which limits the efficiency of certain stream cipher attacks. From the case for n odd, we construct highly nonlinear 1-resilient functions which disprove a conjecture of Pasalic and Johansson for n even. Our constructions do not have a potential weakness shared by resilient functions which are formed from concatenation of linear functions. Second, we give a new construction for balanced Boolean functions with high nonlinearity, exceeding $2^{n-1} - 2^{(n-1)/2}$, which is not based on the direct sum construction. Moreover, these functions have high algebraic degree and large linear span. Third, we construct balanced vectorial Boolean functions with nonlinearity $2^{n-1} - 2^{(n-1)/2}$ and low maximum correlation. They can be used as nonlinear combiners for stream cipher systems with high throughput.

1 Introduction

Boolean functions, when used in cipher systems, are required to have good cryptographic properties. Some of the important properties are balance, high nonlinearity and resiliency. These properties ensure that the functions are resistant against correlation attacks [22] and linear cryptanalysis [12]. In the 1990's, there were many constructions given for resilient functions with maximum nonlinearity $2^{n-1} - 2^{(n-1)/2}$ (n odd) and $2^{n-1} - 2^{n/2}$ (n even) (see [3] for a summary). In 1999, Pasalic and Johansson conjectured that these achieve the maximum nonlinearity for resilient functions [15]. But in 2000, Sarkar and Maitra demonstrated that there exist resilient functions with higher noninearity for both odd and even n [18]. However, their constructions, as well as the many Maiorana-McFarland type constructions (see [3]), are concatenation of linear functions. As pointed out in [3], this may be a weakness as the function becomes linear when certain input bits are fixed. There are other constructions for highly nonlinear resilient functions not based on concatenation of linear functions [3,6,14, 15], which will avoid this potential weakness. It is also desirable for the function to have 3-valued Hadamard transform $0, \pm 2^k$, which limits the efficiency of

R. Safavi-Naini and J. Seberry (Eds.): ACISP 2003, LNCS 2727, pp. 498–509, 2003.
© Springer-Verlag Berlin Heidelberg 2003

the soft output joint attack [11]. For vectorial Boolean functions, it is required that they have low maximum correlation for protection against approximation by nonlinear functions of output bits [23].

In this paper, we present some new constructions for highly nonlinear and resilient Boolean functions, not based on concatenation of linear functions, from the theory of geometric sequences by Klapper, Chan and Goresky [10]. First, we consider the problem of constructing highly nonlinear resilient functions. We look at plateaued$(n-1)$ functions, i.e. functions whose Hadamard transform only takes on the values $0, \pm2^{(n+1)/2}$, n odd. Based on a result of Zhang and Zheng [24], we deduce an efficient test for determining when a plateaued$(n-1)$ function is 1-resilient. From any one such function, we can obtain an infinite number of 1-resilient plateaued$(n-1)$ functions by applying the geometric sequence construction of [10]. These functions have nonlinearity $2^{n-1} - 2^{(n-1)/2}$ (n odd), which is considered high among resilient functions, according to [3]. Moreover, the 3-valued Hadamard transform of our functions limit the number of parity check equations that can be used for the soft output joint attack [11]. By taking the direct sum of our construction for the odd case with the highly nonlinear Patterson-Wiedemann function [16,17], we construct 1-resilient functions with nonlinearity $> 2^{n-1} - 2^{n/2}$ for even number of input bits n. Second, we consider the problem of constructing balanced function with nonlinearity exceeding $2^{n-1} - 2^{(n-1)/2}$ when n is odd. Previous approaches have been to take the direct sum of two highly nonlinear functions, one of which is balanced [18, 20]. Our approach is a new one based on recursive composition of a highly nonlinear balanced function with quadratic functions. By applying our construction to the highly nonlinear balanced Boolean functions of [18,20], we obtain new balanced Boolean functions with high nonlinearity $> 2^{n-1} - 2^{(n-1)/2}$, large linear span and high algebraic degree. Finally, we consider the problem of constructing balanced vectorial Boolean functions to be used as nonlinear combiners in stream ciphers. Such functions will have higher throughput than 1-bit output functions. However, they need to have high nonlinearity to protect against linear approximation attacks [12,22], and low maximum correlation to protect against approximation by nonlinear functions of output bits [23]. Our construction yields balanced vectorial Boolean functions with nonlinearity $2^{n-1} - 2^{(n-1)/2}$ and low maximum correlation.

2 Definitions and Preliminaries

2.1 Polynomial and Boolean Functions

Let $GF(2^n)$ be the finite field with 2^n elements and $GF(2^n)^*$ be $GF(2^n) - \{0\}$. Let $q = 2^n$, the trace function from $GF(q^m)$ to the subfield $GF(q)$ is $Tr_q^{q^m}(x) := \sum_{i=0}^{m-1} x^{q^i}$. When there is no confusion, we denote $Tr_2^{2^n}(x)$ by $Tr(x)$. The *Hadamard transform* of a function $f : GF(2^n) \rightarrow GF(2)$ is defined to be

$$\hat{f}(\lambda) := \sum_{x \in GF(2^n)} (-1)^{Tr(\lambda x)+f(x)}, \lambda \in GF(2^n).$$

A Boolean function is a function $g : \mathbf{Z}_2^n \to \mathbf{Z}_2$. There is a natural correspondence between Boolean functions g and polynomial functions $f : GF(2^n) \to GF(2)$. Let $\{\alpha_0, \dots, \alpha_{n-1}\}$ be a basis for $GF(2^n)$, this correspondence is given by

$$g(x_0, \dots, x_{n-1}) := f(\alpha_0 x_0 + \dots + \alpha_{n-1} x_{n-1}). \tag{1}$$

As defined in [24], a Boolean function $f : \mathbf{Z}_2^n \to \mathbf{Z}_2$ is a *plateaued function of order* r (denoted *plateaued(r)*) if $\hat{f}(w)^2 = 0, 2^{2n-r} \; \forall w \in \mathbf{Z}_2^n$.

The *nonlinearity* of a Boolean function f is defined by

$$N_f = 2^{n-1} - 1/2 \max_\lambda |\hat{f}(\lambda)|. \tag{2}$$

We want the nonlinearity of a function to be as high as possible.

A Boolean function $f : \mathbf{Z}_2^n \to \mathbf{Z}_2$ satisfies the correlation immunity of order k if $\hat{f}(w) = 0$ for all $1 \le wt(w) \le k$. If f is also balanced, then we say f is k-resilient. The *additive autocorrelation* of f at a is defined as:

$$\Delta_f(a) := \sum_x (-1)^{f(x) + f(x+a)}.$$

We say $f : \mathbf{Z}_2^n \to \mathbf{Z}_2$ has a linear structure at a if $\Delta_f(a) = \pm 2^n$. f satisfies the propagation criteria at a if $\Delta_f(a) = 0$. Many useful properties of a Boolean function can be deduced by analysing the relationship between $\Delta_f(a)$ and $\hat{f}(\lambda)$. Some examples include [1,9,14,18,20,21,25,24].

Consider the polynomial function $f(x) = \sum_i \beta_i x^{s_i}, \beta_i \in GF(2^n)$. The *algebraic degree deg(f)* of the corresponding Boolean function is given by the maximum weight of the exponents $\max_i wt(s_i)$ (see [13]). We want it to be high for algebraic complexity. The *linear span* of a polynomial function is the number of monomials x^s in its polynomial expression. We want it to be high to defend against interpolation attack [7].

There is a natural correspondence between Boolean Sboxes $F : \mathbf{Z}_2^n \to \mathbf{Z}_2^m$ and polynomial functions from $GF(2^n)$ to $GF(2^m)$ similar to equation (1). The *nonlinearity* N_F of an S-box is $N_F = min_{b \neq 0} N_{b \cdot F}$ where $b \cdot F$ consists of all linear combination of output bits. When n is odd and $m \ge 2$, $N_F = 2^{n-1} - 2^{(n-1)/2}$ is considered high. The *maximum correlation* [23] of F at w is

$$C_F(w) = \max_g [Prob(g(F(x)) = w \cdot x) - Prob(g(F(x)) \neq w \cdot x)]. \tag{3}$$

where the maximum is taken over all $g : \mathbf{Z}_2^m \to \mathbf{Z}_2$.

Proposition 1 *(Zhang-Chan [23, Theorem 4]) Let $F : \mathbf{Z}_2^n \to \mathbf{Z}_2^m$, the maximum correlation of F satisfies*

$$C_F(w) \le 2^{m/2 - n} max_v |\sum_x (-1)^{v \cdot F(x) + w \cdot x}|$$

Proposition 1 imples that a high nonlinearity will guarantee low maximum correlation.

2.2   Hadamard Transform of Cascaded Functions

We derive a useful result on cascaded function that will be applied to construct cryptographic Boolean functions later. Let $I(f) = \sum_{x \in GF(2^n)} (-1)^{f(x)}$ be the imbalance of f and the correlation between polynomial functions f and g at $\lambda \in GF(2^n)$ be $C_{f,g}(\lambda) = \sum_{x \in GF(2^n)} (-1)^{f(\lambda x) + g(x)}$.

Lemma 1. *(Klapper, Chan, Goresky [10, Theorem 3]) Let $q = 2^n$, consider $g, h : GF(q) \to GF(2)$. The correlation between the pair of functions*

$$g(Tr_q^{q^m}(x)) \text{ and } h(Tr_q^{q^m}(x^{q^i+1}))$$

at $\Lambda \in GF(q^m)^*$ takes on the values:

1. $q^{m-2} I(g) I(h)$
2. $(q^{m-2} - q^{m-(m-d)/2-2}) I(g) I(h) \pm q^{m-(m-d)/2-1} C_{g(x), h(x^2)}(\lambda)$, $\lambda \in GF(q)^*$.

where $d = \gcd(i, m)$.

By applying induction and properties of finite fields on Lemma 1, we can derive the following result that is basic to all our construction methods.

Theorem 1 *Let $q = 2^n$, n, n_j be odd for $j = 1, \ldots, l$ and let $f : GF(q) \to GF(2)$. Define recursively the functions*

$$f_0(x) = f(x)$$
$$f_j(x) = f_{j-1}(Tr_{q_{j-1}}^{q_j}(x^{k_j})), j = 1, \ldots, l$$

where $q_0 = q$, $q_j = q_{j-1}^{n_j}$, $k_j = q_{j-1}^{r_j} + 1$ and $\gcd(r_j, n_j) = 1$. Then $\widehat{f_l}(\Lambda)$, $\Lambda \in GF(q_l)^*$ takes on the values $0, \pm q^{\frac{n_1 n_2 \cdots n_l - 1}{2}} \hat{f}(\lambda)$, $\lambda \in GF(q)^*$.

Remark 1. In [10], Klapper, Chan and Goresky proved that if $f(x) = Tr(x^{2^i+1})$ where $\gcd(i, n) = 1$, then $f_l(x)$ in Theorem 1 is plateaued$(N-1)$, $N = nn_1 \cdots n_l$. They called their construction a cascaded GMW sequence. Here we gneralise it so that it applies to any function $f(x)$. Note that Theorem 1 only holds for $\widehat{f_l}(\Lambda)$ where $\Lambda \neq 0$. The imbalance of $f_l(x)$, which is $\widehat{f_l}(0)$, is given by $q^{n_1 n_2 \cdots n_l - 1} \hat{f}(0)$.

3   New Construction for Resilient Functions

In this section, we explore constructions for resilient plateaued$(n - 1)$ functions. Such functions have nonlinearity $2^{n-1} - 2^{(n-1)/2}$ which is considered high among resilient functions according to Carlet [3]. Sarkar and Maitra constructed 1-resilient functions with nonlinearity $> 2^{n-1} - 2^{(n-1)/2}$ for odd $n \geq 41$ [18, Theorem 6]. However, their construction [18, Corollary 2], as well as the many Maiorana-McFarland type constructions in the existing literature (see [3]), correspond to concatenation of linear functions. This may be a weakness as the functions become linear when certain input bits are fixed [3]. Our construction will avoid this weakness. Moreover, our functions are 3-valued which makes the soft output joint attack less efficient [11, Corollary 1].

First, we derive an efficient test for 1-resilient plateaued$(n - 1)$ functions based on a result of Zheng and Zhang [24].

Lemma 2. *(Zheng and Zhang [24, Theorem 2]) Let n be odd and $f : GF(2^n) \to GF(2)$ be a balanced plateaued$(n-1)$ function. If f does not have a non-zero linear structure, then the Boolean form of f is 1-resilient for some basis of $GF(2^n)$, which can be found by the method of [6].*

Remark 2. We stated Lemma 2 in a modified form (from the original in [24]) so that it applies to polynomial functions. Lemma 2 has also been proven in a more general form in [1, Theorem 7]. From the proof of Lemma 2, we see that the set $\{\lambda | \hat{f}(\lambda) = 0\}$ contains n linearly independent vectors. Based on these n vectors, Gong and Youssef gave an algorithm to find a basis of $GF(2^n)$ such that the Boolean form of f is 1-resilient in [6].

The equation $1/2^n \sum_\lambda \hat{f}(\lambda)^4 = \sum_a \Delta_f(a)^2$ is well-known, e.g. see [1,24]. It can be used to derive Corollary 1 from Lemma 2.

Corollary 1 *Let n be odd and $f : GF(2^n) \to GF(2)$ be a balanced plateaued$(n-1)$ function. If there exists $a \in GF(2^n)$ such that $\Delta_f(a) \neq 0$ or $\pm 2^n$, then $N_f = 2^{n-1} - 2^{(n-1)/2}$ and the Boolean form of f is 1-resilient for some basis of $GF(2^n)$.*

We demonstrate an application with the following example. We introduce the *cyclotomic coset leaders* modulo $2^n - 1$ which are the smallest elements of the sets $\{2^i \times s \mod 2^n - 1, i = 0 \ldots n - 1\}$.

Example 1. Let $n = 5$. We exhaustively search for balanced plateaued$(n-1)$ functions $f : GF(2^5) \to GF(2)$ of the form $f(x) = \sum_{i \in I} Tr(x^i)$, where I are the cyclotomic coset leaders $\{1, 3, 5, 7, 11, 15\}$. We obtain six non-quadratic plateaued$(n - 1)$ functions (all cubic): $Tr(x^7)$, $Tr(x^{11})$, $Tr(x + x^3 + x^{11})$, $Tr(x + x^5 + x^7)$, $Tr(x + x^7 + x^{11})$, $Tr(x + x^3 + x^5 + x^7 + x^{11})$. Since $\Delta_f(1) = 8$ which is $\neq 0, \pm 2^5$ for all these functions, their Boolean form are all 1-resilient for some basis representation.

Let $n = 11$. We exhaustively search for balanced plateaued$(n - 1)$ functions $f : GF(2^{11}) \to GF(2)$ of the form $f(x) = \sum_{i \in I} Tr(x^i)$, I are the cyclotomic coset leaders modulo 2047, from a restricted search space of size 119446698. We obtain 426 non-quadratic plateaued$(n-1)$ functions. By applying Corollary 1 on these functions, we verified that all these functions are 1-resilient in some basis representation.

Remark 3. The above example seems to suggest that if we randomly choose a balanced non-quadratic plateaued$(n - 1)$ function, there is a high chance it is 1-resilient. Moreover, almost all the functions in our test satisfy $\Delta_f(1) \neq 0, \pm 2^n$, so we can confirm $\Delta_f(a) \neq 0, \pm 2^n$ at the beginning. This seems to suggest Corollary 1 gives a fast test.

Next, we derive a new construction for 1-resilient plateaued$(n - 1)$ functions. Precisely, we show that by composing a 1-resilient plateaued$(n-1)$ function from Corollary 1 with a quadratic function, we can obtain infinitely more functions of the same kind.

Theorem 2 *Let n be odd, $q = 2^n$ and $f : GF(q) \to GF(2)$ be a balanced plateaued($n - 1$) function. If there exists $a \in GF(q)$ s.t. $\Delta_f(a) \neq 0, \pm q$, then $g : GF(2^N) \to GF(2)$, $N = mn$, defined by*

$$g(x) = f(aTr_q^{q^m}(x^{q^i+1})), \; m \text{ odd}, \gcd(i, m) = 1$$

is 1-resilient for some basis of $GF(2^N)$ and plateaued($N - 1$) which implies $N_g = 2^{N-1} - 2^{(N-1)/2}$. Moreover, $deg(g) = 2deg(f)$.

Proof. g is balanced because it is a composition of balanced functions. Therefore $\hat{g}(0) = 0$. For $\hat{g}(\lambda)$, $\lambda \neq 0$, we apply Theorem 1 with $l = 1$ to see that $\hat{g}(\lambda)$ takes on the values: $0, \pm q^{(m-1)/2}2^{(n+1)/2} = \pm 2^{(mn+1)/2}$. Thus g is plateaued($N - 1$). The nonlinearity of g is a consequence of equation (2).

To prove that g is 1-resilient. Let $y = Tr_q^{q^m}(x^{q^i+1})$. Then

$$
\begin{aligned}
g(x + 1) &= f(aTr_q^{q^m}((x + 1)^{q^i+1})) \\
&= f(a(Tr_q^{q^m}(x^{q^i+1}) + Tr_q^{q^m}(x^{q^i}) + Tr_q^{q^m}(x) + 1)) \\
&= f(a(y + 1)), \text{ because } Tr_q^{q^m}(x^{q^i}) = Tr_q^{q^m}(x).
\end{aligned}
$$

From the above identity and the fact that for each $y \in GF(q)$, there are q^{m-1} elements $x \in GF(q^m)$ such that $y = Tr_q^{q^m}(x^{q^i+1})$, we deduce

$$\Delta_g(1) = q^{m-1} \sum_{y \in GF(q)} (-1)^{f(ay)+f(ay+a)}$$

$$= q^{m-1}\Delta_f(a) \neq 0, \pm q^m, \text{ because } \Delta_f(a) \neq 0, \pm q.$$

By Corollary 1, the Boolean form of g is 1-resilient in some basis of $GF(2^{mn})$. The algebraic degree is $2deg(f)$ from Theorem 3 part 3. $\qquad\square$

Useful properties of our construction:

1. New construction for resilient function with nonlinearity $2^{N-1} - 2^{(N-1)/2}$, N odd, for protection against linear and correlation attacks [22,12]. Moreover, it is not based on concatenation of linear functions.
2. Our function has 3-valued Hadamard transform which prevents the use of all even parity check equations in the soft output joint attack [11, Corollary 1]. This will limit the efficiency of that attack.

Pasalic and Johansson conjectured that the highest nonlinearity for 1-resilient functions with even number of input bits n is $2^{n-1} - 2^{n/2}$. We can disprove it by applying Proposition 2 on our previous construction for resilient functions with odd number of input bits. Proposition 2 is easy to prove, e.g. see [19].

Proposition 2 *Let $f : Z_2^n \to Z_2$, n odd, be a k-resilient function with nonlinearity $2^{n-1} - 2^{(n-1)/2}$ and $PW : Z_2^{15} \to Z_2$ be the 15-bit Patterson Wiedemann function with nonlinearity 16276 from [16,17]. Then*

$$g(x, y) := f(x) + PW(y), x \in Z_2^n, y \in Z_2^{15}$$

has $m = n + 15$ (even) number of input bits, is k-resilient and has nonlinearity

$$N_g = 2^{m-1} - 27/32 \times 2^{m/2} > 2^{m-1} - 2^{m/2}.$$

Moreover, $\deg(g) = \max(\deg(f), \deg(PW))$.

Note that Sarkar and Maitra also disproved the conjecture of [15] by concatenation involving linear functions [18, Theorems 7,8 and 9]. The useful property of our construction is:

1. If we use a 1-resilient function $f(x)$ by exhaustive search in Examples 1 or Theorem 2, then both $f(x)$ and the Patterson-Wiedemann function $PW(y)$ are constructed from finite fields which are not concatenation of linear functions. Therefore their direct sum $g(x, y)$ is not one too.

4   Highly Nonlinear Balanced Boolean Functions

In this section, we construct new classes of balanced Boolean functions with high nonlinearity $> 2^{n-1} - 2^{(n-1)/2}$, n odd, high algebraic degree and large linear span. This is achieved by applying Theorem 1 on the highly nonlinear balanced functions of Sarkar and Maitra [18] and Seberry, Zhang and Zheng [20].

Theorem 3 *Let $q = 2^n$ and n, n_j be odd for $j = 1, \ldots, l$. Let $f : GF(q) \to GF(2)$ be a balanced function with nonlinearity $> 2^{n-1} - 2^{(n-1)/2}$ (such as the functions from [18,20]). Define recursively the functions*

$$f_0(x) = f(x)$$
$$f_j(x) = f_{j-1}(Tr_{q_{j-1}}^{q_j}(x^{k_j})), j = 1, \ldots, l.$$

where $q_0 = q$, $q_j = q_{j-1}^{n_j}$, $k_j = q_{j-1}^{r_j} + 1$ and $\gcd(r_j, n_j) = 1$. f_l corresponds to a Boolean function with $N = nn_1 \cdots n_l$ input bits and

1. *f_l is balanced having high nonlinearity*

$$2^{N-1} - 2^{\frac{N-n}{2}-1} \max_\lambda |\hat{f}(\lambda)| > 2^{N-1} - 2^{(N-1)/2}.$$

2. *If the polynomial expression for f is $\sum_i \beta_i x^{t_i}$, then the linear span of f_l satisfies*

$$LS(f_l) = \sum_i (n_1 n_2^2 \cdots n_l^{2^{l-1}})^{wt(t_i)} \tag{4}$$

   Thus $LS(f_l) \geq (n_1 n_2^2 \cdots n_l^{2^{l-1}})^{\deg(f)}$.

3. *The algebraic degree of f_l is $2^l \deg(f)$.*

Proof. 1. f is balanced implies that f_l is balanced since it is a composition of balanced functions. Therefore, $\hat{f_l}(0) = 0$. We apply Theorem 1 to see that $\hat{f_l}(\Lambda)$, $\Lambda \in GF(2^N)^*$ takes on the values:

$$0, \pm(2^n)^{(n_1 \cdots n_l - 1)/2} \hat{f}(\lambda) = 2^{(N-n)/2} \hat{f}(\lambda), \lambda \in GF(q)^*$$

By equation (2), $N_{f_l} = 2^{N-1} - 2^{\frac{N-n}{2}-1} \max_\lambda |\hat{f}(\lambda)|$.

The function f has nonlinearity $> 2^{n-1} - 2^{(n-1)/2}$ implies $\max_\lambda |\hat{f}(\lambda)| < 2^{(n+1)/2}$. This implies $N_{f_l} > 2^{N-1} - 2^{\frac{N-n}{2}-1} 2^{\frac{n+1}{2}} = 2^{N-1} - 2^{(N-1)/2}$.

2. Note that $f_l(x)$ can be written as

$$f_l(x) = \sum_i \beta_i g(x)^{t_i}, \beta_i \neq 0, \beta_i \in GF(2^n)$$

where $g(x) = Tr_{q_0}^{q_1}(Tr_{q_1}^{q_2} \ldots Tr_{q_{l-1}}^{q_l}(x^{k_l}) \ldots)^{k_2})^{k_1}$ is a cascaded GMW function from $GF(2^N)$ to $GF(2^n)$ with known linear span $n_1 n_2^2 \cdots n_l^{2^{l-1}}$ [10]. Applying Lemma 2-(i) in [5] to each term $g(x)^{t_i}$, we deduce that for each $i \neq j$, the monomial terms in $g(x)^{t_i}$ and $g(x)^{t_j}$ are distinct. According to Theorem 1 and Lemma 2-(ii) in [5], the number of distinct monomials of $g(x)^{t_i}$ is $(n_1 n_2^2 \cdots n_l^{2^{l-1}})^{wt(t_i)}$. Thus, equation (4) is established.

The inequality $LS(f_l) \geq (n_1 n_2^2 \cdots n_l^{2^{l-1}})^{deg(f)}$ follows from equation (4) because there is at least a monomial in the expression of f that has exponent $deg(f)$.

3. According to the proof of Lemma 2 in [5], we can deduce that when we recursively expand each trace term of f_l using the relation $(\sum_i x^{s_i}) \sum_j 2^{a_j} = \prod_j \sum_i x^{2^{a_j} s_i}$, there is no cancellation among the resulting sum of monomials. Therefore the maximal exponent is $2^l max_i wt(t_i) = 2^l deg(f)$ which is the algebraic degree of f_l.

□

The following proposition will ensure our function have high algebraic degree.

Proposition 3 *(Sarkar and Maitra [18, Proposition 2 and 3]) Let $f : \mathbf{Z}_2^N \to \mathbf{Z}_2$ be a balanced Boolean function. When we change up to two bits in the Boolean truth table of f such that the top half and bottom half truth tables have odd weight. The new function f will be balanced, $deg(f) = N - 1$ and the nonlinearity will decrease by at most 2.*

Useful properties of our Construction:

1. Theorem 3 gives a new construction for balanced function f_l with high non-linearity $> 2^{N-1} - 2^{(N-1)/2}$ not based on taking direct sum.
2. The function can achieve high algebraic degree and large linear span.

Example 2. We apply Theorem 3 by letting $f(x)$ be the 15-bit balanced function with nonlinearity $2^{14} - 2^7 + 6 = 16262$ from [18], $l = 1$, $n_1 = 3$ and $r_1 = 1$. Then

$$f_1(x) = f(Tr_{2^{15}}^{2^{45}}(x^{2^{15}+1}))$$

is balanced, has 45 input bits and nonlinearity $2^{44} - 2^{(45-15)/2-1} \max_\lambda |\hat{f}(\lambda)| = 2^{44} - 2^{22} + 196608$ where $\max_\lambda |\hat{f}(\lambda)| = 244$. As in Proposition 3, we can change at most 2 bits in the Boolean truth table of f_1 to get a balanced function with nonlinearity $\geq 2^{44} - 2^{22} + 196606$ and algebraic degree 44. To ensure a large linear span, we could also apply Proposition 3 to the 15-bit function f to get a balanced function with nonlinearity $\geq 2^{14} - 2^7 + 4$ and algebraic degree 14. Then f_1 as defined above will have nonlinearity $\geq 2^{44} - 2^{22} + 131072$, algebraic degree $2 \times 14 = 28$ and linear span $\geq n_1^{deg(f)} = 3^{14} = 4782969$ by Theorem 3. The large linear span of f_1 provides protection against interpolation attack [7].

5   Highly Nonlinear Balanced Vectorial Functions with Low Maximum Correlation

We construct a new class of balanced vectorial Boolean functions with n (odd) input bits that have nonlinearity $2^{n-1} - 2^{(n-1)/2}$ through geometric sequences. They have low maximum correlation bounds by Proposition 1.

$$C_F(w) \leq 2^{m/2-n} 2^{(n+1)/2} = 2^{(m-n+1)/2} \text{ for } w \neq 0. \tag{5}$$

In symmetric cipher applications, this ensures that linear approximation and approximation by nonlinear functions of output bits are difficult. We also point out that the maximum correlation can be further reduced by a factor of $\sqrt{2}$.

In Table 1 (from [2]), we list known balanced plateaued$(m - 1)$ functions of the form $Tr(x^k)$, $x \in GF(2^m)$, needed for our construction. Note that when $Tr(x^k)$ is plateaued$(m - 1)$, the function $Tr(x^{k^{-1}})$ is also plateaued$(m - 1)$.

Table 1. k such that $f(x) = Tr(x^k)$ and $Tr(x^{k^{-1}})$ are balanced, plateaued$(m - 1)$ for $x \in GF(2^m)$, m odd.

k	condition
$2^r + 1$(Gold)	$\gcd(r, m) = 1$
$2^{2r} - 2^r + 1$(Kasami)	$\gcd(r, m) = 1$
$2^{(m-1)/2} + 3$(Niho)	none
$2^{2r} + 2^r - 1$(Welch)	$4r + 1 \equiv 0 \pmod{m}$

Theorem 4 *Let $q = 2^m$ and m, n_j be odd for $j = 1 \cdots l$. Let $Tr_2^q(x^k), x \in GF(q)$, be balanced and plateaued$(m - 1)$ (see Table 1). Define recursively the functions*

$$F_0(x) = x^k$$
$$F_j(x) = F_{j-1}(Tr_{q_{j-1}}^{q_j}(x^{k_j})), j = 1 \cdots l$$

where $q_0 = q$, $q_j = q_{j-1}^{n_j}$, $k_j = q_{j-1}^{r_j} + 1$ and $\gcd(r_j, n_j) = 1$. Let $N = mn_1 n_2 \cdots n_l$ and $F(x) = F_l(x)$ where $F : GF(2^N) \to GF(2^m)$. Then

1. F is balanced.
2. The nonlinearity is $N_F = 2^{N-1} - 2^{(N-1)/2}$.
3. The maximum correlation satisfies $C_F(w) < 2^{(m-N+1)/2}$ for all $w \neq 0$.
4. The linear span is $(n_1 n_2^2 \cdots n_l^{2^{l-1}})^{wt(r)}$ and the algebraic degree is $\deg(F) = 2^l wt(r)$.

Proof. 1. F is balanced because it is a composition of balanced functions.
2. Let $f(x) = Tr_2^q(F(x))$. Then f is plateaued($N-1$) by Theorem 1 and the fact that it is balanced. We will prove the nonlinearity of F by showing that all linear combination of output bits given by $Tr_2^q(bF(x))$, $b \in GF(q)$ is plateaued($N-1$). To achieve this, we need the following identity which can be proven by induction on j using the properties of trace function.

$$bF_j(x) = F_j(b^{(kk_1 \cdots k_j)^{-1}} x), \text{ for all } b \in GF(q), \, j = 1, \ldots, l.$$

From this, we deduce that $bF(x) = F(b'x)$ where $b' = b^{(kk_1 \cdots k_l)^{-1}}$. And the Hadamard transform of $Tr_2^q(bF(x))$ is given by:

$$\sum_x (-1)^{Tr(bF(x)) + Tr(\lambda x)} = \sum_x (-1)^{Tr(F(b'x)) + Tr(\lambda x)}, \text{ where } b' = b^{(kk_1 \cdots k_l)^{-1}}$$

$$= \sum_y (-1)^{Tr(F(y)) + Tr((b')^{-1}\lambda y)}, \text{ where } y = b'x$$

$$= \hat{f}((b')^{-1}\lambda) = 0, \pm 2^{(N+1)/2},$$

Thus all linear combination of output bits correspond to Boolean functions with nonlinearity $2^{N-1} - 2^{(N-1)/2}$ by equation (2). Therefore F has the same nonlinearity.
3. The maximum correlation bound is a direct application of Proposition 1, since $v \cdot \widehat{F}(w)$ takes the values $0, \pm 2^{(N+1)/2}$. The inequality is strict because we can deduce from equation (3) that

$$2^N C_F(w) = \max_g \sum_x (-1)^{g(F(x)) + w \cdot x}.$$

This should be an integer while $2^N \times$ upper bound $= 2^{(m+N+1)/2}$ is not.
4. The algebraic degree and linear span can be proven in a similar way to Theorem 3 parts 2 and 3.

$\square$

Remark 4. The upper bound for maximum correlation in Theorem 4 holds for all Sboxes with nonlinearity $2^{n-1} - 2^{(n-1)/2}$. For the case $l = 1$, we can prove $C_F(w) \leq 2^{(m-N)/2}$, i.e. the upper bound for maximum correlation can be reduced by a factor of $\sqrt{2}$ [8, Theorem 2].

6   Conclusion

We have applied the theory of geometric sequences, due to Klapper, Chan and Goresky [10], to construct n-variable resilient Boolean functions with nonlinearity $2^{n-1} - 2^{(n-1)/2}$, n odd. Moreover, the Hadamard transforms of these functions are 3-valued, which provides protection against the soft output joint attack [11]. They can be extended to construct highly nonlinear resilient functions that disprove Pasalic and Johansson's conjecture for n even. These functions do not have a weakness shared by Boolean functions formed from concatenating linear functions. We also applied geometric sequences to give a new construction for balanced Boolean functions having high nonlinearity $> 2^{n-1} - 2^{(n-1)/2}$, n odd. This approach is different from previous constructions, which were based on direct sums of highly nonlinear Boolean functions. Finally, we constructed balanced vectorial Boolean functions with high nonlinearity and low maximum correlation. They can be used as combiners for stream ciphers with high throughput.

Acknowledgement. We would like to thank one of the referees for his/her helpful comments, and also Douglas R. Stinson for proof reading this paper. Research for this paper is supported by NSERC grant RG-PIN 227700-00. Khoongming Khoo's research is supported by a postgraduate scholarship from DSO National Laboratories, Singapore.

References

1. A. Canteaut, C. Carlet, P. Charpin and C. Fontaine, "Propagation Characteristics and Correlation-Immunity of Highly Nonlinear Boolean Functions", LNCS 1807, *Eurocrypt'2000*, pp. 507–522, Springer-Verlag, 2000.
2. A. Canteaut, P. Charpin and H. Dobbertin, "Binary m-sequences with three-valued cross correlation: a proof of Welch's conjecture", *IEEE Trans. Inform. Theory*, vol. 46 no. 1, pp. 4–8, 2000.
3. C. Carlet, "A Larger Class of Cryptographic Boolean Functions via a Study of the Maiorana-McFarland Construction", LNCS 2442, *Crypto'2002*, pp. 549–564, Springer-Verlag, 2002.
4. H. Dobbertin, "Construction of Bent Functions and Balanced Boolean Functions with High Nonlinearity", LNCS 1008, *Fast Software Encryption*, pp. 61–74, Springer Verlag, 1994.
5. G. Gong, "Q-ary Cascaded GMW Sequences", *IEEE Trans. Inform. Theory*, vol.42 no.1, pp. 263–267, Jan 1996.
6. G. Gong and A.M. Youssef, "Cryptographic Properties of the Welch-Gong Transformation Sequence Generators", *IEEE Trans. Inform. Theory*, vol.48 no.11, pp. 2837–2846, Nov 2002.
7. T. Jacobsen, L. Knudsen, "The Interpolation Attack on Block Ciphers", LNCS 1267, *Fast Software Encryption*, pp.28–40, 1997.
8. K. Khoo and G. Gong,"Highly Nonlinear Sboxes with Reduced Bound on Maximum Correlation", in *Proceedings of IEEE International Symposium on Inform. Theory 2003*.

9. K. Kurosawa and T. Satoh, "Design of $SAC/PC(l)$ of Order k Boolean Functions and Three Other Cryptographic Poperties", pp. 434–449, LNCS 1233, *Eurocrypt'97*, Springer-Verlag, 1997.

10. A. Klapper, A.H. Chan and M. Goresky, "Cascaded GMW sequence", *IEEE Transactions on Information Theory*, vol. 39 no. 1, pp. 177–183, 1993.

11. S. Leveiller, G. Zemor, P. Guillot,J. Boutros, "A New Cryptanalytic Attack for PN-Generators Filtered by a Boolean Function", *Proceedings of Selected Areas of Cryptography 2002*, 2002.

12. M. Matsui, "Linear cryptanalysis method for DES cipher", LNCS 765, *Eurocrypt'93*, pp. 386–397, 1994.

13. F.J. McWilliams and N.J.A. Sloane, *Theory of Error-Correcting Codes*, North-Holland, Amsterdam, 1977.

14. W. Millan, A. Clark and E. Dawson, "Heuristic Design of Cryptographically Strong Balanced Boolean Functions", LNCS 1403, *Eurocrypt'98*, Springer-Verlag, 1998.

15. E. Pasalic and T. Johansson, "Further Results on the Relationship between Nonlinearity and Resiliency of Boolean Functions", LNCS, *IMA Conference on Coding and Cryptography 1999*, Springer Verlag, 1999.

16. N.J Patterson and D.H. Wiedemann, "The Covering Radius of the $(2^{15}, 16)$ Reed-Muller Code is at least 16276", *IEEE Trans. Inform. Theory*, vol. 29 no. 3, pp. 354–356, May 1983.

17. N.J Patterson and D.H. Wiedemann, "Correction to – The Covering Radius of the $(2^{15}, 16)$ Reed-Muller Code is at least 16276", *IEEE Trans. Inform. Theory*, vol. 36 no. 2, pp. 443, Mar 1990.

18. P. Sarkar and S. Maitra, "Construction of Nonlinear Boolean Functions with Important Cryptographic Properties", LNCS 1807, *Eurocrypt'2000*, pp. 485–506, Springer-Verlag, 2000.

19. S. Maitra and P. Sarkar, "Modifications of Patterson-Wiedemann Functions for Cryptographic Applications", *IEEE Trans. on Inform. Theory*, vol. 48, pp. 278–284, 2002.

20. J. Seberry, X.M. Zhang, Y. Zheng, "Nonlinearly Balanced Boolean Functions and their Propagation Characteristics", LNCS 773, *Crypto'93*, pp. 49–60, Springer-Verlag, 1993.

21. J. Seberry, X.M. Zhang and Y. Zheng, "Structures of Cryptographic Functions with Strong Avalanche Characteristics", LNCS 917, *Asiacrypt'94*, pp. 119–132, Springer-Verlag, 1994.

22. T. Siegenthaler, "Decrypting a Class of Stream Ciphers using Ciphertexts only", *IEEE Trans. Computer*, vol. C34 no. 1, pp. 81–85, 1985.

23. M. Zhang and A. Chan, "Maximum Correlation Analysis of Nonlinear S-boxes in Stream Ciphers", LNCS 1880, *Crypto'2000*, pp. 501–514, Springer-Verlag, 2000.

24. Y. Zheng and X.M. Zhang, "Relationships between Bent Functions and Complementary Plateaued Functions", LNCS 1787, *ICISC'99*, pp. 60–75, Springer-Verlag, 1999.

25. Y. Zheng and X.M. Zhang, "On Relationship among Avalanche, Nonlinearity and Correlation Immunity", LNCS 1976, *Asiacrypt'2000*, pp. 470–482, Springer-Verlag, 2000.

On Parallel Hash Functions Based on Block-Cipher

Toshihiko Matsuo[1] and Kaoru Kurosawa[2]

[1] Tokyo Institute of Technology,
2-12-1 Ookayama, Meguro-ku, Tokyo, 152-8552, Japan
tossy@crypt.ss.titech.ac.jp
[2] Ibaraki University,
4-12-1 Nakanarusawa, Hitachi, Ibaraki, 316-8511, Japan
kurosawa@cis.ibaraki.ac.jp

Abstract. In this paper, we study variants of the *parallel* hash function construction of Damgård. We first show an improvement such that the number of processors is almost a half if $|M| = (2^s + 1)n$ for some s, where M is the message to be hashed. We next show that there exists a variant of our parallel hash construction such that it is secure even if the underlying compression function is not necessarily collision-free nor one-way. The cost is that some constant times more processors are required.

Keywords: hash function, block cipher.

1 Introduction

Hash functions H are a basic tool of many cryptographic protocols. A secure hash function should be one-way (i.e., preimage resistance) and collision-free. (Note that H is second preimage resistant if it is collision-free, where H is second preimage resistant if for a given M, it is hard to find $M' \neq M$ such that $H(M) = H(M')$.)

Damgård showed two general methods of constructing collision-free hash functions $H : (\{0,1\}^n)^* \rightarrow \{0,1\}^n$ from a collision-free compression function $f : \{0,1\}^{2n} \rightarrow \{0,1\}^n$ [2]. Suppose that a message M has length $L \cdot n$. Then his first construction, the *serial* hash function, uses 1 processor and runs in time linear in L, counting evaluation of f as one step. His second construction, the *parallel* hash function, uses $O(L)$ processors, but runs in time $O(\log(L))$.

Preneel, Govaerts, and Vandewalle (PGV) [4] considered 64 ways to construct compression functions $f_1, \cdots, f_{64}$ from a block cipher $E : \{0,1\}^n \times \{0,1\}^n \rightarrow \{0,1\}^n$. That is, they considered all 64 functions of the form $f(h_{i-1}, m_i) = E_a(b) \oplus c$, where $a, b, c \in \{h_{i-1}, m_i, h_{i-1} \oplus m_i, v\}$ and v a fixed n-bit constant. (See Fig.1.) They then regarded $f_1, \cdots, f_{12}$ as collision-free. They classified another 13 schemes as backward-attackable, which means they are subject to an identified potential attack. The remaining 39 schemes are subject to damaging attacks identified by PGV and others.

R. Safavi-Naini and J. Seberry (Eds.): ACISP 2003, LNCS 2727, pp. 510–521, 2003.
© Springer-Verlag Berlin Heidelberg 2003

i	$f_i(h, m)$	i	$f_i(h, m)$	i	$f_i(h, m)$
1	$E_h(m) \oplus m$	8	$E_m(m \oplus h) \oplus h$	15	$E_m(h) \oplus v$
2	$E_h(m \oplus h) \oplus m \oplus h$	9	$E_{m \oplus h}(m) \oplus m$	16	$E_{m \oplus h}(h) \oplus v$
3	$E_h(m) \oplus m \oplus h$	10	$E_{m \oplus h}(h) \oplus h$	17	$E_m(h) \oplus m$
4	$E_h(m \oplus h) \oplus m$	11	$E_{m \oplus h}(m) \oplus h$	18	$E_{m \oplus h}(h) \oplus m \oplus h$
5	$E_m(h) \oplus h$	12	$E_{m \oplus h}(h) \oplus m$	19	$E_m(m \oplus h) \oplus v$
6	$E_m(m \oplus h) \oplus m \oplus h$	13	$E_{m \oplus h}(m) \oplus v$	20	$E_m(m \oplus h) \oplus m$
7	$E_m(h) \oplus m \oplus h$	14	$E_{m \oplus h}(m) \oplus m \oplus h$		

Fig. 1. Compression Functions

Black, Rogaway and Shrimpton [1] proved that $f_1, \cdots, f_{12}$ are really collision-free in the ideal cipher model. They also clearly showed that $f_{13}, \cdots, f_{20}$ are not collision-free. They next proved that the *serial* hash functions obtained from $f_{13}, \cdots, f_{20}$ are secure even though $f_{13}, \cdots, f_{20}$ are not collision-free. They further showed that the rest 44 *serial* hash functions are not secure in the sense of collision resistance and inversion resistance.

In this paper, we study variants of the *parallel* hash function construction of Damgård. We first show an improvement such that the number of processors is almost a half if $|M| = (2^s + 1)n$ for some s, where M is the message to be hashed.

We next show that there exists a variant of our parallel hash construction such that it is secure even if the underlying compression function is not necessarily collision-free nor one-way. It requires $L/2$ more compression functions than our first construction, but it still takes time $O(\log(L))$ using $O(L)$ processors, where $|M| = Ln$. Indeed, we show that $f_{13}, \cdots, f_{20}$ can be used for our modified construction.

(Remark) As in [2,1], we do not consider free-start attacks in which adversaries can choose an initial value h_0 freely.

2 Preliminaries

We consider a hash function H made of a compression function f. We consider probabilistic polynomial time adversaries A who have oracle access to f.

For each of the following problems, we consider the average complexity. $\mathrm{Adv}(A)$ will denote the success probability of A. $\mathrm{Adv}(q)$ will denote the maximum success probability, where the maximum is taken over all adversaries that ask at most q oracle queries to f.

Without loss of generality, we use the following convention. When an adversary A for H outputs a message M, we assume that A has already computed $H(M)$, in the sense that A has made the necessary f queries to compute $H(M)$.

We write $x \xleftarrow{R} S$ for the experiment of choosing a random element from the finite set S and calling it x.

2.1   Collision Problem

For collision-freeness, we consider the following two problems.

(Collision problem 1:) Given $f : \{0,1\}^{2n} \to \{0,1\}^n$, find $x, x' \in \{0,1\}^{2n}$ s.t.

$$x \neq x' \text{ and } f(x') = f(x).$$

(Collision problem 2:) Given $H : (\{0,1\}^n)^* \to \{0,1\}^n$ find $M, M' \in (\{0,1\}^n)^*$ s.t.

$$M \neq M' \text{ and } H(M') = H(M).$$

Define

$$\mathsf{Adv}_f^{\mathsf{coll}}(A) = \Pr[(x, x') \xleftarrow{R} A^f : x \neq x' \wedge f(x') = f(x)]$$
$$\mathsf{Adv}_H^{\mathsf{coll}}(A) = \Pr[(M, M') \xleftarrow{R} A^f : M \neq M' \wedge H(M') = H(M)]$$
$$\mathsf{Adv}_f^{\mathsf{coll}}(q) = max_A\{\mathsf{Adv}_f^{\mathsf{coll}}(A)\}$$
$$\mathsf{Adv}_H^{\mathsf{coll}}(q) = max_A\{\mathsf{Adv}_H^{\mathsf{coll}}(A)\} \ .$$

2.2   Preimage Problem

For preimage resistance (one-wayness), we consider the following two problems.

(One-wayness problem 1:) Given $f : \{0,1\}^{2n} \to \{0,1\}^n$ and $\sigma \in \{0,1\}^n$, find $x \in \{0,1\}^{2n}$ such that
$$f(x) = \sigma.$$

(One-wayness problem 2:) Given $H : (\{0,1\}^n)^* \to \{0,1\}^n$ and $\sigma \in \{0,1\}^n$, find $M \in (\{0,1\}^n)^*$ such that

$$H(M) = \sigma.$$

Define

$$\mathsf{Adv}_f^{\mathsf{inv}}(A) = \Pr[\sigma \xleftarrow{R} \{0,1\}^n : x \xleftarrow{R} A^f : f(x) = \sigma]$$
$$\mathsf{Adv}_H^{\mathsf{inv}}(A) = \Pr[\sigma \xleftarrow{R} \{0,1\}^n : M \xleftarrow{R} A^f : H(M) = \sigma]$$
$$\mathsf{Adv}_f^{\mathsf{inv}}(q) = max_A\{\mathsf{Adv}_f^{\mathsf{inv}}(A)\}$$
$$\mathsf{Adv}_H^{\mathsf{inv}}(q) = max_A\{\mathsf{Adv}_H^{\mathsf{inv}}(A)\} \ .$$

3   Proposed Parallel Hash Construction

In this section, present an improvement of the Damgård's parallel hash construction [2] such that the number of processors is almost a half if $|M| = (2^s + 1)n$ for some s, where M is the message to be hashed.

Step1: Set $\alpha_1^L \leftarrow m_1, \alpha_2^L \leftarrow m_2, \ldots, \alpha_L^L \leftarrow m_L$ and $j \leftarrow L$.

Step2: While $j \geq 2$, do

    If $j = even$ then

        each P_i $(1 \leq i \leq j/2)$ computes $\alpha_i^{j/2} \leftarrow f(\alpha_{2i-1}^j, \alpha_{2i}^j)$ in parallel.

        $j \leftarrow j/2$

    If $j = odd$ then

        each P_i $(1 \leq i \leq (j-1)/2)$ computes $\alpha_i^{(j+1)/2} \leftarrow f(\alpha_{2i-1}^j, \alpha_{2i}^j)$ in parallel.

        Set $\alpha_{(j+1)/2}^{(j+1)/2} \leftarrow \alpha_j^j$ and $j \leftarrow (j+1)/2$

Step3: Compute $f(len_M, \alpha_1^1)$ and output it as $H(M)$

Fig. 2. Basic Construction

3.1 Description

Let $M = m_1||m_2||\cdots m_L$ be a message to be hashed, where $m_i \in \{0,1\}^n$ and $||$ denotes concatenation. Therefore $|M| = L \cdot n$. Suppose that there are enough number of processors compared to L. Let P_i denote a processor which is used as the i-th compression function from the left in each parallel round. Let

$$A_L = (\alpha_1^L, \cdots, \alpha_L^L) = (m_1, \cdots, m_L)$$

and let $j = L$. If $j = even$, then we apply f to $(\alpha_1^j, \alpha_2^j), \cdots, (\alpha_{j-1}^j, \alpha_j^j)$ and obtain

$$A_{j/2} = (\alpha_1^{j/2}, \cdots, \alpha_{j/2}^{j/2}) .$$

If $j = odd$, then we apply f to $(\alpha_1^j, \alpha_2^j), \cdots, (\alpha_{j-2}^j, \alpha_{j-1}^j)$ and obtain

$$A_{(j+1)/2} = (\alpha_1^{(j+1)/2}, \cdots, \alpha_{(j-1)/2}^{(j+1)/2}, \alpha_{(j+1)/2}^{(j+1)/2}) ,$$

where $\alpha_{(j+1)/2}^{(j+1)/2} = \alpha_j^j$. Finally we compute $H(M) = f(len_M, \alpha_1^1)$, where len_M denotes a hashed value of L which is computed by some collision-free hash function. It takes time $O(\log(L))$ using $O(L)$ processors.

On the other hand, the parallel hash function of Damgård [2] is described as follows. First append 0^i to M so that $|M| + i = 2^s n$ for some s. Then apply the algorithm of Fig.2. (Note that the $j = odd$ part in Step 2 is never executed in this case.)

Therefore, our construction is an improvement over the Damgård's construction [2] because 0^i is not appended to M. Hence the number of processors is almost a half of that of Damgård if $|M| = (2^s + 1)n$ for some s. We present an illustration in Fig.3 for $L = 5$.

3.2 Security Analysis

We prove that the proposed hash function H is collision-free if the underlying compression function f is collision-free, and H is one-way if f is one-way.

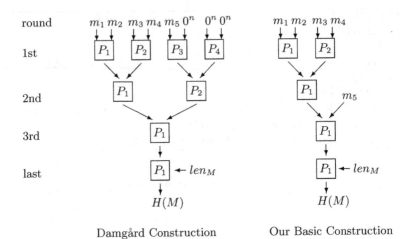

Fig. 3. Comparison.

Theorem 1. *Suppose that no adversary can find (M, M') such that $|M| \neq |M'|$ and $len_M = len_{M'}$ with probability more than τ. Then*

$$\mathtt{Adv}_H^{\mathsf{coll}}(q) \leq \mathtt{Adv}_f^{\mathsf{coll}}(q) + \tau \ .$$

Proof. Let A be a collision-finding adversary for H that takes an oracle f. We construct from A a collision-finding adversary B for f. Adversary B also takes an oracle f.

B runs A. When A makes an f-query, B forwards it to f and return to A the result. For $i \in \{1, \ldots, q\}$, we say that the i-th triple is (x_i^1, x_i^2, y_i) if A's i-th oracle query was an f-query of (x_i^1, x_i^2) and this returned y_i. Algorithm B records the list of triples.

Suppose that A halts with an output (M, M'). Then let B compute $H(M)$ and $H(M')$. All of the necessary queries for B to use in this computation are already recorded in B's list of triples. So no new oracle calls are needed to compute $H(M)$ and $H(M')$. Adversary B inspects its list of triples to see if there exists distinct (x^1, x^2, y) and (x'^1, x'^2, y). If so, B outputs this pair.

Let **BAD** denote the event that A finds (M, M') such that $|M| \neq |M'|$ and $len_M = len_{M'}$. Then

$$\begin{aligned}
&\Pr(\text{A succeeds}) \\
&= \Pr(\text{A succeeds}, BAD) + \Pr(\text{A succeeds}, \neg BAD) \\
&\leq \Pr(BAD) + \Pr(\text{A succeeds} \mid \neg BAD) \Pr(\neg BAD) \\
&\leq \tau + \Pr(\text{A succeeds} \mid \neg BAD) \ .
\end{aligned}$$

Suppose that **BAD** does not happen. Now recall the algorithm in Fig.2. If $len_M \neq len_{M'}$ then B succeed. So, suppose that $len_M = len_{M'}$. In this case, $|M| = |M'|$ from our assumption.

The fact that B records all triples needed to compute $H(M)$ means that she has all intermediate α_{2i-1}^j's, α_{2i}^j's and $f(\alpha_{2i}^j, \alpha_{2i-1}^j)$'s in Fig.2 when $H(M)$ is computed. Similarly, the fact that B records all triples needed to compute $H(M')$ means that she has all intermediate $\alpha_{2i-1}^{\prime j}$'s, $\alpha_{2i}^{\prime j}$'s and $f(\alpha_{2i}^{\prime j}, \alpha_{2i-1}^{\prime j})$'s in Fig.2 when $H(M')$ is computed. Therefore, if A succeeds, then B always finds $(\alpha_{2t}^s, \alpha_{2t-1}^s, f(\alpha_{2t}^s, \alpha_{2t-1}^s)) \neq (\alpha_{2r}^{\prime u}, \alpha_{2r-1}^{\prime u}, f(\alpha_{2r}^{\prime u}, \alpha_{2r-1}^{\prime u}))$ such that $f(\alpha_{2t}^s, \alpha_{2t-1}^s) = f(\alpha_{2r}^{\prime u}, \alpha_{2r-1}^{\prime u})$ in her list. So, we see that B succeeds whenever A succeeds. Hence

$$\Pr(\text{B succeeds}) \geq \Pr(\text{A succeeds} \mid \neg BAD)$$
$$\geq \Pr(\text{A succeeds}) - \tau .$$

Consequently, $\Pr(\text{A succeeds}) \leq \Pr(\text{B succeeds}) + \tau$. $\qquad \square$

Theorem 2. $\mathsf{Adv}_H^{\mathsf{inv}}(q) \leq \mathsf{Adv}_f^{\mathsf{inv}}(q)$.

A proof will be given in the final paper.

4   Using a Block-Cipher for Compression Function

In this section, we show that there exists a variant of our parallel hash construction such that it is secure even if the underlying compression function is not necessarily collision-free nor one-way. It needs $L/2$ more processors but it still takes time $O(\log(L))$ using $O(L)$ processors, where $|M| = Ln$.

4.1   Model

We consider a block cipher E such that $E : \{0,1\}^n \times \{0,1\}^n \to \{0,1\}^n$ where $E_k(\cdot) = E(k, \cdot)$ is a permutation on $\{0,1\}^n$ for each key $k \in \{0,1\}^n$. Let $\mathrm{Block}(n,n)$ be the set of all such block ciphers E. Choosing a random element of $\mathrm{Block}(n,n)$ means that for each $k \in \{0,1\}^n$ one choose a random permutation $E_k(\cdot)$. f_i^E denotes a compression function shown in Fig.1 such that $f_i(h,m)$ is computed by using E as an oracle. H_i^E denotes our modified construction shown in Sec.4.3 which uses f_i^E as a compression function. We sometimes omit the superscript E.

We consider probabilistic polynomial time adversaries A who have oracle access to E and E^{-1}. For the problems of Sec.2, $\mathsf{Adv}(A)$ will denote the success probability of A, where the probability is taken over the random choice of E as well. $\mathsf{Adv}(q)$ will denote the maximum success probability, where the maximum is taken over all adversaries that ask at most q oracle queries to E and E^{-1} in total.

For the collision problem and the one-wayness problem, define

$$\mathsf{Adv}_H^{\mathsf{coll}}(A) = \Pr[E \xleftarrow{R} \mathrm{Block}(n,n); (M, M') \xleftarrow{R} A^{E, E^{-1}} : M \neq M'$$
$$\wedge H^E(M) = H^E(M')]$$

$$\mathsf{Adv}_H^{\mathsf{inv}}(A) = \Pr[E \xleftarrow{R} \mathrm{Block}(n,n); \sigma \xleftarrow{R} R; M \leftarrow A^{E, E^{-1}} : H^E(M) = \sigma]$$

$$\mathsf{Adv}_H^{\mathsf{coll}}(q) = max_A \{\mathsf{Adv}_H^{\mathsf{coll}}(A)\}$$

$$\mathsf{Adv}_H^{\mathsf{inv}}(q) = max_A \{\mathsf{Adv}_H^{\mathsf{inv}}(A)\} .$$

4.2 Can We Use $f_{13}, \cdots, f_{20}$?

$f_{13}, \cdots, f_{20}$ are not collision-free nor one-way [1]. Indeed, $f_{13}, \cdots, f_{20}$ cannot be used for our parallel hash construction as shown below.

Theorem 3. *The proposed hash function H is not collision-free if f is not collision-free.*

Proof. In the basic construction,

$$H(m_1 \| m_2) = f(len_M \| f(m_1, m_2)) \ ,$$

where $M = m_1 \| m_2$. If f is not collision-free, we can find $M = m_1 \| m_2$ and $M' = m_1' \| m_2'$ such that $f(m_1, m_2) = f(m_1', m_2')$. Further, $len_M = len_{M'}$. Therefore, H is not collision-free if f is not collision-free.   □

Hence we cannot use $f_{13}, \cdots, f_{20}$ for the basic construction.

4.3 Modifying Our Parallel Hash Construction

We show that there exists a variant of our parallel hash construction such that it is secure even if the underlying compression function is not necessarily collision-free nor one-way.

The algorithm is illustrated in Fig.4, where $h_0 \in \{0,1\}^n$ is the initial value. The difference from our basic construction is that:

– len_M is not necessary in Step 4.
– The initial value $h_0 \in \{0,1\}^n$ is necessary in Step 1.

It needs $L/2$ more processors than our basic construction, but it still takes time $O(\log(L))$ using $O(L)$ processors.

(Remark)

1. If $|M|$ is not a multiple of n, we can use the same technique as [2] to deal with arbitrary length messages. That is, we pad 0^d to M so that the length of the padded message is a multiple of n. Also, append the binary representation of d. This means that we must hash an extra block.
2. If we use a single processor, the running time of the modified construction is twice as much as our basic construction.

4.4 Security of the Modified Scheme

When f is comp-free: We first prove that our modified construction H is collision-free if the underlying compression function f is comp-free, and H is one-way if f is one-way.

We say that f is comp-free if f is collision-free and h_0-preimage resistant, where h_0 is the initial value used in our modified construction. Formally, we define as follows.

Step1: Set $\alpha_1^L \leftarrow f(h_0, m_1), \ldots, \alpha_L^L \leftarrow f(h_0, m_L)$ and $j \leftarrow L$.
Step2: If $j = 1$ then output α_1^L as $H(M)$, and halt.
Step3: While $j > 2$, do
   If $j =$ even then
     each P_i $(1 \leq i \leq j/2)$ computes $\alpha_i^{j/2} \leftarrow f(\alpha_{2i-1}^j, \alpha_{2i}^j)$ in parallel.
     $j \leftarrow j/2$
   Else if $j =$ odd then
     each P_i $(1 \leq i \leq (j-1)/2)$ computes $\alpha_i^{(j+1)/2} \leftarrow f(\alpha_{2i-1}^j, \alpha_{2i}^j)$ in parallel.
     Set $\alpha_{(j+1)/2}^{(j+1)/2} \leftarrow \alpha_j^j$ and $j \leftarrow (j+1)/2$
Step4: Output $f(\alpha_1^2, \alpha_2^2)$ as $H(M)$

Fig. 4. Modified Construction

(Comp-free problem:)
Instance: $f : \{0,1\}^{2n} \rightarrow \{0,1\}^n$.
Find: $x, x' \in \{0,1\}^{2n}$ such that $f(x) = h_0$, or $x \neq x'$ and $f(x') = f(x)$.
Define

$$\mathsf{Adv}_f^{\mathsf{comp}}(A) = \Pr[(x, x') \xleftarrow{R} A^f : f(x) = h_0 \vee (x \neq x' \wedge f(x') = f(x))]$$
$$\mathsf{Adv}_f^{\mathsf{comp}}(q) = max_A\{\mathsf{Adv}_f^{\mathsf{comp}}(A)\} .$$

Theorem 4. $\mathsf{Adv}_H^{\mathsf{coll}}(q) \leq \mathsf{Adv}_f^{\mathsf{comp}}(q)$.

Proof. Let A be a collision-finding adversary for H that takes an oracle f. We construct an adversary B for f. Suppose that A halts with an output (M, M'). If $|M| = |M'|$, then B always finds a collision pair because $M \neq M'$. Otherwise similarly to the proof of [2, Theorem 3.1], we can show that B finds a collision pair or a preimage of h_0. Therefore, B succeeds whenever A succeeds. □

Theorem 5. $\mathsf{Adv}_H^{\mathsf{inv}}(q) \leq \mathsf{Adv}_f^{\mathsf{inv}}(q)$.

The proof is almost the same as that of Theorem 4.2.

We can therefore use $f_1, \cdots, f_{12}$ as compression functions of our basic construction and our modified construction because they are collision-free, comp-free and one-way in the ideal cipher model [1].

When f is $f_{13}, \cdots, f_{20}$: We next show that $f_{13}, \cdots, f_{20}$ can be used for the modified construction. We use a similar technique to [1].

We assume the following conventions. First, an adversary does not ask any oracle query in which the response is already known. Second, when an adversary A for H outputs a message M, we assume that A has already computed $H^E(M)$, in the sense that A has made the necessary E or E^{-1} queries to compute $H^E(M)$. Similarly, we assume that an adversary A for f computes $f^E(h, m)$ prior to outputting (h, m).

Collision resistance for $f = f_{13}, \cdots, f_{20}$:

Theorem 6. *For any $i \in \{13, \ldots, 20\}$,*

$$\mathrm{Adv}^{\mathrm{coll}}_{H_i}(q) \le 6q(q+1)/2^n \ .$$

Proof. We prove the theorem for H_{13}. The other cases are proved similarly.

Note that f_{13} is defined as

$$f_{13}(h, m) = E_{m \oplus h}(m) \oplus v$$

for some constants h_0 and v. Suppose that an adversary A outputs a collision pair (M, M') such that $H^E(M) = H^E(M')$. Then according to our conventions, A makes all of the queries necessary to compute $H(M)$ and $H(M')$. For example, let $M = m_1 \| m_2 \| \cdots \| m_a$. Then for each $i \in \{1, \ldots, a\}$, A have asked either an E-query (k_i, x_i) or an E^{-1}-query (k_i, y_i).

We say that z is evaluated if z is a constant, or z is queried by A, or $z = E_{k_i}(x_i) \oplus v$ and A asks some corresponding query to E or E^{-1} oracle. By the last query of A, suppose that some c is evaluated such that $c = f_{13}(a, b)$ for some a, b. Then a, b are already evaluated and one of the followings must happen.

(A1) $c = H(M)$ or $H(M')$.

(A2) $c = \beta$ or γ for some $\alpha = f_{13}(\beta, \gamma)$, where α, β, γ are already evaluated.

(A3) In (A2), β was not evaluated if $c = \beta$, and γ was not evaluated if $c = \gamma$.

(A4) $h_0 = f_{13}(h_0, h_0)$. (In this case, $M = h_0$ and $M_1 = h_0 \| h_0$ are a collision pair.)

We consider a directed graph $G = (V_G, E_G)$ as follows. The vertex set is $V_G = \{0,1\}^n \times \{0,1\}^n \times \{0,1\}^n$. The edge set E_G is defined in such a way that there exists an edge $X = (x, k, y) \to X' = (x', k', y')$ iff

$$x' \oplus k' = y \oplus v \text{ or } x' = y \oplus v. \tag{1}$$

We say that X' is a successor of X if there exists an edge $X \to X'$.

- It can be that $X = X'$.
- We consider that there are two edges from X to X' if $x' \oplus k' = y \oplus v$ *and* $x' = y \oplus v$.

We color vertices of G by the following rule. Initially, each vertex is uncolored. We say that:

- $X = (x, k, y)$ satisfies condition 1 if $x \oplus k = h_0$.
- X satisfies condition 2 if
  - X is a successor of X' and X'' which are already colored, or
  - X is a successor of X' which is already colored and there are two edges from X' to X.

Now suppose that the adversary A queries (k, x) to E-oracle and the oracle returns y, or A queries (k, y) to E^{-1}-oracle and the oracle returns x. Then we color $X = (x, k, y)$ and its successors $X' = (x', k', y')$ as follows:

- X is colored red if it satisfies condition 1.
- X is colored white if it satisfies condition 2 and does not satisfy condition 1.
- X is colored black if it does not satisfy condition 1 nor condition 2.
- X' is recolored white if it is black and it satisfies condition 2 owing to the coloring of X.

We say that $X = (x, k, y)$ and $X' = (x', k', y')$ collide if $y = y'$. Define

- A path in G is a RW-path if all their vertices are red or white.
- A set of RW-paths which have a common end vertex (called root) is a RW-tree if all the start vertices of the RW-paths are red and the other vertices satisfy condition 2.
- Two RW-trees collide if their roots collide.

Let C be the event that there are two colliding RW-trees, or there exists a colored $X = (h_0, 0^n, y)$ such that X is a successor of itself. (The latter case corresponds to (A4).)

Then from the rule of our coloring, it is easy to see that C occurs if A outputs a collision pair (M, M') such that $H^E(M) = H^E(M')$. Therefore

$$\mathsf{Adv}^{\mathsf{coll}}_{H_i}(q) \leq \Pr[\mathsf{C}] .$$

We will next prove that

$$\Pr[\mathsf{C}] \leq 6q(q+1)/2^n.$$

Let C_i be the event that C occurs by the i-th query. Define C_0 be the null event. Then $\Pr[\mathsf{C}] = \sum_{i=1}^{q} \Pr[\mathsf{C}_i \mid \neg\mathsf{C}_{i-1} \wedge \cdots \wedge \neg\mathsf{C}_0]$. Given $\neg\mathsf{C}_{i-1} \wedge \cdots \wedge \neg\mathsf{C}_0$, the event C_i occurs in one of the following five ways. Suppose that the adversary A gets the i-th query-answer tuple $X = (x_i, k_i, y_i)$.

Case 1: X is colored white and there exists a successor of X which is recolored.

Case 2: X is colored red and there exists a successor of X which is recolored.

Case 3: X is colored red or white, and there exists a successor of X which is already colored red or white.

Case 4: X is colored red or white, and there exists X' which collides with X.

Case 5: $X = (h_0, 0^n, y)$ and X is a successor of itself.

Case 1 and Case 2 correspond to (A3), Case 3 corresponds to (A2), Case 4 corresponds to (A1) and Case 5 corresponds to (A4), respectively.

We estimate the probability that **Case 1** happens. If **Case 1** occurs via an E-query (k_i, x_i), then y_i is a random value from a set of size at least $2^n - (i-1)$. Therefore

$$\Pr[\text{Case 1 occurs }] \leq \Pr[\text{eq.(1) is satisfied}] \leq \frac{2(i-1)}{2^n - (i-1)} .$$

Alternatively, if **Case 1** occurs via an E^{-1}-query (k_i, y_i), then x_i is a random value from a set of size at least $2^n - (i-1)$. Therefore

$$\Pr[\text{Case 1 occurs }] \leq \Pr[\text{eq.(1) is satisfied}] \leq \frac{2(i-1)}{2^n - (i-1)} .$$

In any case, we obtain that $\Pr[\text{Case 1 occurs}] \leq \frac{2(i-1)}{2^n-(i-1)}$. Similarly, we can show that

$$\Pr[\text{Case } j \text{ occurs}] \leq \frac{2(i-1)}{2^n-(i-1)} \quad \text{for } j \in \{2,3,4\},$$

$$\Pr[\text{Case 5 occurs}] \leq \frac{1}{2^n-(i-1)}.$$

It is clear that **Case 1** and **Case 2** do not occur simultaneously. Therefore, by combining these cases, we have

$$\Pr[C] \leq \sum_{i=1}^{q} \left(\frac{3 \cdot 2(i-1)}{2^n-(i-1)} + \frac{1}{2^n-(i-1)} \right) \leq \frac{6q(q+1)}{2^n}.$$

□

One-wayness for $f = f_{13}, \cdots, f_{20}$: For the message space is $(\{0,1\}^n)^l$, define the success probability of an adversary A as

$$\mathsf{Adv}_H^{\mathsf{owf}}(A,l) = \Pr[E \xleftarrow{R} \mathrm{Block}(n,n); M \xleftarrow{R} (\{0,1\}^n)^l; \sigma \leftarrow H^E(M)$$
$$; M' \leftarrow A^{E,E^{-1}}(\sigma) : H^E(M') = \sigma].$$

Let $\mathsf{Adv}_H^{\mathsf{owf}}(q,l)$ be the maximum of $\mathsf{Adv}_H^{\mathsf{owf}}(A,l)$ over all A that ask at most q queries.

Lemma 1. *For any $i \in \{13,\ldots,20\}$,*

$$\left| \mathsf{Adv}_{H_i}^{\mathsf{inv}}(q) - \mathsf{Adv}_{H_i}^{\mathsf{owf}}(q,l) \right| \leq \frac{(12l-5)(l-1)}{2^{n-1}}.$$

Lemma 2. *Suppose that the message space is restricted to $\bigcup_{l \geq 2}\{0,1\}^{ln}$. Then for each $i \in \{13,\cdots,20\}$,*

$$\mathsf{Adv}_{H_i}^{\mathsf{inv}}(q) \leq 3\mathsf{Adv}_{H_i}^{\mathsf{coll}}(q+2) + (12q-5)(q-1)/2^{n-1}.$$

Proof. Let I be an inverting adversary that attacks H_i on the distribution induced by applying H_i to a random ln-bit string and assume that I makes q oracle queries.

We construct a collision-finding adversary A for H_i as follows;

1. A chooses $M \in \{0,1\}^{2n}$ randomly and computes $\sigma = H_i(M)$.
2. A runs I on σ. When I makes a query to E (resp., E^{-1}) oracle, A forwards the query to its own E (resp., E^{-1}) oracle, and returns to I the result.
3. When I halts with output M', A returns (M, M').

We now analyze the advantage of the adversary A. There are at most $2^n - 1$ points $\sigma \in \{0,1\}^n$ that can have a unique preimage under H_i. Hence there are at least $2^{2n} - 2^n + 1$ massages $M \in \{0,1\}^{2n}$ that hash to range points having at least two preimages. Let N_σ be the number of preimages of σ. Since M is randomly chosen, we have that

$$
\begin{aligned}
\mathsf{Adv}_{H_i}^{\mathsf{coll}}(A) &= \Pr[M' \neq M \mid N_\sigma \geq 2] \cdot \Pr[N_\sigma \geq 2] \cdot \mathsf{Adv}_{H_i}^{\mathsf{owf}}(I) \\
&\geq \frac{1}{2} \cdot \frac{2^{2n} - 2^n + 1}{2^{2n}} \cdot \mathsf{Adv}_{H_i}^{\mathsf{owf}}(I) \\
&\geq \frac{3}{8} \mathsf{Adv}_{H_i}^{\mathsf{owf}}(I) .
\end{aligned}
$$

Rearranging the terms yields that

$$
\mathsf{Adv}_{H_i}^{\mathsf{owf}}(q) \leq 8/3 \cdot \mathsf{Adv}_{H_i}^{\mathsf{coll}}(q+2) \leq 3\mathsf{Adv}_{H_i}^{\mathsf{coll}}(q+2) .
$$

From Lemma 1 we conclude that

$$
\mathsf{Adv}_{H_i}^{\mathsf{inv}}(q) \leq 3\mathsf{Adv}_{H_i}^{\mathsf{coll}}(q+2) + \frac{(12q-5)(q-1)}{2^{n-1}} . \quad \square
$$

We now prove the one-wayness.

Theorem 7. *For any* $i \in \{13, \cdots, 20\}$,

$$
\mathsf{Adv}_{H_i}^{\mathsf{inv}}(q) \leq 42(q+1)(q+3)/2^n .
$$

Proof. From Theorem 6 and Lemma 2, we obtain that

$$
\begin{aligned}
\mathsf{Adv}_{H}^{\mathsf{inv}}(q) &\leq 3\mathsf{Adv}_{H}^{\mathsf{coll}}(q+2) + \frac{(12q-5)(q-1)}{2^{n-1}} \\
&= 3 \cdot \frac{6(q+2)(q+3)}{2^n} + \frac{(12q-5)(q-1)}{2^{n-1}} \\
&\leq \frac{42(q+1)(q+3)}{2^n} . \quad \square
\end{aligned}
$$

References

1. J.Black, P.Rogaway, and T.Shrimpton, "Black-box analysis of the block-cipher-based hash-function constructions from PGV ", In *Advances in Cryptology – CRYPTO '02, Lecture Notes in Computer Science*, pages 320–335. Springer-Verlag, 2002.
2. I.Damgård, "A design principle for hash functions ", In *Advances in Cryptology – CRYPTO '89, Lecture Notes in Computer Science*, pages 416–427. Springer-Verlag, 1990.
3. J.Kilian and P.Rogaway, "How to protect DES against exhaustive key search ", *Journal of Cryptology*, 14(1):17–35, 2001. Earlier version in *CRYPTO '96*.
4. B.Preneel, R.Govaerts, and J.Vandewalle, "Hash functions based on block ciphers: A synthetic approach", In *Advances in Cryptology – CRYPTO '93, Lecture Notes in Computer Science*, pages 368–378. Springer-Verlag, 1994.

Square Hash with a Small Key Size

Swee-Huay Heng[1] and Kaoru Kurosawa[2]

[1] Tokyo Institute of Technology,
2-12-1 O-okayama, Meguro-ku, Tokyo 152-8552, Japan
shheng@crypt.ss.titech.ac.jp
[2] Ibaraki University,
4-12-1 Nakanarusawa, Hitachi, Ibaraki, 316-8511, Japan
kurosawa@cis.ibaraki.ac.jp

Abstract. This paper shows an improvement of square hash function family proposed by Etzel *et al.* [5]. In the new variants, the size of keys is much shorter while the collision probability is slightly larger. Most of the main techniques used to optimize the original square hash functions work on our variants as well. The proposed algorithms are applicable to fast and secure message authentication.

Keywords: Message authentication codes, universal hash, square hash

1 Introduction

Universal hashing is a concept that was introduced by Carter and Wegman [4] in 1979. It has a wide range of applications especially in theoretical computer science. In 1981, the same authors published another new idea that is the universal hash function approach for message authentication codes [15].

Message authentication schemes enable parties in possession of a shared secret key to achieve the goal of data integrity. They have been used for a long time in the banking community. Message authentication assured the receiver that a received message is indeed originated with the purported sender. The setting involves two parties, a transmitter and a receiver who share a secret key x. It consists of two algorithms, an algorithm S_x that applies a tag to a message, and a verification algorithm V_x that validates the correctness of the tag. When a transmitter wants to send a message m to a receiver, she computes a message authentication code, $MAC = S_x(m)$, and sends the pair (m, MAC). Upon receiving the pair, the receiver computes $V_x(m, MAC)$ which returns 1 if the MAC is valid, or returns 0 otherwise. The formal security requirement for a MAC was first defined by Bellare *et al.* [3]. The adversaries are given oracle access to (S_x, V_x). We declared that an adversary is successful if she can output a pair (m^*, MAC^*) such that $V_x(m^*, MAC^*) = 1$ but the message m^* was never input to the oracle S_x. In the universal hash approach, MAC is generated by encrypting $h(m)$, where h is a randomly chosen universal hash function.

Now one of the most important aspects of universal hash functions is that the construction should be easy to implement in software and/or hardware.

R. Safavi-Naini and J. Seberry (Eds.): ACISP 2003, LNCS 2727, pp. 522–531, 2003.
© Springer-Verlag Berlin Heidelberg 2003

Such implementation aspect receives much attention lately, and there are several papers addressing this topic [14,8,12,9,13,7,6,1,5,2,10].

This paper studies fast universal hash functions by using square hash (SQH). Square hash was introduced by Etzel *et al.* [5], it is an improvement on the MMH family construction of Halevi and Krawczyk [6]. Eventually, square hash achieved a significant speedup over MMH based on two new ideas that were being introduced in the construction. However, the implementations of these fast universal hash functions tend to require long keys in order to achieve their impressive speeds. In [5], the key string must be of the same size as the message string in order to achieve fast hash functions. This is in fact a common drawback to all fast universal hash functions.

As mentioned earlier, there have been some previous work on software efficiency of universal hash functions. Some recent papers [7,1,10] are more in line with our direction, focusing on evaluation of universal hash functions with a small key size.

The main contribution of this paper is the improvement upon the work of Etzel *et al.* We prove that the key size can be drastically reduced at the cost of losing some small amount of security. The key is short, independent of the message length. In our construction, we use only a key size that is equivalent to the MAC output or tag size. We formally prove that, despite using a very short key in our construction, the security bound ϵ on the resulting hash function is still low enough to provide for a very secure MAC.

Next, we show that we can make ϵ smaller without increasing the tag size. We can select the key size depending on the desired level of security or collision probability ϵ. That is, there exists trade-off between the key size and the collision bound ϵ.

We can use pseudo-random bit generators (PRG) to generate a key of square hash. In this way, however, the security depends on the security of the underlying PRG. On the other hand, the security of our method holds unconditionally.

The paper is organized as follows. In Section 2 we give the basic definitions and properties of universal hash families and their variants. Section 3 reviews MMH and SQH. In Section 4 we introduce the new approach to the square hash, and we show that most of the main techniques used to optimize the original square hash work on our case as well. A discussion is given in Section 5. Finally, some concluding remarks are made in Section 6.

2 Preliminaries

Let H be a family of functions from a domain D to a range R. Let ϵ be a constant such that $\frac{1}{|R|} \leq \epsilon \leq 1$. The probabilities below, denoted by $\Pr_{h \in H}[\cdot]$, are taken over the choice of $h \in H$.

Definition 1. *H is a universal family of hash functions if for all $x, y \in D$ with $x \neq y$, $\Pr_{h \in H}[h(x) = h(y)] = \frac{1}{|R|}$. H is an ϵ-almost-universal (ϵ-AU) family of hash functions if $\Pr_{h \in H}[h(x) = h(y)] \leq \epsilon$.*

Definition 2. *Let R be an Abelian group and denote by '−' the group subtraction operation. H is a Δ-universal family of hash functions if for all $x, y \in D$ with $x \neq y$ and all $a \in R$, $\mathrm{Pr}_{h \in H}[h(x) - h(y) = a] \leq \frac{1}{|R|}$. H is an ϵ-almost-Δ-universal (ϵ-AΔU) family of hash functions if $\mathrm{Pr}_{h \in H}[h(x) - h(y) = a] \leq \epsilon$.*

Definition 3. *H is a strongly universal family of hash functions if for all $x, y \in D$ with $x \neq y$ and all $a, b \in R$, $\mathrm{Pr}_{h \in H}[h(x) = a, h(y) = b] \leq \frac{1}{|R|^2}$. H is an ϵ-almost-strongly-universal (ϵ-ASU) family of hash functions if $\mathrm{Pr}_{h \in H}[h(x) = a, h(y) = b] \leq \frac{\epsilon}{|R|}$.*

3 MMH and SQH

In this section, we overview MMH and SQH.

3.1 MMH: Multilinear Modular Hashing

MMH is a family of Δ-universal hash functions based on techniques due to Carter and Wegman using modular multilinear functions. Halevi and Krawczyk [6] discovered techniques to enable fast software implementation at negligible costs in the collision probabilities. These hash functions apply to the hashing of variable size data and fast cryptographic message authentication.

We give the description of the basic construction of MMH as follows:

Definition 4. *[6] Let $k > 0$ be an integer. Let $x = \langle x_1, \ldots, x_k \rangle$ and $m = \langle m_1, \ldots, m_k \rangle$ where $x_i, m_i \in Z_p$. The MMH family of functions from Z_p^k to Z_p is defined as follows: $MMH \equiv \{g_x : Z_p^k \to Z_p | x \in Z_p^k\}$ where the functions g_x are defined as*

$$g_x(m) = m \cdot x = \sum_{i=1}^{k} m_i x_i \bmod p.$$

Here is the definition of MMH_{32}, an optimized version of MMH as proposed by Halevi and Krawczyk [6]:

Definition 5. *Set $p = 2^{32} + 15$ and $k = 32$. Let $x = \langle x_1, \ldots, x_k \rangle$ and $m = \langle m_1, \ldots, m_k \rangle$ where $x_i, m_i \in Z_p$. Define the MMH_{32} family of functions from $(\{0,1\}^{32})^k$ to $\{0,1\}^{32}$ as: $MMH_{32} \equiv \{h_x : (\{0,1\}^{32})^k \to \{0,1\}^{32} | x \in (\{0,1\}^{32})^k\}$ where the functions h_x are defined as*

$$h_x(m) = (((\sum_{i=1}^{k} m_i x_i) \bmod 2^{64}) \bmod (2^{32} + 15)) \bmod 2^{32}.$$

Theorem 1. *[6] MMH_{32} is an ϵ-almost-Δ-universal family of hash functions with $\epsilon \leq \frac{6}{2^{32}}$.*

3.2 SQH: Square Hash

Etzel *et al.* proposed a variant of MMH which can be more efficient than MMH in certain settings. The efficiency lies in the fact that whereas other common constructions involve integer multiplications, SQH involves integer squaring.

Definition 6. *Let* $k > 0$ *be an integer. Let* $x = \langle x_1, \ldots, x_k \rangle$ *and* $m = \langle m_1, \ldots, m_k \rangle$ *where* $x_i, m_i \in Z_p$. *The SQH family of functions from* Z_p^k *to* Z_p *is defined as follows:* $SQH \equiv \{g_x : Z_p^k \to Z_p | x \in Z_p^k\}$ *where the functions* g_x *are defined as*

$$g_x(m) = \sum_{i=1}^{k} (m_i + x_i)^2 \bmod p.$$

Theorem 2. *[5] SQH is a Δ-universal family of hash functions.*

SQH is faster than MMH because squaring can be implemented and it requires roughly half the number of basic word multiplications as multiplying two numbers [11]. All the clever optimization techniques of MMH can be applied to SQH as well. Etzel *et al.* further optimized SQH by disregarding many of the carry bits in the computation. The techniques involve ignoring certain parts of the computation while still retaining the necessary statistical properties for secure message authentication.

A fully optimized version of SQH is defined as follows. The notation C and C_2 in the following definition denote the values we get after computing the respective expressions contained within the brackets by ignoring the carry bits between the words. Further explanation about carry bits will be given in the next section.

Definition 7. *[5] Let* l *and* k *be positive integers with* $2^l < p < 2^l + 2^{l-1}$. *Let* $x = \langle x_1, \ldots, x_k \rangle$ *and* $m = \langle m_1, \ldots, m_k \rangle$ *where* $x_i, m_i \in \{0, 1\}^l$. *The SQH$_E$ family of functions from* $(\{0, 1\}^l)^k$ *to* $\{0, 1\}^l$ *is defined as follows:* $SQH_E \equiv \{g_x : (\{0, 1\}^l)^k \to \{0, 1\}^l | x \in \{0, 1\}^l\}$ *where the functions* g_x *are defined as*

$$g_x(m) = (C(\sum_{i=1}^{k} C_2(((m_i + x_i) \bmod 2^l)^2)) \bmod p) \bmod 2^l.$$

Theorem 3. *[5] Let* l *be the word size and* w *is the total number of words needed to store* x_i, *then SQH$_E$ is an ϵ-almost-Δ-universal family of hash functions with* $\epsilon \leq (6 \cdot \prod_{i=1}^{k} (4i + 1)^2)/2^{lw}$.

4   Square Hash with a Small Key Size

The purpose of this section is to slightly modify the key construction in the original square hash, SQH. In our construction, we let $x_1 \in Z_p, x_2 \equiv x_1^2 \bmod p, \ldots, x_k \equiv x_1^k \bmod p$. The difference is essentially that we only use 1 scalar in our key generation whereas SQH uses k scalars chosen from Z_p to form the key $x = \langle x_1, \ldots, x_k \rangle$. In other words, we shorten the key length by k times. The length of the key does not depend on the parameter k, the length of the message-vector. No matter how large the value k, our key size is the same. Notice that the scalars $x_2, \ldots, x_k$ can be precomputed after choosing the first scalar $x_1 \in Z_p$. We formally prove that, despite using a very short key in our construction, the collision probability bound ϵ on the resulting hash functions is still low enough to provide for a very secure MAC. It is mentioned in [6] that depending on the variant and application of MMH one may need long keys (e.g., a few Kbits). Halevi and Krawczyk suggested these keys to be generated using a strong PRG. However, the security must depend on the security of the underlying strong PRG. (For example, the resulting hash is secure against a polynomially bounded adversary only .) In our case, we do not face this problem.

Next, we give the basic construction of our proposed square hash, SQH'.

Definition 8. *Let $k > 0$ be an integer. Let $x = \langle x_1, \ldots, x_k \rangle$, where $x_1 \in Z_p, x_2 \equiv x_1^2 \bmod p, \ldots, x_k \equiv x_1^k \bmod p$ and $m = \langle m_1, \ldots, m_k \rangle, m_i \in Z_p$. The SQH' family of functions from Z_p^k to Z_p is defined as follows: $SQH' \equiv \{g_x : Z_p^k \to Z_p | x \in Z_p^k\}$ where the functions g_x are defined as*

$$g_x(m) = \sum_{i=1}^{k} (m_i + x_i)^2 \bmod p.$$

Theorem 4. *SQH' is an ϵ-almost-Δ-universal family of hash functions with $\epsilon \leq \frac{k}{p}$.*

Proof. Let $m \neq n \in Z_p^k$ with $m = \langle m_1, \ldots, m_k \rangle, n = \langle n_1, \ldots, n_k \rangle$ and $m_i, n_i \in Z_p$. Let $\delta \in Z_p$. Since $m \neq n$ there is some i for which $m_i \neq n_i$. Without loss of generality, suppose $m_1 \neq n_1$. We wish to show that the probability of collision under a randomly chosen hash function from SQH' is at most $\frac{k}{p}$ i.e. to prove that $\Pr[g_x(m) - g_x(n) \equiv \delta \bmod p] \leq \frac{k}{p}$ (where $x = \langle x_1, \ldots, x_k \rangle$, $x_1 \in Z_p, x_2 \equiv x_1^2 \bmod p, \ldots, x_k \equiv x_1^k \bmod p$). So,

$$\Pr[g_x(m) - g_x(n) \equiv \delta \bmod p]$$
$$= \Pr[\sum_{i=1}^{k} (m_i + x_i)^2 - \sum_{i=1}^{k} (n_i + x_i)^2 \equiv \delta \bmod p]$$
$$= \Pr[2\sum_{i=1}^{k} ((m_i - n_i)x_1^i) = \delta + \sum_{i=1}^{k} (n_i^2 - m_i^2) \pmod{p}]$$
$$\leq k/p.$$

The last inequality follows since the congruence equation inside the probability has at most k solutions. This result is due to the Fundamental Theorem of Algebra which states that a nonzero polynomial of degree at most k can have at most k roots. $\square$

4.1 Speeding up SQH'

Next, we present a variant of SQH', called SQH'_{asm}, which is suited for assembly language implementation.

Definition 9. *Let l and k be positive integers with $2^l < p < 2^l + 2^{l-1}$. Let $x = \langle x_1, \ldots, x_k \rangle$, where $x_1 \in Z_p, x_2 \equiv x_1^2 \bmod p, \ldots, x_k \equiv x_1^k \bmod p$ and $m = \langle m_1, \ldots, m_k \rangle, m_i \in Z_p$. The SQH'_{asm} family of functions from Z_p^k to $\{0,1\}^l$ is defined as follows: $SQH'_{asm} \equiv \{g_x : Z_p^k \to \{0,1\}^l | x \in Z_p^k\}$ where the functions g_x are defined as*

$$g_x(m) = ((\sum_{i=1}^{k}(m_i + x_i)^2) \bmod p) \bmod 2^l.$$

Theorem 5. *SQH'_{asm} is an ϵ-almost-Δ-universal family of hash functions with $\epsilon \leq \frac{3k}{2^l}$.*

Proof. Let $\delta \in \{0,1\}^l$ be chosen arbitrarily. Let $m \neq n$ be arbitrary message-vectors. Let x be the key such that $h_x(m) - h_x(n) \equiv \delta \bmod 2^l$, where $h \in SQH'_{asm}$. Equivalently,

$$h'_x(m) - h'_x(n) \equiv \delta \bmod 2^l$$

where $h' \in SQH'$. Now, both $h'_x(m)$ and $h'_x(n)$ are in the range $0, \ldots, p-1$. Therefore, their difference taken over the integers lies in the range $-p+1, \ldots, p-1$. If we denote $p = 2^l + t$ where $0 < t < 2^{l-1}$ then:

$$h'_x(m) - h'_x(n) \in \begin{cases} \{\delta, \delta - 2^l\} & t \leq \delta \leq 2^l - t \\ \{\delta - 2^l, \delta, \delta + 2^l\} & 0 \leq \delta \leq t - 1 \\ \{\delta, \delta - 2^l, \delta - 2^{l+1}\} & 2^l - t < \delta \leq 2^l - 1 \end{cases}$$

That is, if $h_x(m) - h_x(n) \equiv \delta \bmod 2^l$ then the difference $h'_x(m) - h'_x(n)$ can assume at most three values over the integers. Since SQH' is an ϵ-almost-Δ-universal hash function with $\epsilon \leq \frac{k}{p}$, it follows that for any $\delta' \in \{0,1\}^l$ there are at most k choices of the key x for which

$$h'_x(m) - h'_x(n) \equiv \delta' \bmod p.$$

So, for any value of δ, the probability that x solves the equation

$$h_x(m) - h_x(n) \equiv \delta \bmod 2^l$$

is at most three times larger. Therefore,

$$\Pr[h_x(m) - h_x(n) \equiv \delta \bmod 2^l] \leq \frac{3k}{2^l}.$$

$\square$

We have proved that the security bounds in the previous two theorems are only k times larger than the respective security bounds in the original square hash, SQH [5]. Theoretically, these bounds are still low enough to provide for a secure MAC.

4.2   Ignoring Carry Bits in the Computation

Finally, we show that we can further speed up our construction at a small trade-off in the collision probability, as was done in [5]. The idea involves ignoring many of the carry bits in the computation and still get a very strong performance for cryptographic applications.

We describe the notion of carry bits briefly and explain why computation can speed up if we ignore these carry bits. When two words are added, there is usually an overflow or carry that takes place. For example, if the word size is 8 and we get a 9-bit sum after adding two words, then the most significant bit 1 is called the carry or overflow bit. When arithmetic operations are performed on integers that require more than one word to represent, it is necessary to keep track of the carry bits since these carry bits are needed in the subsequent operations. This increases the computation time of arithmetic instructions because it becomes necessary to explicitly keep track of the carry bits. Etzel *et al.* provided a remedy for this dilemma by ignoring the carry bits altogether while still get a quite reasonable trade-off in security.

We show that we can also achieve a further speedup by ignoring the carry bits in the outer summation. Let $C(\sum_{i=1}^{k} a_i)$ denote the value we get when computing the sum $\sum_{i=1}^{k} a_i$ by ignoring the carry bits between the words. We now formally define another new variant of SQH' and show that it still gives us strong performance.

Definition 10. *Let l and k be positive integers with $2^l < p < 2^l + 2^{l+1}$. Let $x = \langle x_1, \ldots, x_k \rangle$, where $x_1 \in Z_p, x_2 \equiv x_1^2 \bmod p, \ldots, x_k \equiv x_1^k \bmod p$ and $m = \langle m_1, \ldots, m_k \rangle, m_i \in Z_p$. The SQH'_c family of functions from Z_p^k to Z_p is defined as follows: $SQH'_c \equiv \{g_x : Z_p^k \to Z_p | x \in Z_p^k\}$ where the functions g_x are defined as*

$$g_x(m) = (C(\sum_{i=1}^{k}(m_i + x_i)^2) \bmod p).$$

Theorem 6. *Let l be the word size of the architecture and let w be the number of words it takes to store x_i. Then the SQH'_c is an ϵ-almost-Δ-universal family of hash functions with $\epsilon \leq \frac{k(2k-1)2^w}{2^{lw}}$.*

Proof. Fix a value $a \in Z_p$ and let $m = \langle m_1, \ldots, m_k \rangle \neq m' = \langle m'_1, \ldots, m'_k \rangle$ be the two message-vectors. We want to prove that

$$\Pr[g_x(m) - g_x(m') \equiv a \bmod p] \leq \frac{k(2k-1)^{2w}}{2^{lw}}.$$

Let

$$C(\sum_{i=1}^{k}(m_i + x_i)^2) = \sum_{i=1}^{k}(m_i + x_i)^2 - c$$

and

$$C(\sum_{i=1}^{k}(m'_i + x_i)^2) = \sum_{i=1}^{k}(m'_i + x_i)^2 - c'$$

where $c, c' \in \{0, 1\}^{2lw + \log_2 k}$ are respectively a "correction vector". We observe that in the ith word of c and c' (counting from the right for $2 \le i \le 2w + 1$), there are 1's in at most the $\log_2 k$ least significant bit positions of that word, the remaining bits must be 0. In other words, only the least significant $\log_2 k$ bits in word i are undetermined. We can show that if the b least significant bits of each of two different words are undetermined, then the difference of those two words can take at most $2^{b+1} - 1$ different values. Therefore

$$\Pr[g_x(m) - g_x(m') \equiv a \bmod p]$$

$$= \Pr[C(\sum_{i=1}^{k}(m_i + x_i)^2) - C(\sum_{i=1}^{k}(m'_i + x_i)^2) \equiv a \bmod p]$$

$$= \Pr[2\sum_{i=1}^{k}((m_i - m'_i)x_1^i) \equiv a + \sum_{i=1}^{k}(m'^2_i - m^2_i) + (c - c')(\bmod p)]$$

$$\le k \cdot (\text{The number of distinct values of } (c - c')) \cdot 2^{-lw}.$$

The last inequality follows since the number of x_1 satisfying the congruence equation inside the probability is at most the product of k multiply with the number of distinct values of $(c - c')$. Next, we show that,

$$\text{The number of distinct values of } (c - c') = (2^{\log_2 k + 1} - 1)^{2w}$$
$$= (2k - 1)^{2w}.$$

This completes the proof. $\square$

Now, we observe that the quantity $\frac{k(2k-1)^{2w}}{2^{lw}}$ is actually rather small. Let us substitute suitable values for the parameters. Suppose the word size l is 32 bits and the length of the message-vector k is 32 ($k = 32$ is the reasonable trade-off value suggested by Halevi and Krawczyk in their paper [6]), then a computationally unbounded adversary can forge a MAC tag of size 2, 3, 4 or 5 words with probability at most $2^{-35}, 2^{-55}, 2^{-75}$ and 2^{-95} respectively. These bounds are still considered as small and fulfilled the condition for a reasonably secure MAC.

5   Discussion

This section shows that we can make ϵ smaller without making the size of MAC larger. In other words, we show that there exists trade-off between the key size and the security bound ϵ in our construction.

If a lower collision probability is desired, one can increase the key size slowly. For example, in the basic construction of SQH' the security bound ϵ is equal to k/p. Depending on the choice of p and the application at hand, collision probability of k/p may be insufficient. In order to reduce the collision probability, we can simply change our key construction. For instance, to reduce the collision bound by half, we choose $x_1, x_2 \in Z_p, x_3 \equiv x_1^2 \bmod p, x_4 \equiv x_2^2 \bmod p, \ldots$, that is we double our key size. This yields a collision probability of $k/2p$ for even k. Similarly, if we want to have a much smaller security bound then we can further increase our key size. It is not difficult to prove this theoretically. We leave it to the reader.

This is a new approach in obtaining a lower security bound. Indeed, the previous approach of reducing ϵ was to make the size of hash values larger. That is, hash the message multiple times using a different key for each message hash and concatenate all the hash values finally. Note that the size of hash values is fixed in our approach.

6   Conclusion

We proposed an efficient variant of square hash with a very short key size which is k times shorter than the one proposed by Etzel *et al*. This is indeed a very significant improvement. We proved that this new variant of square hash still gives a very good security bound in accomplishing the task of fast and secure MAC. It will be a further work to study whether we can ignore the carry bits when squaring as well.

References

1. V. Afanassiev, C. Gehrmann and B. Smeets, "Fast message authentication using efficient polynomial evaluation," Fast Software Encryption, FSE '97, LNCS 1267, pp. 190–204, Springer Verlag, 1997.
2. J. Black, S. Halevi, H. Krawczyk, T. Krovetz and P. Rogaway, "UMAC: Fast and secure message authentication," Advances in Cryptology — CRYPTO '99, LNCS 1666, pp. 216–233, Springer-Verlag, 1999.
3. M. Bellare, J. Killian and P. Rogaway, "The security of cipher block chaining," Advances in Cryptology — CRYPTO '94, LNCS 839, pp. 341–358, Springer-Verlag, 1994.
4. J. L. Carter and M. N. Wegman, "Universal classes of hash functions," Journal of Computer and System Sciences, vol. 18, no. 2, pp. 143–154, 1979.
5. M. Etzel, S. Patel and Z. Ramzan, "Square Hash: Fast message authentication via optimized universal hash functions," Advances in Cryptology — CRYPTO '99, LNCS 1666, pp. 234–251, Springer-Verlag, 1999.
6. S. Halevi and H. Krawczyk, "MMH: Message authentication in software in the gbit/second rates," Fast Software Encryption, FSE '97, LNCS 1267, pp. 172–189, Springer Verlag, 1997.
7. T. Johansson, "Bucket hashing with smaller key size," Advances in Cryptology — EUROCRYPT '97, LNCS 1233, pp. 149–162, Springer-Verlag, 1997.
8. H. Krawczyk, "LFSR-based hashing and authentication," Advances in Cryptology — CRYPTO '94, LNCS 839, pp. 129–139, Springer-Verlag, 1994.
9. H. Krawczyk, "New hash functions for message authentication," Advances in Cryptology — EUROCRYPT '95, LNCS 921, pp. 301–310, Springer-Verlag, 1995.
10. T. Krovetz and P. Rogaway, "Fash universal hashing with small keys and no prepocessing: the polyR construction," International Conference on Information Security and Cryptology — ICISC '00, LNCS 2015, pp. 73–89, Springer Verlag, 2001.

11. A. J. Menezes, P. C. van Oorschot and S. A. Vanstone, Handbook of Applied Cryptography, CRC Press, 1997.
12. P. Rogaway, "Bucket hashing and its application to fast message authentication," Advances in Cryptology — CRYPTO '95, LNCS 963, pp. 15–25, Springer-Verlag, 1995.
13. V. Shoup, "On fast and provably secure message authentication based on universal hashing," Advances in Cryptology — CRYPTO '96, LNCS 1109, pp. 313–328, Springer-Verlag, 1996.
14. D. R. Stinson, "Universal hashing and authentication codes," Designs, Codes and Cryptography, vol. 4, pp. 369–380, 1994.
15. M. N. Wegman and J. L. Carter, "New hash functions and their use in authentication and set equality," Journal of Computer and System Sciences, vol. 22, no. 3, pp. 265–279, 1981.

Author Index

Lecture Notes in Computer Science

For information about Vols. 1–2626
please contact your bookseller or Springer-Verlag

Vol. 2668: V. Kumar, M.L. Gavrilova, C.J.K. Tan, P. L'Ecuyer (Eds.), Computational Science and Its Applications – ICCSA 2003. Proceedings, Part II. 2003. XXXIV, 942 pages. 2003.

Vol. 2669: V. Kumar, M.L. Gavrilova, C.J.K. Tan, P. L'Ecuyer (Eds.), Computational Science and Its Applications – ICCSA 2003. Proceedings, Part III. 2003. XXXIV, 948 pages. 2003.

Vol. 2670: R. Peña, T. Arts (Eds.), Implementation of Functional Languages. Proceedings, 2002. X, 249 pages. 2003.

Vol. 2671: Y. Xiang, B. Chaib-draa (Eds.), Advances in Artificial Intelligence. Proceedings, 2003. XIV, 642 pages. 2003. (Subseries LNAI).

Vol. 2672: M. Endler, D. Schmidt (Eds.), Middleware 2003. Proceedings, 2003. XIII, 513 pages. 2003.

Vol. 2673: N. Ayache, H. Delingette (Eds.), Surgery Simulation and Soft Tissue Modeling. Proceedings, 2003. XII, 386 pages. 2003.

Vol. 2674: I.E. Magnin, J. Montagnat, P. Clarysse, J. Nenonen, T. Katila (Eds.), Functional Imaging and Modeling of the Heart. Proceedings, 2003. XI, 308 pages. 2003.

Vol. 2675: M. Marchesi, G. Succi (Eds.), Extreme Programming and Agile Processes in Software Engineering. Proceedings, 2003. XV, 464 pages. 2003.

Vol. 2676: R. Baeza-Yates, E. Chávez, M. Crochemore (Eds.), Combinatorial Pattern Matching. Proceedings, 2003. XI, 403 pages. 2003.

Vol. 2678: W. van der Aalst, A. ter Hofstede, M. Weske (Eds.), Business Process Management. Proceedings, 2003. XI, 391 pages. 2003.

Vol. 2679: W. van der Aalst, E. Best (Eds.), Applications and Theory of Petri Nets 2003. Proceedings, 2003. XI, 508 pages. 2003.

Vol. 2680: P. Blackburn, C. Ghidini, R.M. Turner, F. Giunchiglia (Eds.), Modeling and Using Context. Proceedings, 2003. XII, 525 pages. 2003. (Subseries LNAI).

Vol. 2681: J. Eder, M. Missikoff (Eds.), Advanced Information Systems Engineering. Proceedings, 2003. XV, 740 pages. 2003.

Vol. 2685: C. Freksa, W. Brauer, C. Habel, K.F. Wender (Eds.), Spatial Cognition III. X, 415 pages. 2003. (Subseries LNAI).

Vol. 2686: J. Mira, J.R. Álvarez (Eds.), Computational Methods in Neural Modeling. Proceedings, Part I. 2003. XXVII, 764 pages. 2003.

Vol. 2687: J. Mira, J.R. Álvarez (Eds.), Artificial Neural Nets Problem Solving Methods. Proceedings, Part II. 2003. XXVII, 820 pages. 2003.

Vol. 2688: J. Kittler, M.S. Nixon (Eds.), Audio- and Video-Based Biometric Person Authentication. Proceedings, 2003. XVII, 978 pages. 2003.

Vol. 2689: K.D. Ashley, D.G. Bridge (Eds.), Case-Based Reasoning Research and Development. Proceedings, 2003. XV, 734 pages. 2003. (Subseries LNAI).

Vol. 2691: V. Mařík, J. Müller, M. Pěchouček (Eds.), Multi-Agent Systems and Applications III. Proceedings, 2003. XIV, 660 pages. 2003. (Subseries LNAI).

Vol. 2692: P. Nixon, S. Terzis (Eds.), Trust Management. Proceedings, 2003. X, 349 pages. 2003.

Vol. 2694: R. Cousot (Ed.), Static Analysis. Proceedings, 2003. XIV, 505 pages. 2003.

Vol. 2695: L.D. Griffin, M. Lillholm (Eds.), Scale Space Methods in Computer Vision. Proceedings, 2003. XII, 816 pages. 2003.

Vol. 2698: W. Burakowski, B. Koch, A. Bęben (Eds.), Architectures for Quality of Service in the Internet. Proceedings, 2003. XI, 305 pages. 2003.

Vol. 2701: M. Hofmann (Ed.), Typed Lambda Calculi and Applications. Proceedings, 2003. VIII, 317 pages. 2003.

Vol. 2702: P. Brusilovsky, A. Corbett, F. de Rosis (Eds.), User Modeling 2003. Proceedings, 2003. XIV, 436 pages. 2003. (Subseries LNAI).

Vol. 2704: S.-T. Huang, T. Herman (Eds.), Self-Stabilizing Systems. Proceedings, 2003. X, 215 pages. 2003.

Vol. 2706: R. Nieuwenhuis (Ed.), Rewriting Techniques and Applications. Proceedings, 2003. XI, 515 pages. 2003.

Vol. 2707: K. Jeffay, I. Stoica, K. Wehrle (Eds.), Quality of Service – IWQoS 2003. Proceedings, 2003. XI, 517 pages. 2003.

Vol. 2709: T. Windeatt, F. Roli (Eds.), Multiple Classifier Systems. Proceedings, 2003. X, 406 pages. 2003.

Vol. 2710: Z. Ésik, Z, Fülöp (Eds.), Developments in Language Theory. Proceedings, 2003. XI, 437 pages. 2003.

Vol. 2711: T.D. Nielsen, N.L. Zhang (Eds.), Symbolic and Quantitative Approaches to Reasoning with Uncertainty. Proceedings, 2003. XII, 608 pages. 2003. (Subseries LNAI).

Vol. 2713: C.-W. Chung, C.-K. Kim, W. Kim, T.-W. Ling, K.-H. Song (Eds.), Web and Communication Technologies and Internet-Related Social Issues – HSI 2003. Proceedings, 2003. XXII, 773 pages. 2003.

Vol. 2714: O. Kaynak, E. Alpaydin, E. Oja, L. Xu (Eds.), Artificial Neural Networks and Neural Information Processing – ICANN/ICONIP 2003. Proceedings, 2003. XXII, 1188 pages. 2003.

Vol. 2715: T. Bilgiç, B. De Baets, O. Kaynak (Eds.), Fuzzy Sets and Systems – IFSA 2003. Proceedings, 2003. XV, 735 pages. 2003. (Subseries LNAI).

Vol. 2716: M.J. Voss (Ed.), OpenMP Shared Memory Parallel Programming. Proceedings, 2003. VIII, 271 pages. 2003.

Vol. 2718: P. W. H. Chung, C. Hinde, M. Ali (Eds.), Developments in Applied Artificial Intelligence. Proceedings, 2003. XIV, 817 pages. 2003. (Subseries LNAI).

Vol. 2719: J.C.M. Baeten, J.K. Lenstra, J. Parrow, G.J. Woeginger (Eds.), Automata, Languages and Programming. Proceedings, 2003. XVIII, 1199 pages. 2003.

Vol. 2721: N.J. Mamede, J. Baptista, I. Trancoso, M. das Graças Volpe Nunes (Eds.), Computational Processing of the Portuguese Language. Proceedings, 2003. XIV, 268 pages. 2003. (Subseries LNAI).

Vol. 2726: E. Hancock, M. Vento (Eds.), Graph Based Representations in Pattern Recognition. Proceedings, 2003. VIII, 271 pages. 2003.

Vol. 2727: R. Safavi-Naini, J. Seberry (Eds.), Information Security and Privacy. Proceedings, 2003. XII, 534 pages. 2003.

Vol. 2731: C.S. Calude, M.J. Dinneen, V. Vajnovszki (Eds.), Discrete Mathematics and Theoretical Computer Science. Proceedings, 2003. VIII, 301 pages. 2003.

Vol. 2734: P. Perner, A. Rosenfeld (Eds.), Machine Learning and Data Mining in Pattern Recognition. Proceedings, 2003. XII, 440 pages. 2003. (Subseries LNAI).